PENGUIN CLASSICS

KRISHNA: THE BEAUTIFUL LEGEND OF GOD

EDWIN BRYANT graduated from Columbia University in 1997, where he taught Sanskrit and Hindi. He was the lecturer in Hinduism at Harvard University for three years, and is presently assistant professor in Hinduism at Rutgers University, New Jersey. His publications include *The Quest for the Origins of Vedic Culture: the Indo-Aryan Invasion Debate* (2002); *The Hare Krishna Movement: The Post-Charismatic Fate of a Religious Transplant* (2004); *The Indo-Aryan Controversy: Evidence and Inference in Indian History* (forthcoming); and *Sources in the Krishna Tradition* (forthcoming). He is presently working on a book, *Quest for the Historical Krishna*, and a translation of the Yoga Sutras.

Krishna: The Beautiful Legend of God

Śrīmad Bhāgavata Purāṇa, Book X

With Chapters 1, 6 and 29–31
from Book XI

Translated with an Introduction and Notes by
EDWIN F. BRYANT

PENGUIN BOOKS

PENGUIN BOOKS

Published by the Penguin Group
Penguin Books Ltd, 80 Strand, London WC2R 0RL, England
Penguin Putnam Inc., 375 Hudson Street, New York, New York 10014, USA
Penguin Books Australia Ltd, 250 Camberwell Road, Camberwell, Victoria 3124, Australia
Penguin Books Canada Ltd, 10 Alcorn Avenue, Toronto, Ontario, Canada M4V 3B2
Penguin Books India (P) Ltd, 11, Community Centre, Panchsheel Park, New Delhi – 110 017, India
Penguin Books (NZ) Ltd, Cnr Rosedale and Airborne Roads, Albany, Auckland, New Zealand
Penguin Books (South Africa) (Pty) Ltd, 24 Sturdee Avenue, Rosebank 2196, South Africa

Penguin Books Ltd, Registered Offices: 80 Strand, London WC2R 0RL, England

www.penguin.com

This translation first published 2003
2

Set in 10.25/12.25 pt PostScript Adobe Sabon
Typeset by Rowland Phototypesetting Ltd, Bury St Edmunds, Suffolk
Printed in England by Clays Ltd, St Ives plc

To my daughter Mohiṇī

Contents

Acknowledgements

To Bhaktivedānta Swāmi, whose devotional rendition of the text was the first to present the Kṛṣṇa story and the path of Kṛṣṇa *bhakti* around the world on a popular level, and in whose works I first encountered the Śrīmad Bhāgavata Purāṇa and the story of Kṛṣṇa. To the Bhaktivedānta Book Trust edition's *padapāṭha*, word-for-word breakdown, which was particularly useful to me for this work. To the American Council of Learned Societies/Social Science Research Council/National Endowment of the Humanities International and Area Fellowship for a 2000–2001 research grant which allowed me to complete this translation. To my father and sister for their unending support and help in ways too numerous to mention. To Mia, for all her support, patience and encouragement, and to her and Matthew Ekstrand, for being always willing to help in matters pertaining to computer problems despite my irritability at such times. To Diana Eck for the wonderful opportunity. To Paul Sherbow, for his Sanskrit editing, and to Janet Tyrrell for transforming a clumsy literal translation into something a good deal more readable. To Satyanārāyaṇa Dāsa of the Jīva Institute in Vṛndāvana for his comments on the introduction and other help. To Ekkehard Lorenz for statistical analysis and other comments. To Michael Moss, who took an independent study with me to learn Sanskrit; together we read some verses from the text.

And finally to all the *bhāgavatas* who have preserved, transmitted and elaborated upon the beautiful story of *Bhagavān* Kṛṣṇa across the ages.

Introduction

THE BHĀGAVATA AS TEXT

Kṛṣṇa (usually anglicized as Krishna) is perhaps best known in the west as the speaker of the Bhagavad Gītā, the Song of God, which is a text located within the narrative of the Mahābhārata Epic. Considered by Hindus to be the incarnation of God, Kṛṣṇa inaugurated the present *yuga*, or world age, by his departure from this world shortly after the great Mahābhārata war. Although Kṛṣṇa's role in the Epic as statesman and friend of the five Pāṇḍavas is pivotal, he is not the protagonist of the story – the Epic gives little information pertaining to other aspects of his life. It is the tenth book of the Śrīmad Bhāgavata Purāṇa, 'The Beautiful Legend of God', generally referred to as the 'Bhāgavata Purāṇa' (or just the 'Bhāgavata'), that has been the principal textual source dedicated to the actual narrative of his incarnation and activities, at least over the last 1,000 years or so.[1] Moreover, it is not Kṛṣṇa's statesmanship in the Mahābhārata that has produced the best loved stories about this deity, nor is it his influential teachings in the Bhagavad Gītā: it is his *līlās* – play, pastimes or frolics – during his infancy, childhood and adolescence in the forests of Vṛndāvana, popularly known as Vraj,[2] among the men and women cowherds, that have been particularly relished by Hindus throughout the Indian subcontinent over the centuries.

In Vraj, Kṛṣṇa sported with his friends, played pranks on his neighbours, and dallied amorously with the young cowherd girls. This very personal depiction of God is the primary subject matter of the tenth book of the Bhāgavata Purāṇa. The stories of Kṛṣṇa in Vraj have been, and, arguably, remain one of the two most influential textual sources of religious narrative in the Hindu religious landscape, along with the stories of Rāma from the Epic Rāmāyaṇa, if we are to judge on the basis of the themes that have surfaced in Hindu drama, poetry, dance, painting, song, literature, sculpture, iconography and temple worship over the last millennium and more. The popularity of the Kṛṣṇa of Vraj has certainly eclipsed the popularity of the Kṛṣṇa of the massive 100,000-verse Mahābhārata Epic, despite its Bhagavad Gītā. Hawley (1979: 202–3), for example, found that of 800 panels depicting Kṛṣṇa to have survived from the period prior to 1500 CE, only three refer with any clarity to the Bhagavad Gītā:

> We are given to understand that for two millennia the *Gītā* has been India's most influential scripture, yet . . . it is remarkable how indifferent sculptors were to this part of Krishna's adult life . . . instead sculptors focus on the events of his youth. The Krishna we see is the cowherdboy who was so fond of butter as a child, [and who] became such an attractive lover as a youth . . . sculpture may at least in some respects be a more accurate index of what people's religious commitments were all along.

T. A. Gopinath Rao (1986) has listed the nine major iconographical forms under which Kṛṣṇa has been worshipped in India, and seven of these relate to his childhood pastimes in Vraj; the remaining two are Kṛṣṇa and his consort Rukmiṇī, the goddess of fortune, and Kṛṣṇa as Pārthasārathi, the charioteer of Arjuna. This latter image is the only representation of Kṛṣṇa in the role of teacher and speaker of the Bhagavad Gītā (Kṛṣṇa had agreed to drive Arjuna's chariot and delivered the Bhagavad Gītā to him on the Mahābhārata battlefield immediately prior to the war). Thus, it is the Kṛṣṇa of Vraj that has most particularly influenced the devotional life of India, and it is the story of this Kṛṣṇa that is the subject of the tenth book of the Bhāgavata Purāṇa.

The Historical Context of the Bhāgavata

The Bhāgavata Purāṇa forms part of a corpus of texts known as the Purāṇas. The word *purāṇa*, in Sanskrit, signifies 'that which took place previously', namely ancient lore or legend. Several Purāṇas list the total number of Purāṇas as eighteen, one of which is the Bhāgavata. As we have them today, these Purāṇas are a vast repository of stories about kings and royal dynasties; the gods and their devotees; sectarian theologies; traditional cosmologies; popular religious beliefs concerning pilgrimages, holy places and religious rites; *yogic* practices; information of social and cultural relevance such as caste duties; and even prophetic statements about the future – almost everything that has come to be associated with 'modern Hinduism' has its roots in the Purāṇas. The eighteen Purāṇas are said to contain 400,000 verses,[3] and are the largest body of writing in Sanskrit.

The three chief gods in the Purāṇas are Brahmā, the secondary creator;[4] Śiva, the destroyer; and Viṣṇu, the maintainer. A number of stories speak of the competition between these three for ultimate supremacy. Brahmā, being himself a mortal created being (albeit with an immense life-span), is never, in fact, a serious contender, and the main rivalry in the Purāṇas is played out between the two transcendent Lords Viṣṇu and Śiva; a later Purāṇa, the Devī Bhāgavata Purāṇa, marks the ascendancy into the Purāṇic genre of Devī, the Goddess, as the supreme matrix.[5] Such usually playful rivalry notwithstanding, the Purāṇas, taken in total, indicate that it is Viṣṇu who as a rule is pre-eminent, especially in the earlier texts.[6]

Despite what sometimes appears to be the partisan nature of the texts associated with one or the other of these two supreme beings (see chapters 63, 66, 88 and 89 in this text for examples), both camps accept and indeed extol the transcendent and absolute nature of the other, and of the Goddess Devī too, merely affirming that the other deity is to be considered a derivative or secondary manifestation of their respective deity, or, in the case of Devī, the *śakti*, or power, of the male divinity. The term 'monotheism', if applied to the Purāṇic tradition, needs to be understood in the context of a supreme being, whether understood as Viṣṇu, Śiva or Devī, who can manifest him- or herself as other supreme beings (albeit all of them secondary to the original Godhead).[7] The metaphysics of the Bhāgavata will be discussed further below.

Although Viṣṇu is a purely transcendent deity (unlike Śiva, who is more terrestrial in the Purāṇas, and typically associated with the Himālayas or the city of Vārāṇasī),[8] he is generally said to have ten principal earthly incarnations,[9] which appear according to time and place, some of them in animal form. The commonly accepted list[10] of these incarnations in the Purāṇas is: Matsya, the fish; Kūrma, the tortoise; Varāha, the boar; Narasiṃha, the man-lion; Vāmana, the dwarf; Paraśurāma, the warrior; Rāma, the prince; Kṛṣṇa, the cowherd boy; Buddha, the founder of Buddhism; and Kalki, the future warrior incarnation who will ride a white horse and terminate the present world age of the *kaliyuga*. The stories of these different incarnations are related in detail in the various Purāṇas. The Bhāgavata Purāṇa occupies itself almost exclusively with Viṣṇu and his incarnations, and most particularly the incarnation of Kṛṣṇa.

The Bhāgavata Purāṇa consists of twelve *skandhas* (cantos, subdivisions or books), of which the tenth book disproportionately comprises about one quarter of the entire text. It is this tenth book that has caused the Purāṇa to be recognized as the most famous work of Purāṇa literature, as evidenced by the overwhelming preponderance of traditional commentaries on the text. Whereas most of the Purāṇas have produced no traditional commentaries at all, and others only one or two, the Bhāgavata has inspired eighty-one commentaries currently available, in Sanskrit alone, as well as others no longer extant.[11] It has been translated into almost all the languages of India, with forty or so translations on record in Bengal alone. It was the first Purāṇa to have been translated into a European language: three different French translations were completed between 1840[12] and 1857, and these were followed in 1867 by a translation of the *pañcādhyāya*, the five chapters of the tenth book dedicated to Kṛṣṇa's amorous pastimes with the *gopīs* (cowherd women), again in French.

Curiously, although a number of English translations by Indian scholars have surfaced from local publishing houses in the subcontinent over the last century, no western scholar has until now undertaken an English translation (with the exception of the disciples of Bhaktivedānta Swami, who completed the latter's in-house translation after his demise), despite the immense importance of the text. This is mainly because the Victorian sensibilities of certain nineteenth-century western (and westernized Indian) critics were offended by the amorous liaisons of Kṛṣṇa in the Bhāgavata, causing the Kṛṣṇa of this text to be passed over in most intellectual circles in favour of the more righteous Kṛṣṇa of the Gītā – a text which has seen hundreds of non-Indian translations. This neglect continues to the present day.

As an unambiguously Vaiṣṇavite text (that is, adhering to Viṣṇu as supreme), the first nine books of the Bhāgavata discuss in greater or lesser detail all the major incarnations prior to Kṛṣṇa. The tenth book, which comprises about 4,000 out of a total of a claimed 18,000 verses of the entire Purāṇa,[13] is dedicated exclusively to Kṛṣṇa and, indeed, it is Kṛṣṇa, under his title of *Bhagavān*, who gives his name to the whole Purāṇa.[14] While the Bhāgavata Purāṇa, then, is a Vaiṣṇavite text in general, it is a Kṛṣṇa-centred text in particular, as the disproportionate size of the tenth book indicates. Indeed, as will be discussed further on pp. xix–xxii, the Kṛṣṇaite theologies that emerged in the sixteenth century, initiated by influential teachers such as Vallabha and Caitanya, suggest that it is not Kṛṣṇa who is an incarnation of Viṣṇu, but Viṣṇu who is a partial incarnation of Kṛṣṇa. These sects extol Kṛṣṇa as the supreme absolute truth from whom all other deities, including Viṣṇu, evolve, the Bhāgavata Purāṇa being presented as the scriptural authority in this regard.

It is an inconclusive task to try to assign specific dates to the Purāṇas, as shown by the considerable variation in the dates proposed by scholars for the Bhāgavata itself. Not the least of the problems is that the Purāṇas are a fluid body of literature that continued to be transformed through the centuries by the process of transmission and adaptation. These texts are composed for public oral recitation, often in specific ritualistic contexts, and their reciters openly modified them in accordance with time and place as well as for sectarian considerations. Any datable piece of information that may be gleaned from the texts may only reflect the historical period in which that section of the text was inserted and may not reflect the date of other sections in the text.

The oldest preserved literatures in India are the four Vedas, which primarily contain hymns recited in the ritualistic context of the ancient Vedic sacrificial cult of the Indo-Aryans. Unlike the Purāṇas, the contents of these texts were fixed at a very early stage by various mnemonic devices such that the different recensions of the Ṛgveda have been transmitted identically across the millennia, despite differences of geographical place. Considered *śruti*, 'that which is heard', or divine revelation not of human authorship, these texts could never be tampered with, particularly since their efficacy as sacred text depended upon the precise preservation and pronunciation of each phoneme. In contrast to these, there are much more flexible expectations associated with the Purāṇas, which are *smṛti*, 'that which is remembered', or indirect revelation, divine in origin, but composed through human agency. While nonetheless sacred and authoritative, the Purāṇas transmit information for the general public and thus adjustments according to the day and age are not viewed askance – indeed, such fluidity is inherent in the claim made by most Purāṇas of presenting the 'essence' of the Veda according to time and place. On the one hand they recognize the need to preserve and transmit faithfully the ancient sacred material intact, and, on the other, they claim to explain, expand upon and even supersede the contents of previous scriptures, by revealing secret truths not contained either in the Vedas or in other Purāṇas. They are thus on-going revelation. In the Bhāgavata (I.5.1ff.), Vyāsa, the traditional author of the text, remained unfulfilled even after compiling all the Vedas as well as the Mahābhārata Epic, until the sage Nārada informed him that the cause of his despondency was that he had not yet described the highest goal of knowledge. The result was the Bhāgavata, the *galitam phalam*, the ripened fruit of the Vedic tree (I.1.3), the essence of all the Vedas, Purāṇas and Ithāsa Epics (I.2.3; I.3.42).

A number of Purāṇas, then, claim to be equal or superior to the Vedas, and thus the Purāṇas are often called the fifth Veda. In Purāṇic narrative, the hymns of the Vedas, along with the Purāṇic stories, were transmitted orally through the first three of the four *yugas*, or world ages – the *satya*, *tretā* and *dvāpara yugas* – and then, with a view to preserving the material from the ravages of time heralded by the beginning of the present fourth world age of *kaliyuga*,[15] the great sage Vyāsa ('the divider') divided the single Veda into four, and then compiled a Purāṇa Saṃhitā, or ur-Purāṇa text, from the tales, lore, anecdotes and songs that had been handed down through the ages. This original Purāṇa text was then further divided by his disciples.

There is little doubt that some of the material in the Purāṇas does indeed go back to the earliest Vedic age. Many of the Vedic hymns assume common knowledge of bygone persons and events to which they briefly allude and which would have been remembered through tradition, and some of these are also mentioned in the Purāṇas.[16] As early as the Atharvaveda of *circa* 1000 BCE, there is a reference to 'the Purāṇa', and numerous references to it in the later Vedic texts. Thus, while the present Purāṇas contain later material that refers to events in historical time, they also contain ancient narratives and anecdotes from the earliest period of proto-history in Southern Asia. Much of the endless conjecture and difference of opinion among scholars results from assigning old dates to an entire text on the basis of an archaic reference, which might simply be an ancient, well-preserved fragment in a later compilation. Equally problematic is the reverse tendency of assigning a much later date to an entire text on the basis of a more recent datable reference such as a dynasty of the historical period, which might in fact be a much later interpolation in an older text. It is thus futile to speak of absolute dates for any Purāṇa as a whole, since one would have to speak of the age of individual sections within particular Purāṇas. Hence Purāṇic scholars such as Rocher (1986) decline even to attempt to date them. Accordingly, I will simply note here that the majority of scholars hold that the bulk of the material in most of the eighteen Purāṇas as we find them today reached its completion by the Gupta period about the fourth to the sixth centuries CE, on the grounds that neither the later dynasties nor later famous rulers such as Harṣa in the seventh century CE are to be found in the king lists contained in the texts.

The date of the Bhāgavata Purāṇa must be charted from within this somewhat nebulous chronological framework. Understandably, there is no consensus regarding the date of the text, that is to say, the final version of the text that has been handed down in its present form. While most specialists of the Purāṇas from India have opted for dates around the Gupta period, the present consensus among most western scholars familiar with the text is that it is the latest of the eighteen Purāṇas written (depending on the scholar) sometime between the ninth and thirteenth centuries CE in the south of the subcontinent. There are a number of significant reasons to question such a time frame, as well as place of origin, which cause me to wonder whether the Bhāgavata might not have reached its final form by the Gupta period, along with the other major Purāṇas. I have outlined my concerns elsewhere in detail (Bryant, 2002), and will only reiterate here that whatever date one assigns to the Bhāgavata applies only to the final date of the *entirety* of the text as we now have it, not to the material contained within it, or even to portions of the text itself. As noted previously with regard to the Purāṇic genre, the upper limit date of the text is one issue, the date of the subject matter recorded in it is another; the story of Kṛṣṇa is far older than the flowering of Purāṇic literature in the Gupta period. The following outline of the earliest historical evidence external to the Bhāgavata pertaining to Kṛṣṇa as a divine being will be limited to evidence datable to before the common era (but I will leave aside the Purāṇic genre and the Mahābhārata Epic because of the problems and differences of opinion involved in dating the Kṛṣṇa narrative in these sources).[17]

Earliest Historical Evidence of Kṛṣṇa as a Divine Being

There is no obvious reference to Kṛṣṇa in the Ṛgveda, the oldest Indic text, although the name does appear occasionally in the hymns. A few scholars have unconvincingly tried to connect these references with Kṛṣṇa, or with some proto-figure from whom he evolved,[18] but most instances of the word *kṛṣṇa* in the Ṛgveda are simply as the adjective 'black', and there is nothing in these occurrences that allows us to connect these references to the Kṛṣṇa of the Purāṇas. The Chāndogya Upaniṣad, a philosophical text of the later Vedic age of about the sixth century BCE, gives us the first plausible, but still questionable, reference to the Purāṇic Kṛṣṇa (III.17.6). The verse in question has provoked considerable debate as to whether or not it refers to an older portrayal of this Kṛṣṇa, a discussion that ultimately remains inconclusive.[19] In any event, indisputable and numerous references to Kṛṣṇa as a divine being occur in a number of subsequent texts in the fifth and fourth centuries BCE,[20] including early Greek sources.

In one such source, Megasthenes, an ambassador of the Seleucid empire (established by one of Alexander's generals from the remains of the Macedonian empire) to the court of the Indian emperor Chandragupta Maurya at the end of the fourth century BCE, provides interesting evidence from outside India that is relevant to the early history of the divine Kṛṣṇa. Megasthenes wrote a book called *Indika*, the original of which has not been preserved, but which was quoted extensively by other ancient classical Greek writers whose works are extant, such as Arrian, Diodorus and Strabo.[21] According to these sources, Megasthenes described an Indian tribe called the Sourasenoi, who worshipped Herakles in particular in their land, which had two great cities, Methora and Kleisobora, and a navigable river, the Jobares. It is well known that the Greeks and other ancients correlated foreign gods with their own divinities, and there seems little reasonable doubt (and almost all scholars agree) that the Sourasenoi refers to the Śūrasenas, a branch of the Yadu dynasty to which Kṛṣṇa belonged; Herakles refers to Kṛṣṇa, or

Hari-Kṛṣṇa; Methora to Mathurā, Kṛṣṇa's birthplace; Kleisobora to Kṛṣṇa pura, 'the city of Kṛṣṇa'; and the Jobares to the Yamunā river, where Kṛṣṇa sported. Quintus Curtius also mentions that when Alexander the Great confronted the Indian king Porus, the latter's soldiers were carrying an image of Herakles at their head.

The Greek connection provides further interesting data: the earliest archaeological evidence of Kṛṣṇa as a divine being (under his name of Vāsudeva) is the Heliodorus column in Besnagar, north-central India, dated to *c.* 100 BCE. The inscription on the column is startling because it reveals that foreigners had been converted to the Bhāgavata religion by this period – Heliodorus was a Greek. This would seem to suggest that the Kṛṣṇa tradition was prominent and prestigious enough to attract a powerful foreign envoy as a convert at the end of the second century BCE. Another interesting feature of the inscription is that it calls Vāsudeva (Kṛṣṇa) the God of gods, suggesting that the cult of Kṛṣṇa's pre-eminence in relation to Viṣṇu, discussed below, might be as old as this column (although this is anyway indicated by the Bhagavad Gītā, commonly dated to around this time, or somewhat earlier). Other archaeological evidence of a divine Kṛṣṇa also surfaces in the first century BCE.[22]

Vāsudeva Kṛṣṇa, then, can first be documented as a divine being at the tail-end of the Vedic period in the fifth to fourth centuries BCE, and heralds the rise of a new theistic religion based on loving devotion to a personal God. While this is much later than the date that the Mahābhārata and Purāṇic tradition assigns to this divinity at the end of the fourth millennium BCE, one must always bear in mind that the earliest date something appears in written or archaeological sources does not necessarily correspond to the actual date of the thing in question: it simply points to the earliest *provable* date that can be assigned to it. In any event, in one regard at least, traditional and academic discourses overlap – Kṛṣṇa appears at the end of one cultural age, and is pivotal to the inauguration of a new one.

THE THEOLOGY OF THE BHĀGAVATA

The Bhāgavata, like the Bhagavad Gītā before it, unambiguously presents Kṛṣṇa as the supreme being. The term *Bhagavān* is the designation most frequently used in the tenth book of the Bhāgavata to refer to Kṛṣṇa as God,[23] and this is illustrated by the very fact that the Bhāgavata Purāṇa, like the Bhagavad Gītā, uses this term in its very title.[24] *Bhagavān* literally means one possessing *bhaga*, a noun that in the Purāṇic and Epic period combines notions such as prosperity, dignity, distinction, excellence, majesty, power and beauty. The Vaiṣṇava schools differ, however, as to whether Viṣṇu is the ultimate and supreme *Bhagavān*, who periodically incarnates into the world in various forms – one of which is Kṛṣṇa – in order to protect *dharma* (righteousness), or whether Kṛṣṇa is the highest being, and Viṣṇu his incarnation for the purpose of the manifestation and maintenance of the cosmic order. The former position is held by the older Vaiṣṇava sects dominant in the south, which attained prominence under the great teachers Rāmānuja and Madhva, and the latter position surfaces most conspicuously across the north of the subcontinent in the sixteenth century, spearheaded by charismatics such as Caitanya and Vallabha. Both schools ultimately hold both Kṛṣṇa and Viṣṇu to be manifestations of the same real, eternal and transcendent personal being who appears in different forms, so, in terms of who came first, the difference is something of a plant and seed situation.

Kṛṣṇa as the Absolute Godhead

In the Mahābhārata, Harivaṃśa[25] and Viṣṇu Purāṇa, there is no doubt that Kṛṣṇa is an incarnation of Viṣṇu.[26] The roles, for the most part, have been somewhat reversed in the Bhāgavata: while there are abundant passages in the text that relate to Viṣṇu without explicitly subordinating him to Kṛṣṇa, particularly in the books prior to the tenth, the general thrust of the tenth book prioritizes Kṛṣṇa. In many ways, the very structure of the Purāṇa culminates in the story of Kṛṣṇa's incarnation, with the first nine books forming a prologue to the full glory of *Bhagavān* in the tenth book, which, as was noted, takes up a quarter of the entire twelve books of the Purāṇa.

The books prior to the tenth teach various aspects of *bhakti yoga*, the path of devotion, and are, in fact, mostly associated with Viṣṇu as the goal of devotion. In the first nine books, the reader of the text encounters prominent features of *bhakti yoga*, as well as the most famous Vaiṣṇava role models: Prahlāda, the child devotee, who shows that by complete faith and surrender to God, Viṣṇu, one can surpass any and all mortal dangers; Dhruva, another child devotee, who demonstrates that one can attain audience of Viṣṇu by unstoppable determination; Gajendra the elephant, who shows that one can attain, and only attain, Viṣṇu's refuge when one finally fully surrenders to him; Ajāmila, who exhibits the power of Viṣṇu's name by attaining liberation simply by chanting it at the moment of death, although accidentally; and Bali, who illustrates that even demons can become perfected devotees. These and other stories familiarize the devotee with the requirements and expectations for the path, while providing illustrations of successful exemplars. The tenth book reveals the goal – Lord Kṛṣṇa himself – and the text makes it clear that those who associate with Kṛṣṇa in his activities during his incarnation are highly elevated and fortunate souls, who have already performed all the requirements of the devotional path in previous lives (X.3.32–8).

Thus the early books prepare the reader for the Bhāgavata's full revelation of God's personal nature that is disclosed in the tenth book. In this, the Bhāgavata, along with the Gītā, which can also be read as promoting Kṛṣṇa as the supreme being, is one of the two primary sources of scriptural authority relied upon by the Kṛṣṇa sects in their prioritization of Kṛṣṇa over Viṣṇu. Understandably, then, the sixteenth-century Kṛṣṇaite theologian Vallabha felt impelled to add the Bhāgavata Purāṇa as a fourth item to the *prasṭhāna traya*, the three traditional primary scriptures used by Vedāntic sects to establish their authenticity – the Upaniṣads, the Vedānta Sūtras and the Bhagavad Gītā – and this in itself speaks to the necessity of this text to Kṛṣṇa-centred theology.[27] While Vallabha himself wrote a commentary on the Vedānta Sūtras (in which he frequently quoted the Bhāgavata), and the Caitanya school eventually produced one under pressure from the other sects, this was primarily in order to gain recognition and acceptance in the intellectual circles of the time. It is the Bhāgavata that really fulfils the theological needs for these schools.

The crucial verse in the Bhāgavata used by the Kṛṣṇa theologians to justify the pre-eminence of Kṛṣṇa over all other manifestations of Godhead is I.3.28. Situated after a number of verses listing previous incarnations, this verse states: 'These [other incarnations] are *aṃśa*, or *kalā* [partial incarnations], but *kṛṣṇastu bhagavān svayam* [Kṛṣṇa is *Bhagavān*, God, himself].' This verse becomes something of a *mahāvākya*, a 'pivotal', 'most important' or 'representational statement' for the theology of the Kṛṣṇa sects. The word *aṃśa* is the crucial term here, and appears frequently throughout the text. It is primarily used in connection with Viṣṇu and Kṛṣṇa,[28] and means a 'portion' or 'partial incarnation'. In ways that roughly approximate the notion of the Christian trinity, the sense of the term is that the supreme Godhead can maintain his (or her) own presence, while simultaneously manifesting some aspect of himself (or herself) elsewhere in a separate and distinct presence (or any number of presences). That secondary, or derivative manifestation, which exhibits a part but not the full characteristics or potency of the source being, is known as an *aṃśa*. A further term, *kalā*, has similar connotations. Verse 28 identifies all other incarnations as *aṃśas* or *kalās*, but sets Kṛṣṇa apart as *Bhagavān* himself, which is taken by the Kṛṣṇa sects to indicate that he is the original being and source of the other incantations.

The importance of I.3.28 for Kṛṣṇaism, then, cannot be overestimated, and it overrides all conflicting statements for the Kṛṣṇa sects.[29] The commentators Viśvanātha and Gaṅgāsahāya consider it to be a *paribhāṣā sūtra*, an exploratory assertion that, while only occurring in one verse, illuminates the entire text, like a lamp that illuminates an entire house, although situated in only one place. Irrespective of this verse, there can be no doubt that Kṛṣṇa is privileged in the Bhāgavata. And there is no doubt that he is God: he assumes the forms of Viṣṇu, Śiva and Brahmā for the maintenance, destruction and creation of the universe (I.2.23); a universe which is situated within him (X.14.22), and constituted from him (X.74.21). Indeed, Brahmā and Śiva are his instruments (X.71.8); together with Śrī, the goddess of fortune, they are only a fraction of a fraction of him (X.68.37). Nothing can be named which is not him (X.46.43), he is the soul of everything (X.40.12), the cause of this world – its creation, maintenance and dissolution – as well as the time factor that moves all things (XI.6.15). Eulogies of Kṛṣṇa as the absolute truth spill out of every page of the Bhāgavata. As in the Gītā, the purpose of his descent to earth is to eliminate the demons and protect the righteous (X.70.27). But, in the Bhāgavata (I.8.35; X.33.36), there is another reason why he incarnates in addition to this mission: Kṛṣṇa descends to engage in *līlā*, or devotional pastimes.

Līlā

The tenth book can be divided into two distinct and equal sections: the childhood pastimes of Kṛṣṇa in Vṛndāvana, or Vraj, called Vraj *līlā*, and the post-Vṛndāvana, adult activities. The moods of the two sections are quite distinct. Many of the chapters in the second section contain stories of Kṛṣṇa's battles with numerous demoniac kings, narrations of his heroic martial exploits, descriptions of his winning the hands of his various wives, and accounts of his statesmanship and lavish life in the royal household. This second section is regal, and resonates far more closely with the tone of the Mahābhārata than does the first section. The stories of the first section, in contrast, paint a delightfully different and far more intimate picture of the supreme being, and it is in this section that the term *līlā*, pastime, occurs most frequently. Here we find God stealing butter from the cowherd women and feeding it to the monkeys, hiding from his mother in fear as she chases him with a stick on account of his mischief, or dallying with the *gopī* cowherd girls in the moonlit forests of Vraj. As has been suggested above, it is the Kṛṣṇa of the first section who has provided the themes that have been the most prominently depicted and represented in the devotional art forms that are so fundamental to Indian culture, not the Kṛṣṇa of the second section, or of the Mahābhārata or Bhagavad Gītā.

The term *līlā* (pastime) first surfaces in literary sources in the Vedānta Sūtra (*circa* third century CE). In II.1.33 of this work, we find the author raising and addressing an opposing atheistic view that a personal God who is in possession of everything does not create, because people create in order to attain possession of something they do not already have. The author's response to this is that 'just as [one finds] in the world, it [creation] is merely *līlā*'. The commentators on this verse compare God to a king who, although completely fulfilled, plays simply as an act of spontaneity, and not out of some hidden need. In explaining this verse, the commentator Baladeva considers God's creation to be an outpouring of joy, as when a man full of cheerfulness, upon awakening, dances without any motive or need, but simply from fullness of spirit. Unlike the term 'sport' or even 'game', then, which might contain a suggestion of drivenness or competition, *līlā* is pure play, or spontaneous pastime.

Thus, although all of God's activities, including creation, are play, the noun *līlā* is especially used in the tenth book of the Bhāgavata when God is enjoying himself as a child in the beautiful and idyllic landscape of Vraj, interacting with his friends and loved ones, free of any sense of mission or purpose. It is rarely used once Kṛṣṇa leaves Vraj and sets out to accomplish his mission and fulfil his promise to Brahmā to kill demons (although sometimes it is used in these contexts in the instrumental case[30] in the sense of 'effortlessly' or 'playfully'), and it is never used in the Bhagavad Gītā. The Gītā gives us Kṛṣṇa as God in the role of teacher imparting spiritual knowledge to humanity, while the Mahābhārata presents Kṛṣṇa as God in the role of diplomat scheming to bring about the destruction of the hosts of unruly armies, which had become a burden on the earth; both depict God with a mission. The Vraj section of Book X presents us with a description of God at play, God with no agenda other than to engage in *līlā* with his most intimate devotees. This observation is further reinforced if we consider the eight or so usages of the word *vihāra*, 'pastime' or 'pleasure', in Book X, all of which occur only in the Vraj section.

This is not to say that demons are not killed by Kṛṣṇa in Vraj in the first part of Book X. But the demons that meet their fate here are intruders into the Kṛṣṇa realm of play – they are not sought after by Kṛṣṇa. With murderous intent they disrupt Kṛṣṇa's carefree frolics in the groves of Vraj and hence are spontaneously killed by the Lord. There are no weapons involved. Moreover, most of the demons that enter Vraj assume the appearance of animals that take enormous forms – Vatsa is a calf, Baka a crane, Agha a serpent, Dhenuka an ass, Kāliya a sea-serpent, and Keśī a horse. Other demons take the form of a witch disguised as a beautiful woman (Pūtanā), of a whirlwind (Tṛṇāvarta), and of a fellow cowherd boy (Pralamba) – all forms that might arise in the imagination of a child. This is in contrast to most of the demons killed later by the adult Kṛṣṇa outside of Vraj, who are kings. Moreover, unlike in Vraj, Kṛṣṇa goes out of his way to seek confrontation with these demons on the battlefield in the second section of Book X, and the showers of weapons released in these encounters closely echo the martial exchanges of the Mahābhārata. The hostile intrusions in Vraj, by contrast, become an extension of Kṛṣṇa's play, and the instrumental form *līlayā* is often used to describe the manner in which Kṛṣṇa playfully rescues his friends from the evil intentions of these demons, whom he effortlessly kills.

A number of the usages of the noun *līlā* in the tenth book, inform the reader that the Lord has assumed a body for the sake of *līlā* (X.23.37; X.45.44; X.52.36; X.58.37). There is no other reason for the Lord's activities in the world than his voluntary decision to engage in pastimes. In this he is different from the *jīvas*, the souls in the world who are helplessly injected into bodies as a result of their *karma*, the reactions to actions performed in previous lives,[31] and who are propelled along by forces beyond their control. This point is continually reinforced throughout the text. At the same time, it is also declared repeatedly that the Lord is *āptarāma*, self-satisfied. The Bhāgavata resonates with the discussion of the Vedāntīs in insisting that God is complete and requires nothing. His decision to engage in *līlā*, then, does not point to a lack or need – it is an expression of his blissful nature. This is not to say that God does not enjoy himself – chapter 33, verse 23 tells us that although Kṛṣṇa is *svaratiḥ*, 'one whose pleasure is self-contained', he still takes pleasure from his *līlā*. Moreover, we are informed that his *līlā* gives pleasure to those devoted to him – the residents of Vraj, including the livestock (X.23.36), the cowherd boys who accompany him on his adventures in the forests (X.12.3), and the elderly *gopīs* who enjoy themselves watching and laughing at his childhood *līlā* (X.8.24). Kṛṣṇa's *līlā* enchants the residents of Vraj (X.8.52). *Līlā*, then, is an opportunity for Kṛṣṇa and his devotees to enjoy themselves in the blissful and spontaneous reciprocation of love.

The great fortune of the residents of Vraj who were able to engage so intimately with Kṛṣṇa in his *līlā* is another theme that surfaces prominently throughout the text; to be an intimate associate of God, particularly one with the intensity of love exhibited by the *gopīs*, is the highest possible perfection of human existence in the Bhāgavata (X.47.58). The ecstatic states of love experienced by the dwellers of Vraj are not paralleled anywhere else in the text; the adult post-Vraj relationships of Kṛṣṇa with his other devotees seem quite formal in contrast. Not surprisingly, the opportunity to participate in *līlā* with God, particularly the Vraj *līlā*, is hard-earned: in their previous lives Kṛṣṇa's parents, Devakī and Vasudeva, worshipped Kṛṣṇa for 12,000 years in order to obtain him as their son, undertaking intensely austere practices by enduring extremes of temperature and subsisting on only leaves and wind (X.3.32–8). The cowherd boys who had the opportunity to roam about with Kṛṣṇa 'had accumulated an abundance of merit' (X.12.11), and the author of the Bhāgavata cannot even describe the penance that must have previously been performed by the queens of Dvārakā who were able to massage Kṛṣṇa's feet (X.90.27). Consequently, the residents of Vraj are the ultimate role models for the devotional path of *bhakti yoga*: on seeing the intense devotion of Kṛṣṇa's devotees, Uddhava yearns to be a shrub or plant in Vraj, so that he might come in contact with the dust of their feet (X.47.61). Entrance into the *līlā*, then, is the supreme goal of life for the Bhāgavata school, a goal unobtainable to all except God's highest and most intimate devotees. The text repeatedly tells us that he who is beyond the reach of the greatest of *yogīs* (X.9.9) is bound by the love of the residents of Vraj even to the point that, 'like a wooden puppet, he was controlled by them' (X.11.7).

Yogamāyā

A further term essential to a discussion of *līlā* is *yogamāyā*, the power of 'divine illusion'. The unqualified term *māyā*, in the Bhāgavata, is generally used in the same way that it is used in the Gītā (VII.14), and in Hindu thought in general, namely, the illusory power that keeps the *jīva* souls bewildered by the sense objects of this world and ensnared in *saṃsāra*, the cycle of birth and death, by their *karma*, or reactions to their previous actions (X.40.23). As we find extensively in Hindu philosophical discourse, the bonds of illusion are typically articulated in terms of attachment to one's body, home, wealth, spouse and offspring (X.48.27; X.60.52; X.63.40). *Māyā* is the force that prevents the *jīva* souls from realizing their true nature as *ātmā*, pure eternal consciousness,[32] and diverts them into identifying with their external bodily covering as well as with the things of this world as objects of desire (X.14.44; X.51.46; X.70.28). As in the Gītā (IX.10), the Bhāgavata specifically and repeatedly subordinates this *māyā* to Kṛṣṇa – it is his *śakti*, power, a force subservient to his will.[33] In consonance with much of the Hindu tradition in general, then, the Bhāgavata portrays *māyā* in negative terms as the ultimate source and cause of bondage of the soul, and, consequently, of all the sufferings of the world.

Māyā has another face in the Bhāgavata, however. This role of *māyā* is especially represented by the name *yogamāyā*.[34] In contrast with the term *māyā*, which is generally used in connection with the *saṃsāric* world, *yogamāyā* is a term that only occurs in the context of Kṛṣṇa's *līlā*. In her personified form, *yogamāyā* is sent by Viṣṇu at the beginning of Book X to help his *līlā* by taking birth in Vraj as his sister (X.2.7). But more importantly, in another capacity, she covers the pure liberated souls participating in the *līlā* with her power of illusion so that they do not perceive Kṛṣṇa as God, but rather as their friend, lover or child, etc. Were *yogamāyā* not to extend her influence in this way, the souls would realize Kṛṣṇa's true nature and consequently be incapable of interacting with him in *līlā* in these intimate modes. Kṛṣṇa relishes these personal associations far more than the conventional formal worship in awe and reverence that results from the awareness of his position as Lord and creator of everything. It is *yogamāyā* who ensures, with her illusory spell, that the *jīvas* in Kṛṣṇa's *līlā* remain unaware of Kṛṣṇa's real nature (X.11.2ff.; X.16.14; X.20.2; X.42.22; X.61.2).[35] Indeed, even Kṛṣṇa himself becomes so involved in his *līlā* that he sometimes seems to prefer to forget his own supremacy (X.12.27–8; X.70.47; X.77.23 and 28).[36] To put it differently, how could God truly play spontaneously and unceremoniously with anyone in the role of a son or friend, if everyone knew he was really God?

Unlike that of her *saṃsāric* counter-role as *māyā*, *yogamāyā*'s power of illusion, then, is a highly desirable and positive one experienced only by the highest *yogīs*. Indeed, the text suggests that Kṛṣṇa's incarnation has, in reality, two motives: one is the 'official' motive expressed in the Mahābhārata, the Gītā and the opening verses of the first book of the Bhāgavata, namely, to protect the righteous and free the earth from the intolerable build-up of demoniac military power. The other is to attract the souls lost in *saṃsāra* to the beauty of *līlā* with God, and thus entice them to relinquish their attachment to the self-centred indulgences of this world of *saṃsāra*, which simply perpetuate the cycle of *karma*, and thus of repeated birth and death (XI.1.6–7).

As both personality and power, *yogamāyā* serves Kṛṣṇa during his *līlās* in this world (and, according to the medieval commentators, in the *brahman* world of Goloka as well),[37] and it is clear that her influence is a positive and highly desirable one. Although even great *ṛṣis* (sages) are anxious to *avoid* the illusory power of the conventional *saṃsāric māyā*, the greatest sage of all, Nārada, by contrast, is very eager to *experience* the power of the divine *yogamāyā* (X.69.19ff.). While the regular *māyā* can only *disappear* by devotion to Kṛṣṇa, the divine *yogamāyā* can only *appear* by devotion to Kṛṣṇa (X.69.38). Just as entrance to the mundane world of *saṃsāra*, an undesirable state of affairs, depends on the pure knowledge of the *jīva* being enveloped by the influence of the *saṃsāric māyā*, entrance into the transcendent world of *līlā*, a desirable state of affairs, depends on the pure knowledge of the *jīva* being enveloped by the influence of the divine *yogamāyā*.

The Bhāgavata vividly illustrates *yogamāyā*'s essential role in the world of *līlā* when Kṛṣṇa's foster-mother, Yaśodā, looks into her son's mouth to see if he has eaten dirt, but sees the entire universe there instead (X.8.36). Becoming enlightened as to the real nature of both herself and Kṛṣṇa, she immediately loses her ability to interact with him as his mother and begins to bow down at his feet, spout Vedāntic-type philosophy, and eulogize him (X.8.40ff.). Kṛṣṇa immediately deludes her with his *yogamāyā*, causing her to lose her memory of the event so that she can again place him on her lap and continue with her maternal duties. He does the same to his real parents, Vasudeva and Devakī, after they too had become aware of his supremacy (X.45.1). Kṛṣṇa doesn't want to be God all the time, he wants to enjoy *līlā* with his friends as an equal, or with his parents as a subordinate. As the text puts it: 'For those who could understand, *Bhagavān* Kṛṣṇa manifested the condition of [submitting] himself to the control of his dependants in this world' (X.11.9).

Being subject to the influence of *yogamāyā* and hence able to play such intimate roles in God's *līlā*, then, is the highest and rarest boon of human existence. The text repeatedly states that not even the gods, or most elevated personalities, or even Viṣṇu's eternal consort, the goddess of fortune herself, enjoy the grace bestowed on the residents of Vraj (X.9.20). Kṛṣṇa's foster-mother Yaśodā was able to chase Kṛṣṇa in anger, to spank him whom the greatest *yogīs* of all cannot reach even in their minds (X.9.9). So elevated are the residents of Vraj that Kṛṣṇa himself becomes subservient to them, 'like a wooden puppet, . . . controlled by them' (11.7). They are able to see Kṛṣṇa, whom *yogīs* cannot reach even after many births of austere disciplines

(X.12.12). All this is possible by the power of *yogamāyā*. Without her, there could be no *līlā*.

The *Yoga* of the Bhāgavata

Kṛṣṇa's *līlā* extends beyond the actual acts performed by Kṛṣṇa. Meditating upon his *līlā* is a process of *yoga*, 'union with the divine'.[38] Five of the seventeen verses where the term *līlā* is used in Book X as a noun occur in the context of the residents of Vraj singing about Kṛṣṇa's *līlā*.[39] Hearing, singing about and meditating upon Kṛṣṇa's *līlā* are the primary *yogic* activities in the Bhāgavata school and, indeed, head the list of the nine standard processes of *bhakti yoga*, the *yoga* of devotion, outlined in Book VII: hearing about Kṛṣṇa, singing about him, remembering him, serving him, worshipping him, making obeisance to him, dedicating all one's actions to him, confiding in him as a friend, and offering one's body and belongings to his service (VII.5.23–4).[40] The entire Bhāgavata Purāṇa is recited because Parīkṣit, who had seven days to live, asked Śuka what a person on the point of death should hear, chant and remember (I.19.38); the answer is the chanting of Kṛṣṇa's names (II.1.11), and meditation upon his personal form (II.1.19). *Bhakti yoga* involves immersing the mind and senses in God; meditation, in this school, does not involve the withdrawal of the senses from their sense objects, or stilling the mind in the manner outlined in the Yoga Sūtras of Patañjali, the founder of one of the six classical schools of orthodox Indic thought.[41]

In Patañjali's yoga system, it is only when distractions from the external objects of the senses are eliminated and internal thoughts stilled that the soul, which is distinct from both the sensual body and the internal mind, can realize itself as pure awareness. *Bhakti yoga*, in contrast, involves saturating the senses with objects connected with Kṛṣṇa's *līlā*, and constantly filling the mind with thoughts of him. It is a process that transforms the focus of the mind and senses, rather than attempting to shut them down, and a saint is one whose mind and senses are used in this fashion (X.13.2). Singing and hearing about Kṛṣṇa's *līlā* with the sense organs of the tongue and the ear are two prime activities in this regard, and the residents of Vraj are constantly engaged in this type of *bhakti yoga*. In fact, in the present world age of *kaliyuga*, the recommended process for worshipping God, *Bhagavān*, is the chanting and hearing of his name (XI.5.24). Indeed, for hundreds of years Kṛṣṇa's names have been recited repetitively all over the Indian subcontinent, either in unison with others, or in personal *mantra* meditation.[42] According to the Bhāgavata, although the present age of *kaliyuga* is a 'storehouse of faults', it has one major redeeming quality: by simply chanting about Kṛṣṇa, one is freed from self-centred attachments, and can attain the highest destination (XII.3.51).

In addition to chanting Kṛṣṇa's name, by simply hearing the stories about Kṛṣṇa one overcomes ignorance (XI.6.48–9), forgets oneself (X.90.46), rejects all other desires (XI.6.44) and attains love for Kṛṣṇa (X.6.44). Echoing the Gītā (VIII.6–7), the Bhāgavata states that anyone whose mind is absorbed in Kṛṣṇa's feet is liberated from the material world at the time of death (X.2.37; X.90.50), does not experience suffering while still within it (X.11.58; X.87.40) and ultimately attains Kṛṣṇa's abode (X.90.50). More than this, those who are absorbed in this way are so satisfied that they do not even desire Kṛṣṇa's abode, let alone Brahmā's position, universal sovereignty or kingship (X.83.41–2). The stories of Kṛṣṇa's *līlā*, even if recited in the household, vanquish lust from the heart (X.33.39), purify (X.15.41), award the highest devotion (XI.31.28) and conquer even the unconquerable Lord (X.14.3). This practice was followed by the great *yogīs* of the past (X.14.5), and anyone rejecting this path toils uselessly (X.14.4). Even Kaṃsa, Kṛṣṇa's mortal enemy, 'whether sitting, resting, eating or moving about the land . . . thought of . . . Kṛṣṇa. He saw the whole universe as pervaded by Kṛṣṇa' (X.2.24). As a result of this, he attained liberation (X.44.39). The highest meditation and goal of life is total absorption in God – even if this is generated out of animosity: 'Those who always dedicate their desire, anger, fear, affection, sense of identity and friendship to Hari [Kṛṣṇa] enter for certain into his state of being' (X.29.15).

After Kṛṣṇa had departed from Vraj, the *gopīs* imitated his *līlā*. In this episode of the text, the *gopīs* used their entire bodies to enact dramas of Kṛṣṇa's pastimes as a result of their perpetual meditation on Kṛṣṇa. In the madness of their love, their acting was not conscious or staged but a spontaneous and irrepressible bodily exhibition of their absolute absorption in thoughts of their Lord, to the amazement of Uddhava, the messenger sent to them by Kṛṣṇa (X.30.14). It is this type of devotional *yoga* – hearing, chanting, imitating and acting the *līlā*, especially of Kṛṣṇa and Rāma, but also of Śiva and Devī, the goddess – that remains the most visible form of Hinduism. It is *bhakti yoga* as evidenced especially in the Bhāgavata and Rāmāyaṇa, but also in the Mahābhārata and other Purāṇas, that has most prominently defined the aesthetic character of Hindu culture in the form of the devotional poetry, drama, dance performances, art, iconography and temple worship of the subcontinent over the centuries.

In the first book of the Bhāgavata, the text is presented as the sun, arisen after Kṛṣṇa departed to his abode, 'for all those who have lost their sight' (I.3.45). A verse in the section of the Padma Purāṇa called the Bhāgavata Māhātmya, 'Glorification of the Bhāgavata', states that the Bhāgavata is the Lord himself in this world (VI.193.20). In other words, the Bhāgavata is a literary substitute for Kṛṣṇa, and by reading, hearing and reciting the text itself one is interacting directly with God. Indeed, the Bhāgavata goes to great lengths to reinforce the point that hearing, chanting and meditating about Kṛṣṇa in his absence are as potent as interacting with Kṛṣṇa in person; Kṛṣṇa goes so far as to attempt to discourage the *gopīs* from personally meeting with him in favour of engaging in *bhakti yoga* at home: 'Love for me comes from hearing about me, seeing me, meditating on me and reciting my glories – not, in this way, by physical proximity. Therefore, return to your homes' (X.29.27). Indeed, Kṛṣṇa later states that the *gopīs* who had been prevented from meeting him in the forest were especially fortunate, because they were united with him by meditating upon him apart, with complete absorption, while those whose lover was on hand did not do so (X.47.35). The importance of meditating upon the stories of the Bhāgavata in isolation is underscored by the fact that the last verse of Book X ends with the following message:

> Therefore, one desiring to surrender to the feet of Kṛṣṇa, the best of the Yadus, should listen to the deeds of the supreme one who has assumed *līlā* forms . . . These deeds destroy *karma* . . .
>
> By thinking about, reciting and hearing the beautiful stories of Mukunda [Kṛṣṇa], which constantly become more in number, a person [attains to] his incomparable abode, and overcomes death. Even rulers of the earth left their communities to go into the forest for this purpose. (X.90.49–50)

Likewise, Book XI, which concludes the narration of the Kṛṣṇa story, ends with the same message in its final verse: 'In conclusion, anyone who recites the delightful deeds of the incarnations of Hari, *Bhagavān* [Kṛṣṇa], and the most auspicious stories of his childhood as are described here and in other sources, achieves the highest devotion for Kṛṣṇa, who is the goal of swan-like devotees' (XI.31.28). The entire Purāṇa concludes by stating that anyone born after the departure of Kṛṣṇa to his abode who is fortunate enough to interact with the Bhāgavata Purāṇa with a devotional attitude will attain the same liberation as those who were fortunate enough to interact with Kṛṣṇa when he was personally present on earth (XII.13.18). By reading, discussing, reciting and meditating upon the Bhāgavata, one can experience the same states of mind as those attained by the actual residents of Vraj in Kṛṣṇa's presence, and reach the same ultimate destination. The text thus presents itself as a fully empowered literary incarnation of Kṛṣṇa for all future generations.

If continuous immersion in Kṛṣṇa's *līlā*, either directly or through the practice of *bhakti* meditation, is the goal of *yoga* and therefore of human life, what experience does this produce? The text is littered with terms such as *paramamudā*, *paramānanda* and *paramāhlāda*, the extremes of bliss experienced by Kṛṣṇa's devotees in their encounters with Kṛṣṇa. Simply from seeing Kṛṣṇa, his devotees are thrown into uncontrollable states of ecstasy, their eyes overflow with tears, and their body hairs stand on end (X.38.26; X.38.35; X.41.28; X.71.25). Bliss spreads throughout the three worlds (X.27.25), and, in some of the most beautiful verses of the text, even the natural world is thrown into a stunned rapture simply by the sound of Kṛṣṇa's flute:

> O *gopīs* . . . The rivers manifest bliss through their surfaces, and the trees shed tears . . .
>
> The cows, their ears pricked, were also drinking the nectar of the flute music coming from Kṛṣṇa's mouth. The calves stood transfixed with their mouths full of milk from the dripping udders. With tears in their eyes, they embraced Govinda [Kṛṣṇa] within their hearts . . .
>
> The rivers found their force disrupted by their state of mind after hearing the sound of Mukunda's [Kṛṣṇa's] flute, as could be seen from their whirlpools. Bearing offerings of lotus flowers, they grasped the two lotus feet of Murāri [Kṛṣṇa] and embraced them closely with their arms in the forms of waves . . .
>
> O girlfriends, when those two [Kṛṣṇa and his brother], conspicuous by their cords and ropes for tying cows, lead the cows and cowherd boys into nearby forests, those embodied beings who are capable of movement are made motionless by the sounds of that renowned flute, with its sweet harmonies. The trees bristle with ecstasy – it is a wonderful thing. (X.21.9–19; see also X.35.4–9)

When Nārada entered one of Kṛṣṇa palaces, it was as if he had entered the bliss of *brahman*. Kṛṣṇa, after all, is *brahman*, the supreme bliss (X.12.11). This rapturous experience is not available only for those fortunate enough to have been born during Kṛṣṇa's incarnation, but also for anyone immersed in thought of Kṛṣṇa – Śuka, the narrator of the Bhāgavata, enters into a state of ecstatic trance simply from remembering Kṛṣṇa when questioned by king Parīkṣit (X.12.44). The experience of *bhakti yoga* is not the detached self-awareness of *puruṣa* (*ātmā*),[43] devoid of content, that is indicated in Patañjali's Yoga Sūtras. It is continuous blissful immersion in God's *līlā*, either directly by the inhabitants of Vraj, or, in Kṛṣṇa's absence, through meditation on his *līlā* as described in the Bhāgavata, and through the repetition of his name.

Ultimately, however, *bhakti yoga* is a religion of surrender and grace. Whenever the residents of Vraj encounter any difficulty, they instantly take complete refuge in Kṛṣṇa and receive full protection. When the Vraj community was being inundated with cataclysmic rain by an infuriated Indra, king of the celestials, their reaction was immediate: '"Kṛṣṇa, most virtuous Kṛṣṇa, master – you are compassionate towards your devotees. Please protect Gokula, which accepts you as Lord, from the wrath of this divinity"' (X.25.13). When Kṛṣṇa's *gopa* friends encountered the huge demon Agha stretched out on the ground preparing to devour them with his massive gaping jaws, their innocent sense of assurance in Kṛṣṇa's complete protection is absolute: '"Will it devour us as we enter it? If so, it will be destroyed in an instant by Kṛṣṇa as Baka [the crane demon] was." Thinking thus, the boys glanced at the beautiful face of Kṛṣṇa, the enemy of Baka, and ventured in, laughing and clapping their hands' (X.12.24).

Kṛṣṇa not only protects his devotees from physical dangers, but delivers them from the clutches of *māyā* (illusion). Hearing and chanting about Kṛṣṇa purify the devotee and free him or her from the sufferings of *saṃsāra* because Kṛṣṇa is situated in the heart of the devotee and it is he who 'cleanses away all inauspicious things' (I.2.17). Unlike the Pātañjalian system where *samādhi*, the enlightened state, can be obtained by the personal prowess of the meditator, the Bhāgavata advocates a grace-based system: it is Kṛṣṇa who bestows liberation (X.60.52). But, more important than liberation, it is devotion, the ultimate goal for the human soul, that is bestowed by Kṛṣṇa. The Bhāgavata does not deny that the individual *ātmā* (the innermost self) can be realized through the mechanical self-discipline of Pātañjalian-type practice, but the supreme self, Kṛṣṇa, God himself, can only be attained by devotion, surrender and grace. Even the mighty Brahmā himself, the most powerful *jīva* soul in the universe, notes that 'one who has received even a trace of grace from your two lotus feet understands the nature of the greatness of God, *Bhagavān*; no other individual will do so, despite searching at length.' He prays that 'either in this life, or in another, or in one among the animals, may that great fortune occur through which I, though just an individual, may become one of your devotees, and worship your blossom-like feet' (X.14.29–30). Without such devotion and grace, the *yogīs* with controlled minds cannot obtain the dust from Kṛṣṇa's lotus feet even after many births of discipline and austerities (X.12.12); on the other hand, one who has attained this dust does not desire the mystic powers of *yoga*, freedom from rebirth or even the highest situation of Brahmā (X.16.37).

It is important to bear in mind that the devotees of Kṛṣṇa have no desire for liberation or self-realization, but are fully satisfied with their immersion in the stories of Kṛṣṇa's *līlā* (X.87.21). There are five types of liberation in Bhāgavata theology,[44] but pure devotion entails renouncing even the desire for these. And as was discussed above, even those who are self-realized – like Śuka, the narrator of the Bhāgavata, and other sages who have realized the *ātmā* – are attracted to Kṛṣṇa. In other words, if one is not a devotee and has not received the Lord's grace one can be self-realized and liberated (that is, be fully immersed in the pure awareness of the *ātmā* [soul] and thus detached from the cycle of *saṃsāra* and situated in *brahman*), without knowing anything about the personal aspect of Kṛṣṇa. Therefore, as will be discussed further in the next section, *brahman*, for the Bhāgavata, is multi-dimensional and not a monolithic or standardized experience for all *yogīs*.

A conspicuous symbol of the concomitant notions of surrender and grace in the Bhāgavata, as illustrated in Brahmā's prayers above, is that surrender is often directed to Kṛṣṇa's lotus feet. Kṛṣṇa's feet are present within the hearts of his devotees (X.6.37). They are the object of the devotees' meditation (X.72.4), and of that of the *yogīs* (X.38.6). People cross over this world of darkness through the lustre of the nails of his feet (X.38.7). They purify the three worlds (X.48.25), and are worshipped by all the major deities (X.38.8; X.38.25; X.69.18).

Those who have attained their shelter desire neither universal sovereignty, nor mystic power, nor even liberation (X.16.37). Even Kṛṣṇa's own consort, the goddess of fortune, undertakes austere disciplines to achieve Kṛṣṇa's lotus feet (X.16.36). What is considered the lowest part of the anatomy in India, the polluted feet, becomes the most desired and esteemed part in the case of God, thus stressing his absolute and complete purity and auspiciousness.

Another striking feature of the *yoga* of Book X is that not only are Kṛṣṇa's devotees awarded liberation, but so too are his enemies. Pūtanā, a devourer of children, attained liberation because she offered her breast to Kṛṣṇa, even though she had smeared it with poison in an attempt to murder him (X.6.35). When the serpent demon Agha was killed, 'an amazing great light rose up from the thick coils of the snake, illuminating the ten directions with its splendour. It waited in the sky for the Lord to emerge, and then entered into him before the very eyes of the residents of the celestial realms' (X.12.33). The same happens with demons such as Śiśupāla (X.74.45) and Dantavakra (X.78.9–10). Kṛṣṇa's mortal enemy Pauṇḍraka, like Kaṃsa, had his bondage destroyed 'through his unceasing meditation on *Bhagavān*'. He was awarded the liberation known as *sārūpya*, having the same form as the Lord, simply by coming into contact with Kṛṣṇa, because 'even Kṛṣṇa's sworn enemies, attain the highest destination' (X.66.24; X.87.23). Not surprisingly, if even those inimical to Kṛṣṇa are involuntarily liberated just by coming into contact with him, irrespective of their motives, then, as will be discussed in the section on the sociology of the Bhāgavata, anyone and everyone is eligible to engage voluntarily in the process of *bhakti yoga* and attain the goal of pure devotion, irrespective of caste, social status, race or gender.

Kṛṣṇa's Form and Abode

Of great importance to the compiler of Book X of the Bhāgavata, given the authoritative nature of the Upaniṣads (the earliest philosophical texts of the late Vedic period) and the Vedānta Sūtras (one of the six classical treatises of orthodox Indic philosophy), is to stress that Kṛṣṇa is *brahman*, the term given in these sources to the absolute truth beyond matter (X.3.13; X.10.33; X.13.61; X.14.32, etc.). The text also states that Kṛṣṇa's body is not made of the elements of *prakṛti* (matter) like the forms of this world (X.14.2). Kṛṣṇa is beyond the permutations of the *guṇas*, which, as will be discussed in detail in the next section, are the activating forces and essential ingredients in the production of the *prakṛtic* bodies of earth, water, fire, air and ether (X.3.19; X.3.24; X.27.4; X.29.14, etc.). Although *brahman* is acknowledged as being beyond matter and thought, and thus beyond description and conceptualization, Hindu texts such as the Bhāgavata attempt to illustrate it by such words as *sat*, *cit*, *ānanda* (eternity, knowledge and bliss) (X.3.24; X.13.54; X.14.22; X.38.7).

It is also important, here, to note that the tenth book of the Bhāgavata does not present Kṛṣṇa's form or personal characteristics as secondary derivations from a higher impersonal absolute. It is never stated that Kṛṣṇa's form and personality ultimately merge or dissolve into some supreme formless truth devoid of personality and qualities; after he had completed his mission on earth, Kṛṣṇa returned to his abode in his same body. While *brahman* is described in the usual impersonal Upaniṣadic phraseology in many sections of the text, particularly in the earlier books, the indications from the tenth book are that *brahman* also contains an eternal personal element, a realm where Kṛṣṇa and his form are eternal.

The transcendent abode of Kṛṣṇa is not described in detail in the tenth book, even though Kṛṣṇa reveals it to the *gopas* (X.28.14), but we are told that it is beyond darkness, and is pure, eternal, unlimited, conscious and effulgent *brahman*. Kṛṣṇa is worshipped there by the Vedic hymns, and the *gopas* were overwhelmed with the highest ecstasy upon seeing it (X.28.14–17). Elsewhere in the Bhāgavata, the text speaks of Vaikuṇṭha, adorable to all the worlds (X.12.26), as the highest realm where Viṣṇu resides (XII.24.14). This, too, is the highest region (IV.12.26); beyond the world of darkness and *saṃsāra* (the cycle of birth and death) (IV.24.29; X.88.25); the destination of those who have transcended the three *guṇas* (see p. xl), even while they are still alive (XI.25.22); and beyond which there is no higher place (II.2.18; II.9.9). The peaceful ascetics who reach that place never return (IV.9.29; X.88.25–6). The residents of Vaikuṇṭha do not have material bodies, but have pure forms (VII.1.34). These forms are like that of Viṣṇu (III.15.14ff.), also known as Nārāyaṇa. Viṣṇu/Nārāyaṇa resides in Vaikuṇṭha with Śrī, the goddess of fortune, in palaces with crystal walls. The parks there shine like final liberation itself, and contain wish-fulfilling trees,[45] which blossom all the year round. There are fragrant winds, and creepers dripping with honey near bodies of water. Cries of exotic birds mingle with the humming of bees, and magnificent flowers bloom everywhere. Devotees of Viṣṇu along with their beautiful wives travel in aerial vehicles[46] made of jewels, emeralds and gold, but the beautiful smiling residents of this realm cannot distract the minds of the opposite sex, since everyone is absorbed in Kṛṣṇa (III.15.14–25).

The text says nothing about a separate realm called Goloka within *brahman*, exclusive to Kṛṣṇa himself as the Kṛṣṇa-based sects believe (the Viṣṇu-centred Vaiṣṇava sects would say Kṛṣṇa is the immanent aspect of Viṣṇu when he incarnates on earth, and who otherwise resides in Vaikuṇṭha in his transcendent aspect as Viṣṇu). However, all Vaiṣṇava commentators unanimously agree that Viṣṇu/Kṛṣṇa is an eternal transcendent being whose body is made of *brahman*, and who resides in an eternal personal *brahman* abode with his devotees. As will be discussed in the next section, they also agree that this personal aspect of *brahman* is the highest dimension of absolute truth, and not secondary to or derivative from some higher non-personal truth, a view that can be supported by the Bhāgavata. The text also speaks of Kṛṣṇa eternally residing on earth in Mathurā (X.1.28), where he took birth during his incarnation; as well as Dvārakā (XI.31.24), the city he established as his capital when on earth. These statements inform Vaiṣṇava belief that Kṛṣṇa's abode is not only in a transcendent *brahman* realm, but also simultaneously in the places where he enacted his *līlā* pastimes in this world (and hence it is highly desirable for aspiring devotees to live in such places, XI.29.10).

Kṛṣṇa, then, is presented in the Bhāgavata as the absolute and ultimate Godhead who descends from his eternal realm and enjoys *līlā* in this world with his intimate associates while also accomplishing his mission on earth. While the Bhāgavata introduces some unique theological concepts to the religious landscape of Purāṇic Hinduism, it is also very consciously appropriating established philosophical categories and vocabulary to do so. There are entire sections of the Bhāgavata dedicated to metaphysical exposition, and even the playful narratives of the tenth book are permeated with technical philosophical discourse. The author of the Bhāgavata is deeply schooled in Hindu thought and, as will be outlined below, devotes a good deal of attention and energy to grafting the theological Kṛṣṇa on to a metaphysical infrastructure incorporating the most established and dominant schools of thought prevalent in the Epic and Purāṇic periods.

THE PHILOSOPHY OF THE BHĀGAVATA

The Bhāgavata is not only sacred history and a theological treatise, but a philosophical text. Traditional sources name six schools of thought that emerged from the Upaniṣadic period of the late Vedic age, several in tension with the other schools, and each with its own focus and preference for a certain set of metaphysical terms. A basic understanding of at least three of these, which provide terms and concepts that pervade the entire text, is unavoidable in order to understand fully the theology of the tenth book of the Bhāgavata. One of these three, the Sāṅkhya school, posited a dualistic metaphysical system in which the created world evolved out of primordial matter, *prakṛti*, from within which the *puruṣa*, or soul (corresponding more or less to the *ātmā* of the Upaniṣads and *jīva* or *dehī* of the Bhagavad Gītā), must extricate itself. Another school, Vedānta, concerned itself with the relationship between *brahman*, the supreme truth of the Upaniṣads; *ātmā*, the soul or individualized feature of *brahman*; and the perceived world as a whole. Finally, Yoga is listed as one of the six schools, although it is less a philosophical school than a practical psychosomatic technique through which the *puruṣa* (soul) can realize itself as distinct from *prakṛti* (matter).[47] The philosophy of the Bhāgavata is a mixture of Vedānta terminology and Sāṅkhya metaphysics, which will be discussed below, and devotionalized *yoga* practice, which was discussed above.

The Sāṅkhya of the Bhāgavata

Scholars hold that the Bhāgavata Purāṇa has preserved an older, more theistic Sāṅkhya than that preserved by the founder of the Sāṅkhya school, Īśvarakṛṣṇa, which took an atheistic turn.[48] The Sāṅkhya (literally 'numeration') system as outlined by Īśvarakṛṣṇa perceives reality as the product of two distinct ontological categories: *prakṛti*, or the primordial material matrix of the physical universe, and *puruṣa*, the term used in this text for the soul, or conscious innermost self. As a result of the contact between these two entities, the material universe evolves in a sequential fashion. The catalysts in this evolutionary process are the three *guṇas*, literally strands or qualities, which are inherent in *prakṛti*. These are: *sattva*, goodness; *rajas*, action; and *tamas*, inertia. These *guṇas* are mentioned frequently throughout the text, as are the various substances evolving from *prakṛti*, and thus require some attention.

In and of themselves, the *guṇas* are influences, which are usually portrayed – and perhaps most easily understood – by their psychological manifestations; Sāṅkhya is both a cosmology and a psychology. Among a number of things, *sattva*, the purest of the *guṇas* when manifested in the mind, is typically characterized by tranquillity, happiness, discernment, detachment and performance of activity out of duty rather than personal gain; *rajas*, by hankering, energetic endeavour, power and the performance of activity according to duty, but with a desire for personal gain; and *tamas*, the least desired *guṇa*, by ignorance, lack of interest, lethargy and disregard for the performance of duty and constructive activity in general. The Gītā (chapters 14, 17 and 18) presents a wide range of symptoms connected with each of these three *guṇas*.[49] In cosmological terms, *sattva* is associated with Viṣṇu and the maintenance of the universe, *rajas* with Brahmā and its creation, and *tamas* with Śiva and its destruction.[50]

In terms of the evolution of the world from *prakṛti*, the primordial material matrix, just as the three primary colours intermix to produce an unlimited variety of colours, so the activation and interaction of these *guṇa* qualities in *prakṛti* result in the production of the entirety of physical forms and psychological dispositions of all manifest reality. The evolution of the universe from *prakṛti* can perhaps be likened to the churning of milk: when milk receives a catalyst and is churned, yogurt, curds or butter are produced, and these, in turn, can be further manipulated to produce tertiary derivative products – toffee, milk desserts, cheese, etc.[51] Similarly, according to the Bhāgavata, the first substance evolving from *prakṛti* is *ahaṅkāra*, or ego. When ego is 'churned' by the *guṇa* of *sattva*, *manas* (the mind), which engages in the functions of thinking, feeling, desiring, willing and the direction and motivation of the senses, is produced. From ego stirred by *rajas* comes *buddhi* (intelligence), which produces the functions of judgement, discrimination, doubt and memory. In the Sāṅkhya of the Bhāgavata, the powers behind the five senses – sight, taste, hearing, smell and touch – and the five organs of action – hand, leg, tongue, genitals and anus – also evolve from the interaction of ego and *rajas*. From the ego stirred by *tamas*, the powers behind the five senses – sound, sight, smell, taste and touch – are produced, and these, in turn, sequentially produce the five *bhūta*, or gross elements – ether, air, fire, water and earth. The Sāṅkhya system is classified in Indian thought as *satkārya*, namely, that the effect is present in the cause. Each category, except for *puruṣa* and *prakṛti* – the ultimate causes – at one end, and the gross elements – the final products – at the other, are both evolved and evolvers: they both have a subtler cause and produce effects grosser than themselves.

There are minor differences of evolutionary sequence between the Sāṅkhya of the Bhāgavata, and the classical Sāṅkhya of Īśvarakṛṣṇa,[52] but the Bhāgavata (XI.22.2–3) recognizes several different schools of Sāṅkhya that define the categories slightly differently, so there seems to have been some taxonomical variation in circulation. A far more significant difference between the two Sāṅkhya systems is that the Bhāgavata presents a third ontological entity as the ultimate cause of both the *puruṣa* (souls) and *prakṛti* (matter) and of their union. This is *Īśvara*, God, and the text identifies this being as Kṛṣṇa. The term *Īśvara* – from the root *īś*, to have extraordinary power and sovereignty – is already used six times by the Atharvaveda, in *circa* 1000 BCE, and refers in the oldest texts to a personal but unnamed God. It is the term often preferred in philosophical discourse in debates over the validity of the concept of a personal creator and, in partial contrast to the term *Bhagavān*, is often associated more with a philosophical category in these contexts, rather than the specific personalities of supreme beings such as Viṣṇu and Kṛṣṇa. In the Bhāgavata, however, *Īśvara* is Kṛṣṇa, and it is he who propels the *puruṣa* – generally referred to as *ātmā* or *jīva* in this text – into the *prakṛtic* matrix at the beginning of each cosmic cycle, reactivating its specific *guṇa* disposition, as well as its inherited *karma* – the accumulated reactions to its previous activities – from its last birth in the previous cycle.[53]

In addition to injecting the *jīvas* into *prakṛti*, Kṛṣṇa also agitates the *guṇas* to start the evolutionary process of material creation, as discussed above, and this culminates in the various forms of the world which accommodate the myriad *jīvas*. It is Kṛṣṇa's *śakti* (power – also known as *māyā*), in the form of time, that causes the stirrings of the *guṇas*. Each *jīva* is thus provided with a particular gross body (a set of sense and action organs) and subtle body (mind, intelligence and ego) that is appropriate to the *karma* and *guṇic* disposition with which it ended its previous life. The freedom of the pure transcendent *jīva* is thus delimited and curtailed when enveloped by these two extraneous and temporary bodies. Its liberation from this encapsulation from the perspective of the Bhāgavata was discussed in the previous section.

God is not only the efficient cause of creation, but also the material cause: the *jīvas* ultimately emanate from him, as does *prakṛti*. Thus all the main ingredients of reality – time, the mover of all things; *prakṛti*, the substratum for all material creation; and the souls who activate the forms that evolve from *prakṛti* –

are all energies, powers or expansions of Kṛṣṇa. God produces everything out of himself just as a spider spins a web (II.5.5). In this sense, all that exists is a transformation of a single cause, hence the *advaita*, monistic (or, more accurately, non-dualistic) element of the text, which will be discussed below: 'From myself I create, maintain and destroy myself in myself by means of myself in the form of the *guṇas*, senses and elements, through the power of my own *māyā*' (X.47.30). The *Īśvara* of the old theistic strains in Indic thought, then, is correlated with Viṣṇu and Kṛṣṇa by Vaiṣṇava texts such as the Bhāgavata, and, as will be discussed below, these personal beings, in turn, are correlated with the highest aspect of *brahman*, the absolute truth of the Upaniṣads and Vedānta.

The Vedānta of the Bhāgavata

The Vedānta Sūtra (Veda+anta: 'conclusion of the Vedas'; Sūtra: 'threads', or aphorisms) is a text written by Bādarāyaṇa to clarify, or harmonize, the disparate and seemingly conflicting statements of the Upaniṣads, the philosophical texts of the late Vedic period (although, in a sense, it achieved the opposite effect and spawned a new era of philosophical debate among different schools). If we posit that the goal of Indian philosophy is to account for the relationship of the visible world of change, both animate and inanimate, with the ultimate and absolute reality of existence, the Vedānta discusses the relationship between *brahman*, the supreme absolute truth; *ātmā*, the soul, or individualized feature of *brahman*; and manifest material reality. But, not surprisingly, this relationship has been construed variously by the principal Vedāntic commentators. Since the Bhāgavata is considered as Vyāsa's own commentary on the Vedānta Sūtra by certain traditional commentators,[54] and the text is permeated by Vedāntic terms and concepts, a brief outline of the Vedāntic tradition is essential in attempting to understand the metaphysical infrastructure of the tenth book.

The first extant commentary on the Vedānta, that of Śaṅkara in the eighth–ninth centuries CE, posited a monistic philosophy of radical *advaita*, or non-duality. For Śaṅkara, the entire world of change is an illusory superimposition upon an unchanging, formless, qualityless and impersonal *brahman*, the ultimate reality.[55] Thus, everything in the realm of *prakṛti* is illusory, *māyā*;[56] the changing world of forms simply does not exist from the perspective of absolute reality – or, perhaps more accurately, everything that exists is in reality the changeless *brahman*. Similarly, the individuality of the *ātmā* is also illusory; there is not an infinite number of living entities: in reality there is only the undivided, all-pervading *brahman* – hence the name, *advaita*, of this school of philosophy. For Śaṅkara there is only one underlying truth and all apparent dualities perceived in existence – the world of forms and individuals – are the product of illusion, or *māyā*.

A number of later Vaiṣṇava commentators on the Vedānta Sūtra vigorously critiqued Śaṅkara's views. Rāmānuja in the twelfth century presented a position of *viśiṣṭādvaita*, 'differentiated non-duality', which modified the basic metaphysical concept of *advaita* by proposing that there were differentiations within ultimate reality. Rāmānuja posited a basic and eternal tripartite subdivision within *brahman*: *brahman* as supreme personal being, or *Īśvara*, whom he identified as Viṣṇu (also known as Nārāyaṇa); *prakṛti*; and the *jīvas*. These are eternal and real ontological categories for Rāmānuja, not illusory superimpositions on an undifferentiated *brahman*, as Śaṅkara had claimed, but they do not compromise the essential non-duality of the absolute since everything emanates from, and remains dependent upon, *brahman* as Viṣṇu. In one of Rāmānuja's analogies, the relationship of the supreme *brahman*, Viṣṇu, with *prakṛti* and *jīva* is like that of the body and the possessor of the body; although in one sense they are one, the latter is dependent upon, and supported by, the former. Madhva, in the thirteenth century (who wrote a commentary on the Bhāgavata), emphasized the divisions between these categories even further. In his system of *dvaita*, 'duality', Madhva posited five eternal and essential differences: between God and the souls, between God and matter, between souls and matter, between individual souls, and between individual atoms of matter. Both of these philosophers took great pains to oppose Śaṅkara's extreme *advaita* non-dualism. Other Vaiṣṇava commentators on the Vedānta added their particular sectarian perspectives on the issue,[57] but, despite differences of nuance, they all shared the basic position of a *brahman* which incorporated *Īśvara*, God, the supreme personal being – Viṣṇu or, depending on the sect, Kṛṣṇa – a world of matter, and eternal, subordinate individualized souls who, in the liberated state, could interact with God in devotion and service. All these commentators drew upon the Upaniṣads, the Vedānta Sūtra and the Bhagavad Gītā as sources of authority.

Some scholars have attempted to correlate the *advaita* non-duality of the Bhāgavata with that of Śaṅkara, but this may have been at the expense of other ways of reading the non-duality promoted by the text, such as those understood by the Vaiṣṇava tradition of commentary (Sheridan, 1986). The tenth book of the Bhāgavata certainly does not promote the view that *prakṛti*, the manifest world, has no ultimate reality beyond the illusion of the individual as does Śaṅkara: *prakṛti* may be illusory in the sense that the forms of the world are temporary and ultimately dissolve back into the primordial matrix, but although it may not be the ultimate or ideal situation or destination of the *jīva*, it is nevertheless very real. The relationship between God and his *śaktis* (energies), such as inanimate *prakṛti* and animate *jīva* (soul), is one of possession and dependence: God is *śaktimān*, the possessor of *śakti*, and all *śakti* is produced from him.[58]

Herein lie two fundamental differences between the *jīva* and *Īśvara*, God. *Īśvara*, who, as noted, is identified with the personal figure of Kṛṣṇa in the tenth book of the Bhāgavata, is *śaktimān*, the possessor and support of his *śakti* powers, whereas the *jīva* is a *śakti* that is supported. In other words God is independent, and both manifest reality and the *jīva*, although distinct, are dependent upon him. Rāmānuja's analogy is useful: the unit of body and soul are one, in a certain sense, but also different, the former being dependent on the latter, but not vice versa. Another major difference between the *jīva* and *Īśvara* is that the latter can never be subject to *māyā* (ignorance or illusion), whereas the *jīva* can. *Īśvara*, God, namely Kṛṣṇa – who is synonymous with *brahman* in the Bhāgavata – remains absolute and unaffected by *māyā* (X.28.6); the latter is his *śakti* power, and it can affect the recalcitrant *jīva*, but never the *śaktimān* who possesses them (X.87.38). Thus, on this level, there is a clear distinction between God himself and the souls manifested from him, even as, in so far as everything emanates from God, they are one in quality, that is, one *ātmā*. In this way, the essential non-duality of the text is not compromised, but neither is the reality of the world and the individuality of the soul denied.

An analogy that helps explain the concept of 'differentiated oneness', or 'oneness-in-difference', between God and his creations and emanations is that of the sun and sunlight. In one sense the sun and its light and heat are one, but in another they are different. We may sit on our veranda and enjoy the light and heat of the sun, but would soon be incinerated if the actual sun itself were to descend on to the veranda. The heat and light are *śaktis* (energies) of the sun, and are dependent on and produced by the sun, but the reverse is not the case. Similarly, the *jīva* and *prakṛti* are *śaktis* of God, one, yet different. One may extend the analogy further and note that the sun's energies produce clouds and fog which then obscure the sun from the vision of the creatures of the world, but the sun itself is never actually obscured. Similarly, God produces *māyā* (illusion), and this bewilders the *jīvas* of this world and prevents them from seeing God and perceiving things as they really are – emanations from God – but God himself is never actually obscured by his *māyā*.

This distinction between God and individual souls is not just maintained in the illusory embodied state, as Śaṅkara's *advaita* school and other monistic philosophies would hold,[59] but in some types of liberation as well. The great devotee Nārada, upon attaining perfection and becoming a spotless soul (*amalātmā*), gave up his body made of the material elements, and received a 'pure divine body' (I.6.29). Likewise, the child devotee Dhruva assumed a form 'brilliant like gold' before being transported to Viṣṇu's divine realm (IV.12.29). As was discussed in an earlier section (pp. xxxvii–xxxviii), Vaikuṇṭha, the pure abode of Viṣṇu beyond *saṃsāra*, is a *brahman* realm of pure non-*prakṛtic* forms[60] where the devotees and the Lord reside eternally as individuals, and this is presented as the highest destination of the human soul. From the five types of liberation in Bhāgavata theology noted earlier, four explicitly involve the maintenance of a distinct individuality. Liberation, then, in the tenth book of the Bhāgavata, as in all Vaiṣṇava traditions, is not generic or one-size-fits-all; there are options. *Sāyujya*, impersonal liberation, or dissolving one's individuality and merging into God's body,[61] is considered the lowest or least desired form of liberation by Vaiṣṇava sects. In fact, the Bhāgavata minimizes the very concept of liberation, the goal of almost all Indic philosophical traditions: those who have developed an attraction for Kṛṣṇa lose interest in personal liberation altogether (X.87.21).

In addition to the different types of liberation, there are indications in the text of different gradations of *brahman* realization as well: Śuka, the narrator of the entire Bhāgavata Purāṇa, despite being beyond all dualities and the influence of the *guṇas* and thus already a self-realized soul liberated from *saṃsāra* (I.4.4–5; II.1.9), was attracted to Kṛṣṇa's personality and activities, as were other sages who had attained the state beyond *saṃsāra* and realized their own *ātmā* (I.7.9–10; II.1.7). As was discussed earlier, the Bhāgavata does not deny that the *ātmā* can be realized through the mechanical self-discipline of *yoga* practice, but the supreme self, Kṛṣṇa, God himself, is another matter. Although ultimately non-dual, *brahman*, for the Bhāgavata, appears to be multi-dimensional; it is not a monolithic or universalized experience for all *yogīs*: 'The knowers of truth speak of that non-dual truth as *brahman* [the impersonal aspect of the absolute], *paramātmā* [the localized aspect of the absolute], and *bhagavān* [the personal aspect of the absolute]' (I.2.11). Those who have realized their own *ātmā*, and thus an aspect of *brahman* beyond *saṃsāra*, still consider the personal aspect of *brahman* as *Bhagavān* Kṛṣṇa to be higher, and yearn for it; it is Kṛṣṇa's consorts the *gopīs* who are promoted by the Bhāgavata as the highest embodied beings (X.47.58), not the liberated *yogīs* who have realized their personal *ātmās*.

Although the Bhāgavata takes an extremely non-dualistic (or monistic) tone in some passages[62] (which some see as a result of different chronological strata in the text),[63] its highest teachings are the performance of personal devotion to Kṛṣṇa both in the state of bondage and in the state of liberation. If there is any loss of the individualized self, it is not an ontological or metaphysical one, but a forgetfulness of one's own self through complete blissful absorption in meditation on God (X.90.46). *Bhakti* is not a means towards some higher monistic goal, but continues in the liberated state: the highest goal of life for the Bhāgavata is to reside as an eternal individual in an eternal divine abode, rendering loving devotion to an eternal personal supreme being, Viṣṇu/Kṛṣṇa. The distinction between God and devotee inherent in the act of devotion in liberation qualifies the text's non-dualism irrespective of any philosophical formulation.

Despite a number of passages that can be read from an *advaita* standpoint (for example III.7.6–12), a 'non-dualism-with-qualities', or 'difference-in-oneness' philosophy as proposed by the various Vaiṣṇava commentators, coupled with a plurality of eternally individual *jīvas*, is the philosophy most easily construed from the Bhāgavata as a whole, and certainly from the tenth book. However, an insistence on too specific a metaphysical system in these matters is likely to be more revelatory of the sectarian concerns of the commentator than of the author of the Bhāgavata. One would have to conclude that the philosophical specificities that became so important to later Vedāntic exegesis were not of such importance to the final redactor of the Bhāgavata. As we have seen, later Vaiṣṇava scholastics attempted a coherent philosophical understanding of this paradox of difference-in-oneness and, depending on the predilection of the interpreter, a system of 'qualified non-dualism', 'dualism in non-dualism', outright 'dualism', 'pure non-dualism' or 'inconceivable difference-in-identity' was the result. While the exact sectarian specifics of these various interpretations may not be explicit in the Bhāgavata itself, their basic thrust is certainly more compatible with the general philosophy of the text than is the philosophy of Śaṅkara. The *māyā* doctrine of Śaṅkara was undoubtedly a major influence on all the Vaiṣṇava commentators themselves, since they all post-dated Śaṅkara and united in opposition to it, but the doctrine is alien to the text itself. Moreover, the very fact that almost all of the eighty-one commentators on the Bhāgavata have read the text from the perspective of one of the 'difference-in-identity' viewpoints speaks for itself (although the most influential of the commentators, Śrīdhara, in the fourteenth century, whose commentary is drawn on in the present translation, was in point of fact aligned with the *advaita* non-dualist school, even if he softened and devotionalized his non-dualist approach in the Bhāgavata).

In conclusion, then, the tenth book co-opts Vedāntic, Sāṅkhyan and Yogic terms and categories in promoting the person *Īśvara*, *Bhagavān* Kṛṣṇa, as the highest, absolute aspect of *brahman*. The theological Kṛṣṇa is thus embedded in a sophisticated philosophical treatise. That the endeavours of the author were successful in bolstering Kṛṣṇa's claim to supremacy by appropriating the metaphysical tools of the day is amply evidenced by the widespread popularity of this Purāṇa. Unlike most philosophical texts, however, which were typically the exclusive prerogative of the intellectuals among the elite *brāhmaṇa* priestly caste, it is the Bhāgavata's universal message that, as will be discussed below, has been especially instrumental in generating the immense appeal which the text still enjoys.

THE SOCIOLOGY OF *BHAKTI* IN THE BHĀGAVATA

The tenth book of the Bhāgavata, like the Gītā (IV.13), does not question the validity of the *varṇa* social system in terms of its everyday functional value (X.24.20; X.80.33). The *varṇa* system consisted of four occupations: that of the *brāhmaṇas*, a caste of teachers, priests and scholars; of the *kṣatriyas*, a caste of warriors and administrators; of the *vaiśyas*, a caste of merchants and landowners; and of the *śūdras*, a caste of labourers. The gender and caste affiliation of the redactor of the text is not in doubt. Apart from the fact that the Sanskrit literati were *a priori* male *brāhmaṇas* (and the author of the Bhāgavata is particularly conspicuous in the Purāṇic genre in terms of his erudition), the *brāhmaṇas* are presented as the most exalted individuals in the Bhāgavata, at least in terms of the conventional *varṇa* social order. Kṛṣṇa himself says in the tenth book that he repeatedly offers homage to the *brāhmaṇa* caste, since they are the best friends of living entities (X.52.33). Moreover, Kṛṣṇa is the foremost of those devoted to *brāhmaṇas*, for they are the source of scripture and thus of his very abode (X.84.20). Indeed, the *brāhmaṇas* are the masters of himself, Kṛṣṇa, the highest deity (X.81.39), and dearer than his own four-armed form (X.81.39; X.86.54). Thus the Bhāgavata prioritizes and idealizes the *brāhmaṇa* caste in a number of passages.[64]

The *kṣatriyas* are portrayed as useful and dear to Kṛṣṇa when they use their perishable bodies in the service of the *brāhmaṇas* (X.72.26), and when the citizens within their domains are protected and happy (X.73.21). But the text has a more ambiguous opinion of this caste, and warns against the illusory nature of hankering after kingdoms and profit, against the cruelty inflicted by kings on their citizens in their quest for personal aggrandizement, against the tendency of royal opulence to ensnare kings in *māyā*, and against the inclination of kings towards pride (X.73.10–14).[65] Overall, like the Purāṇic genre in general (and, for that matter, most Sanskrit literature), the stories in the tenth book are centred in the idealized world and lifestyles of the *brāhmaṇas* and *brāhmaṇa*-friendly *kṣatriyas*, but portray little of the actual life-experiences of *śūdras*. However, the world of the *vaiśyas* is amply portrayed in the Bhāgavata in so far as Kṛṣṇa's entire childhood is spent within the cowherding community. This fact, in itself, makes a unique and powerful statement about *bhakti yoga*.

Moreover, and very importantly, although accepting the divisions of labour expressed by the classical *varṇa* social system, the Bhāgavata does not accept that one is bound to the occupation of the caste into which one happens to be born; it explicitly undermines caste by birthright by noting that caste should be determined according to one's innate nature, even if this nature involves performing the function of a caste other than the one in which one happens to find oneself by birth (VII.2.31 and 35). This notion of a caste system determined by quality rather than birth can be read as implied in the Gītā (IV.13), but it is explicit in the Bhāgavata. The Bhāgavata thus radically goes against the dominant current of the times, which restricted individuals to activities prescribed for the caste into which they were born, irrespective of personal innate nature, propensities or inclination. The enormous significance of this should not be underestimated, given the context of the day.

Also of great significance is the fact that even while the Bhāgavata accepts the basic social order, albeit specifying that the division of labour should be determined by natural quality rather than birth, it elevates *bhakti*, or devotion to God, above it. This, of course, is a conspicuous feature of Hindu *bhakti* in general, but the Bhāgavata goes to some lengths to underscore this. Despite the prioritization of the *brāhmaṇas* noted above, the text considers a *cāṇḍāla*, outcaste, who is dedicated to Kṛṣṇa, to be superior to a *brāhmaṇa* who is not, even if the latter is endowed with all the ideal *brāhmaṇical* qualities (VII.9.10). No one is exempt from attaining the highest destination of life, devotion to God: the outcastes who live on the outskirts of town are also purified by hearing, glorifying and meditating on Kṛṣṇa (X.70.43). Kṛṣṇa specifically instructs Uddhava to speak of his teachings to all those who are devoted, 'even if they be from the *śūdra* caste' (XI.29.31). To appreciate the universality of the Bhāgavata one need only compare this to statements in the *dharma* texts that the Veda should not even be recited in the presence of a *śūdra* (Manu Dharmaśāstra, IV.99) or, worse still, that if a *śūdra* intentionally listens to the Veda, his ears should be filled with molten lead; if he recites it, his tongue should be severed; and if he has mastered it, his body should be hacked to pieces (Gautama Dharmaśāstra, XII.4).

Elsewhere in the Purāṇa (II.4.18), it is stated that even foreign tribes such as the Hūṇas, Yavanas and other non-Āryan[66] people are all purified if they take refuge with Kṛṣṇa. This is not mere rhetoric: we should recall, here, that one of the earliest pieces of archaeological evidence for the worship of Kṛṣṇa was the column erected by Heliodorus, a Greek devotee of *Bhagavān*. The Bhāgavata is quite serious about promoting the transcendence of *bhakti* to the social order: Sūta, the narrator of the entire Purāṇa, is born of a lowly mixed caste; Prahlāda, one of the foremost exemplars of *bhakti*, is the son of a demon and describes himself as of despicable birth (VII9.12); and Nārada, the most distinguished of saintly devotee sages, is the son of a *śūdra* woman. One need only consider that Kṛṣṇa himself chose to share his most intimate *līlās* with a lowly cowherding community to realize how far the Bhāgavata tradition has gone in this direction. One can read such characteristics as indicating that the Bhāgavata may have been written by learned ascetics outside mainstream priestly or scholarly circles who drew mass support from the lower urban classes and thus offset the opposition of established orthopraxy (Hopkins, 1966).

The treatment of women follows similar lines. On the one hand, the secular expectations of women revealed in the text do not depart from those in the conventional texts dealing with *dharma*, or religious and social duties, such as the orthodox social codes given by Manu, the principal lawgiver in classical Hinduism. When Kṛṣṇa attempts to send the *gopīs* back to their husbands after they had abandoned everything to be with him in the forest, for example, he points out that:

> The highest *dharma* [duty] of a woman is to serve her husband faithfully, to ensure the well-being of her relatives, and to nourish her children.
>
> A husband who is not a sinner, even though he be of bad character, ill-fated, old, dull-headed, sick or poor, should not be abandoned by women who desire to attain heaven.
>
> Without exception, the adultery of a woman of good birth does not lead to heaven. It is scandalous, fear-laden, worthless, fraught with difficulty and abhorrent. (X.29.24–6)

Similarly, when the *brāhmaṇa* women likewise abandon their duties to be with him, Kṛṣṇa, after assuring them that they could still be united with him in thought, sends them back to their husbands on the grounds that their presence at home is required in order for their husbands to complete their sacrifices (X.23.19–34). Here, too, the Bhāgavata does not challenge the norms of its day in terms of the conventional expectations of gender roles.

Where the Bhāgavata dramatically departs from such roles is, again, in the context of *bhakti*, and this is best illustrated in the narrative above concerning the *gopīs*. Although Kṛṣṇa attempts to send the *gopīs* back to their husbands and domestic duties, they will hear nothing of it (unlike the *brāhmaṇa* wives, who return once Kṛṣṇa assures them that their families will not be angry with them). The *gopīs* call his bluff:

> You, the knower of *dharma*, have declared that the occupational *dharma* of women consists of attending to friends, husbands and children. Then let this be our *dharma* when it comes to you, the source of this advice, O Lord – after all, you are the soul within all. (X.29.32)

Here and elsewhere the Bhāgavata gives a novel meaning to the traditional concept of *dharma*, normally understood as social and familial duty, by constructing it in the context of *bhakti* as denoting unalloyed devotion and service to Kṛṣṇa: 'Whatever activity is dedicated to me, the supreme, without self-interest, even if it be useless and performed out of fear or other such things, is *dharma*, O best of saintly persons' (XI.29.21).[67]

In his famous concluding words in the Gītā (XVIII.66), Kṛṣṇa instructs Arjuna to abandon all conventional *dharma*, and simply surrender exclusively to him. He assures Arjuna that he will free him from any sinful reaction incurred from doing this, and thus he need not fear any consequences. The Bhāgavata chooses to illustrate this principle dramatically by having the *gopīs* abandon their husbands and even their children to be with him:

> [T]he women of Vraj, enchanted by Kṛṣṇa, came to their lover, their earrings swinging in their haste, and unknown to one another.
>
> Some, who were milking cows, abandoned the milking and

they dropped everything and followed him ..

approached eagerly. Others had put milk on the fire, but then came without even removing [the milk or] the cakes [from the oven].

Others interrupted serving food, feeding their babies milk, and attending to their husbands. Still others were eating, but left their food. Others were putting on make-up, washing, or applying mascara to their eyes. They all went to be near Kṛṣṇa, their clothes and ornaments in disarray.

Their hearts had been stolen by Govinda [Kṛṣṇa], so they did not turn back when husbands, fathers, brothers and relatives tried to prevent them. They were in a state of rapture.

Some *gopīs*, not being able to find a way to leave, remained at home and thought of Kṛṣṇa with eyes closed, completely absorbed in meditation ... [T]hey immediately left their bodies made of the *guṇas*. (X.29.4–11)

The theological message here is clear: the text portrays the *gopīs* as prepared to surrender everything in order to attain Kṛṣṇa, and as such they are exemplars of the highest possible achievement of the human soul. Since, in the mundane world, the love of the paramour is forbidden, ostracized and dangerous, the *gopīs* exemplify the highest attainable intensity of love for God – a love that totally disregards all repercussions; that cannot be bound by any material ethical convention; that transcends regulatory institutions such as that of matrimony; that pays no heed to social criticism; that is oblivious to personal danger, risk and censure; and that is prepared to sacrifice everything for the ultimate beloved, God. Just as in the Abrahamic tradition, Abraham was expected to be prepared to commit an immoral deed – the sacrifice of his own son Isaac – in order to demonstrate his total commitment to God, so the *gopīs* illustrate that the soul must be prepared to renounce conventional notions of duty and morality for the same end. They have thereby attained the highest goal of life, complete surrender to God.

Thus, while the conventional roles of women in everyday society are not challenged by the Bhāgavata, the text allows them to discard these roles in the context of *bhakti yoga* and, having done so, is ground-breaking in the Purāṇic genre by its promotion of women as not just eligible devotees, but the *highest* of all *yogīs*. Uddhava, Kṛṣṇa's personal messenger, is so awed by the intensity and absoluteness of the *gopīs*' surrender to Kṛṣṇa that he wishes to become a shrub so that he might come in contact with even the dust from their feet:

'These *gopī* women are the highest embodied beings on the earth: their love for Govinda [Kṛṣṇa], the soul of everything, is perfected. Those who are fearful of the material world aspire to this, and so do the sages, and so do we ourselves . . .

Aho! May I become any of the shrubs, creepers or plants in Vṛndāvana that enjoy the dust of the feet of these women. They have renounced their own relatives, who are so hard to give up, as well as the Āryan code of conduct and worshipped the feet of Mukunda [Kṛṣṇa], the sought-for goal of the sacred texts of revelation . . .

I pay eternal homage to the dust from the feet of the women of Nanda's Vraj.' (X.47.58–63)

The *gopīs* are certainly more elevated than dutiful *brāhmaṇas*: the wives of the *brāhmaṇas*, who had risked everything by turning their backs on their husbands in order to be with Kṛṣṇa, are presented as being far more spiritually advanced than their ritualistically meticulous *brāhmaṇa* husbands:

Seeing the supreme devotion of the women to *Bhagavān* Kṛṣṇa, they [the *brāhmaṇas*] lamented about their own lack of it, and rebuked themselves:

'Curses on that birth which is threefold,[68] curses on vows, curses on extensive learning, curses on our family lineage, curses on skill in rituals: we still remain averse to Adhokṣaja [Kṛṣṇa] . . .

Aho! See the unlimited devotion of these very women to Kṛṣṇa, the *guru* of the world. It has pierced the fetters of death under the guise of household life.

Neither the *saṃskāra* purificatory rites of the twice-born,[69] nor

> residence in the house of the *guru*, nor austerity, nor inquiry into the self, nor rites of cleanliness, nor auspicious rituals were [practised] by these women.
>
> Nonetheless, they were constant in devotion to Kṛṣṇa, the Lord of the lords of *yoga*, whose glories are renowned. This was not the case with us, even though we have undergone the *saṃskāra* and other such rites . . .[70]
>
> *Aho!* How fortunate we are to have wives such as these! Their devoutness has given rise to unwavering devotion to Hari in us.' (X.23.38–49)

The Bhāgavata thus both dismisses the myopic pettiness of ritualistic *brāhmaṇism* devoid of devotion, and clearly prioritizes the spiritual qualification of devotee women over the activities of the male twice-born *brāhmaṇas*. But more than this, in accepting women as the highest of all *yogīs*, including even all other *bhakti yogīs*, the Bhāgavata significantly surpasses the Gītā's mere acceptance of women devotees as qualified for liberation (IX.32), a statement which itself was radical for the times. And its teachings certainly contrast with the view expressed in *dharma* texts such as that of Manu, the principal Hindu law-giver, that 'it is a firmly established point of law that there is no ritual with Vedic verses for women' (Manusmṛti, IX.18).

It was, incidentally ignorance of the theological content of these very *gopī* passages that caused the Bhāgavata to be disparaged by a number of western missionaries and scholars in the colonial period, resulting even now in a continuing neglect of the text.[71] It is thus important to draw attention to the fact that, while the theologies of Kṛṣṇa's amorous affairs with the *gopīs* are unique to the Kṛṣṇa tradition,[72] the remainder of the tenth book, along with the entire Bhāgavata, shares the disdain for mundane sensuality that is so typical of the Hindu ascetic traditions: 'That woman is extremely foolish who, without smelling the honey of [Kṛṣṇa's] lotus feet, picks a lover who is a living corpse enveloped in nails, skin, and facial, body and head hair; and containing gas, bile, phlegm, stool, bowel worms, blood, bone and flesh inside' (X.60.45). Nothing can 'give happiness to those who do not know the truth and are wandering about in this world after sex-pleasure' (X.87.34).

Such admonitions are not just directed at extra-marital relationships, but even to sensual attachments within marriage: 'Those who worship me [Kṛṣṇa] . . . and yet desire enjoyment in the relationship of marriage, are bewildered by my *māyā*' (X.60.52). There are numerous statements reiterating the point that service to Kṛṣṇa is obtained by the 'renunciation of worldly attachments' (X.83.39), and aspiring devotees free from desires beg Kṛṣṇa for deliverance from 'the dark well of the household' (X.85.45), as well as 'the bonds of illusion in the form of body, home, good company, wealth, wife and offspring, and such things' (X.48.27). The text takes pains to inform us that 'Anyone who has even once offered their mind to you [Kṛṣṇa] . . . does not again become attached to the household' (X.87.35), and 'ascetics [who] do not tear out the roots of lust in their hearts [are] . . . contemptible' (X.87.39). Whatever one may make of Kṛṣṇa's affairs with the *gopīs*, the text is extremely clear that any form of mundane sensuality is illusory, as it is based on a misidentification of the *ātmā*, or self, with the temporary material body and its extensions in the form of family, etc.

Thus, the overall theology seems clear: the exchange of mundane sexual pleasure between a man and a woman is looked down upon (X.60.38), but union between anyone and Kṛṣṇa is the highest goal in life; the Bhāgavata is not encouraging its readers to imitate Kṛṣṇa's activities. Indeed, as noted earlier, the concluding verse of the five *gopī* chapters states that a faithful person who hears of these *līlās* of Kṛṣṇa with the *gopīs* gains devotion for the Lord and is quickly freed 'from lust, the disease of the heart' (X.33.39). The bottom line is that the goal of *bhakti* is to immerse the mind, whether in a mood of love or hate, in Kṛṣṇa, because by doing so one becomes purified and attains liberation. As the Bhāgavata puts it: 'the king of the Cedis, Śiśupāla, attained perfection despite hating Hṛṣīkeśa [Kṛṣṇa]. What then of those dear to Adhokṣaja [Kṛṣṇa]?' (X.29.13). Śiśupāla, Kaṃsa and other demons immersed their mind in hatred, and the *gopīs* in amorous affection. Both were fully immersed in thoughts of God, the culmination of devotional meditation. The goal of life is to become completely absorbed in Kṛṣṇa, and the means to accomplish this are secondary to the end. The Bhāgavata is unique in choosing simple women from a lowly cowherding community as the highest exemplars in this regard.

In conclusion, then, the Bhāgavata is radical in its validation of female spirituality, its undermining of caste by birthright, the extent of its elevation of low-caste devotees, and its implicit criticism of *brāhmaṇical* orthopraxy. The foregoing discussion has focused on the devotional implications of this stance for a present-day audience, since a deconstructive reading envisaging the text's own contemporary audience is beyond the scope of this introduction, but the historical milieu of the times must be kept in mind. It is only by envisaging the extent of *brāhmaṇical* hegemony, the actual day-to-day lot of low castes and outcastes, and the nature of the power imbalance in the conventional gender dynamics of orthodox Hinduism of the period, that the extent to which the Bhāgavata adjusted and redefined the socio-political order of its day can be appreciated. By claiming to be a literary substitute for the supreme Godhead, Kṛṣṇa, for all time subsequent to his incarnation, the author of the text is appropriating the spiritual cachet of a highly revered figure to gather the strength and authority realistically to challenge aspects of the social and cultural milieu of the day. Thus, irrespective of its theological, philosophical or, as will be discussed below, literary features, the Bhāgavata provided – and still provides – significant resources for potentially revolutionary social change.

THE BHĀGAVATA AS LITERATURE

The philosophical and literary erudition of the final redactor of the Bhāgavata is encyclopaedic. The text contains numerous references to the Vedic literature, exact paraphrases of Upaniṣadic verses, and explicit references to supplementary Vedic texts.[73] It is well aware of the two great Epics, the Rāmāyaṇa and Mahābhārata, as well as other Purāṇas, and is replete with statements from the Dharmaśāstra law books. The six philosophical schools are well known, especially, as has been noted, the Vedānta, Sāṅkhya and Yoga systems, which inform the metaphysics of the entire text.[74] Indeed, the philosophical sections can be so terse (and in some places, unintelligible) that the maxim *vidyāvatāṃ bhāgavate parīkṣā*, 'the Bhāgavata is the testing ground of scholars', was coined.[75] But, despite the obscurity of style in places, the final redactor of the text is not only a philosopher or theologian, but an epic poet; there are entire sections of the text, particularly the *pañcādhyāya*, the five chapters of the tenth book dedicated to Kṛṣṇa's amorous pastimes with the *gopīs*, that exhibit all the characteristics of exquisite *kāvya* poetry (see Schweig, forthcoming, for an extensive analysis of the *pañcādhyāya*). Indeed, although categorized as a Purāṇa, the tenth book of the Bhāgavata fulfils the requirements of, and has received recognition as, a *mahākāvya*, or epic poem, both as outlined in the fourteenth-century Sanskrit literary treatise, the Sāhityadarpaṇa (VI.559),[76] and in accordance with the criteria associated with the epic in western literary theory.[77]

The sheer quantity of metres adopted by the Bhāgavata perhaps most amply testifies to the literary erudition and ambition of the author: with thirty-five metres used, the text clearly aspires to distinction in the epic genre (Vyas, 1974).[78] But, ultimately, the poetic quality of exceptional lyrical passages of the text, particularly in the tenth book, speak for themselves. Some of the most exquisite and heartfelt poetry is found in the songs of separation expressed by the *gopīs* after Kṛṣṇa has left them:

> 'O *aśvattha* tree! O *plakṣa* tree! O *nyagrodha* tree! Have you seen the son of Nanda at all? He has stolen our minds with his glances and smiles of love, and has gone.
>
> O *kurabaka*, *aśoka*, *nāga*, *punnāga*, *campaka* trees! Has the younger brother of Balarāma [passed] by here? His smile steals away the pride of haughty women.
>
> O auspicious *tulasī* plant, you who are dear to Govinda [Kṛṣṇa]!

Have you seen your most beloved, Acyuta [Kṛṣṇa], wearing you [as a garland covered] with swarms of bees?

O *mālatī* plant! O *mallikā* plant! O *jāti* plant! O *yūthikā* plant! Has Mādhava [Kṛṣṇa] passed by, awakening your love with the touch of his hand? Have you seen him?

O *cūta* [mango], *prīyāla*, *panasa* [bread-fruit], *asana*, *kovidāra*, *jambū* [rose-apple], *arka*, *bilva* [wood-apple], *bakula*, *āmra* [mango], *kadamba* and *nīpa* trees, and those others which grow on the shore of the Yamunā river and which exist to benefit others! Point us to the path [taken] by Kṛṣṇa. We have lost our hearts.

O earth, you are beautiful in that the hairs of your body [the trees] stand up from the bliss of the touch of the feet of Keśava [Kṛṣṇa]. What ascetic practice have you performed? . . .[79]

O wife of the deer, has Acyuta [Kṛṣṇa] passed by here with his beloved, his limbs giving pleasure to your eyes? O friend, the scent from the jasmine garland of the Lord of our group is wafting here – a garland coloured with breast saffron contracted from the body of his lover.

O trees, did the younger brother of Balarāma wander here? Was he followed by swarms of bees, blinded with intoxication, on his *tulasī* [garland]? With his arm placed on the shoulder of his beloved, he [must have been] holding a lotus flower. And did he acknowledge with glances of love your bowing down?

Ask these creeping plants! Just see, although they are embracing the arms of the forest tree, they surely must have been touched by his fingernails for they are bristling with ecstasy.' (X.30.5–13)

These are beautiful verses, and scholars of the text have every right to say that 'the Bhāgavata can be ranked with the best of the literary works produced by mankind' (Vyas, 1974: 19).

The Sanskrit literary tradition's extensive analysis of the constituents of good poetry is a well-developed, rich and sophisticated one, as is the tenth book's adoption of many such qualities. Hence, irrespective of its other distinctive features, the tenth book merits the attention of literary specialists as an outstanding piece of poetic craftsmanship, particularly in its evocation of *rasa*. As understood in literary and dramaturgical usage, *rasa* is the experience of a mood, or emotional sensibility, such as love or heroic vigour, that is generated by a well-crafted poem or performance and aroused in the mind of the qualified reader or listener. There are eight *rasas* identified in the earliest dramaturgical treatise, the Nāṭyaśāstra of Bharata (VI.39ff.): *śṛṅgāra*, eroticism; *vīra*, heroism; *raudra*, terror; *bībhatsa*, disgust; *hāsya*, humour; *karuṇa*, compassion, pathos; *adbhuta*, wonder; *bhayānaka*, fear, dread. Bharata states that 'there is no drama without *rasa*', and the literary treatise, the Sāhityadarpaṇa (I.3), states that 'poetry is a sentence, whose soul is *rasa*'. According to Bharata (VI.31–3), just as various condiments, sauces, herbs and other ingredients combine to produce different satisfying, pleasurable tastes which are distinct from the flavour of any one of these ingredients individually, and which can be enjoyed by the gourmet, so the various emotions expressed through the disparate elements of a skilful play or piece of literature – the actors, protagonists, dialogue, character interaction, language, gestures, emotional expressions, scenery, and other ingredients of drama or poetry – combine together to be experienced and enjoyed by aesthetic connoisseurs as *rasa*. For the remainder of this section, we will note a few such literary features of the text, with a view to exposing the reader to some sense of the text as a poem.[80]

The author of the Bhāgavata has made generous use of 'natural description' (*svabhāvokti*), and the entire story bears evidence of his skill in this regard. In *kāvya* (poetry) a poet describes natural settings not as a historian or geographer would, but in order to enhance the *rasa*, as the following exceptionally beautiful example illustrates:

> Even *Bhagavān*, God himself, beholding those nights, with autumnal jasmine [*mallikā*] flowers blossoming, called upon his divine power of *yogamāyā*, and turned his thoughts towards enjoying love.
>
> At that time, the moon, king of the constellations, arose in the east, covering the face of the heavens with its copper-coloured soothing rays. It wiped away the cares of the onlookers, like a

> lover who has been absent for a long time wipes away the cares of his beloved.
>
> Seeing that full disc, heralder of the white night-lilies, reddened with fresh vermilion powder, its splendour like the face of Lakṣmī, the goddess of fortune, and seeing the forest coloured by its silky rays, Kṛṣṇa played [his flute] softly, capturing the hearts of the beautiful-eyed women. (X.29.1–3)

People are likewise depicted in vivid detail:

> Yaśodā churned, swaying back and forth. Her bracelets were moving on her arms, which were tired from pulling the rope, and her earrings were swinging to and fro. *Mālatī* [jasmine] flowers dropped from her hair, and her face, with its beautiful eyebrows, was sweating. She wore a linen cloth bound by a girdle on her broad sloping hips, and her quivering breasts were leaking milk out of affection for her son. (X.9.3)

This description is quite elaborate, and not only brings to life the figure, dress and activities of Yaśodā, but reveals her state of mind. Skill in representing emotional states is obviously important for generating *rasa*, and the Bhāgavata has some superb verses in this regard, such as the following lines describing the state of mind of the *gopīs*:

> Hearing Govinda [Kṛṣṇa] speak these unwelcome words, the dejected *gopīs* had their aspirations dashed and were inconsolable in their distress.
>
> They stood silently, their red *bimba*-fruit-coloured lips faded by their sighs, and the vermilion powder on their breasts smeared by the mascara carried by their tears. Casting down their faces out of sorrow and scratching the ground with their feet, they became weighed down by extreme unhappiness. (X.29.28–9)

Inanimate natural objects are also commonly endowed with feelings in the tenth book, a literary device known as 'pathetic fallacy' in western literature. The Bhāgavata has some beautiful examples of this in the songs of the *gopīs*, noted earlier, as well as in those of Kṛṣṇa's wives, the queens of Dvārakā, who also utter some of the most exquisite lines in the text:

> '*Bho! Bho!* You thunder continuously, O ocean. You are not able to sleep, and have fallen into a state of insomnia. Or have your personal possessions been taken away by Mukunda [Kṛṣṇa]?[81] You have entered the state in which we find ourselves – it is impossible to overcome.
>
> O moon! You have been seized by powerful consumption, and do not dispel the darkness with your rays! Have you forgotten the words of Mukunda [Kṛṣṇa] like we have? *Bho!* You appear to us to be dumbstruck! . . .
>
> O noble-minded mountain, supporter of the earth, you do not move, you do not speak! Are you thinking about some grave matter or, alas, do you yearn to place the lotus feet of the son of Nanda on your breast, as we do?
>
> O rivers, wives of the ocean! Alas, your lakes are dry and you are much reduced. Desiring your Lord, your beauty in the form of lotuses has vanished now. You are just like us: our hearts have been stolen, and we are quite withered due to being deprived of the loving glance of Kṛṣṇa, the Lord of Madhu.' (X.90.17–23)

In addition to its ability to evoke *rasa*, good poetry, in Hindu aesthetics, is distinguished by its *alaṅkāras*, embellishments, or literary adornments. Defined variously by theorists as beauty (Vāmana), that which adds grace to poetry (Daṇḍī), and the poetic equivalent of ornaments on the body of a person (Mammaṭa), *alaṅkāra* has been conceptualized as taking many forms. Understandably, many *alaṅkāras* can only be appreciated in the original Sanskrit, and the following examples can simply serve to alert the reader that the author of the tenth book is expertly adopting sophisticated poetic techniques, especially in the *pañcādhyāya*, the five chapters of the tenth book dedicated to Kṛṣṇa's amorous pastimes with the *gopīs*.

The most common *alaṅkāra* is *rūpaka*, the simile. Similes are too numerous to need exemplification – there are about 1,800 of them throughout the Purāṇa (Prasad, 1984) – nearly one in every ten verses – and they are especially visible in the tenth book. Nature is frequently invoked as the *upamāna*, the object of comparison; in the description of autumn in chapter 20 of the present text, for example, every verse from 4 onwards contains similes, and the passage is remarkable because nature is used to deliver a moral discourse on life. Perhaps the most common similes in Book X feature the lotus – lotus eyes, lotus face, lotus feet, etc. Some of these similes reveal a distinct skill of composition:

> The boys of Vraj sat in many rows encircling Kṛṣṇa, with their faces turned towards him. Their eyes were wide with joy, and they glowed like petals round the pericarp of a lotus flower. (X.13.8)

Alaṅkāras can take many forms: *yamaka* (chime), for example, although sometimes considered to be somewhat artificial and laboured, is an *alaṅkāra* that consists of the repetition in a verse of the same word (or similar sequence of letters), but in different meanings.

> *vilokya dūṣitām kṛṣṇām kṛṣṇaḥ kṛṣṇāhinā vibhuḥ*
> *tasyā viśuddhim anvicchan sarpam tam udavāsayat.* (X.16.1)

'After seeing the [river] Yamunā [Kṛṣṇā] polluted by the black [*kṛṣṇa*] snake, Kṛṣṇa, the Almighty Lord, desired to purify it, and so banished that serpent.' The word Kṛṣṇa is used three times consecutively in this passage to denote the river Yamunā, the black snake, and Kṛṣṇa himself. Another interesting *alaṅkāra* is *virodhābhāsa*, or contradiction, when two things appear, on one level, to be contradictory, yet in fact they are not. For example, Pradyumna is described as *anaṅga aṅgayutaḥ*, 'the reincarnate Kāma himself'. In Sanskrit, there is an apparent contradiction in terms between the name of Kāma as *an-aṅga*, literally, the one without limbs, and the term used for embodied or reincarnated, *aṅga-yutaḥ*, literally, endowed with limbs (Pradyumna was a reincarnation of Kāma, who was sometimes called *an-aṅga*, because his body was once consumed by the fire of Śiva's anger). *Virodhābhāsa* is also invoked to remark that Kṛṣṇa, who is the eternal unborn, undergoes birth (e.g. X.3.5). Another *alaṅkāra* is *bhrāntimān* (the mistaken), when something is perceived as being other than it is, such as in the following beautiful example:

> Peacocks danced there on the diverse pinnacles of the houses. Seeing the aloewood incense billowing forth from the holes [in the latticed windows], dear Parīkṣit, they thought them to be clouds and cried out. (X.69.12)

Dhvani (suggestion) is another essential feature of good poetry that has been discussed extensively by the theoreticians. Mammaṭa's Kāvyaprakāśa (I.4) states that poetry is at its most distinctive when the expressed meaning of a word or phrase is superseded by its suggested one. Indeed, just as the Sāhityadarpaṇa considered *rasa* to be the soul of poetry, according to another literary treatise, Ānandavardhana's Dhvanyāloka (1.1), *dhvani* is to be considered *kāvyasyātmā* (the soul of poetry). The Bhāgavata's tenth book has numerous instances of *dhvani*, the recognition and appreciation of which require a certain level of literary sophistication in the reader or listener.

Consider the following verses in chapter 47 where the *gopīs*, in the madness of their love when separated from Kṛṣṇa, chastise a bee, thinking it to be Kṛṣṇa's messenger:

> The *gopī* said:
> 12. 'O keeper of honey, your friend is a cheat. Don't touch our feet with your whiskers – they are [tinged] with the *kuṅkum* powder from the garlands in disarray on the breasts of our female rivals. Let the Lord of the Madhu dynasty carry the remnants [*prasāda*][82] of those haughty women [himself]. One who employs a messenger such as you would be ridiculed in the assembly of the Yadus.
> 13. He made us drink the bewildering nectar of his lips once, and then abandoned us – just like you immediately abandon flowers. How can the lotus-like goddess of fortune keep serving his lotus

feet? Surely her mind has also been stolen by the flattery of Uttamaśloka [Kṛṣṇa].

14. Why do you sing about that ancient One, the ruler of the Yadus, here in front of us, O six-legged one – we who are homeless? Let your fondness for Kṛṣṇa, that friend of the unconquerable Arjuna, be sung to his women companions. Since they are his beloveds, the pain in their breasts has been removed – let them provide you with what you desire.' (X.47.12–14)

The term used for bee in verse 14, *ṣaḍaṅghri*, means six-limbed (that is, a six-legged creature). Since four-legged animals are considered to be ignorant in comparison to two-legged humans, referring to the bee as six-legged implies the bee's even greater stupidity (hence, the *gopīs* add that anyone employing a messenger such as a bee would be the subject of ridicule in the assembly of the Yadus). The idea is that anyone who is a friend of the fickle Kṛṣṇa is very foolish indeed. Moreover, in verse 12 Kṛṣṇa is referred to by his name of Madhupati, the Lord of the Madhus, and the bee by another name, *madhupa*, the keeper of honey. The implication here is that just as the bees abandon flowers once they have tasted their nectar, so Kṛṣṇa has abandoned the *gopīs* after enjoying them (this play of words between Madhupati and *madhupa* is another example of the *alaṅkāra* of *yamaka* [chime], noted above). The tenth book of the Bhāgavata is rich with such literary features.

The characters of the Bhāgavata are all historical (in the sense that their stories are extensively described in the Mahābhārata and other Purāṇas, especially the Viṣṇu Purāṇa and Harivaṃśa), and hence the author is portraying them from within the well-known parameters of traditional history. The characters are fatalists, and almost all are gifted with a sophisticated philosophical outlook. Even creatures such as the serpent Kāliya are quite lucid, and the eulogy of the serpent's wives to Kṛṣṇa is philosophically elaborate, and succinctly summarizes the main contours of the philosophy of the Bhāgavata (X.16.34–53).

I hope these brief illustrations have given the reader some sense that, in addition to its theological and other distinguishing qualities, the Bhāgavata can be appreciated simply on its literary merits, and, from this perspective alone, deserves close attention. This discussion has focused on the merits of the text – known as *guṇas*, distinctive qualities – but, as with any piece of literature, faults can be found. The word for these is *dosas*, debilitating distractions, or deficiencies that destroy distinctiveness in poetry. For example, excessive exaggeration is a *doṣa* – the poet may be trying too hard for distinction, with more energy than skill, and the language may become too ornate, or so erudite that it requires philosophical clarification (one of the qualities of good poetry is *prasāda*, or clarity). Or the language may be clumsy, so that the play on words is compromised.[83] The identification of both *guṇas* and *doṣas* requires a certain level of erudition, and there is as much room for differences of opinion among Sanskrit literati as among connoisseurs of any other literary tradition. One can find laboured verses in the tenth book, and sections so terse and incomprehensible that commentators differ considerably as to their meaning. And there are the regular faults inevitable in any text of such size, such as the distortion of words to fulfil the necessities of metre. But, overall, the tenth book of the Bhāgavata ranks as an outstanding product of Sanskrit literature. Perhaps more significantly, it has inspired more derivative literature, poetry, drama, dance, theatre and art than any other text in the history of Sanskrit literature, with the possible exception of the Rāmāyaṇa.

CONCLUDING COMMENTS

However one reads the Bhāgavata – as scripture, epic, poetry, theology, philosophy or literature – one should keep in mind, as one embarks upon reading the text, that it claims to be sacred history. For most western scholars, the tenth book is likely to be read as a mythological or religio-allegorical story composed to impart a specific set of philosophical views, theological beliefs and socio-cultural values. But it is important to bear in mind that Kṛṣṇa is not viewed as a symbolic figure by his devotees – or, if the Bhāgavata's depiction of Kṛṣṇa's earthly *līlā* is to be considered allegorical in so far as it points to an ultimate, transcendent blissful state of divine interaction between the perfected soul and a personal God, then, for the devotee, it is historically real allegory. From the perspective of generations of devotees all over the Indian subcontinent across the ages who have imbibed and perpetuated the story in so many different forms, the incarnation of Kṛṣṇa is not a myth: 'the life of Krishna to the Hindu . . . is as historical as the life of Jesus the Christ to the Christian' (Abhedananda, 1967: 31). However our modern, rational, post-enlightenment sensitivities might prefer to intellectualize and interpret the story, one should not forget that the Bhāgavata itself claims to be a record of the events that transpired when the absolute Godhead personally appeared in the world, a real-life divine being – the supreme being, no less – who broke into human time, space and history, and performed superhuman deeds.

Moreover, as a text, the Bhāgavata presents itself not just as a record of sacred history, but as a literary substitute for Kṛṣṇa after his departure from the world – the *vāṅmayāvatāra*, or literary incarnation of God. Therefore, as noted earlier, just as those who were fortunate enough to encounter Kṛṣṇa personally when he was on earth were awarded liberation, the concluding verses of the entire Purāṇa claim that those born after the departure of Kṛṣṇa to his abode who are fortunate enough to encounter the Bhāgavata Purāṇa, listen to it, read it and contemplate it constantly with a devoted heart, will likewise attain liberation (XII.13.18).

Whether one reads the text as literary allegory or real-life allegory, with a view to liberation or out of cultural curiosity, it is hard to resist the appeal of the blue, lotus-eyed Lord. The irresistible call of Kṛṣṇa's flute has enticed numerous Hindus (and, more recently, people all over the world)[84] to sacrifice everything in order to attain his lotus feet, and drawn countless more throughout the ages to participate in the process of *bhakti yoga*. The tenth book of the Bhāgavata has inspired generations of artists, dramatists, musicians, poets, singers, writers, dancers, sculptors, architects and temple-patrons across the centuries. Its stories are well known to every Hindu household across the length and breadth of the Indian subcontinent, and celebrated in regional festivals all year round. As such, the lotus-eyed Lord merits a unique and illustrious presence on the religious landscape of the world's great traditions, and the Bhāgavata a distinguished place among the masterpieces of world literature.

NOTES

1. There are two other important sources containing the story of Kṛṣṇa's life: the Harivaṃśa, a sizeable appendix to the Mahābhārata, and another Purāṇa, the Viṣṇu Purāṇa. Scholars (e.g. Sheth, 1984, and Matchett, 2001) generally consider the Harivaṃśa to be the older of these sources, followed by the Viṣṇu Purāṇa and then the Bhāgavata Purāṇa. However, at least over the last millennium, the Bhāgavata Purāṇa has eclipsed these other two sources in popularity, as attested by the sheer number of commentaries written on this text. This will be discussed further below.
2. Present-day Vraj is located between Delhi and Agra in the state of Uttar Pradesh, in the northwest of the Indian subcontinent.
3. Bonazzoli (1979) has determined that the actual number of verses in the Purāṇas is, indeed, almost 400,000.
4. Brahmā is the creator of all the forms in the universe in the sense of being their engineer, but he is not the creator of the primordial universal stuff itself. He is born from the lotus stemming from Viṣṇu's navel, and thus is himself a created being with a finite life-span.
5. Indeed, followers of this Purāṇa claimed that it is the Devi Bhāgavata that is referred to by the reference to 'the Bhāgavata' in the list of eighteen Purāṇas (see Brown, 1983; and Bryant, 2002).
6. See Rocher (1986: 105) and Gonda (1954: 194) for discussion. The fact is that Viṣṇu is associated with the *guṇa* of *sattva*, the influence of goodness and enlightenment, and Śiva with that of *tamas*, the influence of ignorance and bondage. Even if the later Śiva-centred texts attribute to Śiva the roles of creator and preserver, in the broader Purāṇic scheme he is the destroyer.
7. Thus, in the Bhāgavata, Viṣṇu, in addition to being able to become manifest in unlimited other identical Viṣṇu forms (e.g. chapter 13 of the present text), produces from himself the form of Śiva for a specific function – to perform the task of destruction at the end of the universe (Book X, chapter 71, verse 8; Book I, chapter 2,

verse 23 – hereafter, for this text, X.71.8 etc.); and into the Goddess, Devī, or Śakti, for another function – to reveal the actual stuff of the universe, *prakṛti*, and perform other tasks such as cover the souls with illusion in her capacity of *Māyā* (see p. xxvii). Viṣṇu also produces the *jīvas*, or *ātmās* (souls), who populate the world, and he can also empower certain *jīvas* to perform extraordinary tasks, such as those performed by Brahmā, who creates the actual forms in the world out of *prakṛti*. Such *jīvas* are considered empowered incarnations.

8. See X.88.3–5, where Śiva is associated with the *guṇas* and material prosperity, while Viṣṇu is associated with transcendence and the state beyond the *guṇas*.
9. The Bhāgavata Purāṇa, while mentioning twenty-two principal incarnations, states that they are actually innumerable (I.3.26).
10. There are some minor variations between lists, chiefly in connection with the Buddha.
11. Madhva, in the thirteenth century, refers to some commentaries that are not presently available, as does Jīva Gosvāmī in the sixteenth century.
12. An English translation of the Viṣṇu Purāṇa by H. H. Wilson also appeared in 1840.
13. The Bhāgavata is said to have 18,000 verses, both in its own colophons, and in other Purāṇas. In fact it has 16,256.
14. *Bhagavān*, as will be discussed further on p. xix, literally means possessor of *bhaga*, fame, majesty or prosperity. While it is a title sometimes used for other gods, and even on occasion powerful mortals, when used with Kṛṣṇa it means God. Bhagavad Gītā means the song of God, and Bhāgavata Purāṇa means the story, legend or history of God.
15. The *kaliyuga* is the last and most degenerate of the four world ages in terms of human religiosity. Purāṇic narrative holds that, prior to this age, people's intellectual abilities were such that they could easily remember the sacred texts, and thus there was no reason to codify them or preserve them in writing. At the onset of the fourth age, however, people's ability to remember began to wane, and so Vyāsa compiled both the Vedas and the Purāṇas, and committed them to writing.
16. Examples in the Bhāgavata include the stories of Purūravas and Urvaśī (LX.14.15ff.), and of Indra and Vṛtra (V.10–14).
17. For overviews of the development of the Kṛṣṇa tradition see Bhandarkar (1913); Jaiswal (1967); Raychaudhuri (1975); and Preciado-Solis (1984). The earliest evidence pertaining to the

figure of Viṣṇu need not detain us here, but for an overview of Viṣṇu in the Vedic period see Gonda (1954).

18. See Preciado-Solis (1984) for an overview.
19. The reference is plausible because it describes Kṛṣṇa as Devakīputra, the son of Devakī, who is indeed Kṛṣṇa's mother in the Purāṇas; while the names Kṛṣṇa and Devakī may not have been uncommon in this period, their combination as mother and son certainly reduces the odds of a chance correspondence. But the correspondence nonetheless remains questionable, because this Upaniṣadic Kṛṣṇa is the recipient of some esoteric teachings from the sage Ghora Āṅgirasa. There are no stories connecting the Purāṇic and Epic Kṛṣṇa (whose boyhood teacher was Sāndīpani Muni, and whose family *guru* was Garga Muni) with Ghora Āṅgirasa, or with such teachings.
20. These include: Yāska's Nirukta, an etymological dictionary of *circa* the fifth century BCE; the famous Sanskrit grammar, the Aṣṭādhyāyī of Pāṇini, dated *circa* the fourth century BCE; the Baudhāyana Dharma Sūtra, *circa* the fourth century BCE; the Arthaśāstra, also *circa* fourth century BCE; and the Mahānārāyaṇa Upaniṣad of the Taittirīya Āraṇyaka, *circa* third century BCE.
21. These references have been culled by Dahlquist (1962).
22. See Preciado-Solis (1984) for references.
23. Although the term *Bhagavān* is mostly associated with Kṛṣṇa, it is also used in the tenth book for Śiva (X.62.5; X.89.3), and even for other powerful but not supreme beings such as Kṛṣṇa's eagle carrier Garuḍa (X.17.5); the powerful sages Vyāsa (X.87.48) and Nārada (X.36.16); the narrators Sūta (X.52.19) and Śuka (X.75.1–2; X.80.1); Kṛṣṇa's son Pradyumna (X.55.20); and even for a lowly *brāhmaṇa* (X.89.30).
24. The 'n' of *Bhagavān* is transformed into the 'd' and 'ta' in 'Bhagavad' and 'Bhāgavata' respectively, for grammatical reasons; likewise with the difference in vowel length between 'a' and 'ā'.
25. As noted earlier, the Harivaṃśa, which also narrates the story of Kṛṣṇa, is a sizeable appendix to the Mahābhārata.
26. Thus Rāmānuja, an important Vaiṣṇava theologian, prioritized the Viṣṇu Purāṇa and does not even refer to the Bhāgavata despite the fact that it seems highly unlikely that he was unaware of it (Bryant, 2002: 52–3).
27. Although there were six schools of orthodox thought in ancient India (and they all survive in various forms at the present day), it has been Vedānta that has emerged as the school that has had the

most influence on philosophical thought over the last millennium (this school will be discussed more fully on pp. xliii–xlix). Therefore, the founders of the most enduring new schools of thought over the last millennium have primarily been Vedāntīs – interpreters of the Vedānta. Vedāntīs have traditionally given special recognition to the *prasṭhāna traya*, and any new theology was expected to account for itself from within the parameters of these primary sources. While the Gītā is undoubtedly a Kṛṣṇa-centred text, the Upaniṣads and Vedānta Sūtras do not even mention Kṛṣṇa (except, questionably, for the brief cryptic reference in the Chāndogya Upaniṣad mentioned earlier), hence Vallabha's inclination to expand the corpus to include the Bhāgavata.

28. The concept of *aṃśa* can be used in connection with other personal aspects of Godhead such as the goddess: Rukmiṇī, one of Kṛṣṇa's wives, is called an *aṃśa* of Śrī, the goddess of fortune, in this text.

29. There are, in fact, other verses in the tenth book which specifically refer to Kṛṣṇa as an *aṃśa*. In X.38.32 and X.41.46, both Kṛṣṇa and his brother Balarāma are together described as having descended as *aṃśas*. In X.89.59, Kṛṣṇa and Arjuna are referred to by Viṣṇu himself as *kalāvatīrṇau*, 'incarnated as *kalas̄* [partial incarnations]'. In X.20.48, Kṛṣṇa and Balarāma, again together, are referred to as *kalābhyām hareḥ* '[partial incarnations] of Hari', where Hari refers to Viṣṇu. See chapter 2, note 1 for related discussion and Sheth (1982) for a fuller treatment of this issue, and the means taken by the commentators of the Kṛṣṇa sects to account for such statements. Such tension, understandably, allows the Viṣṇu sects to insist that Viṣṇu is the supreme, and Kṛṣṇa Viṣṇu's *aṃśa*. These seemingly conflicting statements also support the view of those who see the text as consisting of chronological strata rather than being a consistent whole.

30. In Sanskrit, unlike classical Greek or Latin, there is a separate case called the instrumental, which denotes, among other things, the means or manner by which an action is accomplished.

31. Every action plants a seed, in Indic thought, and this seed eventually bears the fruit of a corresponding reaction. Since actions with their inherent reactions are generated at every instant, and the fruit of these reactions provokes further actions with new seeds of reactions, the planting and coming to fruition of *karma* is unlimited, and spills over from one lifetime to the next. Hence *saṃsāra*, the cycle of birth and death, is potentially eternal, and the

goal of most Indic religious and philosophical systems is to break free from this self-perpetuating situation and attain liberation.

32. *Jīva* is the term usually used for the soul in the context of its bondage in matter and in *saṃsāra*, the cycle of birth and death, and *ātmā* the term used for the soul in the context of its pure ultimate nature as the innermost eternal self, the source of consciousness. A further term, *puruṣa*, is also used for *ātmā*.

33. E.g., X.1.25; X.14.9; X.16.58; X.23.51; X.37.23; X.38.11; X.40.23; X.47.30; X.48.27; X.49.29, etc.

34. The regular term *māyā* is occasionally also used interchangeably with *yogamāyā*.

35. At times, however, Kṛṣṇa's associates seem to express some awareness of Kṛṣṇa's real nature (X.3.12ff.; X.8.19ff.; X.19.14; X.28.11; X.29.41; .85.18).

36. Even though the residents of Vraj and even Kṛṣṇa himself are lulled in these ways by *yogamāyā* for the sake of enjoying *līlā*, the author of the Bhāgavata takes pains to keep the reader, at least, reminded of Kṛṣṇa's supremacy, by frequently interjecting such asides as: 'The two boys, the sole keepers of the whole universe, became keepers of calves' (X.11.45). On occasion, such interjections are quite forceful (e.g. X.77.30–32).

37. The Kṛṣṇa-centred theologies of Vallabha and Caitanya hold that Kṛṣṇa's *līlās* in this world are replicas of the *līlās* that are eternally ongoing in the divine *brahman* realm – Kṛṣṇa's abode of Goloka – and it is *yogamāyā* that determines and arranges the scenery, landscape and activities in this divine realm. As will be discussed below, *brahman* is not an impersonal, formless and non-active state in the Bhāgavata, but a dynamic realm with form and personal interactions between God and his consort and their devotees. The forms and substances constituting that realm are not made of the earth, water, fire, air, ether, etc., of this world of *prakṛti*, but of *brahman*, which is described as consisting of *sat*, *cit* and *ānanda* – eternity, knowledge and bliss. These medieval commentators refer to *yogamāyā* as Kṛṣṇa's 'internal' power of illusion, active in the internal realm of *brahman*, which serves Kṛṣṇa by facilitating his personal *līlā*, as opposed to Kṛṣṇa's 'external' power of *māyā*, active in the external realm of *saṃsāra*, which serves him by facilitating the world of birth and death.

38. The word *yoga* comes from the root *yuj*, 'to join', and is cognate with the English verb 'to yoke'. The term means 'union with the divine', or a spiritual path, and there are a number of different *yoga* systems outlined in different Hindu texts. The Bhagavad

Gītā, for example, discusses several *yoga* paths including *jñāna yoga*, the path of knowledge; *karma yoga*, the path of action; and *bhakti yoga*, the path of devotion.

39. X.11.33; X.35.1; X.35.26; X.47.54; X.69.39. The term is used more frequently in the instrumental case (see note 30 above).

40. Along these lines, in Book X, two gods who were fortunate enough to encounter Kṛṣṇa state: 'May our speech be engaged in the narration of your qualities, our two ears in your stories, our two hands in your work, our mind in the remembrance of your feet, our head in obeisance to the universe which is your residence, and our eyes in the observing of the saints, who constitute the body of your Lordship' (X.10.38).

41. Patañjali's is the classical text outlining the eight steps of the psychosomatic *yogic* process of realizing the *puruṣa*, the term used in this text for the innermost self (*ātmā*). His is one of the six schools of Hindu philosophy that will be discussed on pp. xxxix ff.

42. Congregational chanting, *kīrtana* and *bhajana*, in the Kṛṣṇa tradition, generally consists of a lead singer singing some simple devotional hymn, or a name or series of names of Kṛṣṇa (such as Hari, Govinda, Vāsudeva, etc.), part or all of which are then repeated back in unison by the congregation. Personal *mantra* meditation involves softly repeating to oneself a *mantra* containing Kṛṣṇa's names, using standard meditational practices in order to focus the mind on the *mantra* without distractions; '*oṃ namo bhagavate vāsudevāya*', which is the opening invocation of the Bhāgavata, is a Kṛṣṇa *mantra*, as is the popular and by now commonly known Kṛṣṇa *mahāmantra*: '*Hare Kṛṣṇa, Hare Kṛṣṇa, Kṛṣṇa, Kṛṣṇa, Hare, Hare; Hare Rāma, Hare Rāma, Rāma, Rāma, Hare, Hare*', which followers of the Caitanya school hold to be particularly potent.

43. Patañjali uses the term *puruṣa* for the soul, or innermost conscious self, in his Yoga Sūtras, where the Upaniṣads and Vedānta Sūtras prefer the term *ātmā*.

44. These five types of liberation are: *sārūpya*, having the same form as the Lord; *sārṣṭi*, having the same opulence as the Lord; *sālokya*, living in the same abode as the Lord; *sāmīpya*, living close to the Lord; and *sāyujya*, merging with the Lord. Several of these are referred to in the present text of the Bhāgavata (X.12.38; X.41.42; X.44.39; X.90.47).

45. The trees in Kṛṣṇa's abode provide the residents of that realm with any item asked for.

46. The residents of Kṛṣṇa's abode travel in vehicles that traverse the sky.
47. The other three schools are the Mīmāṃsā school, which formulated a rationale for perpetuating the old Vedic sacrificial rites; the Nyāya school, which excelled in developing rules of logic so that the debates between the various schools could be conducted according to conventions about what constituted valid argument; and the Vaiśeṣika school, which provided a metaphysics that perceived the created world as ultimately consisting of the combination of various eternal categories such as atoms.
48. See Sheridan (1983 and 1986) and Dasgupta (1922). The sage Īśvarakṛṣṇa, who wrote the Sāṅkhya Kārikās, has no connection with the Kṛṣṇa of the Bhāgavata (although the latter is also referred to as *Īśvara*, 'controller' or 'Lord').
49. These cover such things as: prescribed duty and its mode of performance, worship, diet, charity, sacrifice, austerity, knowledge, activity, understanding, determination, attainment of happiness, and future birth. See also chapter 4, note 11 in the present text.
50. See, in this connection, chapter 4, note 10 in the present text.
51. The analogy of milk only holds good in terms of the production of by-products. Where *prakṛti* differs from milk is that it and the substances evolving from it maintain their own separate identity while simultaneously producing further substances (unlike milk, which is itself fully transformed when producing yogurt).
52. In the Sāṅkhya of Īśvarakṛṣṇa, intelligence is the first product of *prakṛti*, and ego is a derivative of intelligence. Also, mind, the five senses and the organs of action come from the interaction of ego and *sattva*; ego and *rajas* do not give rise to products (the five subtle elements come from ego and *tamas* in both these systems).
53. Creation is cyclical in Purāṇic Hinduism.
54. E.g. Madhva's commentary on the Bhāgavata (I.1.1) as well as Jīva Gosvāmī's Tattva Sandarbha (10).
55. The example typically given by Śaṅkara's school to illustrate the concept of 'superimposition' is that of the snake and the rope. A person walking along at dusk sees a rope lying on the road, and mistakes it for a snake. Superimposing the idea of a snake upon what is in reality a rope, the person experiences fear and other negative reactions born of illusion (which are dispelled as soon as the rope is seen for what it is). Likewise, this world is in reality *brahman*, but because of illusion we superimpose the world of forms and dualities upon it, and thus experience fear and other

negative consequences such as the cycle of birth and death. This, in parallel fashion, can be dispelled by right knowledge.

56. The term *māyā* is sometimes used in the Bhāgavata to refer to *prakṛti* (matter), and sometimes to the power of illusion. For Śaṅkara, the two are one and the same – *prakṛti* is *māyā*.

57. Nimbārka's school was called *dvaitādvaita*, 'dualism in non-dualism', Vallabha's, *śuddhādvaita* or 'pure non-dualism'; and Caitanya's, *acintyabhedābheda*, 'inconceivable difference and non-difference'.

58. 'The powers of such things as the vital airs, and of the creators of the universe, are powers of the supreme being, because they are dependent [on him], as well as different [from him]' (X.85.6). There are numerous references in the tenth book to *māyā*'s existence as Kṛṣṇa's *śakti* (X.1.25; X.14.22; X.16.58; X.23.51; X.37.23; X.38.11; X.40.23; X.47.30; X.48.27; X.49.29; X.70.37; etc.).

59. While in opposition to Śaṅkara by holding *śakti* (and her different manifestations of *māyā* and *prakṛti*) to be real, most goddess-based *Śākta* sects and some Śiva-based Śaivite schools hold that, to reach the enlightened state, the *jīva* must transcend all notions of separate individuality and realize its absolute oneness with and non-difference from Devī or Śiva.

60. These forms are made from pure *sattva*, which is synonymous with *brahman* in Book X.

61. See X.12.33; X.74.45; and X.78.9–10 for examples of *sāyujya*.

62. This is particularly so in the second, third and eleventh books.

63. E.g. Dasgupta (1922). However a number of scholars have argued that, of all the Purāṇas, the Bhāgavata is the only one that displays the consistency of style that might point to a single author.

64. Elsewhere in Book X, it is stated that unlike gods and sacred places, which only purify after some time, a mere glance from a *brāhmaṇa* purifies instantly. Ultimately, by worshipping the *brāhmaṇas*, Kṛṣṇa himself is worshipped (X.86.57), since they are the best of all living beings by birth (X.86.53). An entire story proclaims the evils and negative *karmic* consequences accruing from stealing a *brāhmaṇa*'s property (X.64.32–43).

65. The worst censure is reserved for those *kṣatriyas* who attempt to deprive the *brāhmaṇas* of their property (X.64.32–8; X.89.29); indeed, even if others do so in the kingdoms under their jurisdiction, kings are 'like actors dressed up as kings who exist simply to support themselves' (X.89.29).

66. The term Āryan, despite the extremely unfortunate history of its

appropriation in Europe, is an ancient Sanskrit word which refers to the followers of the Vedic culture.

67. See Dasgupta (1922: vol. IV, 3–9) for a discussion of *dharma* in the context of the Bhāgavata.
68. See chapter 23, note 9.
69. See chapter 23, note 10.
70. See chapter 23, note 10.
71. For a discussion of the theology of the five *gopī* chapters see Schweig (forthcoming); for a discussion of the tension in the commentaries over the theologizing of this section of the narrative see Sheth (1982).
72. Although some later Rāma sects were affected by the theologies of the sixteenth-century Kṛṣṇa sects.
73. These include the Nirukta, a traditional etymological work; the Upavedas, supplements to the Vedas – on medicine, archery, music and arms; and the six *vedāṅgas*, limbs of the Vedas – on astronomy, etymology, phonetics, grammar, metre and knowledge of the sacrificial ceremonies.
74. Terms from the Nyāya and Vaiśeṣika schools are also used, and there are references to the Mīmāṃsā School and a wide variety of other systems such as the Pañcarātra.
75. I have been unable to locate the origin of this maxim, although it is quoted repeatedly, without reference, in much of the secondary scholarship on the text from India. I thus infer that it is of relatively recent coinage.
76. According to the Sāhityadarpana, to qualify as an epic a work must have: a hero who is divine or of noble *kṣatriya* lineage; a principal *rasa*, mood or sentiment, which is either amorous, neutral or heroic, the other *rasas* being supplementary to it; a plot based on history; one or all of the four *puruṣārthas*, or goals of life (religious duty, material prosperity, sensual enjoyment and liberation from the cycle of birth and death), as its object; a beginning with an invocation to a deity, a benediction, or simply with the mention of the subject matter (and sometimes a preamble censuring the wicked and extolling the righteous); more than eight canto divisions, which are neither too long nor too short; one particular metre, although it should end in a different metre (sometimes, however, a variety of metres are used); and the subject matter of a following canto, division, indicated at the end of the preceding canto. Moreover, an epic should contain descriptions of the sun, the moon, day, night, morning, evening, twilight, darkness, the ocean, the mountains, woods, hunting, seasons,

enjoyment and separation of lovers, sages, celestial regions, cities, Vedic sacrifices, military expeditions, marriages, counsels and the birth of a son. These are to be described in accordance with the occasion, and in conjunction with relevant incidents and circumstances. The entire work is to be named after the poet, the hero, or the story, and each individual canto division is to be named according to its principal subject matter.

77. See Vyas (1974) for discussion.
78. According to Vyas (1974), only the poet Māgha has used more metres in the history of Sanskrit poetics – as a point of comparison, the well-known poets Kālidāsa, Bhāravi and Śrīharṣa use nineteen different metres.
79. See chapter 30, note 1.
80. See Prasad (1984) for further discussion.
81. See chapter 90, note 4.
82. See chapter 47, note 5.
83. Moreover, the theoretician Bhāmaha's literary treatise, the Kāvyālaṅkāra, considers *vaidika* words, archaic Vedicisms, to be a fault, and the Bhāgavata is conspicuously replete with these (see Bryant, 2002, for a discussion of the implications of these archaisms).
84. The Hare Krishna Movement, registered as ISKCON – the International Society of Krishna Consciousness – and its growing number of disaffiliated off-shoots is a monotheistic Kṛṣṇa-centred tradition stemming from the Caitanya school of Vaiṣṇavism that has branches all over the world (see Bryant, 2004).

Note on Translation and Method

I use the Chaukhambā Saṁskṛit Prathiṣṭhān's edition of the Bhāgavata Purāṇa for this translation, since it is probably the most commonly used in India. There are very few differences in the manuscripts I have examined (with the exception of Vijayadhvaja's text).

I have adopted a literal translation of the text, with a few minor exceptions noted below:

1. I have supplied proper names for pronouns where their referents are unclear in an English translation. Sanskrit prose in translation is otherwise replete with what would be considered 'dangling pronouns'.

2. I have retained all epithets, since these are often used deliberately in specific contexts to which they add nuances of meaning. At the same time, since this translation is for the educated but non-specialized public, I have also added the most common generic name for personalities after these epithets, even if these do not occur in the original (e.g. I have translated 'Parīkṣit, son of Bharata' for 'son of Bharata', etc.). Since there are a considerable number of epithets for Kṛṣṇa used frequently throughout the text, such as Hari, Acyuta, Mukunda, etc., I have inserted the name Kṛṣṇa after them in square brackets for the first five occurrences of each epithet, after which I assume the reader will have become familiar with them. These names are listed in bold in the glossary for ease of reference. On occasion I add an explanatory phrase (e.g. Śrī, the goddess of fortune, for Śrī, etc.). I provide the literal meaning for these epithets in notes upon their first occurrence.

3. I have retained the Sanskrit for a few words that are by now

standard or quasi-common in the English language and words that, in my opinion, are destined or deserve to become so (e.g. *karma*, *yoga*, *saṃsāra*, *bhakti*, *dharma*, etc.).

4. I have retained the Sanskrit for a very few words for which there exists no adequate or convenient English word or phrase (e.g. *guṇa*, *sattva*, *rajas*, *tamas*). Explanations for these are provided in the introduction, notes or glossary.

5. The verses are often replete with long strings of laudatory epithets in the vocative and I sometimes represent these in the nominative (e.g., 'Your majesty never fades', for 'O you whose majesty never fades').

6. I have construed some of the passive constructions, for which Sanskrit has such a proclivity, into the active voice: 'The forest was entered into by Kṛṣṇa' does not make for the smoothest reading in English!

7. On occasion I have interjected into the text a few clarificatory words that are not in the original Sanskrit. I have kept such additions to the absolute minimum, only providing them if the meaning is otherwise unclear, or if the syntax demands them. I indicate that these insertions are my own by placing them in square brackets.

8. As is described in the introductory paragraphs to chapter 1, the Bhāgavata is recited by the sage Sūta to the sages assembled in the forest of Naimiṣa. Sūta is actually narrating what he had heard from the lips of Śuka when the latter had related the Bhāgavata to king Parīkṣit in the presence of another assembly of sages, including Sūta. As a narrative within a narrative, the tenth book is primarily set as a dialogue between Śuka and king Parīkṣit, although on occasion Sūta directly addresses the sages at Naimiṣa. Śuka's narration, in turn, contains numerous other dialogues between personalities involved in the events he is describing, so there are multiple layers of narrative. Technically speaking, single quotation marks should be used only for the dialogue between Sūta and the sages at Naimiṣa, which is where the present Bhāgavata is set, but Sūta personally interjects so infrequently that I have also used single quotation marks for the dialogue between Śuka and king Parīkṣit, since this encompasses perhaps 99 per cent of the actual frame dialogue present in the

text. For dialogues within this dialogue I use double quotation marks.

9. The ninety chapters of Book X deal exclusively with the story of Kṛṣṇa, with the exception of Kṛṣṇa's departure from this world, which is described in Book XI. I therefore include in the present translation the four chapters from Book XI that describe this. Book XI also contains a lengthy philosophical discourse of over twenty chapters spoken by Kṛṣṇa to Uddhava, known as the Uddhava Gītā. I have included only the last chapter from this, since it presents Kṛṣṇa's ultimate and final instructions.

10. I have attempted to draw almost all of the examples to various theological or literary points in the introduction from the tenth book of the Bhāgavata, although on occasion I have drawn on other essential verses from other books. These quotations are listed according to book, chapter and verse number (e.g. X.25.15).

11. This translation is meant both for the educated lay reader and the specialist. With these two readerships in mind, I have relegated all technical information to endnotes, where they can be accessed by the latter without burdening the former.

12. I have frequently provided clarifications of difficult passages in notes from the fourteenth-century commentary written by Śridhara Svāmī. This is the earliest extant commentary, and held in high regard by subsequent commentators from all schools.

13. There are a number of verses in the text that are almost identical with or very similar to verses from the Gītā, and, on occasion, the Upaniṣads. I provide these latter verses from these other texts in notes for the interested reader.

Table of Contents†

BOOK X

PART ONE

†There are no titles to the chapters in the Bhāgavata itself. I have adopted the titles used by Śrīdhara at the end of each of his chapters. On the occasion that he does not provide a title, I provide one of my own, which will be indicated by an asterisk.

PART TWO

BOOK XI

THE TENTH BOOK

PART ONE

CHAPTER I

The Prelude to Kṛṣṇa's Incarnation

The recitation of the Bhāgavata is set in the forest of Naimiṣa.[1] *Because of the onset of the inauspicious age of* kaliyuga, *which had begun after Kṛṣṇa had returned to his own divine abode, the sages were performing a 1,000-year sacrifice in order to attain Viṣṇu's divine abode. During the proceedings, they invite the sage Sūta to relate to them narrations concerning the appearance and activities of Lord Kṛṣṇa, since one is liberated even by uttering his name. Sūta narrates the Bhāgavata Purāṇa, which he had heard from the lips of Śuka when the latter had related it to king Parīkṣit, grandson of Arjuna and grand-nephew of Lord Kṛṣṇa.*

King Parīkṣit was the last surviving member of the Yadu clan after the carnage of the Mahābhārata war, but had been cursed by a brāhmaṇa *boy to die within seven days. As a result of this, he renounced his kingdom and sat down on the banks of the Ganges to fast till death. All the great sages arrived at the scene in order to witness the event, including the greatest sage of them all, Śuka. King Parīkṣit poses the following question to Śuka: 'What is the ultimate duty of a person about to die? Please tell me what should be heard, what should be recited, what should be performed, what should be remembered, what should be worshipped, and what should be avoided.' Śuka then recites the Bhāgavata to Parīkṣit in the presence of the assembled sages, including Sūta.*

As a narrative within a narrative, the tenth book is primarily set as a dialogue between Śuka and king Parīkṣit, although on occasion Sūta directly addresses the sages at Naimiṣa. In the previous books, Śuka had covered numerous topics, including descriptions of previous dynasties, as well as the deeds of previous incarnations of Viṣṇu and his devotees.

1. The king said:

'You have described the accounts of the sun and of the moon dynasties, as well as the amazing exploits of the kings of both dynasties.
2. You have also described the lineage of Yadu, whose nature was extremely pious, O best of the sages. Now describe to us the great deeds of Viṣṇu,[2] who incarnated in that lineage along with his *aṃśa* [partial incarnation],[3] Balarāma.[4]
3. Narrate to us in detail those deeds performed by the almighty Lord, the creator of all living beings and soul of the universe, when he incarnated in the lineage of Yadu.[5]
4. Who, other than a slaughterer of animals, would be indifferent to the unceasing narrations of the qualities of Uttamaśloka [Kṛṣṇa]?[6] These glories are supreme and are the remedy for the material predicament [of *saṃsāra*, the cycle of birth and death]. They are relished through the ears and in the minds of those who have renounced lust, and they are recited by them.[7]
5. My grandfathers [the five Pāṇḍavas] crossed the ocean of the army of the Kauravas. This was difficult to cross because of the great whale-like chariot warriors such as Bhīṣma and others who could defeat the gods in battle. With Kṛṣṇa as their boat, they reduced that ocean to the size of a calf's footprint.
6. That wielder of the discus,[8] Kṛṣṇa, entered into the womb of my mother, who had approached him for shelter. He protected this body of mine, the seed for the continuation of the Kuru and Pāṇḍava dynasty, from the scorching of Aśvatthāmā's weapon.[9]
7. O learned one, narrate the wondrous deeds of Kṛṣṇa, who is inside and outside of all embodied beings. As the supreme being in the form of time, he is the bestower of death as well as

liberation. He has assumed the form of a human through his divine power called *māyā*.[10]
8. You said that Saṅkarṣaṇa [Balarāma] was the son of Rohiṇī. How could he have been inserted in the womb of Devakī without having taken another body?[11]
9. Why did Lord Mukunda [Kṛṣṇa][12] leave his father's house in Vraj? And where did the Lord of the Sātvatas [Kṛṣṇa],[13] along with his relatives, make his residence?
10. Living in Vraj and in Mathurā, what did Keśava [Kṛṣṇa][14] do? And why did he kill Kaṃsa, his mother's brother, who surely did not deserve such a thing?
11. After accepting a human form, for how many years did he live in the city of the Yadus, Dvārakā, along with the Vṛṣṇi [Yadu] clan? And how many wives of the Lord were there?
12. Please speak in detail to me of these things, and of everything else performed by Kṛṣṇa, O all-knowing sage. I am a faithful soul.
13. This fast, which is extremely difficult to maintain, does not torment me even though I have abstained even from water. I am drinking the nectar of the stories of Hari [Kṛṣṇa][15] which are flowing from your lotus-like mouth.'
14. Sūta said:

'O Śaunaka, descendant of Bhṛgu, hearing these virtuous words, Śuka, the worshipful son of Vyāsa and best of the devotees, offered respects in turn to Parīkṣit, blessed of Viṣṇu, and began to tell of the activities of Kṛṣṇa. These narrations can destroy the sins of the age of *kali*.[16]
15. Your mind has been completely absorbed in the stories of Vāsudeva [Kṛṣṇa],[17] O best of saintly kings. Because of this, unwavering devotion has grown in you.
16. Questions about the stories of Vāsudeva purify the three parties involved – the speaker, the inquirer and the listeners – just like the Ganges water, flowing from the feet of Viṣṇu, purifies [the three worlds].
17. Once, the earth, overwhelmed by the great burden of innumerable hosts of demons in the guise of proud kings of the earth, approached Brahmā the creator,[18] for protection.

18. Assuming the form of a cow, and weeping piteously for mercy with tears in her eyes, she presented herself in distress before Brahmā and told him of her unfortunate plight.
19. Brahmā, reflecting on this, went with her and the gods to the ocean of milk[19] accompanied by Śiva, the three-eyed God.[20]
20. After he had arrived there, with his mind fully focused, Brahmā prayed to Viṣṇu, the supreme being, the Lord of the universe, the God of all gods, with the *Puruṣa-sūkta* prayer.[21]
21. Then, after hearing a voice emanate from the heavens, Brahmā, in a state of *yogic* trance, said to the celestials: "O immortals, listen to me repeat the words of the supreme Person. You should definitely implement them scrupulously and without delay.
22. In actual fact, the afflictions of the earth were already known to the supreme Lord. For as long as the Lord of lords [Kṛṣṇa] will wander on the earth, diminishing the burden of the world through his power of time,[22] you should all take birth through your *aṃśa*, or partial incarnations, in the clan of the Yadus.
23. God himself, the supreme person, will accept birth in the house of Vasudeva.[23] The wives of the demigods should accept birth for his pleasure.
24. The self-effulgent thousand-faced Lord Ananta,[24] who is an *aṃśa* [partial incarnation] of Vāsudeva, imbued with the desire to please Hari [Kṛṣṇa] will be born first.
25. *Māyā*, the supreme potency of Viṣṇu by whom the whole world is deluded, upon being instructed by the Lord, will undergo birth through her *aṃśa* for the sake of this mission."
26. When he had advised the assembly of immortals and consoled the Earth with his words in this way, the all-powerful Brahmā, lord of the *prajāpatis*,[25] the progenitors of mankind, retired to his own exalted abode.
27. Formerly, Śūrasena, the chief of the Yadus, ruled the kingdoms of Mathurā and Śūrasena, while living in the city of Mathurā.
28. From that time onwards, Mathurā became the capital of all the kings of the Yadu dynasty. Lord Hari is eternally present in that city.[26]
29. Once, in that same city, Vasudeva, a descendant of Śūra,

who had just completed his marriage ceremony, mounted a chariot accompanied by his new bride Devakī in order to leave.
30. Desiring to please his sister Devakī, Kaṃsa, the son of Ugrasena, surrounded by hundreds of golden chariots, took the reins of the horses.
31–32. At her departure, Devaka,[27] who was fond of his daughter, presented her with a dowry of 400 elephants decorated with golden neck ornaments, 15,000 horses, 18,000 chariots, and 200 well-adorned, beautiful young maidservants.
33. My dear son, conch shells, trumpets and *mṛdaṅga* drums along with kettledrums resounded to bring good fortune for the bride and groom at the time of their departure.
34. On the journey, an unembodied voice addressed Kaṃsa, who was holding the reins, and said: "The eighth offspring of the woman whom you are transporting will kill you, you fool."
35. Addressed in this way, the sinful wretch Kaṃsa, disgrace of the Bhoja dynasty, grabbed Devakī's hair. With sword in hand, he prepared to kill his sister.
36. To pacify that shameless and cruel perpetrator of evil deeds, the illustrious Vasudeva spoke as follows:
37. "You are the source of fame for the Bhoja dynasty, your qualities are worthy of praise by heroes. How can such a person kill a woman, his very own sister, at the time of her marriage?
38. Death is born along with the body for those who have taken birth, O hero. The death of all living beings is fixed, whether it occurs today or after a hundred years.
39. When the body returns to the five elements,[28] the soul – the possessor of the body – leaves the body and helplessly obtains another form in accordance with the laws of *karma*.[29]
40. Just as a person who is walking stands with one foot and moves with one foot, and just as a caterpillar moves between leaves, so the possessor of the body, the soul, goes on to its *karmic* destination.[30]
41. This is like someone who becomes rather forgetful of himself when thinking in his mind of things that he may have seen or heard. Conjuring up that situation in dream later on, that person's mind becomes absorbed in fantasy, and he imagines [himself in] a body corresponding to that situation.[31]

42. The mind is fickle by nature and is impelled by destiny. The embodied soul, absorbed in the *guṇas*[32] created by *māyā*, is born with such a mind, and materializes in the five elements whatever state the mind flows to at the time of death.[33]
43. Just like the light of the moon or sun [reflected] in earthen vessels of water is made to change state when disturbed by the force of the wind, so a person, disturbed by desires, is bewildered by the *guṇas* created by his own *māyā*.[34]
44. Therefore, on account of being subject to all this, and desiring the welfare of the soul, one should not act with enmity towards anyone. Truly, the fear of other people besets a person who is violent.
45. This distraught woman is your younger sister who is just like a daughter. As one compassionate to those in need, you should not kill this worthy lady." '
46. *Śrī* Śuka said:

'Despite being enlightened with these penetrating and appeasing words, the ruthless Kaṃsa did not desist, O scion of the Kuru dynasty, but persisted on the path of the man-eating demons.
47. Vasudeva, son of Ānakadundubhi, perceiving this resolve of Kaṃsa, thought that fate was imminent. He pondered on how to deter this act in a situation such as this:
48. "Death should be warded off by an intelligent person for as long as strength and intelligence are vigorous. But if it cannot be prevented, then there is no fault on the part of the embodied soul.
49–50. If sons are born, and if death [in the form of Kaṃsa] himself does not die first, I will ensure that this poor woman will be set free by offering my sons to death [Kaṃsa] – provided some contrary consequence does not occur. The ways of fate are unfathomable; what is impending may be averted, and what has been averted may again suddenly reappear.
51. Just as [in a forest fire], there is no other cause apart from Fate for the fact that fire engulfs a tree or bypasses it, so, in the same way, the cause of living entities obtaining and relinquishing physical bodies is difficult to fathom."
52. After deliberating to the best of his ability to reason in this

way, Vasudeva, son of Śūra, presented himself respectfully in front of the sinful Kaṃsa, and went so far as to pay him honour.
53. Smiling, and adopting a beaming, lotus-like countenance, but with a mind consumed with distress, Vasudeva spoke these words to the shameless, cruel Kaṃsa.
54. *Śrī* Vasudeva said: "This fear of yours which the unembodied voice spoke about is not on account of this woman, O gentle one. I will offer up her sons. It is on account of them that your fear has arisen."'
55. *Śrī* Śuka said:

'Perceiving the validity of those words, Kaṃsa refrained from murdering his sister. Vasudeva, clearly relieved, praised him, then entered his residence.
56. Thus, in due course of time, Devakī, the embodiment of all the gods, gave birth to eight sons and a daughter, year by year.
57. Vasudeva, son of Ānakadundubhi, was very troubled by the idea of dishonesty, and so he surrendered his first-born, Kīrtimān, to Kaṃsa with great difficulty.
58. Truly, is there anything that a saint cannot bear? Is there anything for which the wise crave? Is there anything out of bounds for the miserly? Is there anything difficult for the determined to give up?
59. King Kaṃsa was pleased to see such equanimity and commitment to truth from Vasudeva, son of Śūra. Smiling, he spoke these words:
60. "This child should return back home; my fear is not from this one. In fact, it was ordained that the eighth offspring of you and your wife would be the agent of my death."
61. Taking back his son, therefore, Vasudeva departed. But he did not rejoice at these words since they came from an unrighteous person lacking self-control.
62–63. The *gopas*, cowherd men, in Vraj, headed by Nanda, along with their wives also – together with the Vṛṣṇi clan [Yadus][35] headed by Vasudeva, along with the wives of the Yadus headed by Devakī – are almost all gods, O Parīkṣit, descendant of Bharata. So are the relatives, kinsmen and well-wishers in both dynasties, as well as the followers of Kaṃsa.

64. The greatly renowned sage Nārada[36] approached Kaṃsa and informed him about the plan to destroy the demons who were burdening the earth.
65. As a result of this, after the departure of the sage, Kaṃsa reflected upon the fact that the Yadus were gods and that Viṣṇu had been born from the womb of Devakī,[37] and was intent on his destruction.
66. Fearful of Viṣṇu, the unborn one, Kaṃsa imprisoned Devakī and Vasudeva in their home with chains, and killed each of their sons at birth, one after the other.
67. As a general rule, avaricious kings on the earth, who are addicted to life's pleasures, can kill mothers, fathers, brothers and well-wishers.
68. Kaṃsa, knowing that he himself had previously been born on earth as the great demon Kālanemi who had been killed by Viṣṇu, was hostile to the Yadus.[38]
69. The immensely powerful Kaṃsa imprisoned his father Ugrasena as well as the kings of the Yadu, Bhoja and Andhaka dynasties. He then ruled the Śūrasena kingdoms himself.'

CHAPTER 2

Prayers Offered to Brahmā and the Other Gods to Viṣṇu who had Entered the Womb

1–2. *Śrī* Śuka said:

'Joining forces with Pralamba, Baka, Cāṇūra, Tṛṇāvarta, the great devourer Agha, Muṣṭika, Ariṣṭa, Dvivida, Pūtanā, Keśī and Dhenuka, as well as other demoniac kings such as Bāṇa and Bhauma, the mighty Kaṃsa, allied with Jurāsandha the king of Magadha, embarked on the destruction of the Yadus.
3. Being harassed, the Yadus emigrated to the kingdoms of the Kuru, Pāñcāla, Kekaya, Śālva, Vidarbha, Niṣadha, Videha and Kosala clans.
4–5. Some Yadu kinsmen were captured and entered into

Kaṃsa's service. After six of Devakī's children had been killed by Kaṃsa, the son of Ugrasena, she became pregnant for the seventh time. This embryo, known as Ananta [Balarāma], was a manifestation of Viṣṇu's power. He increased both Devakī's happiness and her sorrow.

6. God, *Bhagavān*, the soul of the universe, understood the fear instilled in the Yadus – who had accepted him as their Lord – by Kaṃsa. He instructed Yogamāyā:

7. "Go, O auspicious Goddess, to Vraj, picturesque with *gopas* and cows. There, in the kingdom of Nanda, resides Rohiṇī, the wife of Vasudeva. Others, terrified of Kaṃsa, also live there in hidden places.

8. The embryo in the womb of Devakī is my own *śakti* [power], known as Śeṣa. After you have extracted him, transfer him into the womb of Rohiṇī.

9. Then I, with my *aṃśa* [partial incarnation],[1] will appear as the son of Devakī, O auspicious one, and you will manifest in Yaśodā, the wife of Nanda.

10. People will honour you as the supreme controller and bestower of all favours and desires, and will worship you with incense, offerings and sacrifices.

11–12. They will erect temples for you on earth known by such names as Durgā, Bhadrākālī, Vijayā, Vaiṣṇavī, Kumudā, Caṇḍikā, Kṛṣṇā, Mādhavī, Kanyakā, Māyā, Nārāyaṇī, Īśānī, Śāradā and Ambikā.

13. Because of being removed [*saṅkarṣaṇa*] from the womb, people in the world will call Śeṣa Saṅkarṣaṇa; because of his giving pleasure [*ramaṇa*] to the world they will call him Rāma,[2] and because of the intensity of his strength [*bala*] they will call him Balabhadra."

14. Directed in this way by the Lord, Yogamāyā accepted his instructions, saying: "What you say will be done." After circumambulating the Lord she returned to the earth and did as he had instructed.

15. When the embryo was transferred from Devakī to Rohiṇī by Yogamāyā, all the citizens cried out: "*Aho!*[3] the embryo has miscarried!"

16. Then the Lord, the Soul of the universe and bestower of

fearlessness on his devotees, also entered the mind of Vasudeva, with his *aṃśa* [partial incarnation].

17. Shining like the sun, Vasudeva carried the splendour of the supreme person. He became invincible and unapproachable by all living entities.

18. In due time, queen Devakī bore the manifestation of the infallible Lord, the source of auspiciousness for the whole world, and the soul of everything, who was contained within her. He had been deposited there by Vasudeva, the son of Śūra, by mental transmission.[4] Devakī looked like the [eastern] quarter which bears the pleasure-giving moon.

19. Devakī became the abode of the one who is the abode of all living creatures. But she could not shine with her full potency in the house of Kaṃsa, and remained like a flame which is contained [by a pot], or like Sarasvatī, the goddess of learning, contained by one miserly with his knowledge.

20. Kaṃsa saw Devakī, who was bearing the invincible Lord within her, smiling radiantly and illuminating the house with her effulgence. He said: "The one who is to deprive me of life, Hari [Kṛṣṇa], has surely taken refuge in her womb, because Devakī was not previously like this.

21. What immediate steps should I take in this matter? One who accomplishes his purposes does not stray from his goals. But the opportunistic murder of a woman, a pregnant sister, destroys fame, prosperity and length of life.

22. Anyone who subsists by excessively injuring people undoubtedly lives as if dead. People curse him when his body dies, and he will certainly go to the dark hell for those people who consider their selves to be this body [and nothing more]."

23. Restraining himself from this most abominable intention, the powerful Kaṃsa waited for the birth. But he maintained his enmity towards Hari [Kṛṣṇa].

24. Whether sitting, resting, eating or moving about the land, Kaṃsa thought of Hṛiṣīkeśa [Kṛṣṇa]. He saw the whole universe as pervaded by Kṛṣṇa.

25. Brahmā and Śiva went there accompanied by all the sages such as Nārada, along with the gods and their followers. They

worshipped Kṛṣṇa, the bestower [of everything], with their words:

26. "We take shelter of you. You are the soul of truth, the guide of right and truth, the truth of truth, the source of truth, the vow of truth, beyond truth, the truth of the threesome,[5] and committed to truth.

27. This world is the original tree [of existence] wherein there are two birds.[6] This tree has one support, two fruits, three roots, four juices, five divisions, six characteristics, seven layers, eight shoots, nine outlets and ten leaves.[7]

28. You are the sole truth of this existence. You are the source, you are the support and you are the final repository. Those who are not wise, whose minds are covered by your *māyā*, see you as manifold.

29. You are fully enlightened *ātmā* [soul], but you continually adopt forms for the well-being of all moving and non-moving entities. These forms are constituted of *sattva* [goodness].[8] They bring happiness to righteous people, and misfortune to the wicked.

30. You are the support of all existence, O lotus-eyed one. Some, their consciousness merged in you through meditation, turn this ocean of material existence into the size of a calf's hoofprint by means of your feet, which are like a spaciously built boat.

31. You are merciful to the righteous. Those most affectionate beings, who have crossed over this fearful ocean of existence, which is so hard to cross, and have passed beyond it, leave behind in this world the boat of your lotus feet.

32. Others, O lotus-eyed one, consider themselves liberated, but their minds are impure because of turning away from you. They attain the highest destination with difficulty, but, since their minds are indifferent to your lotus feet, they fall back down.

33. Your followers, bound by affection for you, do not ever fall from your path in that way, O Mādhava [Kṛṣṇa].[9] Protected by you, they trample fearlessly over obstacles and upon the heads of the commanders of armies, O Lord.

34. For the maintenance [of the world] you assume a form constituted of pure *sattva* [goodness], which bestows auspiciousness on all embodied beings. People strive to worship

you through this form by means of Vedic rituals,[10] *yoga*, austere practices and *samādhi* [meditative absorption].[11]

35. If this personal form of yours had not been made of the quality *sattva*, O creator, then pure knowledge, which destroys ignorance, would not exist.[12] Your existence can be inferred from the light of this *guṇa* [quality]. Because it is yours, the *guṇa* [of *sattva*] illumines through your agency.

36. The path [that leads] to you can be inferred by words and by the mind. But your name and form, along with your qualities, birth and activities, cannot be perceived by anyone through the eyes. Therefore, O God, people approach you in acts of worship.

37. They recite, remember and think about your auspicious forms and names. Anyone whose mind is absorbed in your lotus feet during the performance of these acts of worship is no longer a candidate for the material world of birth and death.

38. By good fortune, O Lord, the burden of the earthly realm has been removed by your Lordship's birth. We will see the earth marked with good fortune by your beautiful feet, and heaven blessed by your mercy.

39. You are unborn, O Lord, so we cannot ascertain any cause for your birth other than that of pastime. Birth, together with survival and death, are experienced by the *jivātmā*[13] because of ignorance of you, O abode of fearlessness.

40. You have assumed incarnations as a god [Vāmana], *brāhmaṇa* [Paraśurāma], *kṣatriya* [Rāma], swan [Haṃsa], boar [Varāha], man-lion [Nṛsiṃha], tortoise [Kūrma], horse [Hayagrīva] and fish [Matsya].[14] Now protect us and the three worlds[15] in the same way, O Lord; remove the burden of the world. Homage to you, O best of the Yadus.

41. By good fortune, O mother, the supreme person, *Bhagavān*, God himself, has entered your womb with his *aṃśa* [partial incarnation] for our prosperity. Have no fear of Kaṃsa, king of the Bhoja dynasty – he is courting death. The protector of the Yadus will be born as your son."

42. After they had eulogized the supreme person, whose form is different from the normal forms of this world, the gods, headed by Brahmā and Śiva, returned to the celestial realms.'

CHAPTER 3
Kṛṣṇa's Birth

1. 'In due time, an extremely auspicious moment endowed with all good qualities arrived. At the time of [Kṛṣṇa's] birth, the constellations and the stars were all favourable. The constellation was Rohiṇī, which is presided over by Brahmā.
2. The directions[1] were clear and the sky covered with clusters of visible stars. On the earth there was a happy abundance of mines, pastures, villages and towns.
3. The rivers contained crystal clear water and the ponds were beautiful with lotuses. Lines of trees offered eulogies with the loud sounds of bees and birds.
4. A fresh breeze blew in that region, pleasing the senses and bearing pleasant scents, and the sacred fires of the *brāhmaṇas*[2] blazed forth, undisturbed.
5. The minds of the ascetics and the gods were peaceful, and kettledrums resounded in unison at the moment of birth of the unborn one.
6. The *kinnaras* and *gandharvas* burst into song, the *siddhas* and *cāraṇas* offered prayers, and the *vidyādharas* joyfully danced along with the *apsaras*.[3]
7. The sages and demigods, overflowing with happiness, showered flowers, and the clouds rumbled gently, resonating with the ocean.
8. At midnight, when deep darkness had fallen, Janārdana [Kṛṣṇa],[4] was born. Viṣṇu, who dwells in the heart of everyone, appeared in Devakī, who resembled a goddess, like the full moon appearing in the eastern direction.
9–10. Vasudeva saw that amazing, lotus-eyed child, his four arms wielding the weapons of the conch, club, lotus and disc.[5] He bore the mark of *śrīvatsa*, and the Kaustubha jewel was radiant on his neck.[6] Clad in a yellow garment, he appeared as beautiful as a dark rain-cloud. He was resplendent with a magnificent belt, and arm and wrist bracelets, and his profuse

locks were encircled with a lustrous helmet and earrings made of valuable *vaidūrya* gems.

11. Upon seeing his son, Hari, Vasudeva was overwhelmed by the auspicious occasion of Kṛṣṇa's incarnation. His eyes were wide with amazement. Overcome with joy, he bestowed 10,000 cows on the *brāhmaṇas*.

12. Vasudeva understood that this was the supreme being illuminating the birth chamber with his radiance, O Parīkṣit, descendant of Brahmā. Realizing his majesty, Vasudeva's fear was dispelled. He praised Kṛṣṇa with body bowed, hands joined in supplication, and concentrated mind.

13. Vasudeva said: "It is clear that you are *Bhagavān*, God himself, the supreme being beyond the material world. You are the knower of the minds of everyone. Your form is pure bliss and majesty.[7]

14. It was you, in the beginning, who created this world, comprising the three *guṇa* qualities, out of your own nature. Then, although not actually entering into it, you nonetheless make it seem that you have entered it.

15–16. This is like these material elements: although full of potency, they do not produce form when existing separately. Yet, when they combine and interact together, they produce the manifold universe with all its forms. They appear to enter into this world, but actually this is not the case since they existed beforehand.

17. In the same way you exist, along with the *guṇas*. These can be perceived by their characteristics, which are recognizable by the intelligence. You, however, cannot be perceived by these *guṇas*, due to being concealed. There is no inside and outside of you. You are the universal soul of everything, and the essence of the soul.

18. One who considers the external manifestation of the *ātmā* [soul] in the form of the *guṇas* [i.e. the body] to have existence separate from oneself is foolish.[8] Such an analysis is incorrect and without foundation. Consequently, such a person accepts a view which has been refuted.

19. O all-pervading Lord, they say that the origin, maintenance and destruction of this world is from you. Yet you do not

exert effort, are devoid of the *guṇas*, and are not subject to transformation. But this is not contradictory for you – you are *brahman*,[9] the controller, and all this is performed by the *guṇas* under your auspices.

20. Through your divine potency, you, the Lord, produce from yourself a white colour for the maintenance of the three worlds [Viṣṇu], then a red colour infused with power for creation from *rajas* [Brahmā], and then a black colour for the dissolution of all creatures from *tamas* [Śiva].

21. O Lord of everything and omnipresent one, desiring to protect this world you have incarnated in my house. You will destroy the armies arrayed for battle with millions of demoniac leaders masquerading as kings.[10]

22. But when the barbaric Kaṃsa heard that your birth was to be in our house, he murdered all your brothers born before you. Hearing the reports of your incarnation from his servants, he is rushing here even now, weapons in hand."'

23. *Śrī* Śuka said:

'Then, Devakī, seeing this son of hers displaying the characteristics of the supreme being, went towards him in great astonishment. She was afraid of Kaṃsa.

24. *Śrī* Devakī said: "That form which they call *brahman*, unmanifest, original, the light, devoid of the *guṇas*, unchanging, pure being, undifferentiated and devoid of activity is you. You are Viṣṇu himself, the light of the self.

25. When, through the force of time, the universe is destroyed at the end of two *parārdhas*,[11] when the great elements have entered into their elemental matrix, and when the manifest has withdrawn into the unmanifest,[12] your Lordship alone remains. You are known as all-inclusive.

26. O supreme spirit and friend, they say that this time factor of Lord Viṣṇu, from the twinkling of an eye up to the period of a year, is your activity. As a result of it, this universe acts. I surrender to you, who are that mighty controller, O refuge.

27. Mortal beings, fearful of the serpent of mortality, do not attain fearlessness, despite escaping to all corners of the world.

But now, after serendipitously obtaining your lotus feet, they can sleep peacefully. Death escapes from them.
28. You are he, the Lord. Protect us from Kaṃsa, the fearsome son of Ugrasena. We are terrified. But do not reveal this form as the supreme being, the object of meditation, to ordinary sight.
29. Let that sinful one not know about your birth in me, O Madhusūdana [Kṛṣṇa].[13] My mind is disturbed and I am trembling with fear of Kaṃsa on account of you.
30. O Lord of the universe, withdraw that transcendent form. It has four arms and is adorned with the splendour of lotus, club, disc and conch.
31. That supreme person who, at the appropriate occasion at the end of Brahmā's night,[14] bears this entire universe within his own body, is your Lordship, the same person who has entered my womb. How wonderful is this imitation of the human [ways] of the world."
32. *Śrī Bhagavān* said: "You, in a previous creation, during the era of Svāyambhuva Manu,[15] were Pṛśni, O chaste lady, and this Vasudeva was a faultless *prajāpati*[16] called Sutapā.[17]
33. After you were both instructed by Brahmā in the creation of progeny, you restrained your senses and underwent extreme ascetic practices.
34. You endured the various features of the seasons – heat, cold, sunshine, wind and rain. The impurities of your minds were removed by breath control.[18]
35. You endeavoured to worship me, desiring benedictions from me, your minds appeased by a diet of wind and fallen leaves.
36. In this way, absorbed in me and performing extreme and very arduous disciplines, 12,000 divine years passed by for you both.
37. Then, fully satisfied with your continual austerity, faith and devotion, I manifested in your heart in this form, O sinless one.
38. Being asked to choose a boon, you requested a son like me. So I, the Lord of boon-givers, have become manifest out of a desire to satisfy your desire.
39. You were childless as husband and wife, and had not

indulged in sexual intercourse. Deluded by my divine *māyā*, you did not choose liberation.

40. After I had departed, you received the blessing of a son such as me. Having fulfilled your heart's desire, you enjoyed the pleasures of sexual intercourse.

41. Not finding anyone else in the world who was my equal in the qualities of magnanimity and virtue, I became your son, known as Pṛśnigarbha, born of Pṛśni.

42. As Upendra, I was again born from both of them – that is, you both – of Kaśyapa in the womb of Aditi. Because I was a dwarf, I became known as Vāmana [the dwarf].[19]

43. In this third appearance, I have now again taken birth from you both through that same form [of Viṣṇu]. I have stated the facts, O chaste lady.

44. This form was shown to you to remind you of my previous birth. Otherwise, knowledge of my real nature would not arise, because of my appearance as a mortal.

45. Both of you, constantly thinking affectionately of me in my nature as *brahman*, as well as in my nature as a son, will attain my supreme destination."

46. After speaking in this way, Lord Hari [Kṛṣṇa] fell silent and immediately changed into an ordinary child through his *yogamāyā* power of illusion[20] while his parents were watching.

47. Vasudeva, the son of Śūra, removed his son from the room of the birth as had been directed by the Lord. Then, just at the time that he wanted to leave, Yogamāyā was born to the wife of Nanda.

48–49. As Vasudeva approached carrying Kṛṣṇa, all the entrances, which had been securely shut with huge doors and iron bolts and chains, opened of their own accord through Yogamāyā's influence, just as darkness [disappears] before the sun. Meanwhile, all of the doorkeepers and citizens slept, their consciousness and all their functions overcome [by sleep]. The clouds, rumbling mildly, showered rain. Śeṣa followed, warding off the water with his hoods.[21]

50. While Indra was pouring down rain incessantly, the river Yamunā, younger sister of Yama, the lord of death,[22] foaming

with the force of waves from its mass of deep water, became agitated with hundreds of fearful whirlpools. But she gave passage, as the ocean did to Rāma, the husband of Sītā, the goddess of fortune.[23]

51. On reaching Nanda's Vraj, Vasudeva found all the cowherd men there fast asleep. Putting his son down on Yaśodā's bed and picking up her daughter, he again returned home.

52. Vasudeva then put the infant girl down on the bed of Devakī, refastened his leg-shackles, and remained as he was before.[24]

53. Afterwards, Yaśodā, Nanda's wife, aware of the birth but exhausted, and with her memory stolen by sleep, could not recall the gender of the child.'

CHAPTER 4

*Kaṃsa's Encounter with the Goddess and his Council with his Ministers**

1. *Śrī* Śuka said:

'The doors of the house, both inside and outside, were closed as they had been previously. Then the doorkeepers, hearing the cries of a child, sprang to their feet.

2. They hurriedly approached Kaṃsa, the king of the Bhojas, and informed him of Devakī's delivery, which he had been anxiously awaiting.

3. He got up from his bed quickly, thinking "Death is here!" Stumbling along with his hair loose, he came in haste to the delivery room.

4. That pious divine and wretched lady spoke to her brother piteously: "You should not kill a female – she will be your daughter-in-law, O auspicious one.

5. Impelled by fate, you killed many infants, who were radiant as fire, O brother. You should leave me one daughter.

6. Truly, I am your younger sister, a desperate woman whose

children have all been killed, O master. You should give me this last female infant, O sibling. I am a pitiful soul." '

7. *Śrī* Śuka said:

'Devakī clung on to her infant like a wretched creature. Although implored by his sobbing sister, that brute reviled her and tore the infant from her clasp.

8. Having seized his sister's newborn infant by the feet, Kaṃsa dashed it against the surface of a rock, his [brotherly] affection displaced by self-interest.

9. Flying up immediately from his grasp, the younger sister of Viṣṇu rose into the sky and manifested herself as the goddess, bearing weapons in her eight mighty arms.

10. She was decorated with divine garlands, garments, ointments, jewels and decorations, and bore the bow, trident, arrows, shield, sword, conch, disc, and club.[1]

11. As she was being praised by the *siddhas*, *cāraṇas*, *gandharvas*, *apsarās*, *kinnaras* and *uraga* serpents, and propitiated by extravagant offerings, she spoke the following words:

12. "What will be achieved by killing me, you fool? Your enemy from a former life, the bearer of your death, has already been born somewhere else. Do not kill helpless creatures capriciously."

13. The illustrious goddess Māyā spoke in this way to Kaṃsa. She became known by many names on the earth in many different places.

14. Hearing what she had spoken, Kaṃsa was astonished. Freeing Devakī and Vasudeva, he addressed them courteously:

15. "Alas, O sister! Shame on me, O brother-in-law! Like a cannibal [eating] his own offspring, I have killed many sons. I am an evil person.

16. I am a reprobate who has abandoned pity and cast off affection for my relatives. To which future worlds will I go? Like a *brāhmaṇa*-killer, I am as good as dead, although still breathing.

17. Even gods speak lies, not only mortals.[2] As a result of putting faith in them, I, a sinful being, have killed the offspring of my sister.

18. Do not grieve for your children, O most noble ones – they are suffering the fruits of their own deeds. Subject to the will of providence, no living entities can remain together in one place for ever.

19. Just as in this world things produced from earth emerge [from earth] and then return [to earth], so, in the same way, this *ātmā* does not change, just as the earth does not change.

20. The notion of difference arises for one who does not understand this truth.[3] As a result, there is misunderstanding about the soul and about the process of acquiring and relinquishing physical bodies.

21. Because of this, O auspicious lady, do not grieve for your offspring who were destroyed by me, because everyone cannot help but obtain the fruit of their own deeds.

22. For as long as one who does not see his real self thinks that the self is killed or is the killer, he remains an ignorant person.[4] Because of this, one who has misconceptions remains in the state of being either the oppressor or the oppressed.

23. O saintly people, you are compassionate to the unfortunate, forgive my wickedness." After saying this, Kaṃsa, his face covered with tears, grasped the feet of his sister and brother-in-law.

24. Trusting the words of the goddess, Kaṃsa freed Devakī and Vasudeva from their chains and offered them his warm affection.

25. Devakī, her anger against her repentant brother pacified, forgave him and so did Vasudeva. Smiling, Vasudeva said to him:

26. "O noble one, things are indeed as you say. The consciousness of 'I-ness' and 'other-ness' is due to the influence of ignorance. As a result of this, there is discrimination among living entities.

27. Those people with discriminating vision are influenced by lamentation, joy, fear, hatred, greed, illusion and intoxication. Because of such attitudes, they do not perceive that it is this very mentality that is causing them to kill each other."

28. Kaṃsa accepted this virtuous response from Devakī and Vasudeva, who had become mollified. With their permission, he entered his residence.

29. When the night had passed, Kaṃsa summoned his ministers and told them everything that Yogamāyā had said.
30. Hearing these words of their master, the incompetent demons, who were enemies of the demigods and bore grudges against them, replied:
31. "If this is the case, O king of the Bhojas, then we will today kill all the babies who are ten days old, as well as those who are not yet ten, in all the towns, villages and pastures.[5]
32. What can the gods do by their efforts? Their minds are always terrified by the sounds of the string of your bow, and they are cowards in battle.
33. Beset on all sides by the multitudes of your arrows, which you discharge in all directions, they surrender and flee, intent upon escape.
34. Some celestial residents throw down their weapons and remain in a pathetic state with hands folded in submission; others, with hair and garments in disarray, exclaim: 'We are terrified.'
35. You do not kill those who either have forgotten the science of warfare; are deprived of their chariot; are filled with fear, distracted and intent on something else; or, their bows broken, have stopped fighting.[6]
36. What can the pampered gods do? They are only roused and boastful when away from the field of battle. And what is the use of Hari [Viṣṇu], who resides in hidden places?[7] Or of Śambhu [Śiva], who lives in the forest? And what of Indra, whose potency is limited, or Brahmā, who is engaged in ascetic disciplines?
37. Nevertheless, we are of the opinion that the gods, because of their enmity, should not be disregarded. Therefore, engage us, your followers, in uprooting them.
38. Just as a disease in the body which is neglected becomes more pervasively rooted and cannot be cured, and just as the five senses, if unrestrained, [become impossible to control], so, an enemy whose strength becomes deeply rooted cannot be dislodged.
39. Wherever there is *sanātana dharma* [the eternal religion], Viṣṇu, who is the root of the demigods, is present. This *dharma*

consists of the Vedas,[8] *brāhmaṇas*, cows, austerities and sacrifices with remuneration for the priests.
40. Therefore, O king, using all of our resources, we will kill the *brāhmaṇas*, the ascetics, the reciters of the Vedas, the performers of sacrifice and the cows, who provide milk for sacrifice.
41. The *brāhmaṇas*, cows, the Vedas, austerity, truth, self-control, peace of mind, faith, compassion, tolerance and sacrifices are the body of the Lord.
42. The Lord is the overseer of the gods and the enemy of the demons. He dwells concealed in the heart. All the gods, including Śiva and the four-headed Brahmā, have him as their root. Clearly, such aggression against the sages is the means to vanquish him." '
43. *Śrī* Śuka said:

'After holding council with his ministers in this fashion, the wicked-minded Kaṃsa, a demon trapped in the snare of destiny, decided that persecution of the *brāhmaṇas* was the solution.
44. He commanded the demons, who could assume any form at will,[9] and who were by nature inclined to killing, to engage in the wholesale slaughter of saintly people. Then Kaṃsa entered his residence.
45. The demons, who had *rājasic* dispositions,[10] and whose minds were bewildered by *tamas*,[11] undertook a campaign of enmity against saintly people. The deaths of these demons were imminent.
46. The harassment of the great destroys all good fortunes – length of life, beauty, fame, religious practice, heaven and blessings.'

CHAPTER 5

The Meeting of Nanda and Vasudeva

1. *Śrī* Śuka said:

'After his son had been born, the noble-minded Nanda's joy blossomed. Bathed, purified and decorated, he summoned *brāhmaṇas* who knew the Veda.
2. When he had arranged for the recitation of benedictory Vedic *mantras* and the birth ceremonies for his son, he also performed the worship of the gods and the ancestors, according to the appropriate injunctions.
3. He gave 200,000 well-decorated cows, and seven mountains of sesame, decorated with gold cloth and streams of jewels, to the *brāhmaṇas*.
4. Things become purified through time, through bathing and cleansing, through rites of passage, through austerities, through oblations, through charity and through contentment. The soul becomes purified through knowledge of the self.
5. *Brāhmaṇas*, together with *sūta*, *māgadha* and *vandī* bards,[1] and with singers, recited auspicious blessings, and drums and kettledrums resounded.
6. The gateways of Vraj [were decorated with] various leaves, pieces of cloth, garlands, banners and flags. Inside the houses, the courtyards and doors were sprinkled with water and cleansed.
7. The cows, bulls and calves were smeared with oil and turmeric, and [decorated with] garlands of gold, wreaths of peacock tail-feathers and various minerals.
8. The *gopas* were decorated with very valuable cloth, ornaments, garments and turbans, and arrived bearing various gifts, O king.
9. The *gopīs* were delighted when they heard of the birth of Yaśodā's son. They decorated themselves with garments, ornaments and mascara.
10. The happiness of their lotus faces [was enhanced] with lotus

blossoms and fresh saffron. They hastened along with their presentations, their full hips and breasts swaying.

11. The *gopīs* glittered with earrings of sparkling jewels, ornaments at their necks, bracelets and various garments. Showers [of flowers] from their wreaths fell from the tops of their heads as they were going along the path. They looked elegant with necklaces down to their breasts, and dangling earrings.

12. They sang loudly, bestowing the blessing "Protect him for a long time" on the boy, and sprinkling the unborn one [Kṛṣṇa] with oil and ground turmeric.

13. Various instruments were played on the great occasion when Kṛṣṇa, the limitless Lord of the universe, came to Nanda's Vraj.

14. The joyful cowherd men pushed each other over, drenching one another with water, ghee, milk and curds, and smearing fresh butter on each other.

15. The noble-minded Nanda gave charity in the form of garments, ornaments and cows to those *sūta*, *māgadha*, and *vandī* bards and to whomever else subsisted by learning.

16. In order to propitiate Lord Viṣṇu and for the prosperity of his son, magnanimous Nanda worshipped them appropriately with their desired objects.

17. The most-fortunate Rohiṇī was welcomed by Nanda the *gopa* and wandered about, adorned with garments, garlands and throat ornaments fit for the gods.

18. From that time on, the Vraj of Nanda was full of prosperity. By virtue of the fact that it was the personal abode of Hari [Kṛṣṇa], it became the pleasure ground of Ramā, the goddess of fortune,[2] O king.

19. After assigning the protection of Gokula to the *gopas*, Nanda went to Mathurā to pay the yearly tax, O Parīkṣit, descendant of the Kurus.

20. When he heard that his brother Nanda had arrived and learnt that he had paid his taxes to the king, Vasudeva went to Nanda's residential quarters.

21. Seeing him, Nanda immediately sprang up like a body that has regained its vital airs. Delighted and overwhelmed with love, he embraced his dearest Vasudeva with both arms.

22. Vasudeva was worshipped and honoured and seated

comfortably, O sovereign of the people. After inquiring as to Nanda's health, Vasudeva spoke the following words, his mind fixed on his two sons:

23. "O brother, it is by good fortune that a child was born to you. Advanced in years, you had been childless up to now, and had given up hope for a child.

24. You were wandering in this cycle of *saṃsāra*,[3] but by good fortune you have now regained life anew. Meeting dear ones is a rare thing.

25. Loved ones and friends have different *karmas*, and their cohabitation in one place is not to be. They are like boats separated by the rapid flow of the current.

26. I hope that the place where you now live surrounded by your friends is rich in forests, favourable to cattle, free from disease and abundant in water, grass and plants?

27. O brother, my son, Balarāma, thinks of you as father. Is he, along with his mother, Rohiṇī, being cherished by you both in your Vraj?

28. The three prescribed aims of life, *dharma*, *artha* and *kāma*,[4] are attained for the sake of friends. But the three aims do not accomplish their purposes when these friends are experiencing distress."

29. *Śrī* Nanda said: "Alas, many of your sons born of Devakī were killed by Kaṃsa. Only the youngest one survived, a girl, and even she ascended into heaven.

30. People are undoubtedly subject to destiny. Such destiny is supreme. One who knows that destiny is the reality for the self is not bewildered."

31. *Śrī* Vasudeva said: "The yearly tax has been given to the king, and we have seen each other. Do not stay here for too many days. There are portents in Gokula."'

32. *Śrī* Śuka said:

'Addressed thus by Vasudeva son of Śūra, the *gopas*, headed by Nanda, with Vasudeva's permission set out for Gokula with their carts yoked to the oxen.'

CHAPTER 6

*Pūtanā's Arrival in Vraj**

1. *Śrī* Śuka said:

'On his journey, Nanda, worried about impending calamities, decided that the words of Vasudeva might not have been spoken idly and took shelter of Hari [Kṛṣṇa] [in his mind].
2. The dreadful Pūtanā, slaughterer of children, had been dispatched by Kaṃsa, and was roaming about devouring infants in towns, villages and pastures.
3. Evil beings exist wherever people do not perform their duties, nor engage in devotional activities beginning with hearing about Viṣṇu, the Lord of the Sātvatas.[1] These activities can destroy all evil beings.
4. Pūtanā roamed about freely and was able to fly. One day, after changing herself into a woman by her own mystic power, she flew to Nanda's Gokula [Vraj], and entered it.
5–6. The *gopīs*, the cowherd women, saw a shapely, attractively dressed woman with flowers entwined in her braid. Her waist was heavy with voluptuous hips and breasts, and her face and hair were bright with shining ear-ornaments. The male residents of Vraj, their mind's bewitched by her sideways glances and beautiful smiles, thought that she was like Śrī, the goddess of fortune, coming to her husband with a lotus flower in her hand.
7. Then, with her mind intent on infants, that abductor of children came by chance upon the house of Nanda, and saw the child, the scourge of the wicked, on the bed. His vast powers were concealed, just like fire is concealed in ash.
8. Knowing her to be a compulsive killer of children, Kṛṣṇa, the soul of all moving and non-moving beings, closed his eyes. She lifted the infinite Lord, who was to be her destruction, on her lap, just as a fool lifts a sleeping serpent thinking it to be a rope.
9. The two mothers, overcome by her influence, saw that this

distinguished woman was inside, and stood watching her. Like a sword covered in a sheath, her heart was razor-edged – but she was careful to appear exactly the opposite.

10. The dreadful ogress placed Kṛṣṇa on her lap there, and gave the infant her breast, covered with deadly poison. Squeezing it tightly with both hands, the furious Lord sucked it, along with her life breath.

11. With all her vital parts under stress, her body drenched in sweat, writhing with convulsions, rolling her eyes and thrashing her legs and arms about incessantly, Pūtanā cried out, "Stop! Release me, release me."

12. The earth with its mountains, and space with its planets, trembled at that powerful, reverberant sound. The nether worlds and all the directions[2] reverberated. People fell to the ground fearing that thunderbolts were falling.

13. Being tormented at her breast in this way, that roamer of the night reassumed her original form, O king. Opening her gaping mouth wide, she toppled down like Vṛtra struck by the thunderbolt.[3] Her hair, legs and arms splayed out over the pastures.

14. Even while falling, her body pulverized the trees within a twelve-mile radius, O king. It was a wondrous thing.

15–17. The *gopīs* and *gopas*, whose heads, ears and hearts had just been shattered by that sound, were petrified when they saw that terrifying body with its reddish hair scattered. Its mouth had fearsome teeth the size of ploughs; nostrils like mountain caves; breasts like hillocks; eyes like deep dark wells; a hideous waist like a sandbank; feet, thighs and arms like embankments; and a belly like a waterless lake.

18. Seeing the child playing fearlessly on her bosom, the *gopīs* were panic-stricken and hastily rushed forward and snatched him up.

19. The *gopīs*, along with Yaśodā and Rohiṇī, took elaborate precautions for the protection of the boy from all sides by, for example, waving a cow's tail around him,[4] etc.

20. They bathed the child with cow's urine, and then again with cow dust. They protected him with names [of Viṣṇu, written] with cow dung on twelve different parts of his body.[5]

21. The *gopīs* sprinkled water on both hands, and on the different parts of their bodies, and then performed the application of *bīja* seed *mantras*[6] on the boy, after they had applied them on themselves:

22. "May the unborn one protect your feet;[7] Maṇimān, your knees; Yajña, your thighs; Acyuta, your loins; Hayāsya, your belly; Keśava, your heart; Īśa, your chest; Ina, your throat; Viṣṇu, your arms; Urukrama, your mouth; and Īśvara, your head.

23. May the wielder of the disc protect you in front; Hari, the bearer of the club, from behind; the killer of Madhu and the unborn one, bearers of the bow and the sword, on the sides; Urugāya, the bearer of the conch, on the corners; Upendra, from above; Tārkṣya, on the ground; and the supreme person, the bearer of the plough, on all sides.

24. May Hṛṣīkeśa protect your senses and Nārāyaṇa your vital airs. May the Lord of Śvetadvīpa protect your consciousness, and the Lord of *yoga*, your mind.

25. May Pṛśnigarbha protect your intelligence; the supreme *Bhagavān*, your soul; may Govinda protect you while you are playing; and Mādhava while you are sleeping.

26. May Vaikuṇṭha protect you while roaming about; the husband of the goddess of fortune while sitting; and the enjoyer of sacrifice, the terror of all evil spirits, while eating.

27–29. Those snatchers of infants, the *ḍākinīs*, *yātudhānīs* and *kuṣmāṇḍās*, the ghosts, departed spirits and *piśācas*, the *yakṣas*, *rākṣasas* and *vināyakas*,[8] those such as Koṭarā, Revatī, Jyeṣṭhā, Pūtanā the Mātṛkās, those who are mad, have lost their memory, are hostile to the body, vital airs and senses, who are old, seen in dreams, and are seizers of children, may they all, as well as great portents, be destroyed, fearful of the uttering of Viṣṇu's name."

30. The *gopīs*, who were bound with ties of affection, performed Kṛṣṇa's protective rites in this manner, and then his mother breast-fed her son and put him to rest.

31. In the meantime, the *gopas*, headed by Nanda, had reached Vraj from Mathurā. Seeing the body of Pūtanā they were flabbergasted:

32. "*Aho!* Ānakadundubhi [Vasudeva] has surely become a great sage or else has behaved like a master of *yoga*. This calamity was predicted by him."

33. The people of Vraj cut up the body with axes and deposited it at a distance. Then they covered it with wood and burnt it piece by piece.

34. The smoke rising from the burning body had the pleasant smell of aloe; its sins had been instantly destroyed when suckled by Kṛṣṇa.

35. Pūtanā, the devourer of people's children, was a demoness whose sustenance consisted of blood. But she offered her breast to Hari and so, despite intending to kill him, she attained *sadgati*, the destination of saints.[9]

36. What to say of those, then, who offer something of the highest value to Kṛṣṇa, the supreme soul, with faith and devotion, like his mothers did?

37. The Lord stepped upon Pūtanā's limbs as well as on her breast with his feet. These feet are meditated upon in the hearts of his devotees.[10] They are worthy of worship by those who are themselves worshipped by others.

38. Even though she was a demoness, Pūtanā attained *svarga*, the celestial realm of the gods, the destination of mothers. What need be said about the cows who act like mothers and the milk of whose udders was enjoyed by Kṛṣṇa?

39. The Lord, the son of Devakī, the bestower of all things, including liberation into the oneness of the absolute, drank until he was satisfied the milk flowing from those mothers out of their affection for their son.

40. *Saṃsāra* [the cycle of birth and death], which is produced by ignorance, will never affect these mothers who continually cast motherly glances at Kṛṣṇa.

41. When the people of Vraj smelt the fragrance of the smoke from the cremation ground, they approached Vraj, saying: "What is this? And from where does it come?"

42. After hearing the description of the arrival of Pūtanā, her subsequent acts and her death from the *gopīs* there, they were struck with great amazement and performed rites of blessing for the baby.

43. The noble-minded Nanda took up his son who had come close to death, smelt his head, and felt extreme joy, O best of the Kurus.
44. Any human being who faithfully hears about the liberation of Pūtanā, and about the wonderful deeds of Kṛṣṇa, attains love for Govinda [Kṛṣṇa].'[11]

CHAPTER 7

Deliverance from Tṛṇāvarta

1. The king said:

'Whatever Hari, who is God and Lord, does through any of his incarnations, O master, is delightful to our ears, and pleasing to our minds.
2. Frustration and craving are banished in those who hear these [deeds], their existence is quickly purified, and devotion to Hari and friendship with his followers [develop]. Speak of those captivating [deeds] if it pleases you.
3. Now [please speak about] some other marvellous childhood adventure of Kṛṣṇa, who, after descending into the human world, behaved as humans do.'
4. *Śrī* Śuka said:

'Once, during the constellation of his birth star, the chaste Yaśodā performed the bathing ceremony of the infant, conducted to the sound of *mantras* from the *brāhmaṇas*, songs and musical instruments. She was in the company of women on the occasion of Kṛṣṇa's [first] sitting-up.
5. When the bathing, and other such rites, had been completed, benedictions were performed by the *brāhmaṇas*. These received grains, and were sumptuously honoured with garments, garlands and desirable cows. Then the wife of Nanda gently laid the infant down; sleep had arisen in his eyes.
6. In high spirits, her mind excited about his sitting-up, Yaśodā

honoured the assembled residents of Vraj. But she did not hear her son. Desiring her breast, he kicked up his feet and cried.
7. The cart was struck by the tiny, tender, shoot-like feet of the infant who was lying underneath, and overturned. Its yoke was broken, its wheels and axle inverted, and its metal pots containing various liquids were scattered.
8. Assembled there for the ceremony of the sitting-up occasion, the women of Vraj, headed by Yaśodā, as well as Nanda and the others, were bewildered by this amazing sight: "How on earth could the cart have overturned by itself?"
9. The children told the perplexed *gopas* and *gopīs* that the cart had definitely been upset by the foot of the crying child.
10. The *gopas* did not believe it: "This is certainly foolish talk," they said. They did not understand the immeasurable strength of that boy.
11. Auspicious benedictions and Vedic hymns were invoked by the *brāhmaṇas*. Yaśodā, anxious about the influence of the planets, took up her son and breast-fed him.
12. The cart with its paraphernalia was arrayed as it had been before by the strong *gopas*. After they had offered oblations to the sacrificial fire, the *brāhmaṇas* performed worship with yogurt, unhusked barley, *kuśa* grass and water.
13. These *brāhmaṇas* have cast off envy, falsity, pride, impatience, violence and arrogance. The benedictions of those who are truthful by nature are never fruitless.
14–15. After this, Nanda the *gopa*, with attentive mind, picked up the child, and sprinkled him with water and pure herbs consecrated by hymns from the Sāma, Ṛg and Yajur Vedas. Then he had benedictions uttered by the best of the twice-born,[1] offered oblations to the fire, and gave high-quality grain to the twice-born.
16. He gave cows endowed with all good qualities, garments, garlands and golden necklaces, for the prosperity of his son. And the *brāhmaṇas* then bestowed [benedictions].
17. The *brāhmaṇas* are expert in *mantras*, and absorbed in meditation. Any benedictions uttered by them are potent and never fruitless.
18. On another occasion, the chaste Yaśodā was cuddling her

son. He had been lifted on to her lap, but she was not able to bear the weight of her infant, which seemed like that of a mountain peak.

19. Amazed and overwhelmed by the burden, the *gopī* put him down on the ground, and meditated on the supreme Being of all the worlds. She then tended to her chores.

20. There was a demon named Tṛṇāvarta, who was a servant sent by Kaṃsa. [Assuming] the form of a whirlwind, he seized the sitting child.

21. Enveloping the entire Gokula and obscuring the eyes [of the inhabitants] with dust, he made the directions and quarters resound with a terrifying sound.

22. For a moment the cattle pasture was enveloped in darkness from the dust. Yaśodā could not see her son where she had placed him.

23. Bewildered and oppressed by the grit unleashed by Tṛṇāvarta, nobody could see themselves or any one else.

24. The mother could not see any trace of her son in the sandstorm caused by the fierce whirlwind. The poor woman lamented pitifully, and fell on the ground thinking of Kṛṣṇa, like a cow whose calf had died.

25. When the whirlwind and the fury of its sandstorm had abated, the *gopīs* heard the wailing. Not finding the son of Nanda there, they burst into lamentation; their minds were very troubled and their faces were covered with tears.

26. Assuming the form of a hurricane, Tṛṇāvarta ascended into the sky carrying Kṛṣṇa. But his progress was checked and he could not continue bearing that tremendous weight.

27. He thought Kṛṣṇa was a boulder because of the heaviness of his body, but he could not cast off that amazing child, who was clasping him by the neck.

28. Incapable of motion because of the grasp on his neck, the demon fell down lifeless with the boy on Vraj, his eyes protruding and his cries stifled.

29. The weeping *gopīs*, who had assembled, saw Tṛṇāvarta fall from the sky on to a rock, like when Rudra pierced the city with an arrow.[2] Tṛṇāvarta's fearful limbs were all smashed.

30. The stunned *gopīs* and *gopas* led by Nanda retrieved Kṛṣṇa,

who was dangling from the chest of that [demon], and returned him to his mother. After regaining [him], they became blissful. That fortunate boy had surely been freed from the jaws of death after being borne through the sky by that man-eater.

31. "O! *Aho!* This is amazing! The child who came near to death at the hand of a demon has returned again. The murderous and wicked one has been destroyed by his own sins, and the righteous one has been freed from fear as a result of his equanimity of mind," they said.

32. "What austere practices have been performed by us? What worship of Adhokṣaja [Viṣṇu]?[3] What meritorious work, sacrifice and charity? What friendship towards living beings such that this boy, who [appeared to have] died, is again by good fortune present before us, bringing love to his relatives?"

33. The astonished *gopa* Nanda, after seeing these amazing things again and again in the big forest, continued to value the words of Vasudeva.

34. On one occasion, picking up the child and raising him on to her lap, the beautiful Yaśodā suckled him at her lactating breast, full of affection.

35–36. When her son had almost finished drinking, the mother began caressing his sweetly smiling mouth. As he yawned, O king, she saw in there the sky, heaven and earth, the host of stars, space, the sun, the moon, fire, air, the oceans, the continents, the mountains and their daughters [the rivers], the forests, and moving and non-moving living things.

37. Seeing the universe so suddenly, O king, she began to tremble. Closing her two eyes, the doe-eyed woman was completely astonished.'

CHAPTER 8

The Vision of the Universal Form

1. *Śrī* Śuka said:

'On being invited by Vasudeva, Garga, the *purohita* [family priest] of the Yadus, went to Nanda's Vraj, O king. He was a very austere person.
2. Seeing him, [Nanda] was overjoyed, considering him to be [equal to the supreme Lord] Adhokṣaja [Viṣṇu]. Nanda rose up to greet him with folded hands, and worshipped him by falling down in full obeisance.
3. The sage was comfortably seated and given a hospitable reception. After pleasing him with agreeable and honest words, [Nanda] said: "What arrangements can we make for one who is already fully complete, O *brāhmaṇa*?
4. The wanderings here and there of great souls, O Lord, are for the ultimate benefit of the common people, who are householders and poor in spirit. It never has any other purpose.
5. That knowledge of astrology, the movement of the stars, has been composed by yourself, Sir, and is beyond sense perception. By this knowledge, a person becomes aware of both imminent and distant events.
6. You are certainly the most eminent of the knowers of *brahman*. You should please perform the purificatory rites of these two boys. The *brāhmaṇa* is the *guru* of men, by birth."
7. *Śrī* Garga said: "I am well known everywhere on the earth as the spiritual preceptor of the Yadus. If your son is consecrated by me he will be revealed to be the son of Devakī.
8–9. Kaṃsa has a sinful mind. He has heard the words of Devakī's daughter, and his suspicions are aroused. After deliberating on your friendship with Vasudeva, and on the fact that the eighth pregnancy of Devakī was not supposed to be a female, he will kill [your son]. This might, therefore, be a bad course of action for us."
10. *Śrī* Nanda said: "Perform the purificatory rites of the twice-

born and utter words of blessing in this cow-pen in secret. It will not be observed even by my own relatives." '
11. *Śrī* Śuka said:

'Appealed to in this way, the *brāhmaṇa*, unrecognized, secretly performed the name-giving ceremony of the two boys. He had in any case wanted to perform it personally.
12. *Śrī* Garga said: "This one, the son of Rohiṇī, gives pleasure [*rama*] to his loved ones by his qualities, and so will be known as Rāma. Because of his excessive strength [*bala*], he will be known as Bala, and, because of his association with the Yadus, he will also be named Saṅkarṣaṇa [the uniter].
13. Bodies of three different colours, according to the *yuga*[1] – white, red and then yellow – were accepted by this other one. Now he has come with a black [*kṛṣṇa*] complexion.
14. Previously, this son of yours was born of Vasudeva, and that is why the learned refer to him as beautiful Vāsudeva.[2]
15. There are many names and forms of your son, according to deed and quality. I know them, but common people do not.
16. This boy, who is the delight of Gokula and the *gopas*, will bring good fortune. Because of him, you will all easily overcome every obstacle.
17. Previously, O lord of Vraj, in times of anarchy the righteous were harassed by bandits. Protected by him, they were strengthened and conquered the bandits.
18. People who are very fortunate place their affection in this boy. Enemies cannot overpower them, just as the demons cannot overpower those who have Viṣṇu on their side.
19. Therefore, O Nanda, this son of yours is equal to Nārāyaṇa[3] in qualities, splendour, fame and authority. Protect him with great diligence." '
20. *Śrī* Śuka said:

'After he had been instructed about himself in this way and Garga had gone to his own home, Nanda was filled with joy. He considered himself full of good fortune.
21. After a short time had passed, Balarāma and Keśava [Kṛṣṇa] roamed about Vraj, crawling around on their hands and knees.

22. The two of them crawled in the dust of Vraj like snakes, dragging their legs, which [from their anklets] gave off sweet sounds and tinkling noises. They delighted in that sound, and so they followed people, but then scurried back to their mothers as if frightened and confused.
23. Their two mothers, whose breasts were seeping milk from affection, picked their two boys up in their arms. The boys looked adorable with the mud smeared on their bodies. After offering their breasts and gazing at their faces and their tiny teeth as they suckled, the mothers fell into a blissful state.
24. When the women found their childhood *līlā*[4] worth watching, the ladies of Vraj would leave their households and enjoy themselves, looking and laughing as the two were dragged hither and thither by the calves whose tails they had grasped.
25. The two boys were very active and their play [sometimes] took them out of bounds. When their mothers could not safeguard their sons from horned or fanged animals, fire, swords, water, winged creatures and thorns, nor even perform their household duties, they became very anxious.
26. After a short time, O kingly sage, Balarāma and Kṛṣṇa were walking easily in Gokula and no longer had bruised knees.
27. Thereafter, *Bhagavān* Kṛṣṇa, along with Balarāma, played with the boys of Vraj of the same age, arousing rapture in the women of Vraj.
28. Observing the delightful childish activity of Kṛṣṇa, the *gopīs* gathered and spoke tongue-in-cheek as follows [in the presence] of his mother, who was listening:
29. "Sometimes, he releases the calves at the wrong time, and laughs when cries [of protest] are raised. Moreover, he eats the tasty milk and whey that he steals by means of his thieving devices. He divides [the curds and whey] and feeds the monkeys. If he does not eat, he breaks the pot. When there is nothing available, and he leaves angry with the household, he blames the children.
30. When he cannot reach, he devises a system [to get things] by arranging benches and rice-husking mortars. Knowing what has been placed inside the pots hanging on rope slings, the cunning boy [makes] a hole [in them] at that time of day when

the *gopīs* are absorbed in household chores. His own body, which bears clusters of precious jewels, functions as a light in the dark house.

31. While he is engaged in such audacities, he passes urine and other things in our houses. Although his deeds are carried out by theft, he outwardly appears virtuous." In this way these affairs were related by the women as they gazed at Kṛṣṇa's beautiful face with its fear-stricken eyes. With a smile on her face, Yaśodā did not want to scold Kṛṣṇa.

32. Once, when Balarāma and the other cowherd boys were playing, they complained to mother Yaśodā: "Kṛṣṇa has eaten mud."

33. Yaśodā was concerned for his welfare, and scolded Kṛṣṇa, whose eyes seemed to be full of fear. Grasping him in her hand, she said to him:

34. "Why have you secretly eaten mud, you unruly boy? These young friends of yours are saying so, and so is your elder brother."

35. "Mother, I didn't eat any mud. They are all spreading false accusations. If you think they are speaking the truth, then you look into my mouth yourself."

36. "If that is the case, then open wide," she said. Lord Hari [Kṛṣṇa], whose supremacy cannot be constrained, but who is God assuming the form of a human boy for play, opened wide.

37–38. Yaśodā saw there the universe of moving and non-moving things; space; the cardinal directions; the sphere of the earth with its oceans, islands and mountains; air and fire; and the moon and the stars. She saw the circle of the constellations, water, light, the wind, the sky, the evolved senses, the mind, the elements, and the three *guṇa* qualities.[5]

39. She saw this universe with all of its variety differentiated into bodies, which are the repositories of souls. She saw the time factor, nature and *karma*. Seeing Vraj as well as herself in the gaping mouth in the body of her son, she was struck with bewilderment:

40. "Is this actually a dream? Is it a supernatural illusion, or is it just the confusion of my own intelligence? Or is it, in fact, some inherent divine power of this child of mine?

41. Therefore, I offer homage to his feet, which are the support of this world. From them, and through their agency, this world manifests. Their true nature cannot be known by the senses nor by reason. They are very difficult to perceive by thought, words, deeds or intellect.
42. He is my refuge. Through his illusory power arise ignorant notions such as: 'I am me; he over there is my husband; and this is my son; I am the virtuous wife, protectress of all the wealth of the ruler of Vraj; and all the *gopīs* and *gopas*, along with the wealth derived from the cattle, are mine.'"
43. Then the omnipotent supreme Lord cast his *yogamāyā* [divine power of illusion] in the form of maternal affection over the *gopī*, who had come to understand the truth.
44. Immediately, the *gopī*'s memory was erased. She sat her son on her lap and returned to her previous state of mind, with her heart full of intense love.
45. She considered Hari [Kṛṣṇa], whose glories are sung by the three Vedas, the Upaniṣads, Sāṅkhya *yoga* and the *Sātvata* sages,[6] to be her very own son.'
46. The king said:

'O supreme *brahman*, what did Nanda do, to obtain such great fortune? And what did the greatly fortunate Yaśodā do, that Hari drank from her breast?
47. His mother and father did not fulfil their desire of experiencing the wonderful childhood activities of Kṛṣṇa. These can eradicate the sins of the world. Even to this day, sages sing of them.'
48. *Śrī* Śuka said:

'Once, previously, Droṇa, best of the Vasus, accompanied by his wife Dharā, said to Brahmā: "I will follow the orders of Lord Brahmā.
49. When we are born on earth, supreme *bhakti* [devotion] to Hari, the Lord of the universe, and the supreme God on earth, will flourish. Through this *bhakti*, one can easily overcome the miseries of this world."
50. "Let it be so," was the reply. He, the greatly fortunate

Droṇa, of wide renown, was born in Vraj and became known as Nanda, and she, Dharā, became Yaśodā.[7]

51. Thereafter, O Parīkṣit, descendant of Bharata, eternal devotion to Lord Janārdana [Kṛṣṇa], who had become their son, was manifest in the husband and wife and in the *gopīs* and *gopas*.

52. In order to fulfil the order of Brahmā, Lord Kṛṣṇa resided in Vraj together with Balarāma, and enchanted them by his *līlā*.'

CHAPTER 9

Kṛṣṇa's Favour to the Gopī *Yaśodā*

1. 'One time, when the house servants were busy with other chores, Yaśodā, the wife of Nanda, churned the milk herself.

2. Remembering the songs about the activities of her child, she sang them while she was churning yogurt.

3. Yaśodā churned, swaying back and forth. Her bracelets were moving on her arms, which were tired from pulling the rope, and her earrings were swinging to and fro. *Mālatī* [jasmine] flowers dropped from her hair, and her face, with its beautiful eyebrows, was sweating. She wore a linen cloth bound by a girdle on her broad, sloping hips, and her quivering breasts were leaking milk out of affection for her son.

4. Hari approached his mother as she was churning, desiring to drink her breast milk. Grasping the stirring stick, he obstructed her, demanding her love.

5. He climbed on her lap. Looking at his smiling face, she allowed him to drink from her breast, which was leaking milk from affection. But before he was satisfied she put him down in a hurry and rushed off when the milk that had been on the fire boiled over.

6. Furious and biting his quivering red lower lip with his teeth, Kṛṣṇa broke the butter churning-pot with a stone. With false tears in his eyes he went inside to a hiding place, and ate the freshly churned butter.

7. Yaśodā removed the boiling milk and came in again. Noticing the broken vessel she saw what her son had done. Not finding him there, she laughed.
8. She spied him standing on top of the base of a rice-husking mortar. He was wantonly giving fresh butter to a monkey from a hanging pot, looking anxious on account of his thieving. She approached her son stealthily from behind.
9. Seeing her with stick in hand, Kṛṣṇa hastily climbed down from there and fled, as if in fear. The *gopī* ran after him whom the minds of *yogīs*, directed by the power of asceticism, are not able to reach.
10. The slender-waisted mother chased Kṛṣṇa, her progress slowed by the burden of her broad, moving hips. A trail of flowers falling from her loosened plait in her wake, she seized him.
11. Grasping his arm she chastised him, scaring him. Looking up with eyes agitated with fright, the guilty boy was crying and rubbing his eyes, smearing the mascara with his hands.
12. Yaśodā was fond of her child, and so threw away the stick when she realized her son was frightened. Unaware of the power of her son, she wanted to bind him with a rope.
13. Kṛṣṇa has no beginning and no end, no inside and no outside. He is the beginning and end and inside and outside of the universe. He is the universe.
14. The *gopī* tied him with a rope to the mortar as if he were a common being. She considered Kṛṣṇa, who is the unmanifest truth beyond sense perception in the form of a human, to be her own son.
15. The rope for binding her guilty child was short by two fingers. So the *gopī* joined another one to the first.
16. When that also was too short, she joined another one to it, but however many ropes she brought out, they were always two fingers lacking.
17. In this way, while all the *gopīs* chuckled with amusement, Yaśodā joined together all the ropes in her household. Smiling, she was struck with wonder.
18. Seeing the efforts of his mother, whose limbs were sweating and whose wreath of flowers had fallen from her hair, Kṛṣṇa became compliant in his own binding.

19. Indeed, by this act, dear Parīkṣit, the quality of submission to [his] devotee was demonstrated by Hari [Kṛṣṇa] despite the fact that he is only constrained by his own free will. By him this universe, along with those who control it, is controlled.
20. Neither Brahmā, nor Śiva, nor even Śri, the goddess of fortune, despite being united with his body, obtained the benediction which the *gopī* obtained from Kṛṣṇa, the giver of liberation.
21. God, this son of the *gopī*, is not attained as easily in this world by embodied beings, nor by the wise, nor by the knowers of the self, as he is by those who have devotion.
22. On another occasion, while his mother was distracted by household chores, Lord Krishna noticed that the two *arjuna* trees before him had formerly been two *guhyakas*, sons of Kubera.[1]
23. They had previously been forced to take on [the forms of] trees through the curse of Nārada because of drunkenness. They were known as Nalakūvara and Maṇigrīva and were endowed with great opulence.'

CHAPTER 10

The Curse of Nārada

1. The king said:

'Please describe the cause of the curse of those two, O Lord, and tell what was that reprehensible act as a result of which the *tamas* [anger] of the divine sage was invoked.'
2. *Śrī* Śuka said:

'On becoming the companions of Śiva, the two sons of Kubera the treasurer had become very proud. On one occasion they became completely intoxicated in a delightful grove of Kailāsa called Mandākini.[1]
3. After drinking *vāruṇī*, [an alcoholic drink],[2] their eyes were

rolling from intoxication and they wandered in the flowery garden along with singing groups of females.
4. They went in to the Ganges, splendid with clusters of lotus flowers, and sported with the maidens, just like two bull elephants with female elephants.
5. By chance, the illustrious divine sage Nārada saw the two gods there, O descendant of Kuru, and noticed that they were drunk.
6. Seeing Nārada, the celestial damsels, who were naked, were ashamed and afraid of his curse. They hurriedly put on their clothes. But the two Guhyakas did not, and remained naked.
7. When he saw the two sons of the demigods intoxicated by liquor, and blinded with the pride of wealth, Nārada prepared to utter a curse for their benefit, and proclaimed the following words.
8. *Śrī* Nārada said: "There is no other quality of *rajas*, including such things as good birth, that ruins the intelligence of a person who indulges in pleasurable things, more than the pride of riches. Wherever wealth exists, there women, gambling and liquor are to be found.
9. Wherever there is pride of riches, animals are slaughtered by cruel people whose minds are unrestrained, and who think that this perishable body is without disease and immune from death.
10. Even though it is considered to be sacred, this body, in the end, is treated as dust, excrement and worms. What does one who injures living beings understand about his own self-interest? Hell accrues from such acts.
11. Does the body belong to oneself? Or to the provider of nourishment? Or to the inseminator? Or rather to the mother? Or to the mother's father? Or to the aggressor? Or to the purchaser? Or to the [cremation] fire? Or rather to the dogs?
12. In this way, the body, which is common property, has its origin and its dissolution in the *avyakta*.[3] What learned person other than a rascal who takes the body to be his own self, kills animals?
13. Poverty is the best eye-salve for rascals who are blind from the pride of wealth. A poor person views living things clearly by comparison with himself.

14. Just as one whose limbs have been pricked by thorns does not desire that pain for others – being in a state of equanimity towards living entities because of their [common] natures – so, a person who has not been pricked by thorns, does not [empathize with others' pain].
15. A poor person, devoid of the arrogance of ego, and free from all kinds of pride, obtains with difficulty whatever comes in this world providentially. This [existence] is undoubtedly one of great hardship for him.
16. The senses of a poor person who always craves food and whose body endures hunger become weakened and shun violence.
17. *Sādhus*[4] see all beings equally and only mingle with the poor. Through [association with] such saintly persons, one eradicates craving. Thereafter, one becomes purified in a short time.
18. *Sādhus* possess equanimity and desire the lotus feet of Mukunda [Kṛṣṇa] – what do they [have to do with] those who are proud of their wealth and who are dependent on unrighteous people who deserve to be shunned?
19. Therefore I will take away the pride born of ignorance of these two who are blind with the pride of riches. Their minds are uncontrolled, they are drunk with the intoxicating liquor *vāruṇī*, and they are manipulated by women.
20. Due to being the sons of the protector of the world [Kubera], those two are immersed in ignorance. Completely drunk, they do not even realize that their bodies are naked.
21. Therefore, they deserve to experience a state of immobility so that they may not again find themselves in such a condition as this. But by my mercy and favour their memory will be preserved even in that state.
22. When 100 celestial years have passed, their devotion will be restored after encountering Vāsudeva, and they will regain their personal abodes."'
23. *Śrī* Śuka said:

'After uttering this, Nārada, the divine sage, went to the ashram of Nārāyaṇa, and Nalakūvara and Maṇigrīva became a pair of *arjuna* trees.

24. Hari [Kṛṣṇa], in order to validate the words from the mouth of the all-powerful sage, went slowly to the place where the twin *arjuna* trees were situated.
25. "Since he is most dear to me, I shall now fulfil whatever was sung by that great-souled divine sage with regards to these two sons of Dhanada, the Treasurer [Kubera]."
26. [Thinking] this, Kṛṣṇa went between the twin *arjuna* trees. The mortar fell crossways as soon as his body passed through.
27. The two trees were forcibly uprooted by the boy as he dragged the mortar behind him with a rope tied around his abdomen and they fell as a result of the passage of the supreme one [between them]. They made a tumultuous sound, their branches, leaves and trunks quivering wildly.
28. On that very spot two celestial *siddhas*[5] emerged from the trees, illuminating all directions with intense brilliance. After bowing their heads down to Kṛṣṇa, the Lord of the entire universe, those two perfect beings spoke as follows, hands folded in supplication:
29. "O Kṛṣṇa! Kṛṣṇa! Supreme *yogī*! You are the primordial supreme being. The *brāhmaṇas* know that this universe, both manifest and unmanifest, is your body.
30. You are one. You are the controller of the senses, souls, vital airs and bodies of all living entities. You yourself are time. You are God, *Bhagavān*, Viṣṇu, the imperishable controller.
31. You are the *mahat*.[6] You are the subtle *prakṛti* consisting of *rajas*, *sattva* and *tamas*. You are the supreme person, the overseer, and the knower of the changes in all fields of activity.[7]
32. You cannot be captured by those who are themselves captured by the modifications of the *guṇas* of *prakṛti*. Therefore, who in this world, overwhelmed by the *guṇas*, is capable of knowing him who is prior to that which is created?
33. Homage to that person, who is you, God, *Bhagavān*, the virtuous Vāsudeva, *Brahman*. Your glory is hidden by the brilliant qualities of your own self.
34. His incorporeal incarnations are identified in corporeal bodies by those who are enmeshed in bodies, by means of the various incomparable, pre-eminent, valorous deeds of such incarnations.

35. He is your Lordship, the Lord of blessings. You have presently descended with your *aṃśa*, for the welfare and liberation of the whole world.
36. Homage, most virtuous one. Homage, supremely auspicious one. Homage to the tranquil Vāsudeva, Lord of the Yadus.
37. Grant us leave to depart, O Lord of everything. We are the servants of your devotee. This vision of your Lordship was through sage Nārada's favour.
38. May our speech be engaged in the narration of your qualities, our two ears in your stories, our two hands in your work, our mind in the remembrance of your feet, our head in obeisance to the universe which is your residence, and our eyes in seeing the saints, who constitute the body of your Lordship."'
39. *Śrī* Śuka said:

'Glorified in this manner by those two, *Bhagavān*, who was at the same time Lord of Gokula and he who was bound to the mortar, spoke to the two *guhyakas* with a smile.
40. *Śrī Bhagavān* said: "Sage Nārada is a merciful soul – you were both blinded by opulence, and so your downfall was grace bestowed by him through his words. I already knew about it.
41. Bondage cannot exist after seeing *sādhus* with non-discriminating minds whose selves are completely dedicated to me, just as darkness cannot exist in the eyes of a person after seeing the sun.
42. Therefore, Nalakūvara, now that you two are completely devoted to me, go to your abode. You aspired to [develop] love for me, which is beyond worldly existence, and it has become manifest in you."'
43. *Śrī* Śuka said:

'Being addressed in this fashion, the two circumambulated Kṛṣṇa, who was tied to the mortar, and repeatedly offered obeisance. Then, after taking their leave, they went off in a northern direction.'

CHAPTER 11

The Killing of the Crane and Calf Demons

1. *Śrī* Śuka said:

'After hearing the thundering sound of the falling trees, all the *gopas*, headed by Nanda, approached the place full of fear of an earthquake, O Parīkṣit, best of the Kurus.
2–3. There, they saw the pair of *arjuna* trees fallen on the ground. They were bewildered, unable to understand the cause of their fall even though it was in plain view – the child, bound by a rope and dragging the rice-husking mortar. But they were doubtful, saying: "Whose [work] is this? How has this amazing calamity come about?"
4. The boys said: "[It was done] by Kṛṣṇa over there as he was going through, dragging the mortar, which then fell crossways. And we also saw two beings."
5. The *gopas* were unable to accept what was said: "That could not have happened," they declared. Some found it incredible that such an uprooting of the trees could be caused by the small boy.
6. Naturally, after seeing his own son bound and dragging the mortar by a rope, Nanda, smiling, freed him.
7. Applauded by the *gopīs*, *Bhagavān* Kṛṣṇa would sometimes dance like a child, and sometimes sing innocently. Like a wooden puppet, he was controlled by them.
8. Sometimes, on command, he would carry a stool, measure or slippers, or he would sometimes throw his arms about, arousing the love of his relatives.
9. For those who could understand, *Bhagavān* Kṛṣṇa manifested the condition of [submitting] himself to the control of his dependants in this world. Truly, he brought joy to the residents of Vraj by his childhood activities.
10. [Once], upon hearing: "Hey! Come and buy fruits!", Acyuta [Kṛṣṇa],[1] the bestower of all fruits, grabbed some grains [as exchange] and rushed out, desiring fruit.

11. As the grain was falling from his hands, the woman fruit-seller filled both of Acyuta's [Kṛṣṇa's] hands with fruit, and Kṛṣṇa filled the fruit container with jewels.
12. [On another occasion] Kṛṣṇa, who had shattered the trees, went to the bank of the river and was absorbed in playing with the boys. After some time, Queen Rohiṇī called both him and Balarāma.
13. The two boys did not present themselves when called, because of their absorption in the game. So Rohiṇī sent Yaśodā, who had great affection for her son.
14. Yaśodā called her son, who, along with his elder brother, was still playing with the boys even though their time for play had run out. Her breasts were leaking milk out of love for her son:
15. "Kṛṣṇa, lotus-eyed Kṛṣṇa, my young one, come, drink from my breast. Enough games! You are hungry and exhausted from playing, O son.
16. Hey, Balarāma, my son, the darling of the family, come quickly with your younger brother. You have had only breakfast early in the morning, so you must eat.
17. O Dāśārha [Kṛṣṇa],[2] the chief of Vraj is waiting for you, wishing to eat. Come, bring us both your love. Boys – return to your own homes.
18. Your body is black with dust, my son. Come and take your bath. Today is your birthday; clean up and donate cows to the *brāhmaṇas*.
19. Look, look at the boys your age – they are scrubbed clean by their mothers and adorned beautifully. You, too, should enjoy yourself after you are bathed, nicely adorned and well-fed."
20. In this way, Yaśodā, her mind bound by affection, considered Kṛṣṇa, who is the absolute truth, to be her son. Grasping Acyuta [Kṛṣṇa] along with Balarāma by the hand, she led them to their own compound, and then performed the rites for prosperity.'
21. *Śrī* Śuka said:

'After experiencing the great disturbances in Bṛhadvana,[3] the great forest, the elders of the cowherd men, led by Nanda, gathered together and deliberated on the affairs of Vraj.

22. In that gathering, a *gopa* by name of Upananda, who was advanced in age and knowledge, spoke up. He was a well-wisher of Kṛṣṇa and Balarāma, and someone who understood time, place and the cause of things:

23. "We, who desire the welfare of Gokula, should depart from this place. Major calamities are on their way here aimed at the destruction of the boys.

24. Somehow or other, that boy was saved from the child-slaughtering demoness. What is more, by the grace of God, the cart did not fall on top of him.

25. Then he was whisked up to disaster in the sky by the demon in the form of a whirlwind. He fell on a rock over there, but was saved by the powerful demigods.

26. That this boy or someone else was not killed after finding himself between the two trees is also owing to the protection of Acyuta [Viṣṇu].

27. For as long as such calamitous misfortunes overrun Vraj, let us take the boys away from here and go somewhere else along with our followers.

28. There is a forest called Vṛndāvana,[4] which is fit for habitation by the *gopas*, *gopīs* and cows. It has fresh groves, plants, grass and sacred mountains.

29. Therefore, if this is pleasing to you all, let us go there this very day. Yoke the carts without delay. Our herds of cows should set out and go in front."

30. When they heard this, the *gopas* unanimously declared: "Well said! Well said!" They fastened together their respective cow-pens and set out, laden with their domestic chattels.

31–32. After placing the elderly, the children, women and chattels on the carts, and with their cows in front, the cowherd men set out with their priests, O king. Fully alert with bows in hand, they blew their horns in every direction and made loud trumpet sounds.

33. Seated on the carts, the *gopīs* looked beautiful. Dressed attractively with golden ornaments at their necks, and with fresh

kuṅkum powder on their breasts, they took pleasure in singing about Kṛṣṇa's *līlā*.
34. Yaśodā and Rohiṇī were seated on the same cart. They were delighted by Kṛṣṇa and Balarāma, and eager to hear those narrations.
35. They entered Vṛndāvana, and set up their cowherd camp there, with their carts [arranged] like a half moon. It was a place which brings happiness in all seasons.
36. Seeing Vṛndāvana, Mount Govardhana and the sandbanks of the Yamunā river, Balarāma and Mādhava [Kṛṣṇa] experienced great joy.
37. The two boys became, in time, caretakers of the calves, amusing the residents of Vraj with their childish antics and unformed words.
38. Accompanied by the cowherd boys and [equipped] with paraphernalia for different games, they grazed the calves nearby, in the land of Vraj.
39–40. Imitating the animals with their cries, they roamed about like two mortals. Sometimes, they played flutes, sometimes they let fly with slings, sometimes [they played] with their feet, their ankle bells [jingling], and sometimes, acting like bulls with other pretend bulls and cows, they fought each other, roaring.
41. One time, a demon came to the banks of the Yamunā, intending to kill Kṛṣṇa and Balarāma while they were grazing their cows with their young friends.
42. Seeing the demon, in the form of a calf, enter the herd of calves, Hari slowly approached, pretending to be unaware, while pointing him out to Balarāma.[5]
43. Seizing him by his rear legs and his tail, Kṛṣṇa whirled him around and hurled him lifeless to the top of a *kapittha* tree.[6] Assuming a huge body, the demon fell, along with the *kapittha* trees, which he brought crashing down.
44. Seeing that, the boys were amazed and praised Kṛṣṇa: "Well done! Well done!" The gods, showering them with flowers, were also delighted.
45. The two boys, the sole keepers of the whole universe, became

keepers of calves. Taking their breakfast with them, they roamed here and there, grazing the calves.

46. Once, all of them went near a reservoir, wanting to water their respective herds of calves. They made their calves drink, and then drank themselves.

47. The boys saw a huge creature standing there, and became frightened. It was like the fallen peak of a mountain that had been cut through by a thunderbolt.

48. It was in fact a powerful demon called Baka, who had assumed the form of a crane with a sharp beak. Approaching suddenly, the demon swallowed up Kṛṣṇa.

49. When they saw Kṛṣṇa swallowed by the great Baka, the boys, headed by Balarāma, fainted, like senses deprived of their vital airs.

50. Baka immediately disgorged the son of a cowherd, who was burning like fire in the depths of his throat. Kṛṣṇa, who is the father of Brahmā, the *guru* of the world, was uninjured but utterly furious. Baka approached again, in order to kill him with his beak.

51. As the cowherd boys looked on, the Lord of the righteous seized Baka, the friend of Kaṃsa, as he was rushing towards him, and effortlessly tore him apart by his two beaks like a blade of *vīraṇa* grass, to the joy of the residents of the celestial worlds.

52. At this, the inhabitants of the worlds of the gods rejoiced, [offering] homage with conches and drums, and showering the enemy of Baka with *mallikā* [jasmine] flowers from Indra's garden Nandana. Seeing this, the sons of the cowherd men were struck with wonder.

53. The boys, headed by Balarāma, retrieved Kṛṣṇa once he had been released by Baka, and embraced him, just like the five senses embrace the life force when it has been restored. Their spirits tranquil, they led the calves off, returned to Vraj and reported what had happened.

54. When they heard this, the astonished *gopas* and *gopīs* gazed with eager eyes on Kṛṣṇa with great affection because of their concern. It was as if he had returned from the dead:

55. "This is astonishing! Many causes of death have presented

themselves to the boy. Yet disaster fell on the very ones who provoked fear in the first place.
56. Moreover, even those who looked terrifying and who approached with murderous intent could not overpower this boy. They were destroyed, like moths in a fire.
57. It is wonderful that the words of the knowers of *brahman* are never untruthful! That very thing which the great soul, *Bhagavān*[7] Garga said, has truly come to be."
58. The *gopas*, headed by Nanda, engaged joyfully in *kathā*,[8] narrations about Kṛṣṇa and Balarāma in this manner. Delighting thus, they did not experience the suffering of material existence.
59. In this way, the two boys passed their childhood in Vraj in youthful games such as playing hide-and-seek, building dams and jumping about like monkeys.'

CHAPTER 12

The Killing of the Demon Agha

1. 'One day, Hari decided to have breakfast in the forest. After arising at dawn and waking up his *gopa* friends with the pleasant sound of his horn, he set out, herding the calves in front.
2. Thousands of comely boys, equipped with flutes, bugle-horns, staffs and slings, joined him. Accompanied by thousands of calves, the boys, each driving his own before him, set out merrily.
3. Joining their own calves with the numberless calves of Kṛṣṇa, the cowherd boys diverted themselves in *līlā* while they grazed their cows here and there.
4. Although they were decorated with gold, jewels, *guñjā* berries and crystals, the boys adorned themselves with minerals, peacock feathers, bunches of flowers, young shoots and fruits.
5. They stole each other's slings and various objects and, when detected, threw them at a distance, from where others then threw them further still. Eventually they returned them, laughing.
6. If Kṛṣṇa went far off to view the beauty of the forest, they

would enjoy themselves by [running up and] touching him, saying "I was first, I was first!"

7. Some played their flutes, some blew their horns. Others hummed with the bees and still others cooed with the cuckoos.

8. They chased the shadowless birds, moved gracefully with the swans, seated themselves with the cranes and danced with the peacocks.

9. Tugging at the young monkeys, they climbed the trees with them. Then, imitating them, they joined them in swinging through the trees.

10. Jumping about with the frogs, they got soaked by splashes from the river. They laughed at their own shadows and hurled abuse at their echoes.

11. Thus, those boys who had accumulated an abundance of merit roamed about joyfully with Kṛṣṇa.[1] He is the experience of the bliss of *brahman* for the wise, the supreme Deity for those who are dedicated to his service, and the child of a human being for those who are absorbed in ignorance.

12. Although the dust of his feet is not obtained by *yogīs* with disciplined minds, even after many births undertaking ascetic practices, he has personally become an object of vision for the people of Vraj. How, then, can their fortune be described?

13. At that time, a great demon named Agha rushed out. Wanting to protect their own lives, the immortals constantly longed for his death, even though they had drunk the nectar of immortality. Agha could not tolerate the sight of the boys' happy games.

14. The demon Agha was the younger brother of Baka and Bakī [Pūtanā], and had been dispatched by Kaṃsa. He saw that the boys were led by Kṛṣṇa: "This is undoubtedly the one who brought destruction to my siblings. I will kill him, with his friends, as retribution for those two [siblings] of mine," he said.

15. "When they have been made into sesame and water[2] for my kinsmen, then the residents of Vraj will be as good as finished. When the vital airs have left, what need is there to worry about the body? Children are the very breath of all beings that possess vital airs."

16. After thus resolving, the evil-doer assumed the spectacular

body of a huge boa-constrictor. It extended for one *yojana*,[3] was as dense as a mountain, and had a mouth like a gaping cave. Agha then lay on the path in the hope of swallowing [the children].

17. His lower lip was the ground, and his upper lip the clouds. The inside of his mouth was a cave, his teeth the peaks of mountains, and there was darkness inside his jaws. His tongue was an extended highway, his breath a pungent wind, and the glow of his glare was like fire.

18. After seeing this thing there in such a form, everyone thought it to be one of Vṛndāvana's attractions, and playfully imagined that it resembled the mouth of an extended boa-constrictor.

19. "Hey, friends, say: does this heap of a creature lying ahead resemble the mouth of a snake stretched out to devour us, or not?

20. In truth, the cloud reddened by the sun's rays is like its upper jaw, and the bank, copper-coloured by its reflection, is like its lower jaw.

21. Look – the two mountain caves on the left and the right resemble the corners of its mouth, and even these high mountain peaks resemble its teeth.

22. Moreover, this highway in length and breadth seems like a tongue, and this darkness within it is like the inside of a mouth.

23. Look – this pungent air, hot with fire, seems like breath, and this foul odour of burnt creatures is just like the smell of dead flesh inside it.

24. Will it devour us as we enter it? If so, it will be destroyed in an instant by Kṛṣṇa as Baka was." Thinking thus, the boys glanced at the beautiful face of Kṛṣṇa, the enemy of Baka, and ventured in, laughing and clapping their hands.

25. *Bhagavān* heard the discussion among the boys about this spurious [creature] – even though they were unaware of what it actually was. Since he is situated in the hearts of all creatures, he knew that it was really a demon pretending to be what it was not, and so decided to hold his friends back.

26. Meanwhile, however, the boys, along with their calves, had already entered the belly of the demon. But they were not devoured by him since he, remembering his intimate friends

who had been killed by Kṛṣṇa, the enemy of Baka, was awaiting Kṛṣṇa's arrival.

27. Kṛṣṇa, who bestows fearlessness on everyone, saw that the poor boys, who knew no Lord other than him, had slipped beyond his control and were like grass in the fire of the stomach of death. He was surprised at the workings of fate, and was filled with compassion.

28. What was to be done in this situation? Kṛṣṇa wondered how two purposes could be achieved – how to kill the wicked one without harming the innocent boys. He deliberated, made a decision, and entered that mouth.

29. At this the gods, hiding in the clouds, exclaimed "Alas! Alas!" from fear, but the corpse-eating demon friends of Agha, such as Kaṃsa, were filled with joy.

30. When he heard this, the imperishable *Bhagavān* swelled up in the throat of the demon, who was intent on crushing him as well as the boys and calves.

31. At this, the vital airs of the demon's huge body were blocked, and filled the interior of the body; but the outlets were stopped up, and so the eyes popped out and rolled here and there. Then the vital airs burst out of the hole in the top of the head, and escaped outside.

32. As all the vital airs were seeping out, *Bhagavān* Mukunda [Kṛṣṇa] brought his dead friends and the calves back to life with his glance. Then he re-emerged from the mouth, together with them.

33. An amazing great light rose up from the thick coils of the snake, illuminating the ten directions[4] with its splendour. It waited in the sky for the Lord to emerge, and then entered into him before the very eyes of the residents of the celestial realms.

34. Everyone was overjoyed at this, and they all offered worship with their own particular activities – the gods with flowers; the *apsarās* with dance;[5] those who sang beautifully with songs; musicians with instrumental music; the *brāhmaṇas* with hymns of praise; and the crowds with the sound of "Victory!"

35. The unborn Brahmā heard those many celebrations of wonderful hymns, beautiful music, songs and [sounds of] "Victory!" and hastened there from his abode, which was nearby. Seeing the greatness of the Lord, he was struck with wonder.

36. The amazing dry skin of the boa became an amusement-cave in Vṛndāvana for the residents of Vraj for many months.
37. This deed – Hari's escape from death[6] by the serpent – occurred during the *kaumāra* period of life [1–5 years]. Yet the boys who had seen it related it in Vraj during the *paugaṇḍa* period [6–16 years].
38. There is nothing in this that is astonishing for Kṛṣṇa. By his *māyā* potency, he [appeared] as a small human boy, but he is the supreme creator of both the highest and the lowest. Even Agha had his sins cleansed by Kṛṣṇa's touch, and achieved *ātmasāmya* liberation – attaining the same form as God[7] – which is very difficult for the sinful to achieve.
39. Kṛṣṇa bestows the devotional path [to one who] once internalizes a mental image of Kṛṣṇa's body. Such a one is completely freed from *māyā*, and experiences the eternal happiness of the *ātmā*. What is there to say, then, when [the Lord] has entered inside a person?'
Śrī Sūta said:

40. 'In this way, O *brāhmaṇas*, Parīkṣit heard about the wonderful activities of his benefactor. With his mind focused, he again asked Vaiyāsaki [Śuka] about Kṛṣṇa's purifying activities.'
41. The king said:

'How can something relating to a particular period of time be performed in another period of time, O *brāhmaṇa*? That which the boys related in the *paugaṇḍa* period was performed by Hari in the *kaumāra* period.
42. Tell me this, O great *yogī*. I am extremely curious, O *guru*. Surely this must be nothing other than the *māyā* of Hari?
43. Although we only pose as *kṣatriyas*, we are in fact the most fortunate people in the world, because we continually drink the purifying nectar of the stories [about Kṛṣṇa] from you.'
44. *Śrī* Sūta said:

'When he was questioned in this way, O most eminent of devotees, Śuka, son of Bādarāyaṇa, lost the functions of all his senses in remembering Ananta [Kṛṣṇa].[8] He then regained awareness of his surroundings with difficulty, and slowly replied to the king.'

CHAPTER 13

*Kṛṣṇa Manifests as the Calves and Cowherd Boys**

1. *Śrī* Śuka said:

'You have raised an appropriate question, O greatly fortunate Parīkṣit. Although we hear the narrations of the Lord repeatedly, you make them fresh, O best of devotees.
2. This is the natural mentality of saintly persons who cultivate only the essence [of truth]; their minds, ears and voices are used only for that purpose. This is because pure discussion about Acyuta [Kṛṣṇa] always seems fresh, just like discussion about women is always fresh for debauchees.
3. Listen attentively, O king, and I will tell you even though it is confidential. Actually, *gurus* explain even confidential things to their affectionate disciples.
4. After saving the calf-keepers from death in the mouth of Agha, *Bhagavān* Kṛṣṇa led them to the sandy bank of the river, and spoke as follows:
5. "Hey, friends, the sandy beach is really delightful and covered with soft, clear sandbanks for our play. It is filled with trees reverberating with the sounds and echoes of birds, and of bees attracted by the scent of lotuses in flower.
6. The day is advanced: we should eat our meal here. The calves, who are hungry, may graze at leisure nearby, after they have drunk water."
7. "Let's do it," the boys said. After the boys had watered the calves, they climbed on to the grassy place, opened their sling bags and enjoyed their meal, together with the happy *Bhagavān* Kṛṣṇa.
8. The boys of Vraj sat in many rows encircling Kṛṣṇa, with their faces turned towards him. Their eyes were wide with joy,

and they glowed like petals round the pericarp of a lotus flower.
9. Some of them made plates from petals and flowers, and others used shoots, sprouts, fruits, slings, bark and rocks; then they ate.
10. All of them showed each other the different samples of the things they each were eating. Laughing and making each other laugh, they ate their food along with the Lord.
11. While the residents of *svarga* [the celestial region] looked on, Kṛṣṇa, the enjoyer of sacrifices,[1] took pleasure engaging in childish play. He carried a flute in the garments around his stomach, and a horn and a staff in his belt. In his left hand was a tender morsel of food, and in his fingers were pieces of fruit. Standing in the middle of his circle of intimate friends, he made them laugh with his games.
12. However, O Parīkṣit, descendant of Bharata, while the keepers of the calves, whose very soul was Acyuta [Kṛṣṇa], were eating in this fashion, the cows wandered far into the forest, tempted by grass.
13. Seeing the boys struck by fear, Kṛṣṇa, who is the fear of the fears of this world, said to them: "Do not stop eating, friends. I will fetch the calves back myself."
14. Having said this, *Bhagavān* Kṛṣṇa, a morsel of food in his hand, went off to look for their calves in mountains, caves, groves and thickets.
15. Meanwhile, the lotus-born Brahmā came to see yet another pleasing wonder of the Lord who had become a boy by his *māyā*. Previously he had been greatly astonished after descending from the celestial realms and seeing the liberation of Aghāsura by the eminent Kṛṣṇa. He led the calves and calf-herders away from there to some other place, O best of the Kurus, and then disappeared.
16. Failing to find the calves after some time, or, after going to the river bank, the calf-herders either, Kṛṣṇa searched thoroughly for both in the forest.
17. Needless to say, not finding the calves and the calf-keepers anywhere inside the forest, Kṛṣṇa, the knower of the universe, immediately understood everything that had been done by Brahmā.

18. Thereupon Kṛṣṇa, the Lord and maker of the universe, transformed his own self into both [the calves and the boys] in order to give pleasure to the mothers of those [calves and calf-herders] as well as to Brahmā.
19. He took the form of as many little bodies of calves and calf-herders as there were calves and calf-herders, with as many hands and feet and bodily parts. He assumed the shape of as many staffs, horns, flutes, petals, slings, ornaments and garments, and adopted as many behaviours, qualities, names, appearances and ages, and as many playful personalities. The unborn one, who is the form of everything, became as if an affirmation of the saying "everything is the *māyā* of Viṣṇu".[2]
20. Then Kṛṣṇa took care of his calves, who were his own self, by himself in the form of the calf-herders. The Self of everything entered Vraj, playing games with himself [in the form of the calves and boys].
21. After leading each and every one of the calves separately, Kṛṣṇa made them enter into their respective cowsheds and he then entered into each and every house. He existed as each and every entity, O king.
22. Their mothers hastily rose up at the sound of the flutes, picked [the boys] up in their arms and embraced them profusely. Thinking the supreme *brahman* to be their sons, they then made them drink the nectar of their breast milk, which was flowing from love.
23. Thus Mādhava [Kṛṣṇa], after engaging in the regular schedule of the day, came to the evening, O king, giving joy with his activities. He was then tenderly attended to with massage, a bath, the application of scents, ornaments, protective *mantras*, sacred clay, food and other things.
24. Meanwhile the cows hurried towards the cowsheds and suckled their respective calves, who had assembled there, summoned by the sounds of the cows' mooing. The cows licked the calves repeatedly, milk flowing from their udders.
25. The motherliness of the cows and the *gopīs* towards Kṛṣṇa was just the same as [it had been for their own calves and sons] previously, except that now there was an increase in affection, and the filial behaviour of Hari towards them was the

same [as that of the real calves and sons], except without the illusion.[3]

26. The affection of the people of Vraj for their own sons grew gradually, like a creeping plant, day by day throughout the year. It was not the same as before; it was without limits, just as it had been for Kṛṣṇa.[4]

27. In this way, Kṛṣṇa, the supreme soul as a cowherd boy, herded himself by means of himself through the assumed forms of the calves and calf-herders, and sported in the forests and cow-pastures for an entire year.

28. On one occasion, when five or six nights remained to complete the year, the unborn Kṛṣṇa, who was grazing the calves with Balarāma, entered the forest.

29. At that time, the cows who were grazing on the grass at the top of Mount Govardhana saw the calves grazing far away near Vraj.

30. On seeing them, the cows were overcome with love for their calves. Forgetting themselves, they hastened along on two [pairs of] legs by a path that was hard going even for their own keepers. Their heads and tails were raised, their necks were [stretched back] on to their humps, they were making lowing sounds, and their milk was flowing.

31. After meeting the calves below, the cows made them drink milk from their own udders, even though they possessed calves [of their own]. They also licked their limbs as if they were going to swallow them.

32. The *gopas* were furious with embarrassment at the failure of their efforts to prevent them. They approached by the same arduous route with difficulty, and saw their sons with the calves.

33. Their hearts were overwhelmed by a loving surge of *rasa*[5] at seeing them. Affection was kindled and their anger was dispelled. They lifted up the boys, embraced them with their arms, and experienced the highest ecstasy by smelling their heads.

34. After this, the adult *gopas* departed slowly and with difficulty. Their minds were happy from embracing their children and tears welled up at the memory of them.

35. Balarāma noticed the Vraj community's constant longing for their offspring because of this increase in love, even though

these offspring had been weaned. Not knowing the cause, he thought:

36. "What is this amazing thing? The love of the community of Vraj, and of myself, for the children is growing as it never has before, as if it were for Vāsudeva, the soul of everything.

37. Who is this being [who has caused this] and why has she created this condition?[6] Is she a divine being, a woman, or even a demoness? In all probability it is the *māyā* [illusion] of my Lord Kṛṣṇa. There is no other entity that can bewilder even me."

38. Thinking this, Balarāma understood with the eye of knowledge that the calves and all the companions as well were Kṛṣṇa, the Lord of Vaikuṇṭha:[7]

39. "These are not lords of the demigods, nor are they sages; it is you yourself, O Lord, who are manifest in these individual forms. Tell me briefly – how did their separate existence come about?" Balarāma eagerly absorbed the turn of events from the Lord whom he had addressed in this way.

40. Meanwhile, Brahmā, the self-generated god, returned after a period of time which, by his standards, was merely an instant.[8] He saw that Hari had been playing throughout the year with himself transformed [into the forms of his companions] just like before:

41. "However many boys and their calves there were in Gokula, that same number are all sleeping in the bed of my *māyā*. To this very day, none of them has reawakened.

42. So where do these boys who have been playing here together with Viṣṇu for one year come from? They are different from those there [in the hiding place] who are bewildered by my *māyā*, although they are certainly the same in number."

43. After pondering thus on these differences for a long time, the self-generated Brahmā was not able to understand in any form or fashion which of the two [sets of boys and calves] was real, and which not.

44. Thus, in causing illusion for Viṣṇu, who is free from illusion and who deludes the whole universe, even the unborn Brahmā was in fact himself deluded by his very own *māyā*.

45. Inferior *māyā* used on a superior person destroys the power

of the person invoking it, just like the darkness of fog is destroyed in the night, or the light of a glow-worm in the day.

46. Meanwhile, as the unborn Brahmā was watching, all the calves and herders suddenly became dark as rain clouds and appeared wearing yellow silk garments.

47. They had four arms and held the conch, disc, club and lotus in their hands. They wore helmets, earrings, pearl necklaces and garlands of forest flowers.

48. They were adorned with the *śrīvatsa* [tuft of hair], arm-bracelets and two jewelled conch bangles and bracelets on their wrists. They glittered with foot-bracelets, arm-bracelets, belts and finger rings.

49. Their bodies were covered from head to toe with soft garlands of fresh *tulasī*, which is offered by those who excel in piety.

50. With radiant, moon-like smiles, and glances from the reddish-coloured corners of their eyes, they looked like the creators and protectors of the needs of their devotees by means of *sattva* and *rajas*.[9]

51. They were venerated in various ways by many forms of worship. These included singing and dancing by all moving and non-moving embodied entities – from the first being, Brahmā, down to the clump of grass.

52. They were surrounded by the mystic powers such as *aṇimā* [minuteness]; the potencies such as that of *māyā*; and the twenty-four elements such as the *mahat*.[10]

53. They were worshipped by time, nature, the *saṃskāras*,[11] desire, *karma*, and the *guṇas*, and so forth, all of them possessing form. Their greatness was eclipsed by the personal greatness of Viṣṇu.

54. The forms were only of one *rasa*, essence: truth, knowledge and unlimited bliss.[12] Their unlimited glory had not been experienced even by the seers of the Upaniṣads themselves.[13]

55. In this fashion, Brahmā, the unborn one, saw everything simultaneously as the personal self of the supreme *brahman*, from whom the appearance of everything in this world, moving and non-moving, manifests.[14]

56. Then Brahmā, the unborn one, opened his eyes wide with

amazement, his eleven senses[15] stunned, and fell silent before that majesty. He was like a doll before the local goddess of a town.

57. Thus he was unable to understand that [absolute truth] which is beyond reason, which is self-manifest, which stands in its own glory, and which is established in the principal Vedic texts by the elimination of that which it is not.[16] "What is this?" he thought. When Brahmā, the lord of Irā [Sarasvatī], was bewildered in this way, Kṛṣṇa, the transcendental, unborn, supreme being, understood and instantly concealed his *māyā*.

58. Then, Brahmā, who had regained his material vision, stood up like a corpse [that had come back to life]. Opening his eyes with difficulty, he saw the entire universe, along with his own self.

59. Immediately looking around in all directions, he saw Vṛndāvana in front of him. It was spread with trees, which afford a livelihood for the inhabitants, and with other desirable things.

60. In Vṛndāvana, those who by nature live in enmity such as man and deer, lived together like friends. Craving and anger, and other such negative qualities, dissolved in the abode of Ajita [Kṛṣṇa].[17]

61. There, Brahmā, the supreme deity, saw Kṛṣṇa, the absolute *brahman*, continuing to act as a child in the family of cowherd folk. The one supreme eternal being, who is without a second[18] and whose knowledge is without limit, was searching all over for his friends and his calves, with a tasty morsel in his hand, just as before.

62. Seeing this, Brahmā quickly got down from his vehicle, and prostrated himself upon the ground like a golden rod. He touched Kṛṣṇa's two feet with the crest of his four crowns, and worshipped him with a bathing ceremony performed using auspicious tears of joy.

63. He continued rising repeatedly and then falling at the two feet of Kṛṣṇa for a long time, remembering again and again the grandeur that he had just seen.

64. Then, getting up slowly in humility and wiping his eyes, Brahmā gazed at Mukunda [Kṛṣṇa]. Stammering and trembling, he worshipped Kṛṣṇa with a stream of prayers, his neck bent in

submission, his hands folded in supplication, and his mind intent.

CHAPTER 14

Brahmā's Eulogy

1. '*Śrī* Brahmā said: "I offer you homage, O praiseworthy one. You have two soft feet, your body is the colour of clouds and your garment the colour of lightning. Your face glitters with peacock feather ornaments and *guñjā* berry ear-ornaments, and you wear a garland of forest flowers. You are the son of a cowherd, and your beauty is enhanced by your flute, horn, staff and morsel of food.

2. Although I am Brahmā, O God, I am still unable to understand the greatness of this, your body, that is before my very eyes, even with my mind directed inward. It was manifest out of your own desire as a favour to me. It is not made of material elements. What can I know of your experience of happiness within yourself?

3. Although unconquered within the three worlds, you are often conquered by those who, having given up the pursuit of knowledge entirely, remain at home and live simply by worshipping the stories of your Lordship with their minds, words and bodies. These stories can be known by being heard, and are recited by pious people.

4. O Lord, those who have rejected *bhakti*, the most beneficial path, toil hard to obtain knowledge exclusively. For them, toil itself is the only outcome, nothing else, just like those who thresh the coarse outer husks of grain.

5. In the past, there were many *yogīs* in this world, who attained your supreme destination, O universal one. With their efforts dedicated to you, they became enlightened through *bhakti*, which is produced from stories of you and gained through one's own work, O imperishable Acyuta [Kṛṣṇa].

6. Nevertheless, O universal one, it is possible for you, whose

greatness is free from the *guṇas*, to be known from personal experience by those whose souls are pure. This is accomplished through the essential nature of the self [*ātmā*], which can be known only by itself, and by no other means, for it is unchangeable and formless.[1]

7. The sand of the earth, the snow in the sky and the rays of light in the heavens can be counted, in the course of time, by those who are highly skilled. But, although you are the essence of all qualities, who is able to count your qualities? You have descended [to earth] for the welfare of this world.

8. Therefore, one who contemplates your compassion accepts the ripened fruits of personal *karma* that have been accumulated; offers obeisance to you with heart, words and body; receives your mercy and lives in a state of liberation.

9. Just see, O Lord, my un-Āryan behaviour towards you who are the original, unlimited supreme soul. You are the supreme possessor of *māyā* from all those who possess *māyā*. See how much I desired to see your own potency, like a spark before the fire.

10. Therefore, forgive me, imperishable Acyuta [Kṛṣṇa]. I am born from *rajas*. Being ignorant, I considered myself a lord independent of you. My eyes are blind from ignorant pride of being the unborn one. A person such as I who has accepted you as Lord should be shown compassion. [Please be compassionate] to me.

11. Who am I, but a person with a body measuring seven hand-spans within the container of an egg-like universe which is enveloped by ignorance in the form of earth, water, fire, air, ether, ego and intelligence?[2] And what is this compared to your greatness? You are endowed with such a form that the pores of your skin are the air passageways through which innumerable egg-like universes are moving like tiny atoms.[3]

12. O Adhokṣaja [Kṛṣṇa],[4] is the kicking of the feet of the embryo considered an offence by the mother? Doesn't everything designated as existing and non-existing exist within your belly? What is there that is not contained within you?

13. But the statement, 'On the water from the oceans which merged at the end of the three worlds, Brahmā, the unborn one,

issued from the stalk on the navel of Nārāyaṇa' is not false.[5] Have I not sprung forth from you, O Lord?

14. Are you not Nārāyaṇa, indeed? You are the witness of all the worlds, O supreme Lord. You are the soul of all embodied beings. [It is said that] 'Nārāyaṇa is a subordinate being because he is the source [*ayana*] of the water arising from the original man [*nāra*]'[6] – but this cannot be true – it must certainly be your *māyā*.

15. If this were true, O *Bhagavān*, if your form positioned on the water within the universe really exists, then why was it not seen by me then? Why, rather, was it clearly seen in my heart at that same time? And why, furthermore, did it immediately disappear again?[7]

16. Indeed, it is here, in this very incarnation, O dispeller of *māyā*, that the *māyā*-like nature of this entire, external, visible and phenomenal universe was revealed by you to your mother, in your stomach.[8]

17. Just as this entire universe, along with you yourself, is manifest within your stomach, so, although it is within you, it appears in its totality here [outside of you]. How is this possible except through *māyā*?

18. Have you not demonstrated to me this very day the *māyā* nature of this universe – with the exception of yourself? First you were alone, then you were with all your friends and calves from Vraj as well. Then you became the corresponding number of four-armed forms, which were worshipped by everyone, including myself. Then you became the corresponding number of universes. You are the immeasurable *brahman* without a second.

19. For those who are ignorant, your nature is not spiritual. After expanding your *māyā* from yourself, you appear as me, for the creation of the universe, as you yourself, for the maintenance of the universe, and as Śiva, the three-eyed one, for the destruction of the universe.[9]

20. Although you are unborn, O Lord, your birth has occurred among gods and sages, as well as among humans too. It has also taken place among animals and aquatics.[10] Your birth is in order to curb the pride of the unrighteous, and to bestow favour on the righteous, O master and Lord.

21. O universal One, God, supreme soul, master of *yogīs*, who in the three worlds understands the play of your Lordship or where, how, how many times, or when you extend your *yogamāyā* and play?
22. This entire universe, therefore, has a nature that is false and dream-like, although, arising from *māyā*, it appears real. It is devoid of knowledge and replete with great difficulties. Yet it is actually situated in you. Your body is eternal bliss and knowledge, and you are unlimited.
23. You are the one self, the supreme being, ancient, the truth, self-effulgent, unlimited, original, eternal, imperishable, perpetually happy, immaculate, complete, without a second, and free from limitations and death.
24. Those who clearly perceive you in this way as being their own soul, as well as the very soul of everything, cross the ocean of false material existence. They perceive through the essence of the soul, and through the eyes of the Upaniṣadic texts, which are received from the *guru*, who is like the sun.
25. The entire material manifestation arises for those who do not recognize their own soul by means of the soul's nature of self-awareness, as a result of that very [ignorance]. But it disappears again through knowledge, just like the appearance and disappearance of the coils of a snake [superimposed] on a rope.[11]
26. The terms 'liberation' and 'bondage in *saṃsāra*' are ignorant labels. From the perspective of knowledge of the truth, these two are actually not different when they are perceived by the pure transcendent soul whose consciousness is unobstructed, just as night and day are not different from the perspective of the sun.
27. Just see the ignorance of ignorant people who persist in thinking that the self is to be sought externally. They consider you to be something other than the real self, and consider something else [the body] to be their actual self.
28. The saints, rejecting that which is false, seek for your Lordship within, O unlimited one. Surely, without realizing the false nature of the snake nearby, how can saintly persons realize its true quality [as a rope]?

29. Therefore, O God, one who has received even a trace of grace from your two lotus feet understands the nature of the greatness of God, *Bhagavān*; no other individual will do so, despite searching at length.
30. Therefore, O master, either in this life or in another, or in one among the animals, may that great fortune occur through which I, though just an individual, may become one of your devotees, and worship your blossom-like feet.
31. See how very fortunate are the young women and the cows of Vraj; the milk/nectar from their breasts and udders was fully drunk with great delight by you in your form as the sons and the calves. Until now, even, Vedic sacrifices have not provided you with the same degree of satisfaction.
32. See the good fortune, O just see the good fortune of Nanda the *gopa* and the residents of Vraj! Their friend is the supreme bliss, the eternal absolute *brahman*!
33. Let the greatness of their good fortune be what it is, O infallible Acyuta; to be honest, we, the eleven [presiding deities of the sense organs], are also certainly very fortunate. We – Śiva and the rest of us – repeatedly drink the nectar of the sweetness flowing from your feet through the cups that are the sense organs of those residents.[12]
34. The most fortunate of births would be any birth whatsoever here in this forest – especially in Gokula – where there is bathing in the dust from any [of the residents of Vraj].[13] Their entire life is *Bhagavān*, Mukunda [Kṛṣṇa]. Even up to the present, the dust of his feet is sought after by the Vedas themselves.
35. What, O God, can you bestow on these residents of the cowherding communities? They have dedicated their homes, wealth, friends, loved ones, selves, bodies, vital airs and minds to you. Our mind is bewildered even by simply wondering where on earth could there be any reward other than you yourself, the highest reward in the universe? Even Pūtanā, in the guise of a good person, along with her family, attained you, O God.
36. So long as people do not become your devotees, O Kṛṣṇa, qualities such as attachment [that steal away their lives] act as thieves, the house is a prison, and illusion remains a foot-shackle.

37. Although you are transcendent to whatever is materially manifest, you imitate that which is material on this earth in order to spread an abundance of bliss among your submissive devotees, O master.
38. As for those who [think they] know [you], let them know. As far as I am concerned, what is the use of many words, O master? Your glory is not within the reach of my mind, body or words.
39. Grant me leave to depart, O Kṛṣṇa. You know everything, O universal seer. You alone are the master of the universes, and so this universe is offered to you.
40. Reverence to you until the end of the duration of the universe, and for as long as the sun exists, O *Śrī* Kṛṣṇa. You are the giver of pleasure to the lotus-like dynasty of the Vṛṣṇi clan, and you cause the earth, immortals, *brāhmaṇas*, animals and oceans to prosper. You are the dispeller of the darkness of heresy, and the enemy of the demons on the earth. It is you who are worthy of praise."'
41. *Śrī* Śuka said:

'After offering praise to the all-encompassing one in this fashion, Brahmā, the creator of the universe, circumambulated him three times, made obeisance at his feet, and returned to his own pleasant abode.
42. *Bhagavān* gave leave to the self-generated Brahmā [to depart], and then led the calves, who found themselves as they had been before, back to the sandy bank of the river. There his own friends were waiting, as they had been earlier.
43. Although one year had passed in separation from the Lord of their life, the boys thought it had been half a moment, O king. They had been overcome by Kṛṣṇa's *māyā*.
44. What can those whose minds are bewildered by *māyā* not forget? After all, this entire deluded world has consistently forgotten its own self.
45. Kṛṣṇa's friends said to him: "Welcome back! [You have returned] with great speed! Not a single morsel has been eaten. Come on over and eat to your heart's content!"
46. At this, Hṛṣīkeśa [Kṛṣṇa],[14] smiling, took his lunch with the

boys. He showed them the skin of the boa-constrictor and then returned to Vraj from the forest.
47. Summoning the cows, he entered the cow-compound accompanied by much merry noise from the clamour of horns and split bamboos. His limbs were decorated with minerals from the forest, flowers and peacock feathers. His glories, which purify [those who hear them], were celebrated in song by his followers, and the sight of him was a feast for the eyes of the *gopīs*.
48. In Vraj the children sang: "Today a great snake was killed by the son of Nanda and Yaśodā, and we were saved from it."'
49. The king said:

'O *brahman*, explain how [the residents of Vraj] exhibited a degree of love for Kṛṣṇa, who was born from someone else, that was unmatched even for their own children.'
50. *Śrī* Śuka said:

'One's own self is the dearest thing for all living beings, O king. In fact, it is because of the love of one's self that other things such as offspring and wealth, etc., exist.
51. Therefore, O Parīkṣit, lord of kings, there is less attachment for the things that sustain one's self-interest – sons, wealth, home and other worldly assets – on the part of living beings than there is for one's own individual self.
52. [Acceptance of] the body as the most precious thing surpasses [acceptance] of things that are subordinate to the body [sons, wealth, etc.]. This is the case even for those persons who believe that the self is the body, O best of kings.
53. Even if the body is [accepted as only] a part of "that which is mine", then it is still not as dear as the self. Indeed, when this body grows old, the aspiration for life becomes stronger.
54. Therefore one's self is the dearest thing for all embodied beings. It is for its sake that this whole universe of moving and non-moving entities exists.
55. You should understand that this Kṛṣṇa is the self of all selves. Through his *māyā*, he appears like an embodied being in this world for the benefit of the universe.

56. For those who understand Kṛṣṇa in truth, everything in the realm of mobile or immobile entities is the manifest form of God. There is nothing else anywhere in this world.
57. The cause of all things exists as their essence. [The cause] of that cause is *Bhagavān* Kṛṣṇa. Let anyone give evidence of anything that is not him.
58. For those who have taken refuge in the vessel of the lotus feet of Murāri [Kṛṣṇa][15] of virtuous fame, which are the abode of great souls, the ocean of material existence becomes like the hoof-print of a calf. They attain the supreme destination. This world, with its miseries at every step, is not for them.
59. Whatever you have asked me in this regard has been fully explained to you. What Hari did in his *kaumāra* period of life [1–5 years], was related in his *paugaṇḍa* period [6–16 years].[16]
60. Any person hearing and recounting this adventure of Murāri [Kṛṣṇa] with his friends – the slaying of Agha, the meal in the meadow, the super-normal manifest forms, and the prolific eulogies by Brahmā – [will fulfil] all his desires.
61. In this way, the two boys passed their childhood in Vraj in youthful games such as playing hide-and-seek, building dams and jumping about like monkeys.'

CHAPTER 15

The Killing of Dhenuka

1. *Śrī* Śuka said:

'Thereafter, when they had attained the age of *paugaṇḍa* [6–16 years], the two boys were approved as cowherd men in Vraj. Herding the cows along with their friends, the two made Vṛndāvana sacred with their footprints.
2. At that time, looking for sport, Mādhava [Kṛṣṇa], accompanied by Balarāma and with his cows in front, entered a forest that was suitable for cattle and covered with flowers. He was

playing his flute and was surrounded by *gopas* telling of his glories.
3. Seeing the forest full of the delightful sounds of bees, deer and birds, *Bhagavān* turned his mind to pleasure. The forest was enticing, abounding as it did with ponds whose water was as clear as the minds of great souls, and [swept] by a wind scented by hundred-petalled [lotuses].
4. Kṛṣṇa, the original person, saw the forest trees, beautiful with reddish buds, their tops [bent down] to touch his two feet everywhere through the weight of their abundant flowers and fruits. Smiling a little with delight, he spoke to his elder brother.
5. *Śrī Bhagavān* said: "Just see, O best of Gods! After gathering offerings of jasmine flowers and fruits, these trees are bowing down their heads to your lotus feet, which are worshipped by immortals. This is in order to terminate their birth as trees, which was attained through ignorance.
6. These bees are singing of your glories, which are the subject of veneration for the whole world. As they pursue you along the way, they are worshipping you, O original person! They are mostly the hosts of sages, your most fervent devotees [from past lives]. Although deep in the forest, they do not abandon the Lord of their heart, O one without sin.
7. The forest-dwellers are truly fortunate. These peacocks are dancing, O praiseworthy one, and the does are joyfully soliciting your affection with glances as if they were *gopīs*. The flocks of cuckoos [welcome] you with Vedic hymns, since you have come to their home. Such is the greatness of the nature of saints.
8. Fortunate is the earth, today: the grass and plants have been touched by your feet and the trees and creepers have been brushed by your nails. The rivers and mountains, birds and animals [have been embraced] by your merciful glances, and the *gopīs* have [been enfolded] in your two arms, which are desired even by Śrī, the goddess of fortune."'
9. *Śrī* Śuka said:

'In this way Kṛṣṇa enjoyed beautiful Vṛndāvana, happy in spirit, grazing the cows on the mountain river banks together with his friends.

10. Sometimes, when the bees sang, blinded with intoxication, Kṛṣṇa, whose deeds are sung, would sing along the way with his followers. He was accompanied by Saṅkarṣaṇa [Balarāma].
11. Sometimes he would honk in imitation of the honking swans. Sometimes he would dance in imitation of the dancing peacocks, giving rise to laughter.
12. Sometimes, in a voice that was pleasing to the cows and cowherd boys and was as deep as the rumbling of a cloud, he would call by name the cows who had strayed far off.
13. He would imitate the sounds of birds such as the *cakora*, *krauñca*, *chakravāka*, *bhāradvāja* and peacock, as if afraid of the tigers and lions from the animal kingdom.
14. At other times he would give relief to his elder brother by personally massaging his feet, etc., as Balarāma, fatigued from playing, used the lap of a *gopa* as a cushion.
15. Sometimes, holding hands and laughing, the two boys would urge on the cowherd boys in their dancing, singing, jumping about and wrestling with each other.
16. Sometimes, exhausted from the effort of wrestling, Kṛṣṇa would lie down on a bed of buds. Taking shelter at the base of a tree, he would use the lap of a *gopa* as a pillow.
17. Some great souls would massage his feet and others, whose sins had been eradicated, cooled him with fans.
18. Others, their hearts moved with love, would softly sing songs for that great soul that were appropriate to the occasion and pleasing to the mind.
19. In this way, Kṛṣṇa concealed his personal nature by his own *māyā*, and imitated the nature of the son of a cowherd man by his activities. Although he can conduct himself as the supreme Lord, and his bud-like feet are caressed by the goddess of fortune, he can nonetheless enjoy himself like a villager in the company of villagers.
20. [Once], the cowherd boy called Śrīdāmā, a friend of Balarāma and Keśava [Kṛṣṇa], and of the *gopas* such as Subala and Stokakṛṣṇa, spoke lovingly as follows:
21. "O Balarāma, Balarāma! O mighty-armed Kṛṣṇa, scourge of miscreants! Not far from here is a huge forest full of rows of palmyra trees.

22. Abundant fruits have fallen and keep falling there, but they are guarded by that evil soul Dhenuka.
23. O Balarāma! O Kṛṣṇa! He is an extremely powerful demon who has assumed the form of a donkey. He is surrounded by many other kinsmen whose strength is equal to his.
24. The forest is not frequented by humans and herds of cows because they are terrified of him, O destroyer of enemies – he has devoured human beings. It is even shunned by the flocks of birds.
25. Fragrant fruits that have never before been eaten are found there. In fact, this all-pervading fragrance [of the fruits] can be detected at this moment.
26. Obtain those fruits for us, Kṛṣṇa – our minds are disturbed by their smell. Our desire is great, Balarāma, so if you like, let us go."
27. After hearing these words from their friends, the two lords laughed. Surrounded by their friends, they went to the palmyra forest, desiring to please them.
28. Balarāma entered, and then, with strength like an elephant, shook the palmyra trees violently with his arms, making the fruit drop.
29. When he heard the sound of the falling fruit, the donkey demon came rushing up, making the surface of the earth as well as its mountains quake.
30. Encountering Balarāma, that mighty one turned around and struck him on the chest with two of his legs. The wicked fellow circled Balarāma, making a *kā*-sound.
31. The enraged ass attacked again. Rump-first, it kicked furiously at Balarāma with its two hind legs, O king.
32. Balarāma seized the donkey by two legs and whirled him around with one hand. When the donkey had died from the whirling, Balarāma hurled him on to the top of a palm tree.
33. Struck by the donkey, the great palmyra tree with its huge top trembled, causing its neighbouring tree to shake. This latter tree broke and made the next tree shake, and that tree did likewise to another.
34. Thus, struck by the dead body of the donkey hurled effortlessly by Balarāma, all the trees shook as if agitated by a great wind.

35. This is not remarkable for *Bhagavān*, who is, after all, the unlimited Lord of the universe. By him, this universe is woven lengthwise and crosswise, like a cloth on threads, my dear Parīkṣit.[1]

36. Then all the donkeys of Dhenuka rushed towards Kṛṣṇa and Rāma, furious that their relative had been slain.

37. Kṛṣṇa and Rāma seized each one of them by their rear legs as they came hurtling forward, and threw them effortlessly into the palm trees, O king.

38. The ground was coloured with heaps of bodies of dead demons, tops of trees, and fruit strewn about. It resembled the surface of the sky coloured by clouds.

39. When they heard of the pair's marvellous feat, the gods released a shower of flowers, played instruments and offered eulogies.

40. Thus, people ate the fruit of the palm trees and the cows grazed on the grass in the forest of the dead Dhenuka without fear.

41. After this, lotus-eyed Kṛṣṇa returned home to Vraj to the praise of his followers, the *gopas*. Hearing and reciting about him are means to purification.

42. The *gopīs* came forward in a body, their eyes hungry for a sight of him. Smeared with the dust of cows, Kṛṣṇa had a charming smile and delightful eyes. Forest flowers and a peacock feather were attached to the locks of his hair. He was playing his flute and his glories were being sung by his followers.

43. After drinking the honey of Mukunda's face with their bee-like eyes, the women of Vraj cast off their fever born of separation during the day. After accepting that welcoming reception, conveyed from the corners of the *gopīs*' eyes with modesty, giggles and bashfulness, Kṛṣṇa entered the cow-compound.

44. Yaśodā and Rohiṇī were affectionate towards their boys, and heaped their best blessings for the occasion upon their two sons, to their hearts' content.

45. At home, the boys' weariness from the road was removed by bathing and massage, and so forth. They then dressed in

beautiful clothes and were adorned with lovely garlands and scents.

46. The two pampered boys ate the food offered to them by their mothers, lay down on the best quality beds, and went happily to sleep in the land of Vraj.

47. Kṛṣṇa *Bhagavān* wandered around Vṛndāvana in this way, O king. One time he went without Balarāma to the river Kālindī, surrounded by his friends.

48. There, the cows and the *gopas*, stricken by the heat of the summer and afflicted with thirst, drank the contaminated water of that river; but it had been polluted by poison.

49. They all fell lifeless by the side of the river after touching the poisonous water, O uplifter of the Kurus, their consciousness overpowered by fate.

50. Seeing those who had accepted him as their master in this condition, Kṛṣṇa, the Lord of the lords of *yoga*, revived them with his glance, which is a shower of nectar.

51. Their memories were restored, and they rose up from the side of the water. Looking at each other, all were very surprised.

52. They acknowledged that they had departed to the other world after drinking the poison, and that their resurrection was due to the merciful glance of Govinda [Kṛṣṇa], O king.'

CHAPTER 16

The Banishment of Kāliya

1. *Śrī* Śuka said:

'After seeing the Yamunā polluted by the black snake, Kṛṣṇa, the Almighty Lord, desired to purify it, and so banished that serpent.'

2. The king said:

'How did *Bhagavān* subdue the serpent in the depths of the

waters? How had the snake come to reside there for so many ages? Please relate how this took place, O *brāhmaṇa.*
3. Who could be satiated from tasting the nectar of the exalted pastimes of the all-pervasive Gopāla [Kṛṣṇa], O *brāhmaṇa*? He acts according to his own pleasure.'
4. *Śrī* Śuka said:

'In the Yamunā river there was a pool which was boiling from the fire of Kāliya's poison. Birds flying overhead plummeted into it.
5. All moving and non-moving living entities in the vicinity of the shore died when touched by the spray borne by the wind from the poison-laden waves of the pool.
6. Seeing the contaminated river and the potency of that highly toxic poison, Kṛṣṇa, whose incarnation was to subdue the wicked, climbed a very high *kadamba* tree. With his belt well-fastened, he slapped his arms and jumped into the poisonous water.
7. The serpent was greatly provoked by the force of the supreme being's plunge. He exhaled poison into masses of matter, which overflowed in waves on all sides of the serpent's pool. Lethal from the toxicity of the poison, these waves flooded for a distance of over one hundred bows.[1] But what is this for Kṛṣṇa, who has unlimited power?
8. Kāliya, whose eyes were his ears, heard the commotion of the water churned by the mighty arms of Kṛṣṇa, who was sporting in the pond, as powerful as a mighty elephant, O king. Observing such a lack of respect for his abode, Kāliya came forth, unable to tolerate it.
9. Kṛṣṇa was playing without fear of anyone. Dressed in yellow, and bearing the mark of *śrīvatsa*, he was delicately youthful, gorgeous to behold and luminous as a cloud. His beautiful face was smiling, and his feet resembled the inside of a lotus. Kāliya furiously bit Kṛṣṇa's tender parts and wrapped his coils around him.
10. Seeing Kṛṣṇa apparently motionless and enveloped by the coils of the serpent, his dear friends the *gopas* collapsed in great distress, their minds overcome by fear, sorrow and pain. They

had dedicated their desires, their wives, their wealth, their relatives and their own selves to Kṛṣṇa.

11. The cows, bulls and female calves were greatly distressed. With their eyes fixed on Kṛṣṇa, they were bellowing fearfully and stood as if weeping.

12. Then three kinds of extremely terrifying and ominous portents – on the earth, in the sky, and on people[2] – arose in Vraj. They forewarned of imminent danger.

13. Learning that Kṛṣṇa had gone to graze the cows without Balarāma, the *gopas*, led by Nanda, were struck with fear on seeing these portents.

14. Because of the inauspicious signs, and unaware of who Kṛṣṇa really was, the *gopas* thought Kṛṣṇa had met his death. Their minds were absorbed in Kṛṣṇa and they had surrendered their life to him, and so they were struck by fear, distress and pain.

15. All the cowherd folk, from children to elders and women, O king, feeling miserable, left Gokula anxious for a sight of Kṛṣṇa.

16. Seeing them despairing in this way, Lord Balarāma, the descendant of Madhu, laughed, knowing the power of his younger brother. But he said nothing.

17. Searching for their beloved Kṛṣṇa along the path by means of his footprints, which were marked with the signs of God,[3] the cowherd folk went to the banks of the Yamunā.

18. Seeing the footsteps of the Lord of their community here and there mixed in with the other footprints of the cows on the path, O king, they rushed along. These footprints bore the marks of the flag, the thunderbolt, the goad, the barley and the lotus.

19. Seeing Kṛṣṇa motionless in the body of water in the distance and enveloped in the coils of the serpent in the lake, and seeing the cows and cowherd men in distress everywhere, the cowherd folk were struck with utter despair and cried out in anguish.

20. The *gopis*' minds were attached to the unlimited Lord. Remembering his affectionate smiles, glances and words, they were overcome with utter grief as their beloved was being seized

by the serpent. They perceived the three worlds as void without their dear one.[4]

21. They prevented Kṛṣṇa's mother from following her child [into the lake], although they were as distressed as she. Pouring out their sorrow, and telling stories about the darling of Vraj, each one remained still as a corpse, their eyes fixed on the face of Kṛṣṇa.

22. Lord Balarāma was aware of the potency of Kṛṣṇa. Seeing Nanda and the others, for whom Kṛṣṇa was their very life, about to enter the lake, he restrained them.

23. Kṛṣṇa remained for some time, assuming the behavior of a human being in this manner. Then, seeing that his own Gokula community, including women and children, which had no shelter other than in him, was in great distress, he realized that it was on his account and rose up from the bonds of the serpent.

24. The serpent, his coils tormented by the extended body of Kṛṣṇa, released him. Enraged, the serpent raised his hoods and drew himself erect as he looked at the Lord. His face had unmoving eyes like burning charcoal and he was breathing through his nostrils as from pots of poison.

25. Kṛṣṇa circled around him, toying with him. Like Garuḍa [Suparṇaka], the king of birds,[5] Kṛṣṇa manoeuvred around waiting for his opportunity. The serpent had eyes fiery with dreadful poison and repeatedly licked the two corners of his mouth with his forked tongue.

26. Bending the raised neck of the serpent, whose strength had been depleted by this circling around, Kṛṣṇa, the original being, climbed on to its massive hoods. Then, the original teacher of all art forms danced, his lotus feet made red by contact with the heaps of jewels on the serpent's head.[6]

27. Then his followers – the celestial *gandharvas*, *siddhas*, sages, *cāraṇas*, and young wives of the gods – seeing that Kṛṣṇa had begun to dance, immediately approached in delight with eulogies, offerings, flowers, songs, musical instruments and various types of drums such as *mṛdaṅgas*, *paṇavas* and *ānakas*.

28. Kṛṣṇa, chastiser of the wicked, crushed whichever head of that hundred-and-one-headed snake would not bend with blows

of his feet, O king. The snake's span of life was running out and he was whirling around. He vomited blood profusely from his nose and mouth and was overcome by utter desperation.

29. The serpent was breathing fiercely from anger and was discharging poison from his eyes. Whichever head he raised up, Kṛṣṇa forced him to bow low, striking it with his feet as he danced. As he was being worshipped with flowers, that most ancient being forced the snake to submit in the lake.

30. The serpent, his body broken, and his 1,000 hoods battered by that extraordinary dancing, was spewing blood from his mouths, O king. He remembered that most ancient being, Nārāyaṇa,[7] the teacher of all moving and non-moving entities, and surrendered to him in his mind.

31. The wives of the snake, whose hood umbrellas had been smashed by heel blows, saw that he had been crushed by the extreme weight of Kṛṣṇa, who bears the universe in his abdomen. They approached the original being in distress, with the locks of their hair, ornaments and clothing loosened.

32. Deeply agitated in mind and with their children placed in front of them, they prostrated their bodies on the ground, and offered obeisance to Kṛṣṇa, the Lord of creatures. These righteous ladies folded their hands in supplication and approached the giver of shelter for shelter, desiring the liberation of their wicked husband.

33. The serpent's wives said: "Punishment is certainly fitting for this offender. Your incarnation is for the subjugation of the wicked.[8] You view sons and even enemies with impartiality. In fact, you mete out punishment after considering its benefits.

34. In fact, what has happened to us is your Lordship's blessing. Your punishment of the unrighteous is undoubtedly that which destroys their sin. Even your anger is considered really to be a blessing for this embodied soul who has found himself in the form of this snake.

35. He has renounced his pride and paid his respects – what austere practice did he previously perform so that your Lordship, who is the life of everything, is satisfied? Or was it his righteous and compassionate behaviour towards all living entities?

36. We do not know what were the grounds of his qualification for contacting the dust from your feet, O Lord. The goddess of fortune, a lady, undertook ascetic practices out of a desire for those feet – she gave up pleasures, and maintained her vow for a long time.
37. Those who have attained the dust of your feet do not desire the highest heaven, nor sovereignty over the earth, nor the highest situation [of Brahmā], nor lordship over the lower worlds, nor the mystic powers of *yoga*, nor freedom from rebirth.
38. This lord of serpents, although *tāmasic* in birth after birth and controlled by anger, has obtained that which is difficult for others to obtain, O master. Abounding wealth appears before the eyes of the embodied soul, wandering in the cycle of *saṃsāra*, who desires to obtain this.
39. Reverence to you, *Bhagavān*. You are the great soul, the supreme being, the abode of the world, the world, transcendence, and the supreme soul.
40. Reverence to you, *brahman*. You are the storehouse of knowledge and wisdom, unlimited in powers, without qualities, changeless and original.
41. You are time, the hub of time, the witness of the phases of time, the universe, its observer and maker, and the cause of the universe.
42. You are the soul in the heart, the mind, the vital airs, the senses and the subtle elements. The ability to see you in person is hidden by [people's] pride and the three *guṇas*.
43. You are unlimited, subtle, pre-eminent, wise, the fulfilment of different doctrines, the potency of the speaker and that which is spoken.
44. You are the root of all epistemology, the author and source of scripture. Reverence again and again to you who are the Veda and who are activity and inactivity.
45. Reverence to you Kṛṣṇa, son of Vasudeva. Reverence to Rāma, Pradyumna, Aniruddha, Lord of the Sātvatas.
46. Reverence to you who are the light of the *guṇas*, who cover yourself with the *guṇas*, who can be inferred from the activity of the *guṇas*, who are the witness of the *guṇas* and who are self-knowing.

47. Your pastimes are unfathomable, and you are the conclusion of everything that has been expounded. You are a sage accustomed to silence[9] – let there be obeisance unto you, O Hṛṣīkeśa [Kṛṣṇa].
48. Reverence to you. You know the workings of that which is superior and that which is inferior. You are the overseer of everything, you are transcendent as well as immanent, and you are the witness as well as the cause of this world.
49. Although you are neutral, it is actually you, O omnipresent one, who have brought about the birth, maintenance and destruction of this world by means of the *guṇas*. You are the upholder of the power of time. Through your glance, you awaken the latent dispositions of each of the *guṇas*, within everything that exists.[10] Your pastimes are infallible.
50. The bodies of whatever exists in the three worlds are from you. They are born of those beings who are peaceful [*sāttvic*], agitated [*rājasic*] as well as ignorant [*tāmasic*]. The peaceful ones are the ones who are dear to you. As the Lord, you now wish to protect the righteous out of a desire to preserve *dharma*.
51. The master should tolerate a solitary transgression performed by his own subject. You have a peaceful nature, so please forgive this fool who is ignorant of you.
52. Be merciful, O *Bhagavān*. This serpent is giving up his life. Our husband is our life – please return him to us. We are women, and should be pitied by those who are righteous.
53. We are your servants: tell us what we should do. One is undoubtedly freed from all kinds of fear by complying with your command with faith." '
54. *Śrī* Śuka said:

'When he was extolled in this way by the wives of the serpent, *Bhagavān* released the broken-headed snake, who was unconscious from the blows of his feet.
55. The wretched Kāliya slowly regained his vital airs and senses. Breathing again with difficulty, he spoke to Hari with his hands joined in submission.
56. Kāliya said: "We are miscreants, full of wrath and *tāmasic*

from birth. One renounces one's personal nature with difficulty, O Lord, because it clings to falsehood.
57. This universe is an emanation of the *guṇas*, and has been generated by you, O creator. It contains a variety of natures, potencies, powers, wombs, latent dispositions and forms.
58. And in this universe, O *Bhagavān*, we serpents are extremely wrathful as a species. How can we, who are deluded, shake off your *māyā* by ourselves? It is so hard to cast off.
59. Your Lordship is the means to do this. You are the all-knowing Lord of the universe. Bestow either compassion or chastisement on us as you see fit."'
60. *Śrī* Śuka said:

'After listening to this, *Bhagavān*, who took human form for a purpose, spoke these words: "You should not remain here, serpent. Go to the ocean with your relatives and wives. Do not delay. Let the cows and people enjoy the river.
61. Any mortal being who remembers my command to you, and recites it at the two junctures of day and night, will never experience fear of you.
62. Whoever fasts and bathes here, the place of my pastime, or satisfies the gods with water, or worships while remembering me, is freed from all sins.
63. You left the island of Ramaṇaka out of fear of the eagle, Garuḍa, and took shelter of this lake. He will not eat you. You have been marked by my feet."'
64. The sage said:

'When he had been let free by Kṛṣṇa *Bhagavān*, whose activities are marvellous, the snake, along with his wives, worshipped Kṛṣṇa with joy and with respect.
65–66. He worshipped and pleased the Lord of the universe, whose banner is Garuḍa, with celestial clothes, garlands, jewels, outstanding ornaments, divine scents, ointments and a magnificent garland of blue lotuses. When he was granted leave to go, he circumambulated Kṛṣṇa and saluted him in good spirits.
67. Then he left for an island in the ocean with his wives, friends and sons. From that time on, the nectarean water of the Yamunā

became free from poison through the mercy of *Bhagavān*, who had assumed a human form for sport.'

CHAPTER 17

Deliverance from the Forest Fire

1. The king said:

'How did the serpent Kāliya leave his residence at Ramaṇaka, and why was Garuḍa hostile only against him?'
2–3. *Śrī* Śuka said:

'Whatever sacrificial offerings had formerly been allotted here for the snakes each month, and placed as oblations at the foot of the tree by the snake-worshippers, were now all for Garuḍa, O mighty-armed king. Each and every month the snakes offered him their own portions to ensure their personal protection, O noble soul.
4. But Kāliya, the son of Kadru, puffed up and intoxicated by the potency of the poison, disregarded Garuḍa and enjoyed the offerings himself.
5. After hearing this, O king, the illustrious [*Bhagavān*] Garuḍa,[1] beloved of *Bhagavān*, rushed forth desiring to kill Kāliya. He was enraged and extremely agitated.
6. Kāliya's eyes were fearsome, he was hissing through his dreadful tongues, and his many heads were erect. Armed with his fangs and poison, he charged Garuḍa, who was rushing towards him, and bit him with his teeth.
7. Garuḍa, son of Tārkṣya, is the carrier of Viṣṇu and has formidable force and overwhelming power. Filled with rage, he repelled Kāliya, the son of Kadru, with his left wing, which had the lustre of gold.
8. Struck by Garuḍa's wing, Kāliya became distraught and entered a lake in the Kālindī [Yamunā] river. It was well-hidden and inaccessible to Garuḍa.

9. Once in the past, Garuḍa, feeling hungry, had forcibly snatched up a fish, his favourite food, from there, despite being barred by the sage Śaubhari.
10. Śaubhari saw that the fish were very unhappy when that particular fish, their leader, was killed. Acting out of compassion and in the interests of the inhabitants of that place, he proclaimed:
11. "If Garuḍa enters here again and eats fish he will immediately forfeit his life. I declare this to be immutable."
12. Only Kāliya, and no other serpent, knew this. So he lived there free from fear of Garuḍa, until he was expelled by Kṛṣṇa.
13–14. Beholding Kṛṣṇa step forth from the lake, all the people sprang up, like senses that have retained their vital airs. Kṛṣṇa was wearing divine garlands, fragrances and garments, was laden with heaps of giant gems and was adorned with gold. The *gopas* embraced him lovingly, and their hearts were filled with joy.
15. Yaśodā, Rohiṇī, Nanda, the *gopīs* and the *gopas* approached Kṛṣṇa, O descendant of Kuru. Even the dried-up trees were restored to life.
16. Balarāma embraced Acyuta and laughed, knowing Kṛṣṇa's potency. The trees, cows, bulls and calves experienced utter bliss.
17. The *brāhmaṇas* and *gurus* approached with their wives and said: "Your son was freed by good fortune after being seized by Kāliya.
18. Give alms to the twice-born in honour of Kṛṣṇa's deliverance." At this, Nanda gave gold and cows with a happy mind, O king.
19. The chaste and very fortunate Yaśodā also embraced Kṛṣṇa and lifted him on her lap. Her son had been retrieved from death, and so she wept without ceasing.
20. The residents of Vraj and the cows, worn out by hunger, thirst and exhaustion, spent that night there near the bank of the Kālindī, O king.
21. Then, in the middle of the night, a forest fire burst out in the woods all around, caused by the hot season. It surrounded the sleeping folk of Vraj, and began to rage.

22. Panicked and scorched by the fire, the people of Vraj sprang up and, for refuge, approached Kṛṣṇa, the Lord, who had assumed a human form through his *māyā*:
23. "Kṛṣṇa, O most-fortunate Kṛṣṇa! Hey, Rāma of immeasurable prowess! This fierce conflagration is consuming us. We are your [devotees].
24. Save us from this insurmountable fire, O master. We, your friends and kinsmen, are incapable of abandoning your feet, which remove fear from all quarters."
25. The Lord of the universe saw the helplessness of his devotees in this situation, and swallowed the raging fire. After all, he is infinite and possesses infinite power.'

CHAPTER 18

The Killing of Pralamba

1. *Śrī* Śuka said:

'One day, surrounded and glorified by his relatives, who were in a joyful mood, Kṛṣṇa entered Vraj. It was picturesque with herds of cows.
2. While the two boys were sporting in Vraj in the *māyā* guise of cowherd boys, the summer season came, a season that is not very pleasant for embodied beings.
3. However, because of the special features of Vṛndāvana – *Bhagavān* himself, Keśava [Kṛṣṇa], was there with Balarāma – it exhibited the qualities of spring.
4. In Vraj, the sound of waterfalls drowned the chirping crickets. Spray from these waterfalls constantly fell on groups of trees.
5. There were abundant pastures there, and the forest-dwellers did not experience the heat produced by the sun, fires and summer. This was because of the breeze from the waves of waterfalls, streams and brooks that carried pollen from the blue lotuses, bowers and water lilies.
6. The fierce rays of the sun, terrible as poison, did not drain

the juice and verdancy from the land there. With sandbanks everywhere, the soil was saturated with waves from the shores of the deep-water rivers.

7. The forest was beautiful, full of flowers and echoing with the sounds of various animals and birds, singing peacocks and bees, and the noises of cuckoos and cranes.

8. Preparing to play, *Bhagavān* Kṛṣṇa entered that forest vibrating his flute. He was accompanied by Balarāma and surrounded by the *gopas* and their cows, which were their riches.

9. The *gopas*, led by Balarāma and Kṛṣṇa, were decorated with ornaments made from minerals, garlands, clusters of blossom, peacock feathers and fresh leaves. They danced, wrestled and sang.

10. While Kṛṣṇa danced, some *gopas* sang, some made sounds with horns and hand-claps, while others applauded.

11. The gods, disguised as members of the cowherd clan, praised Kṛṣṇa and Balarāma, who had assumed the forms of cowherd men, like dancers praise [other] dancers, O king.

12. Sporting sidelocks, the two boys played by whirling, jumping, hurling, slapping, dragging, and sometimes by wrestling.

13. And sometimes the two boys themselves became the singers and players while others danced, O great king. They gave encouragement, saying: "Bravo! Bravo!"

14. Sometimes [they played] with *bilva* fruits, sometimes with *kumbha* fruits, and sometimes with handfuls of *āmalaka* fruits. Sometimes they bound their eyes, and [played] at not being touched, and other such games, and sometimes they pretended to be animals and birds.

15. Sometimes [they played] leap-frog or practical jokes, sometimes on swings and sometimes at acting as kings.

16. In this way, the two [played] games that were familiar to people. They wandered about the forest, rivers, mountains, valleys, bowers, woods and lakes.

17. While Balarāma and Kṛṣṇa were grazing the animals with the *gopas* in the forest, a demon called Pralamba, in the guise of a *gopa*, advanced with the intention of seizing them.

18. Although he knew who he was, Kṛṣṇa, the descendant of Daśārha, who is *Bhagavān*, God, the seer of everything,

welcomed him into their fellowship, all the while considering how to exterminate him.

19. Kṛṣṇa was expert at playing, and called the *gopas* there: "Hey, *gopas*, let us divide fairly into two [groups], and play."

20. At this, the *gopas* made Balarāma and Kṛṣṇa the two leaders. Then some became followers of Kṛṣṇa, and others of Balarāma.

21. They organized various types of games that involved winners and losers. In these games, the winners would mount [on the backs of the losers], and the losers would carry [them].

22. Carrying and being carried piggy-back while they grazed the cows, the boys were led by Kṛṣṇa to a banyan tree called Bhāṇḍīraka.

23. When Balarāma's followers such as Śrīdāmā and Vṛṣabha emerged victorious in the games, Kṛṣṇa and the others carried each of them, O king.

24. When he lost, *Bhagavān* Kṛṣṇa carried Śrīdāmā; Bhadrasena carried Vṛṣabha; while Pralamba carried Balarāma, the son of Rohiṇī.

25. Thinking Kṛṣṇa to be invincible, the foremost of demons carried Balarāma and quickly went beyond [the appropriate point] for letting him dismount.

26. By carrying Balarāma, whose weight equalled that of Meru, king of mountains,[1] the great demon's motion was checked and he assumed his own real form. Covered with gold, he shone like a cloud illuminated with lightning flashes and carrying the moon, lord of constellations.

27. Seeing that form moving skilfully in the sky, the plough-bearing Balarāma became a little frightened. It had a burning gaze, terrible teeth, a furrowed brow and hair of fire. The glitter of earrings, helmet and bracelets was startling.

28. But then Balarāma regained his wits and became fearless. With his clenched fist, he furiously struck the enemy who, pretending to separate him from his group of companions, was in fact kidnapping him. Balarāma was like Indra, the chief of the gods, striking the mountain forcefully with his thunderbolt.

29. Upon being struck, the demon at once fell down unconscious and gave forth a great sound. His head was shattered, he vomited

blood from his mouth, and he lost his life. He resembled the mountain struck by the weapon of Indra.
30. Seeing Pralamba killed by Balarāma, who is by nature strong [*bala*], the *gopas* were flabbergasted and cried: "Bravo! Bravo!"
31. Showering blessings on Balarāma, the *gopas* praised that praiseworthy one. Their minds were overcome with love, and they embraced him as if he had come back from the dead.
32. When the sinful Pralamba was killed, the gods were greatly satisfied and showered Balarāma with garlands of flowers. They praised him: "Well done! Well done!"'

CHAPTER 19

Consuming the Forest Fire

1. *Śrī* Śuka said:

'While the *gopas* were intent on playing, their cows strayed far away. Wandering about unchecked, they strayed into a remote place, looking for grass.
2. The goats, cows and buffaloes wandered from forest to forest and entered a thicket of reeds, crying out from thirst because of a fire.
3. When they could not find the animals, the *gopas*, led by Kṛṣṇa and Balarāma, were filled with remorse. Searching around, they could not discover the direction taken by the cows.
4. They became dispirited, for their source of livelihood was lost. They followed the path of the cows by their hoofprints, as well as by the grass that had been severed by their hooves and teeth.
5. The cows who had lost their way were thirsty and tired, and so were lowing. The boys recovered them in the Muñja forest, and turned them back.
6. When they were called by *Bhagavān* in a voice as deep as a cloud, the cows were overjoyed. After hearing the sound of their own names, they lowed in reply.

7. Then, by accident, a huge forest fire broke out on all sides, wreaking destruction on the residents of the forest. Fanned by its helper [the wind], it consumed all things moving and non-moving with terrible fiery embers.
8. Seeing the forest fire hurtling towards them, the *gopas* and cows were terrified. Just as people afflicted by the fear of death take shelter of Hari, they took shelter of Kṛṣṇa and Balarāma. They said:
9. "Kṛṣṇa! Kṛṣṇa, great hero! Hey, Balarāma, we have taken refuge [with you]. Your prowess is never thwarted; you should protect us – we are being burned by the fire.
10. You are the knower of all *dharma*, Kṛṣṇa – surely your friends do not deserve to perish. We have accepted you as our Lord, and have surrendered to you."'
11. *Śrī* Śuka said:

'When he heard the piteous words of his friends, Hari, *Bhagavān*, said: "Close your eyes and don't be afraid."
12. "All right," [the boys replied]. When they had closed their eyes, *Bhagavān*, the supreme Lord of *yoga*, consumed the terrible fire with his mouth, and freed them from danger.
13. Then, after they had opened their eyes, they saw that they had been saved, and that they and the cows had been brought back to Bhāṇḍīra [the banyan tree] again; they were astonished.
14. Remarking on that *yoga* power of Kṛṣṇa, produced by *yogamāyā*, as well as on their own deliverance from the forest fire, the boys decided that Kṛṣṇa was an immortal.
15. In the evening, Janārdana [Kṛṣṇa], along with Balarāma, turned the cows around and returned to the cowherd community as he played his flute and was extolled by the *gopas*.
16. The *gopīs* were filled with utter bliss on seeing Govinda. Without him, a moment was like a hundred *yugas* for them.'

CHAPTER 20

Description of Autumn

1. *Śrī* Śuka said:

1. 'The *gopas* told the women about the amazing acts of Kṛṣṇa and Balarāma – their rescue from the forest fire as well as the killing of Pralamba.
2. Hearing that, the senior *gopas* and the *gopīs* were amazed. They thought that Kṛṣṇa and Balarāma were two important gods who had come to Vraj.
3. In due course, the rainy season, the revival of all living beings, began. The surface of the sky thundered and the horizon flashed.
4. The sky [was replete] with dense blue clouds and thunder and lightning. It was covered with a hazy light, like *brahman* with the *guṇas*.
5. When the appropriate time came, the sun began to release the earth's riches, in the form of water, which it had drunk for eight months by means of its rays.
6. Huge, fierce, lightning-bearing clouds, driven by the wind, released their pleasing water, just like merciful people.
7. Watered by the gods, the earth, which had been parched by heat, became fertile, just like the body of one undergoing austere practices with desires in mind, when it has obtained the fruit of these practices.
8. Because of the darkness, it is the fireflies that shine at the onset of night, not the planets, just as, because of sinfulness, it is the heretical doctrines that shine in the *kaliyuga* and not the Vedas.
9. After hearing the rumbling of the clouds, the frogs, who had previously been resting silently, gave out their calls, just like *brāhmaṇas* at the conclusion of their religious observances.[1]
10. The small rivers, which had dried up, turned into rivers that strayed from their course [through excess water], just like the body, wealth and possessions of a person who is not self-controlled.

11. The earth became transformed into green from the green sprouting grass, red from the red *indragopa* insects, and into a range of colours from being covered with sprouting mushrooms, just like the opulence of men.
12. The fields with their wealth of grain gave joy to the ploughmen, but sorrow to the proud, who were ignorant of their subservience to providence.
13. The inhabitants of the water and the land displayed pleasing forms as a result of the contributions of the new water, just as [the devotees do] from the service of Hari.
14. The ocean, abounding with waves and wind and joined by rivers, was agitated, like the resolution of a neophyte *yogī* when it is driven by lust and influenced by the *guṇas*.
15. The mountains did not flinch when pounded by the water-bearing clouds, just as those whose minds are dedicated to Adhokṣaja [Kṛṣṇa] do not flinch when assailed by adversities.
16. The thoroughfares, overgrown and covered with grass, became obscured, just as the Vedas, not being practised by the twice-born, have become defunct through the influence of time.[2]
17. The lightning, fickle in its friendship, did not remain fixed among the clouds, who are friends of the world, as lusty women do not remain fixed among men who are endowed with good qualities.
18. Indra's bow [the rainbow], which is without qualities, appears in the sky, which possesses qualities, just like the supreme being, who is without *guṇas*, appears in the manifest world, which consists of a mixture of *guṇas*.
19. The moon, covered by clouds and illuminated by its own light, did not shine, like the soul, covered by the concept of ego and illuminated by its own light, does not shine.[3]
20. The peacocks welcomed the arrival of the clouds and were joyful, like those who are depressed and unhappy at home become joyful when the devotees of Acyuta arrive.
21. The trees, who drink through their feet, become transformed after drawing in water through their roots, like those who had previously suffered and became exhausted by austere practices become transformed through indulging in pleasures.

22. The cranes inhabited the lakes, dear Parīkṣit, although the banks were not peaceful, just like vulgar, evil-minded people inhabit households where the activities are not peaceful.
23. When Lord Indra rains, the dams are breached by floods of water, just as in *kaliyuga* the paths of the Veda are breached by the false beliefs of heretics.
24. And the clouds, propelled by the winds, released nectar for living beings, just like chieftains, prompted by the twice-born, release favours from time to time.
25. So Hari, accompanied by Balarāma and surrounded by the cows and cowherders, entered that immense forest to play. It contained ripe dates and *jambu* fruits.[4]
26. Cows move slowly by reason of the excessive weight of their udders, but they arrived quickly when called by *Bhagavān*, their udders flowing out of love.
27. Kṛṣṇa noticed the happy female forest-dwellers, the trees dripping with honey, the nearby caves and, from the sound on the mountain, the streams.
28. Sometimes, when it rained, *Bhagavān* Kṛṣṇa entered caves and hollows of trees, and sported, eating fruits and radishes.
29. In the company of Saṅkarṣaṇa [Balarāma] and the cowherd boys who were ready to eat, he ate upon a rock near the water the rice cooked in yogurt that he had brought along.
30–31. *Bhagavān* Kṛṣṇa observed the cows, made tired by the burden of their udders, as well as the bulls and calves lying down satisfied on a grassy spot, chewing the cud with their eyes closed. He also observed the beauty of the rainy season, invigorated by his own *śakti* [power of a male divinity], which brings happiness every year. He honoured them.
32. In due course, while Balarāma and Keśava were living there in Vraj, autumn arrived with gentle breezes, clear waters and cloudless skies.
33. The waters returned to their natural state by reason of the lotus-bearing autumn season, just like the consciousness of those who have fallen [from their *yogic* path] returns through taking up again the practice of *yoga*.
34. The autumn removed the debris from the water, the mud from the earth, the intermixing of the elements, and the clouds

from the sky, just as devotion to Kṛṣṇa removes impurities from those who follow the *āśrama*.[5]
35. The clouds shone with a magnificent hue after giving up all they were holding, like sages become peaceful and free from sin after giving up their desires.
36. The mountains sometimes released pure water and sometimes did not, like the wise on occasion give, or do not give, the nectar of knowledge.
37. The fish moving in shallow water certainly did not realize that the water was diminishing, just as foolish people, immersed in their families, do not realize the dwindling of their life-span day by day.
38. The fish moving in the shallow water experienced misery by reason of the autumn sun, just as poor wretched people, whose senses are uncontrolled, experience misery in daily life.
39. The dry land gradually became free of mud, and the plants of their unripeness, just like those whose minds are fixed become free of concepts of "I-ness" and "my-ness" with regard to their bodies, which are not their real selves.
40. Upon the arrival of autumn, the ocean becomes quiet and its waters still, just as, finding quietude in the self, a *yogī* completely refrains from the *āgama* ritualistic texts.[6]
41. The farmers contain the waters from the fields by solid dams, just as the *yogīs* prevent the loss of wisdom from flowing out through the senses by controlling the senses.
42. The moon removes the distress generated by the rays of the autumn sun from living entities, just like Mukunda [Kṛṣṇa] removes conceit generated by pride in the physical body from the women of Vraj.
43. The cloudless sky, replete with clear autumn stars, shone beautifully, just as the mind, perceiving the meaning of *śabdabrahman*[7] from its association with *sattva*, shines forth.
44. The moon, its disc unbroken, shone forth with the constellations of stars, just as Kṛṣṇa, the Lord of the Yadu dynasty, shone forth on earth surrounded by the circle of the Vṛṣṇi clan.
45. The people, embracing the wind from the forest flowers, which is constant in cold or heat, let go of their distress – except for the *gopīs*, whose hearts had been stolen by Kṛṣṇa.

46. Because of the autumn, the cows, deer, birds and women became fertile and were followed by their males, just like acts performed for God are followed by their results.
47. The lotuses opened on the rising of the sun, with the exception of the [night-blooming] *kumuda* lotuses, O king, just as people are without fear on account of a monarch – with the exception of thieves.
48. In towns and villages, the earth shone on account of *āgrayaṇa* ceremonies,[8] great festivities which were pleasing to the senses, ripe grass and so forth, and especially on account of the two *kalās* [partial incarnations] of Hari.[9]
49. Merchants, sages, kings and *snāta* students[10] who had been hindered by the rains, attained the goals that they had set, just as the accomplished *siddha yogis* attain their respective bodies when the appropriate time comes.'[11]

CHAPTER 21

*The Vision of Kṛṣṇa**

1. *Śrī* Śuka said:

'Thus, Acyuta entered the [forest of Vṛndāvana] with the cows and cowherders. Its waters were clear because it was autumn, and it was cooled by breezes bearing the pleasant scents of lotuses.
2. Kṛṣṇa, the Chief of the Madhus,[1] along with the cowherding boys, penetrated deep into [the forest] while grazing the cows. Its mountains, rivers and lakes reverberated with the sounds of flocks of birds and of restless bees in the flowering trees. Kṛṣṇa played his flute.
3. The women of Vraj heard that flute music – music which incites Kāma.[2] Some of them described Kṛṣṇa to their confidantes in private.
4. Remembering the activities of Kṛṣṇa, they began to describe them, but their minds became so agitated with the power of Kāma that they were unable [to continue], O king.

5. As his glories were being sung by the band of *gopas*, Kṛṣṇa entered the forest of Vṛndā, which was pleasantly transformed by [the touch of] his feet. His form was that of a superb dancer. He wore a peacock feather head ornament, pericarps of lotus flowers on his ears, garments of a reddish-gold colour, and a *vaijayantī* garland.[3] The nectar of his lips filled the holes of his flute.
6. The sound of the flute steals the minds of all living things, O king. After hearing and describing it, the women of Vraj embraced each other.
7. The beautiful *gopīs* said: "We do not know of any higher reward for those who have eyes than this [sight of] the faces of those two sons of the chief of Vraj as they, with their companions, make the animals follow them, O girlfriends. With their two flutes their faces are enchanting, and they cast loving glances which are absorbed by those [who have eyes].
8. Dressed in a variety of garments twined about with garlands of lotuses, lilies, clusters of blossoms, peacock feathers and mango tree sprouts, they are unmistakable as they shine amidst the assembly of cowherders. They are like two actors sometimes singing on a stage.
9. O *gopīs*, what auspicious deed did this flute perform? It personally enjoys the *rasa* nectar from Dāmodara's [Kṛṣṇa's][4] lips – which should belong to the *gopīs*; whatever flavour is left over is all that remains [for us]. The rivers manifest bliss through their surfaces, and the trees shed tears,[5] just like noble Āryan people.[6]
10. O girlfriends, Vṛndāvana, which has acquired the riches of the lotus feet of the son of Devakī, is spreading the glories of the earth. All other living beings are stunned after seeing the ecstatic peacocks from the mountain ridges dance to Govinda's [Kṛṣṇa's] flute.
11. These female does are lucky, even though they are in an ignorant birth. When they hear the flute-playing of the beautifully dressed son of Nanda, they, along with the spotted antelopes, offer worship with glances of love.
12. Kṛṣṇa's nature and form are a delight for women – the celestial women became captivated when they saw it and heard

the distinctive tunes played on his flute. The flowers from their braids dropped out, and the belts from their waists slipped off as they went about on celestial air-vehicles,[7] their hearts agitated by Kāma.

13. The cows, their ears pricked, were also drinking the nectar of the flute music coming from Kṛṣṇa's mouth. The calves stood transfixed with their mouths full of milk from the dripping udders. Shedding tears, in their hearts they caressed Govinda with their eyes.

14. It is a wonderful thing, O mother! In all probability, the birds in this forest are sages. They fly up to the branches of the trees that are covered with sweet fresh leaves, and, with unblinking eyes, listen to the melodious tunes of the flute coming from Kṛṣṇa. They make no other noise.

15. The rivers found their force disrupted by their state of mind after hearing the sound of Mukunda's flute, as could be seen from their whirlpools. Bearing offerings of lotus flowers, they grasped the two lotus feet of Murāri [Kṛṣṇa] and embraced them closely with their arms in the form of waves.

16. The water-bearing cloud saw Kṛṣṇa playing the flute as he was herding the animals of Vraj with Balarāma and the *gopas* in the heat. Bursting with love, it ascended with streams of flowers [in the form of rain],[8] and with its own body spread out a large umbrella for its friend.

17. The Pulinda women experienced the pain of Kāma from seeing Kṛṣṇa. Taking up from the grass the beautiful *kuṅkum* powder that had decorated the breasts of the women and was red from the lotus feet of Urugāya [Kṛṣṇa], they smeared it on their faces and breasts, let go of their distress and became contented.[9]

18. Look at this mountain, O women. It is overjoyed to be touched by Balarāma's and Kṛṣṇa's feet! It is the best of the servants of Hari because it honours those two, as well as the herds of cows, by [gifts] of radishes, caves, good pasturage and water.

19. O girlfriends, when those two, conspicuous by their cords and ropes for tying cows, lead the cows and cowherd boys into nearby forests, those embodied beings who are capable of

movement are made motionless by the sounds of that renowned flute with its sweet harmonies. The trees bristle with ecstasy – it is a wonderful thing."
20. Discussing in this way the pastimes of *Bhagavān*, who was wandering around in Vṛndāvana, the *gopīs* entered into a state of complete absorption in him.'

CHAPTER 22

Kṛṣṇa Steals the Gopīs' *Clothes**

1. *Śrī* Śuka said:

'In the first month of the *hemanta* [winter season], the young girls of Nanda's Vraj observed the vow to worship the goddess Kātyāyanī by eating sacrificial food.
2–3. After bathing in the waters of the Kālindī river at sunrise, they made an image of the goddess from sand near the water, O king. Then they worshipped it with scents, fragrant garlands, offerings, incense, fire lamps, both simple and costly gifts, fresh shoots, fruits and rice.
4. "O goddess Kātyāyanī, great Māyā, great *yoginī*,[1] supreme Lord; honour to you! Please make the son of Nanda, the *gopa*, my husband, O Goddess." Uttering this *mantra*, those young girls performed *pūjā* worship.[2]
5. The young girls had their hearts fixed on Kṛṣṇa. They performed this vow in this fashion for a month and worshipped the goddess Bhadrakālī[3] in the same way: "Please let the son of Nanda be my husband!"
6. They arose at dawn every day by [calling out] each other's family names. Then they sang loudly about Kṛṣṇa while going to the Kālindī to bathe, with their arms intertwined.
7. Once, arriving at the bank of the river, they threw down their clothes as usual and sported happily in the water, all the while singing about Kṛṣṇa.
8. *Bhagavān* Kṛṣṇa, the Lord of the lords of *yoga*, surrounded

by his companions, arrived at that place. He had come to fulfil those rites.

9. Gathering up their garments, he quickly climbed a *kadamba* tree. Laughing along with the snickering boys, he said jokingly to the girls:

10. "Ladies, you are all exhausted from your vow. Come forward, ladies, and take your own clothes, if you wish. This is not a joke – I am speaking seriously.

11. These [boys] know that I have never uttered a falsehood. Collect your clothes [by coming] one by one, or even all together, O slender-waisted ones."

12. Seeing such jesting, the *gopīs*, who were deeply in love with Kṛṣṇa, were embarrassed. Exchanging glances with each other, they started to giggle, but did not go.

13. When Govinda had spoken in this way, the *gopīs* were flustered by his joking. Immersed in the cold water up to their necks, and shivering, they spoke to him:

14. "Do not behave in this way. You are the son of Nanda the *gopa*, and have a good reputation in Vraj! We regard you as our beloved, so give us back our clothes, dear one – we are shivering.

15. Syāmasundara [Kṛṣṇa]![4] We are your servants and do whatever you want. Give us our clothes – you know what *dharma* is. If you do not, hey, we will tell the king!"

16. *Śrī Bhagavān* said: "You girls have bright smiles! If you really are my servants, or will do whatever I have said, then come here and each take your own clothes."

17. At this, all the young girls, trembling from the cold, emerged from the pool of water. Covering their genitals with their hands, they were stricken by the cold.

18. Seeing that they were virgins,[5] *Bhagavān* was pleased with their pure state of mind. He placed the clothes on his shoulder, and addressed them with a smile. He was satisfied:

19. "Intent on your vow, you all bathed in the waters without clothes, and that is an offence against the gods. Offer obeisance with your folded hands on your head in expiation for this sin, and then take your lower garments."

20. The women of Vraj conceded that, as Acyuta had pointed out, bathing without clothes was a deviation from their vow.[6]

Because they wanted that vow and all of its rites to come to fruition, they offered obeisance to Kṛṣṇa, who was before their eyes, because he is the remover of imperfection.
21. Seeing them bow down in this way, *Bhagavān*, the son of Devakī, was satisfied. Being compassionate, he gave them back their clothes.
22. The girls were cheated, deprived of their modesty, derided and made to perform like puppets. Moreover, their clothes were stolen. Yet, they were not really upset with Kṛṣṇa. They were delighted to be in the company of their darling.
23. When they had on their clothes, the *gopīs* could not move. Their hearts had been captured, and they were attached to the company of their dear one. So they cast bashful glances at him.
24. Dāmodara [Kṛṣṇa] understood their intent – they had undertaken the vow out of the desire to touch his feet. He spoke to the women:
25. "You are chaste ladies and your intention was to worship me. I understand and approve of this. It deserves to be fulfilled.
26. The desire of those whose minds are absorbed in me does not produce desire, just as grain which is cooked or fried is generally not capable of sprouting.[7]
27. Go to Vraj fulfilled, ladies. You will enjoy the nights to come in my company. It was with this intention that you performed this vow by worshipping the goddess Āryā [Kātyāyanī], O chaste ones."'
28. *Śrī* Śuka said:

'When they were instructed by *Bhagavān* in this way, the young girls returned to Vraj reluctantly, meditating on his lotus feet. But their desires had been fulfilled.
29. After some time, *Bhagavān*, the son of Devakī, accompanied by his elder brother and surrounded by the *gopas*, went some distance out of Vṛndāvana while grazing the cows.
30. He saw that in the scorching heat of the summer sun the trees were acting as umbrellas for him with their shade, and so he addressed the people of Vraj thus:
31. "Hey Stokakṛṣṇa, hey Aṃśu, Śrīdāmā, Subala, Arjuna, Viśāla, Vṛṣabha, Ojasvī, Devaprastha and Varūthapa!

32. Look at these lucky trees. They live exclusively for the benefit of others. Tolerating wind, rain, heat and snow, they provide cover for our benefit.
33. *Aho!* Their birth provides sustenance for all living things and so is a distinguished one. The needy never leave them disappointed, just as they never leave a saintly person disappointed.
34. The trees bestow benefits in the form of young shoots, coal, ashes, sap, fragrance, wood, bark, roots, shade, fruits, flowers and leaves.
35. Activities in the form of words, knowledge, wealth and life, which are always conducive to the welfare of living beings in this world, [indicate] a successful birth among living beings."
36. Speaking thus among the trees, whose branches were weighed down with an abundance of leaves, flowers, fruit, clusters of blossoms and fresh shoots, Kṛṣṇa came to the Yamunā river.
37. After letting the cows drink the clean, cool and nourishing water, the *gopas* themselves drank their fill of the sweet-tasting water, O king.
38. As they were leisurely grazing their cows in a grove by the river, they were suddenly hungry, O king. They approached Kṛṣṇa and Balarāma and spoke as follows.

CHAPTER 23

The Deliverance of the Wives of the Sacrificers

1. 'The *gopas* said: "Balarāma, mighty-armed Balarāma! Kṛṣṇa, the annihilator of the wicked! Our hunger is really troubling us; please satisfy it."'
2. *Śrī* Śuka said:

'*Bhagavān*, the son of Devakī, was feeling pleased with his devotees, the wives of the *brāhmaṇas*. When he was appealed to in this way, he spoke as follows:
3. "Go to the sacrificial arena. Desiring to attain *svarga* [the

celestial abode of the gods], the *brāhmaṇa* reciters of the Vedas are taking part in a sacrifice called *āṅgirasa*.
4. Go there and request some cooked rice, mentioning the names of the worthy *Bhagavān* Balarāma, and of me myself; say that you have been dispatched by us."
5. Directed thus by *Bhagavān*, the boys went and asked as suggested. They fell on the ground before the *brāhmaṇas* like sticks,[1] their hands cupped in supplication:
6. "You are gods on earth, please listen. May good fortune be with you. Please know that we *gopas* have been despatched by Balarāma and come to you to execute Kṛṣṇa's instructions.
7. Balarāma and Acyuta have become hungry while grazing the cows not far from here, and desire cooked rice from you. You are distinguished in the knowledge of *dharma*, and if you have any respect for them, give them cooked rice. They entreat you, O *brāhmaṇas*.
8. The eating of food, even from a person who has been consecrated for the performance of sacrifice, is not defiling, O most noble ones, the exception being during the consecration ceremony, the slaughter of the sacrificial animal, and the *sautrāmaṇi* sacrifice."[2]
9. Although they heard *Bhagavān*'s request, the *brāhmaṇas* did not listen to it. They had petty aspirations. They thought themselves distinguished, but despite the fact that they performed numerous rituals, they were ignorant nevertheless.
10–11. Kṛṣṇa is *Bhagavān*, Adhokṣaja, the supreme *brahman* in person. The place, time, sundry utensils, *mantras*, *tantra* rituals, *ṛtvik* priests,[3] fires, gods, sacrificer, offering, and the results accrued [from the sacrifice], are constituted by him. But the *brāhmaṇas*' intelligence was perverted; thinking their bodies to be their real selves, they did not show him courtesy, perceiving him to be a mortal.
12. When they did not respond with either a "yes" or a "no", the *gopas* returned dejected and reported what had happened to Kṛṣṇa and Balarāma, O scorcher of enemies.
13. After listening to this, *Bhagavān*, the Lord of the universe, laughed, pointing out the materialistic ways of the world. He then spoke again to the *gopas*:

14. "Inform the wives that I have arrived, along with Saṅkarṣaṇa [Balarāma]. They will give you as much food as you wish. They are affectionate, and their minds dwell in me."
15. So, the *gopas* went to the *patnīśālā* [women's quarter],[4] where they saw them sitting down, prettily bedecked. They humbly paid homage to the wives of the *brāhmaṇas* and spoke as follows:
16. "Greetings to you, O wives of *brāhmaṇas*; please listen to what we have to say. We have been sent by Kṛṣṇa, who is passing by not far from here.
17. He has come from afar, and has been grazing the cows with Balarāma and the *gopas*. Please give food to him. He and his companions desire to eat."
18. The women had always been eager for a glimpse of Acyuta, because they had been captivated by accounts of him. When they heard that he had arrived nearby, they became flustered.
19. Taking along a great variety of the four types of food[5] in pots, they surged forth to meet their beloved, like rivers to an ocean.
20. [Although] they were obstructed by their husbands, brothers, relatives and sons, their hopes [of meeting Kṛṣṇa] had long been sustained by hearing about him. He is *Bhagavān*, who is praised in the best of hymns.
21. The women saw Kṛṣṇa surrounded by the *gopas* and wandering about with his elder brother in the grove on the Yamunā, which was a picturesque sight with fresh buds of *aśoka* trees.
22. He was dark blue in colour, and wearing a golden garment. He was dressed like an actor with fresh shoots, minerals, a peacock feather and a forest garland. One hand was placed on the shoulder of a companion, the other was twirling a lotus flower. His smiling lotus face had curls on the cheeks and lotuses behind the ears.
23. The women had heard so much about their beloved, and his celebrity had so filled their ears, that their minds had become absorbed in him. Now, they drew him into [their hearts] through the openings of their eyes. They embraced him for a long time and cast off their distress, just like false notions of the self are cast off after wisdom is embraced.

24. Kṛṣṇa is the seer who discerns everything, and so understood that they had arrived in this fashion, giving up all false aspirations out of a desire to see him. He spoke to them smiling:
25. "Welcome. You are very fortunate women! Please be seated. What can I do for you? You have come desiring to see us, which is certainly worthy of you.
26. There is no doubt that those who are learned and who understand their self-interest engage in selfless, uninterrupted *bhakti* to me, because I am the one who is dear to their souls.
27. The vital airs, intelligence, mind, body, wife, children, wealth and other worldly assets, become dear because of contact [with me]. Therefore, what else is there that is dear in actuality?
28. So, go to the sacrificial arena. Your *brāhmaṇa* husbands are householders, and can only complete their sacrifice with your participation."[6]
29. The wives replied: "You should not speak to us in such a cruel fashion, O Lord! Abide by your own doctrine![7] We have transgressed against all our relatives and have arrived at your lotus feet to wear on our hair the *tulasī* garland discarded by your feet.
30. Our husbands, parents, sons, brothers, relatives and friends, not to speak of others, will not accept us. We are souls who have fallen down at your lotus feet, so there can be no other destination for us. Therefore, grant [us your shelter]."
31. *Śrī Bhagavān* said: "Neither your husbands, fathers, brothers, sons or other relatives, nor people in general, will be angry with you. Even the gods will approve, as they take shelter of me.
32. Physical contact between people in this world does not [produce] joy or affection. Therefore, fix your mind on me, and you will obtain me without delay."'
33. *Śrī* Śuka said:

'When they had been addressed in this way, the wives of the *brāhmaṇas* returned to the sacrificial enclosure.[8] The [*brāhmaṇas*] were not displeased with them, and completed the sacrifice with their wives.
34. One woman there, who had been impeded by her husband,

embraced *Bhagavān* in her heart – as she conceived of him from what she had heard – and gave up her body, the product of *karma*.
35. So *Bhagavān*, Govinda, the Lord, fed the *gopas* with the four kinds of foodstuffs, and then he himself ate.
36. Imitating the world of men in a human body for the purpose of *līlā*, he brought pleasure to the cows, *gopas* and *gopīs* through his deeds, words and beauty.
37. Later, those *brāhmaṇas* repented in retrospect: "We have committed an offence because we ignored the request of the two lords of the universe. They are playing the role of mortals."
38. Seeing the supreme devotion of the women to *Bhagavān* Kṛṣṇa, they lamented their own lack of it, and rebuked themselves:
39. "Curses on that birth which is threefold,[9] curses on vows, curses on extensive learning, curses on our family lineage, curses on skill in rituals: we still remain averse to Adhokṣaja [Kṛṣṇa].
40. Truly, the *māyā* of *Bhagavān* bewilders even the *yogīs*. Because of it, we *brāhmaṇas*, the *gurus* of humanity, are confused about our own self-interest.
41. *Aho!* See the unlimited devotion of these very women to Kṛṣṇa, the *guru* of the world. It has pierced the fetters of death under the guise of household life.
42. Neither the *saṃskāra* purificatory rites of the twice-born,[10] nor residence in the house of the *guru*, nor austerity, nor inquiry into the self, nor rites of cleanliness, nor auspicious rituals were [practised] by these women.
43. Nonetheless, they were constant in devotion to Kṛṣṇa, the Lord of the lords of *yoga*, whose glories are renowned. This was not the case with us, even though we have undergone the *saṃskāra* and other such rites.
44. *Aho!* Through the words of the *gopas*, Kṛṣṇa reminded us about the path of the virtuous, but we were deluded about our self-interest and heedless because of our domestic activities.
45. Otherwise, what was the purpose of this play-acting with us by the Lord, the controller who grants blessings such as that

of liberation? His own desires are fulfilled, but we are meant to be controlled [by him].

46. His begging [for food] bewilders people, since the goddess of fortune, spurning others and relinquishing the faults of her own nature,[11] worships him constantly with the desire to touch his feet.

47. The place, time, sundry utensils, *mantras*, *tantra* rituals, *ṛtvik* priests, fires, gods, sacrificer, offering, and the results accrued [from the sacrifice], are constituted by him.

48. He, indeed, is *Bhagavān* himself, Viṣṇu, the Lord of the lords of *yoga*, born amongst the Yadus. Although we had heard this, being fools, we did not understand.

49. *Aho!* How fortunate we are to have wives such as these! Their devoutness has given rise to unwavering devotion to Hari in us.

50. Homage to him, *Bhagavān*, Kṛṣṇa, whose intelligence is ever fresh. We are wandering on the path of *karma*, our intelligence bewildered by his *māyā*.

51. He is the primeval person and so should graciously forgive our offence. Our minds are confused by his *māyā* and we are ignorant of his might."

52. Reflecting on their offence in this way, the [*brāhmaṇas*], who had been contemptuous of Kṛṣṇa, desired to see Vraj; but they did not go, out of fear of Kaṃsa.'[12]

CHAPTER 24

*Kṛṣṇa Diverts Indra's Sacrifice**

1. *Śrī* Śuka said:

'As he was residing there in Vraj with Balarāma, *Bhagavān* Kṛṣṇa saw the *gopas* making preparations for Indra's sacrifice.

2. *Bhagavān* Kṛṣṇa is the seer of everything as well as the soul of everything; despite knowing all about it, he bowed down reverentially and inquired of the elders headed by Nanda:

3. "Tell me, father, what is this bustle that has arisen? Why is this sacrifice being performed, from what incentive and by whom?
4–5. Explain this to me, father – I am curious to hear about it and my desire is great. Surely, the deeds of *sādhus* are not secret. They see the *ātmā* within everything in this world. They do not distinguish between what is their own and what is another's, and they have no friends, enemies or neutral relationships. It is said that a neutral party is to be avoided like an enemy, but a friend is like one's own self.
6. These people perform actions [the purpose of which] they either understand or do not understand. Success in action will be granted to the one who has knowledge, but not for the one who is ignorant.
7. This being so, is this act of *yoga*[1] something that has received careful deliberation, or is it popular practice? This should be clearly explained to me, for I am asking."
8. *Śrī* Nanda said: "*Bhagavān* Indra is the rain. The clouds are the manifestations of his being. They release water, the nourishing life-force of living things.
9. He is the lord and master of the clouds, my son; other people also worship him, just as we do, by sacrifices of the products of his flow of water.
10. They subsist with the remnants in order to accomplish the threefold goals of life.[2] The rain-god produces fruit for people engaged in human undertakings.
11. The person who neglects this duty handed down by tradition, out of lust, animosity, fear or greed, definitely does not achieve auspicious results." '
12. *Śrī* Śuka said:

'After hearing the words of Nanda and the other residents of Vraj, Keśava spoke to his father, provoking the indignation of Indra.
13. *Śrī Bhagavān* said: "The living entity is born because of *karma* and perishes because of *karma*. Happiness, distress, fear and security all arrive because of *karma* alone.
14. Even if there is some kind of a controller who awards the

fruit of the *karma* of other people, he can only interact with a person engaged in action. He is certainly not the master of one who does not engage in action.

15. What can Indra do to living beings who are following their own *karma*? He is incapable of doing anything other than what has been determined as a result of people's own nature.

16. People are actually controlled by their own nature and they act according to their own nature. This whole universe with gods, demons and humankind exists in its own nature.

17. It is as a result of *karma* that the living being accepts and then gives up higher and lower bodies. It is *karma* alone that is the enemy, friend or impartial observer, the *guru* and the lord.

18. One's deity is actually that through which one is able to subsist easily. Therefore, grounded in one's own nature and performing one's duty, one should worship *karma*.

19. If one entity is the means of subsistence, while another entity is dependent on something else, then one cannot find security in the latter, just as an unfaithful woman will not find security in a paramour.

20. A *brāhmaṇa* should subsist by means of the Veda, the *kṣatriya* by the protection of the earth, the *vaiśya* by business, and the *śūdra* by service to the twice-born.[3]

21. There are four types of business: agriculture, trade and cow-protection, as well as money-lending, which is said to be the fourth. From these, we have always taken subsistence from the cows.

22. The causes of maintenance, production and destruction are *sattva*, *rajas* and *tamas*. *Rajas* produces the entire universe, which is given shape by mutual interaction.[4]

23. The clouds are propelled by *raja*, and they shower water everywhere. Living beings prosper as a result of clouds alone. What can the mighty Indra do?

24. Cities are not for us, father, nor are inhabited countries, villages and homesteads. We are forest-dwellers, living in forests and hills.

25. Therefore, let us begin a sacrifice for Mount Govardhana,

the *brāhmaṇas* and the cows. Let this sacrifice be accomplished with these very utensils that are for Indra's sacrifice!

26. People should prepare various types of cooked food, starting with soup and ending with a pudding made from rice, as well as *saṃyāva*, *āpūpa* and *śuṣkalī* cakes. And all the milk-products should be collected.

27–28. The sacrificial fires should receive oblations from the *brāhmaṇas* who recite the Veda. All of you should give many kinds of food and donations of cows to the *brāhmaṇas*, as well as to others also, up to the *cāṇḍālas* [outcastes], and dogs, as is appropriate. And, after grass has been given to the cows, offerings should be made to the mountain.

29. Then, when you are nicely adorned, adequately smeared [with sandalwood paste], handsomely dressed and well fed, walk round the cows, the *brāhmaṇas*, the fire and the hill in a clockwise direction.

30. This is my opinion, father, which can be followed if it is approved. Such a sacrifice will be pleasing to the cows, the *brāhmaṇas* and the mountains, and to me as well."'

31. *Śrī* Śuka said:

'Hearing those words spoken by *Bhagavān* Kṛṣṇa, who, in the form of time, desired to destroy the pride of Indra, Nanda and the others accepted his words as appropriate.

32–33. They prepared everything just as Madhusūdana [Kṛṣṇa] had said. Auspicious blessings were chanted, and offerings presented with full respect to the twice-born and to the hill with those same utensils, as well as grass to the cows. Then, they circumambulated the hill, with their riches – their cattle – in front.

34. The beautifully adorned *gopīs* mounted the carts, which were yoked to the oxen. They were singing of the exploits of Kṛṣṇa in harmony with the uttering of blessings of the twice-born.

35. Then Kṛṣṇa transformed himself into another body to gain the confidence of the *gopas*. Saying: "I am the mountain!" the huge form ate the lavish offering.

36. Together with the people of Vraj, Kṛṣṇa prostrated himself

before that form – which was really himself – saying: "*Aho!* Look – this mountain is assuming a form! It has bestowed its favour upon us.
37. Assuming any form at will, it kills the human residents of the forest who disregard it. We should prostrate ourselves before it for the protection of our cows and ourselves."
38. After performing the sacrifice to the twice-born, the cows and the hill, as directed by Vāsudeva in this fashion, the *gopas* went to Vraj along with Kṛṣṇa.'

CHAPTER 25

Kṛṣṇa Lifts Mount Govardhana

1. *Śī* Śuka said:

'At this, O king, Indra understood that his own worship had been abandoned, and became enraged with the *gopas*, led by Nanda, who had accepted Kṛṣṇa as their Lord.
2. Considering himself Lord, Indra summoned the host of clouds called Saṃvartaka which bring about the annihilation of the universe.[1] Furious, he spoke the following words:
3. "Just see how intoxicated the forest-dwelling *gopas* are because of the wealth [of the forest]. They have taken refuge with Kṛṣṇa, a mortal, and now they neglect the gods.
4. Abandoning meditative knowledge, they desire to cross over the ocean of material existence through ritualistic so-called sacrifices which are like unstable boats.
5. By taking refuge with Kṛṣṇa, a boastful, childish, stubborn, ignorant mortal who thinks himself to be a great scholar, the *gopas* have made an enemy of me.
6. Destroy the arrogance of these people caused by the conceit of riches. They are steeped in wealth and their egos have been inflated by Kṛṣṇa. Bring destruction to their livestock.
7. As for me, I will mount my elephant Airāvata,[2] and follow

you to Vraj accompanied by the immensely powerful host of Maruts,[3] with the intention of destroying the cattle station of Nanda." '

8. *Śrī* Śuka said:

'Ordered on this way by Indra, the clouds, unleashed from their moorings, deluged rain on Nanda's Gokula.

9. Flashing forth with lightning and roaring with claps of thunder, they showered down hail, urged on by the fierce hosts of Maruts.

10. The clouds released incessant torrents of rain as thick as pillars, and the earth became inundated with floods. Low ground could not be distinguished from high ground.

11. The livestock, shivering because of the high wind and rain, and the *gopas* and *gopīs*, afflicted by cold, approached Kṛṣṇa for protection.

12. Covering their heads and shielding their children with their bodies, shivering and tormented by the rain, they approached the soles of the feet of the Lord:

13. "Kṛṣṇa, most virtuous Kṛṣṇa, master – you are compassionate towards your devotees. Please protect Gokula, which accepts you as Lord, from the wrath of this divinity."

14. Seeing them pounded unconscious by the excessive wind and hail, Lord Hari reflected on what Indra had done in his fury:

15. "Indra unleashes rain full of hail and mighty winds out of season in order to destroy us because we neglected his offering.

16. Consequently, I will employ suitable countermeasures through my mystic power. I will destroy the ignorance and pride born of opulence of those who, out of stupidity, think of themselves as lords of the world.

17. The bewilderment caused by thinking of oneself as lord is inappropriate for the demigods, who are endowed with a godly nature. If I break the pride of the impure for their peace of mind it is an appropriate thing to do.

18. Therefore, I make this pledge: I shall protect the cowherd community by my own mystic power. They accept me as their Lord, their shelter is in me and they are my family."

19. Saying this, Viṣṇu lifted up the mountain of Govardhana with one hand and held it effortlessly, as a child holds a mushroom.
20. Then the Lord spoke to the cowherds: "Mother, father and residents of Vraj, enter the cavity under the mountain with your herds of cows whenever you wish.
21. Do not be afraid that the mountain might fall from my hand during this time. Enough of your fear of the rain and wind! I have arranged shelter from them for you."
22. At this, reassured by Kṛṣṇa, they entered the cavity with their wealth, their herds and dependants as far as there was room for them.
23. Giving up concern for hunger and thirst, and any expectation of comfort, Kṛṣṇa held up the mountain for seven days. Watched by the residents of Vraj, he did not move from the spot.
24. Subdued and helpless, and with his plan thwarted, Indra reined in his clouds. He was awed by Kṛṣṇa's mystic power.
25. When he saw that the sky was cloudless, the fierce rain and wind had ceased, and that the sun had arisen, Govardhanadhara [Kṛṣṇa], he who lifted Mount Govardhana, spoke to the *gopas*:
26. "Don't be afraid, O *gopas*, and come out with your wives, possessions and children. The wind and rain have ceased, and the rivers are for the most part without [flood] water."
27. At this, the *gopas*, women, children and elders each took their own cows and their utensils, which had been loaded on to carts, and came out slowly.
28. While all watched, *Bhagavān*, the Lord, effortlessly put back the hill where it had been.
29. The people of Vraj were filled with the force of love, and came to embrace him, or whatever was appropriate. And with joy the *gopīs* offered auspicious blessings, and with love worshipped him with offerings of yogurt and unhusked barley, and other such items.
30. Overcome with love, Yaśodā, Rohiṇī, Nanda and Balarāma, best of the strong, embraced Kṛṣṇa and offered blessings.
31. The hosts of gods, the *siddhas*, *sādhyas*, *gandharvas* and

cāraṇas in the heavens, satisfied, praised Kṛṣṇa and let fall showers of flowers, O Parīkṣit, descendant of Pṛthu.
32. Directed by the gods, they played conches and kettledrums in heaven, while the leaders of the *gandharvas*, headed by Tumburu, sang.[4]
33. Then, O king, Hari, together with Balarāma, went to his own cow-pen surrounded by the friendly cowherders. The *gopīs* happily went on their way singing about such deeds as this. Their hearts were touched.'

CHAPTER 26

*Kṛṣṇa Kills the Baka Demon**

Śrī Śuka said:

1. 'After seeing deeds of Kṛṣṇa such as this, the *gopas* were amazed. Unaware of his power, they approached [Nanda] and said:
2. "Given the astonishing feats of this boy, how did he merit a birth among vulgar folks who are unworthy of him?
3. How could this boy, at the age of seven, effortlessly lift up the biggest mountain with one hand, like the king of elephants lifts a lotus flower?
4. The breast of the immensely powerful Pūtanā, along with her vital airs, was sucked by the infant with his eyes closed, just as the strength of the body is sucked out by the force of time.
5. When he was one month old, his toe struck a cart beneath which he was lying, crying and kicking his two feet upwards. It overturned and collapsed.
6. At the age of one, as he was sitting down, he was carried through the sky by a demon. He killed Tṛṇāvarta, tormenting him by grasping him at the neck.
7. One time, when he was bound to a mortar by his mother for stealing butter, he crawled on his hands [and knees] between two *arjuna* trees and brought them down.

8. Grazing the calves in the forest with Balarāma and surrounded by the boys, he tore the hostile Baka apart at the beak with his arms when Baka tried to kill him.
9. He killed with ease the demon in the form of a calf who had infiltrated the calves with murderous intent, and he made the *kapittha* fruits fall down with him.
10. Accompanied by Balarāma, he killed the donkey demon and his friends, and made safe the Tālavan forest, heavy with well-ripened fruits.
11. He made the powerfully built Balarāma kill the fierce Pralamba and then he liberated the animals of Vraj and the *gopas* from the forest fire.
12. He forcibly subdued the chief of snakes, who had extremely poisonous fangs, expelled him from the lake, and cleared the poison from the waters of the Yamunā.
13. Moreover, how is it, Nanda, that we all, residents of Vraj, feel such affection for this son of yours, as he also does for us? It has existed since his birth, and cannot be shaken off.
14. How can a seven-year-old boy and the carrying of a big mountain fit together? Therefore, we begin to have doubts about your son, O chief of Vraj."
15. *Śrī* Nanda said: "Listen to my words, *gopas*, and your doubts about this boy will be dispelled. Garga told me the following regarding this child:
16. 'The truth is that he has previously assumed bodies of three different colours – white, red and then yellow – according to the *yuga*. Now he has come with a black [*kṛṣṇa*] complexion.
17. Previously, this son of yours was born of Vasudeva. Hence, the learned refer to him as beautiful Vāsudeva.
18. There are many names and forms of your son, according to deed and quality. I know them, but common people do not.
19. This boy is the delight of Gokula and the *gopas*. He will bring good fortune, and through him you will overcome all obstacles with ease.
20. Previously, O lord of Vraj, in times of anarchy the righteous were harassed by robbers. But they became empowered and conquered the robbers because they were protected [by him].

21. Those same persons, who are very fortunate, place their affection in this boy. Enemies cannot overpower them, just as the demons cannot overpower those who have Viṣṇu on their side.
22. Therefore, Nanda, this son of yours is equal to Nārāyaṇa in qualities, splendour, fame and authority. There should be nothing surprising about his acts.'
23. When Garga had gone back to his own home, after advising me clearly in this way, I decided that Kṛṣṇa, who brings us freedom from distress, must be an *aṃśa* of Nārāyaṇa."
24. After hearing Garga's statement repeated by Nanda, the residents of Vraj were happy to honour Nanda, and their wonder at Kṛṣṇa was dispelled.
25. When the demigod Indra unleashed rain, angry at the disruption of his sacrifice, young Kṛṣṇa felt pity when he saw the cowherds, animals and women who had taken shelter of him tormented by the lightning, hailstones and wind. Smiling, the destroyer of the great Indra's pride plucked up and without effort held the mountain with one hand, as if it were a mushroom, and protected the cowherd community. May Indra, the lord of cows, be pleased with us.'

CHAPTER 27

Indra's Eulogy

1. *Śrī* Śuka said:

'When Mount Govardhana was held up and Vraj protected from the rainstorm, Indra, along with Surabhi, the divine cow from Goloka,[1] approached Kṛṣṇa.
2. The offender, ashamed, appeared in a private place and touched Kṛṣṇa's feet with his helmet, which was as brilliant as the sun.
3. Kṛṣṇa's potency is without limit, and his power had been witnessed and reported. Indra's pride at being the ruler of the

three worlds had been destroyed, and he approached with folded hands and spoke as follows.

4. Indra said: "Your *dhāma* [form][2] is unchanging pure *sattva*, composed of virtue,[3] and devoid of *rajas* and *tamas*. This flux of *guṇas*, composed of *māyā* and bound up in ignorance, is not to be found in you.

5. O Lord, greed, and other such negative qualities, the symptoms of an ignorant person, are undoubtedly the causes of this entire world, and the products of it. In any event, *Bhagavān* dispenses discipline for the protection of *dharma*, and the suppression of miscreants.[4]

6. You are the father, the *guru* and the supreme Lord of the universe. You are insurmountable time, and the dispenser of discipline. Moving about in the forms that you assume at will, you occupy yourself with good works and with [the suppression of] the pride of those who fancy themselves lords of the world.

7. Foolish people like me who consider themselves lords of the universe quickly abandon their pride after seeing you fearless in the face of fate. They then humbly honour the path of the Āryas. Your activities are for the control of wrongdoers.

8. You should therefore forgive me, O master. Deeply intoxicated by sovereignty and ignorant of your power, I committed an offence. My mind was bewildered; let my mind never become impure again, O Lord.

9. O Adhokṣaja [Kṛṣṇa], your incarnation in this world is for the well-being of those faithful to your feet, and for the destruction of the warlords. These latter are burdens whose birth has been a great strain on the earth, O God.

10. Homage to you, *Bhagavān*, supreme being, great soul. Homage to you, Vāsudeva, Lord of the Sātvatas.

11. Obeisance to you. Your form is pure knowledge, and your bodies are assumed for the delight of your devotees. You are the seed of everything, as well as the soul in all beings. You are everything.

12. Arrogant and in a blind rage, I attempted to destroy the cowherd community by rain and wind when my sacrifice was abandoned.

13. Be kind and show your favour to me; my endeavour was in

vain and my pride is crushed. You are the Lord, the *guru*, the self, and I have approached you for shelter." '
14. *Śrī* Śuka said:

'When he was glorified in this way by Indra, Kṛṣṇa *Bhagavān*, smiling, spoke to him as follows in a voice as deep as the clouds:
15. *Śrī Bhagavān* said: "The disruption of the sacrifice was orchestrated by me acting in your interests, O Maghavān,[5] so that you would remember me always. You were exhilarated by the power of being Indra.
16. One who is blinded by the intoxication of wealth and sovereignty does not perceive me, rod in hand. I cause whomever I choose to favour to fall from prosperity [and thus become humble].
17. You may take leave, O Indra; follow my instruction, and good fortune to you. You should perform your responsibilities, diligently and free from pride."
18. Then the wise cow Surabhi, along with her offspring, respectfully addressed Kṛṣṇa, who was in the guise of a *gopa*. She saluted him and spoke.
19. Surabhi said: "Kṛṣṇa, Kṛṣṇa, great *yogī*, soul and origin of the universe. You are our master, and the master of the world, O Acyuta.
20. You are our supreme God. You should become our Indra, for the welfare of the cows, *brāhmaṇas* and gods, as well as for those who are holy *sādhus*, O Lord of the universe.
21. Under Brahmā's supervision, we will crown you as our Indra. You have descended to remove the burden of the earth, O soul of the universe."
22–23. After addressing Kṛṣṇa thus, Surabhi consecrated him with her own milk, and Indra did likewise with water from the celestial Gaṇgā river sucked up by the trunk of his elephant, Airāvata. In the company of Surabhi, and under the direction of the mothers of the gods, Indra gave Kṛṣṇa, the descendant of Daśārha, the name "Govinda".
24. The *gandharvas*, *vidyādharas*, *siddhas*, *cāraṇas*, Tumburu, Nārada and others came there. They sang about Hari's glories,

which remove the impurities of the world, while the celestial women joyfully danced together.
25. The most eminent members of the assembly of gods glorified him, and showered him with exotic flowers. The three worlds experienced complete bliss, and the cows transformed the earth into a place flowing with milk.
26. The rivers flowed with waters of different tastes, and the trees with streams of honey. Uncultivated plants ripened, and the mountains bore gems on their surface.
27. When Kṛṣṇa was consecrated, O my dear Parīkṣit, beloved of the Kuru dynasty, all beings became free from enmity, even those who were fierce by nature.
28. Thus Indra consecrated Govinda, the master of the cows and of Gokula. Then Indra was given leave, and departed to heaven surrounded by the gods and other celestial beings.'

CHAPTER 28

*Kṛṣṇa Reveals his Abode**

1. *Śrī* Śuka, the son of Bādarāyaṇa, said:

'After worshipping Janārdana [Viṣṇu] on *ekādasī*, the eleventh day of the lunar month, Nanda, who was fasting, entered the waters of the Kālindī on the twelfth day to bathe.
2. A demon servant of Varuṇa, lord of the waters,[1] seized him and brought him into the presence [of his master]. Nanda had ignored the inauspicious time and entered the water at night.
3. Unable to find Nanda, the *gopas* cried out: "Kṛṣṇa, Balarāma!" When he heard that his father had been seized by Varuṇa, Lord Kṛṣṇa, who is God, the giver of fearlessness to his devotees, went to Varuṇa.
4. When the guardian of the world[2] saw Kṛṣṇa arrive, he worshipped him with great reverence. Overjoyed at seeing Kṛṣṇa, he spoke.
5. *Śrī* Varuṇa said: "Today, my body has been fulfilled; indeed,

today, I have obtained the goal of life. Those who worship your feet have attained the supreme path, O *Bhagavān*.
6. All homage to you. One does not hear about *māyā*, which arranges the creation of the worlds, [affecting] you. You are God, *brahman*, the supreme soul.
7. Your father, here, was brought by my ignorant and foolish servant who does not know his proper duty. Please forgive him.
8. You should also kindly bestow mercy on me, Kṛṣṇa. You are the witness of everything. Please take your father home, Govinda. You feel affection for your father."'
9. *Śrī* Śuka said:

'Mollified by this, Kṛṣṇa *Bhagavān*, Lord of lords, took his father and left, bringing joy to his relatives.
10. Seeing the wonderful and vast wealth of the guardians of the world, and the humility they showed to Kṛṣṇa, Nanda was amazed and told his kinsfolk.
11. The *gopas* thought Kṛṣṇa to be the Lord, O king, and said: "The supreme Lord might even take us to his own transcendental abode," at which they became excited.
12. *Bhagavān*, who sees everything, understood his devotees' [thoughts]. In order to grant their desires and feeling compassion, he deliberated as follows:
13. "Because of *karma*, desire and ignorance, people are wandering in this world in higher or lower states; they do not know their own destination."
14. Thinking thus, *Bhagavān*, the most merciful Hari, revealed to the *gopas* his own abode beyond *tamas*.
15. It was the pure, eternal, unlimited, conscious effulgence of *brahman* which the sages see with tranquil minds when the *guṇas* have subsided.
16. They were transported by Kṛṣṇa to *Brahmahrada*,[3] immersed, and then brought back to normal consciousness.[4] Then they saw the abode of *brahman*, Vaikuṇṭha,[5] where Akrūra had previously had a vision of Kṛṣṇa and Balarāma.[6]
17. Nanda and the others were overwhelmed with supreme ecstasy after seeing this, and also Kṛṣṇa being praised there with Vedic hymns. They were utterly overcome.'

CHAPTER 29

The Description of the Rāsa *Pastime*[1]

1. *Śrī* Śuka, the son of Bādarāyaṇa, said:

'Even *Bhagavān*, God himself, beholding those nights, with autumnal jasmine [*mallikā*] flowers blossoming, called upon his divine power of *yogamāyā*, and turned his thoughts towards enjoying love.
2. At that time, the moon, king of the constellations, arose in the east, covering the face of the heavens with its copper-coloured soothing rays. It wiped away the cares of the onlookers, like a lover who has been absent for a long time wipes away the cares of his beloved.
3. Seeing that full disc, heralder of the white night-lilies, reddened with fresh vermilion powder, its splendour like the face of Lakṣmī, the goddess of fortune, and seeing the forest coloured by its silky rays, Kṛṣṇa played [his flute] softly, capturing the hearts of the beautiful-eyed women.
4. The music aroused Kāma.[2] When they heard it, the women of Vraj, enchanted by Kṛṣṇa, came to their lover, their earrings swinging in their haste, and unknown to one another.
5. Some, who were milking cows, abandoned the milking and approached eagerly. Others had put milk on the fire, but then came without even removing [the milk or] the cakes [from the oven].
6–7. Others interrupted serving food, feeding their babies milk, and attending to their husbands. Still others were eating, but left their food. Others were putting on make-up, washing, or applying mascara to their eyes. They all went to be near Kṛṣṇa, their clothes and ornaments in disarray.
8. Their hearts had been stolen by Govinda, so they did not turn back when husbands, fathers, brothers and relatives tried to prevent them. They were in a state of rapture.
9. Some *gopīs*, not being able to find a way to leave, remained

at home and thought of Kṛṣṇa with eyes closed, completely absorbed in meditation.

10–11. [The *karma*] from their impious deeds was destroyed by the intense and intolerable pain of separation from their lover, and their auspicious deeds were diminished by the complete fulfilment resulting from the intimate contact with Acyuta that they obtained through meditation.[3] Their bondage was destroyed, and they immediately left their bodies made of the *guṇas*. Uniting with the supreme soul, they considered him their lover.'

12. *Śrī* Parīkṣit said:

'O sage, they related to Kṛṣṇa as their supreme lover, not as *brahman*, the absolute truth. So how did the flow of the *guṇas*, in which their minds were absorbed, cease for the *gopīs*?'

13. *Śrī* Śuka said:

'This was explained to you previously: in the same way as the king of the Cedis, Śiśupāla, attained perfection despite hating Hṛṣīkeśa.[4] What then of those dear to Adhokṣaja [Kṛṣṇa]?

14. God appears for the supreme good of humanity, O king. He is immeasurable and eternal. As the controller of the *guṇas*, he is beyond the *guṇas*.

15. Those who always dedicate their desire, anger, fear, affection, sense of identity and friendship to Hari enter for certain into his state of being.

16. You should not show such surprise at Lord Kṛṣṇa. He is unborn and the master of all masters of *yoga*. From him the whole universe attains liberation.

17. The Lord saw that the women of Vraj had arrived in his presence. Being the best of speakers, he addressed them, captivating them with the charm of his words:

18. "Welcome – you are most fortunate. What can I do to please you? Is everything well in Vraj? Tell me the purpose of your coming.

19. This fearsome dark night is frequented by ferocious creatures. Go back to Vraj, O slender-waisted ones; this place is not fit for women.

20. Your mothers, fathers, sons, brothers and husbands are worried because they cannot find you. Do not cause your relatives concern.
21–22. You have seen the forest, adorned with flowers, coloured by the rays of the full moon, and made beautiful by the blossoms of the trees quivering playfully in the breeze of the Yamunā river. Therefore hurry now to the cow-pen and serve your husbands – you are chaste ladies. The babies and calves are crying; suckle them and milk them.
23. Or perhaps your hearts are captivated, and you have come out of love for me. This is commendable of you – living beings delight in me.
24. The highest *dharma* [duty] of a woman is to serve her husband faithfully, to ensure the well-being of her relatives, and to nourish her children.
25. A husband who is not a sinner, even though he be of bad character, ill-fated, old, dull-headed, sick or poor, should not be abandoned by women who desire to attain heaven.
26. Without exception, the adultery of a woman of good birth does not lead to heaven. It is scandalous, fear-laden, worthless, fraught with difficulty and abhorrent.
27. Love for me comes from hearing about me, seeing me, meditating on me and reciting my glories – not in this way, by physical proximity. Therefore, return to your homes."
28. Hearing Govinda speak these unwelcome words, the dejected *gopīs* had their aspirations dashed and were inconsolable in their distress.
29. They stood silently, their red *bimba*-fruit-coloured lips faded by their sighs, and the vermilion powder on their breasts smeared by the mascara carried by their tears. Casting down their faces out of sorrow and scratching the ground with their feet, they were weighed down by extreme unhappiness.
30. Wiping their eyes, and having checked their tears somewhat, the *gopīs* spoke to Kṛṣṇa, their beloved, with voices faltering with agitation. They were utterly devoted, and had sacrificed all desires for his sake, but he had replied to them as if he were anything but their beloved:
31. "You should not speak to us in such a heartless fashion, O

Lord. Renouncing all enjoyments of the senses, we are devoted to the soles of your feet. Reciprocate, you obstinate one, just as the Lord, the original being, reciprocates with those who desire liberation. Do not reject us.

32. You, the knower of *dharma*, have declared that the occupational *dharma* of women consists of attending to friends, husbands and children. Then let this be our *dharma* when it comes to you, the source of this advice, O Lord – after all, you are the soul within all relatives. Indeed, you are the most dear of all embodied beings.

33. You are the eternal beloved, O soul of all, and so the learned place their affection in you. What is the use of husbands and children who simply cause problems? Therefore, O supreme Lord, be pleased with us. Do not dash our hopes. They have been sustained by you for such a long time, O lotus-eyed one.

34. Our hearts, which were absorbed in our households, have been stolen away with ease by you, as have our hands from domestic chores. Our feet cannot move one step from the soles of your lotus feet. How can we go to Vraj? And, besides, what would we do there?

35. O beloved, pour the nectar of your lips on the fire dwelling in our hearts which has been kindled by your musical harmonies, your glances and your smiles. If you do not, we will traverse the path to your feet through meditation, our bodies consumed by the fire born of separation.

36. Lotus-eyed Kṛṣṇa, you are dear to the forest-dwelling hermits. Somewhere or other, for a moment, we providentially touched the soles of your feet, which belong to the goddess of fortune. Alas, from that moment, instantly enamoured of you, we became incapable of remaining in the presence of any other man.

37. The goddess of fortune aspires to the dust of those lotus feet which is worshipped by your servants, even though she has obtained a place on your chest along with Tulasī.[5] Other gods, even, strive to attract her personal glance. In the same way, we solicit the dust of your feet.

38. It is you who banish distress – therefore be compassionate to us. In the desire to worship you, we have given up our homes

and arrived at the soles of your feet. Allow us, whose hearts are burning with intense desire born from your beautiful smiles and glances, to be your servants, O ornament of men.

39. We have gazed on your face covered with curls, with its smiles and glances, and on your honeyed lips placed between your cheeks made beautiful with earrings. And we have beheld your two strong arms, which bestow fearlessness, and your chest, which is the exclusive delight of the goddess of fortune. After this, we have become your servants.

40. Dear Kṛṣṇa, what women in the three worlds would not stray from the behaviour proper to Āryans, when thrown into turmoil by the melodies of your flute, which vibrates harmoniously? And what woman would not stray after seeing this, your form, which brings good fortune to the three worlds and causes the hair of cows, birds, trees and deer to stand on end with bliss?

41. It is clear that you have accepted birth to remove the tribulations and fears of Vraj just as the Lord, the primeval person, protects the denizens of heaven. Therefore, since you are the friend of the afflicted, place your lotus hands on the burning breasts and heads of your servants."'

42. *Śrī* Śuka said:

'The master of the masters of *yoga*, hearing their despairing words, laughed and engaged in amorous pleasures from compassion, even though his satisfaction is self-contained.

43. Kṛṣṇa, the infallible one, whose conduct is upright, shone forth with the assembled *gopīs*, who were dazzling with jasmine teeth and broad smiles. As the *gopīs*' faces blossomed from the glances of their beloved, Kṛṣṇa appeared like the moon surrounded by stars.

44. Praised in song, and singing loudly himself, the Lord of hundreds of women, wearing a garland of *vaijayantī* flowers, frolicked in the forest, making it beautiful.

45–46. Accompanied by the *gopīs*, Kṛṣṇa approached the bank of the river. Its cool sand was swept by a wind bearing the scent of *kumuda* flowers and refreshing from its contact with the waves. Arousing Kāma in the young women of Vraj with jokes, smiles and glances, playfully scratching their breasts, girdles, thighs, hair and hands with his nails, and embracing them with outstretched arms, he gave them pleasure.

47. Such attention from Kṛṣṇa *Bhagavān*, the supreme soul, made the *gopīs* proud. Indeed, they thought themselves to be the best of women on earth.

48. Keśava saw their pride, which was born from the exhilaration of their good fortune, and vanished from the spot out of kindness, in order to moderate [their pride].'

CHAPTER 30

Searching for Kṛṣṇa in the Rāsa *Pastime*

1. *Śrī* Śuka said:

'When *Bhagavān* suddenly vanished, the women of Vraj were filled with remorse at his disappearance. They were like female elephants who had lost sight of the leader of the herd.

2. Intoxicated by the pleasing gestures, playfulness and words, as well as by the quivering glances, smiles of love and movements of Kṛṣṇa, the husband of Ramā, the goddess of fortune, their minds were overwhelmed. They acted out each of those behaviours, their hearts [dedicated] to him.

3. Those beloved women were so bewildered by Kṛṣṇa's pastimes that their bodies imitated their darling in the way they moved, smiled, glanced, spoke, and so forth. With their hearts [dedicated] to him, the women declared: "I am he!"

4. Singing loudly in unison only about him, they searched from grove to grove, like mad women. They asked the trees about the supreme being who, like space, is inside and outside living creatures:

5. "O *aśvattha* tree! O *plakṣa* tree! O *nyagrodha* tree! Have you seen the son of Nanda at all? He has stolen our minds with his glances and smiles of love, and has gone.

6. O *kurabaka*, *aśoka*, *nāga*, *punnāga* and *campaka* trees! Has

the younger brother of Balarāma [passed] by here? His smile steals away the pride of haughty women.

7. O auspicious *tulasī* plant, you who are dear to Govinda! Have you seen your most beloved, Acyuta, wearing you [as a garland covered] with swarms of bees?

8. O *mālatī* plant! O *mallikā* plant! O *jātī* plant! O *yūthikā* plant! Has Mādhava [Kṛṣṇa] passed by, awakening your love with the touch of his hand? Have you seen him?

9. O *cūta* [mango], *priyāla*, *panasa* [bread-fruit], *asana*, *kovidāra*, *jambū* [rose-apple], *arka*, *bilva* [wood-apple], *bakula*, *āmra* [mango], *kadamba* and *nipa* trees, and those others which grow on the shore of the Yamunā river and which exist to benefit others! Point us to the path [taken] by Kṛṣṇa. We have lost our hearts.

10. O earth, you are beautiful in that the hairs of your body [the trees] stand up from the bliss of the touch of the feet of Keśava [Kṛṣṇa]. What ascetic practice have you performed?[1] Is the cause of this these very feet [of Kṛṣṇa]? Or is it because of the step of Urukrama?[2] Or rather from the embrace of the body of Varāha?[3]

11. O wife of the deer, has Acyuta passed by here with his beloved, his limbs giving pleasure to your eyes? O friend, the scent from the jasmine garland of the Lord of our group is wafting here – a garland coloured with breast saffron contracted from the body of his lover.

12. O trees, did the younger brother of Balarāma wander here? Was he followed by swarms of bees, blinded with intoxication, on his *tulasī* [garland]? With his arm placed on the shoulder of his beloved, he [must have been] holding a lotus flower. And did he acknowledge with glances of love your bowing down?

13. Ask these creeping plants! Just see, although they are embracing the arms of the forest tree, they surely must have been touched by his fingernails, for they are bristling with ecstasy."

14. The *gopīs*, [uttering] these crazed words, became perplexed in their search for Kṛṣṇa. With their hearts [dedicated] to him, each of them imitated the *līlā* of *Bhagavān*.

15. One, who was acting as if she were Kṛṣṇa, suckled the breast of someone else, who was playing the part of Pūtanā. Another

became an infant, began crying, and then kicked another one, who was acting as a cart, with her foot.
16. After changing into a demon, one *gopī* kidnapped another, who was imagining herself to be the child Kṛṣṇa. Yet another crawled around, dragging her two feet, accompanied by the sounds from her jewellery.
17. Two *gopīs* enacted the roles of Kṛṣṇa and Balarāma, and others behaved as *gopas*. Yet another struck a *gopī* who had become Vatsa, the calf demon, while someone else there struck the *gopī* who was playing the role of Baka, the crane demon.
18. One called the cows who were far away, as Kṛṣṇa would have done. Others praised one *gopī* who was sporting and playing the flute in imitation of him: "Bravo!"
19. Another, wandering about, placed her arm on someone else, and said: "There can be no doubt that I am Kṛṣṇa. Look at how gracefully I move." Her mind was intent on him:
20. "Do not fear the wind and the rain. I have arranged protection." Saying this, one *gopī*, exerting herself, lifted up her garment with one hand.
21. Another *gopī* mounted and stepped on the head of another with her foot, O king, and said: "Go, wicked snake! There is no doubt that I have undertaken birth as the chastiser of the wicked."
22. Someone there said: "Hey *gopas*, look at the terrible forest fire! Close your eyes, I will with ease arrange for your protection!"
23. One slender-waisted *gopī* was tied to a mortar with a flower garland by another one. The former, her beautiful eyes afraid, covered her face and adopted a posture of fear.
24. Inquiring thus after Kṛṣṇa from the creeping plants and trees of Vṛndāvana, the *gopīs* noticed the footprints of the supreme soul in a certain part of the forest:
25. "These footprints are certainly those of the great soul, the son of Nanda," they said. "They are recognizable from such marks as the flag, the lotus flower, the thunderbolt, the goad and the barley."
26. Following Kṛṣṇa's tracks further, footprint by footprint, the

women noticed that they were clearly interspersed with the footprints of a young woman. They discussed this together in distress:

27. "Whose footprints are these? She is going with the son of Nanda, his forearm placed on her shoulder, like a female elephant with a male elephant.

28. She has worshipped[4] *Bhagavān* Hari, the Lord. Consequently, Govinda was pleased, and so has abandoned us and led that *gopī* to a secluded place.

29. Just see, O friends, how fortunate are these particles of dust from the lotus feet of Govinda. Brahmā, Śiva and the goddess of fortune, Ramā [Śrī], place them on their heads to remove their sins.

30. The footprints of that woman are causing us great distress because she alone of the *gopīs* is enjoying the lips of Acyuta in a secluded place.

31. Now, right here, her footprints are no longer visible: the lover has lifted up his beloved, whose feet with their delicate soles are bruised by the blades of grass.

31a.[5] Look, *gopīs*, at these deeper footprints of lusty Kṛṣṇa weighed down by carrying the young woman. And here the beloved has been put down by that great soul in order to [gather] flowers.

32. Look, here the lover plucked flowers for the beloved: these two footprints are incomplete because he stood on tip-toe.

33. Here, lusty Kṛṣṇa decorated that lusty woman's hair. Surely he sat here while making his lover a crown with those [flowers].'"

34. [*Śrī* Śuka said]:

'Kṛṣṇa took pleasure with that *gopī*, although he is complete, content within himself and delights in his own self. He was displaying the wretchedness of lusty men and women because of their depravity.

35–36. The dispirited *gopīs* wandered about pointing [things] out in this way. The *gopī*, whom Kṛṣṇa had taken to the forest after abandoning the other women, then thought that she was the best of all women: "Kṛṣṇa, my beloved, has abandoned the [other] *gopīs* who were impelled by Kāma and dedicated himself to me."

37. Then, after going to a spot in the wood, the proud woman spoke to Keśava [Kṛṣṇa]: "I am unable to walk any further. Take me wherever your mind [desires]."

38. At this request, Kṛṣṇa told his beloved that she should climb on his shoulder, but then he disappeared. The young woman was filled with remorse:

39. "O Lord, lover, dearest! Where are you? Where are you, mighty-armed one? Reveal your presence to me, friend – I am your miserable servant!"'

40. *Śrī* Śuka said:

'The *gopīs*, searching for the path of *Bhagavān*, saw a distressed girl not far away who was disorientated by the separation from her beloved.

41. Hearing her story of how she had first received respect from Mādhava [Kṛṣṇa], and then humiliation because of her bad faith, they were astounded.

42. After this, they went as far into the forest as the moon gave light. Then, seeing that darkness had descended there, the women returned.

43. Their minds absorbed in Kṛṣṇa, the *gopīs*' conversations focused on him, their activities centred on him, and they dedicated their hearts to him. Simply by singing about his qualities, they forgot their own homes.

44. Meditating on Kṛṣṇa, they reached the bank of the Kālindī [Yamunā] river again. Gathering together they sang about Kṛṣṇa, longing for his arrival.'

CHAPTER 31
The Gopīs' *Song in the* Rāsa *Pastime*

1. 'The *gopīs* said: "Vraj has become pre-eminent because of your birth; indeed, Indirā [Lakṣmī] resides there permanently. O loved one, show yourself! Your devotees, whose lives are sustained in you, are searching for you everywhere.
2. You are taking our life, O Lord of autumn; your glance excels in beauty the heart of a beautiful lotus perfectly born in autumn from a pool of water. We are your maidservants [and do not ask for] any payment. Isn't this killing us, O bestower of favours?
3. O bull among men, we have been continuously protected by you from destruction from the poisonous water, from the wicked demon, from the winds and rains, from fire and lightning, from the bull Ariṣṭa, from the son of Maya [Vyomāsura], and from fear from all sides.
4. You are not, in fact, the son of a *gopī*. You are the witness of the inner self of all embodied beings. Being petitioned by Brahmā, you become manifest in the family of the Sātvatas, O friend, for the protection of the universe.
5. Place your lotus hand on the head of those who have approached you out of fear of the material world, O foremost of the Vṛṣṇi clan. Your hand, which holds the hand of Śrī [Lakṣmī], bestows fearlessness and fulfils desires, O lover.
6. You are the hero of women, and you take away the pain of the people of Vraj! The pride of your devotees is annihilated by your smile! Accept your maidservants, friend! Show us your beautiful lotus face!
7. Place your lotus feet upon our breasts. Your feet have been placed on the hoods of the serpent [Kāliya] and follow the animals to the pasture. They are the abode of the goddess of fortune, Śrī, and they remove the sins of submissive embodied beings. Excise Kāma, who dwells within our hearts.
8. O hero, these women obedient to your will are stunned by your sweet voice, your charming words which please the mind

and the intelligence, and your lotus eyes. Reinvigorate us with the intoxicating liquid of your lips.

9. Those who repeat the sweetness of your words in this world are munificent. These words are praised by poets, spread abroad, and are auspicious to hear. They are life-giving for those who are suffering. They remove sins and bring good fortune.

10. Your bursts of laughter, pleasing looks of love, and pastimes are auspicious to contemplate. Those meetings in secret places touch our hearts, you cheater, and perturb us thoroughly.

11. When you go from Vraj grazing the animals, O Lord, your feet, beautiful as lotuses, are troubled by blades of grass and corn stubble, and so we feel distress. You are our beloved.

12. You possess a lotus face, surrounded by blue locks of hair which you constantly display covered with thick dust at the end of the day. You arouse Kāma in the heart, O hero.

13. O lover, place your most beneficent lotus feet on our breasts. They fulfil the desires of the humble and should be meditated upon in trouble, O destroyer of anxiety. They are worshipped by the lotus-born Brahmā, and are the ornament of the earth.

14. Bestow upon us the nectar of your lips, O hero, which have been thoroughly kissed by the flute as it plays music. It destroys sorrow, increases the pleasures of love, and causes men to forget other passions.

15. When you, Lord, go to the forest during the day, a moment becomes a *yuga*[1] for those who do not see you. He who created eyelashes is dull-witted, from the perspective of those beholding your beautiful face, with its curled locks of hair.[2]

16. Acyuta, you are the knower of [people's] movements. Bewildered by your song, we have thoroughly neglected our husbands, sons, family, brothers and kinsfolk, and come before you. Who would abandon women in the night, you rogue?

17. We have become unsettled from contemplating your broad chest, the abode of Śrī, the goddess of fortune, as well as your looks of love, your smiling face and the meetings in secret places which aroused Kāma. We long for you intensely all the time.

18. Your incarnation is for the good of the universe, and dispels the distress of the people of Vraj. Deliver a little of that [medi-

cine] which removes the ailment from the hearts of your devotees to us. Our hearts yearn for you.
19. We gently place your tender lotus feet on our rough breasts with trepidation. You wander in the forest on them and our minds are disturbed: what if they have been hurt by small stones? Your Lordship is our life."'

CHAPTER 32

The Gopīs' *Lamentation in the* Rāsa *Pastime*

1. *Śrī* Śuka said:

'Thus the *gopīs* sang and spoke incoherently in various ways. Longing to see Kṛṣṇa, O king, they wept loudly.
2. Kṛṣṇa, the descendant of Śūra, bewilderer of the mind of the mind-bewilderer Kāma himself, appeared in their midst, his lotus face smiling. He was wearing yellow garments, and bore a garland.
3. Seeing that their beloved had returned, the women, their eyes wide with love, sprang up simultaneously as if the vital air of the body had returned.
4. One ecstatic woman caught hold of Kṛṣṇa's lotus hand in her folded hands. Another placed his arm, decorated with sandalwood paste, on her shoulder.
5. A slender woman accepted his chewed betel nut with folded hands. Another, burning [with desire], placed his lotus feet on her breast.
6. Yet another, trembling with the fury of love, was biting her lips with her teeth, her brows knitted in a frown. She glared at Kṛṣṇa as if she could strike him with a look of rebuke.
7. Another woman dwelt on his lotus face with unblinking eyes. Although she drank it in with her eyes, she was not fully satisfied, just as a saint is not fully satisfied [by meditating on] Kṛṣṇa's lotus feet.
8. Some other woman, drawing Kṛṣṇa into her heart through

the apertures of her eyes and then sealing them shut, stood embracing him [in her heart], like a *yogī* immersed in bliss.
9. All rejoiced at the wonder of seeing Keśava [Kṛṣṇa], and let go the distress they had felt at separation, as people are joyful after encountering a wise man.
10. *Bhagavān*, Acyuta, surrounded by the women who had shaken off their sorrow, shone brilliantly, like the supreme being surrounded by his *śakti* powers.
11–12. The supreme ruler took the women along and enjoyed himself on the auspicious bank of the Kālindī [Yamunā]. There were bees with six legs and a breeze fragrant with blossoming jasmine and *mandāra* flowers. Its soft sands were lapped by waves that were like the hands of the Kṛṣṇa river [Yamunā]. The darkness of the night was dispelled by the full rays from the autumn moon.
13. The heartache of the *gopis* had been assuaged by the bliss of seeing Kṛṣṇa, just as the Vedas attained the culmination of their hearts' desire.[1] The *gopīs* made a seat for the friend of their heart with their outer garments, which were smeared with the *kuṅkum* powder from their breasts.
14. *Bhagavān*, the Lord, whose seat is fixed within the hearts of the masters of *yoga*, sat down there. He was worshipped as he sat in the company of the *gopīs*, and revealed himself in a form that was a unique embodiment of beauty in the three worlds.
15. Those women worshipped that inciter of Kāma by massaging his hands and feet, which they had placed on their laps. They praised him, their eyebrows quivering, with playful looks and laughter. Then they spoke, somewhat angrily.
16. The beautiful *gopīs* said: "Some serve those who serve them. Some do the opposite of this [i.e. serve those who do not serve them]. And some do not serve either. Can you explain this for us clearly?"
17. *Śrī Bhagavān* said: "Friends, there are those who serve each other reciprocally but their exchange is exclusively out of self-interest; there is no *dharma* or friendship there. Personal gain and nothing else is the motive.
18. Those, like mothers and fathers, who serve those who do not

serve [them] are truly compassionate. There is perfect friendship and *dharma* in this, O slender-waisted ones.

19. Some do not serve even those who serve [them], let alone those who do not serve [them]. They include those who take pleasure in their spiritual self, those whose desires are fulfilled, the ungrateful and the *guru*-haters.

20. I do not serve even those beings who serve me to enhance their devotional state of mind, O friends. The case is like that of the poor man who is not conscious of anything else when the wealth that he had gained is lost, but continues to contemplate that wealth obsessively.

21. In this way, O women, when I disappeared from your presence – you who had abandoned relatives, the [injunctions of the] Vedas, and the world for my sake – it was really to further [your dedication] to me. I was serving you. Therefore, beloved ones, you should not be displeased with your beloved.

22. You have broken the enduring shackles of the household, and have served me. You are full of goodness and without fault, and I am unable to reciprocate, even in the lifetime of a god. Therefore, let your reward be your own excellence."

CHAPTER 33

The Description of the Rāsa *Pastime*

1. 'Hearing the Lord's winning words spoken in this way, the *gopīs* relinquished their distress at separation, but their aspirations increased from touching his limbs.

2. Govinda [Kṛṣṇa] began the *rāsa* pastime[1] there, in the company of those devoted jewels of women, who linked arms happily together.

3. The festival of the *rāsa* dance began, featuring a circle of *gopīs*. The Lord of all *yogīs*, Kṛṣṇa, inserted himself between each pair of *gopīs*, and put his arms about their necks. Each woman thought he was at her side only. Meanwhile, the sky was crowded with hundreds of the vehicles of the gods, who

were accompanied by their wives and carried away with excitement.
4. Kettledrums resounded then, streams of flowers fell, and the chiefs of the *gandharvas*[2] and their wives sang of Kṛṣṇa's spotless glories.
5. There was a tumultuous sound of bracelets, ankle-bracelets and the bells of the young women in the circle of the *rāsa* dance with their beloved.
6. Kṛṣṇa *Bhagavān*, the son of Devakī, was radiant in their company, like a great emerald in the midst of golden ornaments.
7. The consorts of Kṛṣṇa, their braids and belts securely fastened, sang about him with hand gestures and dancing feet. Their faces were sweating, their earrings rolling on their cheeks, and the garments on their breasts slipping. Their waists were bent, and they smiled, their eyebrows playful. They shone like lightning in a circle of clouds.
8. They were intent on amorous pleasure and overjoyed by Kṛṣṇa's touch. Their throats decorated with dye, they sang loudly as they danced, and the world reverberated with their songs.
9. One *gopī* led a duet in harmony with Mukunda. Kṛṣṇa was pleased and praised her: "Well done! Well done!" Then she led the refrain and he heaped praises on her.
10. Another, tired by the *rāsa* dance, her *mallikā* [jasmine] flowers and bracelets loosened, laid her arm on the shoulder of Kṛṣṇa, the wielder of the club, who was standing by her side.
11. Kṛṣṇa placed his arm on the shoulder of one of the *gopīs*. Smelling it, fragrant as a blue lotus and smeared with sandalwood, she kissed it, the hairs of her body tingling with rapture.
12. Kṛṣṇa gave his chewed betel nut to another *gopī* as she placed her cheek, adorned with the glitter of earrings in disarray from the dancing, next to his cheek.
13. Yet another *gopī* who was singing and dancing, her belt and ankle-bracelets jingling, became fatigued. She placed the soothing lotus hand of Acyuta, who was at her side, on her breast.
14. The *gopīs* won their lover Acyuta, who is the exclusive

beloved of Śrī, the goddess of fortune. Their necks encircled by his arms, they delighted in him as they sang.

15. The *gopīs*, with glowing faces, cheeks adorned with locks of hair, and lotus flowers behind their ears, were beautiful. They danced with the Lord in the circle of the *rāsa*[3] to the musical accompaniment of the bees complemented by the sound of their anklets and bangles. Wreaths of flowers fell from their hair.

16. Thus Kṛṣṇa, the Lord of Lakṣmī,[4] sported with the beautiful girls of Vraj with freely playful smiles, amorous glances, and with caresses and embraces. He was like a child enraptured by his own reflection.

17. The senses of the women of Vraj were alive with pleasure from the contact of his limbs. Their ornaments and garlands were awry, and the women could not keep their garments or their hair or the cloth covering their breasts in order, O best of the Kuru Dynasty.

18. The women of the celestial realm travelling in the air were stricken with desire at seeing Kṛṣṇa's pastimes, and became entranced. The moon and its entourage [the stars] were full of wonder.

19. Although content within himself, the Lord became manifest in as many forms as there were *gopī* women, and enjoyed himself with them in *līlā* pastimes.

20. With great compassion, Kṛṣṇa lovingly caressed with his very soothing hands the face of those *gopīs* who were exhausted from the pleasures of love.

21. The *gopīs* paid homage to their hero with sideways looks and honeyed smiles. Their beautiful cheeks glowed with locks of hair and the glitter of golden earrings. Thrilled by the touch of Kṛṣṇa's fingernails, they sang of his auspicious deeds.

22. When he tired, Kṛṣṇa went into the water with them. He was pursued by bees, who [sang] like *gandharva*-chiefs, because of his garland. Crushed by contact with the limbs of the *gopīs*, it was stained with the *kuṅkum* powder from their breasts. Kṛṣṇa was like the king of the elephants who had lost all inhibitions with his female elephants.

23. With looks of love, the young women around him laughed and splashed him vigorously, O King! Worshipped with showers

of *kusuma* flowers by the celestial beings in their aerial chariots, Kṛṣṇa disported himself like an elephant in *līlā* pastimes, even though he is content within himself.
24. Later, he strolled in the groves of the Yamunā river, surrounded by groups of young women and bees. The furthest corners of the river, both on land and on the waters, were pervaded by a wind bearing the fragrance of flowers. He was like an elephant exhilarated by the company of his female elephants.
25. Kṛṣṇa's desires are always fulfilled, and his propensity for enjoyment is fulfilled within himself, but during all those nights he participated in this way in the company of throngs of young women. Such nights, brilliant with the rays of the moon, are the setting for *rasa* in both poetry and prose that describe autumn.'
26. Parīkṣit said:

'God, the Lord of the universe, has descended into the world along with his expansion [Balarāma] for the establishment of *dharma*, and for the suppression of *adharma*, non-dharma.[5]
27. He is the original speaker, exemplar and protector of the injunctions of *dharma*. How could he behave in a manner contrary to *dharma*, O *brāhmaṇa*, by touching the wives of others?
28. The Lord of the Yadu dynasty, who is content within himself, has performed an abhorrent deed. What was his purpose? You who are true to your vows, please take away our doubt.'
29. *Śrī* Śuka said:

'Just as fire consumes everything [without being polluted], so it is seen that the blatant transgressions of *dharma* by the more powerful of rulers are not faults.
30. One who is not a powerful being should certainly never behave in that fashion, not even in his mind. Otherwise, acting out of foolishness, he will be destroyed, just as one who is not Śiva will be destroyed [by drinking] the poison churned from the ocean.[6]
31. The words of powerful beings are truth, and so is whatever

is performed by them. The wise will act in accordance with their words.

32. O master, those who are devoid of personal ego do not accrue benefit for themselves through appropriate behaviour, nor undesirable results through its opposite.

33. What then of the applicability of auspiciousness and inauspiciousness to the supreme being of all supreme beings and of all living entities, whether celestial, human or animal?

34. Satisfied by worshipping the dust of Kṛṣṇa's lotus feet, even the sages act according to their own free will. The bondage of all their *karma* has been destroyed through the power of *yoga*, and so they are never bound. How, then, can one speak of bondage for Kṛṣṇa, who accepts forms according to his own will?

35. He lives within the *gopīs*, their husbands and all living beings. He is the supreme witness who has assumed a form in this world for the purpose of sport.

36. Manifest in a human form, he indulges in such pastime as a favour to the devotees. Hearing about these, one becomes fully devoted to him.

37. Confused by his power of illusion, the menfolk of Vraj were not resentful of Kṛṣṇa; each thought his own wife was present at his side.

38. The *gopīs* held the Lord dear. When the duration of Brahmā's night had expired,[7] they went home unwillingly with the approval of Vāsudeva.

39. The sober person who is endowed with faith should hear and describe these pastimes of Viṣṇu with the maidens of Vraj. Achieving supreme devotion to the Lord, one quickly frees oneself from lust, the disease of the heart.'

CHAPTER 34

The Killing of Śaṅkhacūḍa

1. *Śrī* Śuka said:

'One time, the cowherd men, wanting to make a pilgrimage, set out for the Ambikā forest with their carts yoked to oxen.
2. After bathing in the Sarasvatī river there, they worshipped the eminent god Paśupati [Śiva] and the goddess Ambikā with reverence and devotion, O king.
3. They donated cows, gold, clothing, honey and grains mixed with honey to the *brāhmaṇas*, saying: "May the Lord be pleased with us."
4. Drinking only water and blessed with good fortune, Nanda, Sunanda and the others camped that night on the bank of the Sarasvatī. They kept to their vows.
5. By chance, a huge and hungry snake, a creature that moves on its breast, made its way into the forest and began to swallow Nanda.
6. Nanda was held fast in the snake's mouth. He shouted: "Kṛṣṇa! Kṛṣṇa! This huge snake is swallowing me. Free me, my dear child; I am taking refuge in [you]."
7. Hearing his cries, the distraught cowherd men immediately jumped up and saw that he was being swallowed. They beat the snake with fire-brands.
8. Although burned by the fire-brands, the serpent did not release Nanda. *Bhagavān* Kṛṣṇa, the Lord of the Sātvatas, arrived there and touched the serpent with his foot.
9. The serpent's inauspicious [results of past deeds] were destroyed by the touch of the beautiful foot of *Bhagavān* Kṛṣṇa. He abandoned the body of a snake and assumed a form worshipped by the celestial *Vidyādharas*.
10. This being, with a luminous form wearing a golden necklace and standing reverentially, was addressed by Hṛṣīkeśa [Kṛṣṇa] thus.
11. "Who are you, sir, so wonderful to behold and radiating

with majestic splendour? And how did you obtain this loathsome condition unwillingly?"

12–13. The snake said: "I am Sudarśana ['beautiful to behold'], a certain celestial *Vidyādhara*. I am famous for my wealth and the beauty of my personal form. Once, while roaming the quarters in a celestial air-carrier, I mocked the misshapen Aṅgirā sages, out of conceit at my own beauty. For this offence of ridicule, they made me take on this birth.

14. The curse has been brought about for my well-being by those merciful souls [the Aṅgirās] since I have been touched by the foot of the *guru* of the worlds, and my inauspiciousness has been destroyed.

15. You remove the fear of those who take refuge in you, fearful of material existence. I have been freed from the curse by the touch of your foot, O destroyer of distress. I take my leave of you.

16. Give me leave, O God, lord of the lords of the world. I take refuge in you, O great *yogī*, supreme being, Lord of the righteous!

17. I have been freed in an instant from the punishment of the *brāhmaṇas* by seeing you, Acyuta. One is immediately purified by your name, as are all those who hear it. How much more again is one purified if one has actually been touched by your feet?"

18. Taking leave in this way from Dāśārha [Kṛṣṇa], Sudarśana circumambulated Him, paid his respects and departed to heaven. And Nanda was released from his predicament.

19. When they saw that display of Kṛṣṇa's personal power, the people of Vraj were struck with awe. After completing their ritual observances there they returned to Vraj, O king, relating that event with great reverence [as they went along].

20. On another occasion, the mighty Govinda and Balarāma left for the forest at night, in the company of the women of Vraj.

21. Their limbs were smeared [with fragrances], they were beautifully adorned, and they wore immaculate garments and garlands. The beautiful women, bound to them with love, sang their praises.

22. They delighted in the onset of the night with the risen moon and stars, with bees intoxicated by the fragrance of jasmine, and with the breeze of lotus flowers.
23. The two sang songs in unison, giving pleasure to the ears and minds of all living things, which was enhanced by their harmonies.
24. The *gopīs* swooned at hearing their song, and so did not notice that their garments were slipping from their bodies, and that their hair and their garlands were unravelling.
25. While they were playing and singing freely in this way, as if intoxicated, a follower of Kubera, the treasurer of the celestials, known as Śaṅkhacūḍa, approached.
26. While Kṛṣṇa and Balarāma were looking on, O king, he brazenly herded the womenfolk away to the north. The women look on those two as their masters, and so cried out.
27. Seeing their own followers crying out: "Kṛṣṇa! Balarāma!" and seized by robbers as if they were cows, the two brothers ran in pursuit.
28. Inspiring courage by shouting "Do not fear!", and moving rapidly with a *śāla* tree in hand, Kṛṣṇa and Balarāma quickly approached that vilest of the *guhyakas*[1] as he was hastening away.'
29. *Śrī* Śuka said:

'The fool saw them bearing down like Time and Death personified. He abandoned the womenfolk and fled in terror, desiring to live.
30. Wherever he ran, Govinda [Kṛṣṇa] pursued him, intending to take the jewel from his head. Balarāma remained behind, protecting the women.
31. The Lord sprang forward from nowhere and, with his fist, knocked off the head of that wicked man, along with the jewel on his crest, dear Parīkṣit.
32. After killing Śaṅkhacūḍa in this way, Kṛṣṇa seized the brilliant gem and gave it fondly to his elder brother while the women watched.'

CHAPTER 35

The Song of a Pair of Gopīs

1. *Śrī* Śuka said:

'When Kṛṣṇa went to the forest, the *gopīs* spent their days despondently, attending him in their minds and singing about his *līlā*.

2–3. The beautiful *gopīs* said: "O *gopīs*, whenever Mukunda sets his flute on his lower lip, his soft fingers covering the holes, and blows it, with his left cheek placed on his left arm and his eyebrows moving playfully, the celestial women travelling in the sky, along with the *siddhas*, are struck with amazement. When they hear it, their minds become dedicated to the pursuit of love and they become bashful. Oblivious to [the loosening of] their girdles, they experience faintness of mind.

4–5. Just see! The son of Nanda gives delight to people suffering in this world. He has a smile like a garland of pearls, and lightning sits constantly on his chest.[1] Listen to this wonderful thing, O women: the bulls in the pasture, the herds of cows and deer are spellbound, bewitched by the sounds of the flute from afar. With mouthfuls of chewed food between their teeth and ears erect, they remain as still as if in a picture.

6–7. Whenever Mukunda, dressed as a wrestler with leaves, minerals and peacock feathers, along with Balarāma and the *gopas*, summons the cows, O friend, then the river finds her course disrupted. Desiring the wind-borne dust from his lotus feet, she remains, like us of little piety, her arms trembling with love and her waters motionless.[2]

8–9. Kṛṣṇa's powers are immovable, like those of the supreme person. As he roams in the forest, his glories are recited by his followers. When he summons with his flute the cows who are grazing on the mountain slopes, the trees and creeping plants of the forest seem to be manifesting Viṣṇu in themselves. Richly endowed with fruits and flowers, their young branches bowing reverentially with their load and their bodies bristling with the ecstasy of love, they pour forth streams of honey.[3]

10–11. He wears conspicuous *tilaka*.[4] When he shows appreciation for the pleasant songs of the swarms of bees intoxicated with the nectar from the *tulasī* and the heavenly scents of his forest garland, and picks up his flute, the cranes, swans and birds on the lake come near. Their minds are bewitched by his sweet songs, and they worship Hari. Just see: their minds are fixed, their eyes are closed and they are silent!

12–13. Sporting garlands of flowers and ear-ornaments, and accompanied by Balarāma, Kṛṣṇa causes delight on the summits of the mountain, O women of Vraj. When he is joyful, he makes the whole world echo with the sounds of his flute, and the cloud rumbles deeply in response. Preoccupied about committing an offence against a great personality, it rains upon its friend with flowers, and makes a parasol with its shade.

14–15. Kṛṣṇa is skilled in the various activities of the *gopas*, and has taught himself the many flute melodies that he knows. O chaste lady,[5] when your son, his flute against his lips like *bimba* fruit, produces harmonies in a range of notes, the chiefs of the gods, headed by Indra, Śiva and Brahmā, bow their minds and necks and are overcome; although they are poets, they become hesitant about their own compositions.

16–17. He wanders around, his petal-like lotus feet giving relief to the ground of Vraj from the prickling pain caused by hoofs. His feet are marked with the distinct signs of the goad, the lotus, the thunderbolt and the flag. He is renowned for his flute and he moves like an elephant. We are disturbed by the passion aroused by his playful glances, and are reduced to the [motionless] state of trees. Bewildered, we are unaware of our clothing and our hair.

18–19. Wearing a jewel, Kṛṣṇa sometimes counts the cows with a *tulasī* garland which bears the fragrance of a beloved. When he sings, on occasion throwing his arm around the shoulder of an affectionate friend, the does, mates of the black [*kṛṣṇa*] deer, approach and sit near him, the ocean of all qualities. They are carried away by the sound of the flute and, like the *gopīs*, have given up their longings for their homes.

20–21. O sinless one, your son, the charming son of Nanda, dressed in festival attire made of garlands of jasmine, and surrounded by cows and *gopas*, plays [on the banks of] the Yamunā with his friends.
22. A gentle wind, pleasant from the touch of sandalwood, blows, honouring Him. The lesser gods surround him and pay homage with music, songs and offerings.
23. Because he is fond of the cows of Vraj, he held up the mountain. At the end of the day, he herds all the cows, and his feet are worshipped along the way by those who are learned. His flute plays a tune, and his celebrity is praised by his followers. He arrives [home], wearing a garland specked with dust from the hooves, and though apparently tired, he presents a feast for the eyes. He is the moon, king of the stars, appearing from the womb of Devakī in order to fulfil the wishes of his friends.
24. Wearing a garland from the forest, he pays respects to his friends, his eyes rolling a little from excitement. His face is as white as the *badara* tree, and he decorates his soft cheeks with rich gold earrings.
25. He is the lord of the Yadus, sporting like the king of two-tusked elephants. He returns at the end of the day, his face full of joy. He is like the moon, lord of the night, which gives relief from the endless heat of the day for the cows of Vraj."'
26. *Śrī* Śuka said:

'In this way, O king, the women of Vraj, singing to each other about Kṛṣṇa's *līlā*, passed the days happily. The hearts and minds of those fortunate women were absorbed in Kṛṣṇa.'

CHAPTER 36

The Dispatching of Akrūra

1. *Śrī* Bādarāyaṇi [Śuka] said:

'Then a bull demon, Ariṣṭa, in a huge-humped body made its way to the cowherd community. He made the earth tremble as it was rent by his hooves.
2. He raised his tail and bellowed ferociously, scratching the earth with his hooves, and tearing up the embankments with the tips of his horns.
3–4. His eyes were fixed and he was defecating and urinating in small quantities. Humans and animals miscarried prematurely out of fright at this horrific sound. The clouds settled on his hump, making it look like a mountain, dear Parīkṣit.
5. When they saw his sharp horns the *gopīs* and *gopas* were terrified. The animals fled in fear, O king, abandoning Gokula.
6–7. They took refuge with Govinda saying: "Kṛṣṇa, Kṛṣṇa!" *Bhagavān* Kṛṣṇa of course saw that fear-stricken commotion in Gokula. To give them courage, he said: "Do not fear!" Then he challenged the bull demon: "Why have you terrified these cowherders and animals in my presence?
8. You fool! I am the chastiser of evildoers like you, O worst of miscreants." Saying this, Acyuta slapped his arms,[1] angering Ariṣṭa with the sound.
9. Hari then stretched his serpent-like arm on to the shoulder of a friend, and took his stand. Ariṣṭa was clearly angered by this. Scratching the ground with his hoof, the clouds hovering around his upraised tail, he charged Kṛṣṇa in fury.
10. With his blood-red eyes fixed and the tips of his horns lowered, he glanced sideways at Acyuta and charged at speed, like a thunderbolt released by Indra.
11. *Bhagavān* seized him by his horns and drove him back eighteen steps, like an elephant against a rival elephant.
12. Repulsed by *Bhagavān* Kṛṣṇa, the bull quickly got back up

again and rushed forward. His limbs were sweating, and he was snorting and furious with rage.
13. Kṛṣṇa seized Ariṣṭa's horns as he was charging, and hurled him on the ground. Then he stepped on him with his foot, pressed him as if he were a wet cloth and struck him with one of his horns [which he had pulled out]. Ariṣṭa fell prostrate.
14. Vomiting blood, discharging stool and urine simultaneously, and kicking his legs, the bull went painfully to the place of death, his eyes rolling. The gods praised Hari, showering flowers.
15. After killing the evil humped-back bull in this way, Kṛṣṇa was acclaimed by the twice-born and entered the cowherd compound along with Balarāma. He was a feast for the eyes of the *gopīs*.
16. Kṛṣṇa's acts are amazing; after the demon Ariṣṭa had been killed by him, the potent sage Nārada,[2] possessor of divine vision, spoke to Kaṃsa:
17. "The girl was born of Yaśodā, and a son – Kṛṣṇa – was actually born of Devakī; Balarāma was the son of Rohiṇī.
18. These two boys were placed by the fearful Vasudeva in the house of his friend, Nanda. These men of yours have been killed by those two boys."[3] When he heard this, the lord of the Bhojas was enraged.
19–20. He seized a sharp sword intending to kill Vasudeva, but, restrained by Nārada, he bound Vasudeva and his wife in iron shackles. He was aware that Vasudeva's two sons were destined to bring about his death. When the sage had departed, Kaṃsa addressed Keśī:
21–23. "You must kill Balarāma and Keśava," he said, and dispatched him. Then the king of the Bhojas summoned his ministers such as Muṣṭika, Cāṇūra, Śala, Tośalaka, along with the elephant-keepers. He said: "*Bho! Bho!*[4] Listen to this, O valiant Cāṇūra and Muṣṭika:
23. It has been proclaimed that Balarāma and Kṛṣṇa will be my death – those two sons of Ānakadundubhi [Vasudeva] are reportedly living in Nanda's Vraj!
24. Therefore, both should be brought here by you, and killed under pretext of wrestling. Various platforms should be built around the wrestling arena. Let all the urban dwellers and

residents of the country see this contest between willing participants.[5]
25. Elephant-keeper – you are the best. Station the elephant Kuvalayāpīḍa near to the gate of the arena. Kill my two enemies with him.
26. The bow sacrifice[6] should begin on the fourteenth day in accordance with the appropriate rites, and sacrificial animals should be slaughtered for Śiva, the bountiful king of ghosts."
27. After issuing these orders, Kaṃsa, who had mastered the art of getting his own way, summoned Akrūra,[7] the best of the Yadus. Taking the latter's hand in his hand, he said:
28. "*Bho! Bho!* master of charity! Please perform an act of friendship on my behalf. You are a respected person; apart from you, there is no one among the Bhoja and Vṛṣṇi clans who is known to act in the best interests [of others].
29. Therefore, since you accomplish your duties conscientiously, O gentle one, I am dependent upon you, just as lord Indra attains his goals after taking shelter of Viṣṇu.
30. Go to Nanda's Vraj. There, the two sons of Ānakadundubhi reside. Bring them here in this chariot. Do not delay.
31. My death has been commissioned by the gods who have taken refuge with Viṣṇu, the Lord of Vaikuṇṭha. Bring those two boys, as well as Nanda and the other *gopas*, along with their tribute.
32. After they have been brought here, I will have them killed by the deadly elephant. If they escape, then I will have them killed by the wrestlers, who are like thunderbolts.
33–34. When they have been slain, I will kill their grieving relatives, headed by Vasudeva – the Vṛṣṇi, Bhoja and Daśārha clans – as well as my old father Ugrasena, who covets the kingdom, his brother Devaka, and all my enemies.
35. As a result, friend, this earth will be rid of her thorns. Jarāsandha is my *guru*, and Dvivida a cherished friend.
36. Śambara, Naraka and Bāṇa have become my friends. After killing the kings on the side of the gods through their agency, I will enjoy the earth.
37. Be clear about all this, and then quickly bring the two boys

Balarāma and Kṛṣṇa here on the pretence of seeing the bow sacrifice and the riches of the city of the Yadus."

38. *Śrī* Akrūra said: "Your intention to eliminate your obstacles is commendable, O king. One should act equally in both success and failure; the fulfilment of one's goals is certainly in the hands of Providence.

39. People create intense desires even when these are thwarted by Providence, and they thus encounter both happiness and distress. Nevertheless, I shall fulfil your order."'

40. *Śrī* Śuka said:

'After instructing Akrūra in this fashion, and dismissing his ministers, Kaṃsa entered his residence, and Akrūra likewise went to his own home.'

CHAPTER 37

The Killing of the Demon Vyoma

1. *Śrī* Śuka said:

'A huge horse, Keśī, was dispatched by Kaṃsa. Moving at the speed of thought, he wore down the earth with its hooves, and brought chaos to the sky by scattering the celestial vehicles and clouds with his mane. Everyone was terrified of the sound of his neighing.

2. Coming forward, *Bhagavān* Kṛṣṇa challenged the horse who was looking for him for combat, since the horse was causing terror in Gokula with his neighing, and had scattered the clouds with his tail. Keśī roared like a lion, king of beasts.

3. Formidable and unassailable, he seemed to drink up the sky with his mouth. He was ferociously fast, and when he saw Kṛṣṇa standing before him he rushed up precipitately and struck the lotus-eyed one with his hooves.

4. Dodging him, Adhokṣaja angrily seized his two legs, whirled him around, hurled him contemptuously to a distance of one

hundred bows, and stood fixed, just as Garuḍa, the son of Tārkṣya, does to a snake.

5. Regaining consciousness, Keśī got up again, furiously opened his mouth, and rapidly threw himself upon Hari. Kṛṣṇa, smiling, thrust his left arm into Keśī's mouth, as if it were a snake in a hole.

6. Keśī's teeth fell out after hitting *Bhagavān* Kṛṣṇa's arm, as if coming into contact with something burning hot. The arm of that great soul, inserted into his body, expanded, just as a disease does when it is neglected.

7. Keśī's breath was obstructed by Kṛṣṇa's expanding arm, sweat broke out on his limbs, and his eyes rolled. Kicking his feet, he fell on the ground lifeless, excreting faeces.

8. The mighty-armed one removed his arm from Keśī's lifeless body, which was like the fruit of the *karkaṭikā* cucumber. Although he had killed his enemy with ease and was being acclaimed by the gods who rained down showers of flowers, he was not proud.

9. Nārada, the divine sage and best of the devotees, appeared on the scene. He spoke privately to Kṛṣṇa, whose activities are effortless, as follows:

10. "Kṛṣṇa, Kṛṣṇa, immeasurable one! Lord of *yogīs* and controller of the universe! Vāsudeva, abode of everything! You are the best of the Sātvata clan! O master!

11. You alone are the soul of all living entities, like fire in fuel. Dwelling in the heart, you are the hidden witness. You are the great being, the controller!

12. You are the refuge of the self, by means of [the powers] inherent in yourself. Previously, he, the controller, created the *guṇas* through *māyā*. By means of them, you create, sustain and consume this world. Your desires materialize.

13. You are he, incarnated for the destruction of the demons and demoniac *pramathas* and *rākṣasas*[1] who are living as kings of the earth, and for the protection of the saintly *sādhus*.

14. By good fortune, this demon in the form of a horse was killed with ease. Terrified by his neighing, the gods[2] were abandoning heaven.

15. O Lord, the day after tomorrow I shall see Cāṇūra and

Muṣṭika and the other wrestlers, the elephant, and Kaṃsa, killed.

16. After that, I will see [the slaying] of Śaṅkha, the Yavana and Mura, the seizing of the *pārijāta* tree and the defeat of Indra.

17. I will see the marriage of the daughters of the heroes,[3] which will be significant by being won by your valour. And I will see the deliverance of Nṛga from the curse in the city of Dvārakā, O master of the universe.

18. I will see you accept the Syamantaka jewel, along with a wife, and retrieve for the *brāhmaṇa* his dead son from your abode [of death].

19. After that I will see the killing of Pauṇḍraka, the torching of the city of Kāśī,[4] and the destruction of Dantavakra in the great sacrifice of the king of the Cedis.

20. While living in Dvārakā, you will perform these and other deeds worthy of being recited publicly by the poets; and I will see them.

21. Then I will see the destruction of the *akṣauhiṇī* battalions[5] by you as Arjuna's chariot-driver, intent on the destruction of this world in the form of time.

22. We submit to your Lordship. You are full of pure knowledge. All your goals are fulfilled by your own nature, and your desires are never unfulfilled. Through your own potency, you are eternally immune from the flow of the *guṇas* of *māyā*.

23. I submit myself to you, the best of the Yadu, Vṛṣṇi and Sātvata clans. You are the self-contained controller. The production of all variety [in this world] has been created out of your personal *māyā*. The human form that you have presently adopted is for the sake of sport." '

24. *Śrī* Śuka said:

'After bowing respectfully in this way to Kṛṣṇa, the Lord of the Yadus, the sage and distinguished devotee Nārada was granted leave and departed, uplifted by the sight of Kṛṣṇa.

25. And Govinda, God, having killed Keśī in battle, tended the cows in the company of the delighted herders, bringing joy to Vraj.

26. Once, while grazing the animals on the mountain ridges, the herders engaged in a game of hide and seek, playing the roles of thieves and guards.
27. Free from care they played, some as robbers, some as guards, and a number of them acting as sheep, O king.
28. The son of Maya, Vyoma, a great magician, carried off many of those acting as sheep by pretending to be a cowherder acting mainly as a robber.
29. The mighty demon brought them one by one, deposited them in a mountain cave, and then sealed up the entrance with a stone. Four or five boys remained.
30. Kṛṣṇa, the giver of shelter to the just, was aware of what Vyoma was doing. He seized him as he was leading away the *gopas*, like a lion seizes a wolf with force.
31. Vyoma assumed his real form, huge as the king of mountains. Although he wanted to free himself, he was in pain from Kṛṣṇa's grasp and could not.
32. Holding him fast with his arms, Acyuta made him fall on to the ground and, while the gods were watching in the heavens, killed him just as an animal is slaughtered.
33. Breaking apart [the stone] sealing the cave and releasing the *gopas* from their predicament, Kṛṣṇa returned to his own Gokula, praised by the gods and the *gopas*.'

CHAPTER 38

The Arrival of Akrūra

Śrī Śuka said:

1. 'Then, the noble-minded Akrūra, after spending that night in the city of Mathurā, mounted his chariot and set out for Nanda's Gokula.
2. Going along, that greatly fortunate one felt intense devotion to the lotus-eyed *Bhagavān* Kṛṣṇa. He thought as follows:
3. "What auspicious act did I perform? What great penance did

I endure? Or what did I give away to a worthy person, such that today I will see Keśava?

4. I am a person [addicted to] the senses, so I imagine that it is as difficult for the likes of me to obtain sight of Uttamaśloka [Kṛṣṇa] as the recitation of the Vedas is for a *śūdra*.

5. But this is not the case. Although I am a vile fellow, there might be an opportunity to see Acyuta even for me; sometimes, being dragged by the river of time, a person might cross over [the ocean of *saṃsāra*].

6. Today my ill fortune has been dispelled, and my existence has certainly borne fruit, because I will offer homage to the lotus feet of *Bhagavān* Kṛṣṇa, the object of meditation for the *yogīs*.

7. Truly, Kaṃsa has shown great favour to me today; dispatched by him, I will see the lotus feet of Hari, who has assumed incarnation. In the past, people transcended *tamas*, which is difficult to overcome, through the lustre of the curves of their nails.

8. His feet are worshipped by Brahmā, Śiva, the gods, the goddess Śrī and the sages, with the Sātvatas [his devotees]. They are marked with the *kuṅkum* powder from the breasts of the *gopīs*, and they wander in the forest with his companions in order to graze the cows.

9. Indeed, the deer are passing me on the right,[1] so I will surely see the face of Mukunda surrounded by locks of hair, with beautiful cheeks and nose, and smiling glances from his reddened lotus eyes.

10. This very day there will be [the opportunity] of seeing Viṣṇu. He has voluntarily assumed a human form, the abode of beauty, for the removal of the burden of the world. Thus I will not be denied the fulfilment of the sense of sight.

11. Although he is without ego, he is the witness of right and wrong. By his own power he has dispelled the ignorance born of error and discrimination. He is perceived [as the soul] in the bodies of those he has created with vital airs, sense organs and intelligence by his own *māyā*. These are created within himself through his glance.[2]

12. Those words, which are dedicated to the highly auspicious

[narrations] of his birth, deeds and qualities – narrations which remove all the distress of this world – enliven, beautify and purify this world. Words which are devoid of these are considered to be ornaments on a corpse.

13. The Lord is living in Vraj, spreading his fame. He has descended [to earth] into the lineage of the Sātvatas, bringing joy to the most eminent of the gods, the keepers of his own laws. The gods sing of this fame, which brings good fortune to everyone without exception.

14. The dawns of my days have become beautiful to behold; today I will actually see Kṛṣṇa! Manifesting in a form that is the abode of preference for Śrī, the goddess of fortune,[3] he is the supreme destination, the *guru*, the beloved of the three worlds, a great feast for the eyes of those who have sight.

15. Then, immediately after descending from the chariot, I will assuredly pay homage to the feet of the two lords, the foremost of beings, and to the friends with them, the residents of the forest. These feet are grasped by *yogīs* in their minds, for their own salvation.

16. The Lord will also surely place his own lotus hand on my head, as I lie prostrate at the soles of his feet. His hand bestows fearlessness from the force of the serpent of time to those terrified people who seek shelter in him.

17. Kauśika, as well as Bali, placed something in that hand, and they obtained sovereignty of the three worlds.[4] Smelling like the fragrant lotus, his hand smoothed away the fatigue of the Vraj women by its touch during the pastimes.

18. Acyuta will not adopt a hostile attitude towards me, even though I have been deputed as Kaṃsa's messenger. He is the seer of everything. As knower of the field of the body,[5] he sees with his faultless vision whatever is desired both within and without the mind.

19. Then, he will smilingly look at me with a glance full of feeling, as I lie prostrate at the soles of his feet, my palms joined in supplication. Instantly, all my sins will be absolved and I shall experience intense bliss, free from fear.

20. With his two mighty arms, he will embrace me as a best friend, a kinsman, and one who has no other deity [than him].

My body will then certainly be sanctified, and my bondage, consisting of *karma*, will be undone.
21. As I remain bowed after achieving physical contact with him, and with my palms joined in supplication, Kṛṣṇa, whose fame is widespread, will say to me 'Dear Akrūra,' and then I will be endowed with [real] life. Wretched is the birth of that person who has not received the attention of the great one.
22. No one is a favourite or best friend for Kṛṣṇa, nor is anyone disregarded, despised or neglected by him. Nonetheless, he reciprocates with his devotees in accordance [with how they interact with him], just like the *kalpavṛkṣa* tree of the gods, which bestows gifts according to how it is solicited.[6]
23. Moreover, his older brother, best of the Yadus, will smilingly embrace me as I bow down [before Him]. Taking hold of my folded hands, he will lead me to his house. After I have received full hospitality, he will ask what has been done to his family members by Kaṃsa."'
24. *Śrī* Śuka said:

'Contemplating Kṛṣṇa on the journey in this way, O king, Akrūra, the son of Śvaphalka, reached Gokula by chariot, as the sun reached the western mountain.
25. In the cowherd community he saw Kṛṣṇa's footprints, distinguished by such signs as the lotus, the barley and the goad. The pure dust of Kṛṣṇa's feet is worshipped by the crowns of the rulers of all the planets[7] and brings happiness to the earth.
26. His eagerness increased from the bliss of seeing those [footprints], his eyes filled with tears, and his hair stood on end out of love. He got down from the chariot and rolled on them, saying: "*Aho!* There are the dust particles from the feet of the master!"
27. This alone is the goal of creatures possessing bodies. From the beginning of Akrūra's mission, he gave up pride, fear and sorrow by such means as hearing about and seeing the signs of Hari.
28. In Vraj, he saw Kṛṣṇa and Balarāma, who had gone to milk the cows. They were wearing yellow and blue garments, and their eyes were like autumn lotuses.

29. They were youths[8] of black and white complexion [respectively].[9] They were the most beautiful of people, with lovely faces, mighty arms and the strength of powerful elephants. They were the shelter of Śrī, the goddess of fortune.
30. Those two great souls, their glances smiling and tender, made Vraj beautiful with their feet that were marked with the flag, the thunderbolt, the goad and the lotus.
31. Their play was delightful and dignified. They were bathed, and their limbs smeared with pure fragrances. They wore garlands, wreaths of forest flowers, and garments free of dust.
32. Balarāma and Keśava are the two original and first beings, Lords of the universe and causes of the universe. They have incarnated through their *aṃśa* for the benefit of the world.
33. They drove the darkness from the quarters by their personal radiance, O king, like a mountain made of emerald and covered with gold and silver dispels darkness.
34. Made anxious by love, Akrūra jumped down hastily from the chariot and fell like a stick near the feet of Balarāma and Kṛṣṇa.
35. His eyes overflowed with tears of ecstasy from seeing *Bhagavān* Kṛṣṇa, and the hairs on his limbs stood on end. He was unable to announce himself because of his longing, O king.
36. *Bhagavān* Kṛṣṇa was delighted. He approached Akrūra, embraced him with a hand marked with the discus, and drew him towards himself. He is affectionate to those who take refuge in him.
37. And the big-hearted Saṅkarṣaṇa [Balarāma] also embraced Akrūra as he was bowing down. Balarāma grasped his two hands with his hand, and took him home with his younger brother, Kṛṣṇa.
38. Then, after inquiring about his coming, Balarāma offered Akrūra the best seat, washed his feet according to custom, and brought an offering of *madhuparka*.[10]
39. He presented Akrūra with a cow, and respectfully massaged him since he was tired. Then the Lord, with reverence, offered many kinds of fresh food.
40. When Akrūra had finished eating, Balarāma, the knower of

the highest *dharma*, accorded him with love the highest favour, by [offerings of] flavoured mouth-washes and sweet-smelling garlands.

41. When he had received these courtesies, Nanda asked Akrūra: "How are you managing to survive while the merciless Kaṃsa still lives, O descendant of Daśārha, like a sheep who has a butcher as a keeper?

42. That selfish villain killed the sons of his own sister while she wept with anguish. What then, we ask, of the welfare of you, his subjects?"

43. Akrūra was treated with honour by Nanda, who inquired with friendly words in this fashion. He forgot about the fatigue of the journey.'

CHAPTER 39

The Return of Akrūra

1. *Śrī* Śuka said:

'Seated comfortably on a couch, and greatly honoured by Balarāma and Kṛṣṇa, Akrūra was granted all the wishes he had made on the road.

2. What is not attainable when *Bhagavān* Kṛṣṇa, the abode of Śrī, the goddess of fortune, is pleased? Despite this, those dedicated to him do not desire anything, O king.

3. When *Bhagavān*, the son of Devakī, had finished his evening meal, he inquired about Kaṃsa's conduct with his friends, and about his other intentions.

4. *Śrī Bhagavān* said: "Dear Akrūra! An auspicious welcome to you. Was your journey comfortable? Are our friends and relatives well and in good health?

5. Should I even ask about the welfare of our relatives and of Kaṃsa's citizens while he, the plague of our family, known by the name 'maternal uncle', prospers?

6. *Aho!* Because of me there was great intrigue against my noble

parents. On account of me their sons were slaughtered, and on account of me both were imprisoned.
7. By good fortune, the long-wished-for meeting with you, from among our kinsfolk, has been fulfilled for me today, O gentle one. Explain the reason for your coming, dear Akrūra."'
8. *Śrī* Śuka said:

'Akrūra, descendant of Madhu, when invited by *Bhagavān* Kṛṣṇa, described everything: the hostile designs against the Yadus and the attempt to murder Vasudeva.
9. [He described] the message, and the purpose for which he had been sent as a messenger, and repeated what had been said by Nārada to Kaṃsa regarding Kṛṣṇa's birth from Vasudeva, son of Ānakadundubhi.
10. After hearing the words of Akrūra, Kṛṣṇa and Balarāma, the slayers of heroic opponents, laughed and explained the orders of the king to their father Nanda.
11. Nanda then instructed the *gopas*: "All the milk products should be collected and the carts yoked, and you should take tribute.
12. We will go to the city of Mathurā tomorrow, we will present the offerings to the king and we will see the great festival. The people of the country will certainly be going." Nanda the *gopa* had an official announce this throughout Gokula.
13. The *gopīs* were very distraught when they heard that Akrūra had come to Vraj to take Balarāma and Kṛṣṇa to the city.
14. The faces of some of them were pale from sighing with the pain this [news] caused them. The braids in the hair of some became slack, as did their bracelets and garments.
15. Others stopped all the activities of the senses through meditating on Kṛṣṇa, and they ceased to be aware of this world as if they had departed into the realm of the self.
16. Still other women, remembering Śauri's [Kṛṣṇa's][1] words spoken with loving smiles in wonderful and moving lines, fainted.
17–18. Thinking about the pleasing gait, the activities, the loving looks and smiles, the pastimes which dispel all distress, and the extraordinary deeds of Mukunda, they became anxious

and fearful about separation. With minds preoccupied with Acyuta, and tears in their eyes, they gathered together in groups, and spoke.

19. The *gopīs* said: "*Aho!* Oh creator! You have no mercy whatsoever! After uniting embodied beings in friendship and love, you separate them for no purpose, with their desires unfulfilled. Your behaviour is like that of a boy playing around.

20. You have been unfair: after displaying Mukunda's face, surrounded by locks of black hair, and with pleasing cheeks, striking nose, and the trace of a beautiful smile which removes all distress, you then make it disappear.

21. Alas! although you [have appeared here] as one named Akrūra [not-cruel], O creator, you are cruel [*krūra*]:[2] you take away from us the eyes which were given by you. You are like someone who is ignorant. With these eyes, we have seen your whole magnificent creation in one tiny part of Kṛṣṇa, the enemy of Madhu.

22. Alas! The son of Nanda, who breaks friendships in a second, does not pay us any heed. After giving up our houses, kinsfolk, sons and husbands, we have submitted ourselves to longing [for him] and have bound ourselves in service to him. But he has new lovers.

23. No doubt this night will turn to dawn agreeably for the city women: after all, their aspirations have been fulfilled. They are the ones who will get to see the face of the Lord of Vraj when he enters [the city], his honeyed smile beginning at the corners of his eyes.

24. Though he is wise and dedicated to others, how will Mukunda return to us again, when he has been enchanted by the illusion of their shy smiles, and his mind captured by their sweet, bewitching words? We are simply village women.

25. Today there is certain to be a festival for the eyes of the Dāśārha, Bhoja, Andhaka, Vṛṣṇi and Sātvata clans. They will see the son of Devakī on the road. He is the consort of Śrī, the goddess of fortune, and the home of all qualities.

26. The name of such a cruel person should not be Akrūra [not-cruel]. He will take away Kṛṣṇa, who is dearer than the

dear, beyond our horizons, without consolation for us who are distraught in the extreme.
27. The hard-hearted one has mounted the chariot, and the foolish *gopas* are hurrying along behind him with their carts, unchecked by the elders. Fate is committed to being unfavourable to us today.
28. We will approach Mādhava and stop him. What can our friends, elders and family do to us? Our hearts are miserable and have been broken by fate because it is difficult to give up the company of Mukunda for even half the blinking of an eye.
29. We were brought to the *rāsa* compound by his embraces and playful looks, his winning words, engaging smiles and love; the night was like a moment for us.[3] O *gopīs*, how can we ever pass beyond the never-ending *tamas* without him?
30. When he enters Vraj at the end of the day playing his flute and surrounded by *gopas*, Kṛṣṇa, the friend of Ananta,[4] his garland and hair covered in dust, melts us with his smiles and his glances. How can we ever exist without him?" '
31. *Śrī* Śuka said:

'As they spoke thus, their minds possessed by Kṛṣṇa, the women of Vraj felt the torment of separation. Casting off any bashfulness, they cried loudly: "Kṛṣṇa, Govinda, Dāmodara, Mādhava!"
32. When the sun had arisen, Akrūra performed his early morning prayer to Mitra[5] and other such rituals, and then started up his chariot, despite the fact that the *gopīs* were weeping.
33. Then, collecting up numerous gifts in the form of pots filled with milk products, the *gopas*, led by Nanda, followed closely with the carts.
34. The *gopīs* followed their beloved Kṛṣṇa. Hoping for a declaration from *Bhagavān*, they remained standing, in anticipation.
35. Then, seeing them lamenting his departure, Kṛṣṇa, the best of the Yadus, sent a messenger with words of love and consolation, saying: "I will return!"
36. The *gopīs*, like painted figures, followed him in their minds for as long as the banner and the dust of the chariot could be seen.

37. They turned back devoid of hope for the return of Govinda. But, singing day and night about the activities of their beloved, they remained free from sorrow.

38. Meanwhile, *Bhagavān* Kṛṣṇa, accompanied by Balarāma and Akrūra, reached the Kālindī [Yamunā] river, O king, on the chariot [travelling] at the speed of thought. The Kālindī absolves sins.

39. He scooped up the pure water there, which sparkled like jewels, and drank it. He visited a grove of trees with Balarāma, and then mounted the chariot.

40. Akrūra took leave of the two of them, got down from the chariot, and went to the pool in the Kālindī. He took his bath as prescribed in the sacred texts.

41. Immersing himself in the water while reciting hymns from the eternal Veda, Akrūra saw the very same Balarāma and Kṛṣṇa, together:

42. "The two sons of Ānakadundubhi [Vasudeva] are on the chariot. How can they be here? Perhaps they are not on the chariot." Thus considering, he looked around.

43. They were sitting there as before. He again plunged into the water: "Was my vision of those two false?"

44. He again saw the lord of serpents[6] in the water, being praised by the *siddhas*, *cāraṇas*, *gandharvas* and *suras*, their necks bowed in submission.

45. The God had 1,000 heads, crowns on his 1,000 hoods, blue garments, and was white like the fibres of the lotus flower. He appeared like Śveta, the white mountain.[7]

46. Akrūra saw Viṣṇu, the four-armed supreme being, on the serpent's lap. He was dark as a cloud, and wearing yellow silk garments. He was peaceful and his reddish eyes were like lotus petals.

47. His face had a pleasant smile, and his eyes were laughing engagingly. He had beautiful eyebrows, a striking nose, pleasing ears and cheeks, and red lips.

48. His long arms hung down, and Śrī, the goddess of fortune, was on his broad-shouldered chest. His throat was like a conch shell, his navel low, and his stomach like a leaf with folds.

49. He was endowed with broad hips and loins, and thighs like

elephant's trunks. He had well-formed knees and shapely calves.
50. His ankles were raised, and his lotus feet were shining with tender, petal-like big toes and smaller toes, and circled by a halo of rays from his reddish toenails.
51–52. He was resplendent with arm-bracelets, wrist-bracelets, a crown with clusters of large and very valuable gems, earrings, foot-bracelets, necklaces, sacred thread[8] and belt. He had a lotus in his hand, and held a conch, a disc and a club. On his chest was the tuft of hair [*śrīvatsa*], and he bore the Kaustubha jewel and a garland of forest flowers.
53–54. He was being extolled with words of praise by his attendants – each one according to his particular devotional mood – headed by Sunanda and Nanda;[9] Sanaka and the others;[10] the lords of the gods, Brahmā and Rudra,[11] and others; the nine eminent twice-born *brāhmaṇas*;[12] and the best of the devotees, Prahlāda,[13] Nārada and Vasu.[14] These are pure souls.
55. He was attended by Śrī, affluence; Puṣṭi, nourishment; Gir, speech; Kānti, beauty; Kīrti, fame; Tuṣṭi, satisfaction; Iḷā, the earth; Ūrjā, vitality; Vidyā, knowledge; Avidyā, ignorance; Śakti, power; and Māyā, illusion.[15]
56. On seeing this, Akrūra became ecstatic and was filled with the most intense devotion. The hair on his body stood on end, and his eyes and body became moist with love.
57. Akrūra, the Sātvata, bowed his head in reverence. Then he regained his presence of mind and slowly and attentively offered praise in a quivering voice, his hands folded in supplication.'

CHAPTER 40

Akrūra's Eulogy

1. '*Śrī* Akrūra said:

"I bow to you, Nārāyaṇa, the imperishable, primordial being, the cause of all causes. Brahmā, from whom this world is produced, appeared from the whirl of the lotus born from your navel.

2. All these causes of the universe – earth, water, fire, air and ether; intelligence, *prakṛti*, mind, and so forth; the senses, all the sense objects,[1] and all the gods – become manifest from your body.
3. Brahmā, the unborn one, and the others definitely do not know the real nature of your *ātmā*, because they are enveloped by that which is not *ātmā* [i.e. matter]. Brahmā, the unborn one, is bound by the *guṇas* of *prakṛti*; he does not know your personal nature, which is beyond the *guṇas*.
4. The *yogīs* and the *sādhus* worship you as the supreme being; the Lord; the *adhyātmā* [supreme spirit]; the *adhibhūta* [the spirit pervading all creation]; and the *adhideva* [the supreme being among the gods].
5. By means of the three Vedas and supplementary bodies of knowledge,[2] some twice-born *brāhmaṇas*, who observe the performance of the three sacred fires,[3] worship you with many sacrifices named after gods of different forms.
6. And some obtain tranquillity after renouncing all ritualistic acts of *karma*. The wise worship you, the personification of knowledge, through the sacrifice of knowledge.
7. And other refined souls, their minds absorbed in you, worship you through the prescriptions presented by you,[4] as the sole form amongst many forms.
8. And still others worship you, *Bhagavān*, in the form of Śiva, through the path outlined by Śiva, which has taken many forms through many teachers.[5]
9. Those who are devotees of other gods, even though their minds are focused elsewhere, all also worship you, O master.[6] You are the Lord who comprises all the gods.
10. Just as the rivers who have their source in the mountains are filled by the rain, O master, and come to the ocean from all sides, similarly all paths come to you in the end.[7]
11. The *guṇas* of *prakṛti* are *sattva*, *rajas* and *tamas*. With them is woven that which is derived from *prakṛti*, from Brahmā to all inanimate entities.
12. I offer homage to you. As the soul of everything and the witness of everyone's mind, your judgement is unbiased. This flow of the *guṇas*, produced by ignorance, exerts itself among beings such as gods, men and animals.

13. Fire is conceived of as your mouth, the earth as your feet, the sun as your eye, the sky as your navel, the directions as your hearing, the heavens as your head, the chiefs of the gods as your arms, the ocean as your abdomen, and the winds as your vital airs.

14. The trees and plants are taken to be your hair; the clouds the hair growing on your head; and the mountains the bones and nails of you, the supreme self. The days and nights are your blinking; Prajāpati, the progenitor of mankind,[8] your penis; and the rain your semen.

15. The planets teeming with the multitude of life forms, along with their rulers, can be thought of as existing in your being, O imperishable soul, just like the fish that move about in the water, or the gnats on the *udumbara* fig.

16. People who sing with joy of your glories have their sorrows wiped away by whatever forms you assume for sport.[9]

17. I offer homage to Matsya, the fish incarnation,[10] the cause [of the world], who moved about in the ocean at *pralaya*, the dissolution of the universe.[11] Homage to you, who appeared with the head of a horse [Hayagriva],[12] and to you, the killer of Madhu and Kaiṭabha.[13]

18. Homage to the huge tortoise [Kūrma] who bore the Mandara mountain.[14] Homage to you in the form of a boar [Varāha], who took pleasure in lifting up the earth.[15]

19. Homage to you, the amazing lion [Nṛsiṃha], the remover of fear for righteous people.[16] Homage to you, Vāmana, who stepped over the three worlds.[17]

20. Homage to the lord of the Bhṛgus [Paraśurāma], who cut down the forest of proud warriors.[18] Homage to the best of the Raghus [Rāma], who brought an end to Rāvana.[19]

21. Homage to you, Vāsudeva, Lord of the Sātvatas. Homage to Saṅkarṣaṇa and to Pradyumna and Aniruddha.[20]

22. Homage to the pure Buddha,[21] the bewilderer of the *daityas* and *dānavas*.[22] Homage to you in the form of Kalki,[23] the killer of the warriors who behave like *mlecchas*.[24]

23. This world of souls is wandering on the path of *karma*, O *Bhagavān*, bewildered by your *māyā* under the false notions of *aham mama* ['I and mine'].[25]

24. And I also am wandering about, bewildered by my body, my children, home, wife, wealth and relatives with the conviction that they are real, O Lord, when they are only as a dream.
25. I am immersed in *tamas* and delight in duality. My intelligence is distorted when it comes to things that produce misery, are not eternal, and are not the *ātmā*. I do not know you, although you are the beloved of my being.
26. Like a fool, who overlooks water concealed by whatever has grown up over it, and pursues a mirage, I have similarly turned away [from you].
27. Being of feeble intelligence, I am not able to restrain the mind, which is afflicted by lust and *karma*, and is pulled hither and thither by the powerful senses.
28. Although I am a person such as this, I have approached your feet, which are difficult to attain for the unrighteous. I believe that this very act is your mercy, O Lord. The cycle of birth and death ceases for one whose mind becomes situated in you through service to the righteous, O lotus-navelled one.
29. Homage to you, who are full knowledge, the source of all awareness and the foremost of the Lords of human beings. You are *brahman*, of unlimited *śakti* power.
30. Homage to you, Vāsudeva, the abode of all living entities. Homage to you, Hṛṣīkeśa. I give myself up to you – please protect me, O master."'

CHAPTER 41

The Entrance into the City

1. *Śrī* Śuka said:

'After revealing his form in the water, Kṛṣṇa *Bhagavān* withdrew it while he [Akrūra] was offering praise, just like an actor removes his costume.
2. After seeing it disappear, Akrūra emerged from the water

hastily, completed the mandatory rites, and returned to the chariot in amazement.

3. Hṛṣīkeśa [Kṛṣṇa] asked him: "Have you seen something wonderful on the earth, in the sky or in the water? I suspect that you have seen some such thing."

4. *Śrī* Akrūra said: "Whatever wonderful things exist on the earth, in the sky and in the water, are in you. You are the soul of the universe, so what is there that has not been seen by men [that can be of interest] when I am observing you?

5. And, besides, what wonderful thing is there for me to see in this world? I am observing you; you are *brahman* – all the wonderful things on the earth, in the sky and in the water exist in you."

6. After saying this, Akrūra, the son of Gāndinī, started the chariot moving and brought Balarāma and Kṛṣṇa to Mathurā by the end of the day.

7. The village folk gathered here and there along the route were delighted and could not take their eyes off the two sons of Vasudeva, O king.

8. Meanwhile, the people of Vraj, led by Nanda, the *gopa*, had gone ahead of them and were camped in a grove, waiting.

9. After joining them, *Bhagavān* Kṛṣṇa, the Lord of the world, grasped the hand of the humble Akrūra, and said, smiling a little:

10. "You, sir, should enter the city and your home ahead of us, with the chariot. We, on the other hand, will unharness here, and then we will see the city afterwards."

11. *Śrī* Akrūra said: "I will not enter Mathurā without you, O Lord. You should not abandon me, your devotee, O master – You who are kind to your devotees.

12. You are the best of friends. Come, let us go to my dwelling together with your elder brother, the cowherders and our friends. Grace it with its master, O Adhokṣaja.

13. We, the people, are absorbed in domestic affairs – please purify our houses. Through such purification the forefathers, the gods and the sacrificial fires will be satisfied.

14. After washing your two feet, the great Bali became praise-

worthy, and obtained unrivalled power as well as attaining the destination of those who have you as their pure goal.[1]
15. The pure waters from the washing of your feet have purified the three worlds. Śiva received them on his head, and the sons of Sagara went to heaven [because of them].[2]
16. Homage to you, O Nārāyaṇa. You are the God of gods, master of the world, and best of the Yadu clan. Reciting and hearing about you are purifying, O Uttamaśloka."
17. *Śrī Bhagavān* said: "I will come to your house accompanied by my elder brother and show affection to my friends after I have killed the enemy of the Yadu circle."'
18. *Śrī* Śuka said:

'Addressed thus by *Bhagavān*, Akrūra, who had entered the city to report the events to Kaṃsa, went home somewhat dejected.
19. Then in the afternoon, *Bhagavān* Kṛṣṇa, together with Saṅkarṣaṇa [Balarāma] and surrounded by the *gopas*, entered Mathurā, wanting to see it.
20. He saw its lofty entrances and gateways made of crystal, and its wide arches and doors of gold. The granaries were made of copper and brass, and it was protected by moats. Its beauty was enhanced by pleasant parks and gardens.
21–22. It was splendid with mansions, craftsmen's guild council chambers, pleasure groves, palaces, and crossroads made of gold. It reverberated with the sounds of peacocks and pigeons perching on the apertures of the inlaid lattice-work of the balconies and turrets. These were adorned with emeralds, pearls, coral, sapphires, crystal diamonds and *vaidūrya* gems. Its crossroads, thoroughfares, markets and highways were sprinkled with water, and the town was strewn with flower garlands, young shoots, parched grain and rice.
23. The doorways of the houses were embellished with full pots smeared with yogurt and sandalwood, and with rows of lamps and blossoms. There were fresh shoots, clusters of flowers, plantain trees, betel nut trees, flags and ribbons.
24. The women of the city hurried forward to see the two sons of Vasudeva as, flanked by their companions, they entered the

city by the royal road. The women even climbed on to their houses in their eagerness, O king.

25. Some of them wore their ornaments and their clothes back to front, while others had forgotten one of a pair of something and had put on only one ear-ornament, or one ankle-bracelet. Still others had failed to put mascara on their second eye [having done the first].

26. Some discarded whatever they were eating in their excitement. Some who were massaging themselves did not complete their bathing, some who were sleeping jumped up after hearing the sounds, while mothers who were breast-feeding put aside their infants.

27. The lotus-eyed Lord captivated them with his glances, his smiling and his confident *līlā*. He had the gait of the leader of excited two-tusked elephants, and his person was a feast for the eyes, the source of pleasure for Śrī, the goddess of fortune.

28. The women had heard about Kṛṣṇa many times, and when they saw him their minds flowed out to him. They were proud that they had been touched by the nectar of his smiles and glances. With the hairs on their skin standing on end, they embraced his blissful form, which they had seen and taken into their hearts, and were relieved of their intense longing [for him], O subduer of enemies.

29. Climbing on to turrets of the houses, their lotus faces blossoming with love, the women joyfully showered flowers on Balarāma and Keśava.

30. Here and there, the delighted twice-born paid homage to Kṛṣṇa and Balarāma with unhusked barley, yogurt, water pots, garlands, scents and offerings.

31. The women of the city said: "*Aho!* What austere practices have the *gopīs* performed that they can gaze upon these two, who are outstanding in the world of men?"

32. Then Kṛṣṇa, the elder brother of Gada,[3] saw a certain washerman, whose occupation was dyeing cloth, coming towards him. He asked the washerman for clean garments that were of the best quality:

33. "Give us some suitable clothes, dear sir. We are worthy, and you as the giver will certainly be accorded the highest benefit!"

34. At this request from *Bhagavān* Kṛṣṇa, who is complete in all things, the washerman was angered. As a servant of the king and full of himself, he replied insultingly:
35. "What impudence to ask for the possessions of the king! Would you who perpetually roam about in the forests and the hills wear garments of such quality?
36. Go quickly if you want to live, you fools. Do not ever make such a request. The king's men arrest and kill those who are arrogant and they plunder [their property]."
37. The son of Devakī was furious. While the washerman was threatening in this way, Kṛṣṇa made the man's head fall from his body with a touch of his fingertips.
38. His attendants all abandoned the containers of clothes on the road and fled in every direction. Acyuta took up the garments.
39. Kṛṣṇa and Saṅkarṣaṇa dressed themselves in the clothes that took their fancy, discarded some on the ground and gave the rest to the *gopas*.
40. Then a weaver, out of affection for the two of them, supplemented their dress with coordinated ornaments made out of cloth of different colours.
41. Kṛṣṇa and Balarāma were brilliant in clothes of different kinds. Beautifully adorned, they were like two young elephants at a festival, one white and the other, by contrast, black.
42. *Bhagavān* Kṛṣṇa was pleased with the weaver, and conferred the liberation of *sārūpya*[4] on him, as well as extreme opulence, strength, vigour, memory and power of the senses of this world.
43. Then they proceeded to the house of a garland-maker, Sudāmā. Seeing them, Sudāmā stood up and then made obeisance with his head on the ground.
44. He brought seats for them and their companions, and water to wash their feet. He paid homage with *arghya* water,[5] presentations, garlands, betel nuts and ointments.
45. Sudāmā said: "Our birth has become meaningful, and our lineage purified by the arrival of you both, O Lords. My forefathers, the gods and the *ṛṣis* [sages] must be satisfied with me.
46. Your lordships are both, in truth, the supreme cause of the entire universe. You have descended to this world through your *aṃśa* for its protection and welfare.

47. You perceive all impartially. Even though you are devoted to those who are devoted to you, you are equitable to all living beings. Both of you are the souls of the universe, and its benefactors.
48. Command me, your servant. What can I do for you both? Great favour is undoubtedly bestowed on that person whom you command."
49. After expressing his intentions thus, Sudāmā took pleasure in presenting them with garlands made with beautiful and fragrant flowers.
50. Kṛṣṇa and Balarāma and their companions were delighted to be thus bedecked. Those bestowers of favours bestowed favours on Sudāmā, who bowed and was humble.
51. For his part, Sudāmā chose unwavering devotion to Kṛṣṇa, the soul of everything; friendship with Kṛṣṇa's devotees; and the utmost compassion for all living beings.
52. After granting this favour to Sudāmā, as requested, as well as wealth that would increase with his descendants, strength, longevity, fame and beauty, Kṛṣṇa and his elder brother left.'

CHAPTER 42

Description of the Wrestling Arena

Śrī Śuka said:

1. 'After this, while walking along the royal road, Mādhava saw a hunchbacked woman going along. She was youthful, with a beautiful face, and was carrying a vessel containing bodily ointments. Smiling, the giver of *rasa*[1] asked:
2. "Who are you, O lady with beautiful thighs? Tell us truthfully, O woman with shapely limbs, whose ointment is this? Give us both the best bodily ointment – good fortune will follow without delay."
3. The maidservant said: "I am the servant girl by name of Trivakrā ['crooked in three places'], well-known to Kaṃsa for

making ointments, O good-looking one. Kaṃsa, the Lord of the Bhojas, takes great pleasure in them when they are prepared by me. But who deserves them better than you two eminent men?"

4. Trivakrā's mind was overwhelmed by Kṛṣṇa's looks, his speech, his smiles and his sweetness, charm and form, and she smeared the concentrated ointment on both of them.

5. They looked gorgeous: their limbs, coloured with the hues [of the ointments] that had been applied to their upper body, appeared beautiful by contrast with their natural colour. They were delighted.

6. *Bhagavān* Kṛṣṇa was pleased, and decided to make the beautiful hunchback Trivakrā straight of form, thus showing what can result from seeing him.

7. Stepping on the front part of her foot with his foot, and grasping her chin with two fingers of his upturned hand, Acyuta lifted up her body.

8. At the touch of Mukunda Trivakrā instantly became a most beautiful young woman, with large hips and breasts, and with her limbs straight and uniform.

9. Endowed with beauty, good qualities and generosity, she then pulled the end of his outer garment and spoke to Keśava [Kṛṣṇa] smiling. Kāma had awoken in her heart.

10. "Come, hero, I am unable to leave you here – let us go home. You are the best of men; oblige a woman whose mind has been aroused by you!"

11. Kṛṣṇa was solicited in this manner by the woman while Balarāma was watching. He looked at Balarāma and then at the cowherd boys and said to Trivakrā as he laughed:

12. "Your house removes the cares of men. I will come there when my goals have been accomplished. You are a woman with beautiful eyebrows and are the best refuge for us travellers who are without our home."

13. Leaving her with sweet words, Kṛṣṇa proceeded along the thoroughfare. He and his elder brother were presented with scents, garlands, betel nuts and various offerings by the merchants along the road.

14. When they saw him, women, aroused by Kāma, forgot themselves [in their excitement]. Their bracelets, plaits and

clothes became dishevelled, and they were [transfixed] like figures in a still-life picture.
15. Then Acyuta asked the citizens the whereabouts of the bow.[2] He entered the place [where it was kept], and saw it. It was as amazing as the bow of Indra.
16. It was worshipped as a source of great supernatural power, and guarded by many men. Although these men tried to prevent him, Kṛṣṇa forcibly seized the bow.
17. He lifted it easily with his left hand. After stringing it in an instant, Urukrama [Kṛṣṇa] drew it while the men were watching, and broke it in the middle just as an elephant in rut breaks a stick of sugar cane.
18. The sound of the breaking bow filled the sky, the earth and the quarters. Hearing it, Kaṃsa was seized with terror.
19. The guardians of the bow became enraged and surrounded Kṛṣṇa and his companions with their weapons drawn. Intent on seizing him, they cried: "He must be seized; he must be killed!"
20. Seeing their evil intentions, Balarāma and Keśava became angry. They took up the two halves of the bow and killed them.
21. When they had also slaughtered the force of soldiers that had been dispatched by Kaṃsa, Kṛṣṇa and Balarāma set out from the entrance of the sacrificial area. They had seen the richness of the city and roamed about merrily.
22. The citizens, having seen the extraordinary heroism, as well as the power, boldness and beauty of those two boys, thought that they must both be distinguished gods.
23. While the two were wandering around as their fancy took them, the sun neared its setting point. Kṛṣṇa and Balarāma, surrounded by the *gopas*, proceeded from the city to their carts.
24. The very blessings the *gopīs* [of Vraj] had predicted when they were distressed by the separation from Mukunda on his departure[3] were realized in Mathurā by those gazing on the bodily beauty of Kṛṣṇa, that ornament among men. Abandoning others who were devoted to her, Śrī, the goddess of fortune, longed for him as her refuge.
25. Kṛṣṇa and Balarāma's feet were washed and they enjoyed a dish of food sprinkled with milk. Then they spent that night

happily, even though they were aware of what Kaṃsa intended to do.

26–27. But Kaṃsa was fearful after hearing about the breaking of the bow, the slaughter of the guards and of his troops, and the unparalleled sporting of Govinda [Kṛṣṇa] and Balarāma, and stayed awake for a long time. That malevolent one saw many evil omens, harbingers of death, both while awake and while sleeping.

28. [For example,] when he saw his reflection there was no head visible, and stars appeared double when there were in fact no second stars there.

29. Holes appeared in shadows, and the sound of his breathing became inaudible. Gold appeared in trees, and he could not see his own footprints.

30. He was embraced by ghosts in dreams, ate poison while riding a donkey, and moved about alone, naked, smeared with oil and wearing a garland of spikenard flowers.

31. Seeing such things and others both when dreaming and awake, Kaṃsa became terrified of death, and could not sleep for anxiety.

32. When the night turned to dawn, O descendant of Kuru, and the sun had arisen from the waters, Kaṃsa made preparations for the great occasion of the wrestling match.

33. The men consecrated the arena, striking their kettledrums and playing instruments. They decorated the platforms with garlands, flags, pieces of cloth and ornamental archways.

34. The city-dwellers and countryfolk, headed by the *brāhmaṇas* and *kṣatriyas*, seated themselves where they wanted on those platforms. The kings also had seats prepared.

35. Surrounded by ministers, Kaṃsa sat on the king's platform. With a troubled heart, he placed himself in the midst of the rulers of countries.

36. As the instruments were sounding, together with the louder sound of the wrestlers slapping their hands on their arms, the proud, well-decorated wrestlers sat down together with their trainers.

37. Cāṇūra, Muṣṭika and Kūṭa, as well as Śala and Tośala, sat down in the assembly, exhilarated by the stirring sounds.

38. Summoned by Kaṃsa, the king of the Bhojas, the *gopas*, led by Nanda, offered their gifts and sat down on one of the platforms.'

CHAPTER 43

The Killing of Kuvalayāpīḍa

1. *Śrī* Śuka said:

'Then Kṛṣṇa and Balarāma, after performing rites of purification, heard the sounds of the kettledrums and wrestlers, and arrived to watch, O destroyer of foes.
2. When he reached the gate of the arena, Kṛṣṇa saw the elephant Kuvalayāpīḍa stationed there, commanded by an elephant keeper.
3. After tightening his waistband and fastening up his curly locks of hair, Śauri [Kṛṣṇa] spoke to the elephant keeper in a voice as deep as the sound of clouds:
4. "Elephant driver, elephant driver! Make way for us. Step aside without delay. If not, I will send you and your elephant to the abode of Yama, lord of death, today."
5. The elephant driver was furious at being threatened thus and urged his enraged elephant, who resembled Yama, the personification of death and time, towards Kṛṣṇa.
6. The king of elephants charged Kṛṣṇa and swiftly seized him with his trunk. Slipping out from his hold, Kṛṣṇa struck him and then disappeared between his feet.
7. Infuriated at not being able to see him, the elephant seized Keśava with his trunk, using his sense of smell. Kṛṣṇa wrenched himself free.
8. Grabbing that most powerful of elephants by the tail, Kṛṣṇa dragged him for twenty-five bow lengths with the ease of Garuḍa dragging a snake.
9. Acyuta dodged to the right and to the left in synchrony with the twirling elephant, like a boy with a tottering calf.

10. Then, he came forward in front of the elephant and struck him with his hand. Running ahead, Kṛṣṇa would allow himself to be overtaken and then made the elephant tumble down at each step.
11. As he was running, Kṛṣṇa fell down in feint and then suddenly jumped up. The infuriated elephant, thinking Kṛṣṇa had fallen, gored the ground with his tusk.
12. His power frustrated, the king of elephants became utterly incensed. Goaded by the elephant keeper, he charged Kṛṣṇa in fury.
13. *Bhagavān* Madhusūdana [Kṛṣṇa], reaching the elephant, who was rushing forward, seized his trunk with his hand and hurled him on to the ground.
14. Stepping effortlessly upon the fallen elephant with his foot like a lion, Hari tore out a tusk and killed the elephant and the elephant keeper with it.
15. He left the dead elephant and entered [the arena], tusk in hand. He looked magnificent, marked with drops of rut fluid and blood, and with the tusk placed on his shoulder. His lotus face had generated drops of sweat.
16. Balarāma and Janārdana [Kṛṣṇa], surrounded by a certain number of *gopas*, entered the arena, O king, with the elephant's tusk – a formidable weapon.
17. Kṛṣṇa went in to the arena with his elder brother. He was perceived by the wrestlers as a lightning bolt; by men as the best of men; by the women as Kāma personified; by the *gopas* as their relative; by the unrighteous rulers of the earth as the chastiser; by his mother and father as a child; by Kaṃsa, the king of the Bhojas, as death; by the ignorant as the manifest universe; by the *yogīs* as the supreme truth; and by the Vṛṣṇi clan as the supreme divinity.
18. When he saw that Kuvalayāpīḍa had been killed and that the two boys were invincible, Kaṃsa was deeply troubled in his mind, O king.
19. The two mighty-armed ones looked dazzling when they arrived in the arena. With their various clothes, ornaments, garlands and garments, they were like two actors wearing the choicest clothes. The onlookers were struck by their radiance.

20. At the sight of those two singular men, the people on the platforms – both country and city folk – drank in their faces with their eyes but remained unsatisfied, O king. Their faces and eyes bloomed with a surge of happiness.
21. It was as if they were devouring [them] with their eyes, licking [them] with their tongues, smelling [them] with their noses, and embracing [them] with their arms.
22. Recalling the boldness, sweetness, qualities and form of those two, the people discussed what they had seen and heard.
23. "Those two boys have descended to this world in the house of Vasudeva as the *aṃśas* of *Bhagavān* Hari and Nārāyana.
24. This one, Kṛṣṇa, was actually born to Devakī and brought to Gokula. Living unknown during this period, he grew up in the house of Nanda.
25. By him, Pūtanā, the demon Cakravāta, the two *arjuna* trees, the *guhyaka* [Śaṅkhacūḍa], Keśī, Dhenuka and others like them were overcome.
26. By him, the cows and the cowherders were delivered from the forest fire, the snake Kāliya was subdued, and Indra was made humble.
27. By him the best of the mountains was held up with one hand for seven days and Gokula saved from rain, wind and lightning.
28. The blissful *gopīs*, constantly seeing his face with its happy smiles and glances, found it easy to let go of their distress.
29. They say that this Yadu dynasty will attain wealth, fame and greatness; his protection has made it legendary.
30. And this other one, his elder brother, is the lotus-eyed Balarāma, possessor of great riches. Pralamba was killed by him, as were others such as Vatsa the calf demon, and Baka the crane demon."
31. While the people were talking thus and the instruments were sounding, Cāṇūra addressed Kṛṣṇa and Balarāma with these words:
32. "Hey son of Nanda! Hey Balarāma! You, sirs, are esteemed as heroes. You have been summoned by the king, who has heard of your skill in martial arts and is keen to witness them.
33. Those citizens who work to please the king with their minds,

their actions and their words have good fortune, otherwise, they have the opposite.
34. It is well known that the *gopas*, the keepers of the calves, are always joyful. They graze the cows in the forest while they play at wrestling.
35. Therefore, let you and us do what is pleasing to the king. Living beings will be pleased with us since the king comprises them all."
36. After hearing this, Kṛṣṇa was in favour of the wrestling, being partial to it himself. He spoke words that were appropriate to the place and time.
37. "Even though we are wanderers of the forests, we are subjects who always act for the pleasure of the king of the Bhojas. This is the greatest benefit for us.
38. We are boys and will compete with boys equal to us, according to the appropriate rules. Let the wrestling take place, but let no transgression of *dharma* taint the judges in the wrestling assembly."
39. Cāṇūra said: "The elephant who possessed the strength of 1,000 elephants was easily killed by you – you are no boy or youth.[1] As for Balarāma, he is the best of boys.
40. Therefore, the wrestling contest will be between you both and strong men – there is certainly no breach of sportsmanship in this. Show your prowess with me, O descendant of Vṛṣṇi, and Muṣṭika with Balarāma."'

CHAPTER 44
The Killing of Kaṃsa

1. *Śrī* Śuka said:

'*Bhagavān* Madhusūdana [Kṛṣṇa] considered this proposal and then squared up to Cāṇūra, while the son of Rohiṇī did the same with Muṣṭika.

2. Locking hands with hands and feet with feet, they grappled fiercely with each other, desiring victory.
3. Elbow with elbow, knee with knee, head with head and chest with chest, each one in the two pairs struck the other.
4. They confronted each other by advancing and backing off, by circling round, and by throwing, clasping and flooring each other.
5. Eager to win, they injured themselves by lifting, hoisting and displacing each other, as well as by standing their ground.
6. The assembled women, feeling pity, spoke to each other in groups about the contest between the weak and the strong, O king:
7. "Alas! This is a great transgression of *dharma* on the part of these judges in the assembly, even as the king watches. They want to have a contest between the weak and the strong.
8. On the one hand there are two wrestlers whose limbs are like the mightiest of mountains. And on the other, two teenagers who have not yet attained puberty, and whose limbs are extremely youthful.
9. There is no doubt that there has been a transgression of *dharma* from this assembly, and one should never remain long in a place where there has been such a violation.
10. A wise person who is aware of the faults of an assembly should never enter that assembly, and a person who refrains from speaking and claims ignorance, or one who speaks falsely, is culpable.
11. Look at the lotus face of Kṛṣṇa as he dances around his enemy. It is covered with drops of perspiration from fatigue, like water on the calyx of a lotus flower.
12. Do you not see the face of Balarāma, with its red-coloured eyes? It is flushed with anger at Muṣṭika, and glows from excitement and laughter.
13. Truly, how blessed are the lands of Vraj that the original being, wearing a garland of various forest flowers, wanders around playfully, grazing the cows with Balarāma and playing his flute. Although he is in the guise of a human being, his lotus feet are worshipped by Ramā, the goddess of fortune, and by Śiva, the protector of the mountains.

14. What severe disciplines must the *gopīs* have performed that they drink in his form with their eyes? It is supremely pleasing, ever-fresh, unparalleled in excellence and unrivalled in perfection. It is difficult to attain, and is the sole abode of fame, fortune and wealth.
15. During milking, threshing, churning, smearing cowdung, rocking the cradles of crying infants, sprinkling water, cleaning, and so on, the *gopīs* sing about Kṛṣṇa choking with sobs and with devotion to him in their hearts. The women of Vraj are blessed: their minds are intent on Urukrama [Kṛṣṇa].
16. The truly blessed women rush out to the road when they hear him play his flute as he sets out with the cows from Vraj at daybreak and returns with them at dusk. They see his smiling face, with its looks of compassion."
17. While the women were talking thus, *Bhagavān* Hari, the lord of *yogīs*, decided to kill his enemy, O Parīkṣit, best of the Bharatas.
18. His mother and father, overwhelmed with anxiety because of their love for their son, were upset at the worried words of the women. They were not fully aware of their son's strength.
19. Just as Acyuta and his opponent used the whole range of techniques to fight, so Balarāma and Muṣṭika fought in exactly the same way.
20. Cāṇūra momentarily reached a state of exhaustion, his limbs broken by *Bhagavān* Kṛṣṇa's blows, which were striking his body as hard as thunderbolts.
21. Enraged, Cāṇūra clenched both of his hands into fists, fell upon *Bhagavān* Vāsudeva with the speed of a hawk, and beat on his chest.
22–23. As an elephant does not flinch from a flower garland, Hari did not flinch from his blows and he seized Cāṇūra by the arms. Whirling him around repeatedly, he hurled him forcefully on to the ground, depriving him of life. Cāṇūra's garland, hair and ornaments were scattered, and he fell like Indra's banner.
24. In the same way, Muṣṭika was violently struck by the palm of the powerful Balabhadra [Balarāma] – who himself had just been struck by Muṣṭika's fist.

25. Muṣṭika quivered in anguish, vomiting blood, and fell lifeless on to the bosom of the earth like a tree struck by the wind.
26. Kūṭa was the next to confront Balarāma, best of fighters, who, with his left fist, killed him easily and with disdain.
27. After that, Śala's head was struck by Kṛṣṇa's toes, O king, and Tośalaka was torn in two. Both of them collapsed.
28. With Cāṇūra, Muṣṭika, Kūṭa, Śala and Tośalaka killed, the remaining wrestlers fled for their lives.
29. After summoning their cowherd boy companions and joining with them, the two celebrated, dancing about with their anklets jingling while the instruments sounded.
30. All the people except Kaṃsa rejoiced at what Kṛṣṇa and Balarāma had done. The leaders of the *brāhmaṇas* and the ascetics cried, "Well done! Well done!"
31. After the most powerful wrestlers had been killed or had fled, Kaṃsa, king of the Bhojas, hushed the musical instruments that were playing for him and spoke these words:
32. "Throw these two reprobate sons of Vasudeva out of the city. Seize their wealth and bind the evil-minded cowherd Nanda.
33. The wicked Vasudeva, worst of wrong-doers, should be killed, and so should Ugrasena with his followers – even though Ugrasena is my father, he has sided with the enemy."
34. While Kaṃsa was ranting in this way, the omnipotent Lord became furious. He swiftly jumped with ease on to the high dais and climbed it.
335. Seeing Kṛṣṇa, his own death, approaching, the quick-witted Kaṃsa immediately arose from his seat and seized his sword and shield.
36. Kaṃsa had his sword in hand and was feinting left and right like a hawk in the sky. Kṛṣṇa seized him fiercely with overpowering force, just as Garuḍa, the son of Tārkṣya, seizes a snake.
37. Grabbing Kaṃsa by the hair, Kṛṣṇa threw him from the high dais into the arena. Kaṃsa's crown tumbled off. Then the lotus-navelled Lord,[1] who is the self-sufficient support of the universe, threw himself on top of him.
38. Kṛṣṇa dragged the dead body along the ground in full

view of everyone, as a lion does an elephant. Then, O king, a tumultuous sound of "O! O!" arose, uttered by all the people!

39. Kaṃsa was troubled by fear, and whenever he drank, ate, moved about, slept or breathed had that Lord, whose weapon is the disc,[2] before his eyes. By this means, he attained the exact same form [as the Lord] – something very difficult to achieve.[3]

40. His eight younger brothers, Kaṅka, Nyagrodhaka and the others rushed up in fury, determined to avenge their brother.

41. They were intent on conflict, but rash and impetuous. The son of Rohiṇī, Balarāma, raising his club, slew them as the king of beasts kills deer.

42. Kettledrums reverberated in the sky. The powerful manifestations of Brahmā, Śiva and all the gods were pleased. They scattered flowers and recited his glories while their wives danced.

43. The wives of Kaṃsa [and his brothers], distressed by the deaths of those close to them, came forward with tears in their eyes, beating their heads, O great king.

44. Grieving, they embraced their husbands, who were lying on the heroes' resting place [the battlefield], and lamented loudly with an endless outpouring of sorrow:

45. "Alas, O kind and beloved master, you are the knower of *dharma*, and compassionate to those with no shelter! With you dead, we, along with your children and households, are finished.

46. Just like us, this city, without you, its lord, no longer shines. It has been deprived of its festivity and good fortune.

47. *Bho!* You brought terrible harm to innocent living beings. As a result you have been reduced to this; how can one who injures living beings attain peace?

48. This Kṛṣṇa is the beginning and the end to all living beings in this world, as he is their protector. No one prospers who disregards him."'

49. *Śrī* Śuka said:

'*Bhagavān*, the creator of the world, consoled the wives of the king and made arrangements for what are known as the customary rites for the dead.

50. After releasing their parents from their imprisonment,[4]

Kṛṣṇa and Balarāma paid them homage, touching their feet with their heads.
51. Devakī and Vasudeva, realizing that the two sons who were paying them homage were the Lords of the universe, were bewildered and did not embrace them.'

CHAPTER 45

The Retrieval of the Guru*'s Sons*

1. *Śrī* Śuka said:

'The supreme person understood that his mother and father had realized the truth and thought: "This should not be." He covered them with his personal *māyā*, which deludes people.
2. Kṛṣṇa, the bull of the Sātvatas, together with his elder brother, approached his mother and father. He bowed humbly and, consoling them, addressed them respectfully as "dear mother" and "dear father":
3. "Because of us, your two sons, our infancy, childhood and youth was not spent with you both, even though it was what you were always longing for, dear father.
4. Deprived by fate, we did not have the experience of living with you, nor the happiness that children who are cherished experience when living in their parents' home.
5. The debt to one's parents is not diminished even in a lifetime of a hundred years. The body, the source of all goals of life,[1] is born from and nourished by one's parents.
6. If a son who was able and rich enough did not provide for his parents, [the servants of Yama, lord of death] would force that son to eat his own flesh after he had died.
7. A person who is able, but who does not support a mother, father, an older person, chaste wife, son, infant, *guru*, *brāhmaṇa* or someone who has approached for shelter, is dead while still breathing.
8. We were unable to do this – we were preoccupied all the time

with Kaṃsa. We spent those days in vain because we were not honouring you.
9. Therefore forgive us, dear father and mother, for we were under the control of others. Greatly harassed as we were by that wicked-hearted Kaṃsa, we were not able to render due service to you."'
10. *Śrī* Śuka said:

'Beguiled thus by the words of Hari, the soul of the universe, who had appeared in a human form through his *māyā*, his parents lifted him on to their laps and embraced him, in a state of extreme joy.
11. Bewildered and in floods of tears, they did not say anything, O king. Caught in the bonds of affection, their throats were [choked] with tears.
12. To console his parents, *Bhagavān* Kṛṣṇa, the son of Devakī, made his maternal grandfather, Ugrasena, king.
13. Kṛṣṇa said: "The Yadus should not sit on the royal throne because of the curse of Yayāti,[2] so you should command us citizens, O great king.
14. While I attend you as your servant, the gods and others will bring offerings – not to speak of other rulers of men."
15–16. All Kṛṣṇa's relatives – the Yadu, Vṛṣṇi, Andhaka, Madhu, Dāśārha, Kukura and other clans – were welcomed from everywhere and Kṛṣṇa consoled them. They had been overwhelmed by fear of Kaṃsa and become debilitated from living in foreign lands. The maker of the universe settled them in their own homes and pleased them with the gift of wealth.
17. Protected by the arms of Kṛṣṇa and Saṅkarṣaṇa [Balarāma], their desires were fulfilled and they became satisfied. Once their grief had been dispelled by Kṛṣṇa and Balarāma, they became contented in their homes.
18. They looked happily on Mukunda's lotus face, day after day. It was always cheerful, with sweet smiles and looks of compassion.
19. Continually absorbing the nectar of the lotus face of Mukunda with their eyes, even the old became youthful with abundant strength and vigour.

20. Then, *Bhagavān* Kṛṣṇa, the son of Devakī, and Saṅkarṣaṇa approached Nanda, embraced him, and spoke as follows:
21. "Father! You have been so loving – we have been nourished and cosseted by you both. Indeed, the love of parents for their sons exceeds even that for themselves.
22. The father and the mother are in fact those who nourish infants who have been abandoned by relatives who are unable to protect and sustain them.
23. Go to Vraj, father, and we will come to see you after we have made our friends happy. You are our relatives and love has made you suffer."
24. After consoling Nanda and the people of Vraj, *Bhagavān* Acyuta, as a mark of respect, gave Nanda garments, ornaments, metal [vessels] and other things.
25. Nanda was overwhelmed with love at being addressed in this way. His eyes filled with tears, and he embraced the two boys. Then he went to Vraj with the *gopas*.
26. After this, Vasudeva, the son of Śūra, made appropriate arrangements through the head priest and the *brāhmaṇas* for the performance of the [sacred-thread] rite for the twice-born.
27. When the *brāhmaṇas* had been well decked out, Kṛṣṇa worshipped them and gave them gifts of cows nicely decorated with garlands of gold, and calves with garlands of linen.
28. The noble-minded Nanda remembered those cows which had been misappropriated by Kaṃsa, and which he had mentally given away on the occasion of Kṛṣṇa's and Balarāma's birthdays, and gave those away too.
29. Then, after fulfilling the rite, the two boys received the status of twice-born *brāhmaṇas* from Garga, the spiritual preceptor of the Yadu lineage, and adopted the vow of celibacy. They are always true to their vow.
30. The two Lords of the universe, all-knowing and the source of all knowledge, hid their absolute knowledge – knowledge which is not acquired from others – through their deeds as men.
31. Then, wanting to live in the *gurukula*, the house of the *guru*, the two Lords went to one known as Sāndīpani. Although from Kāśī, Sāndīpani was residing in the city of Avantī.
32. Kṛṣṇa and Balarāma approached him and rendered him

service with devotion as if he were a god. Since their senses were under control, they conducted themselves faultlessly with the *guru*.

33. The *guru* is the best of the twice-born. Satisfied with their pure-hearted acts of obedience, Sāndīpani explained all the Vedas, along with their supplementary literature,[3] as well as the Upaniṣads.

34. [He explained] the knowledge of warfare, including its secrets; the *dharma* literature;[4] the systems of debate and logic, and the knowledge of polity, which is of six kinds.[5]

35. Kṛṣṇa and Balarāma, those two best of men, immediately assimilated everything merely by its recitation. They are, after all, the originators of all knowledge, O king.

36. Since they are disciplined in mind, in sixty-four days and nights they learned as many arts.[6] They pleased their teacher by offering *gurudakṣiṇā* [the gift offered to the *guru* by the disciple at the end of the period of study], O king.

37. The twice-born *brāhmaṇa* Sāndīpani observed the extraordinary ability and superhuman intelligence of the two boys, O king. After consulting with his wife, he made a request for his son, who had died in the great ocean at Prabhāsa.

38. The two great charioteers,[7] whose power is limitless, said: "So be it." Then they mounted their chariot and set out for Prabhāsa. They went towards the shore and sat down for a moment. The ocean recognized them and gave them offerings.

39. *Bhagavān* said to him: "The son of our *guru* should be returned immediately. He is the young boy you seized here with a huge wave."

40–41. The ocean said: "I did not seize him, O God. There is a mighty demon called Pañcajana who assumes the form of a conch shell and travels through the water. It was definitely he who seized the boy, O Kṛṣṇa." Hearing this, the Lord quickly entered the water and killed the demon. But he did not see the boy in his stomach.

42–44. He took the conch that formed the demon's body and returned to his chariot. Then, with Balarāma, whose weapon is a plough, Janārdana [Kṛṣṇa] went to the city called Saṃyamanī, which is protected by Yama, the god of death, and blew the conch. Hearing the sound of the conch, Yama, the chastiser of living beings, worshipped them lavishly, brimming with devotion. He humbly said to Kṛṣṇa, who dwells in the hearts of all living beings: "O Viṣṇu, what can I do for you both? You are in human form for the purpose of *līlā*."

45. *Śrī Bhagavān* said: "The son of our *guru*, bound by his personal *karma*, was brought here. Obey my command immediately and bring him, great king."

46. Saying: "Let it be so," Yama brought the son of the *guru*. Kṛṣṇa, best of the Yadu dynasty, gave the boy to their own *guru* and told him: "Choose another [favour]."

47. The *guru* said: "You have both fulfilled the gift-offering to the *guru* completely, my son. What is left to desire for the *guru* of one such as you?

48. Go to your own home, O heroes. May your fame purify, and may your Vedic hymns remain potent, both in this world and the hereafter."

49. When they were given leave to go by the *guru* in this manner, dear Parīkṣit, both of them arrived at their own city in their chariot, which reverberated like a thunder cloud and was as rapid as the wind.

50. The citizens, who had not seen them for many days, rejoiced together when they saw Balarāma and Janārdana, like people who had regained a lost treasure.'

CHAPTER 46

The Removal of Nanda's Distress

1. *Śrī* Śuka said:

'The minister Uddhava was a distinguished Vṛṣṇi, a beloved friend of Kṛṣṇa, and a direct disciple of the sage Bṛhaspati.[1] He was also extremely clever.

2. Once, *Bhagavān* Hari, who removes the distress of those who submit to him, took Uddhava's hand in his own. He said to that

most dear of devotees, who was dedicated exclusively to him:
3. "Go to Vraj, gentle Uddhava, and convey our love to our parents. By my messages, free the *gopīs* from the mental pain of separation.
4. Their minds are concentrated on me, their lives devoted to me, and they have given up all bodily needs for me. Their minds are absorbed in me, their most beloved and their life and soul.[2]
5. The women of Gokula remember me as their best beloved, dear Uddhava, although I am far away. Agitated by the grief of separation, they languish.
6. For the most part, the cowherd women somehow or other maintain their lives with great difficulty by my messages about my return. Their hearts are dedicated to me."'
7. *Śrī* Śuka said:

'At this request, O king, the respectful Uddhava took his master's message, mounted his chariot, and set forth for Nanda's Gokula.
8. The fortunate Uddhava reached Nanda's Vraj when the sun was setting. His vehicle was obscured by dust from the hooves of the animals who were returning home.
9. Vraj was filled with the sounds of sexually excited bulls fighting for the cows on heat, and with cows running with their calves and lowing because of the burden of their udders.
10. It was picturesque: white calves frisked here and there, and the place resounded with the sound of flutes and of cows being milked.
11. It sparkled with beautifully decorated *gopas*, and with the *gopīs* singing about the auspicious deeds of Balarāma and Kṛṣṇa.
12. It was picturesque also with the houses of the *gopas*, which bustled with the worship of the gods, the ancestors, *brāhmaṇas*, guests, sun and fire by use of incense, fire-lamps and garlands.
13. Vraj was noisy with swarms of bees and flocks of birds, and pretty with flowering groves everywhere, and with clusters of lotuses, among which were swans and ducks.
14. When Kṛṣṇa's dear friend arrived the delighted Nanda came

to meet him. With his mind on Vásudeva, Nanda embraced Uddhava and honoured him.

15. When Uddhava had been fed with the best food, had rested comfortably on a couch, and been relieved of his fatigue by foot massage, Nanda inquired from him:

16. "Dear Uddhava – you are so fortunate. Is our friend Vasudeva, the son of Śūra, who has been freed, well and united with his offspring, and other family members? He is true to his friends.

17. It is good that the sinful Kaṃsa, along with his followers, has been killed because of his own wickedness. He always hated the *sādhus* and the Yadus who were disposed towards *dharma*.

18. Does Kṛṣṇa even remember us – his mother, his well-wishers, his girlfriends, the *gopas*, Vraj, which has him as its Lord, the cows, the forests of Vṛndāvana, and the mountain [Govardhana]?

19. Will Govinda come even once to see his people? If so, we will see his face, with its beautiful nose and sweet smiling glances.

20. We were protected from the forest fire, the wind, the rain, the bull, the serpent and from inevitable mortal dangers by that great soul, Kṛṣṇa.

21. [The performance of] all our chores has become slack, dear Uddhava, because we remember the prowess of Kṛṣṇa, his playful sideways looks and his words.

22. The minds of those who see the places for play – the river, hill and forest regions – adorned by the feet of Mukunda become absorbed in him.

23. From the words of Garga, I think that Kṛṣṇa and Balarāma are the most eminent of gods, who have arrived here in this world for some great purpose of the gods.

24. In sport those two killed Kaṃsa, who had the strength of 10,000 elephants, as well as the two wrestlers and the king of elephants, just like the lion, king of animals, kills a deer.

25. Kṛṣṇa broke the bow, which was very solid and the size of three *tāla* trees, like the king of elephants breaks a stick. He held up the mountain with one hand for three days.

26. The demons Pralamba, Dhenuka, Ariṣṭa, Tṛṇāvarta, Baka

and others had vanquished both gods and demons, but they were killed by him with ease."'

27. *Śrī* Śuka said:

'Nanda's mind was full of Kṛṣṇa; reminiscing over and over in this way, he then fell silent. He was experiencing extreme longing, and was overwhelmed with the force of love.

28. Yaśodā was listening to the description of the deeds of her son; she shed tears, and her breasts discharged milk from love.

29. At this display of Nanda's and Yaśodā's extreme affection for *Bhagavān* Kṛṣṇa, Uddhava spoke joyfully to Nanda.

30. *Śrī* Uddhava said: "You are both the most praiseworthy of embodied beings in this world, courteous Nanda, because you have expressed such an attitude towards Nārāyaṇa, the *guru* of everyone.

31. The two boys, Balarāma and Kṛṣṇa, are the matrix of the seed of the universe, the supreme being, primordial matter. Accompanying living entities, those two primeval beings control the knowledge and perfection of these entities.[3]

32. A person who has destroyed the stock of *karma* and concentrated their impure mind on Kṛṣṇa even for a moment when they are giving up their last breath, immediately goes to the supreme destination.[4] That person, Nārāyaṇa [Viṣṇu], is the colour of the sun, and is composed of *brahman*.[5]

33. You have both directed your love completely to him, Nārāyaṇa, O great-minded one. Those two boys are the cause and soul of everything and have assumed the form of humans for a purpose. What propitious work remains for you two to do?

34. Acyuta, the Lord of the Sātvatas, who is God, will come to Vraj soon and will show love to his parents.

35. He has killed Kaṃsa, the enemy of all the Sātvatas, in the middle of the arena, and now, reunited with you, Kṛṣṇa will make good whatever he has said.

36. Do not be distressed, O happy ones, you will see Kṛṣṇa in your presence. He is within the hearts of all living entities, just like fire within kindling wood.

37. For him, no one is in favour or out of it. There is no highest or lowest. He is free of pride, and equal to all alike.

38. For him there is no mother, no father, no wife and no sons or other relative. There is no friend, and no foe, nor, indeed, is there a body or birth.

39. There is no work for him to perform in the pure, impure or mixed condition of this world. He becomes manifest for the sake of sport and for the protection of the righteous.

40. Although he is transcendental and free from the *guṇas*, he engages with the *guṇas*, namely, *sattva*, *tamas* and *rajas*, while playing. He also creates, destroys and maintains by means of the *guṇas*.

41. Just as the ground appears to be moving to an eye affected by vertigo, so, because of the sense of 'I-ness', the self considers itself to be the doer in situations when it is [actually] the mind that is doing things.[6]

42. This *Bhagavān*, Hari, is certainly not the son of you both – he is the son, and also the soul, father and mother of everyone. He is the supreme Lord.

43. Without Acyuta, there is nothing at all that can be expressed, seen or heard. There is nothing in the past, the present or the future, nothing stationary or moving, nothing great or small. He alone exists as the supreme soul of everything."

44. That night passed as Nanda and Uddhava, the servant of Kṛṣṇa, were talking thus, O king. The *gopīs* arose, searched for their lamps, performed rites of worship for their homes, and churned the curds and whey.

45. As they pulled the churning rope, the *gopīs* sparkled; there were rows of bracelets on their arms, and their jewels were illuminated by the lamps. Their faces had reddish *kuṅkum* powder on their cheeks, which glittered with earrings. Their buttocks, breasts and necklaces swayed.

46. The sound of the women of Vraj singing about the lotus-eyed Kṛṣṇa mingled with the noise of the churning of the curds and whey and touched the heavens. All ill fortune from the four quarters of the universe was removed by it.

47. After the sun god had arisen, the residents of Vraj saw a golden chariot at Nanda's gate. They said: "Whose is this?

48. Perhaps Akrūra, who carries out Kaṃsa's wishes, has arrived. Lotus-eyed Kṛṣṇa was taken away to Mathurā by him.

49. Will Kṛṣṇa give funerary offerings to his contented master [Kaṃsa] by means of us?"[7] As the women were speaking, Uddhava, who had completed his daily rites, approached.'

CHAPTER 47
Uddhava's Return

1–2. *Śrī* Śuka said:

'The women of Vraj were astonished to see Kṛṣṇa's companion. His arms were hanging down and his eyes were like fresh lotuses. He wore a yellow garment, and a garland of lotuses. His lotus face shone with polished earrings: "Who is this person, looking so handsome?" they wondered. "He is wearing Acyuta's clothes and ornaments. From whence does he come and to whom does he belong?" Saying this, all the *gopīs* eagerly surrounded Uddhava, who had taken refuge at the feet of Uttamaśloka [Kṛṣṇa].
3. They understood that he was the message-bearer of Kṛṣṇa, Lord of Ramā, the goddess of fortune. Humbly bowing down, they questioned him after he had taken a seat in a private place. He was treated with great respect by the women, with modesty, smiles, glances, friendly words and so on:
4. "We know that you have arrived as the messenger of the Lord of the Yadus. You have been sent here by your master through his desire to give pleasure to his parents.
5. The bonds of family affection are difficult to give up, even for sages. Apart from these, we do not see anything worthy of his attention in the cow community of Vraj.
6. Friendship with others is given for a motive. It is a pretence that lasts for as long as that motive lasts. It is like the friendship of men for women, or of bees for flowers.
7. Courtesans abandon those who have no means; citizens, a king who is uncontrolled; graduates, their teacher; and *ṛtvik* [priests], the person who has given them payment.

8. Birds abandon trees that are stripped of fruit, and guests a household after they have eaten. Similarly, deer abandon a forest that has been burnt, and lovers a devoted woman after enjoying her."
9. The *gopīs* spoke these words to Uddhava, the messenger of Kṛṣṇa, when he met them. Their minds, bodies and words were absorbed in Govinda, and they had given up worldly concerns.
10. Their bashfulness disappeared as they wept and sang about their beloved's childhood deeds, and they reiterated them continually.
11. One of them,[1] meditating on her association with Kṛṣṇa, saw a honeybee, which she imagined had been sent by her beloved. She spoke as follows:[2]
12. The *gopī* said: "O keeper of honey,[3] your friend is a cheat. Don't touch our feet with your whiskers – they are [tinged] with the *kuṅkum* powder from the garlands in disarray on the breasts of our female rivals. Let the Lord of the Madhu dynasty [Kṛṣṇa][4] carry the remnants [*prasāda*][5] of those haughty women [himself]. One who employs a messenger such as you would be ridiculed in the assembly of the Yadus.
13. He made us drink the bewildering nectar of his lips once, and then abandoned us – just like you immediately abandon flowers. How can the lotus-like goddess of fortune keep serving his lotus feet? Surely her mind has also been stolen by the flattery of Uttamaśloka.
14. Why do you sing about that ancient one, the ruler of the Yadus, here in front of us, O six-legged one – we who are homeless? Let your fondness for Kṛṣṇa, that friend of the unconquerable Arjuna, be sung to his women companions. Since they are his beloveds, the pain in their breasts has been removed – let them provide you with what you desire.
15. What woman in heaven, the earth or the underworlds can he not obtain with his arched eyebrows and deceptively sweet smile? The goddess of fortune worships the dust of his feet – who then are we [who are so lowly, to think we can obtain him], even if the name 'Uttamaśloka' is intended for lowly beings?
16. Remove your foot from my head. I know all about you. You

know well how to appease through flattery, which you learned from Mukunda by being his messenger. The fickle Kṛṣṇa abandoned those who had abandoned children, husbands and other people in this world for his sake. Why then should I be reconciled with him?

17. His disposition is cruel, like a hunter's – he shot a monkey with his bow.[6] Because he was dominated by a female, he disfigured a woman who lusted after him.[7] After consuming his charity like a crow, he bound Bali.[8] Enough of friendship with that dark-complexioned one. But the treasured stories about him are so hard to give up.

18. The tendencies towards [perceiving reality from the perspective of] duality are at once dispelled by taking in through the ears a drop of the nectar of the *līlā* performed by Kṛṣṇa.[9] Many people abandon their wretched households and families in this world, and then immediately become wretched themselves and pursue a mendicant's life like birds.

19. We were foolish and believed that his deceitful speeches were true, just like the does, the wives of the black deer, trust the notes played by the hunter. Again and again, we have experienced the torment of Kāma brought about by the touch of his nails. So, speak about some other topic, O messenger.

20. Dear friend, have you been sent by our beloved and returned again? You are worthy of honour, dear one. Choose whatever wish you desire from me. How will you lead us from here to the presence of that couple? Śrī, the goddess of fortune, is always united with him on his chest as his consort, O gentle one. It is difficult for her to relinquish that union.

21. Is Kṛṣṇa, an Āryan offspring, presently in Mathurā? Does he remember his father's households and his friends the *gopas*, O gentle one? Does he ever relate stories about us, his maidservants? Will he ever place his arm, exquisitely fragrant with the scent of the *aguru* [aloe] tree, upon our heads?"'

22. *Śrī* Śuka said:

'After Uddhava had heard this, he consoled the *gopīs*, who were so eager to see Kṛṣṇa, with messages from their beloved. He spoke as follows:

23. *Śrī* Uddhava said: "*Aho!* You women have fulfilled the goals of life: your mind is dedicated to *Bhagavān* Vāsudeva in this way, and so people revere you.
24. Devotion to Kṛṣṇa is attained in this world by control of the senses, Vedic study, *mantra* recitation, fire sacrifices, austerity, vows and charity, as well as by other auspicious acts.
25. By good fortune, the highest devotion to *Bhagavān* Uttamaśloka has been kindled in you. This is rarely attained even by those who are sages.
26. By good fortune, you have renounced sons, husbands, relatives, homes and your own bodies, and chosen the supreme person known as Kṛṣṇa.
27. You have done me a great favour: by your [complete absorption in Kṛṣṇa even in] separation [from him], you have shown wholehearted love for Adhokṣaja, and you are very lucky.
28. Listen to the message – it will bring you happiness, O fortunate women. I have come as the confidant of my master, and brought it for you."
29. *Śrī Bhagavān* said: "There can never be any separation between you and myself, because I am the soul of everything. Just as the elements – ether, air, fire, water and earth – exist in all entities, so I am the repository of the *guṇas*, the senses, the elements, the vital airs and the mind.
30. From myself I create, maintain and destroy myself in myself by means of myself in the form of the *guṇas*, senses and elements, through the power of my own *māyā*.[10]
31. The *ātmā* [soul] is pure, distinct, separate from the *guṇas*, and comprised of knowledge. It is perceivable in the states of deep sleep, dream and waking as a result of the fluctuations of *māyā*.[11]
32. When one arises, the mind causes one to meditate uselessly on the objects of the senses (which are like a dream), and, when fully awake, one indulges those senses. One should control that mind.
33. The body of sacred texts of the wise – Yoga and Sāṅkhya[12] – and renunciation, austerity and truth, have this as their goal, just like rivers have the ocean as their goal.
34. That I, your beloved, remain far removed from your vision

is in order to attract your minds; it is because of longing that you meditate upon me.

35. When the beloved is far away, the minds of women who are absorbed in him dwell on him; but the consciousness does not do this when he is near at hand, within the range of vision.

36. Because you remember me always, having become completely absorbed in me, you are freed from all turbulence of mind and will meet me soon.

37. Those who remained in Vraj during that night in the forest, and so did not participate in *rāsa* with me as I was enjoying myself, are fortunate: they attained me by meditating on my heroic deeds."'

38. *Śrī* Śuka said:

'When they heard the instruction from their best beloved, the women of Vraj were delighted, and spoke to Uddhava. Their memories had been reawakened by that message.

39. The *gopīs* said: "By good fortune, the evildoer Kaṃsa, enemy of the Yadus, has been killed together with his followers. By good fortune, Acyuta is now prosperous and is with his friends, who have attained all their goals.

40. Does Kṛṣṇa, the elder brother of Gada, bestow his love – which is rightfully ours – on the women of the city, gentle Uddhava, when he is worshipped by them with gentle glances, laughter, bashfulness and affection?

41. Our beloved is expert in the details of sexual pleasure – how could he not be captivated when they flatter him by their words and coquetry?

42. Does Govinda even remember us when he is in the company of the city women, O *sādhu*, or spontaneously refer to us village girls during his conversations?

43. Does he ever remember those nights when he took pleasure with his lovers in Vṛndāvana, beautiful with the moon, jasmine and lotuses? His charming stories were celebrated by us in the assembly of the *rāsa*, which echoed with the sound of foot bracelets.

44. Will Dāśārha [Kṛṣṇa] come here and restore life to us with

his body, like Indra restores life to a forest with water-giving clouds? We are in torment from the distress he causes us.
45. But why should Kṛṣṇa come here? He has obtained a kingdom, killed his enemy, and married the daughters of rulers. He is happy and surrounded by all his friends.
46. What purpose can be served by us forest dwellers, or by others, for him who is the husband of the goddess of fortune? His desires have been fulfilled, and he is complete within himself.
47. Even the unchaste Piṅgalā stated that the greatest happiness is precisely in renouncing desire.[13] Nonetheless, even though we know this, our desire for Kṛṣṇa is difficult to give up.
48. Who could bear to give up conversing with Uttamaśloka? Even though he is free of desires, Śrī, the goddess of fortune, never moves from his body.
49. These forest areas, hills and rivers, the cows and the sounds of the flute were used by Kṛṣṇa and his companion Saṅkarṣaṇa, O master.
50. They make us remember the son of Nanda the *gopa* again and again. We are unable to forget him because of his footprints, which are the abode of Śrī, the goddess of fortune.
51. Our minds have been stolen by his sweet words, his graceful way of moving, his gentle laughter and playful looks. O how can we ever forget him?
52. O Master! Govinda! Master of Ramā, the goddess of fortune! Master of Vraj! Destroyer of suffering! Raise up Gokula, which is sunk in an ocean of distress." '
53. *Śrī* Śuka said:

'In due course, when the fever of separation had been dispelled by Kṛṣṇa's messages, the *gopīs* recognized that Adhokṣaja was their soul, and worshipped Uddhava.[14]
54. Uddhava stayed with the *gopīs* for several months, driving away their grief. He brought joy to Gokula by singing stories of Kṛṣṇa's *līlā*.
55. Because of the discussions about Kṛṣṇa, the number of days Uddhava resided in Nanda's Vraj seemed like the passing of a moment for the people of Vraj.
56. While viewing the rivers, forests, mountains, valleys and

flowering trees, the servant of Hari took pleasure in making the people of Vraj remember Kṛṣṇa.

57. When he saw how moved the *gopīs* were in their preoccupation with Kṛṣṇa, Uddhava was extremely pleased. Paying homage to them, he sang the following:

58. "These *gopī* women are the highest embodied beings on the earth: their love for Govinda, the soul of everything, is perfected. Those who are fearful of the material world aspire to this, and so do the sages, and so do we ourselves. What is the use of births as Brahmā[15] for one who has a taste for the infinite stories [of Kṛṣṇa]?

59. On the one hand, these women are forest dwellers tainted by deviant behaviour, and, on the other, they have developed a love for Kṛṣṇa, the soul of everything. Truly, the lord personally bestows blessings on the person who worships him even if that person is not learned; it is as if the king of medicines[16] had been consumed.

60. In the *rāsa* festival, he bestowed his favour on the beloved women of Vraj, who were accorded the honour of having their necks embraced by his long arms. That favour was not bestowed on the most loving Śrī, the goddess of fortune, who [resides] on his chest, nor on the celestial women, who have the beauty and the scent of lotuses – not to speak of other women.

61. *Aho!* May I become any of the shrubs, creepers or plants in Vṛndāvana that enjoy the dust of the feet of these women. They have renounced their own relatives, who are so hard to give up, as well as the Āryan code of conduct,[17] and worshipped the feet of Mukunda, the sought-for goal of the sacred texts of revelation.

62. Those lotus feet of *Bhagavān* Kṛṣṇa were placed on their breasts in the assembly of the *rāsa*. They are worshipped by Śrī, the goddess of fortune, by Brahmā and the other [gods] whose desires are fulfilled, and even, in their minds, by the masters of *yoga*. These very women embraced them and let go of their anguish.

63. I pay eternal homage to the dust from the feet of the women of Nanda's Vraj. Their songs about the stories of Hari purify the three worlds."'

64. *Śrī* Śuka said:

'Then, with the permission of the *gopīs* and *gopas*, and of Nanda and Yaśodā, Uddhava, the descendant of Daśārha, prepared to depart. He bid farewell and mounted his chariot.
65. Nanda and the others, with tears of affection in their eyes, approached him with various gifts in their hands as he was setting out. They said:
66. "May the restlessness of our mind rest in the lotus feet of Kṛṣṇa, may our words utter his names, and may our bodies bow to him, and perform other such devotional duties.
67. Wheresoever we are made to wander [in this *saṃsāra*, the cycle of birth and death] by the will of the Lord, or as a result of either our *karma*, our good works or our charitable actions, may our affection rest in Lord Kṛṣṇa."
68. Uddhava was honoured by the *gopas* in this way through their devotion to Kṛṣṇa, O ruler of men, and returned again to Mathurā, which was under Kṛṣṇa's protection.
69. Bowing respectfully to Kṛṣṇa, Uddhava told him about the exceeding devotion of the people of Vraj. Then he presented the gifts to Vasudeva [Kṛṣṇa's father], Balarāma and the king.'

CHAPTER 48

*Kṛṣṇa Satisfies Trivakrā and Meets Akrūra**

1. *Śrī* Śuka said:

'*Bhagavān* Kṛṣṇa is the all-seeing soul of everything; remembering the maidservant Trivakrā, who was burning with desire, he went to her house wanting to satisfy her.
2. It was replete with very costly decorations, and equipped with the appurtenances of sensual pleasure. It was decorated with strings of pearls and banners, with awnings, beds and seats, and with fragrant incense, oil lamps, garlands and scents.
3. When Trivakrā saw him coming to her house, she jumped

up from her seat at once, in a flurry. In the company of her women friends she approached Acyuta and received him respectfully with a good seat, and other such offerings, as was appropriate.

4. Then Uddhava was honoured by her in the same way. As a *sādhu*, he sat down on the ground after touching the seat [respectfully].[1] Kṛṣṇa, on the other hand, imitating the behaviour of worldly people, quickly settled down on a very opulent bed.

5. Trivakrā prepared herself by bathing, and with ointments, fine cloth, ornaments, garlands, perfume, betel nuts and nectarean liquors, and so on. Then she approached Mādhava with coy smiles and coquettish glances.

6. Kṛṣṇa summoned his lover, who was apprehensive and bashful about this new encounter. He pulled her forward by her two hands, decorated with bangles, and placed her upon the bed. Then he enjoyed himself with that beautiful woman, even though she had merely performed a token act of piety by offering him ointment.

7. Trivakrā embraced her lover with her two arms, and eased the pain of desire in her burning breasts, as well as the pain in her chest and eyes, by smelling the lotus feet of Ananta [Kṛṣṇa]. Kṛṣṇa, the embodiment of bliss, placed himself between her breasts, and she gave up the intense yearning she had suffered for so long.

8. *Aho!* The Lord is the master of liberation and so hard to obtain, but Trivakrā won him by offering dye for his body. The unfortunate woman[2] begged as follows:

9. "Let us stay here together for some days, lover. Enjoy yourself with me. I cannot bear to give up your company, lotus-eyed one."

10. The Lord of everything granted her her ardent desire and, since he is the giver of respect, he offered her respect. Then he went to his own opulent abode with Uddhava.

11. One who chooses sensual objects[3] after having worshipped Viṣṇu, the Lord of all lords who is rarely worshipped, is misguided. This is because the nature of sensual objects is illusory.

12. Lord Kṛṣṇa set out for Akrūra's house, along with Balarāma

and Uddhava, with the intention of taking care of some business and wanting to please Akrūra.

13. Akrūra saw those most illustrious men, his own relatives, from a distance and was delighted. He rose up, welcomed them and embraced them.

14. He paid homage to Kṛṣṇa and Balarāma, and was himself greeted by them in turn. When they had accepted a seat, he honoured them according to the appropriate conventions.

15–16. Sprinkling the water used for washing their feet on his head,[4] O king, Akrūra worshipped them with celestial gifts and garments, and with the best quality fragrances, garlands and ornaments. Massaging their feet, which they placed on his lap, Akrūra bowed his head and humbly bent down in reverence. He then spoke to Kṛṣṇa and Balarāma:

17. "By good fortune, the sinful Kaṃsa and his followers have been killed, and this dynasty of ours has been delivered from insurmountable difficulties and made prosperous by you both.

18. You are the original beings. You are the cause of the universe, and the substance of the universe. Without you two there is nothing that exists before or afterwards.

19. This universe was created from yourself [O Kṛṣṇa], after which you subsequently entered it with your own energies. You pervade it in many forms that can be seen and described. You are *brahman*.

20. Just as the elements such as earth, and so on, become manifest in various degrees in [different] species and in moving and non-moving beings, so it is you, Lord, alone, the independent self among selves, who becomes manifest in various degrees in the species which emanate from your own self.

21. Indeed, you create, destroy and protect the universe through your own energies of *rajas*, *sattva* and *tamas*, but you are not bound by these *guṇas* or by *karma*. You are the essence of knowledge – so what could cause your bondage?

22. Because impositions such as the body are not discernible in the soul, there can be no birth or duality in reality.[5] Therefore, there can certainly be neither bondage nor liberation for you. You act out of your own free will.[6] It is our lack of understanding of you [that makes us think otherwise].

23. Whenever the ancient path of the Veda, revealed by you, is obstructed by the false paths of the heretics, your lordship assumes [a form] from *sattva guṇa*.
24. That supreme person is you, O master. You have now become incarnate in the world in the house of Vasudeva with your own *aṃśa* [partial incarnation] in order to remove the burden from the earth by killing hundreds of the battalions of kings who are *aṃśas* of the enemies of the gods, and by spreading the fame of this dynasty.
25. Today, O Lord, our homes have become truly blessed – he who is the embodiment of the Vedas, humankind, living beings, ancestors and all the gods has entered them. The water from washing his feet purifies the three worlds. You are he, the *guru* of the universe, O Adhokṣaja.
26. What wise person would approach someone other than you for shelter? You are a faithful friend because of your gratitude and affection for your devotees. As a friend, you grant all that is desired, even your own self, to one who is devoted to you; but no increase or decrease occurs in you.
27. It is our good fortune to see your Lordship, Janārdana, here, even though you are the goal that is attained with difficulty by the masters of *yoga* and the lords of the gods. Sever quickly our bonds of illusion in the form of body, home, good company, wealth, wife, offspring and such things – these are the *māyā* of your lordship."
28. When *Bhagavān* Hari was honoured and addressed thus by his devotee, he smiled and spoke to Akrūra as if he were casting a spell upon him.
29. *Śrī Bhagavān* said: "You are our *guru* and paternal uncle, and always a respected relative. We are dependants who need to be protected, nourished and shown compassion.
30. The worthiest of righteous people like your own self are most blessed. You deserve to be worshipped always by men who desire the highest goals. The gods are concerned with their own welfare, but saints are not.
31. Holy places containing water, and gods made of earth and stone, purify after a long time, but saints purify simply from being seen.

32. You yourself are such a person. You are the best of our friends. Go to Gajāhvaya [Hastināpura] to make inquiries about the Pāṇḍavas, and out of a desire for their welfare.
33. We have heard that when their father [Pāṇḍu] passed away, the [Pāṇḍava] boys, along with their distraught mother, were brought by king Dhṛtarāṣṭra to his own city.[7]
34. The evil-minded king, son of Ambikā, does not deal equally with the sons of his brother Pāṇḍu. Indeed, that blind man [Dhṛtarāṣṭra] is under the control of his wicked sons.
35. Go, find out if his conduct is at present just or unjust. When we know this we will make arrangements according to the interests of our friends."
36. After instructing Akrūra in this way, *Bhagavān* Lord Hari then went to his own home with Saṅkarṣaṇa and Uddhava.'

CHAPTER 49

*Akrūra Visits Hastināpura**

1. *Śrī* Śuka said:

'After arriving at Hastināpura, made notorious by the rulers of the Pūru dynasty, Akrūra saw Dhṛtarāṣṭra, the son of Ambikā, together with Bhīṣma, Vidura and Pṛthā [Kuntī] there.[1]
2. He saw Bāhlīka and his son; Droṇa, the descendant of Bhāradvāj, together with Kṛpa, the descendant of Gautama; Karṇa; Suyodhana [Duryodhana]; Aśvatthāmā, the son of Droṇa; the Pāṇḍavas and other good friends.[2]
3. After meeting them in the proper fashion, Akrūra, the son of Gāndinī, was solicited by his friends for news of their dear ones, as well as of himself; he inquired after their welfare in turn.
4. He remained for a few months out of a desire to observe the dealings of the king. The latter had little determination, was compliant to the will of reprobates, and had evil sons.
5–6. Pṛthā and Vidura told him all about the unpleasant acts that had been done by the sons of Dhṛtarāṣṭra – such as the

giving of poison[3] – and about their intentions. The sons could tolerate neither the good qualities of the sons of Pṛthā – their prowess, energy, strength, heroism, humility and other positive characteristics – nor the affection that the citizens had for them.

7. Remembering the home of her birth, Pṛthā approached her brother Akrūra when he arrived. With tears in her eyes, she said:

8. "Do my brothers, parents, sisters, brother's sons, female relatives and girlfriends remember us, gentle Akrūra?

9. *Bhagavān* Kṛṣṇa, who gives refuge and is kind to his devotees, is my brother's son. Does he remember his cousins, the sons of his paternal aunts – and does the lotus-eyed Balarāma, too?

10. Will he console me and my fatherless young boys with his words? I grieve in the midst of enemies, like a deer among wolves.

11. Kṛṣṇa, O Kṛṣṇa, great *yogī*, soul and creator of the universe. Protect me and my children; I have taken refuge in you and am sunk in despair, O Govinda!

12. I do not see any other shelter than your lotus feet, which bestow liberation, for people fearful of *saṃsāra*. You are the supreme Lord.

13. Homage to you, Kṛṣṇa. You are the pure *brahman*, the supreme soul, the Lord of *yogīs*, and *yoga* itself! I have come to you for shelter." '

14. *Śrī* Śuka said:

'Remembering in this way her relative Kṛṣṇa, the Lord of the universe, that unhappy woman – your paternal grandmother, O king – began to weep.

15. Akrūra, who was equally unperturbed by both happiness and distress, and the widely renowned Vidura consoled Kuntī by [telling her about] the reasons for the births of her sons.[4]

16. Dhṛtarāṣṭra was partial towards, and fond of, his sons. As Akrūra was about to depart, he went up to the king, who was in the midst of his friends, and told him what had been said in good faith by his relatives.

17. Akrūra said: "*Bho! Bho!* Dhṛtarāṣṭra, son of Vicitravīrya.

Since the death of your brother you have sat upon the throne of the Pāṇḍavas and increased the glories of the Kurus.
18. You will achieve fame and prosperity by protecting the earth through *dharma*, by pleasing the citizens by your qualities, and by remaining equally disposed towards your own relatives.
19. But, by behaving otherwise, you will attain darkness and be censured in the world. Therefore, deal impartially with your own sons and with the Pāṇḍavas.
20. No relationship of one with another lasts for ever in this world, O king, or even [between oneself] and one's own body – let alone with one's wife and children.
21. A living being is born alone, dies alone and enjoys alone the fruits of pious and impious deeds.
22. Other people, with the excuse of needing sustenance,[5] steal the wealth that has been accumulated by non-*dharmic* means from a foolish person, just as fish steal water.
23. Those things which a person nourishes by non-*dharma*, thinking them to be his own – vital airs, wealth, sons and other worldly assets – are the very things that betray the foolish man and leave him with his goals unfulfilled.
24. Carrying his own sins on his own head, he is rejected by other people. Ignorant of the goal of life, and opposed to performing his *dharma*, he enters into blind darkness with his goals frustrated.
25. Therefore, O king and master, after realizing that this world is as a dream, phantasmagoria of the mind, let the self hold the mind in check and become peaceful and in balance."
26. Dhṛtarāṣṭra said: "O master of charity, the more you speak virtuous words, sir, the more I remain unsatiated by them, like a mortal who has obtained nectar.
27. Nevertheless, your kind and true words do not remain fixed in my fickle heart, which favours my sons out of affection, like lightning does not remain fixed.
28. Otherwise, what person would ignore the injunctions of the Lord? He has descended in the dynasty of the Yadus in order to remove the burden from the earth.
29. I offer my homage to him, the supreme Lord. The perpetuation of the cycle of *saṃsāra* is the result of his mysterious

pastimes. He creates this world through his own *māyā*, whose ways are unknowable, and, after entering it, activates the *guṇas*."'

30. *Śrī* Śuka said:

'When he had ascertained the intentions of the king in this way, Akrūra, the descendant of Yadu, took leave of his friends and returned to the city of the Yadus.

31. He told Kṛṣṇa and Balarāma about the conduct of Dhṛtarāṣṭra towards the Pāṇḍavas, O descendant of Kuru – for this was the purpose for which he had been sent.'

PART TWO

CHAPTER 50

Entrance into the Fort

1. *Śrī* Śuka said:

'When their lord was killed, Asti and Prāpti, Kaṃsa's two grief-stricken queens, went to their paternal homes, O bull amongst men.
2. The two unhappy women informed their father, Jarāsandha, the king of Magadha, the reason for their widowhood.
3. At that unpleasant news, O king, Jarāsandha was overcome with sorrow and fury, and embarked upon a massive operation to rid the earth of the Yadus.
4. Surrounded by twenty-three *akṣauhiṇī* battalions, he laid siege from all sides to Mathurā, the capital of the Yadus.
5–6. When *Bhagavān* Hari saw that show of force, like an ocean overflowing its shores, and when he saw his own city besieged by Jarāsandha, and his subjects terror-stricken, he deliberated upon the best course to take according to time and place. He thought also about the purpose of his own descent [to earth], for he had, after all, become a human being for a purpose.
7–8. "I will destroy this force of vassal kings, comprising *aukṣauhiṇī* battalions of soldiers, horses, chariots and elephants, assembled and brought by the king of Magadha. It is a burden on the earth. But the king of Magadha must not be killed, so that he can again make an attempt [to assemble] another force.
9. My incarnation has been accomplished for this purpose – the

removal of the burden of the earth, the protection of the *sādhus* [saints] and the destruction of those who are not *sādhus*.[1]
10. I assumed a different body for the protection of *dharma*, and also for the elimination of non-*dharma* whenever it arises in the course of time."[2]
11. At the very moment that Govinda was deliberating thus, two chariots appeared from the sky. They had charioteers and equipment, and were as splendid as the sun.
12. Ancient divine weapons also appeared spontaneously,[3] seeing which, Hṛṣīkeśa [Kṛṣṇa] spoke to Balarāma:
13. "Just see the calamity that has befallen the Yadus, who are protected by you, O Ārya. And here your chariot has appeared, along with your favourite weapons.
14. Mount your vehicle and deliver your people from this calamity. Our birth was for this purpose, O Lord of the *sādhus*. You are the giver of protection.
15–16. Deliver the earth from its burden in the form of these twenty-three armies." After they had finished consulting about this, the two descendants of Daśārha, armed and mounted on their chariots, sallied forth from the city. They were laden with weapons and surrounded by a smaller force. Hari, with Dāruka as his charioteer, blew his conch as he set out.
17. At this, the hearts of the enemy soldiers trembled with fear. Seeing those two, the king of Magadha said: "Hey, Kṛṣṇa, you are the lowest of men.
18. I do not wish to fight with you out of shame [of fighting with an inferior]. You remained hidden,[4] and are merely a boy and alone, you fool. I will not fight with you, so go, you who murder kinsfolk.
19. Balarāma, if you can fight steadfastly, then muster your courage. Either kill me, or go to the celestial region, leaving behind your body pierced by my arrows."
20. *Śrī Bhagavān* said: "Heroes do not boast, but display their prowess. We do not heed the words of those who are injured, nor those who are about to die."'
21. *Śrī* Śuka said:

'The son of Jarā advanced and surrounded them, their soldiers, chariots, banners, horses and charioteers, with his more powerful force, which was like a great flood. It was as the wind surrounds the sun with clouds or a fire with dust.

22. The women swooned when they could not see in the battle the two chariots of Hari and Balarāma, marked with the banners of Garuḍa and the palm tree. Standing on the watchtowers, palaces and gates of the city, they were overcome with grief.

23. Hari saw his own army continually harassed by the intense torrent of arrows from the clouds of the opposing army and twanged his superb bow, Śārṅga, which is worshipped by gods and demons.

24. Taking arrows from his quiver, Kṛṣṇa fixed them on the bow. Then he drew his bow, releasing a multitude of sharpened arrows and striking without mercy chariots, elephants, horses and foot-soldiers, like a firebrand.

25. Elephants fell, their foreheads cleft, as did great numbers of horses, their necks pierced by arrows. Chariots were struck, and so were horses, banners, charioteers, commanders and foot-soldiers, their necks, thighs and arms sliced.

26. Numerous rivers of blood flowed with the limbs of horses, elephants and men who were being decimated. The rivers were filled with dead elephants [that appeared like] islands; horses [that appeared like] crocodiles; human heads [that appeared like] tortoises; and arms [that appeared like] snakes.

27. They were full of weapons [like] thickets; bows [like] waves; hands and thighs [like] fish; human hair [like] duckweed; wheels [like] dreadful whirlpools; huge jewels and choice ornaments [like] stones and pebbles.

28. They were released by Saṅkarṣaṇa, whose power was immeasurable and who, in the battle, was slaughtering with his club his enemies in their arrogance. These rivers filled the timid with terror, but brought delight to the wise.

29. That limitless force, dear Parīkṣit, a terrible and impassable ocean protected by the king of Magadha, was destroyed by the two sons of Vasudeva. It was no more than sport for the two lords of the universe.

30. Although the annihilation of the opposing army by Kṛṣṇa,

who was conforming to the ways of mortal beings, is not surprising – after all, his qualities are unlimited and he undertakes the maintenance, creation and destruction of the three worlds as his own *līlā* – nevertheless, it has been described.

31. Balarāma forcefully seized the mighty Jarāsandha, like a lion seizes a lion. Without a chariot and with his army slaughtered, Jarāsandha was left with only his breath remaining.

32. Jarāsandha had always put his opponents to death. But, as he was being bound by Balarāma with the fetters both of the god Varuṇa[5] and of humans, Govinda stopped him, out of a desire to accomplish his mission.

33. As one renowned among heroes, Jarāsandha was humiliated. When he had been set free by those two masters of the world, he made up his mind to engage in austere disciplines. But he was intercepted on his way by [friendly] kings.

34. With arguments that were banal, yet packaged in words of spiritual connotation, the kings said: "This defeat by the Yadus was caused by the bondage of your own *karma*."

35. Humiliated by *Bhagavān*, and with his armies annihilated, king Jarāsandha, son of Bṛhadratha, returned to his kingdom of Magadha in a troubled state of mind.

36. Mukunda, on the other hand, who had overcome the ocean of the enemy's force, emerged with his army unscathed. He was applauded by the gods and showered with flowers.

37. He was approached by the joyous people of Mathurā, whose fever had been eased, and his victory was celebrated by bards, heralds and royal minstrels.

38. When the Lord entered the city, conches, drums, kettledrums, musical instruments, stringed *vīṇās*, flutes and *mṛdaṅga* drums resounded in great numbers.

39. Its thoroughfares were sprinkled with water, its citizens were joyful, and it was decorated with banners. It echoed with the sounds of the Vedas, and its arches were festooned with banners.

40. Kṛṣṇa was looked upon with love and showered with garlands, yogurt, unhusked grain and fresh shoots by the women, their eyes wide with love.

41. The Lord bestowed all the wealth that had been abandoned

on the battlefield – the countless ornaments of the heroes – to the king of the Yadus.

42. With a force consisting of the same number of battalions as before, the king of Magadha fought seventeen times with the Yadus, who were protected by Kṛṣṇa.

43. By the power of Kṛṣṇa, the Vṛṣṇi clan destroyed his entire force. [Each time], when his armies were slaughtered, the king would be released by his enemies and would depart.

44. A *yavana* hero[6] appeared in the interval before the eighteenth battle, which was impending. He had been sent by Nārada.

45. Finding no rival in the world of men, he had heard that the Vṛṣṇi clan were his match. So he went to Mathurā, and besieged it with thirty million *mlecchas* [barbarians].[7]

46. When Kṛṣṇa, with his companion Saṅkarṣaṇa, saw the *yavana* he thought: "*Aho!* A great calamity has befallen the Yadus from two sides.

47. This *yavana*, with such a mighty force, is besieging us today, and the Māgadhan also will arrive today, tomorrow or the next day.

48. While we are fighting with the *yavana*, the powerful son of Jarā will kill our kinsfolk or else take them to his own city.

49. Today, therefore, we will construct an impregnable fortress and place our relatives there, and then we will fight the *yavana*."

50. After deliberating thus, *Bhagavān* built a fortress in the middle of the ocean. It was a fabulous, fully self-contained city.

51. The expertise of Tvaṣṭā, specialist in the *śilpa* manuals,[8] was evident there. It was meticulously constructed with streets, crossroads and carriageways.

52–54. The city was replete with groves, parks, creeping plants and trees from the gods. It was designed with gates and watchtowers of crystal with gold spires that touched the sky; granaries of silver and brass decorated [in front] with pots of gold; and houses of gold with jewelled domes and roofs made from huge emeralds, with terraces, and with temples for household gods. It was populated by members of the four *varṇas*,[9] and magnificent with the residences of the rulers of the Yadus.

55. The great Indra gave the assembly hall of the gods, called

Sudharmā, and the celestial *pārijāta* tree, as a gift. Wherever this tree is found, mortals are not subject to natural laws.

56. Varuṇa bestowed pure black as well as white horses, that were as fast as the speed of thought. The lord of wealth, Kubera, gave eight treasures, and the rulers of the planets, their own wealth.

57. Whatever sovereignty had been given to them by *Bhagavān* for the accomplishment of their duties, was all rendered again to Hari, who had come down to earth, O king.

58. After transporting all the people there by the power of *yoga*, Hari consulted with Balarāma, the protector of the people, and set out from the city wearing a garland of lotuses, but without a weapon.'

CHAPTER 51

The Eulogy of Mucukunda

1. *Śrī* Śuka said:

'The *yavana* saw him, going forth like the rising moon. Dark in complexion and wearing yellow silk garments, Kṛṣṇa was very beautiful to behold.

2. The *śrīvatsa* curl of hair was on his chest and his neck was graced with the glittering *kaustubha* gem, his four arms were long and thick, and his eyes were reddish like the fresh lotus.

3. He was in a state of constant bliss, and had beautiful cheeks and a brilliant smile. He had a lotus face, and wore sparkling earrings shaped like alligators.

4–5. "From the characteristics described by Nārada, this person can be no other than Vāsudeva. He is identifiable by his *śrīvatsa* curl of hair, four arms, lotus face and gorgeous forest garland. Since he is proceeding on foot unarmed, I will fight with him unarmed."

6. Thus resolved, the *yavana* rushed forward intending to seize Kṛṣṇa. Although Kṛṣṇa is difficult even for *yogīs* to attain, the *yavana* chased him as he was fleeing.

7. The ruler of the *yavanas* was led far away to a mountain cave by Hari, who made himself appear to be within grasp at each step.
8. As he pursued Kṛṣṇa, the *yavana* taunted him: "You have taken birth in the Yadu dynasty – flight is unbefitting you." But he could not catch Kṛṣṇa because his impurities had not been removed.
9. Despite being insulted in this way, *Bhagavān* entered the mountain cave. The *yavana* also entered, and saw some other person sleeping there:
10. "Just see: after bringing me such a long way, this Kṛṣṇa is sleeping here like a *sādhu*." Taking the other person to be Acyuta in this way, the fool kicked him hard.
11. The man, who had been sleeping for a long time, arose and slowly opened his eyes. Looking all around, he saw the *yavana* standing at his side.
12. From the enraged glance he cast, the *yavana* was incinerated in an instant; he was reduced to ashes by the fire generated from the man's body, O Parīkṣit, descendant of Bharata.'
13. The king said:

'What was the name of that man, O *brāhmaṇa*? Of what [lineage]? And what powers did that killer of the *yavana* possess? Why had he gone into the cave and slept? And what about his fiery glare?'
14. *Śrī* Śuka said:

'He was a mighty son of Māndhātā, born in the dynasty of Ikṣvāku. Known as Mucukunda, he was devoted to *brāhmaṇas* and faithful to his word.
15. He was enlisted by the assembly of gods for their personal protection. Led by Indra, they were terrified of the demons. He provided protection for them for a long time.
16. After the gods had obtained Kārttikeya[1] they sad to Mucukunda, the protector of heaven: "O king! Your lordship should give up the strenuous task of protecting us.
17. You renounced the world of men and a kingdom in which all enemies had been struck down, and you put aside all personal desires while you were protecting us, O hero.

18. Driven forward by the force of time, the sons, queens, kinsfolk, ministers, advisers and citizens who were your lordship's contemporaries are no longer alive.[2]
19. Time is *Bhagavān*, the imperishable Lord, and more powerful than the powerful. It drives creatures forward without effort, like a herdsman drives his herds.
20. May good fortune be with you. Choose any favour from us today except that of liberation – *Bhagavān*, the imperishable Viṣṇu, is the only one capable of [bestowing] that!"
21. Addressed thus, the widely renowned Mucukunda paid reverence to the gods. (The king was exhausted with fatigue, and so chose sleep for his gift: "If anyone breaks my sleep, O eminent gods, let him be reduced to ashes immediately," he requested. "So be it," said the gods.)[3] The king entered a cave, and lay down for the sleep granted by the gods.
22. "If any fool causes you to wake prematurely once you have fallen asleep, he will be reduced to ashes instantly just by your glance," [said the gods].
23. After the *yavana* had been reduced into ashes, *Bhagavān*, the best of the Sātvatas, revealed himself to the clever Mucukunda.
24. Mucukunda saw him, dark as a cloud, wearing garments of yellow silk. Kṛṣṇa bore the *śrīvatsa* curl on his chest, and was dazzling with the glittering *kaustubha* gem.
25. He had four arms, and looked handsome with a *vaijayantī* garland. He had a kind and charming face, and wore glittering earrings shaped like alligators.
26. He was magnificent and in the prime of life, and he captivated people by his smiling and affectionate looks. His gait was broad like that of the proud lion, king of beasts.
27. Overwhelmed by Kṛṣṇa's radiance, the highly astute king was puzzled. He softly questioned this person, who seemed unapproachable because of his brilliance.
28. *Śrī* Mucukunda said: "Who are you, Sir, who have arrived here in this mountain cave from the forest? You walk on the thorny ground with feet like lotus petals.
29. Among powerful beings, are you perhaps *Bhagavān*, the power of the powerful? Or are you Sūrya, the sun god; Soma,

the moon god; or the great Indra? Or are you rather some other ruler of a planet?

30. I consider you to be supreme among the three gods of gods[4] because you are dispelling the darkness of this cave, like a lamp with its effulgence.

31. If it pleases you, tell us the truth about your birth, deeds and lineage. We are anxious to hear, O best of men.

32. As for ourselves, O tiger among men, we are members of the *kṣatriya* caste stemming from Ikṣvāku.[5] I am known as Mucukunda, the son of Yuvanāśva, O master.

33. I was exhausted from staying awake for a long time, and my senses were overcome with sleep. I lay down in this isolated place to sleep my fill and was just aroused by someone.

34. That same person has just been reduced to ashes by his own sinfulness. Right after that, I noticed you, glorious sir. You are the chastiser of enemies.

35. We are deprived of our potency, and so are not able to look at you for long because of your unbearable radiance. You are worthy of respect from embodied beings, O illustrious one."

36. Addressed in this way by the king, *Bhagavān* Kṛṣṇa, the creator of all creatures, responded with a smile in a voice that was as deep as the rumblings of clouds.

37. *Śrī Bhagavān* said: "Dear Mucukunda! My births, deeds and names number in the thousands. In fact, they cannot be counted even by men because they are unlimited.

38. One might, at some point, count all the particles of dust on the earth over a long span of lifetimes, but nobody can count my qualities, deeds, names and births.

39. The great *ṛṣi* sages who enumerate my births and deeds that take place in the three phases of time – past, present and future – do not come to the end of them, O king.

40. Nevertheless, hear me as I recount those that are taking place now, dear Mucukunda. I was earlier requested by Brahmā to protect *dharma*, and to destroy the demons who are burdening the earth.

41. I have descended in the dynasty of the Yadus, in the house of Ānakadundubhi [Vasudeva]. They call me Vāsudeva, since I am the son of Vasudeva.[6]

42. Kālanemi has been killed, as has Kaṃsa, Pralamba and others who are envious of saintly persons. And this *yavana* has been incinerated by your fierce glance, O king.
43. I am that Vāsudeva. Because I care about my *bhaktas* [devotees], I have entered this cave to show mercy on you since in the past you prayed to me at great length.
44. Choose a favour, O kingly sage. I can bestow whatever you desire. Anybody who has pleased me need never worry again." '
45. *Śrī* Śuka said:

'Mucukunda was filled with joy when he was thus addressed. Remembering the words of Garga,[7] he understood Kṛṣṇa to be Lord Nārāyaṇa. After paying homage to Kṛṣṇa, he spoke.
46. *Śrī* Mucukunda said: "People in the world, men and women, are confused by your *māyā*, O Lord; unaware of their real interest, they do not worship you. For the sake of happiness, they cling to their domestic lives. But these are the sources of unhappiness, and so they are cheated.
47. The human body is perfectly formed and difficult to attain in this world. A person who, somehow or other and without effort, has attained a human body but does not worship your lotus feet, O sinless one, has a deluded mind. Such people have fallen into the blind well of domestic life, like an animal.
48. This period of time has passed by uselessly for me, the king of the earth, O unconquerable one. I thought that my body was my real self. Continually anxious, I was attached to land, treasury, wives and sons; I was proud and obsessed by the increase in my wealth and my kingdom.
49. My mind was led astray by this body – which is similar to a pot or wall[8] – and I did not care about you. Surrounded by chariots, horses, foot-soldiers and generals, I roamed the earth thinking: 'I am a god amongst men.' I was drunk with conceit.
50. You are never deluded. [In the form of death] you unexpectedly seize those who are deluded on account of their excessive anxieties about their obligations. Such people have inordinate greed and hanker after sense-objects. You are like a snake, death personified for the mouse, darting out its tongue in hunger.

51. Travelling around with chariots decorated with gold, and with elephants in rut, I was previously known as a god among men. But this very same body, because of the inescapable force of your time, is [eventually] seen to be faeces, worms and ashes.

52. After conquering the [kingdoms] in every direction, and removing all opposition, a man who is seated on the highest of thrones, and honoured by kings who are his peers, is led around like a pet animal of women at home, the place of sexual pleasure.

53. Thinking: 'In comparison to this, I will become even more mighty – I will become the king of heaven,' such a person performs his duties while being extremely diligent in ascetic practices and renunciation of the pleasures of the senses. But his cravings [simply] become inflamed and he does not attain happiness.

54. Someone wandering [in the cycle of *saṃsāra*] who encounters a holy person, O Acyuta, attains the end of material existence. Such an encounter allows an inclination towards you, the destination of the righteous, to take root. You are the Lord of both the mighty and the lowly.

55. I think that the removal of my attachments to my kingdom is a great favour that has been providentially bestowed on me by you, O Lord. *Sādhus*, who desire to live in the forest in solitude, pray for this, and so do the rulers of vast lands.

56. I do not desire any favour other than the service of your feet, the best object of prayer for those who are destitute, O all-pervading Hari. After worshipping you, the very bestower of liberation, what Ārya would choose a favour that would put his soul in bondage?

57. Therefore, having completely renounced all desires – which are the consequences of the *guṇas* of *sattva*, *tamas* and *rajas* – I submit myself to you. You are the primordial person who is free from the *guṇas*, untainted, non-dual, pure knowledge and supreme.

58. I have been afflicted with miseries for a long time in this world, and am consumed with remorse. My six enemies [the senses] are unsatisfied, and I have not obtained peace by any

means. O supreme soul and giver of shelter, I have approached your lotus feet, which are the abode of fearlessness, truth and freedom from sorrow. Give me shelter, O Lord, for I am in distress."

59. *Śrī Bhagavān* said: "O emperor! Your mind is pure and powerful because although you were enticed with gifts, it was not disturbed by desire, O great king.

60. Know that you were enticed with gifts to [show you] equanimity. The intelligence of the *bhaktas*, whose devotion is unwavering, is never disrupted by desires.

61. The minds of non-devotees who are performing *prāṇāyāma*[9] and such things do not have their subconscious memories erased,[10] O king. One sees that they again become reactivated.

62. Roam the earth at will with your mind absorbed in me. Let it always be for you as you have requested: your devotion for me will remain unwavering.

63. Situated in your *dharma* as a *kṣatriya* [warrior], you killed animals in hunting expeditions, and such things. Taking refuge with me and with full awareness, absolve that sin by austere practices.

64. In your next life, O king, after becoming a distinguished *brāhmaṇa*, the best friend of all living beings, you will certainly attain me alone."'

CHAPTER 52

The Marriage of Rukmiṇī

1. *Śrī* Śuka said:

'Blessed in this way by Kṛṣṇa, Mucukunda, the descendant of Ikṣvāku, circumambulated Kṛṣṇa, bowed to him and stepped from the mouth of the cave.

2. Noticing that humans, animals, plants and trees had become diminished in size, Mucukunda concluded that the *kaliyuga* had arrived, and headed for the northern direction.[1]

3. Endowed with discipline and faith, resolute, devoid of attachments and free from doubts, he fixed his mind on Kṛṣṇa and entered Gandhamādana.[2]
4. Peaceful, and tolerant of all dualities, he approached Badarikāśram,[3] the abode of Nara-Nārāyaṇa, and worshipped Hari by undertaking ascetic practices.
5. *Bhagavān* then returned to the city, which was surrounded by Yavanas. He destroyed the *mleccha* army and carried off their wealth to Dvārakā.
6. While the wealth was being carried off by the men and oxen under the direction of Acyuta, Jarāsandha approached, in command of twenty-three armies.
7. When they saw the powerful force of the enemy's armies, Mādhava and Balarāma behaved like humans, and hastily ran away, O king.
8. Although actually fearless, they behaved like frightened cowards. Abandoning the vast amounts of treasure, they went many *yojanas* away on their lotus-petal feet.
9. When he saw the two fleeing, the powerful king of Magadha laughed and pursued them with his chariots and armies. He was unaware of the nature of the two lords.
10. After they had run a long way, the pair became exhausted and climbed a high mountain called Pravarṣaṇa.[4] *Bhagavān* [Indra] always showers down rain there.
11. Jarāsandha knew that the two were hiding on the mountain, but he could not find out where, O king. So he set fire to the mountain with firewood, producing flames on all sides.
12. Kṛṣṇa and Balarāma leapt from the mountain in haste as its sides were burning, and jumped down on to the ground below. It was eleven *yojanas* high.
13. Unseen by the enemy and his followers, O king, those two best of the Yadus returned to their own city, which had the ocean as its moat, O king.
14. The king of Magadha, however, mistakenly thinking that Balarāma and Keśava had been burnt, withdrew his force and returned to the extremely powerful kingdom of Magadha.
15. Under the directions of Brahmā, Raivata, the prosperous

ruler of Ānarta, bestowed his daughter Revatī to Balarāma. This was mentioned earlier.
16. *Bhagavān* Govinda similarly took Vaidarbhī, the daughter of Bhīṣmaka, as wife in a *svayaṃvara* marriage ceremony.[5] She is an *aṃśa* of Śrī, the goddess of fortune.
17. He vanquished with force kings such as Śālva and others who had gone over to the side of Śiśupāla, king of the Cedis, while everyone was watching, O descendant of the Kuru dynasty, just as the son of Tārkṣya, Garuḍa, snatched the nectar."[6]
18. The king said:

'It has been reported that *Bhagavān* married the beautiful Rukmiṇī, the daughter of Bhīṣmaka, through the *rākṣasa* system of marriage.[7]
19. O *Bhagavān* Sūta, I desire to hear about Kṛṣṇa, of immeasurable prowess. How did he defeat the king of Magadha, Śālva and others and then carry off the maiden?
20. The stories of Kṛṣṇa are sweet and pure, O *brāhmaṇa*, and they remove the impurities of the world. What person familiar with oral knowledge could be satiated by hearing them? They are ever-fresh.'
21. Śukadeva, the son of Bādarāyaṇa, said:

'There was a great king by name of Bhīṣmaka, the ruler of the Vidarbha kingdom. Five sons were born of him, and one beautiful daughter.
22. Rukmī was the first-born, and then Rukmaratha and Rukmabāhu, Rukmakeśa and Rukmamālī. The girl, Rukmiṇī, was the chaste sister.
23. After hearing recitations about the riches, qualities, prowess and beauty of Mukunda by people who came to the house, Rukmiṇī decided that he would be a suitable husband.
24. And Kṛṣṇa had also made up his mind to marry Rukmiṇī. As the embodiment of intelligence, distinctive features, magnanimity, beauty, character and good qualities, she was a suitable bride.
25. At this, Rukmī, an enemy of Kṛṣṇa, forbade his family

members from giving his sister to Kṛṣṇa, O king, although they desired to. He had the king of the Cedis, Śiśupāla, in mind [as a bridegroom].

26. Dark-eyed Vaidarbhī [Rukmiṇī] learnt of this and was greatly troubled in mind. After deliberating, she sent a certain trusted twice-born *brāhmaṇa* to Kṛṣṇa.

27. When he arrived at Dvārakā, the *brāhmaṇa* was admitted by the gatekeepers. Then he saw the primordial being seated on a golden throne.

28. The Lord, who is friendly to *brāhmaṇas*, saw him, rose up from his own seat, and then seated the *brāhmaṇa*. He honoured him just as he himself is honoured by the denizens of heaven.

29. Kṛṣṇa, who is the goal of the righteous, approached the *brāhmaṇa* after he had eaten and rested. Massaging the *brāhmaṇa*'s feet with his hands, Kṛṣṇa inquired from him in a relaxed manner:

30. "O best and most distinguished of *brāhmaṇas*, are your duties, sanctioned by the elders, proceeding without excessive trouble? Are you always satisfied in mind?

31. When a *brāhmaṇa* lives faithful to his own duty and remains satisfied with whatever presents itself, a *kāmadhenu* exists for him.[8]

32. When unsatisfied, even if he is the ruler of the gods, he attains to repeated [birth in other] planets. But if he is satisfied he sleeps with his whole being free from distress, even though he be destitute.

33. I offer homage with my head again and again to the *brāhmaṇas* who are satisfied with their own lot. They are *sādhus*, peaceful and free from ego, the best friends of living creatures.

34. Are you well? The king in whose domain the citizens are protected and live happily is dear to me, O *brāhmaṇa*.

35. From whence have you come, after traversing difficult terrain, and with what intent? Tell us everything, if it is not a secret. What service can we perform for you?"

36. When these questions had been put to him by the supreme Lord who assumes bodies in his *līlās*, the *brāhmaṇa* recounted everything to him.

37. *Śrī* Rukmiṇī said: "I have heard of your qualities, O beauty

of the world. Entering the ears of listeners, they remove bodily distress. Your form is the fulfilment of all the desires of the eyes of onlookers. My bashful heart has settled on you, Acyuta!

38. What sensible lady of noble descent would not choose you as a husband at the appropriate time, Mukunda? You alone are your equal in descent, character, beauty, knowledge, vigour, wealth and majesty. You are a lion among men, and a delight to the minds of humankind.

39. Therefore, I have clearly chosen you as husband, dear Kṛṣṇa, and I have hereby surrendered myself to you as wife. Make this happen quickly, my Lord; the king of the Cedis should not touch that which has been set aside for the hero, just like a jackal should not touch the offering for the lion, king of beasts, O lotus-eyed one.

40. If *Bhagavān* the supreme Lord has been sufficiently won over by my meritorious deeds – sacrifices; charity; religious observances; vows; and worship of the *guru*, *brāhmaṇas* and cows – then Kṛṣṇa, the elder brother of Gada, should come and take my hand, not the likes of Śiśupāla, the son of Damaghoṣa.

41. Tomorrow, when the marriage is about to take place, come disguised to Vidarbha surrounded by the leaders of your army, O unconquerable one. After crushing the armies of Magadha and Cedi by force, marry me according to the *rākṣasa* system[9] as the prize for your prowess.

42. You may be thinking: 'How do I carry her away as she goes about inside the women's chambers, without killing her relatives?' I will describe the plan. On the day before [the marriage], there will be a great procession to the household deity. During this, the new bride goes outside and approaches the goddess Girijā.[10]

43. Great souls like Śiva, the husband of Umā, aspire to bathe in the dust of your lotus feet in order to eradicate *tamas* from themselves. If I do not gain your favour, O lotus-eyed one, I shall give up my vital airs, after they have become weakened through the performance of vows. Perhaps [the gaining of your favour] will happen after hundreds of lifetimes."

44. The *brāhmaṇa* said: "These secret messages have been

hereby conveyed by me, O Lord of the Yadus. Reflect on what is to be done in this matter and then let it be done forthwith."'

CHAPTER 53

The Abduction of Rukmiṇī

1. *Śrī* Śuka said:

'Kṛṣṇa, the descendant of Yadu, heard the message of Vaidarbhī [Rukmiṇī], took the *brāhmaṇa*'s hand in his hand, and spoke with a smile as follows:

2. *Śrī Bhagavān* said: "I likewise also have my mind on Rukmiṇī and cannot get to sleep at night. I know that our marriage has been forbidden by Rukmī out of hatred.

3. Rukmiṇī has a perfect body. She is dedicated to me, so I will take her away after destroying the outcaste[1] kings in battle, just like a flame of fire is taken from kindling wood."'

4. *Śrī* Śuka said:

'When Madhusūdana [Kṛṣṇa] had ascertained the favourable astrological constellation for Rukmiṇī's marriage, he told his charioteer, Dāruka, that the chariot should be prepared immediately.

5. Dāruka brought the chariot, yoked with the horses Śaibya, Sugrīva, Meghapuṣpa and Balāhaka, and stood in front with folded hands.

6. Śauri [Kṛṣṇa] mounted his chariot and had the twice-born *brāhmaṇa* climb in. With his swiftly moving horses, Kṛṣṇa arrived in Vidharbha from Ānarta in a single night.

7. The king, ruler of Kuṇḍina, the capital of Vidharbha, had come under the sway of his love for his son. He was about to give his daughter to Śiśupāla, and had made arrangements for the ceremonies.

8. The city had its crossroads, thoroughfares and roads cleansed and sprinkled with water. It was decorated with various flags and banners and with ornamental arches.

9. It contained houses fragrant with incense, and men and women clothed in immaculate garments and adorned with ornaments, garlands, perfumes and necklaces.
10. The king worshipped the forefathers, the gods and the twice-born, and had them fed according to the proper regulations, O king. Then he had propitious *mantras* chanted.
11. The maiden, who had beautiful teeth, had been fully bathed and had undergone the auspicious ceremony of the marriage thread. She was decorated with ornaments of the best quality, and with two unworn cloths.
12. The best of the twice-born *brāhmaṇas* performed rites of protection for the bride with *mantras* from the Sāma, Ṛg and Yajur Vedas. The *purohita*,[2] who was a specialist in the Atharvaveda, offered oblations to appease the planets.
13. The king was without peer among experts in the customary rites, and bestowed cows, gold, silver, garments and sesame seeds mixed with molasses on the twice-born.
14. In the same way, king Damaghoṣa, ruler of the Cedis, had everything customary performed for the good fortune of his son, Śiśupāla, by those expert in *mantras*.
15. Surrounded by armies replete with infantry and horses, chariots [decorated] with golden garlands, and columns of musk-secreting elephants, Kṛṣṇa went to Kuṇḍina.
16. The ruler of Vidarbha went out to meet him, honoured him and joyfully accommodated him in a place that had been specially prepared.
17. Thousands of the king of the Cedis' allies such as Śālva, Jarāsandha, Dantavakra, Vidūratha and Pauṇḍraka went there.
18–19. The enemies of Kṛṣṇa and Balarāma were ready to protect the maiden for the king of the Cedis. They thought: "If Kṛṣṇa, surrounded by Balarāma and others, comes and should seize [the bride] we will unite to fight him." The kings, lords of the earth, all arrived in resolute mood, and with their entire forces and vehicles.
20. *Bhagavān* Balarāma was fearful of confrontation: he had heard both of this resolve of the opposing kings, and that Kṛṣṇa had gone alone to capture the maiden.
21. Full of love for his brother, he hastily set out for Kuṇḍina

accompanied by a mighty army – infantry, chariots, horses and elephants.

22. Bhīsmaka's daughter, Rukmiṇī, who had an exquisite waist, was longing for the arrival of Hari. When she did not see the *brāhmaṇa* return, she thought:

23. "*Aho!* My marriage will take place after the three *yāmas*, or watches[3] of the night. I am unfortunate. The lotus-eyed one does not come and I don't know why; even the *brāhmaṇa* who was bearing my message does not return.

24. After making his preparations, that spotless soul Kṛṣṇa has surely seen something obnoxious in me and no longer comes to take my hand.

25. Woe is me; the creator of Brahmā is not favourably disposed towards me, nor is Maheśvara [Śiva]. Or is it Devī, that chaste, fair, mountain-born wife of Rudra [Śiva], who is averse to me?"

26. With these thoughts, the girl, whose mind had been stolen by Govinda, closed her eyes, which were full of tears. But she knew when the appropriate time would be.[4]

27. As she was waiting in this way for the arrival of Govinda, O king, the left thigh, arm and eye of the bride trembled, the sign of a desirable event.

28. The distinguished *brāhmaṇa*, instructed by Kṛṣṇa, went to visit that worthy princess as she was going about in the women's chambers.

29. The chaste woman observed his delighted face and his relaxed body and gait. Skilled in interpreting signs, she questioned him with an innocent smile.

30. He informed her that Kṛṣṇa, the son of the Yadus, had arrived, and relayed to her Kṛṣṇa's promise concerning his offer of himself.

31. When she understood that Kṛṣṇa had arrived, Vaidarbhī was delighted. Not finding anything appropriate [to give] to the *brāhmaṇa*, she offered reverence.

32. Hearing that Balarāma and Kṛṣṇa had arrived eager to see the wedding of his daughter, [the king] went towards them to the sound of musical instruments and with gifts of respect.

33. He presented them with the *madhuparka* [welcome drink],

spotless garments and desirable gifts, and he honoured them according to the prescribed rites.

34. The noble-minded king prepared pleasant accommodation for Kṛṣṇa, Balarāma and their soldiers and companions, and afforded them appropriate hospitality.

35. According to the prowess, seniority, strength and wealth of the assembled kings, he showed them honour with all manner of desirable things.

36. When the citizens of Vidarbha heard that Kṛṣṇa had arrived they came and drank up his lotus face with their eyes [just as one drinks water] with cupped hands:

37. "Rukmiṇī and no one else ought to be the wife for Kṛṣṇa," they said, "and, likewise, that sublime one is a suitable husband for the daughter of Bhīṣmaka.

38. May the creator of the three worlds be pleased with whatever good deeds we have performed and, satisfied with them, may [he arrange that] Acyuta take the hand of Vaidarbhī [Rukmiṇī]."

39. The citizens spoke in this way, bound by ties of love. Meanwhile, the maiden, protected by soldiers, set out from the women's chambers to the temple of goddess Ambikā.

40. Meditating intently on the lotus feet of Mukunda, she set out to see the blossom-like feet of the goddess Bhavāni [Ambikā].[5]

41. Keeping silent, she was accompanied by her mothers, surrounded by friends, and protected by the valiant royal guards, who were fully armed with weapons at the ready. *Mṛdaṅga* drums, conch shells, drums, musical instruments and kettledrums began to sound.

42–43. Thousands of courtesans were there, with various gifts and offerings, and the wives of the *brāhmaṇas*, resplendent with garlands, perfumes, garments and ornaments, were singing. There were singers and musicians, and bards, minstrels and heralds surrounding the bride and singing her praises.

44. After reaching the temple of the goddess, Rukmiṇī sipped ablution water. At peace and purified, her lotus hands and feet cleansed, she then entered into the presence of the goddess Ambikā.

45. The elderly *brāhmaṇa* wives, who were familiar with the

rites, had the girl offer respects to Bhavānī, who was in the company of Bhava [Śiva], her husband:

46. "I offer homage to you repeatedly, O Ambikā, wife of Śiva, along with your offspring. May *Bhagavān* Kṛṣṇa be my husband; let this [wish] be granted."

47. Rukmiṇī paid homage with water, perfume, unbroken grain, incense, garments, garlands, wreaths and ornaments, with various gifts and offerings, and with rows of lamps, one by one.

48. Then she paid respects to the married wives of the *brāhmaṇas*, with the same articles, and with salty cakes, betel nut, fruit and sugar cane as well as with embraces.

49. The women gave her the remnants [of the offerings][6] and bestowed blessings upon her. The bride offered homage to them and to the goddess, and accepted the remnants.

50. Giving up her vow of silence, Rukmiṇī stepped out of the temple of Ambikā, and took hold of a maidservant with her hand, ornamented with a jewelled signet ring.

51. Rukmiṇī was like Devamāyā, the illusory power of Viṣṇu which bewilders even the sober-minded. She had a beautiful waist, and her face was set off with earrings. Her complexion was dark [*śyāma*],[7] and a jewelled girdle was placed on her hips. She had budding breasts, and her eyes looked timid through her locks of hair.

52. Her smile was innocent, and the jasmine buds of her teeth were reddened by the splendour of the *bimba*-fruits of her lips.[8] Her feet adorned with glittering, well-made and jingling anklets, she walked with the gait of a swan.

53. The assembly of celebrated heroes became captivated at the sight of Rukmiṇī, and were tormented by the lust she aroused in them. Those lords of men, bewitched by her bashful glances and broad smiles, dropped their weapons upon seeing her.

54. From their seats on their horses, chariots and elephants, they fell to the ground in a daze. Under pretext of being in the procession, Rukmiṇī was offering her beauty to Hari. Thus, she was moving her two lotus-bud [feet] slowly forward, while waiting for the arrival of *Bhagavān* Kṛṣṇa.

55. Then, pushing aside her hair with the nails of her left hand, she glanced shyly at the assembled kings from the corner of her

eyes, and saw Acyuta. With his enemies looking on, Kṛṣṇa seized the princess, whose desire it was to mount his chariot.

56. Lifting her up on to the chariot, with its conspicuous insignia of Garuḍa, Mādhava defeated the multitude of kings. Then, he departed slowly, with Balarāma leading the way, like a lion removing its share from the midst of jackals.

57. The proud men on the other side, led by Jarāsandha, could not bear their humiliation and the loss of their reputation: "*Aho!* Shame on us! Although we have bows in hand, our honour has been snatched away by cowherds, like the honour of lions by deer!"'

CHAPTER 54

The Festivities at the Marriage of Rukmiṇī

1. *Śrī* Śuka said:

'Saying this, armed and very angry, they all mounted their conveyances with bows in hand and set off in pursuit, surrounded by their armies.

2. The leaders of the Yādava army saw them rushing forward, O king, and stood facing them, making a twanging sound with their bows.

3. From horseback, from the shoulders of elephants and from the seats of chariots, the experts in weaponry released torrents of arrows, like clouds releasing water on mountains.

4. The beautiful-waisted Rukmiṇī saw the army of her lord hidden by showers of arrows. With eyes full of fear, she looked bashfully at Kṛṣṇa's face.

5. *Bhagavān* Kṛṣṇa laughed and said: "Do not fear, beautiful-eyed one. This force on your side will soon destroy the enemy force."

6. Gada and Saṅkarṣaṇa among the heroes, unable to tolerate the kings' display of prowess, attacked their chariots, elephants and horses with iron arrows.

7. The heads of those on the chariots, horses and elephants, bearing helmets, earrings and turbans, fell to the ground by the millions.
8. Hands holding swords, clubs and bows; elephant trunks; thighs; feet; and the heads of men, donkeys, camels, elephants, mules and horses also fell.
9. The kings, with Jarāsandha at their head, withdrew dejectedly as their armies were being slaughtered by the Vṛṣṇis in their eagerness for victory.
10. They approached Śiśupāla, who was as distressed as if it had been his wife who had been seized. His lustre had been tarnished, his enthusiasm lost, and his face had dried up. They said:
11. "*Bho! Bho!* O tiger among men! Do not be despondent. Pleasant and unpleasant things are never lasting for embodied beings, O king.
12. As a wooden doll dances according to the whim of the puppeteer, so one acts in happiness and distress under the control of the Lord.
13. I [Jarāsandha] was defeated by Kṛṣṇa, the descendant of Śura, seventeen times with my twenty-three armies; I was only victorious once – the last time.
14. Nevertheless, knowing that the world is driven by time in conjunction with fate, I never lament or rejoice.
15. All of us – we leaders of leaders of heroes – have just been defeated by the Yadus under the protection of Kṛṣṇa, with their puny army.
16. With time favourable to them, our enemies are now victorious. When the time is right [for us] we will be victorious."'
17. *Śrī* Śuka said:

'Thus enlightened by his friends, Śiśupāla from Cedi returned to his city with his followers, and the kings who had survived in the midst of the dead also went back to their respective cities.
18. But Rukmī, who hated Kṛṣṇa, could not tolerate this *rākṣasa*-style marriage of his sister. Surrounded by a powerful *akṣauhiṇī* battalion he pursued Kṛṣṇa.
19. The mighty-armed Rukmī, wearing his armour and bearing

his bow, was both impetuous and furious. While all the kings were listening, he vowed:
20. "I will not enter Kuṇḍina without having killed Kṛṣṇa in battle and recovered Rukmiṇī. This is the truth that I declare to you."
21. Uttering these words, he mounted his chariot and told his charioteer: "Urge the horses on with haste to where Kṛṣṇa is – let a confrontation between us take place at once.
22. With my sharpened arrows, I will today remove the arrogance of power from that evil-minded cowherd Gopāla [Kṛṣṇa] who abducted my sister by force."
23. The boasting fool did not know the measure of the Lord; with a single chariot he challenged Govinda: "Stop! Stop!"
24. Drawing his bow with great power, he struck Kṛṣṇa with three arrows and said: "Stop here for a moment, defiler of the Yadu dynasty.
25. Today, I will bring down your pride, fool, wherever you may go after stealing my sister like a crow steals the oblation. You are a trickster and a pretence of a warrior.
26. Release the girl while you can before I strike you with my arrows and lay you low!" Kṛṣṇa, smiling, pierced Rukmī with six arrows and sliced his bow in half.
27. He struck the four horses with eight arrows, the charioteer with two, and the flag with three. Rukmī took up another bow and pierced Kṛṣṇa with five arrows.
28. Struck by the torrents of arrows, Acyuta split Rukmī's bow apart. Rukmī picked up another bow, but the invincible Kṛṣṇa split that as well.
29. Whatever weapons Rukmī picked up – iron club, spear, pike, sword and shield, lance and javelin – Hari sliced them all apart.
30. Furious, Rukmī leapt down from his chariot, sword in hand, determined to kill Kṛṣṇa, and rushed towards him, like a moth into a fire.
31. As Rukmī bore down upon him, Kṛṣṇa cut his sword and shield into pieces as small as sesame seeds with his arrows, and then took up his sharp sword, intent on killing him.
32. Seeing him attempt to kill her brother, the chaste Rukmiṇī,

stricken by fear, fell at the feet of her lord and spoke piteously:
33. "O Lord of *yoga*, immeasurable soul, God of gods, Lord of the worlds! You should not kill my brother, O noble mighty-armed one."'
34. *Śrī* Śuka said:

'As Rukmiṇī caught hold of his feet, the merciful Kṛṣṇa desisted. Her golden necklace had fallen loose in her agitation, her limbs were trembling from fear, her throat was choked, and her face was dry with grief.
35. After binding the evil-doer with a garment, Kṛṣṇa disfigured him by shaving his hair and beard. Meanwhile, the Yadu heroes had crushed the formidable opposing army as an elephant crushes a lotus.
36. Approaching Kṛṣṇa, they saw Rukmī there. The merciful and mighty *Bhagavān* Saṅkarṣaṇa saw him in that condition, almost dead. He loosened Rukmī's bonds and said to Kṛṣṇa:
37. "This unrighteous deed that you have done, Kṛṣṇa – the shaving of the hair and beard – is shameful for us. The disfigurement of an ally is [as good as] killing him.
38. Do not be displeased with us out of sorrow for the disfigurement of your brother, righteous Rukmiṇī, because people reap the rewards of their own deeds; no one else is the source of happiness and distress.
39. An offence by a relative which deserves death should not incur death. By being shunned, he had already been killed simply by his own offence alone. Why should he be killed again?
40. This *dharma* of the *kṣatriyas*, by which a brother should kill even his own brother, has been established by *prajāpati* Brahmā.[1] It is therefore a very demanding *dharma*.
41. Blinded by the arrogance of opulence caused by kingdom, land, wealth, women, honour, power or some other cause, the arrogant commit offences.
42. Your tendency always to wish ill to those who are inimical towards all living beings, and well towards those who are benevolent, is both wrong and ignorant.
43. The illusion of the souls of men who think the body is the

self is produced by the Lord's *māyā*. They think in terms of 'friends', 'enemies' or 'neutral parties'.

44. There is really only one supreme soul of all embodied beings. It is perceived as diverse by the ignorant, just like light or the sky.

45. This body has a beginning and an end. It is composed of material elements, vital airs and the *guṇas*. It is imposed on the soul as a result of ignorance, and causes the embodied being to wander in *saṃsāra*.

46. The soul is neither united with nor separate from anything that is unreal, chaste lady, because the soul is the cause of those things and reveals them, just like the sun [is neither united with nor separate from] the faculty of sight and the objects of forms.[2]

47. The transformations of the body, such as birth, are not those of the soul, just as, among the phases of the moon, the day of the new moon is obviously not the death of the moon.

48. Just as in sleep one experiences oneself, the objects of the senses, and the consequences of actions, although they are unreal [dream] objects, so one who is ignorant undergoes the cycle of birth and death.

49. Therefore, with the knowledge of reality, shake off this sorrow born of ignorance which bewilders and withers you, O lady with the pure smile, and regain your composure."'

50. *Śrī* Śuka said:

'Enlightened thus by *Bhagavān* Balarāma, the slender lady abandoned her despair and calmed her mind with reason.

51. Rukmī was released with only his vital airs intact. His power and strength had been destroyed by his enemies, and his desires thwarted. Brooding on the cause of his disfigurement, he constructed a mighty city called Bhojakaṭa for his residence.

52. Because he had previously stated, "I will not enter Kuṇḍina without having killed Kṛṣṇa and retrieved my younger sister," that evil-minded man lived there in bitterness.

53. After defeating the kings, *Bhagavān* Kṛṣṇa brought the daughter of Bhīṣmaka to his city, and married her according to the appropriate rites, O best of the Kurus.

54. At this, there were great festivities among the people in every

household in the city of the Yadus. Their love for Kṛṣṇa, the Lord of the Yadus, was absolute.

55. The joyful men and women, wearing earrings of polished jewels, presented wedding gifts to the bride and groom, who were decked in brightly coloured clothes.

56. The city of the Vṛṣṇi clan was splendid with upraised banners of Indra, and various arches, jewels, cloth and garlands. There were lamps, *aguru* incense, brimming pitchers and items of good omen displayed at every doorway.

57. The thoroughfares were sprinkled with water, and the city was decorated with plantains and betel-nut trees in the doorways. These had been seized by the elephants in rut belonging to the privileged kings who had been invited.

58. The Kuru, Sṛñjaya, Kaikeya, Vidharbha, Yadu and Kuntī clans enjoyed each other's company amidst the flurry of people running about on that occasion.

59. The kings and the daughters of the kings were astonished at the account of the abduction of Rukmiṇī, which was being talked about everywhere.

60. There was great joy among the citizens in Dvārakā, O king, when they saw Kṛṣṇa, the husband of Śrī, the goddess of fortune, united with Rukmiṇī who is [none other than] Ramā [Śrī, the goddess of fortune].'[3]

CHAPTER 55

Reflections on the Birth of Pradyumna

1. *Śrī* Śuka said:

'Now, Kāma, an *aṃśa* of Vāsudeva [Kṛṣṇa], submitted himself to Kṛṣṇa in order to attain a body again. He had formerly been burnt by the anger of Rudra [Śiva].[1]

2. He was born of Vaidarbhī [Rukmiṇī] and was known as Pradyumna. Conceived from the potency of Kṛṣṇa, he was in no way inferior to his father.

3. Śambara, who could change his form at will, snatched the infant during the ten-day period after childbirth. Knowing that the child would be his enemy,[2] he cast him into the ocean, and went home.
4. A mighty fish swallowed Pradyumna. He was entangled in a large net along with other fish, and caught by fishermen.
5. The fishermen presented the unusual fish to Śambara as a gift. His cooks brought it to the kitchen, and cut it into pieces with a knife.
6. After seeing the boy in the stomach, the cooks delivered him to Māyāvatī. She was alarmed, but Nārada told her all about the boy – his birth and how he got into the fish.
7. Māyāvatī was in fact the well-known wife of Kāma, whose name was Ratī. She was waiting for the creation of a [new] body for her husband, whose [previous] body had been burnt.
8. She had been assigned the preparation of cooked grain dishes by Śambara. When she understood that the infant was the god Kāma, she became fond of the child.
9. After a short time, that child of Kṛṣṇa became a developed youth who caused bewilderment in women who looked at him.
10. Casting glances, with raised eyebrows and bashful laughter, Ratī lovingly approached her husband, intent on love. His eyes were wide like lotus petals, his arms were long, and he was gorgeous in the world of men, dear Parīkṣit.
11. *Bhagavān*, the offspring of Kṛṣṇa, said to her: "Mother! Your mood is inappropriate. You have transgressed the love of a mother, and are acting as if you were my lover."
12. Ratī said: "You are the son of Nārāyaṇa. You were taken from the house by Śambara. You are Kāma, O master, and I am your lawful wife Ratī.
13. Śambara is a demon who threw you into the ocean before you were ten days old. A fish swallowed you and you ended up here from its stomach, O master.
14. Slay your enemy with the confusing magic of *māyā*. He is dreadful, invincible, and expert in hundreds of tricks.
15. Your mother is wailing for you like an osprey whose offspring have left. Full of love for her child, the poor woman is like an afflicted cow without her calf."

16. Ratī was an expert in *māyā* magic. After this speech, she gave to the great-souled Pradyumna knowledge of powerful *māyā* magic that could wipe out all other types of magic.
17. Pradyumna approached Śambara and, provoking a quarrel by hurling intolerable insults at him, challenged him to battle.
18. Stung by those vile words, Śambara emerged like a snake that had been trodden on. His eyes were red with anger, and he bore a club in his hand.
19. Brandishing his club vigorously, he hurled it at the great soul Pradyumna while bellowing with a roar as terrible as a crashing thunderbolt.
20. With his club *Bhagavān* Pradyumna warded off the club which was hurtling towards him. Infuriated, he then threw his own club at his enemy, O king.
21. Śambara resorted to the demoniac *māyā* magic which had been revealed to him by the demon Maya. Hovering in the sky, the demon let loose a torrent of weapons upon the son of Kṛṣṇa.
22. The son of Rukmiṇī was a great warrior. Harassed by this rain of weapons, he [made use of] a powerful science, *sāttvic* in nature, which could annul all *māyā* magic.
23. At this, the demon employed hundreds of [magic spells] used by the celestial *guhyakas*, *gandharvas*, *piśācas*, divine serpents and *rākṣasas*. But the son of Kṛṣṇa deflected them all.
24. Raising a sharp sword, Pradyumna decapitated Śambara with force – separating his head, with its helmet, earrings and red beard, from his body.
25. Showered with streams of flowers by the celestial beings who were praising him, Pradyumna was brought to the city [of Dvārakā] through the sky by his wife, who could travel through the air.
26. With his wife he entered the magnificent inner quarters from the sky, O king, like a cloud with lightning. The quarters were filled with hundreds of women.
27–28. The women saw him, dark as a rain cloud, and wearing yellow silken garments. His arms were long, his eyes reddish, and he was smiling charmingly. His lotus face was graced with layers of curly blue locks, and his countenance was captivating.

Thinking him to be Kṛṣṇa, the women became bashful and hid themselves here and there.
29. Eventually, because of slight differences in characteristics, the women gradually came to realize [their mistake] and approached Pradyumna, who was accompanied by Ratī, that jewel among women, in amazement and delight.
30. Then, because of this situation, sweet-spoken and dark-eyed Vaidarbhī [Rukmiṇī] remembered her own lost son, and her breasts became moist from affection:
31. "Who is this jewel of a man, really? Whose son is this lotus-eyed one? In whose womb was he carried? And who is this woman whom he has accepted [as his wife]?
32. Although my own son was snatched away from the delivery chamber and has perished, he would have been similar to this man in age and appearance, were he alive somewhere.
33. How is it that there is in this man such similarity to Kṛṣṇa, the bearer of the Śārṅga bow, in appearance, bodily limbs and in gait, as well as in tone of voice, smile and glance?
34. He might perhaps even be the child whom I bore in my womb. [I feel] great affection for him, and my left arm is twitching."[3]
35. While Vaidarbhī was entertaining these thoughts, Uttamaśloka [Kṛṣṇa], the son of Devakī, appeared, accompanied by Devakī and Ānakadundubhi [Vasudeva].
36. Although aware of the situation, *Bhagavān* Janārdana remained silent. Nārada recounted everything about the kidnapping by Śambara, and the rest of the story.
37. After hearing that amazing [account], the women in Kṛṣṇa's inner chambers welcomed Pradyumna with joy. He had been lost for many years, but had returned as if from the dead.
38. Devakī, Vasudeva, Kṛṣṇa, Balarāma, the women and Rukmiṇī were ecstatic, and embraced the man and his wife.
39. After hearing that Pradyumna, who had been lost, had returned, the residents of Dvārakā said: "*Aho!* The boy was as good as dead but by good fortune has come back!"
40. It is not surprising that his mothers thought of him as their own husband, since they were unwavering in their devotion to Kṛṣṇa, and Pradyumna had a strong resemblance to his father. Indeed, their love was secretly kindled by Pradyumna, the very

image of Kṛṣṇa, the abode of Ramā, the goddess of fortune. What can then be said about how other women [reacted when they saw him]? It was, after all, Kāma, love personified, who was visible to their eyes!'

CHAPTER 56

The Story of the Syamantaka Jewel

1. *Śrī* Śuka said:

'Satrājit had committed an offence, and so presented his daughter along with the Syamantaka jewel[1] to Kṛṣṇa of his own accord, and gave them [to him].'

2. The king said:

'What offence did Satrājit commit against Kṛṣṇa, O *brāhmaṇa*? Where did his Syamantaka jewel come from? And why was his daughter given to Hari?'

3. *Śrī* Śuka said:

'Satrājit had Sūrya, the sun god [as his deity], and Sūrya was the close friend of his devotee. Being loving and content, Sūrya presented Satrājit with the Syamantaka jewel.
4. Wearing the jewel around his neck, Satrājit entered Dvārakā, shining like the sun. It was impossible to look at him because of the brightness, O king.
5. People saw him from a distance, their eyes dazzled by the light. Assuming him to be Sūrya, they announced his arrival to *Bhagavān* Kṛṣṇa, who was playing with dice:
6. "O Nārāyaṇa! O bearer of the conch, disc and club! O Dāmodara! O lotus-eyed one! O Govinda! O descendant of Yadu! Homage to you!
7. It is Savitā, the sun god, who comes to see you, O Lord of the universe. His rays are fiery, and he dazzles the eyes with the sphere of his rays.

8. It seems that the most eminent gods in the three worlds have realized that you are now hidden among the Yadus, and are tracking you down – the unborn [sun god] is coming to see you, O master!" '

9. *Śrī* Śuka said:

'When he heard these childish words, the lotus-eyed Kṛṣṇa smiled and said: "This person is not the sun god! He is Satrājit, and he shines because of the jewel!"

10. Satrājit entered his own opulent house, where propitious rites had been performed. He had the jewel installed by *brāhmaṇas* in a shrine.

11. It produced eight *bhāras*[2] of gold every day, O master. Wherever the jewel is worshipped, inauspicious things – want, death, calamities, snakes, anxiety, disease and cheats – are not found.

12. Satrājit was once asked by Kṛṣṇa, the descendant of Śūra, for the jewel [in order to give it] to Ugrasena, the king of the Yadus. But, addicted to his wealth, Satrājit did not give it, nor did he reflect upon what his refusal might mean.

13. On one occasion, Prasena [his brother] fastened that brightest of jewels on his neck, mounted his horse, and roamed about in the forest for hunting.

14. A lion killed both Prasena and his horse, and tore off the jewel. Entering a mountain [cave], the lion was killed in turn by the bear, Jāmbavān, who wanted the jewel.

15. Jāmbavān then made the jewel into a plaything for his young daughter in the cave. Satrājit was tormented when he failed to find his brother:

16. "My brother was wearing the jewel on his neck, so he was probably killed by Kṛṣṇa," he said. When the people heard this, it went by whispers from ear to ear.

17. On hearing this, *Bhagavān*, accompanied by the citizens, retraced the path taken by Prasena in order to clear the libellous smear that had been made against him.

18. The people found Prasena and the horse that had been killed by the lion in the forest. Then, on the side of the mountain, they found the lion that had been killed by the bear.

19. *Bhagavān* stationed the people outside and entered the pitch blackness of the terrifying cave of the king of bears alone.
20. There he saw the coveted jewel, made into a child's toy. He stood there in the presence of the child intending to take it away.
21. Seeing the unfamiliar man, the nurse cried out as if frightened. Hearing that, Jāmbavān, the strongest of the strong, ran forwards angrily.
22. He fought with *Bhagavān* Kṛṣṇa, his own master.[3] Jāmbavān was enraged and unaware of Kṛṣṇa's power, thinking him to be an ordinary being.
23. The duel between the two of them, with weapons, rocks, trees and arms, was fierce, with both striving for victory, like two hawks over a piece of carrion.
24. Using blows of the fist as hard as the striking of thunderbolts, the contest between them continued without respite, day and night for twenty-eight days.
26. Jāmbavān's huge muscles and limbs were pounded by the blows from Kṛṣṇa's fists. With his strength ebbing and his limbs sweating, Jāmbavān was utterly confounded. He said to Kṛṣṇa:
26. "I realize that you are Viṣṇu, the primordial being, the overlord and supreme controller. You are the vital air, the energy, the strength and the force of all living beings.
27. You are the creator of the creators of the universe, and also the essence of created things. You are time, the controller of those who set things in motion, and you are also the supreme soul of all souls.
28. Because you cast your glance, which manifested a touch of anger, the ocean, its *timiṅgila* fish and crocodiles disturbed, showed you a way [to cross]. A bridge to mark your fame was built, the city of Laṅkā was set ablaze, and the heads of the demons, severed by your arrows, fell to the ground."[4]
29–30. The lotus-eyed Kṛṣṇa touched his devotee with his hand, which grants good fortune. Then *Bhagavān* Acyuta, the son of Devakī, in a voice full of mercy and as deep as the clouds, O great king, spoke to the king of bears, who had come to realize the truth.
31. "We have come here to the cave on account of the jewel, O

lord of bears. With this jewel, we can remove an accusation falsely made against me."

32. Thus appealed to, the bear happily offered Kṛṣṇa his own daughter, Jāmbavatī, as a gift of honour, along with the jewel.

33. When the people did not see Kṛṣṇa, the descendant of Śūra, coming out of the cave he had entered, they waited for twelve days, and then dejectedly returned to their city.

34. When Devakī, the divine Rukmiṇī, Ānakadundubhi, friends and relatives heard that Kṛṣṇa had not come out of the cave, they were cast down with sorrow.

35. The unhappy citizens of Dvārakā cursed Satrājit, and approached the goddess Chandrabhāgā, Durgā, for the return of Kṛṣṇa.

36. For their worship the goddess granted a blessing, as a result of which Hari appeared with his wife, smiling. His goals had been fulfilled.

37. Everyone was filled with great joy at regaining Hṛṣīkeśa – he had returned as if from the dead with the jewel on his neck, together with his wife.

38. *Bhagavān* Kṛṣṇa summoned Satrājit to the assembly, in the presence of king Ugrasena. He announced that the jewel had been retrieved, and presented it to him.

39. Deeply ashamed, Satrājit took the gem and went home with his head hanging down, tormented by his offence.

40. Contemplating what he had done, and preoccupied by his quarrel with a powerful person, he thought: "How can I remove this stain from myself, and how can Acyuta be pacified?

41. What course of action should I take so that there will be a favourable result for me and people will not curse me? I am short-sighted, despicable, foolish and greedy for wealth.

42. My daughter is a gem among women; I will give her to Kṛṣṇa, together with the gem itself. This is an appropriate solution – there is no other way to appease him."

43. Reasoning thus, Satrājit personally took his beautiful daughter, along with the jewel, and presented them to Kṛṣṇa.

44. *Bhagavān* Kṛṣṇa married the daughter, Satyabhāmā, according to the proper rites. She was endowed with character, beauty, generosity and good qualities, and many had asked for her hand.

45. *Bhagavān* Kṛṣṇa said: "We do not desire the jewel, O king. You are the devotee of the [sun] god – let it stay with you. We will enjoy its fruits!"'

CHAPTER 57

The Story of the Syamantaka Jewel (Continued)

Śrī Bādarāyaṇi [Śuka] said:

1. 'Although he was aware of the truth, when Govinda heard that the Pāṇḍavas had been burnt,[1] he went with Kuntī and Balarāma to the land of the Kurus to carry out family duties.
2. Kṛṣṇa and Balarāma met with Bhīṣma, Kṛpa and Vidura, Gāndhārī and Droṇa.[2] All equally distressed, they exclaimed: "Alas! How painful! Alas!"
3. Availing themselves of this opportunity, O king, Akrūra and Kṛtavarmā said to Śatadhanvā: "Why shouldn't we seize the gem?
4. Satrājit promised the maiden and the gem to us but, disregarding us, he gave them to Kṛṣṇa. Why shouldn't he suffer [the fate of] his brother?"
5. Thus, Śatadhanvā's mind was corrupted by them, and so the wicked fellow, most evil of evil-doers, murdered Satrājit out of greed while he was sleeping. As a result, Śatadhanvā's life span was cut short.
6. As the women were crying out and wailing like widows, Śatadhanvā took the jewel and left, like a butcher after slaughtering animals.
7. When she saw her murdered father, Satyabhāmā was overcome with grief. She wailed: "Father! O father! Alas! I am deprived of life!" and fainted.
8. She threw the corpse in a vat of oil and went to Hastināpura in distress. She related the story of the murder of her father to Kṛṣṇa, who was already aware of it.
9. Hearing this, the two Lords, imitating the ways of men,

lamented with tears in their eyes: "*Aho!* This is so painful for us!"
10. As a result, *Bhagavān* Kṛṣṇa returned to his city with his wife and elder brother, and prepared to kill Śatadhanvā and retrieve the gem from him.
11. Śatadhanvā heard of these preparations and was terrified. Wanting to save himself, he asked Kṛtavarmā for assistance, and said:
12. "I should not commit an offence against the Lords Balarāma and Kṛṣṇa. Who can succeed in intrigue against them?
13. Kaṃsa was abandoned by the goddess of fortune because of his hatred of them, and he and his followers went [to the next world]. Jarāsandha was left without even a chariot after seventeen battles."
14. When he was turned down, Śatadhanvā sought help from Akrūra, his ally. But Akrūra also said: "What sane person would challenge the strength of the two Lords?
15. Kṛṣṇa creates, maintains and destroys this universe with ease. Bewildered by *māyā*, even the creators of the universes do not understand his activities.
16. When he was a child of seven years, he picked up a mountain and held it effortlessly on one hand, like a boy plucks a mushroom.
17. All homage to him, *Bhagavān* Kṛṣṇa – his deeds are wonderful. Homage to the unlimited one, the original being, the supreme soul."
18. Rejected by Akrūra as well, Śatadhanvā deposited the great jewel with Akrūra, mounted a horse which could travel a hundred *yojanas*, and departed.
19. Balarāma and Janārdana mounted their chariot marked with the flag of Garuḍa, and pursued the murderer of their elder, Satrājit, with very swift horses, O king.
20. In a garden in Mithilā, Śatadhanvā abandoned his horse, which had collapsed, and fled, petrified, on foot. Kṛṣṇa [dismounted] likewise, and chased Śatadhanvā furiously.
21. Proceeding on foot, *Bhagavān* decapitated Śatadhanvā with his sharp-rimmed disc as the latter was escaping. He went through Śatadhanvā's two garments for the jewel.

22. Not finding the gem, Kṛṣṇa went to his elder brother and said: "Śatadhanvā has been killed in vain. The gem is not to be found on him."
23. At this Balarāma said: "The gem has obviously been entrusted to someone. Go to the city and seek it.
24. I desire to see the king of Videha [Janaka] – he is very dear to me." Saying this, O king, Balarāma, the descendant of Yadu, entered the city of Mithilā, capital of Videha.
25. On seeing him, the king of Mithilā immediately rose up, delighted. He honoured the worthy Balarāma with respectful offerings according to custom.
26. The Lord lived in the city of Mithilā for several years, honoured by that great soul, Janaka, who was affectionately disposed towards him. It was during this period, that he taught club-fighting to Duryodhana, the son of Dhṛtarāṣṭra.[3]
27. [Meanwhile], Keśava went to Dvārakā. The Lord, the giver of affection, told his beloved, Satyabhāmā, about the death of Śatadhanvā, and about not finding the gem.
28. After this, *Bhagavān* Kṛṣṇa, along with his friends, arranged for the performance of whatever rites were customary for funerary occasions, for his murdered relative.
29. Akrūra and Kṛtavarmā, the instigators, heard of the death of Śatadhanvā and moved away from Dvārakā, petrified with fear.
30. During Akrūra's absence, there were frequent occurrences of inauspicious omens for the people of Dvārakā. These became manifest as physical and mental afflictions caused by both natural and supernatural beings.
31. Those who had forgotten what had been declared previously, dear king, asked: "How can the appearance of inauspicious omens arise in the dwelling-place of Kṛṣṇa, the abode of the wise?
32. When the god [Indra] did not produce rain, the king of Kāsī gave his daughter to Śvaphalka [Akrūra's father], who had arrived there; it then rained in Kāśī.
33. Akrūra is his son and has the same power. Wherever he is, the god [Indra] will send rains, and afflictions and death do not occur there."

34. When he heard these words of the elders, Janārdana understood that they had not reached the bottom of the matter. But he summoned Akrūra.

35. Everything is known to Kṛṣṇa. He paid respects to Akrūra, and chatted with him, discussing pleasant topics. Then the knower of hearts said to Akrūra, smiling:

36. "The fact is, charitable Akrūra, Śatadhanvā deposited the magnificent Syamantaka jewel with you. This was already known to us.

37. Because Satrājit is without heir, his daughter's sons should receive the balance of the inheritance after they have made the offerings of the water and *piṇḍa* oblations,[4] and honoured Satrājit's debts.

38. Having said this, however, the jewel should remain with you; it is difficult for others to look after. You are someone who keeps promises. However, my elder brother is not completely convinced of [the whereabouts] of the jewel.

39. Your sacrifices these days take place on golden altars all the time, greatly fortunate Akrūra. Show the jewel and bring peace to your relatives."

40. Akrūra, the son of Śvaphalka, was touched by these conciliatory words. He took the jewel, which he had hidden in his garments, and handed it over. Its effulgence equalled that of the sun.

41. After showing the Syamantaka jewel to his relatives and thus removing the stain on himself, the Lord returned it to Akrūra.

42. Whoever reads, hears or remembers this narrative about *Bhagavān* Viṣṇu, the Lord, will drive away infamy and danger and attain peace. It is full of potency and good omen, and purges wickedness.'

CHAPTER 58

The Marriage of Eight Princesses

1. *Śrī* Śuka said:

'Once, the glorious and supreme person went to Indraprastha to see the Pāṇḍavas, who had reappeared[1] accompanied by Yuyudhāna [Sātyaki] and others.
2. Those heroes, the sons of Pṛthā, arose simultaneously when they saw Mukunda, the Lord of everything, approaching, like the five vital airs upon the return of the principal [vital air].
3. The heroes embraced Kṛṣṇa, and their sins were removed by contact with his body. Gazing into his face, which was smiling affectionately, they became ecstatic.
4. After offering homage at the feet of Bhīma and Yudhiṣṭhira, and then embracing Phālgunī [Arjuna],[2] Kṛṣṇa received homage from the twins [Nakula and Sahadeva].
5. The faultless Kṛṣṇā [Draupadī], newly wed and bashful, hesitatingly approached Kṛṣṇa, who was sitting on a magnificent throne, and offered her respects.
6. Sātyaki was honoured and respectfully greeted by the sons of Pṛthā in the same way, and took his seat. When the others had also been honoured, they also sat down.
7. Kṛṣṇa approached Pṛthā [Kuntī], the sister of his father. He greeted her respectfully, and was embraced by her, her eyes moist with deep affection. He asked her about her welfare, and about her daughter-in-law Draupadī, and he in his turn was questioned about his relatives.
8. Kṛṣṇa's appearance removes all difficulties. Remembering those numerous difficulties,[3] Pṛthā spoke to him, with tears in her eyes and her throat choked with the emotion of love:
9. "Our good fortune began only when we came under your protection. My brother [Akrūra] was sent by you, Kṛṣṇa, when you remembered us, your relatives.
10. There is no illusion for you regarding 'that which is mine' and 'that which belongs to others', since you are the soul and

benefactor of the universe. Nevertheless, residing within the heart, you destroy the difficulties of those who always remember [you]."

11. Yudhiṣṭhira said: "O supreme Lord, I do not know what virtuous deed we have performed. You are rarely seen by the masters of *yoga*, yet you are visible to us of limited intelligence."

12. Invited by the king in this way, the Lord [remained there] happily for the rainy months, giving joy to the eyes of the residents of Indraprastha.

13. Once, Vijaya [Arjuna] mounted his chariot marked with the flag of a monkey, and took up his Gāṇḍīva bow[4] and his two quivers with their inexhaustible supply of arrows.

14. Wearing armour and accompanied by Kṛṣṇa, the destroyer of enemy heroes entered a great forest full of beasts of prey, in order to hunt.

15. There, with his arrows, Arjuna shot tigers, boars, buffaloes, *ruru* antelopes, *śarabha* deer,[5] *gavaya* oxen, rhinos, deer, hares and porcupines.

16. The servants carried away those [animals] since they were suitable for offering at the approaching sacrifice for the moon's passing into a new constellation, O king. Then, exhausted and overcome by thirst, Arjuna went to the Yamunā river.

17. After bathing in and drinking that pure water, the two great chariot warriors, Kṛṣṇa and Arjuna, saw a young woman wandering along. She was beautiful to behold.

18. Sent by his friend Kṛṣṇa, Arjuna approached the handsome woman. She had a superb waist, beautiful teeth and a charming face. He inquired from her:

19. "Who are you? From whom were you [born], O woman with perfect hips? What are you intending to do? I think you are in want of a husband. Explain everything, O beauty."

20. *Śrī* Kālindī said: "I am the daughter of the sun god Savitā and desire Viṣṇu as a husband. He is most desirable and is the granter of favours, and so I am performing hard ascetic practices.

21. I will choose no husband other than he who is the dwelling place of Śrī, the goddess of fortune, O hero. May he, *Bhagavān*

Mukunda, the refuge for those who have no protection, be pleased with me.

22. I am known as Kālindī, and until I see Acyuta in a house built by my father, I am living in the waters of the Yamunā."

23. Guḍākeśa [Arjuna] reported all this to Vāsudeva, who already knew it. Kṛṣṇa had the woman ascend the chariot and went to Dharmarāj [Yudhiṣṭhira].

24. Kṛṣṇa, on being requested, had a most spectacular and wonderful city constructed by Viśvakarmā, the architect of the gods, for the Pāṇḍavas.

25. *Bhagavān* resided there out of a desire to please his followers. He became Arjuna's charioteer in order to give the Khāṇḍava forest to Agni, the god of fire.[6]

26. When Agni was satisfied, he gave Arjuna a bow, white horses, a chariot, two quivers of arrows, and armour that could not be pierced by weapons, O king.

27. Saved from the fire, Maya presented an assembly hall to his friend Arjuna. Duryodhana's mistaking of water for land happened in that hall.[7]

28. With the permission of Arjuna, and with the approval of his dear friends, Kṛṣṇa again went back to Dvārakā surrounded by [his associates], headed by Sātyaki.

29. Then, when the season and stars were favourable, Kṛṣṇa married Kālindī. Bestowing supreme bliss on his followers, Kṛṣṇa's auspiciousness is unparalleled.

30. Vindhya and Anuvindhya, the rulers of Avantī, who were followers of Duryodhana and under his control, opposed their sister, who was enamoured of Kṛṣṇa, in her *svayaṃvara* marriage.[8]

31. Kṛṣṇa forcibly carried off Mitravindā, the daughter of Rājādhidevī, his father's sister, while the kings were looking on, O king.

32. There was a very righteous king known as Nagnajit in the kingdom of Kosala. His daughter was a chaste maiden, the princess Nāgnajitī.

33. No king could marry her without subduing seven bulls. They had sharp horns, were vicious and invincible, and could not tolerate the smell of warriors.

34. When *Bhagavān*, the Lord of the Sātvatas, heard about this woman who could be won by defeating bulls, he went to the city of Kosala, surrounded by a large army.
35. The ruler of Kosala was pleased, and honoured Kṛṣṇa by rising and [offering him] a seat, and other such gestures of hospitality, as well as with significant gifts. He was respectfully greeted in turn.
36. The daughter of the king saw that a suitable suitor had arrived and desired him, the husband of the goddess of fortune, Ramā [Śrī]: "If my vows have been upheld let this person be my husband; may the fire make my prayer come true," she said.
37. "Śrī, the goddess of fortune, Brahmā, the lotus-born one, Śiva, Lord of the mountains, along with the rulers of the planets, hold the dust from Kṛṣṇa's lotus feet on their heads. At the appropriate time, he has accepted a body for his *līlā* out of a desire to protect the institution [of *dharma*] previously established by him. How might he, *Bhagavān* Kṛṣṇa, be pleased with me?"
38. When Kṛṣṇa had been honoured again, the king said to him: "What can I, a humble person, do for one who is complete in his own happiness, O Nārāyaṇa, Lord of the Universe?"'
39. *Śrī* Śuka said:

'*Bhagavān* Kṛṣṇa was pleased and accepted the seat that had been prepared. With a smile, he spoke to the king in a voice that was as deep as a cloud, O descendant of the Kurus.
30. *Śrī Bhagavān* said: "The wise have forbidden the soliciting of alms for anyone related to the royal order if they are following their own *dharma*, O king. Nevertheless, I am asking for your daughter out of a desire for your friendship. However, we are not offering any dowry."
41. [The king] replied: "Who in this world could be a more excellent or desirable bridegroom than you, O Master? Śrī, the goddess of fortune, dwells on your body, which is the unique reservoir of qualities, and she never leaves.
42. However, we initially established a condition to test the prowess of the men, O bull of the Sātvatas. This was out of a desire to obtain the best suitor for my daughter.

43. These seven bulls, O hero, are almost impossible to tame or control. A great number of princes have been mangled by them, and their limbs have been broken.

44. If you can subdue these, O descendant of Yadu and Lord of Śrī, your Lordship will be the longed-for groom for my daughter."

45. When he heard this condition, the Lord tightened his belt, divided himself into seven forms, and restrained the bulls with ease.

46. He tied them up with ropes and pulled them effortlessly, like a child pulls a wooden toy. Once bound, the bulls' pride was crushed and their vigour destroyed.

47. The king was delighted at this, and presented his daughter to Kṛṣṇa, smiling. *Bhagavān* Kṛṣṇa, the Lord, accepted her as his wife according to the proper rites.

48. The king's wives were ecstatic at receiving beloved Kṛṣṇa as the husband of their daughter, and great celebrations broke out.

49. Conches, drums and kettledrums resounded, along with musical instruments, songs, and the blessings of the twice-born. Both men and women were overjoyed, and they dressed themselves up with beautiful garments and garlands.

50. As a wedding gift, the powerful king gave 10,000 cows and 3,000 beautifully clothed maidens with golden ornaments on their necks.

51. He gave 9,000 elephants, a hundred times as many chariots as elephants, a hundred times as many horses as chariots, and a hundred times as many men as horses.

52. After having the husband and wife mount a chariot surrounded by a great army, the king of Kosala saw to their departure, his heart moved with affection.

53. When they heard this, the [other] kings became very frustrated. Although their strength had previously been crushed by the Yadus, as well as by the bulls, they harried Kṛṣṇa on the road as he was carrying away the maiden.

54. Arjuna, wielder of the Gāṇḍiva bow, supporter of his friend, drove them off as they were discharging volleys of arrows, like a lion drives off puny animals.

55. *Bhagavān* Kṛṣṇa, the son of Devakī, foremost of the Yadus, took his dowry along with Satyā, and went to Dvārakā and enjoyed [conjugal happiness].
56. Kṛṣṇa married Bhadrā, the daughter of his father's sister Śrutakīrti, and Kaikeyī, who was presented by her brothers led by Santardana.
57. He seized Lakṣmaṇā, the daughter of the ruler of Madra, single-handedly, like Garuḍa seized the nectar. She was endowed with good qualities.
58. In a similar fashion, thousands of other wives of great beauty were delivered from captivity by Kṛṣṇa after killing Bhauma.'

CHAPTER 59

The Seizing of the Pārijāta *Jewel and the Killing of Naraka*

1. The king said:

'Please recount the heroic act of *Bhagavān* Kṛṣṇa, the holder of the Śārṅga bow, when he killed Bhauma, and also how those women were held captive by Bhauma.'
2. *Śrī* Śuka said:

'When he was told about Bhauma's [Naraka's] activities by Indra – whose umbrella, [mother's] earrings and residence on Amarā mountain had been seized [by Bhauma][1] – Kṛṣṇa mounted Garuḍa [his eagle carrier] with his wife, and set out for the city of Prāgjyotiṣa, Bhauma's capital.
3. [The city] was surrounded on all sides by mountain forts, armed fortifications, and tens of thousands of vicious snares set by Mura. It was made inaccessible by wind, fire and water [defences].
4. Kṛṣṇa cut through the mountains with his club; the armed fortifications with his arrows and disc; and the water, air and fire with his sword.
5. Kṛṣṇa, the club-bearer, smashed the ramparts with his heavy

club, and shattered the mechanical contrivances, as well as the hearts of those resolute men, with the sound of his conch.
6. The sleeping five-headed demon Mura arose from the water when he heard the sound of the *pāñcajanya* conch,[2] which was as fearsome as the thunderbolts at the end of the *yugas*.
7. It was hard to look at Mura, as his fierce glare was like the sun's fire at the end of the *yuga*, and he seemed to be devouring the three worlds with his five heads. Holding his trident aloft, he rushed forward like a serpent upon Garuḍa, the son of Tārkṣya.
8. Brandishing his trident, he hurled it hard at Garuḍa. Then he roared with his five mouths. That great [sound] filled heaven and earth, all the directions and the sky, and reverberated around the shell of the universe.
9. As the trident was hurtling towards Garuḍa, Hari sliced it into three pieces with two arrows, and struck Mura's faces with arrows. Mura furiously launched his club against Kṛṣṇa.
10. In the battle, Kṛṣṇa, the elder brother of Gada, shattered the oncoming club into a thousand pieces with his club. Then the invincible Kṛṣṇa effortlessly sliced off Mura's heads as he was rushing forward with his arms upraised.
11. Mura fell lifeless into the water, his heads severed, like the mountain whose peak was lopped off by Indra's power. His seven sons, distraught at the slaughter of their father, made ready for action, overcome by a passion for revenge.
12. Directed by Bhauma, the seven – Tāmra, Antariksa, Śravana, Vibhāvasu, Vasu, Nabhasvān and Aruṇa – put their general Pīṭha in front, and sallied forth into battle bearing their weapons.
13. Livid with anger they attacked, hurling arrows, swords, clubs, spears, lances and tridents at the invincible Kṛṣṇa. *Bhagavān* Kṛṣṇa, of course, whose prowess is never thwarted, cut that multitude of weapons into smithereens the size of sesame seeds with his own arrows.
14–15. Thus Naraka [Bhauma], the son of Dharā, the earth,[3] saw the leaders of his army, headed by Pīṭha, dispatched to the abode of Yama, lord of death, with their armour, legs, arms, thighs and heads severed by the arrows and disc of Acyuta.

Finding this intolerable, Naraka marched out with his musk-secreting elephants, who had been generated from the ocean of milk.[4] He saw Kṛṣṇa with his wife, seated upon Garuḍa, like a cloud with lightning upon the sun. Naraka [Bhauma] let fly a *śataghni* [fire weapon] at Kṛṣṇa, and all his soldiers struck Kṛṣṇa simultaneously.

16. Then, with his sharp and colourfully feathered arrows, *Bhagavān* Kṛṣṇa, the elder brother of Gada, reduced Bhauma's army to severed bodies, necks, thighs and arms, and slaughtered the horses and elephants in the same way.

17. Hari sliced each and every weapon and missile discharged by the soldiers with three sharp arrows, O best of the Kuru dynasty.

18–19. He was transported by Suparṇa [Garuḍa], who was simultaneously killing elephants with his wings. The elephants, harassed and slaughtered by the beak and talons of Garuḍa, retreated to the city. Naraka [Bhauma] saw his army routed and oppressed by Garuḍa, but he continued fighting on the battlefield.

20. Bhauma hurled his spear, which had once warded off [Indra's] thunderbolt, at Kṛṣṇa. Like an elephant struck by a garland, Kṛṣṇa, struck by that spear, did not flinch.

21. Bhauma took up his trident to kill Acyuta, but his efforts were futile: before Naraka [Bhauma] could discharge it, Hari beheaded him with the razor-sharp rim of his disc, as Naraka sat astride his elephant.

22. Bhauma's head fell to the ground, gleaming. Decorated with its earrings and beautiful helmet, it glittered. The sages and leaders of the gods scattered garlands on Mukunda and praised him crying: "Alas! Alas!" and "Well done!"

23. After this, the goddess of the earth approached Kṛṣṇa and presented him with the earrings, resplendent with jewels and shining gold; the *vaijayantī* garland;[5] the umbrella of Varuna; and a great jewel [all of which had been stolen by Bhauma].[6]

24. The goddess then praised the Lord of the universe, who is worshipped by the best of the gods, O king. Her mind brimming with devotion, she bowed reverentially with hands folded.

25. The earth said: "All homage to you, O Lord of the lords of

gods, wielder of the club, disc and conch, let reverence be paid to you. You are the supreme soul and you assume [different] forms according to your devotees' desires.
26. Homage to you who have a lotus navel! Homage to you who wear a lotus garland! Homage to you who have lotus eyes! Homage to you who have lotus feet!
27. Homage to you, *Bhagavān*, Vāsudeva, Viṣṇu! Homage, omniscient being, original seed [of existence]!
28. Let homage be paid to you, supreme soul, soul of the living entities and soul of the high and the low. You are the unborn progenitor of this universe and have infinite power.
29. You adopt the powerful *rajas*, when you desire to create, O unborn one, and *tamas*, for destruction, O master – but you remain unaffected [by these]. For maintenance of the universe, you adopt *sattva*, O Lord of the universe. You are time, you are primordial undifferentiated matter, and you are the transcendent being.
30. This illusion – [consisting of] myself, water, fire, air, sky, elements, gods, mind, senses, ego, intelligence, and everything moving and non-moving – is in you, O *Bhagavān*.
31. This frightened person who has been brought to your lotus feet is the son of Bhaumāsura. You remove the affliction of those submissive to you, so please protect him. Put your lotus hand, which removes all sins, on his head."'
32. *Śrī* Śuka said:

'Entreated in these words by the goddess of the earth in devoted humility, *Bhagavān* Kṛṣṇa granted his protection. Then he entered Bhauma's house, which was opulent in the extreme.
33. There, Hari saw 16,000 princesses. Bhauma had captured them from kings he had attacked.
34. The women saw that an outstanding man had entered, and were enraptured. They marked him out in their minds as their longed-for husband, who had been brought by fate.
35. Mentally saying: "May this person be my husband. May the creator allow this," they all separately gave their hearts to Kṛṣṇa.
36. Kṛṣṇa sent them off to Dvārakā on palanquins, wearing

spotless garments, along with great hoards of treasure, chariots, horses and much wealth.

37. Keśava also dispatched sixty-four swift, white, four-tusked elephants that were descended from Airāvata.[7]

38. He then went to the abode of the lord of heaven [Indra] and gave the earrings to Aditi.[8] With His beloved [Satyabhāmā], Kṛṣṇa was worshipped by the thirty-three gods, and by the great wife of Indra.

39. Then, urged on by his wife, Kṛṣṇa plucked up the *pārijāta* tree[9] and placed it on Garuḍa. After defeating the gods, including Indra, he returned to his city.

40. The *pārijāta* tree was planted by Satyabhāmā, and it graced the garden of their dwelling. Attracted by its nectar and its fragrance, the bees from heaven sought it out.

41. *Aho!* There is *tamas* even among the gods! First, the great Indra prostrated himself, touching with the tips of his helmet the feet of Acyuta, and begged for help. Kṛṣṇa fulfilled his wish and then, his goals achieved, Indra fights with Kṛṣṇa. Shame on wealth!

42. After all this, *Bhagavān* Kṛṣṇa married those women in different houses simultaneously, according to the appropriate rites. The imperishable one assumed as many forms as there were women.

43. He lived with them, without leaving, in those incomparable residences. Kṛṣṇa is immersed in his own pleasure, but he took pleasure with his wives, while performing his household duties, just like anybody else. He performs deeds that are beyond reason.

44. Thus, those women obtained Kṛṣṇa, the husband of Ramā [Śrī], as their husband, when even the gods like Brahmā do not understand his status. The women happily enjoyed themselves with him, bashful in conversation and in their glances and smiles, since their association was new, their affection increasing unhindered.

45. Even though there were hundreds of maidservants, the queens ministered to their master with gifts; by bathing him, arranging his bed and combing his hair; with garlands, perfumes, betel-nuts, worship and the best seats; and by

drawing near to him, fanning him, relaxing him, and washing his feet.'

CHAPTER 60

The Conversation between Rukmiṇī and Kṛṣṇa

1. Śuka, the son of Bādarāyaṇa, said:

'Once, Bhaiṣmī [Rukmiṇī], along with her women, was attending to her husband by fanning him. Kṛṣṇa, the *guru* of the universe, was sitting on her bed and smiling happily.
2. The unborn Lord, who playfully creates, secures and devours this universe, has actually been born among the Yadus for the protection of his own codes [of *dharma*].
3–6. Rukmiṇī served her husband, the Lord of the universes. He was sitting happily in the inner quarters on a magnificent bed, which resembled the foam of milk and had the best-quality pillows. The quarters were resplendent with canopies from which shining strings of pearls hung down; with lamps made of jewels; and with the pure rays of the moon, which filtered in through the holes in the lattice. They hummed with swarms of bees on account of the flowers in the jasmine garlands, and were pervaded by the garden breeze [bearing] the strong fragrance of the *pārijāta* groves. *Aguru* incense seeped out through the holes in the lattice, O king.
7. Taking a tail-whisk with a jewelled handle from a girlfriend, the goddess paid service to the Lord, fanning him with it.
8. To the tinkling sound of her jewelled ankle bells, and the rings and bracelets on her fingers and hand [which was holding] the fan, Rukmiṇī appeared radiant next to Acyuta. The lustre of her necklace was reddened with *kuṅkum* powder from her breasts, which were covered by the end of her garment.
9. Hari gazed at her, Śrī, the beautiful goddess of fortune, who has no other refuge [than him]. Her face [was adorned with] locks of hair, earrings, a gold neck ornament and the nectar of

a radiant smile. Her form was an appropriate counterpart for the body assumed [by him] for the sake of *līlā*. Delighted, he spoke to her with a smile.
10. *Śrī Bhagavān* said: "O princess! You were desired by kings, as mighty as the rulers of planets. They had great power, wealth, beauty, generosity, strength and vigour.
11. Why did you reject the king of Cedi and the others who arrived as suitors, maddened by Kāma, to choose me, who is not their equal? You were promised to them by your own brother and your own father.
12. Having made enemies of powerful people and fearing the kings, I more or less gave up the royal throne and sought refuge in the ocean, O beautiful-browed one.
13. Women who follow the path of men whose conduct is controversial, and who follow anti-social ways, usually end up in distress, O beautiful-browed one.
14. I am always destitute, and am dear to destitute people. Therefore, the wealthy generally do not worship me, O beautiful-waisted one!
15. Marriage and friendship are for those whose possessions, birth, riches, appearance and life situation are equal to each other – never between a superior and an inferior.
16. O Vaidarbhī, you did not know this, and so I was chosen by you; in this you are short-sighted. I am devoid of qualities and praised by beggars, but to no avail.
17. Therefore choose an eminent warrior who is a suitable match for you, and with whom you can realize your desires both in this world and in the next.
18. Kings such as Caidya [Śiśupāla], Śālva, Jarāsandha, Dantavakra and others hate me, and so does Rukmī, your elder brother, O woman with beautiful thighs.
19. I carried you away in order to confound the arrogance of the proud, who were blind with the intoxication of power, as well as to strip away the power of the wicked.
20. The fact is, I am indifferent to house and body, and am not desirous of wealth, children or women. I am fulfilled by what is available in myself, just like a lamp which does no work."'

21. *Śrī* Śuka said:

'After speaking in this way to Rukmiṇī, *Bhagavān* Kṛṣṇa, the destroyer of Rukmiṇī's pride, desisted. Because they had never separated, Rukmiṇī had always thought that she was his beloved.
22. But hearing such unpleasant words as had never before been spoken by her beloved, the master of the lords of the universe, Rukmiṇī was afraid and became faint of heart. She started to cry, and was filled with endless anxiety.
23. She stood still with her head down, scratching the ground with her perfectly shaped foot, beautiful with the reddish tint of her nails. Her voice was choked with extreme distress, and she was moistening her breasts, which were smeared with *kuṅkum* powder, with tears that were black with mascara.
24. The bracelets slipped off her hand, and the fan fell from it. Her intelligence was thrown into turmoil by anguish, fear and extreme unhappiness, and her mind was overcome with alarm. Her hair became dishevelled and her body suddenly began to fall into a faint, like a plantain tree struck by the wind.
25. *Bhagavān* Kṛṣṇa is kind and became compassionate when he saw how much his beloved, who did not understand the extent of his joking, was bound by love.
26. [Manifesting] four arms, he immediately climbed down from the bed, picked her up, arranged her hair and wiped her face with his hand.
27. He wiped her eyes, which were full of tears, and her breasts, which were painful with distress. He put his arms around the chaste woman, who had nothing other [than him].
28. The Lord, the goal of the righteous, is expert in consolation, and comforted that poor woman with compassion, O king. She had become confused by the extent of his joking and had not deserved that.'
29. *Śrī Bhagavān* said: "Do not be upset, O Vaidarbhī – I know that you are committed to me. My playful conduct was only out of a desire to see how you would respond, O shapely lady.
30. [I desired] to see your face, its lips trembling with the

agitation of love, the arch of the beautiful curves of your eyebrows, and the glances from the reddish corners of your eyes.
31. This is the greatest boon for householders in their domestic life – that a few hours can pass in sport with their beloved, O timid, angry one."'
32. *Śrī* Śuka said:

'Thus Vaidarbhī [Rukmiṇī] was consoled by *Bhagavān* Kṛṣṇa, O king. When she understood that his words were in jest, she lost her fear of being rejected by her lover.
33. Looking with coy sidelong glances and bashful laughs at the face of *Bhagavān* Kṛṣṇa, the best of men, O Bharata, she spoke.
34. *Śrī* Rukmiṇī said: "Actually, it is as you said, O lotus-eyed one. I am indeed not equal to the mighty *Bhagavān*. Look at the difference between you and me. You are *Bhagavān*, the supreme Lord of the three [Brahmā, Viṣṇu and Śiva], and you delight in your own majesty. I am *prakṛti* [constituted of] the *guṇas*, and my feet are grasped by the ignorant.
35. O Urukrama [Kṛṣṇa], it is true that you lie within the ocean as if from fear of the *guṇas*. You are soul and pure intelligence, and always opposed to the harmful *guṇas* and the senses. Your servants reject positions of royalty as being blind *tamas*.
36. The path followed by the sages, who enjoy the honey of your lotus feet, is not easy to understand; indeed, it is incomprehensible for beast-like men. Because your activities, Lord, are transcendental, so likewise are the activities of those that follow you, O all-encompassing one.
37. You are, indeed, destitute since nothing exists apart from you. It is to you that the unborn Brahmā and other [gods] bring sacrifices, despite the fact that they are the recipients of sacrifice. You are the dearest person for those who receive sacrifice, and they are for you too. Those devoted to worldly happiness, blinded by wealth, do not realize that you are death.
38. It is actually you who are the embodiment of all the goals of human life, and the fruit in the form of the soul. Out of their longing for you, intelligent people renounce everything. Union between you and such people is fitting, O Master, but that

between a man and a woman who are attached to happiness and distress is not.

39. You are the soul of the universe, and the giver of your own soul. Your majesty is talked about by sages who have even renounced their ascetic staffs.[1] You were chosen by me after I rejected the masters of the heavens, Śiva and Brahmā, whose desires are frustrated by the force of time, which is generated from your eyebrows. So what is there to say of others?

40. After putting to flight the protectors of the earth with the twanging sound of your bow, Śārṅga, you carried me away like a lion carries away his share of his prey from other animals, O Lord. Your statement that you took shelter in the ocean out of fear of them is foolish, Kṛṣṇa, elder brother of Gada.

41. The crown jewels among kings – such as Aṅga, Vainya [Pṛthu], Jāyanta [Bharata], Nāhuṣa [Yayāti] and Gaya[2] – renounced the absolute sovereignty of their kingdom and entered the forest, O lotus-eyed one. Committed to following your path, did they perish in this world?

42. After smelling the fragrance of your lotus feet, what mortal woman of discrimination would disregard them and seek refuge with some other person who is forever subject to great fear? You are the repository of good qualities. Your feet bestow liberation on people, are the abode of Lakṣmī, and [their glories] are broadcast by saints.

43. I chose you as suitable. You are the supreme Lord of the universes, the soul, and the fulfiller of desires both here and in the next world. May your lotus feet, which approach the worshipper and bestow liberation from falsehood, grant me shelter; I am wandering about on the paths [of *saṃsāra*].

44. Let those things you mentioned, O Acyuta, belong to women whose innermost ears have not been reached by the stories about you that are sung in the assemblies of Brahmā and Śiva. Those kings are servants, cats, dogs, cows and donkeys in the houses of women, O harasser of enemies.

45. That woman is extremely foolish who, without smelling the honey of your lotus feet, picks a lover who is a living corpse covered in skin, nails, and facial, body and head hair; and with

gas, bile, phlegm, stool, bowel worms, blood, bone and flesh inside.

46. May I be granted affection for your feet, O lotus-eyed Kṛṣṇa. When you employ excessive *rajas* for the development of this universe and you look at me, it is truly the greatest mercy for us – [even though] your glance upon me is brief and your pleasure is self-contained.[3]

47. But I do not think that your words are wrong, O Madhusūdana; a girl's attraction [for someone else] often develops – as once happened with Ambā.[4]

48. Even though she be married, the mind of a harlot seeks new man after new man. A wise person should not maintain an unchaste woman – both become degraded by keeping such a woman."

49. *Śrī Bhagavān* said: "You were deceived by what I spoke because of my desire to hear your words, O saintly lady. Everything that you have said in response is true, O princess.

50. Whatever desires you may have for the purpose of being free from desires are always fulfilled for you, O angry one! You are a devotee who is focused exclusively on me, virtuous lady.

51. Your love for, and firm commitment to, your husband have been demonstrated, O sinless woman! Although you were deceived by those words, your mind could not be moved from me.

52. Those who worship me, the giver of liberation, by the performance of asceticism and the taking of vows, and yet desire enjoyment in the relationship of marriage, are bewildered by my *māyā*.

53. I am the wealth of liberation as well as the Lord of wealth, proud lady. But those who request only wealth from me, after obtaining me, are ill-fated. These things can be found even in hell. Residence in hell for such people is appropriate because of their obsession with money.

54. It is by good fortune, O lady of the house, that you continually submit to me, because this submission grants liberation from material existence. It is a very difficult thing for wrongdoers to do, and especially for women, who are only [concerned with]

maintaining their lives, have wicked intentions and are dedicated to deceitfulness.
55. I cannot find in [other] homes a housewife who is as devoted as you are. You had heard true stories about me, and, at the time of your marriage, after you had disregarded the assembled kings, you sent a *brāhmaṇa* messenger to me secretly.
56. Afraid to lose me, you said nothing about your anguish both at the disfigurement of your brother when he was defeated in battle on the occasion of your marriage, and at his death at the gambling assembly.[5] This won me over to you.
57. You sent a messenger with a well-calculated plan for winning me. When I delayed, you thought of this world as empty and [were prepared to] give up your body as an offering to no one else [except me]. Let this be [a testament] to you; I take you with my whole heart."'
59. *Śrī* Śuka said:

'*Bhagavān*, the Lord of the universe, is self-contained in his pleasure. But, imitating the ways of mortals, he enjoyed amorous banter with Ramā [Śrī].
59. In the same way, Lord Hari, the *guru* of the world, acting as if he were a householder, also performed the duties of a married man in the houses of his other wives.'

CHAPTER 61

Rukmī's Death at Aniruddha's Marriage

1. *Śrī* Śuka said:

'Each and every one of Kṛṣṇa's wives bore him ten sons each. These were endowed with all personal perfections, and were not inferior to their father.
2. Seeing that Acyuta stayed at home and never left the house, each princess regarded her beloved as exclusively her own. These women were not aware of his real nature.

3. They were entranced by *Bhagavān* Kṛṣṇa's pleasing small-talk and his feeling glances, loving laughter, eyes, long arms, and face like a beautiful lotus bud. But they could not capture the mind of the almighty with their own charms.
4. The 16,000 wives could not distract his senses with their actions, nor with Kāma's arrows cast through the arches of their eyebrows. These passionate amorous messages were discreetly revealed through their glances and smiles, and were captivating to the mind.
5. Thus, although even Brahmā and the other [gods] do not know his position, those women obtained Kṛṣṇa, the husband of Ramā [Śrī], as their husband. Eager for his stimulating company, his glances, laughter and love, they enjoyed [his company] uninterruptedly with increasing bliss in various ways.
6. Despite having hundreds of maidservants, they rendered service to the Lord themselves by making arrangements for his feet-washing and bath, for attending to his hair, for sitting, relaxation and rest, and for the best of worship; with offerings of garlands, scents, fans and betel nut; and by going to meet him.
7. From those aforementioned wives of Kṛṣṇa who had ten sons, I shall relate to you the sons of the eight queens, beginning with Pradyumna.
8–9. With Pradyumna as the most prominent, there were Cārudeṣṇa, Sudeṣṇa, Cārudeha the valiant, Sucāru and Cārugupta; followed by Bhadracāru, Cārucandra, Vicāru and Cāru, the tenth. These were born of Hari to Rukmiṇī, and were not inferior to their father.
10–12. The ten born of Satyabhāmā were: Bhānu, Subhānu, Svarbhānu, Prabhānu, Bhānumān, Candrabhānu, Bṛhadbhānu, Atibhānu the eighth son, Śribhānu and Pratibhānu. The sons of Jāmbavatī were: Sāmba, Sumitra, Purujit, Śatajit, Sahasrajit, Vijaya, Citraketu, Vasumān, Draviḍa and Kratu. Beginning with Sāmba, these were favoured by their father.
13. The sons of Nāgnajitī were: Vīra, Candra, Aśvasena, Citragu, Vegavān, Vṛṣa, Āma, Śaṅku, Vasu and the wealthy Kuntī.
14. Of Kālindī were born: Śruta, Kavi, Vṛṣa, Vīra, Subāhu,

the solitary Bhadra, Śānti, Darśa, Pūrṇamāsa and Somaka, the youngest.
15. Praghoṣa, Gātravān, Siṃha, Bala, Prabala, Ūrdhvaga, Mahāśakti, Saha, Ojas and Parājita were the sons of Mādrā.
16. The sons of Mitravindā were: Vṛka, Harṣa, Anila, Gṛdhra, Vardhana, Unnāda, Mahāṃśa, Pāvana, Vahni and Kṣudhi.
17. Of Bhadrā were: Saṅgrāmajit, Bṛhatsena, Śūra, Praharaṇa, Arijit, Jaya, Subhadra, Vāma, Āyu and Satyaka.
18–19. The sons of Hari by Rohiṇī were headed by Dīptimān, Tāmra and Tapta. And the mighty Aniruddha was born from Pradyumna by Rukmavatī, the daughter of Rukmī in the city of Bhojakata. The mothers of Kṛṣṇa's descendants were 16,000, O king, and their grandsons ran into the tens of millions.'
20. The king said:

'How did Rukmī give his daughter to the son of his enemy? He had been defeated in battle by Kṛṣṇa and was waiting for a moment of vulnerability in order to kill him. Tell me how the marriage arrangement between these two enemies took place, O learned one.
21. *Yogīs* see the future, the past and the present perfectly, as well as that which is distant, concealed or beyond the senses.'[1]
22. *Śrī* Śuka said:

'Pradyumna, who is the reincarnate Anaṅga [Kāma] himself,[2] was chosen by Rukmavatī in a *svayaṃvara* marriage. Alone on his chariot, he defeated the assembled kings in battle and carried her away.
23. Rukmī had been humiliated by Kṛṣṇa, but, although his enmity was not forgotten, he gave his daughter to his nephew Pradyumna, thereby pleasing his sister Rukmiṇī.
24. The powerful son of Kṛtavarmā, O king, married the large-eyed maiden Cārumatī, the daughter of Rukmiṇī.
25. Rukmī bestowed his granddaughter, Rocanā, on Aniruddha, out of a desire to please his sister, despite being sworn to enmity and knowing that it was contrary to *dharma*.[3] He was bound by the ties of affection.
26. Rukmiṇī, Balarāma and Keśava, Sāmba, Pradyumna and

the others went to the city of Bhojakaṭa on that occasion, O king.

27. When the marriage ceremonies were over, the arrogant kings, led by the ruler of Kaliṅga, told Rukmī: "You should defeat Balarāma at dice.

28. That Balarāma is not expert at dice, O king, although he is greatly addicted to it." Appealed to thus, Rukmī summoned Balarāma and played dice with him.

29. On that occasion, Balarāma accepted a wager of 100 [coins], then 1,000, and then 10,000. But Rukmī beat him. At this, the king of Kaliṅga laughed loudly at Balarāma, displaying his teeth. Balarāma, the wielder of the plough, found this insupportable.

30. Then Rukmī accepted a wager of 100,000 [coins]. Balarāma won that one. But Rukmī, resorting to cheating, cried: "I won!"

31. Trembling with anger like the ocean at the change of the moon, beautiful Balarāma, whose eyes were red from birth, furiously accepted a wager of 100 million [coins].

32. Balarāma won that one fairly, too. But Rukmī, resorting to trickery, said: "Let these witnesses attest that this one was won by me."

33. Then a voice from the heavens declared: "The wager was won fairly by Balarāma. Rukmī speaks lies."

34. Egged on by the wicked kings, Rukmī the Vaidarbhan ignored that [voice]. Impelled by the force of time, he spoke to Saṅkarṣaṇa, laughing:

35. "You are cowherders who roam the forests; you are not expert at dice – kings play with dice as well as with arrows, but not the likes of you."

36. Insulted by Rukmī thus and ridiculed by the kings, Balarāma became furious. He raised his iron club and killed Rukmī in the middle of that valiant assembly.

37. Furious, he then seized the king of Kaliṅga, who had laughed with his teeth exposed, on his tenth step [as he was fleeing] and knocked his teeth out.

38. The other kings were terrified by Balarāma. Harassed by his club, they fled, splattered with blood, their heads and arms broken.

39. When his brother-in-law Rukmī was killed, O king, Hari

did not express either approval or disapproval, afraid to endanger his [ties of] affection with either Rukmiṇī or Balarāma.
40. After this incident, the descendants of Daśārha, headed by Balarāma, had the groom Aniruddha ascend the chariot along with his bride, and went to Kuśasthalī [Dvārakā] from Bhojakaṭa. With Madhusūdana as their refuge, all their goals had been fulfilled.'

CHAPTER 62

The Binding of Aniruddha

1. The king said:

'Aniruddha, the best of the Yadus, married Uṣā, the daughter of Bāṇa. On that occasion there was a huge and bitter fight between Hari and Śaṅkara [Śiva]. Would you kindly tell us all about that, O great *yogī*?'
2. *Śrī* Śuka said:

'Bāṇa was the eldest of the 100 sons of the great soul Bali, by whom the earth was given to Hari in the form of Vāmana, the dwarf incarnation.[1]
3. Bāṇa, the son born of Bali, was always engaged in devotion to Śiva. He was respected, munificent, intelligent, truthfully disposed and firm in vow.
4. In the past he ruled from the delightful city of Śoṇita. By the grace of Śambhu [Śiva], the immortal gods became as good as his servants – he had pleased Mṛḍa [Śiva] in his dance, by playing musical instruments with his 1,000 arms.
5. *Bhagavān* Śiva, the Lord of all creatures and giver of shelter, is fond of his devotees and granted Bāṇa a favour. Bāṇa chose that Śiva be the protecting sovereign of the city.
6. Once, touching Śiva's lotus feet with a helmet which had the hue of the sun, Bāṇa spoke to the Lord of the mountains, who was standing by his side. He was intoxicated with pride.

7. "I offer my respects to you, O Mahādeva [Śiva]. You are the Lord and *guru* of the worlds, the tree of the immortals that fulfils the desires of men who have unfulfilled desires.
8. The 1,000 arms that you have given me have become a heavy burden. Other than you, I cannot find an equally matched antagonist in the three worlds.
9. Itching to fight with my arms, O original being, I set out towards the elephants [who support] the cardinal points [of the earth],[2] pulverizing mountains [along the way]. But they too fled, terrified."
10. Hearing this, *Bhagavān* Śiva was furious: "When your banner is broken, fool, a battle will take place with someone equal to me who will crush your pride."
11. Thus addressed, that ignorant fool was delighted and entered his residence, O king, waiting for Giriśa's [Śiva's] prediction that his valour would be destroyed.
12. His daughter, the maiden Uṣā, dreamed she had a romantic encounter with a lover. He was Aniruddha, the son of Pradyumna, whom she had neither seen nor heard of previously.
13. She awoke among her girlfriends, saying: "Who are you, lover?" Not seeing him there, she was confused and extremely embarrassed.
14. Kumbhāṇḍa was one of Bāṇa's ministers. His daughter was [Uṣā's] female companion, Citralekhā. Full of curiosity, Citralekhā asked her friend Uṣā:
15. "Whom are you looking for, O beautiful-browed one? What is the nature of your desire? I have not seen anyone take your hand in marriage yet, O princess."
16. Uṣā replied: "Some man appeared in my dream. Dark, with lotus eyes, yellow garments and mighty arms, he touches the hearts of women.
17. Having drunk the nectar of his lips, I am searching for that lover. But he has gone somewhere and cast me, yearning, into an ocean of misery."
18. Citralekhā said: "I will relieve your distress. If he is to be found in the three worlds, I will bring this man who, as a lover, has stolen your heart. Point him out."
19. Saying this, Citralekhā drew pictures of gods, *gandharvas*,

siddhas, *cāraṇas*, *pannaga* serpents, *daityas*, *vidyādharas*, *yakṣas* and humans.

20. Of the humans she drew the Vṛṣṇis, Śūra,[3] Ānakadundubhi [Vasudeva], Balarāma and Kṛṣṇa. Seeing Pradyumna drawn, Uṣā became shy.

21. When she saw Aniruddha, she lowered her head bashfully, O great king. "This is the one, this is the one!" she said, smiling.

22. Citralekhā was a female *yogī* and recognized him as the grandson of Kṛṣṇa, O king. She travelled through the sky to the city of Dvārakā, which was protected by Kṛṣṇa.

23. There she availed herself of her *yogic* powers and transported the son of Pradyumna, Aniruddha, who was sleeping on a beautiful bed, to the city of Śoṇita. She presented her friend with her beloved.

24. Uṣā saw Aniruddha, the choicest of handsome men, and her face became joyful. She enjoyed relations with the son of Pradyumna in her own chambers, which were hidden from the eyes of men.

25. He was honoured with garments of the best quality, garlands, perfumes, incense, lamps, sitting arrangements, drinks, meals, things to eat, words and service.

26. He remained hidden in the maidens' quarters with Uṣā, whose love continued to increase. Aniruddha's senses were bewitched by Uṣā, and he was not aware of the passage of days.

27–28. By her symptoms, which were hard to conceal, the guards noticed at a certain point that Uṣā's chastity had been breached, that she was enjoying relations with the Yadu hero, and that she was full of joy. They reported [to Bāna]: "O king, we notice signs in your daughter, a maiden, that dishonour your family.

29. We guarded her in the residence, O master, and we never left. We do not understand how this violation of the maiden [happened]; she was hidden from the eyes of men."

30. Bāṇa was distressed when he heard that his daughter had been violated and rushed to the maidens' quarters. Arriving there, he saw Aniruddha, the best of the Yadus.

31–32. Bāṇa was amazed when he saw Aniruddha, the son of Kāma. His beauty was unmatched in the world: he was dark, his clothes were yellow, he had lotus eyes and his arms were broad. His face was bright with locks of hair, the lustre of earrings, and with smiling looks. Playing dice with his auspicious beloved, Aniruddha was sitting in front of her, a garland between his arms. It was made of jasmine and, from contact with her body, contained *kuṅkum* powder from her breasts.

33. Aniruddha, the descendant of Madhu, saw Bāṇa enter surrounded by guards and by soldiers with weapons drawn. He raised his iron club and, ready to kill, positioned himself, like death, the bearer of the rod of chastisement.

34. He struck them down as they approached from all sides intent on seizing him, like the leader of a herd of boars strikes down dogs. Having received a beating, they left the mansion and fled, with broken arms, thighs and heads.

35. Bāṇa, the powerful son of Bali, became enraged with Aniruddha, who was striking down his own army, and bound him with serpent fetters. Uṣā was overcome with sorrow and distress when she heard that he had been bound. With tears in her eyes, she wept.'

CHAPTER 63

The Escorting of Aniruddha

1. *Śrī* Śuka said:

'Four months passed as his relatives lamented when they could not find Aniruddha, O Parīkṣit, descendant of Bharata.

2. The Vṛṣṇi clan, who worship Kṛṣṇa as their deity, set out for the city of Śoṇita after hearing from Nārada about the deeds of Aniruddha, and the news that he had been captured.

3–4. Every single eminent hero of the Sātvata clan – Pradyumna, Yuyudhāna, Gada, Sāmba, Sāraṇa, Nanda, Upananda, Bhadra and others – all of them followers of Balarāma and Kṛṣṇa, gathered together and besieged Bāṇa's city from all sides with twelve *akṣauhiṇī* battalions.

5. Seeing the town gates, watchtowers, ramparts and parks of the city being destroyed, Bāṇa was filled with fury and set out with a comparable army.
6. Rudra [Śiva] mounted Nandī the bull, with his son [Kārttikeya],[1] and, surrounded by the *pramathas*,[2] fought on the side of Bāna against Balarāma and Kṛṣṇa.
7. A tumultuous, hair-raising and spectacular battle ensued between Kṛṣṇa and Śaṅkara [Śiva], as well as between Pradyumna and Guha [Kārttikeya], O king.
8. There were clashes between Kumbhāṇḍa and Kūpakarṇa and Balarāma; between Sāmba and the son of Bāṇa; and between Sātyaki and Bāṇa.
9. Led by Brahmā, the rulers of the gods, the sages, the *siddhas*, *cāraṇas*, *gandharvas*, *apsarās* and *yakṣas* came on their celestial air-carriers to spectate.
10–11. Kṛṣṇa, the descendant of Śūra, caused the followers of Śaṅkara – the *bhūtas*, *pramathas*, *guhyakas*, *ḍākinīs*, *yātudhānas*, *vetālas*, *vināyakas*, *pretas*, *mātās*, *piśācas*, *kūṣmāṇḍas* and *brahmarākṣasas*[3] – to scatter by releasing sharp arrows from his Śārṅga bow.
12. Śiva, the wielder of the Pināka bow, discharged various types of weapons against the wielder of the Śārṅga bow. But Kṛṣṇa, the bearer of Śārṅga, was not impressed and countered them with other weapons.
13. *Brahmāstra* [clashed] against *brahmāstra*,[4] wind weapon against mountain weapon, fire weapon against rain weapon, and Paśupati's [Śiva's] weapon against Kṛṣṇa's own personal weapon.
14. Kṛṣṇa, the descendant of Śūra, bewildered Śiva, Lord of the mountains, with a yawning weapon, and Śiva yawned. Then Kṛṣṇa struck Bāṇa's army with his sword, club and arrows.
15. Harassed on all sides by torrents of Pradyumna's arrows, Skanda left the battle on his peacock carrier, blood pouring from his limbs.
16. Kumbhāṇḍa and Kūpakarṇa fell down, struck by the club [of Balarāma]. With their leaders slain, their armies fled everywhere.
17. Seeing that his own army was being scattered, Bāṇa was

utterly enraged. He left Sātyaki in the battle and rushed on his chariot towards Kṛṣṇa.

18. Maddened by the battle, Bāṇa drew his 500 bows simultaneously, and fixed two arrows in each one.

19. *Bhagavān* Hari struck Bāṇa's charioteer, chariot and horses, and then sliced each of those bows simultaneously. He sounded his conch.

20. Wanting to save the life of her son, Bāṇa's mother, known as Koṭarā, stood before Kṛṣṇa naked and with her hair unbound.

21. At this, Kṛṣṇa, the elder brother of Gada, lowered his head to avoid seeing her naked. In that interval, Bāṇa, his bow broken and without his chariot, entered his city.

22. When the multitude of ghosts had been routed, the three-headed and three-footed Jvara, the personification of fever, rushed at Dāśārha [Kṛṣṇa] as if he was burning up [the world in all] ten directions.

23. Seeing him, Lord Nārāyaṇa [Kṛṣṇa] then released [his own] fever. The two fevers – the one belonging to Viṣṇu and the one belonging to Maheśvara [Śiva] – entered into combat.

24. Tormented by the Viṣṇu fever, the Maheśvara one was crying out piteously. Terrified and unable to find shelter elsewhere, the Maheśvara fever stood before Hṛṣīkeśa with folded hands, seeking protection.

25. The fever said: "I offer homage to you. You are the supreme Lord and have infinite power. You are the soul of everything, the absolute. You are pure consciousness, the cause of the creation, maintenance and dissolution of the universe. You are that *brahman* which is indicated by the Vedas. You are tranquil.

26. Time, fate, *karma*, the souls, personality, the material ingredients, the field of nature, the vital air, the self, the transformation [of *prakṛti*], the combination of these things, and the cycle of seed and shoot[5] – these are your *māyā*. You can annul these things, and so I surrender to you.

27. You uphold the *sādhus*, gods and religious principles of the world by assuming various forms in play. You kill those who deviate from the path and who live by violence. This birth of yours is to remove the burden of the world.

28. I am overwhelmed by your power in the form of this

intolerable fever. It is intensely hot and cold. The sufferings of embodied beings continue for as long as they remain bound to their desires and do not worship the soles of your feet."

29. *Śrī Bhagavān* said: "O three-headed Jvara! I am appeased; let your fear of my fever disappear. Whoever remembers our conversation, will not be afflicted by fear of you."

30. Addressed thus, the Maheśvara fever offered homage to Acyuta, and then departed. But Bāṇa mounted a chariot and came forth intending to fight Janārdana.

31. The demon, extremely angry and holding various weapons with his 1,000 arms, let fly arrows against Kṛṣṇa, whose weapon is a disc, O king.

32. As Bāṇa was hurling weapons, *Bhagavān* repeatedly sliced his arms off with the rim of his razor-sharp disc as if they were the many branches of a tree.

33. *Bhagavān* Bhava [Śiva] is compassionate towards his devotees. As Bāṇa's arms were being sliced off, he approached Kṛṣṇa, the wielder of the disc, and spoke:

34. *Śrī* Rudra [Śiva] said: "You are the supreme *brahman*, the light hidden in the Vedas, which are the spoken *brahman*. Those with spotless souls can see you. Like the sky, you are unadulterated.

35–36. He whose navel is the sky, whose mouth is fire, whose semen is the waters, whose head is the heavens, whose hearing is the quarters, whose feet are the earth, whose mind is the moon, whose eye is the sun, whose *ātmā* is I myself, whose belly is the ocean, and whose arm is Indra, whose body hairs are the herbs, whose head hairs are the clouds, whose intelligence is the creator Brahmā, whose generative organ is Prajāpati the progenitor of humankind, and whose heart is *dharma*, that person is you, the supreme being, made manifest in the world.[6]

37. Your majesty never fades, your incarnation in this world is for the protection of *dharma*, and for the benefit of the world. All of us [gods] who become manifest in the seven worlds are empowered by you.

38. You are the unique primordial supreme being without a second. You are the fourth state of consciousness – transcendence.[7] You are self-aware. You are the controller, the cause that

has no cause. Moreover, you are recognized by means of the effects [produced] by your *māyā* through the manifestation of all the *guṇas*.

39. Just as the sun, though covered by its own cloud, illuminates the cloud as well as other objects, so, although covered by the *guṇas*, you illuminate the *guṇas*. You are the light of the soul and the possessor of the *guṇas*. You are all-pervading.

40. Those who are attached to home, wife and sons, their intelligence bewildered by your *māyā*, sink and surface continually in an ocean of distress.

41. One whose senses are unrestrained and does not worship your feet after obtaining the human form of life is a cheater of the soul; such a person is certainly to be pitied.[8]

42. That mortal who rejects you, the *ātmā*, the beloved Lord, for the sake of the perverse objects of the senses ingests poison while rejecting nectar.

43. I, Brahmā, the gods and the pure-minded sages surrender ourselves to you with all our being. You are the *ātmā*, the most dear Lord.

44. We worship you for liberation from the material world. You are the Lord, the one without a second, the cause of the creation, maintenance and destruction of the universe. You are impartial and peaceful, the friend and Lord of the soul. The souls in the universe dwell with you.

45. This person is my favoured and beloved follower. I granted him fearlessness, O Lord. Please bestow your mercy on him, just as you bestowed your mercy on the chief of the demons."[9]

46. *Śrī Bhagavān* said: "We respect whatever was granted by you, O Bhagavān – whatever is pleasing to you. Whatever was determined by you is perfectly acceptable to me.

47. I will not kill this descendant of Virocana [Bali], even though he is a demon. This promise was given to Prahlāda: 'Your lineage will not be killed by me.'

48. I hewed off his arms, and his huge army, which had become a burden on the earth, was destroyed, so as to quell his pride.

49. Four of his arms have been spared. The demon will live as your principal attendant, free from old age and death and without fear from anybody."

50. When he had been granted courage in this way, the demon bowed his head to Kṛṣṇa, had the son of Pradyumna ascend a chariot with his bride, and brought them forward.
51. Arrayed in beautiful garments, and surrounded by an *akṣauhiṇī* battalion, Kṛṣṇa placed Aniruddha and his wife in front and, with the permission of Rudra, took his leave.
52. Kṛṣṇa then entered his capital city, and was welcomed by *brāhmaṇas*, friends and citizens with the sounds of drums and kettledrums. The city was well decorated with flags, arches and with crossroads and thoroughfares that had been sprinkled with water.
53. Whoever gets up at daybreak and remembers the victory of Kṛṣṇa, and his battle with Śaṅkara [Śiva], will never experience defeat.'

CHAPTER 64

The Story of Nṛga

1. Śuka, the son of Badarāyaṇa, said:

'Once, the young boys of the Yadu dynasty – Sāmba, Pradyumna, Cāru, Bhānu, Gada and the rest – went to a grove to play, O king.
2. After playing there for a long time, they were thirsty, and when looking for water they saw an extraordinary creature in a waterless well.
3. The boys saw a lizard that resembled a mountain and they were struck with astonishment. Filled with compassion, they tried to lift it up.
4. The boys tied bonds made of leather and thread round the fallen creature, but they could not lift it out. So in their excitement they reported [the matter] to Kṛṣṇa.
5. Lotus-eyed *Bhagavān* Kṛṣṇa, creator of the universe, went there and saw it. He lifted it up with his left hand with ease.
6. Touched by the hand of Uttamaśloka, it at once discarded

the form of a lizard and turned into a celestial being with the beautiful colour of molten gold, [wearing] magnificent garlands, garments and ornaments.
7. Although he knew all about it, Mukunda asked the being about the cause of his existence in that life-form in order to make it known [to the others]: "Who are you, greatly fortunate one, that you have this distinguished form? You are surely a most eminent god.
8. By what act, exactly, have you attained such a condition? You do not deserve this, O most fortunate one. We desire to know: if you think it is appropriate to speak to us, explain about yourself." '
9. *Śrī* Śuka said:

'Questioned in this way by Kṛṣṇa, whose forms are infinite, the king offered respects to Mādhava [by touching] his helmet, which was as brilliant as the sun, [to the ground]. Then he said:
10. "I am a ruler of men by name of Nṛga, a descendant of the Ikṣvāku dynasty, O master. Perhaps [my name] has reached your ears when [the names] of philanthropists are being recited.
11. What is there that is unknown to you, O master? Your vision is not limited by time and you are the [innermost] witness of the *ātmā* of all living beings. Nonetheless, I will speak as you have commanded.
12. I gave in charity as many cows as there are grains of sand on the earth, stars in the heavens and drops of rain.
13. The cows I gave were young milch-cows, with calf. They were endowed with good qualities, beauty and good nature. They were brown in colour with gold on their horns and silver on their hooves, and [bore] ornaments, garlands and fine cloth. And they were acquired righteously.
14. I gave to distinguished *brāhmaṇas* who were youthful; true to their vows; from stricken families; the possessors of good qualities and character; well-ornamented; [endowed with] righteousness and liberality; [expert in] the Vedas and oral knowledge; and [dedicated to] austere practices.
15. [I gave] cows, land, gold, houses, horses, elephants, maidens with maidservants, sesame, silver, beds, garments, jewels,

furniture and chariots. I did good works and carried out sacred rites with sacrifices.

16. A cow belonging to a certain distinguished *brāhmaṇa* escaped and mixed in with my herd. She was donated by me unawares to [another] twice-born *brāhmaṇa*.

17. Her owner, after seeing her being led away, said: 'She is mine!' The one who had received her said to the former: 'She is mine! Nṛga gave her to me.'

18. One of the two *brāhmaṇas* in the quarrel said to me: 'You are the one who gave her!' The other said: 'You are the one who stole her!' After hearing this, I was thrown into confusion.

19. I entreated the two *brāhmaṇas*: 'I will give you 100,000 first-class cows. Give this one up.' I had fallen into a difficult situation in terms of *dharma*:

20. 'Please treat this unwitting servant kindly. Deliver me from this difficulty – I have fallen into an impure hell.'

21. 'I do not accept, O king,' said the owner, and went off. 'I do not want even 10,000 [more than you are offering] cows,' said the other, and departed.

22. At this juncture, I was brought to the abode of Yama, lord of death, by Yama's messengers, O Lord of the universe and God of gods. There I was questioned by Yama:

23. 'You may first enjoy either your good fortune, or your bad fortune, O king,' he said. 'I see neither the end of your charity and *dharma*, nor of the radiant world [you have earned from them].'

24. 'I will first accept my bad fortune, O god,' I said. 'Fall down,' said he. At that, I saw myself falling as a lizard, O master.

25. Even up until now, O Keśava, the memory of this servant of yours – who is munificent and devoted to *brāhmaṇas* – has not been lost. I have been longing for a vision of your Lordship.

26. He, the supreme soul, is you. You are perceived with the eyes of scripture in the pure heart of the masters of *yoga*, so how is it that you are visible to my eyes, O master – my intelligence is blinded by excessive vice? How is it that you are personally present before me, Adhokṣaja – you are only supposed to be visible in this world to one who is liberated from *saṃsāra*?

27. O Lord of lords, master of the universe, Govinda, supreme

person, Nārāyaṇa, Hṛṣīkeśa, O you of good fame, Acyuta, imperishable one!

28. Allow me to depart, O Kṛṣṇa – I am going to the destination of the gods, O Master. And wherever I may be, may my mind remain on your feet.

29. All homage to you, *brahman*, reality of everything, unlimited power. All homage to you, Kṛṣṇa, Vāsudeva, Lord of *yogīs*."

30. After saying this, Nṛga circumambulated Kṛṣṇa, and touched his feet with his crown. Having been given permission [to leave], he then boarded a distinctive heavenly vehicle, while the humans watched.

31. *Bhagavān* Kṛṣṇa, the son of Devakī, is the soul of *dharma* and favourably disposed to *brāhmaṇas*. He spoke to his entourage, instructing the royal class thus:

32. "Truly, the property of a *brāhmaṇa*, little though it may be, is [seized and] enjoyed with great difficulty even by one who is as powerful as fire. What then of kings, who think they are Lords?

33. I do not think that *hālāhala*[1] is a poison – there is an antidote to it. But it is said that a *brāhmaṇa*'s property is poison. There is no remedy for it in the world.

34. Poison kills him who consumes it and fire is quenched by water, but the fire from the kindling wood of a *brāhmaṇa*'s property burns a family to its roots.

35. A *brāhmaṇa*'s property, enjoyed without permission, destroys three generations. And, if enjoyed after being won by force, it destroys ten previous and ten succeeding generations.

36. Kings, blinded by royal opulence, do not clearly see their own fall. Those who hanker after the property of a *brāhmaṇa*, [earned] virtuously, are foolish; [it leads to] hell.

37–38. Kings and members of the royal household who, beyond restraint, seize the gifts belonging to *brāhmaṇas* who are generous householders, are burned in the Kumbhīpāka hells. If the *brāhmaṇas*' means of support has been seized and they are weeping, such kings are buried for as many years as there are particles of sand touched by the *brāhmaṇas*' tears.

39. He who steals the property of a *brāhmaṇa*, whether it was

given by himself or by someone else, is born as a worm in faeces for 60,000 years.
40. Let the wealth of a *brāhmaṇa* not come to me. By coveting it, men's lives are shortened. Overthrown and deprived of their kingdoms, [in their next life] they become dreadful snakes.
41. My followers should never be hostile towards a *brāhmaṇa* – even if he has committed an offence. They must always offer respects even if he is beating or cursing them.
42. Just as I diligently offer respects to *brāhmaṇas* according to the occasion, so should you do likewise. He who does otherwise will be punished by me.
43. The stolen wealth of a *brāhmaṇa* causes the thief to fall down even if he is unaware, just as this *brāhmaṇa*'s cow caused Nṛga to fall."
44. After obliging the people of Dvārakā to hear this, *Bhagavān* Mukunda, the purifier of all the worlds, entered his own palace.'

CHAPTER 65

The Dragging of the Yamunā at Balarāma's Triumph

1. *Śrī* Śuka said:

'The auspicious Balarāma, best of the Kurus, mounted his chariot and went to Nanda's Gokula, intent on seeing his friends. He was excited.
2. Balarāma was embraced at length by the *gopas* and *gopīs*, who had been pining to see him. He greeted his mother and father and was welcomed with their blessings:
3. "May you, along with your younger brother, the Lord of the universe, protect us for a long time, O Dāśārha [Balarāma]." Saying this, they had Kṛṣṇa sit on their laps, embraced him, and wet him with their tears.
4–5. Then Kṛṣṇa met the cowherders and the elderly *gopas* with smiles and handshakes as was customary, and was greeted respectfully by his juniors according to age, degree of friendship

and relationship. When he had rested and was comfortably seated, they surrounded him and asked him questions.
6. They had given up all their wealth for lotus-eyed Kṛṣṇa, and so were also asked [in turn by Kṛṣṇa], in a voice choking with love, about the health of their families.
7. The cowherd men and women said: "Are all our kinsfolk healthy, Balarāma? Now that you have wives and sons, do you remember us, Balarāma?
8. By good fortune the sinful Kaṃsa has been killed; by good fortune our good friends have been freed; and by good fortune they have taken refuge in a fortress after killing and defeating their enemies."
9. The *gopīs*, honoured by the presence of Balarāma, asked with smiles whether Kṛṣṇa, the beloved of the women of the city, was happy:
10. "Does he remember his relatives, his father and his mother? Will he also ever come to see his mother? Does the mighty-armed one even remember our service?
11. For his sake we abandoned our kinsmen – mothers, fathers, brothers, husbands, sons and sisters – those whom it is difficult to give up.
12. Truly, how can women not believe words such as his? But he is a breaker of friendships – he suddenly abandoned us and left.
13. How can the intelligent women of the city accept the words of such a fickle, ungrateful person? Overcome by Kāma, they are carried away by his bewitching smiles and glances.
14. O *gopīs*, what use is it to talk about him? Speak of other subjects. If his time is spent without us, so will ours be [without him]."
15. Recalling thus the loving embrace, the way of moving, the sweet look, conversation and laughter of the descendant of Śūra [Kṛṣṇa], the women wept.
16. *Bhagavān* Saṅkarṣaṇa [Balarāma] is a practised peacemaker, and consoled them with touching messages from Kṛṣṇa.
17. *Bhagavān* Balarāma lived there for the two months – *Madhu* and *Mādhava*[1] – bringing pleasure to the *gopīs* in the nights.
18. He frequented the groves of the Yamunā river, which was

touched by the full crescent of the moon and by a lotus-scented breeze, and enjoyed himself, surrounded by groups of women.
19. The divine *vāruṇī* liquor, sent by the god Varuṇa, oozed from the hollow of a tree, perfuming the whole of the grove with its fragrance.
20. Balarāma smelt the wind-borne scent of that flow of honey, and went there and drank along with the women.
21. As his deeds were celebrated in song by the women, Balarāma, the bearer of the plough, wandered in the forests in an inebriated state, his eyes rolling from intoxication.
22. He was drunk, with only one earring on, and wearing a garland of *vaijayantī* flowers. The lotus of his face was decorated with dewy drops of sweat.
23. As Lord, he summoned the Yamunā river so that he could sport in the water. Since he was drunk, Balarāma was furious when she did not come, and thought: "She has shown disrespect for my personal command." Then he dragged the river with the tip of his plough.
24. Balarāma said: "O sinful one, you disobeyed me because you did not come when I summoned you. I will bring you here, who flow at will, in a hundred pieces, with the tip of my plough."
25. Threatened thus, the Yamunā river was terrified, O king. She fell trembling at his feet, and spoke these words to Balarāma, the joy of the Yadu dynasty:
26. "O Balarāma, O mighty-armed Balarāma, I did not understand your power. This world is supported by one fraction of you, O Lord of the universe.
27. O *Bhagavān*, please release me – I am ignorant of your Lordship's transcendent nature, O Soul of the universe. You are compassionate towards your devotees, and I submit [to you]."
28. At this supplication, *Bhagavān* Balarāma released the Yamunā and plunged into the water with the women, like the king of tuskers with his elephants.
29. Kāntī[2] presented Balarāma with a garland of good omen, valuable ornaments and a pair of dark-coloured garments when he came out of the water, having had his fill of sport.
30. He dressed himself in the two blue pieces of clothing and put on the golden garland. Smeared [with sandalwood] and

beautifully adorned, he was as magnificent as Airāvata, Indra's elephant.
31. Even today, O king, the Yamunā can be seen to flow where she was dragged, as if manifesting the infinite prowess of Balarāma.
32. In this way, the nights passed for Balarāma as if they were only one. His mind was charmed by the exquisite beauty of the women of Vraj.'

CHAPTER 66

The Killing of Pauṇḍraka and Others

1. *Śrī* Śuka said:

'When Balarāma had gone to Nanda's Vraj, O king, Pauṇḍraka, the foolish overlord of Karūṣa, dispatched a messenger to Kṛṣṇa, saying: "I am Vāsudeva."
2. Egged on by stupid men who said: "You are *Bhagavān* Vāsudeva, the Lord of the universe incarnate," he thought himself to be Acyuta.
3. The idiot sent a messenger to Dvārakā to Kṛṣṇa, whose ways are mysterious. The fool was like a child who had been elected king by children.
4. After arriving in Dvārakā, the messenger relayed the king's message to the lotus-eyed Lord Kṛṣṇa, who was seated in an assembly:
5. "I am the only Vāsudeva, become incarnate out of compassion for living beings – there is no other. You must give up your false title!
6. Give up my insignia[1] which you bear out of foolishness, O Sātvata, and approach me for shelter. If you refuse, then give me battle."'
7. *Śrī* Śuka said:

'When they heard the dull-witted Pauṇḍraka bragging thus,

king Ugrasena and the other assembly members laughed loudly.
8. After some laughter and some talk, *Bhagavān* replied [via] the messenger: "I will hurl [at you] those insignia which you thus boast about, you fool.
9. With your mouth closed shut, you ignoramus, you will lie there dead, circled by herons, vultures and *vaṭa* birds. You will become shelter for the dogs!"
10. The messenger relayed all these insults to his master. Kṛṣṇa then mounted his chariot and he too approached Kāśī [Vārāṇasī].
11. The mighty chariot warrior Pauṇḍraka, in turn, learning of Kṛṣṇa's actions, swiftly ventured forth from the city equipped with *akṣauhiṇī* battalions.
12. Hari saw Pauṇḍraka and his friend, the king of Kāśī, who was following Pauṇḍraka, and threatening from the rear with three *akṣauhiṇīs*.
13. Pauṇḍraka was conspicuous with [the emblems of Viṣṇu] – conch, disc, sword, club, Śārṅga bow, *śrīvatsa*, and so forth. He wore the Kaustubha jewel and was adorned with a forest garland.
14. He had Garuḍa on his banner, was wearing two yellow silk garments, a priceless helmet and glittering crocodile earrings.
15. Seeing him standing in that dress copied from his own, like an actor whose place is on a stage, Hari laughed heartily.
16. The enemy bombarded Hari with tridents, clubs, iron bludgeons, spears, lances, darts, pikes, swords, javelins and arrows.
17. The army of Pauṇḍraka and the king of Kāśī consisted of elephants, chariots, horses and infantry, but Kṛṣṇa harassed it mercilessly with clubs, swords and discs, just as fire, the devourer of oblations, consumes all creatures at the end of the cycle of *yugas*.[2]
18. The battlefield was littered with chariots, horses, elephants, humans, donkeys and camels which had been smashed to pieces by the disc. It shone like the horrific pleasure grove of the Lord of ghosts.[3] It brought pleasure to the wise.
19. Then Kṛṣṇa, the descendant of Śūra, said: "*Bho! Bho!* Pauṇḍraka! I will now hurl those very weapons about which you spoke to me in the words of the messenger!

20. I will make you give up my title which you have falsely assumed, you fool! Today I will submit to you if I do not wish a fight."
21. After insulting Pauṇḍraka with these words, Kṛṣṇa with his sharp arrows deprived him of his chariot, and sliced off his head with his disc, as Indra sliced the mountain with his thunderbolt.
22. Then, with his arrows, he decapitated the king of Kāśī, causing his head to land in the city of Kāśī, like the calyx of a lotus severed by the wind.
23. Having killed the envious Pauṇḍraka and his friend in this way, Hari entered Dvārakā, while the honeyed stories of his deeds were being sung by the heavenly *siddhas*.
24. All Pauṇḍraka's bondage was destroyed through his unceasing meditation on *Bhagavān*. [By] assuming the personal form of Hari, O king, Pauṇḍraka attained to Hari's nature.[4]
25. When they saw the fallen head, complete with earrings, at the royal gate, the people were confused: "What is this? Whose face is this?"
26. The queens, sons and kinsfolk of the king recognized it as the lord of Kāśī, O king. The citizens cried out: "Oh master! Oh master – we are finished!"
27–28. Sudakṣiṇa, Pauṇḍraka's son, performed the customary rites for his father and resolved to himself: "I will kill the murderer of my father, and thus get revenge for him." Sudakṣiṇa, along with his mentor, then worshipped Maheśvara Śiva with deep concentration.
29. The powerful *Bhagavān* Śiva was satisfied and granted him a favour in Avimukta, an area in Kāśī. Sudakṣiṇa made his wish – the means of slaying the killer of his father.
30–31. "Circumambulate the *dakṣiṇa* sacrificial fire, along with the *ṛtvik* priest,[5] according to the rites of black magic, and in the company of *brāhmaṇas*. The fire, surrounded by the *pramathas*,[6] will fulfil your desire when invoked against one who is not favourably disposed to *brāhmaṇas*." Sudakṣiṇa did as he was instructed. After observing his vow, he invoked magic against Kṛṣṇa.
32. Thereupon, the fire arose from the pit, taking on a ferocious

form. His eyes spat out live coal, and his beard and hair were of red-hot copper.
33. He was naked, and his cruel face had stick-like eyebrows and fearsome teeth. He was licking the corner of his mouth with his tongue and shaking his blazing trident.
34. Surrounded by ghosts and burning up the quarters [of the world] with his flames, he rushed towards Dvārakā, causing the surface of the earth to tremble from feet the size of palm-trees.
35. The citizens of Dvārakā saw the conflagration, produced by the black magic, approaching. They were terrified, like deer in a burning forest.
36. Frantic with fear, they said to Kṛṣṇa, who was playing with dice in the assembly hall: "Save, please save the city from the burning fire, O Lord of the three worlds!"
37. Hearing the despair of the population and seeing the terror of his own people, Kṛṣṇa, the provider of shelter, broke out laughing and said: "Do not fear. I am your guardian."
38. The Lord who is the internal and external witness of everything knew that this was the sorcery of Śiva. He dispatched his disc, which stood by his side, to the task of warding off the conflagration.
39. The disc, Sudarśana, resembled 1,000 suns. Blazing, it had the brilliance of the fire of *pralaya* at the annihilation of the universe.[7] It tormented that fire, as well as the sky, space, heaven and earth.
40. The fire raised by black magic was repelled by the potency of the weapon of Kṛṣṇa, the disc-holder, O king. The black magic [produced by Sudakṣiṇa] withdrew with a frustrated face, returned to Vārāṇasī [Kāśī], and burnt Sudakṣiṇa along with his *ṛtvik* priestly class.
41. Viṣṇu's disc entered Vārāṇasī in pursuit of it. Vārāṇasī had markets, dwellings, assembly halls and shops. It was replete with granaries, watchtowers and gateways, and filled with chariots, horses, elephants and depositories.
42. After burning Vārāṇasī in its entirety, Viṣṇu's Sudarśana disc again positioned itself by the side of Kṛṣṇa, whose deeds are effortless.

43. The mortal who attentively hears or recites this heroic deed of Uttamaśloka [Kṛṣṇa], who is praised in the best of verses, is freed from all sins.'

CHAPTER 67

The Killing of Dvivida

1. The king said:

'I wish to again hear about the amazing deeds of the unlimited and immeasurable Balarāma. What else did the Lord do?'
2. *Śrī* Śuka said:

'There was a certain friend of Naraka, a powerful ape by the name of Dvivida. He was an associate of Sugrīva and the brother of Mainda.[1]
3. The ape was carrying out acts of vandalism in the kingdom, kindling fires, and burning the cattle settlements, mines, villages and cities. He was avenging his friend Naraka.
4. In some places he tore up mountains and pulverized the land with them – especially that of the Ānartas where Hari, the killer of his friend, was to be found.
5. In other places, he stood in the ocean and agitated the water with his hands, submerging the kingdoms along their coastlines. He had the vigour of 10,000 elephants.
6. After smashing the trees in the *āśrama* hermitages of prominent sages, the miscreant polluted the sacrificial fires with stool and urine.
7. Arrogantly he threw men and women into caves in the valleys of mountains, and sealed them shut with stones, like a wasp does to an insect.
8. As he was causing mayhem in the lands in this fashion, and polluting women from good families, Dvivida heard the sound of an enchanting song and went to Raivataka hill.
9. He saw there the lotus-faced Balarāma, Lord of the Yadus.

All Balarāma's limbs were beautiful to behold, and he was in the midst of groups of women.

10. Having drunk *vāruṇī* liquor, he was singing and rolling his eyes with intoxication. He was magnificent in physique, like an elephant in rut.

11. Dvivida, that wicked creature of the branches, climbed a branch and caused the trees to shake. He made a sound, "*kilakila*", and became visible.

12. Balarāma's consorts – young ladies who were fickle by nature and fond of laughter – saw the audacity of that monkey, and burst out laughing.

13. While Balarāma was watching, the monkey ridiculed them by gesturing with his eyebrows, confronting them and displaying his rectum to them.

14–15. Balarāma, the peerless fighter, became angry and threw a rock at him. The cunning monkey dodged the rock and grabbed the pitcher of liquor. Laughing at Balarāma, the monkey insulted him, making him furious. The rascal then broke the pitcher and tugged at [their] garments.

16. Being powerful, the monkey was puffed up with pride, took no notice of Balarāma and mocked him. Balarāma saw his rude behaviour, and the destruction he had wreaked on the land.

17. Angered, Balarāma took up his club and plough, eager to kill this enemy. But Dvivida was also extremely powerful, and lifted up a *śāla* tree with one hand.

18. He quickly rushed forward, and struck Balarāma on the head with it. But Saṅkarṣaṇa stood firm as a mountain as it fell on his head.

19. Balarāma grabbed it in turn, and struck Dvivida with his pestle, Sunanda. Struck on the head by the pestle, Dvivida was bright with streams of blood.

20. Oblivious to that blow, Dvivida appeared like a mountain with red chalk. He lifted up another [*śāla* tree] and vigorously stripped it of foliage.

21. He struck Balarāma with it. Enraged, Balarāma smashed it into hundreds of pieces. Then Dvivida struck him powerfully with another one, and Balarāma smashed that one into hundreds of pieces also.

22. Tree after tree was broken while fighting in this fashion with *Bhagavān*. Dvivida made the forest treeless after pulling them up from everywhere.
23. Then Dvivida in a rage unleashed a torrent of rocks over Balarāma. The wielder of the pestle effortlessly smashed them all.
24. The lord of monkeys then made his arms into fists as big as palm trees, attacked Balarāma, the son of Rohiṇī, and pounded him intensely on the chest with them.
25. Balarāma, the Lord of the Yadus, was furious. He discarded his pestle and beat Dvivida on the collar-bone with his two arms.
26. As Dvivida was falling, the mountain, with its peaks and trees, shook because of him, like a boat on the water shakes from the wind, O Parīkṣit, lion of men.
27. The words: "Victory! Honour! Bravo, bravo!" were uttered from the sky, and there was a shower of *kusuma* flowers from the leaders of the sages, the *siddhas* and the gods.
28. Thus, having killed Dvivida who had brought destruction on the world, *Bhagavān* Balarāma entered his city, to the acclamation of the people.'

CHAPTER 68

Saṅkarṣaṇa's [Balarāma's] Victory as Manifested in theDragging of Hastināpura

1. *Śrī* Śuka said:

'Sāmba, Kṛṣṇa's wife Jāmbavati's son, who is victorious in battle, O king, abducted Lakṣmaṇā, the daughter of Duryodhana, when she was taking part in her *svayaṃvara* marriage ceremony.
2. The Kauravas were furious and said: "This boy is impudent. Lacking respect for us, he has abducted the maiden by force against her will.

3. Imprison this impudent person. What can the Vṛṣṇi clan do? They enjoy land we gave them and are prosperous by our grace.
4. If the Vṛṣṇis hear that their son has been caught and they come, they will be defeated and their pride broken, like senses that are brought well under control."
5. Saying this, Karṇa, Śala, Bhūri, Yajñaketu and Suyodhana set out to engage with Sāmba, under the direction of the Kuru elders.
6. The great charioteer Sāmba saw that the followers of Dhṛtarāṣṭra were pursuing him. He took up his magnificent bow, and stood his ground like a solitary lion.
7. Intent on capturing him, the Kauravas said: "Stand still, stand still!" Led by Karṇa, the bowmen attacked him with a shower of arrows.
8. Sāmba, son of the unknowable Kṛṣṇa, best of the Kurus and joy of the Yadus, was pierced [by their arrows]. He did not tolerate this, as a lion would not tolerate [being harassed by] insignificant animals.
9. With a twanging sound of his magnificent bow, the hero pierced them all, beginning with Karṇa, with his arrows, simultaneously running their six chariots through with as many arrows.
10. He pierced the four horses with four arrows, and the chariot drivers with one arrow each. The charioteers and great bowmen were awed by Sāmba's [feat].
11. They deprived him of his chariot. Four men [struck his] four horses, one man [struck] the chariot driver, and the other his bow.
12. After relieving Sāmba of his chariot in the fight and binding him with difficulty, the victorious Kurus entered their city with the youth and their maiden.
13. When they heard about this, the Vṛṣṇis' anger was aroused. They made ready for a counter-expedition under the direction of Ugrasena.
14. But Balarāma pacified the eminent Vṛṣṇis, who had donned armour. He is the remover of the stain of strife, and did not want conflict between the Kurus and the Vṛṣṇis.

15. Balarāma went to Hastināpura in a chariot as brilliant as the sun, surrounded by *brāhmaṇas* and family elders, like the moon accompanied by stars.
16. Reaching Hastināpura, Balarāma remained in a grove outside the city. Wanting to find out about Dhṛtarāṣṭra, he sent Uddhava ahead.
17. Uddhava greeted Dhṛtarāṣṭra, son of Ambikā; Bhīṣma; Droṇa; Bāhlīka; and Duryodhana[1] according to protocol, and informed them of Balarāma's arrival.
18. They were delighted to hear that Balarāma, the best of friends, had come. After honouring Uddhava, they all went with auspicious gifts in hand.
19. They approached Balarāma and presented him with cows and *arghya* according to custom. Those of them who knew Balarāma's power bowed their heads in homage.
20. After they had heard that each other's friends were well, and had asked about their health and welfare, Balarāma spoke these forthright words:
21. "Ugrasena is your master, the lord of the lords of the earth. After listening carefully to what he has ordered, you should carry it out without delay.
22. Out of a desire for harmony between kinsfolk, I am overlooking the fact that many of you, by breaking the codes of *dharma*, defeated one single man who honoured the codes of *dharma*, and then bound him up."[2]
23. The Kurus heard the words of Balarāma, which were as potent as himself, and brimming with strength, heroism and power. They were angry, and declared:
24. "*Aho!* This is indeed very remarkable. Because of the insuperable passage of time, the shoe wishes to climb on to the head bearing the crown.
25. Connected [with us] by marriage ties, these Vṛṣṇis were elevated to a state of equality. They shared our meals, seats and beds, and were given kingly thrones by us.
26. It is because of our indulgence that they enjoy the fly-whisk, fan, conch, white umbrella crown, throne and bed.[3]
27. Enough of the Yadus' kingly insignia – it is being redirected against those who bestowed it, like nectar given to snakes. These

Yadus, who are thriving by our grace, are now giving orders. They have truly lost all shame.
28. How could even Indra keep that which was not given by such Kurus as Arjuna, Droṇa and Bhīṣma, like a sheep keeping the lion's booty?"'
29. *Śrī* Bādarāyaṇi [Śuka] said:

'Carried away by the extent of their wealth, their relationships and birth, O Parīkṣit, best of the Bharatas, those offensive men subjected Balarāma to their wicked words and then entered into their city.
30. When he saw the bad character of the Kurus, and heard their words, the infallible Balarāma was full of wrath, his expression formidable. Laughing repeatedly, he said:
31. "So, inflated by various conceits, these unrighteous people do not desire peace. Punishment will subdue them, as the stick does to animals.
32. *Aho!* It took me some time to pacify the enraged Yadus, as well as Kṛṣṇa, who was furious. Then I came here desiring peace for the Kurus.
33. These dull-witted, arrogant rascals relish strife. They have disregarded me, and uttered harsh words.
34. Is Ugrasena not the master, according to them?! He is the lord of the Bhoja, Vṛṣṇi and Andhaka dynasties, whose order Indra and the other rulers of the planets obey.
35. He who frequents the Sudharmā assembly hall, who brought the *pārijāta* tree of the gods and enjoys it,[4] is he, Kṛṣṇa, not deserving of a throne, according to them?!
36. He whose two feet Śrī, the goddess of fortune and ruler of everything, personally worships, does he, the Lord of Śrī, not deserve the royal insignia of kings, according to them?!
37. Brahmā, Śiva and even I, as well as Śrī – all only a fraction of a fraction of him – constantly carry the dust of his lotus feet. That dust is borne on the crowns of the most eminent rulers of all the worlds, and is the sacred place of all sacred places worthy of worship. What is a royal throne to him?!
38. The Vṛṣṇis enjoy a piece of the world that was given by the

Kurus, according to them?! We ourselves are the shoe and the Kurus are the head, according to them?!

39. *Aho!* What ruler would tolerate such ridiculous, harsh words from arrogant men, who behave as though drunk – and are indeed drunk with riches.

40. Today I will free the world of Kurus," Balarāma said in a rage. Then he seized his plough and stood up, as if burning the three worlds.

41. Furious, he tore up the city of Hastināpura with the tip of his plough, dragged it to the Gaṅgā river and was about to hurl it in.

42. The Kurus saw the city whirling around like a vessel on the water, and falling into the Gaṅgā. They were thrown into confusion.

43. Desiring to save their lives, they placed Sāmba in front, along with Lakṣmaṇā, and approached the master for refuge, their hands folded in supplication:

44. "Balarāma, Balarāma, you are the support of everything. We did not understand your power. Please forgive our offence; we are dull-witted fools.

45. You are without support, and you alone are the cause of the maintenance, creation and dissolution [of the universe]. They say that you are simply playing and that the worlds are playthings for you, O Lord.

46. It is indeed you who playfully bear this globe of the world on your head, O infinite thousand-headed one.[5] And at the end, the world is withdrawn into your own self, and you are left remaining without a second.

47. Your anger is not from envy or hate, but in order to instruct everyone, O *Bhagavān*. You uphold *sattva*, which is dedicated to [the tasks of] maintenance and protection.[6]

48. Homage to you, soul of all creatures, imperishable support of all powers! Let there be homage to you, maker of the universe. We have come to you for shelter." '

49. *Śrī* Śuka said:

'Balarāma was appeased by them. Their world was shaking and,

terrified, they surrendered. Gratified, Balarāma said: "Do not fear," and made them fearless.
50. As dowry [for Lakṣmaṇa], Duryodhana gave 1,200 sixty-year-old elephants, and tens of thousands of horses.
51. [He gave] 6,000 golden chariots as brilliant as the sun, and 1,000 maidservants with golden ornaments on their necks. He held his daughter in great affection.
52. *Bhagavān*, best of the Sātvatas, accepted all this and was applauded by those dear to him. Then he set forth with his son and daughter-in-law.
53. Later, when he had entered his own city, Balarāma, whose weapon is a plough, met his fond relatives. Then, in the centre of an assembly of eminent Yadus, he related all that he had done.
54. Even today, that city still shows evidence of the prowess of Balarāma – it appears raised up on the south side of the Gaṅgā.'

CHAPTER 69

The Vision of Kṛṣṇa's Householder Life

1. *Śrī* Śuka said:

'Hearing that Naraka had been killed, and that one person, Kṛṣṇa, had married many women, Nārada desired to see this:
2. "It is astonishing that one person with one body has married 16,000 women, and lives simultaneously in many houses."
3. Saying this, the eager sage of the gods came to see Dvārakā. It was resonant with swarms of bees and flocks of birds, and had flowery parks and pleasure groves.
4. It was filled with the loud sounds of swans and cranes in lakes blooming with *kumuda* and *kahlāra* [white lotuses], *ambhoja* [lotuses], *indīvara* [blue lotuses] and water lilies.
5. It was endowed with 900,000 mansions made of silver and crystal with adornments of gold and jewels, and was distinctive with great emeralds.
6. Residences of gods, assembly halls and buildings, laid-out

markets, crossroads, paths and thoroughfares were among its delights. Its terraces, streets, courtyards and roads were sprinkled with water, and it was shaded from the heat by flying flags and banners.

7. Hari's private inner city was in Dvārakā; it was beautiful, blessed by the celestial guardians of the quarters of the world, and was evidence of the personal skill of Tvaṣṭā, the architect of the gods.

8. That inner city was beautifully decorated with 16,000 palaces. Nārada entered one of these magnificent houses of [Kṛṣṇa's] wives.

9–11. It was supported with coral pillars with choicest overlays of *vaidūrya* gems, and decorated with walls made of sapphire, and floors whose lustre never faded. There were canopies constructed by Tvaṣṭā, with hanging strings of pearls, and ivory seats and couches embellished with the best-quality jewels. There were women dressed in beautiful garments with golden ornaments on their necks, and men wearing jewelled earrings, turbans, fine clothes and armour.

12. The darkness was dispelled by the light of clusters of jewelled lamps, O dear king. Peacocks danced there on the diverse pinnacles of the houses. Seeing the aloewood incense billowing forth from the holes [in the latticed windows], dear Parīkṣit, they thought them to be clouds and cried out.[1]

13. The sage saw the Lord of the Sātvatas with his wife in that house. She was continually accompanied by 1,000 maidservants who were equal in dress, age, beauty and qualities, and she was fanning Kṛṣṇa with an oxtail fan with a golden handle.

14. *Bhagavān* Kṛṣṇa, the most eminent of those who uphold *dharma*, saw Nārada and immediately rose up from the bed of Śrī, the goddess of fortune. He paid homage to both Nārada's feet with his head, which was graced with a helmet. Then, with his hands folded in respect, he insisted that [Nārada] sit on his own personal seat.

15. Although he is the ultimate *guru* of the world, and the water that washes his feet [the Gaṅgā] is the ultimate holy place, Kṛṣṇa, the Lord of the righteous, washed Nārada's feet and actually carried that water away on his own head. For this

quality [of respect for *brāhmaṇas*] he is called *Brahmaṇyadeva*, "the Lord of *brāhmaṇas*".

16. After worshipping the most eminent of the celestial sages according to the injunctions of the scriptures, Kṛṣṇa, the ancient sage Nārāyana, friend of mankind, spoke measured words as sweet as nectar: "Pray tell, master, what can we do for you?"

17. *Śrī* Nārada said: "O almighty one, it is certainly not surprising that you, the master of all the worlds, are the friend of all creatures, and the chastiser of the wicked. You are widely praised, and we know well that your incarnation is from your own free will. It is for the protection and maintenance of the world, and for [bestowing] liberation.

18. I have seen your two lotus feet, which give liberation to people. Brahmā and the other [gods] of profound intelligence meditate upon them in the heart. They are the grounds of deliverance from those fallen into the well of *saṃsāra*. Grant that my remembrance [of them] will remain, so that I can travel about meditating [on them]."

19. Thereafter, Nārada entered the residence of another of Kṛṣṇa's wives, O dear king, desiring to witness the *yogamāyā* of the Lord of the lords of *yoga*.

20. There, he [saw] Kṛṣṇa again, this time playing dice with his beloved and with Uddhava. Nārada was welcomed with the highest devotion, by [Kṛṣṇa's] rising up to greet him and [offering] him a seat, and other marks of hospitality.

21. Kṛṣṇa, apparently unaware, asked Nārada: "When did you arrive, sir? What can we, who are imperfect, do for those who are perfect?

22. Therefore please tell us, O *brāhmaṇa*, make this birth auspicious for us." Nārada was amazed. He rose silently and went to another residence.

23. There, too, he saw Govinda, who was indulging his infant children. Then, in another residence, Nārada saw that preparations had been made for taking a bath.

24. Elsewhere, Kṛṣṇa was placing oblations in the three sacred fires,[2] worshipping with the five sacrifices,[3] feeding the twice-born and eating their remnants.[4]

25. In another place, Kṛṣṇa was sitting down at dusk and

silently chanting *japa mantras*.[5] In yet another place he was manoeuvring around in the fencing area with sword and shield.
26. Elsewhere, Kṛṣṇa, the elder brother of Gada, was riding horses, elephants and chariots, and, somewhere else again, he was lying on a couch being eulogized by bards.
27. In one place, Kṛṣṇa was consulting with his ministers such as Uddhava, while elsewhere he was enjoying sporting in the water surrounded by women and courtesans.
28. In another place he was giving beautifully bedecked cows to distinguished members of the twice-born castes, and listening to auspicious stories from the Purāṇas and epic histories.
29. At some point, in some other beloved's house, Kṛṣṇa was telling jokes and laughing, while elsewhere he was pursuing *dharma*, *artha* or *kāma*.[6]
30. In some other place he was meditating on the supreme being who is beyond *prakṛti*, and serving his *gurus* with desirable objects, enjoyments and worship.
31. And somewhere else Keśava was preparing for war against certain people, and, elsewhere again, alliances with others. In yet another place, Kṛṣṇa was contemplating the welfare of the righteous, along with Balarāma.
32. [Nārada saw] him making arrangements for traditional marriages with due pomp for his sons and daughters, with suitable brides and grooms at the appropriate time.
33. He saw great celebrations by the Lord of the lords of *yoga* for his children when they were sent off and when they returned. All this astonished the people.
34. In some places, [Nārada saw] Kṛṣṇa offering sacrifices to all the gods with elaborate rituals, or fulfilling his *dharma* by [building] monasteries, groves and wells.
35. In other places, he was roaming around in the hunt, mounted on a horse from the Sindh province, and killing sacrificial animals, surrounded by the Yadu heroes.
36. Elsewhere, the Lord of *yogīs* was wandering about in disguise among his ministers in the inner section of the city, wanting to find out the attitudes of each.
37. After seeing this exhibition of *yogamāyā* by Kṛṣṇa, who was following human ways, Nārada said to Hṛṣīkeśa with a smile:

38. "We know that your *yogamāyā* is hard to perceive, even for magicians. But it will become manifest, O soul of the lords of *yoga*, by service to your lotus feet.
39. Give me your leave, O God – I will wander about the worlds, which are overflowing with your glories, singing about your *līlās*, which purify the earth."
40. *Śrī Bhagavān* said: "O *brāhmaṇa*, I am the speaker, performer and authorizer of *dharma*, and I am present in this world to teach it. Do not be concerned, O son."'
41. *Śrī* Śuka said:

'Nārada saw Kṛṣṇa himself, as one person, performing the righteous and purifying householder *dharmas* in all the houses.
42. After seeing time after time the exhibition of *yogamāyā* by Kṛṣṇa, of infinite power, the sage was amazed and struck with admiration.
43. After being thoroughly honoured by Kṛṣṇa, who was dedicated to *artha*, *kāma* and *dharma*, Nārada was gratified and went on his way, remembering only Kṛṣṇa.
44. Thus, following the ways of humans, Nārāyaṇa manifested his *śakti* powers for the liberation of everyone. He enjoyed himself with 16,000 of the choicest women, O dear king, delighting in their laughter, their glances, their affection and their shyness.
45. Hari, the cause of the manifestation, maintenance and destruction of the universe, did these things; no one else is able to. Devotion for *Bhagavān*, who is the path to liberation, will arise in the person who sings about, hears and rejoices in them, dear king.'

CHAPTER 70

*A Message from the Kings Imprisoned by Jarāsandha**

1. *Śrī* Śuka said:

'As dawn was approaching, Mādhava's wives, in the embrace of their husband, cursed the crowing cocks and were overcome by feelings of separation [from their beloved].
2. While bees hummed, the birds, aroused by the breeze of the *māndara* groves, sang like bards, awakening Kṛṣṇa.
3. Snuggled between the arms of her beloved, Vaidarbhī [Rukmiṇī] did not appreciate the auspicious *brāhmamuhūrta* hour,[1] [fearing] separation from his embrace.
4. After rising at *brāhmamuhūrta*, and touching water [for purification], Mādhava Kṛṣṇa meditated with a tranquil mind on his own being,[2] which is beyond *tamas*.
5. His being is one, luminous within itself, without a second and imperishable. It removes all impurities by its own self-abiding nature. It is known as *brahman*. It is bliss and existence, made manifest through its own *śaktis*, which are the causes of the manifestation and destruction of the world.
6. When Kṛṣṇa had bathed in pure water according to the customary rites, he dressed in two pieces of cloth and performed the full range of rituals of the righteous – the daybreak worship and other such rites, and the sacrificial fire. Then, he silently chanted the *brahman* [*gāyatrī*] *mantra*.[3]
7. Kṛṣṇa, self-possessed, worshipped the rising sun and appeased the gods and the forefathers – who are his own *aṃśa* – and honoured the elders and the *brāhmaṇas*.
8–9. He gave 13,084 cows to well-adorned *brāhmaṇas* every day, along with linen, antelope skin and sesame seeds. The cows had gold on their horns, silver on their hooves and fronts, necklaces of pearls, and were draped with cloth. They were obedient and milk-giving, and each was accompanied by only one calf.

10. Kṛṣṇa offered homage to cows, *brāhmaṇas*, gods, elders, *gurus* and all creatures – all of whom are manifestations of himself – and touched auspicious things.
11. He adorned himself, the adornment of the world of men, with ornaments, as well as with garments, his own personal ointments and a heavenly garland.
12. He looked in a mirror, as well as at ghee, cows, bulls, *brāhmaṇas* and gods.[4] Then he arranged for the satisfaction of the desires of all the castes who frequented the inner quarters and the city, and similarly gratified his ministers [by granting] their desires. He was joyfully received in turn.
13. He distributed ointments, betel nut and garlands first to *brāhmaṇas*, friends and ministers, before taking some for himself.
14. Meanwhile the charioteer brought Kṛṣṇa's striking chariot, yoked with Sugrīva and the other horses. He offered homage, and stood before Kṛṣṇa.
15. Kṛṣṇa grasped the hand of the charioteer, and then climbed on to the chariot accompanied by Sātyaki and Uddhava, like the sun rising on the eastern mountain.
16. Watched by the women of the inner quarters with modest and loving glances, Kṛṣṇa was reluctantly allowed to depart, and set out. With a smile breaking [on his face], he won over their hearts.
17. He entered the assembly hall called Sudharmā surrounded by the Vṛṣṇi clan. The six waves [in the ocean of *saṃsāra*][5] do not exist for those who enter it, dear Parīkṣit.
18. Seated there on a magnificent throne, the Lord lit up the quarters of the heavens with his own brilliance. Encircled by the Yadus, lions among men, the best of the Yadus was like the moon surrounded by clusters of stars.
19. Jesters entertained the Lord there with comedy [performed] in different moods, O king, as did teachers of dance and, separately, female dancers with energetic dance performances.
20. They danced and sang to the sounds of conches, cymbals, flutes, tambourines and *mṛdaṅga* drums, and bards, heralds and minstrels offered praises.

21. Some of the *brāhmaṇas* seated there were specialists in the Vedas, and narrated stories of previous kings of pious fame.
22. [One day], a certain man arrived there, O king, who had not been seen before. He was announced to *Bhagavān* Kṛṣṇa by the door-keepers, and allowed to enter.
23. With folded hands, the man offered homage to Kṛṣṇa, the supreme Lord. Then he informed him about the sufferings of certain kings imprisoned by Jarāsandha.
24. Those kings had not accepted submission to Jarāsandha during his *digvijaya* [conquering of the directions].[6] Twenty thousand of them were forcibly imprisoned by him in Girivraja.
25. The kings said: "Kṛṣṇa, Kṛṣṇa, immeasurable soul, destroyer of the fear of those who are given up to you: we are approaching you for refuge. Our perspective [on the world] is one of duality, and so we are fearful of *saṃsāra*.[7]
26. To the extent that people cannot give up illicit activities, and have disregarded that which is in their own best interests – the activities prescribed by you and the worship of your Lordship – that powerful one [time] suddenly cuts down their hopes for the duration of their life in this world. Let reverence be paid to him who is vigilant time.
27. Your Lordship is the master of the universe. You have descended into the world with your *aṃśa* to protect the righteous and to subdue the wicked. We do not understand how any one else [i.e. Jarāsandha] can transgress your order, O Lord – or is it that people attain [the fruits of] their own deeds?
28. With this corpse [of a body], which is always full of fear, we bear our burden – kingly happiness, which is dreamlike and dependent on others. We have given up the happiness of the self, which is obtained from you by freedom from desire. We are pitiable, and suffering in this world due to *māyā*.
29. Your two feet remove the sorrows of those who take refuge in you; therefore, your Lordship should please release us from the snares of *karma* – namely the king of Magadha [Jarāsandha]. We are imprisoned. That one man possesses the strength of 10,000 excited elephants, and has incarcerated us in his abode, like the lion, king of beasts, [traps] sheep.

30. O Kṛṣṇa – Your disc is upraised! You have unlimited power, and this villain was crushed by you in battle eighteen times. But after defeating you once, when you were absorbed in [affairs] in the world of men, O unconquerable one, he became proud and abuses us, your citizens. Please give us redress."
31. The messenger said: "This is what those imprisoned by the king of Magadha have said. They are desperate for the arrival of your Lordship, and take refuge in the soles of your feet. Bring peace to these unfortunate men."'
32. *Śrī* Śuka said:

'While the kings' messenger was speaking, the sage of the gods [Nārada] appeared like the sun. He shone brilliantly, and wore a mass of matted locks.
33. When he saw the sage [Nārada], *Bhagavān* Kṛṣṇa, the Lord of the lords of all the worlds, rose up with his followers and with the assembly, and joyfully bowed his head in respect.
34. He honoured the sage, who had accepted the seat that had been prepared, and respectfully spoke these friendly words:
35. "Can there be any fear from any quarter in the three worlds, today? It is certainly a great boon that you wander around the worlds yourself.
36. Nothing is unknown to you in the worlds where the Lord is the creator. Therefore we can inquire from you, sir, about the intention of the Pāṇḍavas."
37. *Śrī* Nārada said: "I have witnessed your insuperable *māyā* repeatedly, O Lord. You are the bewilderer of the creator of the universe [Brahmā]. O Lord of everything, you wander among living creatures with your *śakti* powers, like the concealed light of a fire. I am not surprised at [your question].
38. Who is able to understand fully your intention? You create and conceal this world by your own *māyā*; this world becomes manifest on account of its essence, which is real. Homage to you – your own self is undefinable.
39. I submit to you. Your personal glories in the form of your *līlā* incarnations cause a lamp to shine forth for the *jīva* souls who are wandering about in the cycle of birth and death. They

are ignorant about liberation from their bodies, which are the houses of misfortune.

40. Nevertheless, since you are imitating [the behaviour of] men in this world, I shall let you hear about the intentions of the king – the son of your father's sister, and your devotee [Yudhiṣṭhira].[8]

41. The king, son of Pāṇḍu, desiring supremacy, will honour you by means of the *rājasūya*, the chief of sacrifices.[9] Your lordship should please give your approval.

42. In that distinguished ceremony, O God, the gods, and other celestials, as well as famous kings, will gather together, eager to see your Lordship.

43. The outcastes, who live on the edges of towns, are purified by hearing, glorifying and meditating on you, O Lord – your nature is *brahman*. What of those, then, who see and touch you?

44. Your untarnished fame extends across heaven, earth and the lower worlds, O bringer of good fortune to mankind. The water from your feet purifies the universe – it is known as the Mandākinī river in the heavens, the Bhogavatī in the lower regions, and the Gaṅgā here."'[10]

45. *Śrī* Śuka said:

'When his supporters there did not approve of this, out of a desire to defeat [Jarāsandha], Keśava [Kṛṣṇa] spoke delicately and with a smile to his servant Uddhava.

46. *Śrī Bhagavān* said: "You are our friend, our ultimate eye, and an expert in the art of consultation. Therefore, please say what is to be done here. We have faith and will do accordingly."

47. At this request of his master, who, although omniscient, acted as if confused, Uddhava took the order upon himself and responded.'

CHAPTER 71

Kṛṣṇa's Journey to Indraprastha

1. *Śrī* Śuka said:

'After hearing what had been spoken by the sage of the gods, Uddhava, who was highly intelligent and who understood the points of view both of the assembly and of Kṛṣṇa, spoke.
2. *Śrī* Uddhava said: "You should provide both the assistance spoken about by the sage for your cousin, who is intent on performing a sacrifice, O God, and protection for those desiring your shelter.
3. A *rājasūya* sacrifice is to be performed by one who has conquered the circle of directions, O master.[1] Therefore, my view is that victory over the son of Jarā is the objective of both.
4. A major goal of ours will be accomplished by this, Govinda, as well as fame for you when you free the imprisoned kings.
5. The king Jarāsandha is equal in strength to 10,000 elephants, and invincible even by the powerful – with the exception of Bhīma, who is matched in strength.
6. He can be defeated in individual [combat] between two chariots, but not when he is accompanied by his 100 *akṣauhiṇī* battalions. But he is devoted to *brāhmaṇas* and, when solicited by the twice-born, never rejects anyone.
7. Therefore, adopting the dress of a *brāhmaṇa*, the wolf-bellied Bhīma[2] should go to him and beg. Bhīma will kill him in one-to-one chariot [combat] in your presence – there is no doubt.
8. Hiraṇyagarbha [Brahmā] and Śarva [Śiva] are your primary instruments in the creation and destruction of the universe. You are the Lord who exists as formless time.
9. In their homes, the queens of the kings are singing [in anticipation] about the slaying of their enemy [Jarāsandha] and the freeing of [their husbands who are like] their own selves. They are also singing about the freeing of the king of elephants; the freeing of Sītā, the daughter of Janaka; and the freeing of your

parents.[3] The *gopīs* and we sages who have attained your refuge are doing the same.
10. The slaying of Jarāsandha as a result of his *karma* maturing and bearing fruit will accomplish significant goals, O Kṛṣṇa – including, in all probability, your intended sacrifice." '
11. *Śrī* Śuka said:

'Nārada, the sage of the gods, the Yadu elders, Kṛṣṇa and everyone approved of Uddhava's words, since they were foolproof and full of good omen, O king.
12. Consequently, the omnipresent *Bhagavān* Kṛṣṇa, the son of Devakī, took leave of his *gurus*, and instructed his servants, Dāruka and Jaitra and the others, [to prepare] for the journey.
13. After arranging for the departure of his wives, their sons and possessions, Kṛṣṇa took leave of Saṅkarṣaṇa and Ugrasena, the king of the Yadus, O killer of enemies. Then he mounted his chariot, marked with the banner of Garuḍa, which had been brought forward by his charioteer.
14. He set out, surrounded by the commanders of the horsemen, foot-soldiers, elephants and chariots, and by his own formidable army. The quarters of the earth resounded with the tumult of horns, conches, kettledrums, drums and *mṛdaṅga* drums.
15. The faithful wives, along with their children, followed their husband Acyuta in golden palanquins [drawn] by horses and men. They wore garments of the best quality, ornaments, ointments and garlands, and were guarded by men with swords and shields in hand.
16. The beautifully adorned courtesans and retinue loaded their chattels, such as clothes, blankets and straw huts, on to she-elephants, carts, she-mules, donkeys, buffaloes, cows, camels and men and went along on either side.
17. With its flags, cloth, parasols, and fly-whisks, as well as weapons of the best quality, ornaments, helmets and armour, the great army, tumultuous with noise, glittered in the rays of the sun by day.
18. The sage Nārada, honoured by the Yadus, heard what [Uddhava] had resolved. He accepted the honour paid him, offered his homage to Kṛṣṇa, placed him in his heart, [and

departed] to the sky, his senses satisfied by the sight of Mukunda.
19. *Bhagavān* spoke as follows to the kings' messenger, with words which pleased him: "Do not fear, messenger. May there be good fortune for you! I will take care of the killing of the king of Magadha."
20. Addressed thus, the messenger departed and told the kings [everything] exactly as it had taken place. Eager for freedom, they looked forward to seeing Kṛṣṇa, the descendant of Śauri.
21. Hari passed through the Ānarta, Sauvīra, Maru and Vinaśana regions, crossed mountains and rivers and went through cities, villages, pastures and quarries.
22. Then, after crossing first the Dṛṣadvatī and then the Sarasvatī rivers, as well as the Pañcāla and Matsya territories, he arrived at Śakraprastha [Indraprastha].
23. Yudhiṣṭhira, a man without enemies, heard that Kṛṣṇa had arrived. It is rare for people to catch a glimpse of Kṛṣṇa. Yudhiṣṭhira came out surrounded by friends and accompanied by his priests.
24. He went forward with reverence to Hṛṣīkeśa, accompanied by the sounds of songs, musical instruments and Vedic hymns, just as the vital airs go forward to the principal vital air.[4]
25. His heart was touched with love at seeing his beloved Kṛṣṇa, whom he had not seen for a long time. Yudhiṣṭhira, the son of Pāṇḍu, embraced him again and again.
26. With both his arms, the king embraced Mukunda's body, which is the pure dwelling of the goddess of fortune, Ramā, and all his imperfections were destroyed. With tears in his eyes, his body tingling with ecstasy, and the travails of the world forgotten, Yudhiṣṭhira experienced supreme bliss.
27. Bhīma was delighted. He embraced his maternal cousin with a smile,[5] and his eyes filled with tears of love. The twins and Arjuna embraced their dearest friend Acyuta with joy, tears welling up in their eyes.
28. Kṛṣṇa was embraced by Arjuna and respectfully greeted by the twins. He offered homage to the *brāhmaṇas* and elders according to their status.
29–30. He offered respects to the honourable members of the Kuru, Sṛñjaya and Kaikaya clans. Bards, heralds, eulogists,

jesters, *brāhmaṇas* and *gandharva* celestials sang, danced and offered praise to the lotus-eyed one with *mṛdaṅga* drums, conches, kettledrums, *vīṇas*, cymbals and horns.

31. Surrounded and praised by his supporters, *Bhagavān*, the crown jewel of those of renown, entered the city, which had been decorated.

32. The city had roads wetted by the fragrant fluid of elephant musk, and was splendid with a variety of flags, golden arches and full water-pots. There were men and women bedecked with garlands, ornaments, fragrances and new, fine-quality clothes.

33. Kṛṣṇa saw the royal capital of the Kurus. It was decked out with golden pitchers on the roofs, and wide, silver pinnacles. Flags fluttered, and each house looked picturesque, with incense wafting out of the lattices, and flickering sacrifices and lamps.

34. Kṛṣṇa is worthy of being absorbed by the eyes of humans; when the women heard that he had arrived, the clasps of their garments and hair became loosened in their eagerness. They immediately abandoned their housework, left their husbands in bed, and went to see the lord of men on the road.

35. The women climbed on to the tops of the houses, and saw Kṛṣṇa with his wives on the road, which was congested with elephants, horses, chariots and humans. They embraced him in their hearts, scattered flowers on him, and offered him a warm welcome with smiles and glances.

36. The women saw the wives of Mukunda on the road, like the moon accompanied by stars, and said: "What [pious act] was done by these women that the foremost of men bestows pleasure on them with a few playful glances and broad smiles?"

37. Here and there the citizens approached with auspicious things in their hands. The heads of the guilds offered homage to Kṛṣṇa, and their sins were absolved.

38. Mukunda was approached by the people from the inner quarters, who were all in a flurry, their eyes blooming with love. He entered the king's palace.

39. Pṛthā [Kuntī] saw Kṛṣṇa, the son of her brother and Lord of the three worlds, and her heart was delighted. She arose from the couch with her daughter-in-law [Draupadī] and embraced him.

40. With great reverence King Yudhiṣṭhira took Govinda, the Lord of the god of gods, into his home. He was so overwhelmed with love that he could not remember the proper procedures in the worship.
41. Kṛṣṇa paid respects to the wives of his *gurus*, and to his paternal aunt, Kuntī. He himself was offered respect by his sister, Subhadrā, and by Kṛṣṇā [Draupadī].
42–43. Prompted by her mother-in-law Kuntī, Kṛṣṇā [Draupadī] honoured all the wives of Kṛṣṇa – Rukmiṇī, Satyā, Bhadrā, Jāmbavatī, Kālindī, Mitravindā, Śaibyā, the chaste Nāgnajitī, and all the other women who had come – with garments, garlands and ornaments.
44. The king of *dharma*, Yudhiṣṭhira, provided facilities for Janārdana, as well as for his army, followers, wives and ministers, with ever more novel delights.
45. Accompanied by Phālguna [Arjuna], Kṛṣṇa propitiated the god of fire with the Khāṇḍava forest, and freed Maya, the architect of the gods, by whom the divine assembly hall had been built.[6]
46. Kṛṣṇa stayed there for several months, desiring to please the king. Mounted on his chariot and surrounded by soldiers, he sported with Phālguna [Arjuna].'

CHAPTER 72
The Killing of Jarāsandha

1–2. *Śrī* Śuka said:

'Once, standing in the middle of the assembly, and encircled by sages, *brāhmaṇas*, *kṣatriyas*, *vaiśyas*, his brothers, teachers, family elders, clansmen, relatives and friends, Yudhiṣṭhira addressed those in the audience as follows.
3. *Śrī* Yudhiṣṭhira said: "I will worship your Lordship's majesty by means of the king of sacrifices, the *rājasūya* sacrifice.[1] Please make it succeed for us, O Master.

4. Your feet remove ill fortune. Those who are pure are fully and continually absorbed in them, meditate on and glorify them, and obtain liberation from material existence, O Lord, or, if they prefer, the fulfilment of their desires – but others do not.
5. Therefore, may these people see the power of service to your Lordship's lotus feet in this world, O Lord of lords. Show to both the Kurus and the Sṛñjayas the results attained both by those who worship you, and by those who don't.
6. The mentality that discriminates between what is 'mine' and what is 'another's' cannot exist in you – you are *brahman*, the soul of everything; your vision is equal and you experience happiness in your own self. You show mercy according to the service rendered by your servants. There is nothing inappropriate in this – it is like the celestial *kalpataru* tree."[2]
7. *Śrī Bhagavān* said: "What has been resolved by you is perfect, O king, the scourge of enemies. By this sacrifice, your propitious fame will spread across the worlds.
8. This king of sacrifices is desirable for sages, forefathers, gods, our friends and, indeed, also for all living entities, O master.
9. Defeat all the kings and put the earth under your control. Then collect together all the utensils and perform the great sacrifice.
10. Your brothers are born as partial incarnations of the deities of the world.[3] I am won over by the self-controlled, but unobtainable by those whose minds are not fixed.
11. There is no one in this world who can overcome one who accepts me as supreme – either in power, fame, opulence or might – whether he be a god or a king."'
12. *Śrī* Śuka said:

'When he heard the words of *Bhagavān*, Yudhiṣṭhira was pleased, and his lotus face blossomed. Then he entrusted his brothers, empowered with the potency of Viṣṇu, with the conquest of the directions.
13. He assigned Sahadeva, along with the Sṛñjaya clan, to the southern direction; Nakula to the west; Arjuna to the north; and wolf-bellied Bhīma, with the Matsya, Kekaya and Madraka clans, to the east.

14. Those heroes subdued kings with their prowess, O king, and brought abundant wealth from those directions to Yudhiṣṭhira, for he desired to perform the sacrifice.
15. When he heard that Jarāsandha remained undefeated, Hari told the thoughtful king about the strategy that Uddhava had suggested.
16. Bhīmasena, Arjuna and Kṛṣṇa, the three of them in the guise of *brāhmaṇas*, went to Girivraja, O son, where Jarāsandha, the son of Bṛhadratha, was to be found.
17. Jarāsandha was devoted to *brāhmaṇas* and diligent in the performance of domestic sacrifices. At the appropriate time assigned to unexpected guests, the *kṣatriyas*, disguised as *brāhmaṇas*, went to his quarters and petitioned him:
18. "Know that we are here as guests who have come from afar, and that we are beggars. Grant us that which we desire – and may good fortune attend you.
19. What is intolerable for those who are patient? What is an inappropriate deed for those who are wicked? What cannot be given away by those who are charitable? And what is the 'other' for those whose vision is impartial?
20. He who, even though able, fails to achieve with this temporary body lasting fame that is recognized by the righteous is pitiable and blameworthy.
21. Many have attained eternity by means of the temporary: Hariścandra, Rantideva, Uñchavṛtti, Śibi, Bali, and both the hunter and the pigeon."'[4]
22. *Śrī* Śuka said:

'From the sound of their voices, their appearances and their forearms, which had been marked by the strings of bows, Jarāsandha recognized that they were members of the royal caste. He wondered whether they had been seen before:
23. "These are members of the royal caste in the guise of *brāhmaṇas*. But I must give them whatever is requested – even if it be my own body, however difficult to renounce.
24–25. The widespread and spotless fame of Bali is heard across the quarters of the earth, even though he was deprived of his riches by Viṣṇu disguised as a *brāhmaṇa* intent on snatching

back the riches of Indra. The king of the demons nevertheless gave him the earth, although knowing him to be Viṣṇu in the form of a twice-born *brāhmaṇa*, and despite being restrained [by his own *guru*, Śukrācārya].[5]
26. Truly, what is the use of a member of the *kṣatriya* caste who, although alive, does not strive for great fame by [using] this perishable body for the welfare of *brāhmaṇas*?"
27. Saying this, the generous-minded Jarāsandha spoke to Kṛṣṇa, Arjuna and the wolf-bellied Bhīma: "Hey, *brāhmaṇas*, choose your wish; I will even give you the head of my own body."
28. *Śrī Bhagavān* said: "Give us one-to-one combat, O lord of kings, if you care to. We are warriors who have come in order to fight. We do not desire anything else.
29. That one is the wolf-bellied Bhīma, son of Pṛthā, and this one is his brother Arjuna. Know me to be their maternal cousin, Kṛṣṇa – your enemy."
30. Addressed thus, the Magadhan king laughed loudly, and said angrily: "In that case, I will give you combat, fools.
31. I will not fight with you in battle, Kṛṣṇa. You are a coward whose power is dwindling; you abandoned your own city, Mathurā, and took shelter in the ocean.
32. And this Arjuna is not very strong, and is unequal in age; not being equally matched with me he should not be a contender. Bhīma is my equal in strength."
33. When he had spoken, Jarāsandha gave Bhīma a mighty club, took a second one for himself, and went outside the city.
34. Then, on a level piece of ground, the two heroes clashed. Made furious by the combat, they pounded each other with clubs which were as strong as thunderbolts.
35. The combat was spectacular, the two of them manoeuvring dramatically in circles to the left and to the right, like stage actors.
36. The sound of the pounding clubs was like the striking of thunderbolts – "*caṭa caṭa*" – [or] like the noise of two elephants striking tusks, O king.
37. The two clubs kept raining down with the force of their arms, and began to disintegrate from coming into contact with

[the combatants'] shoulders, hips, feet, arms, thighs and collarbones, like two branches of the *arka* tree [in the grasp of] two fighting elephants inflamed with anger.

38. When their clubs were smashed, the two furious heroes pounded away with their own fists, which felt like iron. The sounds that arose from the striking of their blows – as harsh as the thunder of a violent storm – were like those of two clashing elephants.

39. The combat between them was indecisive since they were equal in skill, strength and vigour, but their strength began to wane, O king.

40. In this way, twenty-seven days passed for those two as they were fighting, O Mahārāja. In the nights, they behaved like friends.[6]

41. At one point, O king, wolf-bellied Bhīma finally said to his cousin Kṛṣṇa: "I am unable to defeat Jarāsandha in battle, O Mādhava."

42. Knowing about the birth and death of his enemy, and about how he had been brought back to life by Jarā,[7] Hari considered the situation. Then he invested the son of Pṛthu with his own potency.

43. Kṛṣṇa's foresight is unfailing; after reflecting on the means of killing his enemy, he revealed it to Bhīma by splitting apart a twig as a sign.

44. Bhīma had great strength and was the best of combatants. Understanding this sign, he seized his enemy by his feet and hurled him on to the ground.

45. Stepping on one leg with his leg, Bhīma grasped Jarāsandha's other leg with his two hands and split him from the anus, like a mighty elephant splits a leaf.

46. The citizens saw two halves [of a body], each with one ear, eyebrow, eye, arm, shoulder, nipple, [half of a] back, hip, testicle, thigh and foot.

47. A great cry of "Oh! Oh!" arose when the king of Magadha was slain. Acyuta and Arjuna embraced Bhīma and honoured him.

48. *Bhagavān* Kṛṣṇa arranges for the welfare of living beings. He crowned Jarāsandha's son Sahadeva as the lord of the

Magadhans. Then, the master, the immeasurable *ātmā*, released the kings who had been imprisoned by the king of Magadha.'

CHAPTER 73

Kṛṣṇa's Meeting [with the Kings]

1. *Śrī* Śuka said:

'Those 20,800 kings who had been defeated in battle and imprisoned emerged from Giridroṇī. They were dirty, and their clothes were filthy.
2. Suffering from hunger and emaciated from imprisonment, their faces withered, the kings saw Ghanaśyāma [Kṛṣṇa],[1] who was wearing yellow silken garments.
3. He bore the mark of the *śrīvatsa*, and had four arms and eyes like the calyx of a lotus. There was a charming smile on his face, and he wore glittering alligator-like earrings.
4. He held a lotus in his hand, and was distinctive with his club, conch and disc. He was adorned with upper-arm bracelets, belt, gold bracelets, necklace and helmet.
5–6. A precious gem was sparkling at his throat, and a forest garland was hanging around his neck. The kings appeared to be drinking him with their eyes, licking him with their tongues, smelling him with their noses and embracing him with their arms. They paid homage with their heads to the feet of Hari, and their sins were taken away.
7. Exhaustion from their imprisonment vanished in the joy of seeing Kṛṣṇa. With their hands folded in supplication, the kings extolled Hṛṣīkeśa with their words.
8. The kings said: "All homage to you, immutable Lord of the god of gods. You who remove the sufferings of those who surrender, protect us who surrender, O Kṛṣṇa – we are full of fear of this terrifying material existence.
9. We do not blame this king of Magadha, O master. Our fall from sovereignty was your Lordship's mercy, O Madhusūdana.

10. Shackled by the pride of sovereignty, a king does not achieve what is in his best interest. Forever bewildered by your *māyā*, he believes his wealth to be permanent.
11. Just as fools think a mirage to be a reservoir of water, so the indiscriminate see this fluctuating *māyā* as real.
12. Our clear-sightedness was previously obscured by our pride. We were rivals of one another out of our desire to conquer this world, O master, and we slaughtered our own citizens with great contempt. We are dull-witted and ignored your presence before us as death.
13. Our power was today taken away by your Lordship's grace in the form of time, which is your body. It is mysterious, irresistible and infinitely powerful. Our pride is destroyed and we are keeping your feet in our minds, O Kṛṣṇa.
14. We do not long for our kingdoms any more, O master. They exist in the form of mirages that are served by this body, which is the place of disease and constantly deteriorating. Nor do we hanker for the fruits of our work after departing this world; these sound pleasing [but are not, in reality].
15. Tell us how our remembrance of your lotus feet may never fade in this world, even while we are wandering in *saṃsāra*.
16. Let there be reverence paid to [you], Kṛṣṇa, Vāsudeva, Hari, the supreme soul. Let there be reverence paid to [you], Govinda – you destroy the distress of those who seek refuge in you."'
17. *Śrī* Śuka said:

'Praised by the kings released from captivity, O son, *Bhagavān* Kṛṣṇa, the merciful giver of protection, spoke to them with gentle words.
18. *Śrī Bhagavān* said: "Henceforward, your devotion will certainly flourish as you have requested, O kings – you will remain utterly focused on me, the self, and Lord of everything.
19. You are speaking the truth, O kings, and this resolve of yours is your good fortune. An excess of power and wealth makes people mad.
20. Haihaya, Nahuṣa, Veṇa, Rāvaṇa, Naraka and other rulers of the gods and the demons fell from their positions because of wealth.[2]

21. Understanding that such things as this body are produced and have an end, worship me with sacrifices and, with minds intent, protect the citizens through *dharma*.
22. As you beget generations of offspring, tolerate happiness and distress and birth and death as they occur. With your minds fixed on me, go about your business.
23. Indifferent to such things as the body, and firm in vow, become enjoyers of the *ātmā*, the self. With the mind completely concentrated on me, you will attain me, *brahman*, at the end of life."'
24. *Śrī* Śuka said:

'After instructing the kings in this way, *Bhagavān* Kṛṣṇa, the Lord of the worlds, employed men and women to clean them up.
25. He honoured them with ornaments and garments fit for kings and with garlands and ointments, all gifts of Sahadeva, O Parīkṣit, descendant of Bharata.
26. When they were nicely bathed, well-adorned and supplied with betel nuts and other things suitable for kings, Kṛṣṇa had them fed with food and various tasty things.
27. Freed from their distress, honoured by Mukunda, and with their earrings gleaming, the kings looked magnificent, like the planets at the end of the rainy season.
28. Kṛṣṇa had them mount chariots with fine horses decorated with gold and gems. Then he charmed them with kind words, and had them return to their own countries.
29. Thus freed from difficulty by the great-souled Kṛṣṇa, the kings went on their way meditating upon him, the Lord of the universe, and upon his deeds.
30. They related the deeds of that great being to their ministers and eagerly did whatever *Bhagavān* Kṛṣṇa had instructed.
31. After having Jarāsandha killed by Bhīmasena, Keśava was worshipped by Sahadeva, and then departed, accompanied by the two sons of Pṛthā.
32. When they arrived at Khāṇḍavaprastha [Indraprastha], they blew their conches to show their enemy had been defeated. The conches gave joy to their friends, but distress to their enemies.

33. When they heard [the conches], the people of Indraprastha were pleased for they knew the king of Magadha had been laid low. And king Yudhiṣṭhira had his desire fulfilled.
34. Bhīma, Arjuna and Janārdana greeted king Yudhiṣṭhira respectfully and told him everything they had accomplished.
35. Yudhiṣṭhira, king of *dharma*, heard about the act of kindness that had been performed by Keśava, and shed tears of happiness from love. He could not utter a word.'

CHAPTER 74
The Killing of Śiśupāla

1. *Śrī* Śuka said:

'Thus, king Yudhiṣṭhira heard about the killing of Jarāsandha and the power of Lord Kṛṣṇa. He was delighted, and spoke.
2. *Śrī* Yudhiṣṭhira said: "Those who are the *gurus* of the three worlds carry your order, so rarely obtained, on their heads [as a sign of respect]. So do the powerful deities, as well as [everyone in] all the worlds.
3. That you, the lotus-eyed Lord, accept the bidding of wretches who imagine themselves to be Lords, is the extreme of play-acting, O all-encompassing one.
4. The potency of *brahman*, the supreme soul, who is one without a second, neither increases nor diminishes by activity, just as the potency of the sun does not.
5. The mentality that discriminates between 'I' and 'mine', and 'you' and 'yours' – like the fluctuating state [of mind] of animals – does not exist at all among your devotees, O unconquered Mādhava."'
6. *Śrī* Śuka said:

'At the appropriate time for sacrifice, Yudhiṣṭhira, son of Pṛthā, encouraged by Kṛṣṇa, selected the expert *ṛtvik* priests and *brāhmaṇa* reciters of the Vedas.

7–9. [He chose] Dvaipāyana, Bharadvāja, Sumantu, Gautama, Asita, Vasiṣṭha, Cyavana, Kaṇva, Maitreya, Kavaṣa, Trita, Viśvāmitra, Vāmadeva, Sumati, Jaimini, Kratu, Paila, Parāśara, Garga and Vaiśampāyana, Atharvā, Kaśyapa, Dhaumya, Balarāma, Bhārgava, Āsuri, Vītihotra, Madhucchandā, Vīrasena and Kṛtavraṇa.[1]

10. Others were also invited – such as Droṇa, Bhīṣma and Kṛpa, Dhṛtarāṣṭra with his sons, and the noble-minded Vidura.

11. *Brāhmaṇas*, *kṣatriyas*, *vaiśyas* and *śūdras* went there eager to see sacrifice, as did all the kings and ministers from the various kingdoms, O king.

12. Then the *brāhmaṇas* ploughed the sacrificial area with a golden plough, following sacred tradition, and then consecrated the king there.

13–15. The utensils were made of gold, just as those of Varuṇa had been previously.[2] Indra and the other [gods], along with their entourages, the *siddhas*, *gandharvas*, *vidyādharas*, great serpents, sages, *yakṣas*, *rākṣasas*, [celestial] birds, *kinnaras*, *cāraṇas* and the invited royalty and their wives, assembled from everywhere at the *rājasūya* sacrifice of king Yudhiṣṭhira, son of Pāṇḍu and devotee of Kṛṣṇa. They were joined by Brahmā and Śiva. They all considered it highly appropriate for the occasion and were not surprised [by its grandness].

16. The sacrificers had the potency of gods, and assisted the great king in the *rājasūya* sacrifice as priests, according to the customary rites, just as the immortals had done for Varuṇa.

17. On the day that the *soma* is extracted,[3] the king of the earth attentively and appropriately honoured the exalted sacrificial priests and leaders of the assembly.

18. The members of the assembly were considering which member deserved the first honours but could not reach agreement, because there were so many. Then Sahadeva spoke out:

19. "*Bhagavān* Acyuta, the Lord of the Sātvatas, deserves preeminence. He *is* the gods, as well as everything relating to the time, place and resources, and so forth [of the sacrifice].

20. This universe consists of him and sacrifices consist of him, as do the fire, oblations and *mantras*. The schools of Sāṅkhya and Yoga have him as their highest goal.[4]

21. O members of the assembly, Kṛṣṇa is one without a second. This universe is constituted from him. His refuge is himself. From himself, the unborn one creates, preserves and destroys.
22. This entire world generates various activities with his guidance and strives for its welfare in the form of *dharma*, and so forth.
23. Therefore, you should offer the highest honours to Kṛṣṇa the supreme. If you do so, honour will be [offered] to all living entities, including yourselves.
24. Honour should be offered to Kṛṣṇa by those desiring eternity. Kṛṣṇa exists as the soul of all beings and sees nothing separate [from himself]. He is complete and free from passion."
25. Sahadeva, who understood Kṛṣṇa's feelings, said this and fell silent. When they heard, all those good people offered praise: "Bravo! Bravo!"
26. The king heard what had been uttered by the twice-born, and understood the feelings of the assembly members. Delighted, he paid honour to Hṛṣīkeśa with deep affection.
27. Along with his wife, younger brothers, ministers and family, Yudhiṣṭhira washed Kṛṣṇa's two feet. Then he carried away on his hand the water which purifies the world.
28. After this, he arranged for Kṛṣṇa to be honoured with yellow silk garments and costly ornaments, but, his eyes brimming with tears, he was unable to look at Kṛṣṇa.
29. Seeing Kṛṣṇa honoured in this way, all the people offered him respects with folded hands, saying: "All homage! Victory!" Showers of flowers fell.
30. When Śiśupāla, the son of Damaghoṣa, heard this, he arose from his seat. The descriptions of Kṛṣṇa's qualities had kindled his anger, and he was furious at the assembly. He waved his arms about, and with no fear spoke the following harsh words, making sure that *Bhagavān* heard them:
31. "The Vedas speak truthfully when they say that time, which is insuperable, is the controller [of people's destinies]. Even the intelligence of the elders is diverted by the words of a child.
32. All of you are the most eminent of qualified people, O leaders of the assembly – do not heed these words of a child, that Kṛṣṇa should be chosen in the matter of [receiving] honour.

33–34. You have bypassed the leaders of the assembly – they practise vows, the cultivation of learning and asceticism, and their sins have been removed by knowledge. They are the most distinguished of sages, absorbed in *brahman*, and worshipped by the rulers of planets. Kṛṣṇa is the disgrace of his family, so how is it that he deserves worship, any more than a crow deserves the sacrificial offerings?
35. He has renounced his family and the *varṇāśrama* system, and been excluded from all *dharmas*. He acts without restraint and lacks good qualities – so how is it that he is worthy of worship?
36. Their lineage was cursed by Yayāti,[5] and ostracized by the righteous. They are reckless in their addiction to excessive drinking. So how is it that he is worthy of worship?
37. Abandoning the lands frequented by *brāhmaṇas*, these criminals have taken refuge in an ocean fortress beyond the influence of *brāhmaṇas*, and there they harass the citizens."
38. His [previously acquired] merit destroyed, Śiśupāla uttered these and other offensive words. But *Bhagavān*, like a lion hearing a jackal, did not say a thing.
39. When the members of the assembly heard the criticism of *Bhagavān* Kṛṣṇa they could not bear it, so they covered their ears and walked out, angrily cursing the king of the Cedis.
40. Whoever hears blasphemy of *Bhagavān* or of his devotees and does not leave, falls from his good deeds, and goes to the lower regions.
41. Then the furious sons of Pāṇḍu, and the Matsya, Kaikaya and Sṛñjaya clans, sprang up with weapons raised, intent upon killing Śiśupāla.
42. The king of the Cedis was undismayed at that, O Parīkṣit, descendant of Bharata, and grasped his sword and shield, shouting insults at Kṛṣṇa's supporters and the kings in the assembly.
43. At this, *Bhagavān* Kṛṣṇa got up, restrained his supporters, and decapitated his attacking enemy with the sharp edge of his disc.
44. A great din and uproar erupted when Śiśupāla was killed. The kings who were his followers fled, anxious for their lives.
45. While all the people were watching, a light arose from

Śiśupāla, the king of the Cedis, and entered Vāsudeva, like a meteor fallen to earth from the sky.

46. Meditating [on Kṛṣṇa] for three consecutive births with his mind consumed by hatred,[6] Śiśupāla attained absorption into Kṛṣṇa – one's state of mind determines one's rebirth.[7]

47. Yudhiṣṭhira made generous gifts to the *ṛtvik* priests and the members of the assembly. Then the emperor honoured everyone according to tradition and performed ablutions.

48. After Kṛṣṇa, Lord of the lords of *yoga*, had arranged for the king's sacrifice to be completed, he stayed on for a few months at the request of his friends.

49. Then, despite his reluctance, the Lord, son of Devakī, returned to his own city with his wife and his ministers, having obtained permission from the king.

50. The account of the birth of the two residents of Vaikuṇṭha because of the curse of the *brāhmaṇas* has already been related by me in great detail.[8]

51. When king Yudhiṣṭhira had been bathed during the ablutions for the *rājasūya* sacrifice, he shone in the midst of the assembly of *brāhmaṇas* and *kṣatriyas* like the king of the gods.

52. When all gods, mortals and celestial beings who could travel through space had been honoured by the king, they went happily to their own dwelling places, praising Kṛṣṇa and the sacrifice.

53. All, that is, except the sinful Duryodhana, the [personification of the age of] *kali*, and bane of the Kuru dynasty. After seeing the extensive opulence of the son of Pāṇḍu, he could not tolerate it.

54. Whoever sings about this deed of Kṛṣṇa – the slaying of the king of the Cedis and other such acts, the liberation of the kings, and the sacrifice – is freed from all sins.'

CHAPTER 75

The Crushing of Duryodhana's Pride

1–2. The king said:

'We have heard that, after seeing the great festival of Yudhiṣṭhira's *rājasūya* sacrifice, the assembled *brāhmaṇas*, kings and royalty, along with the sages and gods, were all delighted, O *Bhagavān* [Śuka][1] – with the exception of Duryodhana. Please tell us the reason for that.'

3. *Śrī* Bādarāyaṇi [Śuka] said:

'At the *rājasūya* sacrifice of your noble-souled grandfather [Yudhiṣṭhira], his relatives, bound to him by love, became engaged in serving him.

4. Mighty Bhīma supervised the kitchen; Suyodhana [Durodhana] supervised the treasury; Sahadeva, the worship; and Nakula, the procuring of the materials.

5. Viṣṇu [Arjuna] supervised the service of the *gurus*; Kṛṣṇa, the washing of feet; the daughter of Drupada [Draupadī], the hospitality; and the generous Karṇa, the gifts.

6–7. Yuyudhāna, Vikarṇa, Hārdikya, Vidura and others, Bhūrya and other sons of Bāhlīka, and Santardana were appointed to various duties at the great sacrifice, which they undertook out of a desire to please the king.

8. After Śiśupāla, the king of the Cedis, had merged into the feet of Kṛṣṇa[2] – the Lord of the Sātvatas – the wise *ṛtvik* priests and assembly members, all of whom were [Yudhiṣṭhira's] ultimate well-wishers, were honoured with courteous words, reverence and gifts. Then they performed the ablution, bathing in the celestial river [Gaṅgā].

9. Various musical instruments – *mṛdaṅga*, *paṇava* and *dhundhuri* drums, conches and horns – resounded at the ablution rite.

10. Dancers danced happily, and singers sang in unison. The sound of their clapping, their flutes and stringed instruments [*vīṇas*] reached the heavens.

11. Kings wearing golden necklaces set out with their highly decorated soldiers, their horses, chariots and kingly elephants, and with a variety of prominent flags and banners.
12. Placing the sacrificer [Yudhiṣṭhira] at their head, the Yadu, Sṛñjaya, Kāmboja, Kuru, Kekaya and Kośala clans made the earth tremble with their armies.
13. The eminent members of the assembly, *ṛtvik* priests and twice-born *brāhmaṇas* celebrated with abundant recitations from the Vedas, and the gods, sages, forefathers and *gandharvas* showered flowers.
14. Men and women, beautifully decked out with garments, ornaments, garlands and ointments, disported themselves by smearing and sprinkling [each other] with various liquids.
15. The courtesans were smeared by the men, and smeared [them in turn], with oil, milk, perfumes, water, turmeric and strong vermilion powder.
16. The royal princesses, protected by guards, came out to join in, as did the princesses in the heavens in their beautiful air-carriers. As they were sprayed by the women friends of their maternal cousin Kṛṣṇa, they glowed with their shy smiles and blossoming faces.
17. They sprayed their menfolk and girlfriends from leather pouches containing liquid. With their garments clinging to them, their garlands slipping from their hair loosened from excitement, and their waists, thighs, breasts and limbs exposed, their innocent playfulness disturbed those with unchaste minds.
18. The emperor mounted a chariot [drawn] by sturdy horses with golden necklaces. With his wives he looked magnificent, just like the king of sacrifices with its rituals.
19. The *ṛtvik* priests conducted the ablutions for the *patnīsaṃyāja* ritual.[3] Then, when the king had sipped the purificatory water, they had him take a bath in the Gaṅgā river along with Kṛṣṇā [Draupadī].
20. The kettledrums of the gods resounded along with the kettledrums of humans, and humans, forefathers, *ṛṣis* and gods released showers of flowers.
21. All those belonging to the *varṇāśrama* social system bathed

there. By doing this, even great sinners are immediately released from sin.

22. Then, dressed in fresh linen, the handsomely adorned king honoured the *brāhmaṇas*, assembly members, *ṛtvik* priests and others with garments and ornaments.

23. The king, who was devoted to Nārāyaṇa, repeatedly worshipped his relatives, kinsfolk, friends and well-wishers, the kings and ministers, and all others too.

24. Wearing necklaces of great worth, fine cloth, corselets, turbans, garlands, earrings and gems, the men were as radiant as gods and the women resplendent with their golden girdles, the beauty of their faces enhanced with locks of hair and pairs of earrings.

25–26. After this, the *ṛtvik* priests of noble character, the assembly members, the reciters of the Vedas, the *brāhmaṇas*, *kṣatriyas*, *vaiśyas* and *śūdras*, the assembled princes, the gods, sages, forefathers and ghosts, and the guardians of the world and their followers, were all worshipped. Then, with Yudhiṣṭhira's permission, they returned to their homes, O king.

27. They were not completely satisfied by the great occasion of the *rājasūya* sacrifice of the king, the servant of Hari, just as a mortal is not completely satisfied by drinking nectar.

28. Distressed by separation, king Yudhiṣṭhira lovingly dissuaded his friends, family and kinsmen, as well as Kṛṣṇa [from departing].

29. *Bhagavān* Kṛṣṇa sent the Yadu heroes ahead – Sāmba to Kuśasthalī [Dvārakā], for example – and stayed in Indraprastha himself, dear Parīkṣit, to the contentment of Yudhiṣṭhira.

30. In this way, king Yudhiṣṭhira, son of Dharma, crossed over the great ocean of his desire – which was difficult to overcome – by means of Kṛṣṇa, and was released from his fever.

31. Yudhiṣṭhira's life and soul was Acyuta. On one occasion Duryodhana saw the opulence of Yudhiṣṭhira's inner quarters and became tormented by the splendour of the *rājasūya* sacrifice.

32. There the assorted wealth of the lords of gods, demons and men, accumulated by Brahmā the creator, sparkled, and Draupadī, the daughter of king Drupada, used it in the service

of her husbands. Duryodhana, the Kuru king, was in torment – his heart obsessed with Draupadī.

33. At that time, there were thousands of Madhupati's [Kṛṣṇa's] queens there. Their graceful feet tinkled [from the sounds of bracelets, as they walked] slowly due to the weight of their breasts, and their necklaces were reddened with *kuṅkum* powder from their breasts. They had lovely waists, and beautiful faces surrounded by locks of hair and swinging earrings.

34. On one occasion in that assembly hall built by the celestial architect Maya, the emperor Yudhiṣṭhira, son of Dharma, was surrounded by his followers and relatives, among whom was Kṛṣṇa, his [guiding] eye.

35. Sitting on a golden throne and praised by bards, Yudhiṣṭhira resembled Indra himself. He possessed the riches of Brahmā.

36. The haughty Duryodhana, wearing a helmet and necklace and surrounded by his brothers, entered that place. Sword in hand, he hurled insults angrily around.

37. In one place he gathered up the ends of his garments, thinking [the ground] to be water, and in another place, confused, he fell into the water which appeared to be like ground. He was bewildered by the magic of Maya, the celestial architect.

38. Encouraged by Kṛṣṇa, Bhīma saw him and laughed, as did the women and other kings, despite being restrained by king Yudhiṣṭhira, O dear Parīkṣit.

39. Humiliated and with head bowed low, Duryodhana furiously got out of the water and silently left for Hastināpura. A huge cry of "Alas! Alas!" arose from those who were righteous. Yudhiṣṭhira, who was without enemies, appeared downcast, but *Bhagavān* Kṛṣṇa remained silent – it was by his glance that Duryodhana had been thrown into confusion. Kṛṣṇa desired to remove the burden of the earth.[4]

40. Thus have I explained the ill-feeling of Duryodhana at the great *rājasūya* sacrifice, O king, as was requested by you.'

CHAPTER 76

The Battle with Śālva

1. *Śrī* Śuka said:

'Now hear also about another amazing deed of Kṛṣṇa, whose human form is for the purpose of sport, O king: the slaying of Śalva, the lord of the Saubhas.
2. Śālva was a friend of Śiśupāla who had gone to Rukmiṇī's marriage ceremony. He had been defeated in battle by the Yadus, as Jarāsandha and the others had been.
3. Śālva had made a vow while all the kings were listening: "I will void the earth of Yadus; be witnesses to my valour."
4. Then the fool worshipped Lord Paśupati [Śiva], eating [only] a handful of dust once [a day].
5. *Bhagavān* Śiva, Lord of Umā, is easily pleased. At the end of a period of one year, he gratified Śālva, who had approached him for refuge, with a boon.
6. Śālva chose a vehicle that could move at will. It was to be terrifying for the Vṛṣṇi dynasty, and could not be destroyed by gods, demons, humans, *gandharvas*, celestial serpents or *rākṣasas*.
7. The architect Maya, the conqueror of enemy cities, was instructed by Giriśa [Śiva]: "Do as he has asked." Maya constructed [a vehicle in the form of] a city called Saubha made of iron, and presented it to Śālva.
8. Śālva received the vehicle; it was impenetrable and could move at will. He headed for Dvārakā, harbouring in his mind the memory of the enmity created by the Vṛṣṇi clan.
9–11. After besieging the city with his mighty army, O Parīkṣit, best of the Bharatas, Śālva destroyed the gardens, groves, towers, gateways, palaces, watchtowers, surrounding walls and recreation areas everywhere. Torrents of weapons rained down from the front of that air-borne vehicle. There were stones, thunderbolts, snakes, hailstones and violent whirlwinds – all quarters were covered with dust.

12. Bombarded in this way, the peace of Kṛṣṇa's city was completely shattered by the Saubha vehicle, O king, just as the earth when it was harassed by the three cities.[1]

13. *Bhagavān* Pradyumna saw his own citizens being assaulted. The famous hero said: "Do not fear," and mounted his chariot.

14–15. Sātyaki, Cārudeṣṇa, Sāmba, Akrūra and his younger brothers, Hārdikya, Bhānuvinda, Gada, Śuka and Sāraṇa, as well as other commanders of the chariot chiefs, went forth, armed and protected by chariots, elephants, horses and infantry.

16. At this, the battle between the followers of Śālva and the Yadus commenced, just like the battle between the gods and the demons. It was tumultuous and hair-raising.

17. Then Pradyumna, the son of Rukmiṇī, at once dispelled, with divine weapons, all the magic of Saubha's master, just as the sun destroys the darkness of night.

18. He pierced Śālva's commander with twenty-five arrows that were gold-shafted, iron-tipped and hooked at the end.

19. With 100 of these arrows, he struck Śālva; with one each, Śālva's guards; with ten each, his army chiefs; and with three each, his horses.

20. When they saw the great-souled Pradyumna's prodigious and magnificent feat, the soldiers on his own side as well as on the opposing one all honoured him.

21. The magic vehicle built by the architect Maya was sometimes seen in multiple forms, sometimes in only one, and sometimes was not seen at all. It was difficult for the opposing side to pinpoint it.

22. Sometimes the Saubha vehicle moved around on the ground, sometimes in the sky, sometimes on the top of a mountain, and sometimes in the water. Like a firebrand, it was never still.

23. Wherever Śālva was seen with his Saubha vehicle and army, the Sātvata leaders would discharge arrows at them.

24. Śālva became bewildered. His city and army were overwhelmed by the arrows unleashed by the enemy. These impacted like fire or the sun, and were as intolerable as snake venom.

25. The Vṛṣṇis [in their turn] were severely afflicted by the deluge of weapons from the leaders of Śālva's army, but, desiring

victory over the two worlds, they did not desert their places in the battle.

26. Śālva's powerful minister, Dyumān by name, who had previously been assaulted, attacked Pradyumna. He struck him with an iron club, and roared.

27. Pradyumna's chest was crushed by the club. His chariot-driver, the son of Dāruka, knew his duty, and carried Pradyumna, the subduer of enemies, away from the battle.

28. Regaining consciousness after some time, the son of Kṛṣṇa spoke to his chariot-driver: "*Aho*, chariot-driver! My retreat from the battle is shameful.

29. It is unheard of for one born in the Yadu dynasty to have ever abandoned a battlefield – except, [now,] for me. I have incurred this shame because of my impotent chariot-driver.

30. What exactly shall I say about my worth, when I meet with my fathers, Balarāma and Keśava, and am asked about my flight from the battlefield?

31. My sisters-in-law will no doubt say, mockingly: 'Tell us, O hero, how, O how did you become impotent in the face of your enemies in the battle?!'"

32. The chariot-driver said: "Sir – you are alive. I performed this act, knowing well my *dharma*: the chariot-driver must protect the charioteer who has fallen into danger, and the charioteer must do likewise for the chariot-driver, O master.

33. Knowing this, sir, I removed you from the battle since you were injured by the enemy. I thought that you had been knocked unconscious when you were struck by the club."'

CHAPTER 77

The Destruction of Saubha

1. *Śrī* Śuka said:

'Clad in armour, Pradyumna took up his bow and sipped water. Then he said to his charioteer: "Take me before the hero Dyumān."

2. Pradyumna, the son of Rukmiṇī, retaliated against Dyumān, who was striking his soldiers. Smiling, Pradyumna struck back with eight iron arrows.

3. With four arrows he struck four horses; with one, his chariot-driver; with two, his bow and banner; and with another, his head.

4. Gada, Sātyaki, Sāmba and the others decimated the army of Śālva, the lord of Saubha. The Saubhan men all fell into the ocean, their necks severed [from their bodies].

5. There ensued a tumultuous and ferocious battle lasting twenty-seven nights, during which the Yadus and the followers of Śālva struck at each other.

6. [Meanwhile], after the *rājasūya* sacrifice had been completed and Śiśupāla killed, Kṛṣṇa went to Indraprastha, invited by the son of Dharma, Yudhiṣṭhira.

7. Observing that the omens were very inauspicious, he took leave of the Kuru elders, the sages and Pṛthā [Kuntī] and her sons, and departed for Dvārakā.

8. He said: "I have come here accompanied by the honourable Ārya [Balarāma]. So those on Śālva, the king of the Cedis', side must be attacking my city."

9. When he saw the Saubha vehicle, king Śālva, and the destruction of his people, Keśava saw to the protection of the city and then said to Dāruka:

10. "Bring my chariot at once to the vicinity of Śālva. Make sure you are not bewildered – the lord of Saubha is a magician."

11. Thus commanded, Dāruka mounted the chariot and urged

it forward. Everyone on their side and on the opposing side saw [the emblem of] Garuḍa joining [the battle].

12. Śālva, commander of an army that had been practically exterminated, also noticed Kṛṣṇa on the battlefield. He hurled a spear that made a fierce noise against Kṛṣṇa's son.

13. Śauri [Kṛṣṇa] sliced it into 100 pieces as it hurtled forwards in the sky, illuminating the quarters like a huge meteor.

14. He struck Śālva with sixteen arrows and pierced the Saubha vehicle, which was hovering in the sky, with a mass of arrows, just as the sun pierces the sky with its rays.

15. Śālva hit the Śārṅga bow and the left hand of Śauri [Kṛṣṇa], the wielder of Śārṅga, which fell from Kṛṣṇa's hand. It was an amazing sight.

16. A loud cry of "Alas! Alas!" arose from the people watching there. The lord of Saubha bellowed loudly and said to Janārdana:

17–18. "Because you snatched the bride of your brother and our friend before our very eyes, and because you killed our friend [Śiśupāla] unawares in the midst of the assembly, fool, I will dispatch you today to the place of no return with my sharp arrows, if you stand before me. You fancy yourself to be invincible."

19. *Śrī Bhagavān* said: "You speak frivolously, fool, and do not see death at hand. Heroes demonstrate their prowess – they do not waste words."

20. When he had said this, *Bhagavān* became furious and, with his club, smashed Śālva on his collarbone with ferocious force. Śālva trembled, vomiting blood.

21. When the club was removed, Śālva disappeared. Then, in an instant, a man approached, offered homage to Acyuta by bowing his head, and said these words, crying: "I have been sent by Devakī.

22. O Kṛṣṇa, mighty-armed Kṛṣṇa, you are fond of your parents – your father has been bound and taken away by Śālva, like an animal by a butcher."

23. Hearing this distressing news, Kṛṣṇa took on the nature of a human being. He became troubled and tender with affection, like an ordinary person, and said:

24. "How could the insignificant Śālva defeat the steadfast Balarāma who cannot be defeated by gods or demons, and carry off my father? Fate is powerful."

25. As Govinda was speaking in this way, the lord of Saubha came up, leading Vasudeva, and said this to Kṛṣṇa:

26. "Here is the cherished person who begot you and for whose sake you are alive. I will kill him while you watch. Protect him if you have the power, imbecile."

27. The magician taunted [Kṛṣṇa] in this way, then cut off Ānakadundubhi's [Vasudeva's] head with a sword, and carried it off. Then he entered the Saubha vehicle as it hovered in the air.

28. At this, Kṛṣṇa, holding his followers in affection, was overwhelmed by human sentiment for a moment. But knowing himself and being extremely powerful, he understood this to be demonic *māyā* magic originating from Maya and invoked by Śālva.

29. Fully cognizant, he recognized that, as in a dream, there was no messenger there in the battlefield, nor was the body of his father there. Acyuta saw his enemy sitting in the Saubha vehicle and moving through the sky. He made ready to kill him.

30. This version of events is what those sages who misunderstand say, but their words are self-contradictory. In all probability they do not really remember.

31. How can things born of ignorance – grief, illusion, affection or fear – exist in Kṛṣṇa, the infinite one? His greatness, knowledge and wisdom are infinite.

32. By knowledge of the *ātmā*, fortified by devotion to Kṛṣṇa's feet, [saints] destroy the tendency of clinging to that which is not the *ātmā*, which has existed since time immemorial, and attain their own eternal greatness. How, then, can there be illusion for the supreme being who is the goal of the saints?

33. As Śālva was furiously discharging masses of weapons, Śauri [Kṛṣṇa] pierced him with his arrows, and shattered Śālva's armour, bow and crown jewel. Then he smashed his enemy's Saubha vehicle with his club. Kṛṣṇa's prowess is infallible.

34. The Saubha vehicle fell into the water, smashed into 1,000

pieces by the club hurled from Kṛṣṇa's hand. Śālva abandoned it and stood on the surface of the earth. He picked up a club and swiftly rushed at Acyuta.
35. As he came rushing forwards, Kṛṣṇa cut off his club-wielding arm with a missile. Then he raised his amazing discus, which resembles the sun at the dissolution of the universe, in order to destroy Śālva. He was as radiant as the eastern mountain conjoined with the sun.
36. Hari, who possesses great magic, cut off with the disc Śālva's ear-ringed head, which was wearing a helmet, just as Indra did to Vṛtra with his thunderbolt. At this, the cry of "Alas! Alas!" arose from the men.
37. When that wicked person fell, and the Saubha vehicle was struck by the mace, kettledrums resounded in the sky, vibrated by the hosts of gods. But then, Dantavakra rushed forward furiously, to fulfil his [obligation to] revenge his friends.'

CHAPTER 78

Preparations for the Killing of Balvala and the Adventures of Balarāma

1–2. *Śrī* Śuka said:

'The evil-minded Dantavakra appeared alone, on foot, with club in hand. With his immense strength he made the earth tremble with his steps, O king, and he was enraged. He was fulfilling [the obligations of] his secret friendship for those who had gone to the next world – Śiśupāla, Śālva and Pauṇḍraka.
3. When Kṛṣṇa saw Dantavakra swiftly approaching, he raised his club, jumped down from his chariot and restrained him, as the shore does the ocean.
4. The evil-minded king of the Karūṣas [Dantavakra] raised his club and said to Kṛṣṇa: 'It is really by good fortune that you have crossed my line of sight today.
5. You, our maternal cousin, Kṛṣṇa,[1] are the enemy of my friends

and are intent on killing me. Therefore, fool, I will kill you with my club, which is as powerful as a thunderbolt.

6. I am faithful to my friends. So, after killing my enemy in the guise of a friend, who is like a disease pervading the body, I will fulfil my obligation to my friends."

7. After taunting Kṛṣṇa with harsh words, like an elephant [is taunted] with a goad, Dantavakra struck him on the head with his mace, and roared like a lion.

8. Although he had been hit by the mace in the battle, the best of the Yadus did not flinch. Rather, Kṛṣṇa struck Dantavakra on his chest with his heavy Kaumodakī mace.[2]

9. Dantavakra's heart was shattered by the mace, and he fell lifeless on the ground, vomiting blood from his mouth, and with his hair, arms and legs extended.

10. Then, an astonishing and very subtle light entered Kṛṣṇa while all the people were watching, O king, just as happened at the killing of Śiśupāla, the king of the Cedis.

11. After this, Dantavakra's brother, Vidūratha, approached with sword and shield, overwhelmed with grief for his brother. He was breathing heavily from his desire to kill Kṛṣṇa.

12. As Vidūratha attacked, Kṛṣṇa cut off his head with its helmet and earrings, with his sharp-edged disc, O Parīkṣit, lord of kings.

13–15. After he had thus destroyed the Saubha vehicle, as well as Śālva and Dantavakra, who were invulnerable to others, and their followers too, Kṛṣṇa entered into his decorated city. He was praised by gods, men, sages, *siddha* mystics, *gandharva* angels, *vidyādharas*, celestial serpents, *apsarā* nymphs, hosts of ancestors, *yakṣas*, *kinnara* celestial musicians and *cāraṇas*. His victory was celebrated in song, and he was showered with flowers, and surrounded by distinguished Kurus.

16. Thus, *Bhagavān* Kṛṣṇa, the Lord of *yogīs* and controller of the universe, is victorious. He only appears vanquished by those who have the perception of beasts.

17. When Balarāma, who was a neutral party, heard about the Kuru preparation for war with the Pāṇḍavas, he left on the pretext of performing ablutions in holy places.

18. After bathing in Prabhāsa and satisfying the gods, sages,

forefathers and humans, he set out upstream along the Sarasvatī, surrounded by *brāhmaṇas*.

19–20. He went to Pṛthūdaka, Bindusara, Tritakūpa, Sudarśana, Viśāla, Brahmatīrtha, Cakra, the eastern Sarasvatī, those holy places along both the Yamunā and the Gaṅgā, and Naimiṣa, where the sages were engaging in the sacrifice, O Parīkṣit, descendant of Bharata.

21. The sages performing that long sacrifice approached Balarāma when he arrived. They greeted him as is prescribed, bowed down, and then arose, worshipping him.

22. When he had been honoured along with his retinue, and accepted the seat that had been prepared, Balarāma noticed that Romaharṣaṇa, the disciple of the great sage,[3] remained seated.

23. Mādhava [Balarāma] saw that this charioteer was seated higher than the other *brāhmaṇas*, and that he neither rose nor respectfully joined his hands nor bowed down. Balarāma became angry:

24. "Because this evil-minded person, born from an improper marriage,[4] is seated higher than us, as well as these *brāhmaṇas*, the guardians of *dharma*, he deserves death.

25–26. He became a disciple of the sage *Bhagavān* [Vyāsa] and studied deeply many histories, Purāṇas, and all the treatises on *dharma*. But these did not lead to the development of his qualities, just as they do not for an actor. Foolishly considering himself to be a scholar, he is unrestrained, arrogant and lacking in self-control.

27. It was for this reason that I assumed an incarnation in this world. Those who are the standard-bearers of *dharma* are the most sinful and deserve to be killed by me."

28. *Bhagavān* Balarāma said this much, and although he had given up killing the impious, the Lord killed Romaharṣaṇa with the tip of a blade of *kuśa* grass held in his hand.

29. The sages were distressed in mind and uttered: "Alas! Alas!" They said to Lord Saṅkarṣaṇa [Balarāma]: "You have performed an act contrary to *dharma*, O master!

30. It was we who granted him the seat of the *brāhmaṇa* priest, O son of the Yadus, as well as health and freedom from fatigue for the duration of the sacrifice.

31. You have, albeit unknowingly, committed the murder of a *brāhmaṇa*, even though you are the Lord of *yogīs* and, as preceptor, not subject to sacred precepts.
32. You are the purifier of the worlds, and if your Lordship performs the purification for this killing of a *brāhmaṇa*, it will be as the benefactor of the world. You are not impelled by anything else."
33. *Śrī Bhagavān* said: "I will perform the expiation for murder out of a desire for the welfare of the world. Prescribe whatever is the best atonement as penance.
34. Just let me know; with my *yogamāyā*, I can restore the long life, strength and vitality of the senses that has been bestowed upon Romaharṣaṇa."
35. The sages said: "Act in such a way that the integrity of your weapon and power, as well as the death [inflicted on Romaharṣaṇa], are upheld, O Balarāma, but that our words are too."
36. *Śrī Bhagavān* said: "The teaching of the Vedas is that a son born is the same as one's own self. Therefore, let Romaharṣaṇa's son be the speaker [of the Purāṇas] and the possessor of longevity, vitality of the senses and strength.
37. Tell me what your wish is, O best of sages, and I will fulfil it. Determine an appropriate expiation for me, O wise ones, for I do not know."
38. The sages said: "The terrifying demon son of Ilvala, known as Balvala, comes and contaminates our sacrifice every full and new moon.
39. Kill that evil one, O Dāśārha [Balarāma] – he showers us with pus, blood, faeces, urine, liquor and meat. That will be the best service that you can do for us.
40. After that, fixed in mind, circumambulate the land of Bhārata [India],[5] bathing in the holy places. After travelling around, you will be purified."'

CHAPTER 79

An Outline of Balarāma's Pilgrimage

1. *Śrī* Śuka said:

'Then, when the change of the moon approached, a violent shower of dust and a fearsome wind broke out, O king, and the smell of pus was everywhere.
2. This was followed by a torrent of impure substances produced by Balvala on to the sacrificial area. Balvala subsequently appeared bearing a trident.
3–4. Balarāma looked at him. He had a huge body that resembled a heap of broken charcoal. His beard and headknot were like burnt copper and his face had a terrifying frown and set of teeth. Balarāma summoned his club, the crusher of opposing armies, and his plough, the subduer of demons, both of which speedily presented themselves.
5. Balarāma was furious and, with the tip of his plough, dragged Balvala, who was moving about in the sky. Then he struck that *brāhmaṇa*-hater on the head with his club.
6. Balvala's brow was smashed and he fell on to the ground. Discharging blood and uttering a tormented cry, he was like a red-coloured mountain struck by a thunderbolt.
7. The illustrious sages glorified Balarāma and bestowed propitious blessings on him, consecrating him as the gods did Indra, the killer of Vṛtra.
8. They presented Balarāma with a *vaijayantī* garland of unfading lotuses, which are the abode of Śrī, the goddess of fortune, as well as a set of divine garments and divine ornaments.
9. Then Balarāma was given leave by them [to go] and went to Kāśī accompanied by *brāhmaṇas*. After bathing, he went to the lake from where the Sarayū river flows forth.
10. He approached Prayāga along the flow of the Sarayū, bathed, propitiated the gods and performed other such rites. Then he went to the ashram of Pulaha.[1]
11–12. He bathed in the Gomatī, Gaṇḍakī and Vipāśā, and

immersed himself in the Śoṇa. He continued on to Gayā, offered sacrifice to his forefathers and then bathed at the confluence of the Gaṅgā with the ocean. He saw Balarāma [Paraśurāma] on Mount Mahendra,[2] and greeted him respectfully. Then [he bathed] in the seven [tributaries] of the Godāvarī, as well as in the Veṇā, the Pampā and the Bhīmarathī rivers.

13. After seeing Skanda, Balarāma went on to Śrī Śaila, the abode of Giriśa [Śiva]. Then the Lord saw the very holy Veṅkaṭa mountain in the Draviḍa country.

14. After this, Balarāma went to Kāmakoṣṇī, to the city of Kāñcī, and to the Kāverī, best of rivers. He also went to the most holy Śrīraṅga, where Hari is present.[3]

15. Then he went to Mount Ṛṣabha, the place of Hari, and then to the southern Mathurā. He proceeded on to Setu, the bridge across the ocean[4] which eradicates the most heinous sins.

16. The plough-bearer Balarāma gave 10,000 cows to the *brāhmaṇas* there. Then [he went] to the Kṛtamālā and Tāmraparṇī rivers, and to the Malaya mountain range.

17. He offered homage to Agastya, who was seated there, and greeted him reverently. He was blessed by him and, with his permission, proceeded to the southern ocean, where he saw the goddess Durgā, who is known there as the maiden Kanyā.[5]

18. After this, Balarāma approached Phālguna, the eminent Pañcāpsarasa lake where Viṣṇu is present. After bathing there he gave 10,000 cows in charity.

19. Thereafter, *Bhagavān* Balarāma passed through the lands of Kerala and Trigartaka, and [went to] Śiva's abode called Gokarṇa, where Dhūrjaṭi [Śiva] is present.

20–21. Balarāma saw the island-born Āryā [Pārvatī], and [then went to] Śūrpāraka. He bathed in the Tāpī, Payoṣṇī and Nirvindhyā rivers, and then entered the Daṇḍaka forest. After this he went to the Revā river, where the city of Māhiṣmatī lies. Then he bathed in [the holy place] Manutīrtha and returned again to Prabhāsa.

22. He heard the twice-born *brāhmaṇas* relate the account of the annihilation of all the kings in the encounter between the Kurus and the Pāṇḍavas,[6] and determined that the burden of the world had been removed.

23. Balarāma, the descendant of Yadu, went to Vinaśana, where the river Sarasvatī disappears [Kurukṣetra], desiring to intervene between Bhīma and Duryodhana, who had entered into combat with clubs.
24. Yudhiṣṭhira and the twins, as well as Kṛṣṇa and Arjuna, greeted Balarāma with honour, but remained quiet, [thinking]: "What has he come here intending to say?"
25. Balarāma saw Bhīma and Duryodhana both worked up with anger, each with club in hand. Eager for victory, they were stalking each other with various circular manoeuvres. Balarāma said this to them:
26. "Hey, O king! Hey, wolf-bellied Bhīma! I consider you two heroes to be equal in prowess – one is superior in strength while the other is superior in expertise.
27. You are both equal in power – neither victory nor defeat for either of you seems likely. Therefore, desist from this fruitless fight."
28. But, locked in enmity, and remembering each other's evil deeds and wicked words, the pair did not heed Balarāma's sensible words.
29. Accepting this as destiny, Balarāma went to Dvārakā. He was met by his delighted relatives, headed by Ugrasena.
30. When he returned once again to the Naimiṣa forest, the sages engaged him, the embodiment of sacrifices, to perform sacrifice with all types of rituals. He had abstained from all engagement in the war.[7]
31. *Bhagavān* Balarāma, the Lord, bestowed pure knowledge on the sages, by which they could understand that the universe is within him, and that his self pervades this universe.[8]
32. He bathed and performed the purificatory rites along with his wife, and put on beautiful garments and suitable ornaments. Surrounded by his friends, relatives and kinsmen, he shone like the moon with his own radiance.
33. There are countless things of this sort [performed] by the powerful Balarāma. He is unlimited and immeasurable, and [appears as] a mortal by his *māyā* illusion.
34. Whoever remembers at dusk and at dawn the deeds of Balarāma becomes dear to the unlimited Viṣṇu. His deeds are prodigious.'

CHAPTER 80
The Story of Śrīdāmā

1. The king said:

'O *Bhagavān* [Śuka]. I desire to hear of some other of the great-souled Mukunda's heroic deeds; his heroic deeds are infinite, O master.
2. What judicious person, disillusioned by sensual pursuits and who has repeatedly heard the stories of Uttamaśloka [Kṛṣṇa], O *brāhmaṇa*, could desist [from hearing them]?
3. It is by speech that one praises his qualities, it is hands that perform his deeds, mind that contemplates him dwelling in all that is moving and non-moving, and the ear that listens to his holy stories.
4. It is the head that bows down to his two types of manifestation,[1] the eye that perceives him, and the limbs that always worship the water from the feet of the devotees of Viṣṇu.
5. Sūta said:

'Questioned by Viṣṇurāta [Parīkṣit], *Bhagavān* Bādarāyaṇi [Śukadeva] – whose heart was immersed in *Bhagavān* Vāsudeva – spoke.'
6. *Śrī* Śuka said:

'There was a noble *brāhmaṇa* friend of Kṛṣṇa, a peaceful soul, and knower of *brahman*. He was detached from the objects of the senses, and his senses were disciplined.
7. He was a householder who subsisted on whatever came his way fortuitously. His wife, emaciated by hunger, was in a similar ragged state.
8. The chaste wife, her face drawn, approached her poor husband. Despondent and shaking, she said to him:
9. "*Brāhmaṇa* – you actually are the friend of *Bhagavān* Kṛṣṇa, who is the best of the Satvata clan and the husband of Śrī, the

goddess of fortune herself. He is the giver of shelter and is devoted to *brāhmaṇas*.

10. You are very fortunate. Approach him, for he is the ultimate resort for the saintly. He will give you much wealth since you are a desperate householder.

11. Kṛṣṇa, the Lord of the Andhaka, Vṛṣṇi and Bhoja clans, is now in Dvārakā. He is the *guru* of the world, and gives even his own self to one who remembers his lotus feet – what is it, then, for him to give wealth and worldly desires, which are not very favoured, to his devotee?"

12–13. The *brāhmaṇa* was entreated profusely and repeatedly by his wife. Thinking, "The sight of Uttamaśloka is actually the highest blessing," he made a decision to go: "If there is any gift in the house, give it to me, auspicious lady," he said.

14. She begged four handfuls of flat rice from the *brāhmaṇas*, tied them up in a piece of cloth and gave them to her husband to be used as a gift.

15. The distinguished *brāhmaṇa* took them and set off for Dvārakā, thinking: "Is it possible that I will catch a sight of Kṛṣṇa?"

16. Accompanied by *brāhmaṇas*, he passed three outside walls and three contingents of guards between the unassailable houses of the Andhaka and Vṛṣṇi clans, who followed the laws of Acyuta.

17. There were 16,000 houses for Hari's queens. The *brāhmaṇa* entered one of them, which was magnificent – it was as if he had entered the bliss of *brahman*.

18. Acyuta was seated on a couch with his beloved, but saw the *brāhmaṇa* from a distance. He immediately rose up, went towards the *brāhmaṇa* and embraced him joyfully with two arms.

19. The delighted lotus-eyed Kṛṣṇa was ecstatic from the bodily contact with his dear friend, the *brāhmaṇa* sage, and shed tears from his eyes.

20–21. Then he seated the *brāhmaṇa* on his own couch, and offered his friend gifts. After this, *Bhagavān*, the purifier of the world, washed the *brāhmaṇa*'s feet, and placed the washing water on his head, O king. He then smeared him with heavenly scents, and with sandalwood, aloe and vermilion.

22. With joy he honoured his friend with fragrant incense and rows of lamps, and presented him with betel nut and a cow. Then he welcomed him.

23. The goddess herself attended that weak, dirty, tattered and emaciated *brāhmaṇa*, by fanning him with a whisk.

24. When the people in the inner quarters saw how the ascetic had been worshipped with great love by Kṛṣṇa of spotless fame, they were astonished:

25–26. "What pious deed did this ascetic mendicant perform? He is without wealth, and shunned as the lowest in this world, yet this person is honoured by Kṛṣṇa, the *guru* of the three worlds, and the shelter of the goddess of fortune. Kṛṣṇa left Śrī sitting on the couch and embraced the *brāhmaṇa*, as if he were his elder brother."

27. Kṛṣṇa and the *brāhmaṇa* grasped each other's hands, and talked about pleasing past events that had happened when they were both in *gurukula* school at the house of their *guru*.

28. *Śrī Bhagavān* said: "O *brāhmaṇa*, you are a knower of *dharma*; did you take a wife in marriage when you returned home from the *guru*'s school after he had received the student remuneration from you, or not?

29. I know that your mind is usually focused on your household affairs without craving, and hence you are not gratified by wealth, O learned one.

30. Some people renounce the material world and perform their activities for the welfare of the world – just as I do – with their minds unaffected by lust.

31. Do you remember, O *brāhmaṇa*, our residence in the house of the *guru*? It is there that a twice-born understands that which is to be understood, and experiences that which is beyond *tamas*.

32. The first personification of the *guru* is as the one from whom there is birth in this world. Then, there is the *guru* of the sacred duties of the twice-born, and then there is the *guru* who is the giver of knowledge. I myself am as the latter, dear *brāhmaṇa*.

33. Those among the followers of the *varṇāśrama* social system

who are wise to their own interests cross over the ocean of *saṃsāra* by [following] my words. I am the *guru*.

34. I am not as satisfied by worship, birth, austere practices and tranquillity of mind as I am by obedience to the *guru*.

35. Do you remember, O *brāhmaṇa*, what happened when we were living with the *guru*? Once, we were sent by the *guru*'s wives to fetch kindling wood.

36. We entered an enormous forest at the wrong time of year, O *brāhmaṇa*. There was fierce wind and rain, and harsh thunder.

37. The sun had set at that point, and the quarters were enveloped in darkness. High ground and low ground were covered with water, and nothing could be recognized.

38. Wind and water pounded us continually and relentlessly, and we could not discern the directions in the flood of water. Grasping each other's hands in the forest, we wandered about in distress.

39. When the sun arose, our *guru*, Sāndīpani, who knew all this and was conducting a search, saw us, his distressed disciples. He said:

40. '*Aho!* Hey boys! You have been put to great distress for our sake. Dedicated to me as you are, you have neglected even your own selves, which are so dear to embodied beings.

41. The offering of oneself and all one's possessions with a pure mind to the *guru* is the type of offering the true disciple should make to the guru.

42. I am satisfied with you, O best of the twice-born. May your desires be fulfilled, and may your recitations of Vedic hymns be invocations that remain potent both in this world and in the next.'

43. We [experienced] many such things when we were living in the *guru*'s house. It is by the grace of the *guru* alone that a person succeeds in attaining peace."

44. The *brāhmaṇa* said: "Your desires are fulfilled, O God of gods and *guru* of the universe. What could remain unaccomplished for us when our residence with the *guru* was in your company?

45. Your body is *brahman*, composed of the Vedas, and the

fount of all benefit, O all-pervading one – your residing in the house of the *guru* is the ultimate play-acting."'

CHAPTER 81

The Episode of the Flat Rice

1. *Śrī* Śuka said:

'Hari was chatting in this way with the best of the *brāhmaṇas*. Knowing the minds of all creatures, he addressed the *brāhmaṇa* with a smile.

2. *Bhagavān* Kṛṣṇa, who is the goal of the saintly, and devoted to *brāhmaṇas*, was looking at the dear *brāhmaṇa* with an expression of love. Kṛṣṇa was laughing.

3. *Śrī Bhagavān* said: "What gift did you bring for me from home, O *brāhmaṇa*? Something brought with love by my devotees, even if insignificant, becomes great, while something brought by a non-devotee is not able to give me satisfaction, even if it is great.

4. I accept whatever is presented with love by a devout soul who offers me a leaf, flower, fruit or water with devotion."[1]

5. Although he was questioned in this way, the *brāhmaṇa* did not present Kṛṣṇa, the husband of Śrī, the goddess of fortune, with the handful of flat rice, O king. He held his face down and became embarrassed.

6. Kṛṣṇa directly sees the *ātmā* of all creatures and knew the reason for the *brāhmaṇa*'s coming. He thought: "This *brāhmaṇa* was never desirous of wealth previously.

7. On the contrary, my friend has come to me as a favour to his chaste wife. I will bestow wealth on him that is hard even for the gods to come by."

8. With these thoughts, Kṛṣṇa himself grabbed the flat rice that had been tied up in the strip of cloth from the twice-born *brāhmaṇa*, and said: "What is this?

9. What you have brought for me is delightful, dear friend.

These grains of flat rice will satisfy me, and thus the universe!"
10. Saying this, Kṛṣṇa immediately devoured a handful, and then took a second one to devour. At this, Śrī, who is devoted to him, grasped the hand of the highest God, and said:
11. "This much is enough to grant a person an abundance of all types of prosperity both in this world and the next, O soul of the universe; it is sufficient for your satisfaction."
12. The *brāhmaṇa* ate, drank and resided happily in Acyuta's palace that night; he thought he was in heaven.
13. When the next day arrived, he was respectfully saluted by Kṛṣṇa, the cause of the universe, whose happiness comes from himself, and set out for his own residence. He made the journey blissfully.
14. He went home without having obtained wealth from Kṛṣṇa – since, being embarrassed, he did not solicit it himself – but he was ecstatic from seeing that great being.
15. The *brāhmaṇa* said: "*Aho!* I have seen the devotion to *brāhmaṇas* of the Lord who is dedicated to *brāhmaṇas*. I, the poorest of the poor, have been embraced by him who carries Lakṣmī, the goddess of fortune, on his chest.
16. Who am I but a poor sinner? And who is Kṛṣṇa but the abode of Śrī, the goddess of fortune? Nonetheless I, who can be called a *brāhmaṇa* in name only, was embraced in his arms.
17. I was made to spend the night on the bed enjoyed by his beloved as if I were his brother. When I was tired, I was fanned by his queen, who held a fly-whisk in her hand.
18. I was worshipped like a god by the God of gods and God of *brāhmaṇas* with the highest service – the massaging of feet.
19. Worship of his feet is the root of all perfections, of wealth both in this world and in the lower worlds, and of [the attainment] of the celestial regions and liberation.
20. Thinking, 'This poor person might not remember me if he obtains wealth, but will revel in it excessively,' the merciful [Lord] did not even give me some token wealth."
21. Thinking this inwardly, the *brāhmaṇa* arrived in the vicinity of his home. The area was covered on all sides by palaces that resembled the sun, fire and the moon.
22. It was covered with various parks and groves brimming with

flocks of cooing birds and there were lakes of *ambuja* lotuses, blue *utpala* lotuses, red *kumuda* lotuses and white *kahlāra* lotuses in full bloom.

23. It was populated by handsomely adorned men, and by women with doe-like eyes. "What is this? Whose place is it? How has it become like this?" he thought.

24. While the most fortunate *brāhmaṇa* was thinking like this, the men and women, who were as brilliant as gods, welcomed him with much music and song.

25. When his wife heard that her husband had arrived, she became very excited with joy. She quickly came out of the house, like the beautiful goddess Śrī coming out from her dwelling.

26. The husband saw his chaste wife, who had tears in her eyes from the pain of love. With her eyes closed, she silently offered respect to him and embraced him in her mind.

27. The *brāhmaṇa* saw his wife, who looked like a glittering goddess travelling in a celestial vehicle. She was radiant in the midst of maidservants wearing golden neck ornaments. He was astonished.

28. Delighted, he entered his own palace in her company. It was endowed with 100 jewelled columns, just like the residence of the great Indra.

29. It had ivory beds resembling the foam of milk, couches with golden appendages, and fly-whisks and fans with golden handles.

30. The chairs were golden, with soft cushions, and there were glittering canopies hanging with strings of pearls.

31. The women were adorned with gems, and gem lamps shone in walls of pure crystal containing huge emeralds.

32. The *brāhmaṇa* saw the extravagance of unlimited wealth there and deliberated calmly about his unexpected abundance:

33. "Since I have always been poor and unfortunate, the cause of my prosperity could certainly not have happened other than by the glance of that greatly powerful and eminent member of the Yadu dynasty, Kṛṣṇa.

34. No doubt, Kṛṣṇa, the enjoyer of abundance, without saying anything, personally notices and bestows abundance on a

person present before him who only intends to solicit. My friend Kṛṣṇa, the best of the descendants of Daśārha, is like a rain cloud.

35. Whatever is given by himself, he makes out to be insignificant, and whatever is done by his friend, even if of no consequence, he makes out to be great. I brought a handful of flat rice, and that great Soul accepted it with love.

36. May my service, friendship, camaraderie and affection for Kṛṣṇa continue birth after birth, and may I feel devotion for his followers, who are attached to him, that noble-minded fount of qualities.

37. *Bhagavān* does not personally arrange conspicuous wealth, power or sovereignty for his devotee, whose intelligence is limited. Being wise, the unborn one foresees the downfall of the wealthy brought about by pride."

38. When he had understood this, the *brāhmaṇa*, who was absolutely devoted to Janārdana and not over-lustful, enjoyed relations with his wife while renouncing the objects of enjoyment.

39. *Brāhmaṇas* are the masters for Lord Hari, the God of gods and Lord of sacrifice. There is no deity higher than them.

40. Thus, the *brāhmaṇa*, *Bhagavān*'s friend, saw how the unconquered one becomes conquered by his own servants in this way. The bondage of his *ātmā* was released through the power of his meditation on Kṛṣṇa. He then attained Kṛṣṇa's abode, the goal of the saintly.

41. A person who has heard about the devotion to *brāhmaṇas* by the Lord of *brāhmaṇas* attains love for *Bhagavān*, and is released from the bondage of *karma*.'

CHAPTER 82

The Meeting of the Gopas *and the Vṛṣṇi Clan*

1. *Śrī* Śuka said:

'Once, while Balarāma and Kṛṣṇa were living in Dvārakā, there was a major eclipse of the sun, just like the one at the termination of the *kalpa* world age.[1]
2. The people knew this ahead of time, O king, and went from everywhere to the location of Samantapañcaka, hoping to gain merit.
3. This place is where Paraśurāma, best of weapon-bearers, made huge lakes from the torrents of the blood of the kings, while purging the earth of the *kṣatriya* caste.[2]
4. Although Lord Paraśurāma is *Bhagavān* and untouched by *karma*, he performed sacrifice there for the purpose of removing sins just like anybody else would. He was instructing the world [by his example].
5. Citizens of the land of Bhārata went to that great pilgrimage place, and so did the Vṛṣṇi clan, Akrūra, Vasudeva, Āhuka and others.
6. Gada, Pradyumna, Sāmbha and others, accompanied by Sucandra, Śuka and Sāraṇa, went there desiring to do penance for their own sins, O Parīkṣit, descendant of Bharata.
7–8. Aniruddha remained to protect [the city of Dvārakā] along with Kṛtavarmā, the commander of the army. Wearing golden helmets, the Vṛṣṇi clan shone brightly on the road. They were accompanied by chariots which were like seats of gods, horses that surged forward in waves, trumpeting elephants that resembled clouds, and men that were as luminous as *vidyādharas*.
9. Wearing divine armour, garments and garlands, they were like sky-travelling [celestials] with their wives. After bathing there, those most fortunate people fasted with great diligence.
10. The Vṛṣṇi clan gave cows adorned with golden necklaces, garlands and cloth to the *brāhmaṇas*. Then, they again bathed in Paraśurāma's lakes according to the appropriate prescriptions.

11–12. They gave sumptuous food to the foremost of the twice-born, saying: "May devotion to Kṛṣṇa be bestowed upon us!" Then, with their permission, the Vṛṣṇis, whose Lord is Kṛṣṇa, themselves partook of food. After this, they sat down at leisure at the foot of trees with pleasing shade, and met kings, relatives and dear ones who had come there.

13. [They saw] the Matsya, Uśīnara, Kaikaya, Madra, Kuntī, Ānarta and Kerala clans.

14. [They saw] hundreds of others from their own as well as the opposing side, O king, along with Nanda and the others, their friends the *gopas*, and the *gopīs*, who had been pining for a long time.

15. The beauty of their lotus faces and hearts bloomed with intense joy at seeing each other. With tears flowing from their eyes, their skin tingling with ecstasy, and choked voices, they embraced tightly and entered into a state of bliss.

16. The women looked at each other, smiling with pure glances of deep friendship, their eyes full of tears of love. They embraced with their arms, pressing each other's breasts, smeared with saffron unguents, with their own breasts.

17. Then they greeted the elders respectfully, and were greeted by the juniors. They asked each other about their pleasant journey and their well-being, and then engaged in discussions about Kṛṣṇa.

18. Pṛthā [Kuntī] saw her brothers, sisters, their sons, her parents, her brothers' wives and Mukunda. She let go of her sorrow as a result of their conversations.

19. Kuntī said: "O Ārya! O brother! I feel that I am an unfulfilled person. O righteous ones, you did not remember my welfare in times of calamity.

20. Friends, family, sons, brothers and even parents do not remember their own kin when fate is unfavourable to them."

21. *Śrī* Vasudeva said: "Mother, do not be angry with us. We men are but the playthings of fate. The world is in the control of the Lord, whether it acts or is made to act.

22. Harassed by Kaṃsa, we scattered in every direction. It is only now that we have again been returned to our positions by fate, O sister."'

23. *Śrī* Śuka said:

'The kings were honoured by the Yadus, led by Ugrasena and Vasudeva, and were pacified by the joy of seeing Acyuta.
24–26. They were Bhīṣma, Droṇa, the son of Ambikā, Gāndhārī with her sons, the Pāṇḍavas with their wives, Kuntī, Sañjaya, Vidura, Kṛpa, Kuntibhoja, Virāṭa, Bhīṣmaka, the great Nagnajit, Purujit, Drupada, Śalya, Dhṛṣṭaketu, the king of Kāśī, Damaghoṣa, Viśālākṣa, the kings of Mithilā, Madra and Kekaya, Yudhāmanyu, Suśarmā, Bāhlīka and others, along with their sons.
27. All these as well as the kings who were in allegiance with Yudhiṣṭhira saw the personal form of Śauri [Kṛṣṇa], the abode of Śrī, the goddess of fortune, along with his wives, and were amazed.
28. When they had duly received gifts from Balarāma and Kṛṣṇa, they were overwhelmed with happiness. They praised the Vṛṣṇis, Kṛṣṇa's attendants:
29. "*Aho*, Ugrasena, chief of the Bhojas! You, among the people in this world, [are able to] enjoy life because you see Kṛṣṇa all the time, when it is so hard even for *yogīs* to see him.
30. His fame, celebrated in the Vedas, adequately purifies this world, as does his foot-washing water, as well as the scriptures, which are his words. Previously, the earth had its fortunes destroyed by the force of time but, with its *śakti* powers restored by the touch of Kṛṣṇa's lotus feet, it now showers us with all material goods.
31. Viṣṇu himself, who causes the cessation [of interest in] both heaven and liberation, is present in your household while you live in it, [even though] the household is the path to hell. He is bound to you through your forefathers and your matrimonial connections, as well as through activities involving eating, sitting around, taking rest, chatting, companionship, personal contact and meeting."'
32. *Śrī* Śuka said:

'Then, when Nanda found out that the Yadus had arrived with Kṛṣṇa at their head, he came, eager to see them. He was surrounded by the *gopas* with their utensils loaded on to carts.

33. When the Vṛṣṇis saw Kṛṣṇa, they were delighted and rose up, like bodies [upon the return of] their vital airs. Agitated at seeing Kṛṣṇa after so long, they embraced him vigorously.

34. Vasudeva, delighted and overwhelmed by love, embraced them as he remembered the entrusting of his sons in Gokula [to Nanda], and the difficulties caused by Kaṃsa.

35. Kṛṣṇa and Balarāma embraced and honoured their parents. The Kuru heroes could not utter a single word, choked by tears of love.

36. The most fortunate Yaśodā made her sons climb on to her seat, hugged them and forgot her sorrow.

37. Then Rohiṇī and Devakī also embraced the queen of Vraj. Remembering the friendship extended by her, their throats became choked with tears, and they declared:

38. "Who could forget your unceasing friendship, O queen of Vraj? Even if one obtained the power of Indra, it could not be repaid.

39. These two boys, who had never seen their [real] parents, received protection, nourishment, care and delight from you, and lived with you as their actual parents. They were entrusted to you, O good lady, just as the eyelids are to the eye, and they had no fear from any quarter. For holy people, there is no [distinction between] that which belongs to oneself, and that which belongs to someone else." '

40. *Śrī* Śuka said:

'The *gopīs* obtained their beloved Kṛṣṇa after such a long time. Gazing at him, they cursed the person who had created eyelids on their eyes. They placed him in their hearts and embraced him with their eyes until they had had their fill. They attained the loving state of mind towards him that is difficult even for those who are always engaged in *yoga*.

41. In a secluded spot *Bhagavān* got together with the *gopīs* who were in this state of mind. He embraced them and inquired after their health. Then, smiling, he spoke as follows:

42. "Friends, do you remember us? We were committed to

destroying those on the enemy side, and so went away for a long time wanting to fulfil the needs of our kinsfolk.
43. Still, perhaps you think ill of us, suspecting us of being ungrateful. Actually, it is God who unites and separates living creatures.
44. The creator brings living creatures together and then hurls them apart again, just as the wind does to groups of clouds, or to straw, grass or dust.
45. Devotion to me results in immortality for living creatures. By good fortune, it has developed [in you]; your love for me has resulted in you attaining me.
46. I am the beginning and the end, the inside and outside of all living creatures, just as ether, air, fire, water and earth are of all material things, O beautiful ladies.
47. Consequently, the *ātmā* is diffused within all creatures by its own nature and thus these creatures exist. Understand that both of them abide in me, but, manifested in the imperishable [*brahman*], I am transcendent."'
48. *Śrī* Śuka said:

'When the *gopīs* were instructed by Kṛṣṇa thus in spiritual matters, they became absorbed in him. Meditating on him, the coverings of their souls were destroyed.[3]
49. The *gopīs* said: "O you of the lotus navel! Let your lotus feet be always present in our minds, even though we are absorbed in domestic life. They are the object of meditation in the hearts of the profoundly knowledgeable masters of *yoga*, and are the means of deliverance for those fallen into the well of *saṃsāra*."'

CHAPTER 83

*The Queens Relate their Stories**

1. *Śrī* Śuka said:

'*Bhagavān*, who is the *guru* as well as the refuge of the *gopīs*, showed his kindness in this way. Then he inquired of Yudhiṣṭhira and all his dear friends as to their welfare.
2. Their minds were delighted at being honoured and questioned in this way by the Lord of the worlds, and their cares were dispelled from seeing his feet. They replied:
3. "How can there ever be ill fortune for those who take in the nectar of your lotus feet to their full satisfaction through the apertures of their ears? [This nectar] emanates from the mouths of the noble-minded ones, and destroys ignorance, which is the cause of bodily existence for embodied beings.
4. We offer homage to you. You are the refuge of swan-like ascetics[1] and have assumed a form through *yogamāyā* for the protection of the Veda, which had become obscured by time. Your intelligence is beyond duality and ever fresh. You are a flood of bliss. The three states created by the *ātmā* [wakefulness, sleep and deep sleep] are dispelled by the splendour of your *ātmā*."'
5. The sage [Śuka] said:

'While the people were thus glorifying Kṛṣṇa, the crown jewel among those most worthy of praise, the women of the Andhaka and Kaurava dynasties assembled and related stories of Govinda among themselves. These stories are sung throughout the three worlds. Listen and I will tell them to you.
6–7. *Śrī* Draupadī said: "O wives of Kṛṣṇa – Vaidarbhī, Bhadrā, Jāmbavatī, Kausalā, Satyabhāmā, Kālindī, Śaibyā, Rohiṇī, Lakṣmaṇā – tell us this: how did Acyuta, God himself, marry you, imitating ordinary people through his *māyā*?"
8. *Śrī* Rukmiṇī said: "When the kings had their bows raised ready to give me to the king of the Cedis, Kṛṣṇa carried me off like a lion carries off his spoil from sheep and he-goats. The

dust of his feet [covered] the crowns of those invincible warriors. May those feet, the abode of Śrī, the goddess of fortune, be the objects of my worship."

9. *Śrī* Satyabhāmā said: "He killed the king of bears, seized the jewel, and then handed it over in order to give the lie to the accusation spread by my father, whose heart was grieving over the murder of my brother. Because of this, my father became fearful and gave me to the Lord, even though I had already been committed."

10. *Śrī* Jāmbavatī said: "My father was unaware that this person was Rāma, the husband of Sītā, and his own deity and master, and fought him for twenty-seven days. When his abilities had been put to the test, he realized. Then he grasped Kṛṣṇa's feet, and presented me along with the jewel as an offering. I am Kṛṣṇa's servant."

11. *Śrī* Kālindī said: "Knowing that I was undertaking austere practices in the hope of touching his feet, Kṛṣṇa arrived with his friend and took my hand. I am the cleaner of his house."

12. *Śrī* Mitravindā said: "He came to my *svayaṃvara* marriage ceremony and defeated the kings, as well as my brothers, who were engaged in wrongdoing. Then he took me away to his own city, the residence of Śrī, the goddess of fortune, just as the lion takes away his own spoil which has fallen to a pack of dogs. May the privilege of washing his feet be mine in every birth."

13. *Śrī* Satyā said: "Kṛṣṇa, the destroyer of the arrogance of heroes, swiftly restrained the seven bulls that had been prepared by my father to test the prowess of the rulers of the world. They were extremely strong and powerful, and had very sharp horns, but he light-heartedly bound them like children bind the offspring of goats.

14. Thus, he carried me off as the prize of his valour, with my army of four divisions,[2] after defeating the kings on the way. May I attain service to him."

15. *Śrī* Bhadrā said: "My mind was set on him, so my father personally invited my maternal cousin Kṛṣṇa, and gave me to him, O Kṛṣṇā [Draupadī], along with an *akṣauhiṇī* battalion and my female companions.

16. I am wandering around, birth after birth, because of my

karmas. May I attain the touch of his feet, which is the highest blessing for the *ātmā*."

17. *Śrī* Lakṣmaṇā said: "My heart, too, was [fixed] on Mukunda after repeatedly hearing about the deeds and birth of Acyuta recited in the kingdom by Nārada. Indeed, he was chosen by Śrī, the goddess of fortune, who holds a lotus in her hand, after carefully considering and rejecting the rulers of the worlds.

18. My father, known as Bṛhatsena, holds his daughter in affection, O saintly lady. He knew my aspiration, and devised a strategy to fulfil it.

19. Just as a fish was used in your *svayaṃvara* marriage ceremony, O queen, out of your desire for Arjuna [so it was in mine], except that the fish was concealed from the outside and only [its reflection] was visible in water.[3]

20. After hearing this, kings came to my father's city in their thousands, from everywhere. They were experts in all the sacred manuals on weaponry and were accompanied by their teachers.

21. All were honoured by my father according to their prowess and their seniority. Then with minds intent on [winning] me, they took up the bow with its arrow in the assembly hall, so as to pierce [the target].

22. Some discarded the bow after picking it up, unable to string it. A few pulled the bowstring as far as their stomachs, but then were struck by it and tumbled down.

23. Other heroes – the kings of Magadha (Jarāsandha), Ambaṣṭha (Śisupāla) and Cedi; Bhīma; Duryodhana and Karṇa – strung it, but could not figure out the location of the fish.

24. Arjuna, son of Pṛthā, saw the reflection of the fish in the water, and understood its location. He released an arrow, but merely grazed the fish; he did not pierce it.

25. The proud kings were humbled in their pride. After they had given up, *Bhagavān* Kṛṣṇa took up the bow and effortlessly strung it.

26. As the sun was situated in the constellation of Abhijit, he fixed an arrow in the bow, instantly saw the fish in the water, pierced it with the arrow, and made it fall.

27. Kettledrums resounded in the heavens, blending with cries of

'victory' on the earth. Overwhelmed with joy, the gods released showers of flowers.

28. Then I put on and fastened fresh, best-quality cloth, took a garland of dazzling jewels and gold,[4] and entered the arena on foot, my golden anklets making a melodious sound. I wore a wreath on my braided hair, and had a bashful smile on my face.

29. I raised my face, its cheeks glittering with earrings and abundant locks of hair, and observed the kings all around by casting sidelong glances and cool smiles at them. Then, with a loving heart, I gently placed my own garland on the shoulders of Murāri [Kṛṣṇa].

30. At that, *mṛdaṅga* and *paṭaha* drums, conches, kettledrums and *ānaka* military drums resounded, male and female dancers danced, and singers sang.

31. When *Bhagavān*, the Lord, was chosen by me in this manner, O Draupadī, the leaders of the kings could not tolerate it. Full of lust, they became contentious.

32. Thereupon, the four-armed Kṛṣṇa had me mount the chariot with its four gems of horses. Then he raised his Śārṅga bow and took his position, fully armed.

33. Dāruka the charioteer drove the chariot, with its golden decoration, forward, O queen, before the very eyes of the kings, [with Kṛṣṇa looking] like a lion, king of beasts, before [other] animals.

34. In order to block Kṛṣṇa's path, some of the kings followed behind with their bows and arrows raised, ready for battle, just as dogs follow a lion.

35. They tumbled down on the battlefield, their necks, feet and arms severed by a flood of arrows from Acuta's Śārṅga bow. Some gave up and fled.

36. After this, Kṛṣṇa, the Lord of the Yadus, entered his city, Kuśasthalī [Dvārakā], like the sun entering its abode. The city is glorified in the heavens and on earth. It was highly decorated, and its splendid arches, banners and flags obscured the sun.[5]

37–38. My father honoured his dear friends, family and relatives with costly garments, ornaments, couches, seats, articles, highly skilled maidservants, horses, chariots, soldiers and elephants.

He gave valuable weapons to the all-perfect Lord out of devotion.
39. It is clear that by ascetic practices and the renunciation of worldly attachments, we here have become household servants of the self-fulfilled Kṛṣṇa."
40. The queens said: "Although his desires are all fulfilled, Kṛṣṇa killed Bhauma and his followers in battle. Then, since he knew that we were the daughters of defeated kings and had been imprisoned by Bhauma during his conquest of the world, he released and married us. We were meditating on his lotus feet, which give liberation from worldly existence.
41–42. We do not desire empire, dominion or even kingship, universal sovereignty, the position of Brahmā, eternity, or Hari's abode. We desire to carry on our heads the dust from the beautiful feet of the wielder of the club, Kṛṣṇa, which is redolent with the scent of saffron powder from the breast of Śrī, the goddess of fortune.
43 The women of Vraj, the cowherd boys who graze the cows, the Pulinda tribal women, the plants and the grass yearn for the touch of the feet of that great-souled one."'

CHAPTER 84

Description of the Pilgrimage

1. *Śrī* Śuka said:

'Pṛthā [Kuntī], the daughter of Subala [Gāndhārī], Yājñasenī [Draupadī], Mādhavī [Subhadrā], the wives of the kings, as well as Kṛṣṇa's own *gopīs*, their eyes full of tears, were deeply astonished at this loving attachment to Kṛṣṇa, Hari, the soul of everything.
2. While the women were discussing with each other in this way, and the men with the men, the sages arrived, wanting to see Kṛṣṇa and Balarāma.
3–5. They were: Dvaipāyana [Vyāsa], Nārada, Cyavana, Asita,

Viśvāmitra, Śatānanda, Bharadvāja, Gautama, *Bhagavān* Paraśurāma with his disciples, Vasiṣṭha, Gālava, Bhṛgu, Pulastya, Kaśyapa, Atri, Mārkaṇḍeya, Bṛhaspati, Dvita, Trita and Ekata, the [Kumāra] sons of Brahmā, Aṅgirās, Agastya, Yājñavalkya, Vāmadeva and others.[1]

6. When they saw these universally respected sages, Kṛṣṇa and Balarāma, the Pāṇḍavas and the other kings and dignitaries, who had until then been seated, immediately stood up and offered homage.

7. All the kings venerated them in an appropriate manner. Acyuta also, along with Balarāma, showed them deference with paste, incense, garlands, mouthwash, footwash, seats and words of welcome.

8. As that great assembly listened, *Bhagavān* Kṛṣṇa, who is a measured speaker and the embodiment of the protection of *dharma*, addressed them when they were sitting comfortably.

9. *Śrī Bhagavān* said: "*Aho!* Our lives have become completely fulfilled. We have attained the fruit which is difficult even for the gods to obtain: a vision of the lord of *yogīs*.

10. How did the opportunity to see you, touch you, inquire from you, bow to you, worship your feet, and other such devotional activities, arise for men of little austerity whose vision [is limited] to seeing the divine in the form of a deity?

11. Holy places are more than bodies of water, and divinities are more than things made of earth and stone. But they purify only after a long time, while saints purify simply from being seen.

12. Neither fire, the sun, the moon, stars, earth, water, sky, breath, nor thought, the speech of the mind, dissolve sins when worshipped – they create dissension. But the wise destroy sins after being served for a short time.

13. One who identifies this corpse made of the three elements to be the *ātmā*, considers one's wife and so forth to be one's own, holds the earth to be worthy of worship, understands water to be sacred, but does not accept those who are wise, is truly a donkey or a cow.""

14. *Śrī* Śuka said:

'After hearing such words, which were difficult to fathom, from the perfectly wise *Bhagavān* Kṛṣṇa the sages fell silent, confused in their minds.

15. The sages pondered over this humility shown by the Lord for some time: "This is for the welfare of people," they said. Then, smiling, they spoke to Kṛṣṇa, the *guru* of the universe.

16. The sages said: "We are distinguished knowers of truth, and foremost among the creators of universes, but we are bewildered by Kṛṣṇa's *māyā*. Concealed by his activities, he acts as if subordinate. *Aho!* The behaviour of God is wondrous.

17. Single-handedly and time after time he creates, animates and devours this universe effortlessly out of his own self – just as the earth creates an abundance of earthly substances and forms – but he is not bound [by it].

18. Nonetheless, at the appropriate time, you accept a [form of] *sattva* for the protection of your own devotees and the suppression of wrongdoers, and uphold the eternal path of the Vedas by your own *līlā*. You, Lord, are the supreme being.

19. The Veda is your pure heart. By means of discipline of the senses, study and austerity, the manifested and unmanifested existence, as well as the transcendent, can be understood from it.

20. It is because of this that you honour the *brāhmaṇa* caste, O absolute truth. *Brāhmaṇas* are the venerable abode of your very self, and you are the source of the scriptures.[2] Therefore, you are the foremost of those devoted to *brāhmaṇas*.

21. Today is the culmination of our birth, erudition, asceticism and faculty of sight – we have come into contact with you, the goal of the virtuous. You are the greatest of boons, the final destination.

22. Homage to you, Kṛṣṇa, *Bhagavān*. You are the supreme soul, of perfect wisdom. Your greatness is covered by your *māyā*.

23. These kings, as well as the Vṛṣṇi clan who have [you] as their only object of pleasure, do not know you. You are the Lord of time, but your true self is covered by the screen of *māyā*.

24–25. A person who is sleeping sees reality through the *guṇas*; because of the disruption of memory, he does not remember his other self [when awake], which is distinct from the ephemeral, sensual appearance [of the dream self]. In the same way, by the agency of *māyā*, a person whose consciousness is bewildered by sensual engagement with ephemeral sense objects does not know you.

26. Today we have seen your feet. They are the seat of the holy places which absolve masses of sin, and are placed in the heart by those whose *yoga* practice is mature. Those who have destroyed the mental covering of the soul[3] by being saturated in *bhakti* have attained you as their goal. Therefore, bestow favour on your devotees."'

27. *Śrī* Śuka said:

'Saying this, the sages took leave of Dāśārha [Kṛṣṇa], Dhṛtarāṣṭra and Yudhiṣṭhira, O kingly sage, and turned their thoughts towards returning to their own *āśramas*.

28. When he saw them approaching, Kṛṣṇa's father, the highly renowned Vasudeva, offered homage and touched their feet. With a composed appearance, he addressed them:

29. *Śrī* Vasudeva said: "Homage to you, O sages. You are the gods of everyone. Please listen. Please inform us as to how *karma* can be eradicated by the performance of *karma*."

30. *Śrī* Nārada said: "This is not so very surprising, O sages, that Vasudeva, who thinks Kṛṣṇa is a boy, asks us about the welfare of the *ātmā* out of a desire for knowledge.

31. Familiarity between people breeds contempt. This is like someone who lives near the Gaṅgā river, but who goes to some other body of water for purification.

32. Kṛṣṇa's knowledge is not destroyed by time, by such things as the dissolution or creation of the universe, by the *guṇas*, by itself, or by anything else from any quarter.

33. The Lord is one without a second, and his consciousness is never affected by the flow of the *guṇas*, or by the ripening of *karma*, or by distress. But someone may think that he is covered by his own emanations in the form of the vital airs and so forth, just as someone may believe that the sun is covered by clouds, snow or eclipses."

34. After he had said this, the sages again addressed Ānakadun-

dubhi [Vasudeva], while Acyuta, Balarāma and all the kings were listening:

35. "It has been determined by the *sādhus* that *karma* can be eradicated by *karma* if one faithfully worships Viṣṇu, the Lord of all sacrifices, with sacrificial oblations.[4]

36. This *yoga* controls the mind. By using the eye of sacred scripture, the learned have shown that it is easily performed. It is *dharma*, and it brings happiness to the *ātmā*.

37. This path, by which the supreme person is worshipped faithfully with one's wealth obtained by pure means, brings good fortune to the householders of the twice-born castes.

38. A wise person should renounce the desire for wealth by performing sacrifice and giving charity, should renounce the desire for wife and children by undertaking household affairs, and should renounce the desire for the celestial realms by [understanding the workings of] Time, O worthy Vasudeva. All those in the past who renounced their desires for everyday life headed off to the forest to practise austere disciplines.

39. A twice-born is born with three debts – to the gods, to the sages and to the ancestors, O master. A person who renounces [these obligations] without fulfilling these debts by means of sacrifice, study and the begetting of children falls down.

40. But you, O great soul, have now been freed from two debts – to the sages and to the ancestors. After freeing yourself from the debt to the gods by the performance of sacrifice, you will become free from debt and support systems.

41. It is clear that you, Vasudeva, had previously worshipped Hari, the Lord of the universe, with the highest devotion, such that he has come as the son of you both."'

42. *Śrī* Śuka said:

'When he heard these words, the noble-minded Vasudeva bowed his head, made arrangements for the satisfaction of the sages, and chose them as his *ṛtvik* officiating priests for the sacrifice.

43. On being selected, those sages supervised the righteous Vasudeva in the sacrifice. It was performed on the field [of Kurukṣetra] with unprecedented ritualistic ceremonies.

44–45. While the initiation ceremony[5] was proceeding, O king, the Vṛṣṇi kings, who had bathed and were wearing lotus garlands, choice garments and appropriate ornaments, along with their joyful queens, who had been anointed and wore special garments and golden ornaments on their necks, approached the initiation hall with articles in hand.

46. *Mṛdaṅga*, *paṭaha*, *bherī* and *ānaka* drums resounded, along with conches; male and female performers danced; bards and minstrels recited eulogies; and sweet-voiced female celestial *gandharvas* sang songs along with their husbands.

47. When Vasudeva had been daubed [with mascara] and smeared [with butter],[6] according to custom, the *ṛtvik* priests consecrated him for the sacrifice, along with his eighteen wives. He was like the moon with the stars.

48. Consecrated for the sacrifice, and wrapped in the skin of an antelope, he looked radiant with his beautiful wives, who were decorated with earrings, anklets, necklaces, bracelets and fine cloth.

49. His *ṛtvik* priests, wearing jewels and silk clothes, O king, along with the assembly members, shone brilliantly, as at the sacrifice of Indra, the slayer of Vṛtra.

50. Balarāma and Kṛṣṇa, the Lords of the *jīva* souls, in the company of their respective relatives, wives and children, were resplendent in their own majesty.

51. With each sacrifice, Vasudeva honoured the Lord of the ritual act, the knowledge [of the *mantras*], and the ritual paraphernalia, by the performance of routine as well as specialized sacrifices. These sacrifices were characterized by various oblations such as those to Agni, the god of the sacred fire, and performed according to the appropriate rules and regulations.

52. Then, at the appropriate time and according to the injunctions of the scriptures, Vasudeva decorated the already lavishly bedecked *ṛtvik* priests, and bestowed remuneration on them in the form of great wealth, cows and maidens.

53. After conducting the post-sacrifice *avabṛtha* ablutions and the *patnīsaṃyāja* sacrifices,[7] the great *brāhmaṇa* sages put Vasudeva, the sponsor of the sacrifice, at their head, and bathed in Paraśurāma's lake.

54. When Vasudeva had bathed, he gave ornaments and garments to the bards, and so did the women. Then, beautifully adorned, he honoured all the castes – including the dogs – with food.

55–56. He honoured his relatives with their wives and sons; the members of the Vidarbha, Kosala, Kuru, Kāśī, Kekaya and Sṛñjaya clans; assembly members; *ṛtvik* priests and hosts of gods; as well as humans, ghosts, forefathers and *cāraṇa* celestials, with abundant gifts. After taking leave of Kṛṣṇa, the abode of Śrī, the goddess of fortune, they all departed, praising the sacrifice.

57–58. Dhṛtarāṣṭra, his younger brother Vidura, Bhīṣma, Droṇa, Pṛthā [Kuntī], the two twins Nakula and Sahadeva, Nārada, *Bhagavān* Vyāsa, friends, relatives and kinsmen embraced their relations the Yadus, their hearts tender with affection. Feeling the pain of separation, they and all the other people set out for their own lands.

59. But Nanda, who held his family in affection, stayed, and so did the cowherd men. He was honoured with respect by Kṛṣṇa, Balarāma, Ugrasena and the others.

60. Having crossed over the great ocean of his desire with ease, and surrounded by his well-wishers, Vasudeva was contented in his mind. He spoke to Nanda, touching him with his hand.

61. *Śrī* Vasudeva said: "O brother, what people call 'affection' is a God-made bond for people. It seems to me that it is hard even for *yogīs* and heroes to renounce it.

62. Saints extend friendship to people like us, although we do not appreciate what has been offered. Despite the fact that it is unreciprocated and bears no fruit, this friendship is never withdrawn.

63. Previously we did not act on your behalf, O brother, because of our inability to do so. And now, our eyes blinded by riches, we [still] do not notice you standing in front of us.

64. May royal opulence not befall a person who desires his own best interest. It brings pride. One's vision is blinded by it, and one overlooks one's own family and friends.'

65. *Śrī* Śuka said:

'Ānakadundubhi [Vasudeva] wept as he remembered the friendship extended by Nanda. His heart became tender with affection and his eyes filled with tears.
66. Nanda showed fondness for his friend, and, out of love for Govinda and Balarāma, said: "[I will leave] today or tomorrow." But he stayed for three months, honoured by the Yadus.
67–68. Then, laden with desirable things – priceless furnishings and exceptionally valuable ornaments and linen – he was allowed to depart. He accepted the gifts offered by Vasudeva, Ugrasena, Kṛṣṇa, Uddhava, Balarāma and others, and set off with his family and the people of Vraj.
69. Nanda, the *gopas* and the *gopīs* proceeded to Mathurā. Their minds were fixed on Govinda's lotus feet and could not be diverted.
70. After their relatives had left, the Vṛṣṇi clan, whose Lord was Kṛṣṇa, saw that the rainy season was approaching and set out once more for Dvārakā.
71. They told the people about the great Yadu festival, about events occurring on the pilgrimage, about the encounter with their loved ones, and about everything else.'

CHAPTER 85

Fetching the Deceased Elder Brothers

1. *Śrī* Bādarāyaṇa [Śuka] said:

'Once, Vasudeva greeted his two sons, Saṅkarṣaṇa and Acyuta, when they came to meet him and had paid respects at his feet. He greeted them affectionately and spoke to them.
2. He had heard the words of the sages, which revealed the true nature of his two sons, and his conviction [about them] had grown [from seeing] their deeds. He addressed them, saying:
3. "O Kṛṣṇa, Kṛṣṇa, great *yogī*, O eternal Saṅkarṣaṇa! I realize that you two are the supreme beings, the original sources of this world in person.

4. Where, by whom, from whom, of whom, for whom, in whatever fashion, whenever, and however this universe might come into being, it is *Bhagavān*, God, the Lord, the supreme being and original source in person.
5. This diverse universe was created from your *ātmā*, O Adhokṣaja. After entering it with your *ātmā*, you maintain it, O *ātmā*. You are the vital air and the *jīva* soul, O unborn one.
6. The powers of such things as the vital airs, and of the creators of the universe, are powers of the supreme being, because they are dependent [on him], as well as different [from him]. So, too, is the activating force of those who are active among both [moving and non-moving entities].
7. The splendour, brilliance, radiance and existence of the moon, fire, sun, stars and lightning; the firmness of the mountains; and the fragrance existing in the earth are, in actuality, your Lordship.
8. You are the nourishing and life-giving qualities of the waters, O God, their flavour, and water itself. You are vitality, power, strength, endeavour and the movement of the wind, O Lord.
9. You are the space encompassing the quarters of the world, the quarters, the ether and the substratum [of sound]. You are the eternal *sphoṭa* sound, the *nāda* sound, the *om* sound, and phonemic sound which differentiates into syllables.[1]
10. You are the power of the senses, and the gods that uphold them. You are the faculty of awareness of the intelligence, and the power of memory present in the *jīva* [soul].
11. You are the essence of the material elements; the illumination of the senses; the transforming ability of the gods; and the underlying *pradhāna*, the primordial matter.[2]
12. You are the imperishable entity behind perishable substances, just as it is seen that matter is behind the modifications of matter.
13. The *guṇas* – known as *sattva*, *rajas* and *tamas* – and their activity occur within you, the supreme *brahman*, under the jurisdiction of *yogamāyā*.
14. Therefore, these substances do not exist until they are arranged in you. It is you who exist in these transformations. Otherwise you remain unmanifest.

15. Those who are ignorant of the subtle presence of the universal soul in this flow of *guṇas* transmigrate in this world with their *karmas* because of their ignorance.
16. Having obtained a rare and competent human birth in this world by chance, O Lord, the life of a person neglectful of his real interest is lost by your *māyā*.
17. Your Lordship binds this entire universe with the chains of affection. [Thus, people think]: 'I am such and such a person, and these bodies belong to me as family members and other relatives.'
18. You two are not our sons; you are the Lords of *pradhāna* [material nature] and the *puruṣa* [soul].[3] You have stated that you have descended to destroy the earth's burden in the form of military power.
19. Therefore, today I have come for refuge at your lotus feet; they remove the fear of transmigration [of the soul] for those who resort to them, O friend of the downtrodden. Enough, enough, of such intense longing of the senses, as a result of which I conceive of you, the supreme being, as being my child, and regard my *ātmā* as being the mortal [body].
20. In the room of your birth, your Lordship told us that you were actually unborn, but had taken birth in order to protect *dharma*, which is your own. You adopt various bodies like a cloud, and then you relinquish them. You are all-pervading and greatly renowned – who can understand the magnificence of your *māyā*?" '
21. *Śrī* Śuka said:

'When he heard these words of his father, *Bhagavān*, foremost of the Sātvata clan, bowed respectfully. Smiling, he responded in a tender voice.
22. *Śrī Bhagavān* said: "We consider these words that you have explained to us, your sons, to be full of meaning, dear father; you have set forth an abundance of truth.
23. I, you, he – my elder brother – as well as these citizens of Dvārakā, indeed everyone – all moving and non-moving entities – should be regarded in this way, O best of the Yadus.
24. The *ātmā* is really one. It is self-effulgent, eternal, distinct,

and free from the *guṇas*. As a result of the *guṇas* created from the *ātmā*, it appears manifold in the entities created by it.
25. Ether, air, fire, water and earth are either visible or invisible, and either small or great in quantity in the things made from them, according to the receptacle [wherein they are found]. In the same way, the *ātmā* is one, but becomes manifold." '
26. *Śrī* Śuka said:

'When Vasudeva was addressed in this way by *Bhagavān*, O king, his conception of reality as being manifold was destroyed, and he fell silent, his mind content.
27. Then, Devakī, the goddess of all, who was present, was astonished at hearing that the *guru*'s son had been brought back by her sons, O best of the Kurus.
28. Remembering her own sons who had been murdered by Kaṃsa, she told Kṛṣṇa and Balarāma about them. Then, with tears of sorrow in her eyes, she spoke piteously.
29. *Śrī* Devakī said: "O Balarāma, Balarāma, immeasurable Soul! O Kṛṣṇa, Kṛṣṇa, Lord of the lords of *yoga*! I know that you both are the original beings, Lords of the creators of the universes.
30. Indeed, you have now descended through me on account of the kings who are creating a burden for the earth. Their good qualities have been destroyed by time, and they act outside the injunctions of the scriptures.
31. The creation, perpetuation and dissolution of the universe evolve from a fraction of a part of a part of a part of you. Today I have come to you for refuge, O soul of the universe.
32. It has been said that you were dispatched by your teacher to retrieve his sons who had long been dead. You brought them from the abode of the forefathers as *gurudakṣiṇā* [remuneration of the teacher].
33. You are both the Lords of the lords of *yoga*: fulfil my desire in the same way. I desire to see my sons, who were killed by Kaṃsa, the king of the Bhojas, restored." '
34. The sage [Śuka] said:

'Implored in this way by their mother, Balarāma and Kṛṣṇa took

recourse to *yogamāyā*, and entered the planet Sutala, O Parīkṣit, descendant of Bharata.
35. Once they had entered, Bali, the king of the demons, understood them to be the Lord and soul of the universe, and, even more so, of his own self. His heart overflowing with joy at seeing them, he immediately arose along with his family and offered homage.
36. Joyfully, Bali brought a magnificent seat for them. When those two great souls had settled down on it, he washed their feet and then, along with his retinue, carried the water. That water purifies [everything] up to Brahmā, the creator.
37. He worshipped them with his riches – extremely costly garments, ornaments and ointments, betel nut, lamps, nectar, food and other such offerings – and by surrendering all his family's wealth as well as his own self.
38. Bali, who had an army like that of Indra, repeatedly clasped the lotus feet of *Bhagavān*, his thoughts disturbed by love. He spoke faltering words, his eyes filled with tears of ecstasy and his hair standing on end, O king.
39. Bali said: "Homage to you, O great unlimited one! Homage to you, O Kṛṣṇa, creator, disseminator of the Sāṅkhya yoga system, *brahman*, supreme soul!
40. The vision of you both is rare and difficult to come by for entities whose nature is *rājasic* and *tāmasic*. But we have obtained it – by good fortune you have both come.
41–42. We – the *daityas*, *dānavas*, *gandharvas*, *siddhas*, *vidyādharas*, *cāraṇas*, *yakṣas*, *rākṣasas*, *piśācas*, *bhūtas*, *pramathas*, *nāyakas*[4] – and other similar characters are always bound by enmity to you, who are undoubtedly the embodiment of the scriptures and the abode of pure goodness.
43. Some are bound by enmity and some by devotion born of lust; but those such as the gods who are immersed in *sattva* are not intimately connected [with you] to the same extent [as those bound by hate].[5]
44. The Lords of *yoga* generally do not know the length and breadth of *yogamāyā*, O Lord of the lords of *yoga* – what then of us?
45. Therefore, be merciful to us: deliver us from the dark well

of the household, which is different from the abode of your lotus feet, which are sought after by those free from desire. I will subsist on whatever is available at the foot of trees, which give shelter to the world. I will wander about peacefully alone, or in the company of those who are friends to everyone.

46. Instruct us, O Lord of those who are to be lorded over. Make us sinless, O master! A person following you with faith is freed from the injunctions of the scriptures."

47. *Śrī Bhagavān* said: "There were six sons begotten of [his wife] Ūrṇā by the sage Marīci during the first *manvantara*.[6] These gods laughed when they saw Brahmā the creator intent on copulating with his daughter.[7]

48–49. On account of that blameworthy act, they entered into a demoniac womb; they were transported by *yogamāyā*, and took birth from Hiraṇyakaśipu. Then they were born from the womb of Devakī and murdered by Kaṃsa. Devakī is lamenting for them as her own offspring. These same sons are now living nearby.

50. We will take them from there in order to dispel our mother's grief. Then, freed from the curse, they will be freed from affliction and go to their abode.

51. By my grace, these six – Smara, Udgitha, Pariṣvaṅga, Pataṅga, Kṣudrabhṛt and Ghṛṇī – will again return to the destination of the righteous."

52. Having said this, Balarāma and Kṛṣṇa took the sons, after they themselves had been honoured by Bali. They then returned again to Dvārakā and presented them to their mother.

53. When goddess Devakī saw those boys, her breasts flowed with affection for her sons. Embracing them, she lifted them on to her lap and smelled their heads repeatedly.

54. She was delighted, and had them drink from her breast, which was producing milk [stimulated by] the touch of her sons. She was bewildered by Viṣṇu's *māyā*, by which the creation is set in motion.

55. They drank that honeyed milk – the remnant of that which had been drunk by Kṛṣṇa, the wielder of the club. Then, by touching the body of Nārāyaṇa, they gained the realization of their real selves.

56. They offered homage to Govinda and Balarāma, and to Devakī and their father. Then, while all beings looked on, they went to the dwelling of the residents of the celestial realm.
57. After seeing their return from the dead and their subsequent departure, goddess Devakī was amazed and decided that this had been produced by Kṛṣṇa's *māyā*, O king.
58. There are innumerable deeds performed by Kṛṣṇa, the supreme Soul, which are just as amazing as this – his deeds are infinite, O Parīkṣit, descendant of Bharata.'
59. *Śrī* Śuka said:

'He who listens to, or recites, this story of Murāri [Kṛṣṇa] of undying fame, which has been described by the son of Vyāsa [Śuka], will attain the happiness of that final abode, with his mind fixed on *Bhagavān* Kṛṣṇa. This story is sufficient to destroy the sins of the world, and is an ornament of truth for the ears of the devotees.'

CHAPTER 86

Grace Bestowed on Śrutadeva

1. The king said:

'I would like to know about how Vijaya [Arjuna] married my grandmother [Subhadrā], the sister of Balarāma and Kṛṣṇa.'
2. *Śrī* Śuka said:

'When the mighty Arjuna was wandering about the earth on pilgrimage, he arrived at Prabhāsa and heard about his maternal uncle's daughter.
3. Convinced that Balarāma would give her to Duryodhana and no one else, Arjuna desired to win her hand. After transforming himself into an ascetic bearing a *tridaṇḍa* staff,[1] he went to Dvārakā.
4. He resided there for the rainy season in order to accomplish

his goal, and was constantly revered by the citizens, including Balarāma, who was unaware of who he was.

5. Once, Arjuna was invited and brought by Balarāma to his own house as a guest, and offered food with devotion. He ate it.

6. He saw there that noble maiden who captivated the minds of heroes. His eyes wide with love, he surrendered to her his heart, which was disturbed by love.

7. She, in turn, saw Arjuna, who moved the hearts of women, and desired him. Smiling, and casting sidelong glances, she fixed her eyes and heart on him.

8. Thinking only of her, Arjuna was anxious to find an opportunity to win her for himself. With his mind distracted by intense desire, he was not able to find peace.

9. With the permission of her parents and of Kṛṣṇa, the great charioteer abducted her when, seated on a chariot, she came out for a major pilgrimage to the gods.

10. Standing on his chariot as her relatives protested, he took up his bow and scattered the heroes and guards who impeded him, just as a lion [seizes] his share.

11. Balarāma, when he heard about this, was disturbed, just like a great ocean when the moon changes. But he was pacified when Kṛṣṇa and his dear friends took hold of his feet.

12. Balarāma joyfully bestowed goods upon the bride and groom – gifts of great value, elephants, chariots, horses, and male and female servants.'

13. *Śrī* Śuka said:

'There was a distinguished *brāhmaṇa* devoted to Kṛṣṇa known as Śrutadeva. His goals were all fulfilled by exclusive devotion to Kṛṣṇa. He was a wise, peaceful and chaste soul.

14. Śrutadeva was a householder and lived in the city of Mithilā in the land of Videha. He carried out his personal duties with whatever sustenance came his way without endeavour [on his part].

15. By good fortune, day after day, as much as was required for his livelihood presented itself, and no more. Śrutadeva was satisfied with that much, and carried out his duties in the appropriate manner.

16. The guardian of that country was known as Bahulāśva, dear Parīkṣit, a man free of ego. Both of them were dear to Acyuta.
17. Being pleased with both of them, Lord Kṛṣṇa, *Bhagavān*, mounted the chariot that was brought by Dāruka and set out for the kingdom of Videha, accompanied by sages.
18. These included myself, Nārada, Vāmadeva, Atri, Kṛṣṇa, Balarāma, Asita, Āruṇi, Bṛhaspati, Kaṇva, Maitreya, Cyavana and others.
19. In each place [along the way], the citizens and country-dwellers approached Kṛṣṇa with offerings in hand, as he was arriving like the rising sun with the planets.
20. The men and women from the lands of the Ānarta, Dhanva, Kuru, Jāṅgala, Kaṅka, Matsya, Pāñcāla, Kuntī, Madhu, Kekaya, Kośala, Arṇa and others drank in the loving glances and broad smiles of his lotus face with their eyes.
21. Kṛṣṇa, the *guru* of the three worlds, slowly proceeded towards the kingdom of Videha, bestowing an awareness of truth as well as liberation upon them, so that their deluded perspectives were banished by his glances. Meanwhile, he was listening to the songs of the gods about his glories, which destroy sins and purify the ends of the quarters.
22. When the Videhan citizens and country-dwellers heard that Acyuta had arrived, O king, they came towards him joyfully, bearing gifts in their hands.
23. Seeing Uttamaśloka, their faces and hearts swelled with joy. With their hands extended over their heads they offered homage to him, as well as to the sages, about whom they had previously heard.
24. The king of Mithilā [Bahulāśva] as well as Śrutadeva fell at the feet of the Lord, each thinking that the *guru* of the universe had arrived to bestow mercy on himself [exclusively].
25. The king of Mithilā and Śrutadeva, their hands joined, simultaneously invited Kṛṣṇa, the descendant of Dāśārha, as guests, along with the *brāhmaṇas*.
26. Desiring to please, *Bhagavān* accepted the invitations of them both. He entered the houses of both of them, but this was unnoticed by both.
27–29. The noble-minded Bahulāśva, the descendant of Janaka,

bowed down to them when they arrived from afar, rather tired, at his house. His eyes filled with tears and his heart was ecstatic from a surge of devotion. When they were sitting happily on special seats, he, along with his family, washed their feet. Then, carrying that water, which purifies the worlds, on his head [as a sign of respect], he worshipped those lords with sandalwood paste, garlands, garments, ornaments, incense, lamps, *arghya* offering water, cows and bulls.

30. Pleasing them with sweet words once they had been satisfied with food, he joyfully spoke the following words while slowly massaging Viṣṇu's feet, which were placed on his lap.

31. *Śrī* Bahulāśva said: "Your Lordship is the soul of all entities, the self-realized witness, the Lord. You have now become manifest visibly before us, who remember your lotus feet.

32. You have stated: 'Śrī, the goddess of fortune, Brahmā the unborn one, and Ananta [Balarāma] are not as dear to me as my faithful devotee.' In order to make good your own word, you have become visible to our senses.

33. What person knowing this would give up your lotus feet? You give your own self to the peaceful sages who have no possessions.

34. You have incarnated in the Yadu dynasty in order to put an end to [the predicament] of those who are wandering in *saṃsāra* in this world, and you spread your glories, which remove the sins of the three worlds.

35. Homage to you, *Bhagavān* Kṛṣṇa of infinite intelligence. You are the sage Nārāyāṇa, who engages in very peaceful ascetic practices.

36. O all-pervading one. Stay in my residence for some days in the company of the sages, and purify our dynasty of king Nimi[2] with the dust of your feet."

37. Thus invited by the king, *Bhagavān* Kṛṣṇa, the benefactor of the world, remained there, bestowing blessings on the men and women of Mithilā.

38. Śrutadeva [also] received Acyuta in his house just as Janaka had done. He offered respects to the sages, and then danced about waving his cloth in ecstasy.

39. He seated them on mats and seats made of dried grass that

he had brought, and honoured them with words of welcome. Then, along with his wife, he joyfully washed their feet.
40. After this, he sprinkled himself, his house and his family with that water. He was ecstatic, and all his desires were fulfilled.
41. Śrutadeva honoured them with homage, *sattva*-enhancing nourishment, lotuses, *kuśa* grass, *tulasī* leaves, fragrant clay, pure honeyed water, the *uśīra* plant, offerings, fruit, and with whatever was available.
42. He pondered: "How have I, who am fallen into the blind well of household life, attained association with Kṛṣṇa, and with the *brāhmaṇas* whose hearts are his dwelling, and the dust of whose foot is the source of all the holy places?"
43. Śrutadeva, with his wife, kinsmen and children, approached his guests when they were comfortably seated and had received hospitality. As he was massaging Kṛṣṇa's feet, he spoke.
44. Śrutadeva said: "O supreme person. The vision [of you] that we have received today is not the only one: when this world is created by your powers, it is permeated by your very being.
45. This is like a sleeping person who, out of his own *māyā*, creates a different world with his imagination and then enters this dream [world] and appears real [in it].
46. You shine forth in the hearts of those pure-minded people who hear, speak and talk together about you, and who always worship you, and honour you.
47. Although you reside in the heart, you remain very far from those whose minds have been bewildered by *karma*, work performed out of personal desire; you cannot be attained by their personal prowess. However, you are near to those souls who are absorbed in [thinking about] your qualities.
48. Homage to him, who is the highest soul for those who understand the supreme soul. He is death to those who are indifferent to their own real self, and are destitute of knowledge of the self. He combines together the caused and uncaused characteristics.[3] He either obstructs or uncovers [people's] vision by his personal *māyā*.
49. You are he. Instruct your servants; what should we do, O Lord? Your Lordship has become visible to the eyes, and this puts an end to the miseries of human beings."'

50. *Śrī* Śuka said:

'When *Bhagavān*, who removes the afflictions of the meek, heard the words spoken by Śrutadeva, he took Śrutadeva's hand in his own hand and spoke, with a smile.
51. *Śrī Bhagavān* said: "You should know that these sages have come in order to bestow their kindness on you, O *brāhmaṇa*. They travel around with me, purifying the worlds with the dust of their feet.
52. The gods, sacred places and holy spots purify gradually over time as a result of being seen, touched and worshipped. That same result [is attained] by a glance from the eminent sages.
53. A *brāhmaṇa* is the best of all living beings by birth, quite apart from his practice of ascetic disciplines, his knowledge, tranquillity and mindfulness of me.
54. This four-armed form of mine is not dearer to me than the *brāhmaṇa*. The *brāhmaṇa* comprises all the Vedas, as I comprise all the gods.
55. Foolish, envious people do not understand this. They treat the *brāhmaṇa* – who is me myself, the *guru*, the very self – with contempt. They only recognize the deity and suchlike as worthy of worship.
56. A *brāhmaṇa*, by focusing on me, accepts in his mind that all objects, as well as this universe, with its moving and non-moving entities and its causes, are forms of me.
57. Therefore, worship these *brāhmaṇas* and sages with faith in me, O *brāhmaṇa*. If you do so, I am thereby worshipped, otherwise I am not, even with abundant riches." '
58. *Śrī* Śuka said:

'Thus instructed by the Lord, Śrutadeva worshipped the distinguished *brāhmaṇas* along with Kṛṣṇa in the conviction that they were one and the same entity. He and the king of Mithilā attained the destination of the righteous.
59. *Bhagavān* Kṛṣṇa is committed to his devotees. He lived in this way with his two devotees and instructed them on the saintly path. Then he returned again to Dvārakā.'

CHAPTER 87

The Praise by the Vedas in the Exchange Between Nārada and Nārāyaṇa

1. *Śrī* Parīkṣit said:

'O *brāhmaṇa*, how can the revealed scriptures, whose domain is the *guṇas*, directly reveal the indescribable *brahman*, which is devoid of *guṇas* and transcends that which is true or false?'

2. *Śrī* Śuka said:

'The Lord created the intelligence, senses, mind and vital airs of living creatures for the material world and for *saṃsāra*, as well as for liberation.

3. This is the [secret teaching of the] Upaniṣads which deal with *brahman*, and was practised by those born even before our ancestors. One who, without possessions, practises it faithfully attains liberation.

4. Now I will relate to you an ancient song about Nārāyaṇa. It is a conversation between Nārada and the sage Nārāyaṇa Ṛṣi.

5. Once Nārada, who is dear to *Bhagavān* Kṛṣṇa, was wandering about the worlds, and went to the *āśrama* [hermitage] of Nārāyaṇa to see that eternal sage.

6. For the benefit and well-being of people in this land of Bhārata, Nārāyaṇa had been practising austere disciplines coupled with sense-control, knowledge and *dharma* from the beginning of the *kalpa* world age.

7. He was seated and surrounded by the sages who lived in the village of Kalāpa. Bowing down to him, Nārada asked the very same thing [that you asked], O best of the Kurus.

8. While the sages listened, *Bhagavān* Nārāyana told Nārada about a discussion on the topic of *brahman* between the residents of the planet Jana in ancient times.

9. *Śrī Bhagavān* Nārāyaṇa said: "O Nārada, son of the self-born Brahmā, there was once a discussion about the Vedas on the

planet Jana between the celibate sages residing there who were born from the mind [of Brahmā].[1]

10. When you went to Śvetadvīpa to see the Lord in whom the Vedas repose, a vigorous discussion on the Veda arose. There, you asked the very question that you are asking me now.

11. Although they were equal in learning, discipline and character, and impartial towards kinsmen, enemies and neutral parties, the [sages there] appointed one person as speaker; the rest became an eager audience.

12. *Śrī* Sanandana said: 'The supreme being, along with his *śakti* powers, sleeps after withdrawing into himself this universe that he had previously created.[2] At the end of this period, the Vedas awoke the supreme being with [hymns about] his qualities.

13. This is just like the court bards who approach the sleeping emperor every morning, and awaken him with beautiful verses praising his heroism.'

14. The Vedas said: 'Victory, victory to you. By your very nature, you embody all excellences. Please withdraw [your] *māyā* – she has used the *guṇas* to impede [the soul], O unconquered one. By means of all your *śakti* powers, you awaken those who inhabit moving and non-moving forms.[3] Sometimes the Veda can keep up with you as you move about as your own self with your *māyā* power.

15. The sages understand that this visible world is *brahman* by the fact that the latter remains [after the dissolution of the world]. It is from *brahman* that creation and dissolution take place, but it remains unchanged by the transformations – just like clay.[4] How can people's footsteps not be accepted as being placed on the earth?[5] Therefore the sages dedicate their minds, words and actions to you.

16. In this way, the wise give up their suffering and plunge into the nectarean ocean of narrations about you, which destroy the impurities of the whole world, O supreme master of the three [worlds]! What, then, of those who have freed themselves from the influence of time and of the mind by their own potency? They attain the supreme destination, where one experiences eternal happiness.

17. Unless they obey you, living beings simply breathe like

bellows. It is from your grace that primordial intelligence and ego create this egg of a universe.[6] You are intimately connected with the different forms of people and, in that regard, you are the highest of the five sheaths of the soul, such as *annamaya*.[7] You are beyond both being and non-being[8] – you are the divine truth which remains in all these things.

18. From the paths presented by the sages, those with gross vision[9] concentrate on the abdomen; the Āruṇis focus on the heart, which is the subtle terminal for the arteries. From there, they ascend to the head, which is your abode, the highest destination.[10] After attaining that, they never fall down into the mouth of death in this world.

19. Because you are their material cause, it seems as if you enter into the various wombs of creatures created by you, and shine forth to a greater or lesser degree in proportion to your own creation, like fire [shines variously in proportion to the firewood]. Those whose intelligence is pure, and who are absolutely indifferent [to material attractions], strive for your undifferentiated and unchanging abode, which is the reality among these unreal things.

20. The sages say that the soul, existing in these bodies which have been made by its own [*karma*], is not [actually] enveloped [by such bodies, which are the product of such] cause and effect. It exists as an *aṃśa* part of you, since you possess all *śakti* powers. They have determined that your Lordship's feet are the seed from which the Vedas sprouted, the cause of liberation in the world, and the goal for humankind; and so they worship them confidently.

21. Some do not desire liberation, O Lord. Free from all distress, they immerse themselves in the great nectarean ocean of stories about the forms you have assumed in order to teach truth about the self, which is so hard to understand. They renounce their households due to their association with the flocks of swan[-like devotees][11] who [take refuge with] your lotus feet.

22. When it follows your path, this body, in which the *ātmā* dwells, acts like a well-wisher and as a friend to the soul. *Aho!* Unfortunately, those who do not take pleasure in the *ātmā* –

which is you, the well-disposed and affectionate benefactor – harm their own selves by worshipping that which is unreal. Because of their attachment to the unreal, they are furnished with miserable bodies and wander around in the terrifying [cycle of *saṃsāra*].

23. Engaged in *yoga* with determination, and with their senses, mind and breath under control, the sages focus in their heart on the same thing that even [your] enemies attain by concentrating [on you]. You are impartial: the women, their minds fixed on your trunk-like arms, which are like the coils of a mighty serpent, and we [Vedas] too, are equal for you, since we all [relish] the nectar of your lotus feet.

24. Who in this world knows him who preceded all? People's births and deaths come after [him]. The sage [Brahmā, the original created being] came forth from him, and both hosts of gods came after Brahmā, in turn.[12] When he lies sleeping after withdrawing [the universe within himself], neither being nor non-being, nor their combination, nor the movement of time remains there, nor certainly the [Vedic] scriptures.

25. Those who declare that there is production from non-being, destruction of being, differentiation in the *ātmā*, and truth in the business transaction [of *karma*][13] teach erroneously.[14] The idea of differentiation, such as thinking that a person is comprised of the three *guṇas* [rather than being pure soul], is the result of ignorance about you. Such ignorance cannot exist in you, who are the essence of knowledge.

26. The unreal, including everything [in the world] up to human beings, appears as if real when [superimposed] on you by the threefold [*guṇas*] of the mind. Nonetheless, those who are self-realized consider this entire world to be real because of its essential nature as *ātmā*. People do not discard an object that is a transformation of gold, since, after all, it does have the same essential nature as gold.[15] Because of its essential nature as *ātmā*, this universe is considered to have been created, and subsequently entered, by him.

27. Those who worship you on the grounds that you are the refuge of all beings disregard death, and step on its head with their feet. You bind the learned with your words [in the Vedas].[16]

Those who have established friendship with you purify [others], but those who are averse to you do not.

28. Although you yourself are without senses, you sustain the powers of all those who act [with their senses]. Out of illusion, the gods consume the oblations offered to you, but they also carry them [to you], just like rulers of tracts of lands do to the emperors of the whole earth. Fearful of you, the creators of the universes govern wherever they have been appointed to do so.

29. Moving and non-moving beings come into existence only when the play of the supreme being with *prakṛti* [material nature] takes place through his glance.[17] They are connected with their causes [their previous *karma*], which are activated, O liberated one. You are supreme, and for you no one can be superior or inferior. You appear neutral – just like the sky, which has no fixed abode.

30. If embodied beings were unlimited, permanent and all-pervading then there could not be any restrictions [imposed on them], O permanent one, and so one could not say that there was any sovereignty [over them].[18] On the other hand, a person must be the controller of a product that is made from himself and is not separate from him.[19] Because of the defective nature of understanding, those who [claim to] know him [God] do not understand.[20]

31. It is not possible that there is birth of *prakṛti* and of the soul, since both of them are birthless. Yet life-forms arise from the union of these two, just like bubbles in water. And then, with their various characteristics and names, these life-forms dissolve back into you, the supreme being, like rivers into the ocean, or like all the juices [collected by bees from different flowers] into honey.[21]

32. Those with pure intelligence understand the great illusion [imposed] on these people by your *māyā*, and so they offer you, the bestower of liberation, their intense love. How can there be fear of *saṃsāra* for those who follow you? However, your triple-rimmed frown [time][22] constantly creates fear among those who do not take refuge with you.

33. Addicted to hundreds of vices, those in this world who neglect the *guru*, and who attempt to control the wild horse of the unsubdued and very fickle mind with control of the breathing

and of the senses,[23] become frustrated with their methods. They are like a merchant on the ocean who has not taken on a helmsman, O unborn one.

34. What is the use of vehicles, vital air, land, homestead, wealth, wife, body, offspring and kinsmen for one who has taken refuge with you, the embodiment of all *rasa*, who exists as the *ātmā* of people? Similarly, what can give happiness to those who do not know the truth and are wandering about in this world after sex-pleasure? This world is perishable and devoid of good fortune by its very nature.

35. Free from pride, and with your Lordship's lotus feet in their hearts, sages [frequent] temples and holy places of great merit. The water from their feet destroys sins. Anyone who has even once offered their mind to you, the forever happy *ātmā*, does not again become attached to the household, which robs people of their essence.

36. To say that this world is real because it has arisen from that which is real is a false argument. It cannot be true because such an argument sometimes proves to be faulty, and sometimes false.[24] The world is a combination of both [the real and the illusory]. The false notion is promoted by a tradition of blind people for the sake of [carrying on their] mundane affairs.[25] The rhetoric [of the Vedas], with its elaborate use of words, deludes the dull-witted through its sacrificial utterances.[26]

37. This universe did not exist in the beginning, and it will not exist after its dissolution. In the interim, it falsely appears to be displayed within you, whose essence[27] is unchanging. It is then observed through its various combinations of different types of matter. Those who are ignorant consider this figment of the mind to be true.

38. When the soul settles into *māyā* and by its affluence embraces the *guṇas*, it obtains a state of embodiment. At this point, its majesty disappears, and it [is subject to] death. You, on the other hand, discard *māyā* like a snake discards its skin, and preserve your majesty. You are exalted in your greatness, with your eight [mystic] qualities,[28] and infinite majesty.

39. If ascetics do not tear out the roots of lust in their hearts, you, even though situated within the hearts of such contemptible

men, remain inaccessible, just like a forgotten jewel on the neck. O *Bhagavān*, the frustration of *yogīs* who indulge their senses is twofold: from death, because it is ever-present, and from you, because your feet remain unattained.

40. One who has realized you does not experience the good and bad effects [that accrue] from the auspicious and inauspicious actions that are prescribed by you, and is uninterested in the verses [of the Vedas] which are for embodied beings. Such a person is absorbed daily in hearing the sacred songs [about you] that are handed down through the generations in every *yuga*. Thus, you are the goal of liberation for mankind.

41. Indeed, these lords of the celestial regions cannot attain the limits [of you] – nor can even you yourself do so – because [you are] unlimited. Multitudes of egg-shaped universes, along with their coverings,[29] whirl around inside you by the force [of time], just like particles of dust in the sky. Accordingly, in reality, the Vedas culminate in you by eliminating that which is not truth.[30] You are their conclusion.' "

42. *Śrī Bhagavān* said: "After the sons of Brahmā, who were perfected beings, had heard this instruction about the *ātmā* and understood the goal of the *ātmā* as expressed above, they worshipped Sanandana.

43. Thus, the essence of the Upaniṣads, Purāṇas, and all the sacred texts was extracted by the great souls born in previous times, who could travel through the sky.

44. And you, O son of Brahmā, should wander about the earth at will, meditating on the instructions about the *ātmā* with faith. They destroy the desires of people." '

45. *Śrī* Śuka said:

'Directed in this fashion by Nārāyaṇa *Ṛṣi*, O king, sage Nārada, who was self-possessed, perfect and firm of vow, faithfully retained what he had heard, and replied.

46. *Śrī* Nārada said: "Homage to you, *Bhagavān* Kṛṣṇa of unsullied fame. You manifest your incarnations, which are assumed for the sake of [bestowing] freedom from material existence, to all living entities.

47. After thus venerating that original sage Nārāyaṇa, as well

as the great souls who were his disciples, Nārada went from there directly to the *āśrama* of my father, Dvaipāyana [Vyāsa].
48. He was worshipped by *Bhagavān* Vyāsa, and accepted the seat that was provided. Then he repeated what he had heard from the mouth of Nārāyaṇa.
49. Thus the question you posed to me as to how the mind can access *brahman* – despite the fact that it is indescribable and devoid of *guṇa* qualities – has been answered, O king.
50. He who is the observer of this world, its beginning, middle and end, and is the Lord of souls and of unmanifest matter, creates this world, enters it along with the souls, creates bodies and controls them. Because of his transcendence, he has no connection with birth in a womb. When one has surrendered to him, one gives up *māyā*, just as a person lying down asleep gives up the physical body. One should continually meditate upon Hari, who is fearlessness."'

CHAPTER 88

The Release of Rudra

1. The king said:

'Those among the gods, demons and mortals who worship the austere Śiva are often wealthy and lead a life of enjoyment. Hari is the Lord of Lakṣmī, the goddess of fortune, but this is not the case with those who worship him.
2. I wish to understand this – actually, I have some serious misgivings about this matter. The end results are different for the worshippers of these two Lords, whose personalities are so opposite.'
3. *Śrī* Śuka said:

'Śiva is always connected with his *śakti* power. He is enveloped by the *guṇas*, with their three characteristics. He is ego in its three divisions of *sattva*, *rajas* and *tamas*.[1]

4. The transformations from this have resulted in the sixteen ingredients of this world. Anyone having recourse [to Śiva] enjoys the acquisition of all riches.
5. Hari, however, is untouched by the *guṇas*. He is the supreme person beyond *prakṛti*. He is the witness, the seer of everything. One who worships him becomes free from the *guṇas*.
6. When the *aśvamedha* sacrifices[2] had been completed, king Yudhiṣṭhira, your grandfather, upon hearing the teachings about *dharma* from *Bhagavān* Kṛṣṇa, asked Acyuta the very same question [that you have asked].
7. *Bhagavān* Kṛṣṇa is the Lord incarnated into the Yadu dynasty for the ultimate benefit of humans. He was pleased, and replied as follows to Yudhiṣṭhira, who was anxious to hear.
8. *Śrī Bhagavān* said: "I will deprive the person whom I favour of his wealth. At this, his own family members abandon this person, who has become poverty-stricken and afflicted by suffering.
9. When his endeavours come to nothing, and he becomes despondent in his attempts to [gain] wealth, then I bestow my favour on him, once he has formed friendships with those devoted to me.
10. That supreme *brahman* is pure consciousness, subtle, eternal and unlimited. Because I am so hard to worship, people reject me and worship other [gods].
11. Then, arrogant with the royal wealth obtained from the other [gods], who are easily pleased, these people become heedless and unrestrained. In their pride, they treat with contempt those others who grant boons."'
12. *Śrī* Śuka said:

'Brahmā, Śiva, Viṣṇu and others are capable of blessing or cursing, dear Parīkṣit. Śiva and Brahmā bestow blessings and curses immediately, but Acyuta does not.
13. People relate the following event from ancient times as an example of this. Śiva, Lord of the mountains, once granted the demon Vṛka a boon, but then found himself in a crisis.
14. Once, that evil-minded demon called Vṛka, son of Śakuni,

saw Nārada on the road, and asked him who was most easily pleased of the three gods.

15. Nārada replied: "Worship Lord Śiva, and you will quickly attain success. He can be easily pleased or easily angered by a small amount of either merit or fault.

16. He was satisfied by the ten-headed Rāvaṇa and by Bāṇa,[3] both of whom praised him like minstrels. After he had bestowed unparalleled opulence on them, Śiva found himself in a severe crisis."[4]

17. Thus advised, the demon worshipped Śiva by offering the flesh from his own limbs as an oblation to the sacrificial fire, the mouth of Śiva.

18. After seven days, Vṛka became despondent at not attaining a sight of the god, and so, his hair wet because he was in a sacred place, he slashed his head, with a knife.

19. At this, the matted-haired Śiva, who is very merciful – just as I am – emerged from the fire, like Agni, the god of fire. Grasping Vṛka's two arms with his own arms, he restrained him. The demon's body was rendered whole from that touch.

20. Śiva said to him: "Enough! Enough, dear Vṛka! I will grant you a boon: ask for something from me according to your desire. *Aho!* I am pleased by [merely an offering of] water from people who surrender to me – you have tortured your body too much and unnecessarily."

21. The sinful Vṛka chose a favour from Lord Śiva, who is the remover of fear from living creatures: "On whomever's head I place my hand, that person should die," said he.

22. Hearing this, *Bhagavān* Rudra's [Śiva's] spirits sank. Laughing, and uttering "*Oṃ*",[5] he granted this favour to Vṛka, like poison to a snake.

23. The demon then actually began to place his own hand on the head of Śambhu [Śiva], O Parīkṣit, descendant of Bhārata, in order to test the favour out. Śiva was afraid of what he himself had done.

24. Terrified and with Vṛka hot on his heals, Śiva fled trembling all the way to the ends of the earth, the heavens and the quarters, and went up towards the north.

25. The rulers of the gods did not know of a remedy and remained silent. Then, Śiva arrived at shining Vaikuṇṭha,[6] beyond *tamas*.

26. There, Nārāyaṇa resides, the supreme goal of peaceful, non-violent ascetics. One who goes there never returns.[7]

27. *Bhagavān* is the remover of distress, and when he saw Śiva in this predicament, he rose and approached from a distance, after transforming himself into a small [*brāhmaṇa*] boy by his *yogamāyā*.

28. He shone like fire with his potency, and with his prayer beads, staff, antelope skin and girdle. With an appearance of humility, he greeted Vṛka with *kuśa* grass in hand.

29. *Śrī Bhagavān* said: "It appears that you are tired, O Vṛka, son of Śakuni. Why have you come from afar? Rest for a while. This human body fulfils all a person's desires [and should therefore be taken care of].

30. If your intention is worthy enough for us to hear, then tell us, O master. One usually accomplishes one's personal goals by means of assistants." '

31. *Śrī* Śuka said:

'Thus questioned by *Bhagavān* with this shower of words, which were like nectar, Vṛka's fatigue disappeared, and he told him what had transpired up to then.

32. "If this is what has happened, then we do not place much faith in Śiva's words. He became a *piśāca* [demon] on account of Dakṣa's curse,[8] and is the king of *piśācas* and ghosts.

33. If you have faith in him as the *guru* of the world, O king of the demons, then place your hand on your own head, dear Vṛka, and you will immediately be certain.

34. If the words [of Śiva] are untruthful in any way, O best of the demons, then kill the liar so that he will never again speak falsely."

35. The wicked Vṛka was confused by such fanciful and crafty words of *Bhagavān* and he became forgetful. He touched his head with his own hand.

36. Then, in an instant, his head burst apart and he fell down

as if struck by a thunderbolt. The sounds of: "Victory! Homage! Well done!" arose from the heavens.
37. When the sinful Vṛka was killed, the gods, sages, forefathers and *gandharvas* released showers of flowers, and Śiva was freed from danger.
38–39. *Bhagavān*, the supreme being, spoke to the freed Śiva, Lord of mountains: "*Aho*, Lord Mahādeva [Śiva]! This sinful person has been killed by his very own sins. No creature who has committed an offence against great souls, even, can feel secure, O Lord, let alone if the offence has been committed against you, the Lord of the universe and *guru* of the world."
40. Therefore, one who recites or hears about Hari's release of Śiva, the protector of mountains, is released from *saṃsāra* and also from his enemies. Hari is an ocean of indescribable *śakti*, the transcendent Lord and supreme soul in person.'

CHAPTER 89

Retrieving the Sons of the Brāhmaṇa

1. *Śrī* Śuka said:

'The sages once performed a sacrifice on the banks of the Sarasvatī river, O king, and a controversy sprang up as to which of the three supreme Lords of all creatures was the greatest.
2. Out of a desire to resolve this, they dispatched Bhṛgu, son of Brahmā, to settle this matter, O king. He set out for Brahmā's assembly.
3. In order to test Brahmā's qualities of *sattva*, Bhṛgu did not offer him homage or laudatory prayers. *Bhagavān* Brahmā became furious with Bhṛgu, and glowed with fiery energy.
4. The self-begotten Lord controlled the anger that had arisen within himself against his own son, by [restraining] himself, just as fire is controlled by water, which is produced from itself.[1]
5. Then Bhṛgu went to Kailāsa, Śiva's abode. Lord Maheśvara [Śiva] joyfully arose and started to embrace his brother.[2]

6. But Bhṛgu did not allow him: "You are a transgressor of the [religious] path," he said. The God became furious. With fiery eyes, he picked up his trident and prepared to kill Bhṛgu.
7. The goddess fell at Śiva's feet and appeased him with her words. Then, Bhṛgu went to Vaikuṇṭha, where Lord Janārdana [Viṣṇu] lives.
8. He kicked Viṣṇu on the chest with his foot, while Viṣṇu was lying on the lap of Śrī, the goddess of fortune. At this, *Bhagavān*, the goal of the saintly, arose along with Śrī.
9. He got up from his couch and offered homage to the sage with his head. Then he said: "Welcome, *brāhmaṇa*: please sit down here on this seat for a while. Please forgive us – we were not aware of your arrival, O master.
10. Dear great sage! Your feet are very delicate!" continued Kṛṣṇa as he was massaging the feet of the *brāhmaṇa*.
11. "Please purify me, along with the planets and the rulers of the planets who are devoted to me, with your foot-washing water. This water is the source of the sacredness of sacred places.
12. Today, *Bhagavān* [Bhṛgu], I have become the exclusive abode of Lakṣmī [Śrī]. The goddess of fortune will settle on my chest because my sins have been destroyed by the touch of your lordship's feet."'
13. *Śrī* Śuka said:

'Bhṛgu fell silent as the Lord of Vaikuṇṭha was speaking in this way. He was delighted, and fully satisfied with these charming words. His eyes filled with tears, and he was overcome with *bhakti*.
14. Bhṛgu then returned again to the sacrifice of the sages, who were well-versed in the Vedas, and recounted in detail what had happened to him, O king.
15–16. The sages were flabbergasted when they heard him. Freed from doubts, they placed their faith in Viṣṇu. He is the source of peace and fearlessness. *Dharma* comes from him personally, as do knowledge linked with renunciation, opulence and the eight *siddhis*.[3] His glory removes any impurities from the soul.
17. Viṣṇu is known as the supreme goal of the sages, who

are non-violent, peaceful, impartial *sādhu* ascetics without possessions.
18. His cherished form is made of *sattva*, and the *brāhmaṇas* are his favoured deities. Those who are without desire and peaceful, and whose intelligence is sharp, worship him.
19. He has three forms: *rākṣasa* demon [*tamas*], *asura* demon [*rajas*] and demigod [*sattva*]. These are created by *māyā*, which consists of the *guṇas*. *Sattva* is the means of attaining the goal of Viṣṇu.'
20. *Śrī* Śuka said:

'The *brāhmaṇas* from the Sarasvatī river reached this conclusion for the benefit of people, and attained the goal of Viṣṇu through service to the lotus feet of the supreme being.'
21. *Śrī* Sūta said:

'A traveller who continually drinks this fragrant nectar about the supreme person from the lotus mouth of Śukadeva through the vessels of the ears shakes off the fatigue of travelling. This nectar is renowned, and destroys the fear of material existence.'
22. *Śrī* Śuka said:

'Once, an infant boy, who had just been born of the wife of a *brāhmaṇa* in Dvārakā, died as soon as he touched the ground, O Parīkṣit, descendant of Bharata.
23. The *brāhmaṇa*, distressed and mournful, took the corpse and placed it at the king's door. Lamenting, he said the following words:
24. "My son has returned to the five elements because of shortcomings in the performance of duty by a fallen *kṣatriya* who is an enemy of the *brāhmaṇas*, and who is avaricious, addicted to sensual pleasure and of deceitful intelligence.[4]
25. Citizens who are unfortunate enough to serve a king who is of bad character, has uncontrolled senses and takes pleasure in violence are always miserable and are doomed."
26. The *brāhmaṇa* sage sang that song after leaving a second child at the king's door, followed by a third child in the exact same manner.

27. At a certain point, after the ninth boy had died, Arjuna heard that song in the presence of Keśava and said to the *brāhmaṇa*:
28. "Are there no fallen members of the royal class who can hold a bow here in your house, O *brāhmaṇa*? These *kṣatriyas* are [as good as] *brāhmaṇas* at a sacrifice.[5]
29. Wherever *brāhmaṇas* are deprived of their children, wives or wealth, the kings are like actors dressed up as kings who exist simply to support themselves.
30. I will protect your offspring, O *Bhagavān*, since you are in despair. If my promise is not kept, I will enter fire, so that my sin can be expiated."
31. The *brāhmaṇa* said: "Saṅkarṣaṇa, Vāsudeva, Pradyumna, who is the best of bowmen, and Aniruddha, who is unrivalled on the chariot, could not protect him.
32. Why should you, out of immaturity, wish to perform a feat which is beyond the power of the lords of the world? We do not put any faith in this."
33. *Śrī* Arjuna said: "I am not Saṅkarṣaṇa, O *brāhmaṇa*, nor even Kṛṣṇa or his descendant. I go by the name of Arjuna, and my bow is the Gāṇḍīva.
34. Do not treat my prowess with contempt, O *brāhmaṇa* – it impressed the three-eyed Śiva. I will defeat death in battle, and recover your offspring, O master."
35. So, O Parīkṣit, scorcher of the enemy, the *brāhmaṇa* placed his trust in Phālguna [Arjuna], and went happily to his own home, hearing about the prowess of Arjuna, son of Pṛthā.
36. When the time of birth came for his wife, the distinguished *brāhmaṇa* said to Arjuna in distress: "Protect, please protect my offspring from death."
37. Arjuna touched pure water, offered homage to Maheśvara [Śiva], invoked his divine weapons and strung his Gāṇḍīva bow.
38. The son of Pṛthā surrounded the delivery room above, below and across with arrows that contained various warheads. He made a cage of arrows.
39. Then, with a continuous wail, the baby boy was born to the wife of the *brāhmaṇa*. Suddenly he physically disappeared into the sky.

40. Then the *brāhmaṇa*, criticizing the unconquerable Arjuna in the presence of Kṛṣṇa, said: "Just see my foolishness! I placed my faith in the boasting of a coward!
41. If neither Pradyumna, nor Aniruddha, nor Balarāma, nor Keśava is capable of saving someone, then who else is competent to protect him?
42. Shame on the useless braggart, Arjuna. Shame on the bow of that self-promoter, that wicked-minded one, who foolishly desired to bring back what had been claimed by fate."
43. When the *brāhmaṇa* sage cursed him in this manner, Arjuna resorted to [mystic] science and immediately went to the city of Saṃyamanī, where *Bhagavān* Yama, Lord of death, resides.
44. When he did not find the child of the *brāhmaṇa* there, Arjuna went on to Indra's city, and then to the cities of Agni [the fire god]; Nairṛti [a subordinate god of death]; Soma [the moon god]; Vāyu [the wind god]; and Varuṇa [the god of the waters]. Then, with weapons in hand, he went to the subterranean region, the uppermost celestial region and other regions.
45. Thus, when he could not find the son of the *brāhmaṇa*, it meant that Arjuna's promise was broken and he prepared to enter the fire. But he was checked by Kṛṣṇa, who prevented him:
46. "I will show you the *brāhmaṇa*'s son," he said. "Do not lose respect for yourself by [destroying] your body. Those people[6] will establish our stainless reputation."
47. Then, *Bhagavān*, the Lord, took Arjuna along, and, mounting his personal chariot, approached the western quarter.
48. After crossing the seven islands, the seven oceans, the seven mountains and the Lokāloka mountain range,[7] he entered a great dense darkness.
49. In that area, the horses – Śaibya, Sugrīva, Meghapuṣpa and Balāhaka – lost their way in the dark, O best of the Bharata dynasty.
50. *Bhagavān* Kṛṣṇa, master of the masters of *yoga*, saw them and let fly his disc ahead. It was equivalent to 1,000 suns.
51. At the speed of thought, the Sudarśana disc penetrated that dense and utterly terrifying darkness, which was the product of *mahat* [primordial matter],[8] and dispersed it with an abundance

of light, just like Rāma's arrows, discharged from his bowstring, penetrate an army.

52. Through the passage made by the wake of the disc, Arjuna saw a transcendental, pervading light of infinite expanse beyond that darkness. His eyes were struck and so he closed them.

53. Then he went into water that was agitated by a mighty wind and formidable waves. An astonishing and resplendent palace glimmered there, embellished with thousands of jewelled pillars.

54. Ananta, the fabulous great serpent, was inside.[9] He shone with the radiance of the jewels on the hoods of his 1,000 heads, and looked awesome with his 2,000 eyes. He resembled a white mountain; his tongue and throat were dark blue.

55. He [Arjuna] saw the almighty Lord, the highest of supreme beings, reclining happily on that serpent. He resembled a dense rain cloud, and wore a beautiful yellowish garment. His countenance was smiling, and his beautiful eyes were elongated.

56. His abundant locks of tousled hair were made beautiful with earrings and a helmet containing clusters of valuable gems. He had eight long and graceful arms. He wore the Kaustubha gem, bore the mark of *śrīvatsa*, and was draped with a garland of forest flowers.

57. The Lord of the highest gods was being served by Puṣṭi, the goddess of grace; Śrī, the goddess of fortune; Kīrti, the goddess of Fame; Māyā, the unborn one; all the [eight] mystic powers; his personal weapons such as the disc in personified form; and by his own associates, headed by Nanda and Sunanda.

58. Acyuta offered respects to the infinite one, who was actually himself, as did Arjuna, who was struck with alarm at the sight of him. The all-pervading one, master of the chief gods, smiling, spoke to them in a deep voice as they stood with hands folded in supplication:

59. "I brought the sons of the *brāhmaṇa* here out of a desire to see you both. You have descended on the earth as *kalās* [partial incarnations] for the protection of *dharma*.[10] Once you have killed the demons who are a burden on the earth, return here again quickly.

60. You are the sages Nara and Nārāyaṇa,[11] the best of men.

Although your desires are fulfilled, you wander around in order to establish *dharma* and for the welfare of the world."

61. Kṛṣṇa and Arjuna were thus instructed by *Bhagavān* Viṣṇu, the supreme, and replied: '*Om*.'[12] Then they offered their respects to the Almighty, and took the sons of the *brāhmaṇa*.

62. Delighted, they returned to their own dwelling by the same way that they had come. Then they gave the *brāhmaṇa* his sons in the same bodies and at the same ages [as they had been when they died].

63. After seeing the dwelling place of Viṣṇu, Arjuna, son of Pṛthā, was amazed. He decided that whatever heroism people possess, it is by the grace of Kṛṣṇa.

64. Exhibiting many such feats, Kṛṣṇa enjoyed everyday sensual pleasures, and performed powerful sacrificial rites.

65. Secure in his supremacy, *Bhagavān* Kṛṣṇa, in accordance with the appropriate occasion, and like Indra, showered living beings, such as the *brāhmaṇa* and others, with all desirable things.

66. After [either personally] killing the heretic kings, or ensuring that they were killed by Arjuna, Kṛṣṇa without difficulty enabled the performance of *dharma* by Yudhiṣṭhira, the son of Dharma, and others.'

CHAPTER 90

Description of Kṛṣṇa's Activities

1–2. *Śrī* Śuka said:

'The Lord of Śrī lived happily in his city of Dvārakā. It was thriving and prosperous, and was enjoyed by the distinguished members of the Vṛṣṇi clan, and by their women. Dressed in choice garments, these women had the beauty of fresh youth. Playing in the palaces with balls and other playthings, they were like streaks of lightning.

3. The roads were always jammed by elephants oozing musk,

handsomely bedecked soldiers, horses, and chariots of shining gold.

4. Dvārakā abounded in gardens and parks, and echoed on all sides with the sounds of birds and bees who settled on the rows of flowering trees.

5. Kṛṣṇa enjoyed himself as the sole beloved of 16,000 wives. He assumed as many different forms as there were mansions for these women.

6–7. The Lord sported by plunging into the rivers, whose pure waters were fragrant with the pollen from blooming lotuses – blue lotuses and *kumuda* and *kahlāra* white lotuses – and where flocks of birds sang. He was embraced by the women, his limbs smeared with saffron powder from their breasts.

8. He was extolled in song by *gandharvas* playing *mṛdaṅga*, *paṇava* and *ānaka* drums, and by bards, heralds and minstrels who were happily playing *vīṇas* [stringed instruments].

9. Squirted from syringes by the laughing women, and responding in kind, Acyuta would play, like the kings of the *yakṣas* with the female *yakṣīs*.

10. After being squirted, the women embraced their lover, intending to take away his syringe. Their breasts and thighs were exposed by the wet cloth, and the flowers from their abundant braids of hair were thrown into disarray. They shone radiantly, their faces glowing with smiles born of Kāma.

11. And Kṛṣṇa, who was continually spraying, was sprayed in return by the women, and the knot of his abundant hair was loosened as he took part in the game. With saffron powder from the breasts of the women clinging to his garland, he enjoyed himself like the lord of elephants surrounded by female elephants.

12. Kṛṣṇa gave the clothes and ornaments [worn] during these games to the male and female performers who earned their livelihood from singing and playing instruments, and the women did likewise.

13. The women were completely won over by the embraces, games and pastimes, as well as by the smiles, glances, talk and movements of Kṛṣṇa, as he diverted himself with pleasure.

14. With minds focused exclusively on Mukunda, the women

uttered words as though possessed or overwhelmed by thinking of the lotus-eyed Aravinda [Kṛṣṇa].[1] Listen to me speak about them.

15. The queens said: "O *kurari* bird, the Lord is sleeping in the world at night, his consciousness overtaken [by sleep], but you do not rest. You have been deprived of sleep and are lamenting. Has your mind been deeply wounded like ours, O friend, by the noble, playful glances and smiles of the lotus-eyed Lord?

16. Alas, O *cakravākī* bird, your friend is not to be found at night, and so you close your eyes and wail piteously.[2] Have you become a servant [of the Lord] like us? Or is it that you wish to wear the garland that has touched Acyuta's feet on your braid of hair?[3]

17. *Bho! Bho!* You thunder continuously, O ocean. You are not able to sleep, and have fallen into a state of insomnia. Or have your personal possessions been taken away by Mukunda?[4] You have entered the state in which we find ourselves – it is impossible to overcome.

18. O moon! You have been seized by powerful consumption, and do not dispel the darkness with your rays! Have you forgotten the words of Mukunda like we have? *Bho!* You appear to us to be dumbstruck!

19. What have we done that is displeasing to you, O Malayan breeze? You are arousing lust in our hearts, which have been pierced by Govinda's glances.

20. O beautiful cloud! You must certainly be dear to the Lord of the Yādavas. Bound by love, you meditate on Kṛṣṇa, who bears the *śrivatsa* on his body, just as we do. Remembering him again and again with an anguished heart, like us you pine intensely and release endless torrents of tears. Attachment to Kṛṣṇa brings unhappiness.

21. O cuckoo! You utter such melodious sounds about my beloved with words that can animate the dead. Tell me, what nice thing can I do for you today? You utter such pleasing sounds.

22. O noble-minded mountain, supporter of the earth, you do not move, you do not speak! Are you thinking about some grave

matter or, alas, do you yearn to place the lotus feet of the son of Nanda on your breast, as we do?
23. O rivers, wives of the ocean! Alas, your lakes are dry and you are much reduced. Desiring your Lord, your beauty in the form of lotuses has vanished now. You are just like us: our hearts have been stolen, and we are quite withered from being deprived of the loving glance of Kṛṣṇa, the Lord of Madhu.
24. Welcome, O swan, and be seated! Drink milk and tell us stories about Śauri [Kṛṣṇa]. We know that you are the messenger of Kṛṣṇa. Is the invincible one well? Does our fickle friend remember the words he spoke to us before? Why should we worship him, O [messenger of] a cruel person? He fulfils desires, but speak to him when Śrī, the goddess of fortune, is not present – she among women is exclusively devoted to him, without a doubt."'
25. *Śrī* Śuka said:

'By engaging in these types of *bhāvas* [loving emotional states of mind] for Kṛṣṇa, the Lord of the lords of *yoga*, the wives of Mādhava attained the supreme destination.
26. Kṛṣṇa is widely praised in many songs. By merely hearing about him, the mind becomes irresistibly attracted – so what about those who actually see him?
27. The queens lovingly ministered to the *guru* of the world in such ways as massaging his feet and other such devotional acts, keeping in mind that he was their husband. How can one describe the penance [they must have performed in previous lives]?[5]
28. Thus, Kṛṣṇa, the goal of the righteous, by following the strictest standards of *dharma* as expressed in the Veda, continually demonstrated that the household is the place for pursuing *dharma*, *artha* and *kāma*.[6]
29. While following the strictest *dharma* for householders, Kṛṣṇa had 16,100 queens.
30. Eight of those jewels of women, headed by Rukmiṇī, were previously described, O king, as were their sons in order.
31. Kṛṣṇa begot ten sons from each and every one of his wives. His activities are never unfruitful.

32. These sons were extraordinarily heroic. Out of them, eighteen were mighty *mahārathas* [chariot warriors] of widespread fame. Listen to me tell their names:
33. Pradyumna, Aniruddha, Dīptimān, Bhānu, Sāmba, Madhu, Bṛhadbhānu, Citrabhānu, Vṛka, and Aruṇa.
34. Puṣkara, Vedabāhu, Śrutadeva, Sunandana, Citrabāhu, Virūpa, Kavi and Nyagrodha.
35. Out of these sons of Kṛṣṇa, the enemy of Madhu, O chief of kings, Pradyumna, son of Rukmiṇī, was the oldest. He was just like his father.
36. That great *mahāratha* married the daughter of Rukmī. By her he begot Aniruddha, who was endowed with the strength of 10,000 elephants.
37. Rukmī's daughter's son married Rukmī's granddaughter. His son was Vajra, who survived the club battle.[7]
38. From him came Pratibāhu, and his son was Subāhu; from Subāhu, Śāntasena, whose son was Śatasena.
39. No one born in the dynasty was poor, childless, short-lived, weak or inimical to the *brāhmaṇas*.
40. Even in tens of thousands of years, one would not be able to count the celebrated deeds of the men born in the Yadu dynasty.
41. I have heard that there were 38,800,000 teachers for the youth of the Yadu dynasty.
42. Who can count all the great-souled Yadus – among them Ugrasena alone had billions [in his entourage].
43. The vicious demons killed in the battle between the gods and the demons were born among human beings. They were arrogant and harassed the citizens.
44. The gods were instructed by Hari to incarnate in the dynasty of the Yadus in order to suppress them. There were 101 families of them, O king.
45. By his very Lordship, *Bhagavān* Hari was their authority. All of the Yadus who were his followers prospered.
46. While engaged in the activities of sleeping, sitting, wandering about, chatting, playing and bathing, the Vṛṣṇis, whose minds were absorbed in Kṛṣṇa, forgot their own existence.
47. He who took birth among the Yadus, O king, surpassed [in

potency] the heavenly Ganga which washes his feet. Enemies and friends attained *svarūpya* [liberation].[8] The unconquerable and transcendent Śrī, the goddess of fortune, for whose favour people strive, [is his consort]. His name, when heard and recited, removes ill fortune. Family duties were created by him. There is, therefore, nothing remarkable about the removal of the burden of the earth by Kṛṣṇa, the wielder of the wheel of time.

48. He is victorious. He is the refuge of people. He is reputed to have been born of Devakī. Surrounded by the eminent Yadus, he banishes irreligion with his two arms. He destroys the sins of all moving and non-moving entities, and he increases Kāma in the women both of Vraj and of the cities with his beautiful face with its bewitching smiles.

49. Therefore, one desiring to surrender to the feet of Kṛṣṇa, the best of the Yadus, should listen to the deeds of the supreme one who has assumed *līlā* forms out of a desire to protect his own path [of *dharma*]. These deeds destroy *karma* and are imitations [of human behaviour] appropriate to each *līlā*.

50. By thinking about, reciting and hearing the beautiful stories of Mukunda, which constantly become more in number, a person [attains to] his incomparable abode, and overcomes death. Even rulers of the earth left their communities to go into the forest for this purpose.'

This concludes the tenth book of the Śrīmad Bhāgavata Purāṇa.

THE ELEVENTH BOOK

CHAPTER 1

*The Curse of the Sages**

1. *Śrī* Śuka said:

'After Kṛṣṇa and Balarāma in the company of the Yadus had removed the burden of the earth, they caused a sudden quarrel to break out.
2. The Lord used the sons of Pāṇḍu as the immediate cause, since they had been made furious by the grabbing of [Draupadī's] hair, the insults, the cheating in gambling and other such acts of their enemies. He removed the burden of the earth after killing the kings from both sides as they confronted each other.
3. After removing the armies of the kings, who were a burden to the earth, by means of the Yadus, who were protected by his own arms, the Lord, who is beyond human comprehension, deliberated: "Now it may be said that the burden of the earth has gone, but I think it is not so, because the Yadu dynasty itself remains and is intolerable.
4. The downfall of the Yadus, with their unlimited power, cannot come from any outside source because they have taken eternal refuge with me. I will arrange an internal quarrel within the Yadu dynasty, like fire within a clump of grass. Then I will return to my [transcendent] abode in peace."
5. When he had thus determined, O king, the almighty Lord, whose resolutions are always fulfilled, removed his own dynasty on the pretext of a curse by the *brāhmaṇas*.

6–7. He decided that with his personal form, which eclipses the beauty of the world, he had spread his illustrious glories by captivating the eyes of people; with his words he had captivated the minds of those who remembered them; and with his feet he had captivated the activities of those who saw them. Since people on the earth can easily transcend ignorance by means of his glories, the Lord went to his [transcendent] abode.
8. The king said:

'How did the *brāhmaṇas*' curse against the Vṛṣṇi clan come about? The Vṛṣṇis were devoted to *brāhmaṇas*, generous, always serving the elders, and their minds were fixed on Kṛṣṇa.
9. What kind of a curse was it, and what was its cause? How could there be division among those who were of one mind? Please tell us all about this, O best of the *brāhmaṇas*.'
10. *Śrī* Śuka, the son of Bādarāyaṇa, said:

'The highly renowned Kṛṣṇa possessed a form that was the culmination of all beauty. Although his desires are all fulfilled, he wandered around the earth performing deeds of great good omen. He lived in his city [Dvārakā], enjoying himself. But one outstanding task remained, and so he desired to eliminate the dynasty.
11–12. Kṛṣṇa performed deeds that are extremely auspicious and earn merit. Chanting about them destroys the sins of the world in the age of *kali*. The sages Viśvāmitra, Asita, Kaṇva, Durvāsā, Bhṛgu, Aṅgirā, Kaśyapa, Vāmadeva, Atri, Vasiṣṭha, Nārada and others were given leave [to go] by Kṛṣṇa, the soul of time, who was residing in the house of the Lord of the Yadus [Vasudeva]. They went to the holy place of Piṇḍāraka.
13–15. While the young sons of the Yadu dynasty were playing, they dressed Sāmba, the son of Jāmbavatī, in women's clothes and approached the sages. Although the boys were impudent, they feigned humility and clasped [the sages' feet]. They asked: "This dark-eyed lady, who is pregnant, has a query for you, O sages, but she is too shy to ask you directly. Your vision is infallible, so pray tell: she is about to deliver and desires a son; to a child of what [sex] will she give birth?"

16. The sages became angry at the deception, O king. They replied: "She will beget a club for you, fools, that will destroy your dynasty!"
17. Hearing this, the boys were terrified. They immediately uncovered Sāmba's belly and saw that there was, indeed, a club made of iron there:
18. "We are so unlucky – what have we done? What will people say to us?" they said. Taking the club, they went to their homes, trembling.
19. They brought the club into the assembly; the beauty of their faces faded. Then they related [what had happened] to the king in the presence of all the Yadus.
20. When they heard about the unavoidable curse of the *brāhmaṇas*, and saw the club, O king, the people of Dvārakā were overcome and paralysed with fear.
21. Āhuka [Ugrasena], the king of the Yadus, had the club ground up, and then hurled it into the waters of the ocean, along with the piece of iron that remained from it.
22. A certain fish ate the iron piece, and the ground-up particles were carried by the waves to the shore, where they became absorbed into *eraka* grass.
23. The fish was caught by a fisherman from the ocean in a net, along with other fish, and a hunter made an arrowhead from the piece of iron that had entered its stomach.
24. *Bhagavān* knows the essence of everything. Although he is the supreme Lord, he did not wish to arrange things otherwise. In his form of time, he gladly permitted the *brāhmaṇas*' curse.'

CHAPTER 6

*The Gods Visit Kṛṣṇa**

1. *Śrī* Śuka said:

'In due course, Brahmā, accompanied by his own sons as well as by the gods and the progenitors of mankind, went [to Dvārakā].

Śiva, the Lord of past and future, also went, surrounded by hosts of ghosts.

2–4. *Bhagavān* Indra, together with the *maruts*, the *ādityas*, the *vasus*, the two *aśvins*, the *ṛbhus*, the *aṅgirās*, the *rudras*, the *viśvadevatas*, the *sādhyas*, other gods, the *gandharvas*, the *apsarās*, the *nāgas*, the *siddhas*, *cāraṇas* and *guhyakas*, the sages and forefathers, the *vidyādharas* and *kinnaras*, went to Dvārakā desiring to see Kṛṣṇa. *Bhagavān* Kṛṣṇa bewitches human beings by his beautiful form, and spreads his fame, which removes the impurities of all people, across the [three] worlds.

5. In that resplendent city, abundantly prosperous, they gazed with insatiable eyes upon Kṛṣṇa, who is wonderful to behold.

6. They covered Kṛṣṇa, the best of the Yadus, with garlands of flowers obtained from gardens in the celestial realms, and praised the Lord of the Universe with words full of wonderful meanings:

7. "We bow down, master, at your lotus feet with our words, minds, vital airs, senses and intelligence. Those filled with love, who desire freedom from the great snares made of *karma*, meditate upon your feet in their hearts.

8. You create, protect and annihilate this incomprehensible manifest world in yourself by means of your *māyā* composed of the three *guṇas*. But, although you situate yourself in the *guṇas* of this world, you are definitely not affected by these acts because you delight in your own uninterrupted bliss. You are beyond reproach, O unconquerable one.

9. The purification of people with impure minds does not occur by means of works, austere disciplines, charity, study of the Vedas or learning – to the extent that it does among pure souls by means of mature faith nourished by hearing about your glories.

10. May your feet be the fire that burns the impurities in our minds. They are carried in the tender hearts of sages for the purpose of liberation; they are worshipped by the Sātvata saints by means of the *vyūha* forms[1] for the purpose of attaining *sārṣṭi*, equal opulence [with you];[2] and they are worshipped by the self-controlled at the three junctures of the day, for the purpose of passing beyond the celestial realms.[3]

11. Your feet are the object of meditation for those who have taken oblations in their outstretched hands for the *adhvara* sacrificial fire[4] as instructed in the three Vedas and Niruktas.[5] They are worshipped by *yogīs* desiring to know about your *māyā* by means of spiritual *yoga*, and by the foremost devotees.
12. May your feet always be the fire that burns the impurities in our minds. Śrī, the goddess of fortune, is like a female rival, who vies with your faded garland, O master. But you accept this garland as worship that has been sincerely offered by us.
13. We are your worshippers, O *Bhagavān*. May your feet purify our sins. With their three steps, they are worshipped as a flag, a banner flowing over the three worlds [the Ganges].[6] They inspire fear and fearlessness for the armies of the demons and gods, and [lead] the *sādhus* to heaven and the wicked to hell, O mighty One.
14. Living entities, beginning with Brahmā, harass each other. They are under your control, just like cows tied through their nostrils. You are time, transcendental to the *puruṣas* and to *prakṛti*. You are the highest being. May your feet bestow peace upon us.
15. You are the cause of this world – its creation, maintenance and dissolution. They say that you are time for the undifferentiated *prakṛti*, the soul and *mahat*.[7] As time, your swift action is unpredictable, and you engage in the decay of everything through your three wheels.[8] You are the highest being.
16. The original being, whose potency is infallible, obtained his potency from you. Then, along with *māyā*, he generates the *mahat*, which is like the womb of this world. That very *mahat*, in conjunction with *māyā*, generated from itself the golden egg [of the universe] with its external coverings.[9]
17. Therefore, your Lordship is the controller of all moving and non-moving entities. O Lord of the sense organs, although you enjoy the sense objects, which are produced from the modification of the *guṇas* that originate in *māyā*,[10] you are not tainted. Other entities, on the other hand, are fearful because of renouncing [these sense objects] by their own efforts [since they may again fall under their control].[11]
18. Sixteen thousand wives were unable to distract his senses in

any way. Sending arrows of love steeped in seductive charms through the curves of their enchanting eyebrows, their love was discreetly revealed through glances and smiles.
19. The honeyed streams of your stories, and the rivers produced from washing your feet,[12] are both able to destroy the impurities of the three worlds. Those who live a pure life contact those two holy bodies of water produced from your feet, by hearing with their ears, and by immersion of their bodies." '
20. *Śrī* Bādarāyaṇi [Śuka] said:

'When Brahmā, who was present in the sky with Śiva and the other gods, had in this manner praised Hari, Govinda, he offered homage and spoke.
21. *Śrī* Brahmā said: "O master, we previously asked you to remove the burden of the earth, a task which has now been accomplished, O unlimited soul.
22. You have established *dharma* for righteous people who are true to their promise, and your fame, which removes the impurities of all the worlds, has been spread through all the quarters.
23. Assuming an incomparable form, you incarnated in the Yadu dynasty and performed extraordinary deeds for the benefit of the world.
24. In the age of *kali*, human beings and the pious can easily cross over *tamas* [ignorance] by hearing and reciting those stories, O Lord.
25. O master, O supreme being, more than 125 years have passed by since you incarnated in the Yadu dynasty.
26. Nothing of the work of the gods remains to be done, O support of everything. Moreover, this dynasty has been almost destroyed by the curse of the *brāhmaṇas*.
27. Therefore, return to your supreme abode, if you care to, and protect us, the rulers of the worlds, along with the worlds. We are the servants of Viṣṇu, the Lord of Vaikuṇṭha."
28. *Śrī Bhagavān* said: "I understand what you are saying, O lords of the gods. Your task has been accomplished – the burden of the world has been removed.
29. The Yadu dynasty, which had become unrestrained through

its wealth, heroism and power, was about to devour the world. So it was checked by me, like the ocean is by the shore.
30. If I were to leave without restraining the great dynasty of proud Yadus, this world would be destroyed by their excess.
31. As we speak, the destruction of the dynasty, provoked by the curse of the *brāhmaṇas*, has begun. After this is complete, I will go to your residence, O sinless Brahmā."'
32. *Śrī* Śuka said:

'Thus addressed by the Lord of the worlds, the self-born god Brahmā offered homage to Kṛṣṇa, and then returned to his own dwelling along with the other gods.
33. Then *Bhagavān* Kṛṣṇa saw that powerful portents had arisen in the city of Dvārakā. He addressed the assembled Yadu elders.
34. *Śrī Bhagavān* said: "These most powerful omens are breaking out here everywhere. There has been a curse on our dynasty by the *brāhmaṇas* which is impossible to overcome.
35. We should not live here if we desire to survive, O Āryans. Let us go today to the very holy place Prabhāsa, without delay.
36. The moon was once afflicted by consumption because of Dakṣa's curse. After bathing in Prabhāsa, it was immediately freed from its sins and returned to waxing in due sequence.[13]
37. We will bathe there, satisfy the forefathers and the gods, and feed worthy *brāhmaṇas* with a variety of tasty foods.
38. Then we will distribute abundant wealth to those worthy persons with faith. By means of charity, we will sail over our sins like a boat over the ocean."'
39. *Śrī* Śuka said:

'Thus advised by *Bhagavān*, the Yadus decided to go to the holy place, O joy of the Kuru dynasty. They harnessed their chariots.
40–41. When Uddhava, an eternal follower of Kṛṣṇa, saw this and heard what had been said by *Bhagavān* Kṛṣṇa, O king, and when he saw the terrifying omens, he approached the Lord of the lords of the universe in a private place. After offering homage [by touching] Kṛṣṇa's feet with his head, Uddhava, hands folded in supplication, addressed him.
42. *Śrī* Uddhava said: "O God of gods, Lord, master of *yoga*,

hearing and reciting about you are purifying. It seems evident that your Lordship will withdraw your family and depart from this world. You did not counteract the *brāhmaṇas'* curse, O Lord, although you could have done.

43. I am unable to give up your lotus feet for even half a second, O Keśava. Take me also with you to your abode, O master.

44. Your pastimes, Kṛṣṇa, are supremely auspicious for human beings. People reject all other desires after receiving the nectar [of their recitation] through their ears.

45. We are your devotees [and serve you] while sleeping, sitting, walking, being still, playing, eating and other such activities. How can we give you up – you are our dear soul?

46. We are your servants, and overcome *māyā* by eating the remnants of your [food], and adorning ourselves with the ornaments, garments, perfumes and garlands that you have enjoyed.[14]

47. Those pure and peaceful *sannyāsī* sages who are *śramaṇa* ascetics,[15] retain their semen and dress only in air go to your abode known as *brahman*.

48–49. But we, on the other hand, are wandering on the paths of *karma*, O great *yogī*. We will cross over formidable *tamas* [darkness] by talking about you with your followers, and by remembering and reciting your deeds, words, games, glances, smiles and movements, which imitate the world of men." '

50. *Śrī* Śuka said:

'Addressed thus, O king, *Bhagavān* Kṛṣṇa, the son of Devakī, spoke to his dear and unalloyed servant Uddhava.'

A second Bhagavad Gītā, generally known as the Uddhava Gītā, is spoken at this point, by Kṛṣṇa to Uddhava. The topics covered range from metaphysics to social duties, the practice of the various types of yoga, liberation, the nature of saṃsāra *and a host of other subjects. Included here is the last chapter of this Gītā, which takes up thirteen chapters of the eleventh book, since it presents the final teachings of Kṛṣṇa to Uddhava and, by extension, to all those desiring to know how to practise devotion to Kṛṣṇa after his departure from the world.*

CHAPTER 29

*Kṛṣṇa's Final Instructions to Uddhava**

1. [*Śrī* Śuka said:] '*Śrī* Uddhava said: "I think that this practice of *yoga* is extremely difficult to perform for one whose mind is undisciplined, O Acyuta.[1] So please tell me in simple terms how a person can easily accomplish it.
2. Usually, *yogīs* who [try to] fix their minds became wasted from disciplining their minds, and despondent because of not being fixed in contemplation.[2]
3. Therefore swan-like people take refuge joyfully with your lotus feet, which bestow happiness, O lotus-eyed Lord. These others are deluded by your *māyā* and become proud because of their practice of *yoga* and *karma*, O Lord of the universe.
4. You are the friend of everyone, so what is so surprising about this intimacy with your servants? – they have no other refuge than you. Although your footstool is frayed at the edges from the fabulous helmets of the great lords [when they bow down], you yourself take pleasure from [being with] the animals.[3]
5. You are the beloved Lord and soul of all, and the bestower of everything on those who have taken refuge with you. What person who knows what you have done [for them] could abandon you? Who would indulge in wealth, which brings forgetfulness [of you]? What is there that is not available for us who have taken refuge with the dust of your feet?
6. Those who are learned overflow with happiness when they remember what you have done; they are not able to begin to repay their debt to you, O Lord, even with the lifespan of Brahmā. Removing ill fortune, you manifest your own nature inside all embodied beings, in the form of the inner Lord,[4] and outside, in the form of the *guru*."'
7. *Śrī* Śuka said:

'When he was questioned in this way by Uddhava, who was deeply devoted to him, the Lord of lords, who has assumed the three forms[5] by his own *śaktis*, and for whom the universe is a plaything, gave an affectionate, engaging smile, and replied.

8. *Śrī Bhagavān* said: "Ah! I will tell you about the *dharma* [duty] that is the most auspicious to me. By following it faithfully, a person will conquer death – that which is so difficult to overcome.

9. A person should perform all *dharmas* for my sake.[6] Surrendering the mind and thoughts to me, one should delight in doing *dharma* to me.[7]

10. One should reside in holy places, and associate with *sādhus*, who are my devotees. One should [follow] the behaviour of my devotees, who exist among the gods, demons and humans.

11. Either as an individual, or in association with others, one should arrange for the performance of great festivities on calendar occasions with song, dance and such activities, [presented] with royal extravagance.

12. One should see that it is actually I who am present both within and without, just like the sky, and one should see the *ātmā* within the body.

13. Therefore, one who has submitted himself to absolute knowledge accepts all living beings as having me as their essence, and honours them, O radiant Uddhava.

14. A *paṇḍita*, or learned person, is considered to be one who sees everything equally whether it be a *brāhmaṇa*, a member of the *Pukkasa* tribe,[8] a thief, one devoted to *brāhmaṇas*, the sun, a spark of fire, the gentle or the cruel.[9]

15. Rivalry, envy, abuse and ego quickly disappear from a person who constantly reflects upon the essence of all people as being me.

16. Ignoring one's relatives who mock, and renouncing any sense of embarrassment and identification with the body, one should offer homage even to dogs, *cāṇḍāla* outcastes, cows and asses [by falling] like a stick on the ground.[10]

17. Until [the ability to see] me as the essence of all living beings develops, one should worship me with the activities of the body, mind and speech.[11]

18. Completely freed from doubt, and seeing with knowledge

and self-reflection that the nature of everything consists of *brahman*, one should cease from action.
19. I definitely consider this [attitude] – that the essence of all living entities is me – to be the most efficacious of all practices involving the activities of one's body, speech and mind.
20. There is not the slightest loss, even in the least attempt to perform *dharma* for me, my dear Uddhava.[12] It has been prescribed by me, and is devoid of yearning because it is free from the *guṇas*.
21. Whatever activity is dedicated to me, the supreme being, without self-interest, even if it be useless and performed out of fear or other such things, is *dharma*, O best of saintly persons.
22. This is intelligence for the intelligent, and wisdom for the wise. One can attain me, the immortal truth, by means of this mortal body.
23. What has been spoken to you, both in detail and in brief, is the sum total of the teachings of the Vedas. It is difficult even for the gods to understand.
24. This knowledge has been given to you repeatedly with clear reasoning and argument. Understanding it, a person's doubts are destroyed and he is liberated.
25. I have carefully responded to your question. One who fixes his mind upon this eternal secret of the Vedas attains to the supreme *brahman*.
26. I give myself out of my own free will to anyone who transmits this knowledge of *brahman* and who liberally propagates this [teaching] among my devotees.[13]
27. One who recites this holy, sanctifying and supreme [teaching], revealing me with the lamp of knowledge, becomes purified day by day.[14]
28. And the person who continually hears it faithfully and without distraction, engaging in supreme *bhakti* to me, is not bound by *karma*.[15]
29. So, Uddhava, my friend, have you understood *brahman*? Has your illusion and sorrow, born of the mind, been dispelled?[16]
30. You should not pass on this teaching to those who do not

want to listen, who are not humble, or who are hypocrites, atheists, cheats and non-devotees.[17]

31. You should tell it to those free from these faults: those disposed towards the *brāhmaṇas*, well-wishers, *sādhu* ascetics, the pure and the devotees – even if they be from the *śūdra* caste, or women.[18]

32. When this is known by a curious person, nothing remains to be known. When this delicious nectar has been drunk, nothing remains to be drunk.

33. Whatever goals [are achieved] by men through the pursuit of knowledge, work, *yoga*, business and political power – the four goals of life[19] – I am those for you, my dear Uddhava.

34. When a mortal gives up all *karma*, surrenders himself to me, and desires to act for me, he achieves immortality and attains to my same nature." '[20]

35. *Śrī* Śuka said:

'When he had heard the words of Uttamaśloka, and had been shown the path of *yoga* outlined above, Uddhava stood with hands folded in supplication. His throat was choked with love, his eyes were overflowing with tears, and he was unable to say anything.

36. With an effort, he composed his mind, which was disturbed by love, O king. With a feeling of gratitude, he stood with hands folded in supplication and spoke to Kṛṣṇa, the most eminent hero of the Yadu dynasty, touching his lotus feet with his head.

37. *Śrī* Uddhava said: "The illusion and great ignorance in which I was immersed have been dispelled by your presence. How can cold, darkness and fear have influence over one who has approached the sun, O original, unborn Lord?

38. Your Lordship has kindly reciprocated with me, your servant, by giving the torch of knowledge. How could any grateful person abandon the soles of your feet and approach anyone else for refuge?

39. The very strong ropes of attachment for the Dāśārha, Vṛṣṇi, Andhaka and Sātvata clans have been severed by the weapon of true knowledge. They were cast by you through your *māyā* for the purpose of procreating and expanding [the dynasties].

40. All homage to you, great *yogī* – I cast myself upon you; please purify me so that I may have undeviating attachment to your lotus feet."

41. *Śrī Bhagavān* said: "You have received instruction from me, Uddhava. Now go to my *āśrama* known as Badarī[21] and receive purification there by touching and bathing in the water, which was sanctified by [contact with] my feet.

42. All sins are absolved from simply glancing at the Alakanandā river. Wearing bark and subsisting on the produce of the forest, my dear Uddhava, be happy and free from desire.

43. With disciplined senses and exemplary character, tolerate the dualities of matter, and be peaceful, steady in intelligence and absorbed in knowledge and realization.

44. Reflecting with discrimination upon what I have taught you, devote yourself to my *dharma*, with your mind and words absorbed in me. Then you will surpass the three conditions [of the *guṇas*], and attain me, the supreme."

45. Addressed in this way by Hari in his wisdom, Uddhava circumambulated Kṛṣṇa to the right. Even though he had gone beyond all dualities, his mind was full of feeling on his departure, and he placed Kṛṣṇa's two feet on his head, and then drenched them with his tears.

46. Feeling distressed and irresolute at separation, out of a love which it was impossible to relinquish, Uddhava could not leave Kṛṣṇa. He set out after paying homage again and again, and slowly departed, carrying Kṛṣṇa's two sandals on his head.

47. After installing Kṛṣṇa within his heart, that great devotee Uddhava went to Viśālā, as directed by the sole friend of the universe. After undertaking austere disciplines, he went to the destination of Hari.

48. Whoever faithfully honours this nectar of knowledge containing an ocean of bliss, spoken by Kṛṣṇa, whose feet are worshipped by the lords of *yoga*, to his devotee, is liberated, along with the world.[22]

49. I offer homage to him who is known as Kṛṣṇa, the original eminent being, author of the Vedas. In order to dispel fear of *saṃsāra*, he collected like a bee the essence of the Vedas – the

essence of knowledge and wisdom – from the ocean of nectar, and gave it to his groups of devotees to drink.'

CHAPTER 30

The Destruction of the Yadu Dynasty

1. The king said:

'So, when the great devotee Uddhava had gone to the forest, what did *Bhagavān* Kṛṣṇa, the creator of all living beings, do?
2. When his own dynasty had been devastated by the curse of the *brāhmaṇas*, how did the Lord relinquish his body, which is so dear to the eye?
3. Once their eyes were fixed on him, women could not withdraw them. Once he had entered the ears of the saintly, he remained in their hearts and would not depart from there. His beauty produces delightful words, not to mention fame, for poets. Those who saw him on Arjuna's chariot attained the same [form] as him.'[1]
4. The sage [Śuka] said:

'When he saw that great portents had sprung up in the sky, on land, and in space, Kṛṣṇa spoke the following words to the Yadus, who were seated in the Sudharmā assembly hall.
5. *Śrī Bhagavān* said: "These are fearsome, death-foreboding portents in Dvārakā. We should not remain here for a moment longer, O best of the Yadus.
6. The women, children and elderly should go to Śaṅkhoddhāra, and we should go to Prabhāsa, where the Sarasvatī river flows to the west.
7–8. When we are purified from bathing there and fasting, we will worship deities with concentrated minds by bathing them, smearing them [with sandalwood paste] and making offerings. We will recite the *mantras* invoking good fortune, and then

worship the auspicious *brāhmaṇas* with cows, land, gold, garments, elephants, horses, chariots and houses.

9. This is the remedy that will ward off the bad omens; it is the best way [to accomplish] our welfare. Worship of the gods, *brāhmaṇas* and cows [is the means of attaining] the highest state of being."

10. All the Yadu elders heard this from Madhudviṭ [Kṛṣṇa],[2] and said: "Let us do this." Then they crossed [the sea] in boats, and proceeded to Prabhāsa in chariots.

11. There, the Yadus performed with the utmost devotion whatever they had been instructed to do by *Bhagavān* Kṛṣṇa, Lord of the Yadus, accompanied by all the auspicious rites.

12. Then, deprived of reason by the force of destiny, they drank great quantities of the sweet beverage called *maireyaka*, the alcoholic potency of which confuses the mind.

13. A great quarrel broke out among those heroes. Bewildered by Kṛṣṇa's *māyā* and intoxicated from enormous quantities of the beverage, they became arrogant.

14. Incensed with anger and with bows drawn, the Yadus fought on the seashore with bows, swords, arrows, clubs, spears and lances.

15. Wholly intoxicated and riding on chariots with banners flying, and on elephants, donkeys, camels, cows, buffaloes, donkeys and even men, they challenged and assailed each other with arrows, tusks and other weapons.

16. Pradyumna and Sāmba confronted each other in the battle, their hostility aroused, as did Akrūra and Bhoja; Aniruddha and Sātyaki; the vicious Subhadra and Saṅgrāmajita; the two Gadas; and Sumitra and Asuratha.

17. The others, too, attacked each other: Niśaṭha and Ulmaka, as well as others led by Sahasrajit, Śatajit and Bhānu. Thoroughly bewildered by Mukunda and blinded by drunkenness, they slaughtered each other.

18. Casting their friendship to the winds, the Dāśārha, Vṛṣṇi, Andhaka, Bhoja, Sātvata, Madhu and Arbuda clans, the citizens of Mathurā and Śūrasena, the Visarjana, Kukura and Kunti clans slaughtered each other.

19. In a state of confusion, sons fought with fathers, brothers,

nephews, grandsons and paternal and maternal uncles. Friends fought with friends, well-wishers with well-wishers, and relatives killed their kinsmen.

20. When the arrows had all been discharged, the bows shattered and the weapons depleted, they seized the *eraka* grass in their fists.

21. These had turned into iron bars that were like thunderbolts. The men clasped them in their fists and attacked their enemies. When Kṛṣṇa obstructed them, they attacked him, too.

22. Deprived of their senses, they also became determined to kill Balabhadra [Balarāma], thinking him to be on the opposing side, and assailed him with drawn bows, O king.

23. This provoked Kṛṣṇa and Balarāma to fury also, O son of the Kurus, and they manoeuvred about in the combat striking out, with the iron bars of the *eraka* grass in their clenched hands.

24. Anger born of rivalry brought death to those whose minds had been covered by Kṛṣṇa's *māyā*, and upon whom the *brāhmaṇa*'s curse had been unleashed, just as fire does to a bamboo forest.

25. When his entire dynasty had been destroyed in this way, Keśava felt that the remaining burden upon the earth had been removed.

26. On the shore of the ocean, Balarāma resorted to *yoga* [by fixing his mind on] the supreme being, merged his *ātmā* in the *ātmā*, and departed from the world of mortals.

27–28. *Bhagavān* Kṛṣṇa, the son of Devakī, saw the departure of Balarāma and placed himself down upon the lap of the earth. He sat quietly under a *pippala* [banyan] tree, and became manifest in his four-armed form, dispelling the darkness of the quarters by his radiance.

29. He was as dark as a cloud, and had the lustre of burnt gold. Displaying the *śrīvatsa* mark on his body, and dressed in a set of silken garments, he was most auspicious.

30. His lotus face had a beautiful smile, and was adorned with blue-black hair. His lotus eyes were captivating and he had glittering alligator-shaped earrings.

31. He was splendid with waist belt, *brāhmaṇa* thread, helmet,

gold bracelets, arm ornaments, necklaces, anklets, insignia and the Kaustubha gem.
32. His body was encircled with a forest garland, and [he was surrounded by] his personal weapons in personified form. As he sat, he placed his reddish lotus foot on his right thigh.
33. Confusing it with a deer, Jarā the hunter pierced that deer-like foot with an arrow made from the piece of iron that was left over from the club.
34. When he saw that it was a four-armed being, he was terrified at the sin he had committed, fell down with his head at the feet of the Lord, the killer of demons, and said:
35. "This deed was done by an ignorant sinner, O Madhusūdana. You should be merciful and forgive me, a sinful wretch, O sinless Uttamaśloka.
36. They say that by remembering you, O Viṣṇu, the darkness of ignorance is dispelled. I have committed a terrible deed, O master.
37. I am a sinful hunter of animals, so kill me at once so that I may never again commit such an offence against a saintly person, O Lord of Vaikuṇṭha.
38. Brahmā, and his sons such as Rudra, as well as the masters of the sacred words, do not understand that which is created by your personal *yoga* [*māyā*], because their intelligence is covered by your *māyā*. Therefore, what can I say about me – my birth is impure?"
39. *Śrī Bhagavān* said: "Get up and do not fear, O Jarā. This deed was actually desired by me. Go with my permission to the celestial realm of *svarga*, the destination of the righteous."
40. On these instructions of Kṛṣṇa *Bhagavān*, who assumes a body at will, Jarā circumambulated him three times, offered obeisance, and then went to the heavenly realms in a celestial vehicle.
41. Kṛṣṇa's charioteer, Dāruka, searching for the place where Kṛṣṇa was, came upon it after he smelt a breeze fragrant with *tulasī* leaves. He went towards it.
42. He saw his master at the foot of the *aśvattha* [banyan] tree, surrounded by his dazzlingly bright weapons. His heart

overwhelmed with love and his eyes full of tears, Dāruka jumped down from his chariot, fell down at Kṛṣṇa's feet, and said:
43. "My sight was lost and enveloped in darkness when I could not find your lotus feet, O master, just like when the moon disappears at night. I could not find my way, nor obtain peace of mind."
44. While the charioteer was speaking thus, Kṛṣṇa's chariot, marked with the insignia of the eagle Garuḍa, rose up into the sky before his very eyes, along with its horses and banner.
45. Viṣṇu's divine weapons then followed it. Janārdana spoke to his charioteer, who was astounded by this:
46. "Go to Dvārakā, charioteer, and tell our relatives about the internecine destruction of our kinsmen, the departure of Saṅkarṣaṇa, and my condition.
47. You all, along with your families, should not remain in Dvārakā. The ocean will submerge the city once it has been abandoned by me.
48. You should all bring along your respective families as well as my parents, and, protected by Arjuna, head for Indraprastha.
49. As for you, when you have situated yourself in my *dharma*, are fixed in knowledge, are unattached and have understood that this world is simply the creation of my *māyā*, then go your way with a peaceful mind."
50. Addressed thus, Dāruka circumambulated Kṛṣṇa, offered homage again and again, placed Kṛṣṇa's two feet upon his head and then set out for the city with an unhappy mind.'

CHAPTER 31

*Kṛṣṇa Returns to his own Abode**

1. *Śrī* Śuka said:

'Then, Brahmā, Śiva, along with his consort, the gods, led by the great Indra, the sages and the progenitors of the universe came there. So did the forefathers, *siddhas*, *gandharvas*, *vidyād-*

haras, mighty serpents, *cāraṇas*, *yakṣas*, *rākṣasas*, *kinnaras*, *apsaras* and the twice-born *brāhmaṇas*.

3. Singing and reciting the birth and deeds of Śauri [Kṛṣṇa], they were highly excited and eager to witness the departure of *Bhagavān*, God [to his transcendent abode].

4. Crowding the sky with rows of celestial vehicles, and filled with great devotion, they showered down streams of flowers.

5. When *Bhagavān* Kṛṣṇa saw grandfather Brahmā and [the gods] who were manifestations of his own power, he closed his eyes and fixed his mind on himself.[1]

6. Without burning his body – which is pleasing to the whole world and the object of meditation and trance – with the fire of *yogic* concentration,[2] Kṛṣṇa entered his own abode.

7. Kettledrums resounded in the heavens, and flowers fell from the sky, and Truth, Dharma, Resolution, Fame and Opulence followed him.

8. The gods and everyone, headed by Brahmā, were dumbfounded, but they were not able to see Kṛṣṇa entering his abode, since his path is unknown.

9. As mortals cannot trace the path of a moving lightning flash which has left a ring of clouds, so the path of Kṛṣṇa could not be traced by the gods.

10. Brahmā, Rudra and others who had witnessed Hari's *yogic* method were full of amazement and returned to their respective planets, glorifying him.

11. O king, you should consider the activities of birth and of departure of the supreme among human beings to be the role-playing of *māyā*, just like that of an actor. After creating this world from himself, he enters it, sports in it and, in the end, withdraws from it and remains retired in his own glory.

12. Kṛṣṇa, the giver of protection, brought the *guru*'s son from the abode of Yama, Lord of death, in his mortal body; he saved you when you were burned by the ultimate weapon;[3] he defeated Lord Śiva, who is death even for death himself; and he brought the hunter Jarā to the celestial world – how could he be incapable of protecting his own self?

13. Although he is the sole cause of the origin, maintenance and disappearance of everything, and the wielder of all *śakti* powers,

he did not desire to leave his form behind in this world – since what is the use of this world? – but demonstrated the path of those who are situated in the self.

14. One who rises early in the morning, and glorifies Kṛṣṇa's supreme departure in a devotional frame of mind, also attains to that highest destination.

15. Dāruka went to Dvārakā and fell at the feet of Vasudeva and Ugrasena, soaking their feet with his tears because of the separation from Kṛṣṇa.

16. He told of the total destruction of the Vṛṣṇi clan, O king. When they heard this, the people felt faint at heart, and swooned with grief.

17. Overwhelmed at the loss of Kṛṣṇa, his relatives rushed to that place, beat their faces and fell down unconscious.

18. Devakī, Rohiṇī and Vasudeva were overcome with grief at not finding their two sons, Kṛṣṇa and Balarāma, and fainted.

19. Overwhelmed by separation from *Bhagavān* Kṛṣṇa, they relinquished their lives on the spot. The women embraced their husbands and climbed upon the funeral pyre, Parīkṣit, my dear son.

20. The wives of Balarāma, too, embraced his body and entered the flames. The wives of Vasudeva embraced his body, as did Hari's daughters-in-law [the bodies of their husbands] such as Pradyumna and others, as they entered the fire. Kṛṣṇa's wives Rukmiṇī and the others, for whom Kṛṣṇa is their life and soul, did the same.

21. Arjuna was stricken by the loss of his dear friend Kṛṣṇa, but consoled himself by the words of truth spoken by Kṛṣṇa.

22. Arjuna made arrangements, according to custom and seniority, for the funerary rites of his deceased relatives whose family lineages had been destroyed.

23. The ocean immediately submerged Dvārakā when it was abandoned by Hari, O great king, leaving only the residence of the beautiful *Bhagavān* Kṛṣṇa.

24. *Bhagavān* Madhusūdana is eternally present there. It is the most auspicious of auspicious places, and removes all impurities simply by remembrance of it.

25. Dhanañjaya took the survivors of those who had been

slaughtered – the women, children and elders – and settled them in Indraprastha. Then he consecrated Vajra, the son of Aniruddha, on the throne there.

26. When your grandfathers [the Pāṇḍavas] heard about the destruction of their friends, O king, they made you the preserver of the dynasty, and then they all set out on the great journey.[4]

27. Any mortal who recites these birth and deeds of Viṣṇu, the Lords of lords, with faith, is freed from all sins.

28. In conclusion, anyone who recites the delightful deeds of the incarnations of Hari, *Bhagavān*, and the most auspicious stories of his childhood, as are described here and in other sources, achieves the highest devotion for Kṛṣṇa, who is the goal of swan-like devotees.'

This ends the translation of the beautiful story of Kṛṣṇa.

Notes

PART ONE

CHAPTER 1
The Prelude to Kṛṣṇa's Incarnation

1. *Naimiṣa*: Modern Nimsar, is on the banks of the Gomatī in the Sītāpur district of the state of Uttar Pradesh, in India.
2. *Viṣṇu*: Viṣṇu and Kṛṣṇa are the same being – the supreme God of all gods – in different contexts. Followers of Viṣṇu/Kṛṣṇa are called Vaiṣṇavas. As noted in the Introduction, depending on the Vaiṣṇava sect, either Kṛṣṇa is considered the ultimate Godhead, and Viṣṇu his secondary manifestation, or Viṣṇu the ultimate Godhead, and Kṛṣṇa his derivative incarnation.
3. *aṃśa [partial incarnation]*: Deities can remain in their abodes and simultaneously produce incarnations of themselves that embody a portion or aspect of their powers or attributes to descend upon the earth. These are called *aṃśa*.
4. *Balarāma*: Balarāma plays the role of Kṛṣṇa's brother during his incarnation.
5. *Yadu*: Yadu was one of the five sons born to Yayāti, whose story is described in Book IX of the Bhāgavata, chapters 18–19.
6. *Uttamaśloka [Kṛṣṇa]*: Uttamaśloka is a name of Kṛṣṇa, meaning one who is praised in the best of verses.
7. *They are relished . . . recited by them*: The process of *bhakti yoga*, or the *yoga* of devotion, involves always remembering Kṛṣṇa by hearing and reciting the stories of his different incarnations (see Introduction, p. xxix ff.).
8. *That wielder of the discus*: Viṣṇu always carries a *cakra*, or discus-like weapon, which Kṛṣṇa summons at will.
9. *He protected . . . Aśvatthāma's weapon*: Parīkṣit, although still within the womb of his mother, was the last remaining male in

the Pāṇḍava dynasty after the Mahābhārata war. Aśvatthāmā, who had sided with Duryodhana, the commander of the Kuru army opposing the Pāṇḍavas, attempted to murder him by hurling a formidable heat weapon, released by *mantra*, against the embryo. Kṛṣṇa intervened and saved the embryo.

10. *māyā*: *Māyā* is the power of illusion that ensnares all entities in the world, causing them to identify with their temporary material bodies and circumstances, and forget their spiritual nature. In another capacity, *māyā*, or *yogamāyā*, is the power that serves Kṛṣṇa during his incarnations. Kṛṣṇa controls *māyā*; all other living entities are under *māyā*'s control. *Māyā* is a feminine entity.
11. *You said that Saṅkarṣaṇa . . . another body*: Devakī is Kṛṣṇa's mother. Balarāma was Devakī's seventh pregnancy (and hence Kṛṣṇa's elder brother). However, Balarāma was transferred into the womb of Vasudeva's second wife, Rohiṇī, and it thus appeared that Devakī had a miscarriage.
12. *Mukunda [Kṛṣṇa]*: Mukunda is a name of Kṛṣṇa that means 'the giver of liberation'.
13. *Sātvatas*: The Sātvatas are a tribe who are devotees of Kṛṣṇa.
14. *Keśava [Kṛṣṇa]*: Keśava is a name of Kṛṣṇa that means 'having beautiful hair'.
15. *Hari [Kṛṣṇa]*: Hari is a name of Kṛṣṇa, which can be derived from the root *hṛ*, to take away (evil, or sin).
16. *the age of kali*: *Kaliyuga*, the present world age, is the last and most degenerate of the four ages. The devotional path of *bhakti yoga* – hearing and reciting the activities and pastimes of Kṛṣṇa and the other incarnations of Viṣṇu – are the primary activities prescribed by the Bhāgavata for liberation in this age.
17. *Vāsudeva [Kṛṣṇa]*: Vāsudeva is a patronymic name for Kṛṣṇa as the son of Vasudeva (the difference is in the length of the first vowel).
18. *Brahmā the creator*: The four-headed Brahmā, although not the supreme being, is the creator god whose duty it is to engineer the forms of this world.
19. *the ocean of milk*: In Hindu cosmography, the earthly realm consists of concentric rings of earth. Each ring of earth is surrounded by a concentric ring of ocean, each of which contains different liquids. Viṣṇu reclines upon the ocean of milk.
20. *Śiva, the three-eyed God*: Śiva has three eyes, the third being on his forehead and made of fire. Flames issue from this when he becomes infuriated, such as when he burnt up Kāma, the god

of desire, when the latter attempted to distract him from his meditations.

21. *the Puruṣa-sūkta prayer*: The *Puruṣa-sūkta* is an ancient Ṛgvedic hymn to *Puruṣa*, the primordial being, often recited by Vaiṣṇavas, who equate the primordial *Puruṣa* with Viṣṇu.
22. *his power of time*: Time is a potency of Kṛṣṇa, often used in the text in the sense of death, or the force that moves all beings inexorably towards their imminent demise.
23. See note 17.
24. *Lord Ananta*: Ananta, also known as Śeṣa, is a thousand-headed snake upon which Viṣṇu rests as he reclines on the ocean of milk. Each head is continually reciting the glories of Viṣṇu. Ananta/Śeṣa incarnates as Balarāma, Kṛṣṇa's brother.
25. *Brahmā, lord of the prajāpatis*: The *prajāpatis* are beings created by Brahmā for the purpose of facilitating creation.
26. *Mathurā . . . in that city*: Mathurā is about 100 miles south of Delhi, on the Agra road. It is adjacent to Vṛndāvana, where Kṛṣṇa spent his childhood. Devotees consider that Kṛṣṇa is eternally present in such holy places, and that he is forever enacting his *līlās*, or pastimes, there, which those advanced on the path of *bhakti yoga*, or devotion, can experience even while in the embodied state. Such places are thus potentially epiphanic, and pilgrimage to such places is an important feature of Hindu religious practice.
27. *Devaka*: Devaka is the father of Devakī and brother of Ugrasena, Kaṃsa's father. Devakī and Kaṃsa are thus cousins, strictly speaking, but are referred to as brother and sister in this text.
28. *the five elements*: The five elements are earth, water, fire, air and ether.
29. *karma*: *Karma* is from the root *kṛ*, to 'do' or 'make'. *Karma* literally means 'work', but inherent in the Indic concept of work, or any type of activity, is the notion that every action breeds a reaction. Thus *karma* refers not only to an initial act, but also to the reaction that generates from it (even though this may come to fruition at some later time). In accordance with their *karma*, or pious and impious activities in this life, souls are awarded a good or bad body and set of circumstances in the next life.
30. *Just as a person . . . karmic destination*: This verse is from the Bṛhadāraṇyaka Upaniṣad (IV.4.3).
31. *This is like someone . . . to that situation*: The sense here is that just as a person forgets his or her real self when dreaming and identifies with some fantasy self, so, in everyday life, the *ātmā*,

the real self, forgets its essential spiritual nature and identifies with the temporary material body.

32. *guṇas*: *Prakṛti*, the primordial matter from which the entire creation evolves in Purāṇic thought, consists of three qualities, or *guṇas*: *sattva*, 'goodness'; *rajas*, 'action'; and *tamas*, 'inertia'. Just as the three primary colours intermix to produce an unlimited variety of colours, so the intermingling of these qualities results in the production of the variety of physical forms and psychological dispositions of all animate and inanimate beings (see Introduction, pp. xl–xliii).

33. *whatever state the mind flows to at the time of death*: According to the Bhagavad Gītā (VIII.6), whatever state one remembers at the time of death will determine one's next birth. At death, the soul leaves behind the gross body made of the five elements, but, except for liberated souls, is still encapsulated in the subtle body made of mind, intelligence and ego. At the time of death, the soul and subtle body are projected into the womb of a creature – human or non-human – that can provide a gross body most appropriate for the dominant state of mind of that particular person.

34. *Just like the light . . . by his own māyā*: Just as the moon, which is pure and transcendent, appears agitated when reflected in water ruffled by the wind, so the soul, which is pure and transcendent, identifies, due to illusion, with the forms of the world created by the *guṇas* when disturbed by desires.

35. *the Vṛṣṇi clan [Yadus]*: Vṛṣṇi was a king in the Yadu dynasty. The term 'Vṛṣṇis' is used more or less synonymously with 'Yadus' in the text.

36. *Nārada*: Nārada is a sage who travels through space visiting his disciples in the various realms and planets of the universe. He plays a *vīnā*, a stringed instrument, and constantly chants the names of Viṣṇu. Although a great devotee of Viṣṇu, he often spurs on the Lord's mission, as illustrated in these verses.

37. *born from the womb of Devakī*: The 'unborn' being born is a conscious usage of the *alaṅkāra* of *virodhābhāsa*, contradiction, when two things appear, on one level, to be contradictory (see p. lxiv of Introduction).

38. *Kaṃsa . . . Yadus*: Kaṃsa was a demon called Kālanemi in his past life. Since he had been killed by Viṣṇu in that life his enmity carried over into his present life as Kaṃsa.

CHAPTER 2

Prayers Offered by Brahmā and the Other Gods to Viṣṇu who had Entered the Womb

1. *Then I, with my aṃśa [partial incarnation]*: *Aṃśena* can be translated as either 'with my *aṃśa*', or 'through my *aṃśa*'. The theological implication of opting for either of these two possible translations is potentially significant. Followers of Viṣṇu believe that Kṛṣṇa is a manifestation of Viṣṇu. They would understand the speaker of verse 6, God, the soul of the universe (*Bhagavān, viśvātmā*), to be Viṣṇu, who is to appear in Devakī through his partial incarnation, *aṃśabhāgena*, namely, Kṛṣṇa. However, the Kṛṣṇa sects consider Kṛṣṇa to be supreme. They read this phrase as stating that Kṛṣṇa appears with his *aṃśa*, namely his brother Balarāma. I follow Śrīdhara in taking it in this latter sense.
2. *Rāma*: Rāma as Balarāma is not to be confused with the incarnation of Viṣṇu called Rāma. There is also a third Rāma, who is Paraśurāma.
3. *Aho!*: *Aho!* is a common exclamation meaning a variety of things depending on the context, such as Alas! Hey! Just see!
4. *He had been deposited . . . by mental transmission*: This is a mentally transmitted type of immaculate conception by which Kṛṣṇa was placed in Devakī's womb via the projection of a thought from Vasudeva's mind, rather than through the normal forms of insemination.
5. *the threesome*: Commentators have understood this 'threesome' variously as referring to: regular time – past, present and future; the three Vedas; the three ingredients of reality –time, the souls and matter; or the three phases of cosmic time – creation, before creation and after creation.
6. *This world . . . two birds*: In the Muṇḍaka (III.1.1) and the Śvetāśvatara (IV.4.6) Upaniṣads, two birds are sitting in a tree; one of them is eating the fruits of the tree, the other looks on. One bird is understood as being the soul in *saṃsāra* who is enjoying the fruits of the world (i.e., experiencing the results of its good and bad *karma* and producing more *karma*), while the other bird, depending on the theistic or monistic predilections of the commentator, is either God or the liberated soul, who is uninterested in such fruits and merely observes the endeavours of his companion.
7. *one support . . . ten leaves*: These numbers have been interpreted variously by Śrīdhara and other commentators as follows: one

support is *prakṛti*, from which the world evolves (or, according to some commentators, God, the support of everything); the two fruits are pleasure and pain; the three roots are the *guṇas*; the four juices are the four goals of human life – religion, wealth, enjoyment and liberation (or heaven, hell, darkness and emancipation); the five divisions are the five sense organs (or the five vital airs); the six characteristics are the six waves of existence – cold, heat, greediness, illusion, hunger and thirst (or according to others, the afflictions of hunger, thirst, grief, delusion, old age and death; or, again, birth, existence, growth, ripeness, decay and destruction; or the six coverings of the self [Śrīdhara does not enumerate these]); the seven layers are skin, blood, flesh, muscle, bone, marrow and semen; the eight shoots are the elements of *prakṛti* – earth, water, fire, air, ether, mind, ego and intelligence; the nine outlets are the genitals, anus, mouth, and the two eyes, ears, and nostrils; and the ten leaves are the ten vital airs (or the ten objects of the senses).

8. *sattva [goodness]*: Pure *sattva* is synonymous with *brahman* in the Bhāgavata.
9. *Mādhava [Kṛṣṇa]*: Mādhava is a name of Kṛṣṇa that means 'descendant of Madhu'.
10. *Vedic rituals*: The ancient Vedic religion, the matrix from which and against which Hinduism, Buddhism and Jainism evolved, consisted primarily of elaborate ritual sacrifices where items such as animals and *ghee* were offered to the gods through the sacrificial fire.
11. *samādhi [meditative absorption]*: *Samādhi* is the eighth and final stage of the eight-limbed path of Patañjali's *yoga* system. It culminates in complete detachment from the mind and senses, and full absorption in the *ātmā*, the self or soul (called *puruṣa* by Patāñjali).
12. *pure knowledge . . . would not exist*: Pure *sattva* is correlated with pure knowledge and enlightenment.
13. *jīvātmā*: The soul is referred to as *jīva*, *ātmā*, *jīvātmā* (or, in Patañjali, *puruṣa*). The term *jīva* (or *jīvātmā*) is usually used in the context of the soul embodied in *saṃsāra*.
14. *You have assumed . . . fish [Matsya]*: Viṣṇu incarnates in all of these forms in previous ages. These incarnations are described in earlier books of the Bhāgavata Purāṇa.
15. *the three worlds*: In Hindu cosmography, there are upper, middle and lower realms in the universe.

CHAPTER 3
Kṛṣṇa's Birth

1. *The directions*: There are ten directions in Hindu cosmography: eight cardinal points on the horizontal plane (N, S, E, W, NE, NW, SE, SW), and the up and down directions on the vertical plane.
2. *brāhmaṇas*: There are four castes in the Hindu social system. The *brāhmaṇas* are the scholarly and priestly class.
3. *The kinnaras ... apsaras*: These are different types of celestial beings, most of whom are renowned for their singing, music and dancing.
4. *Janārdana [Kṛṣṇa]*: Janārdana is a name of Kṛṣṇa meaning 'one who stimulates men'.
5. *four arms ... and disc*: Kṛṣṇa is here exhibiting his form of Viṣṇu.
6. *śrīvatsa ... on his neck*: *Śrivatsa* is a tuft of hair on Viṣṇu's chest. The Kaustubha jewel was obtained after the ocean of milk was churned by the gods and the demons. Both are characteristic of Viṣṇu/Kṛṣṇa.
7. *Your form is pure bliss and majesty*: The Bhāgavata states that the body of God is not made from *prakṛti*, or matter, but from *brahman*. The ingredients of *brahman*, from at least the time of the Upaniṣads, are said to be *sat*, *cit* and *ānanda*, eternity, bliss and knowledge (see Introduction, pp. xxxvi ff.).
8. *One who considers ... is foolish*: This abstruse verse seems to be stating that matter has no existence separate from *ātmā*. Patañjali's Yoga Sūtras (II.18) state that *prakṛti*'s sole function is to provide either enjoyment or liberation to the *puruṣa* soul, and thus does not exist separately.
9. *you are brahman*: *Brahman* is the name for the absolute truth throughout Hinduism from at least the times of the Upaniṣads. Kṛṣṇa/Viṣṇu is understood as the highest aspect of *brahman* by Vaiṣṇavas.
10. *You will destroy ... masquerading as kings*: The main reason why the earth approached Brahmā in the first chapter was because she was afflicted by the burden of the tremendous build-up of military might in the world.
11. *parārdhas*: A *parārdha* is 100,000 billion human years. This period of time corresponds to fifty years, or half of Brahmā's life.
12. *when the manifest ... the unmanifest*: In Sāṅkhya, the metaphysical system accepted by the Purāṇas, the elements of creation evolve sequentially from undifferentiated primordial *prakṛti*, or

the material matrix (see Introduction, pp. xl–xliii). At the time of the dissolution of the universe, the process is reversed, and the elements withdraw again into undifferentiated *prakṛti*.

13. *Madhusūdana [Kṛṣṇa]*: Madhusūdana is a name of Kṛṣṇa that means 'killer of Madhu'. Madhu was a demon who was killed by Viṣṇu for attempting to steal the Vedas.
14. *at the end of Brahmā's night*: There is a partial dissolution of the universe at the end of each of Brahmā's days and nights, and a complete one at the end of his life of 100 years (see footnote 11, above).
15. *the era of Svāyambhuva Manu*: Each day of Brahmā is divided into fourteen periods, each one ruled by a different Manu.
16. *prajāpati*: The *prajāpatis* are progenitors of mankind.
17. *Sutapā*: Sutapā means one who performs ascetic disciplines.
18. *breath control*: The fourth limb of the eight-limbed path of *yoga* as outlined by Patañjali is *prāṇāyāma*, breath control.
19. *Vāmana [the dwarf]*: Vāmana is the dwarf incarnation of Viṣṇu who approached Bali in the guise of a young boy mendicant. Although Bali was king of the demons, and had usurped Indra's command of heaven, he was also respectful to *brāhmaṇas*, and offered Vāmana any favour he cared to choose. Vāmana asked for a mere three steps of land. However, when this was granted by Bali, he covered the whole earth with his first step, and the entire heavens with his second. When there was no place left to place the third step, Vāmana had Bali arrested for not fulfilling his promise. Bali then requested Vāmana to put his third step on his head, in an act of devotional submission. This story is narrated in the Bhāgavata (VIII.15–23), its theological message being that no one is barred from becoming a devotee of Viṣṇu, since even demons can do so.
20. *his yogamāyā power of illusion*: *Yogamāyā* is the power of illusion exerted by Kṛṣṇa such that the inhabitants of Vraj do not realize that he is the supreme Lord (see Introduction, pp. xxvi–xxix).
21. *Śeṣa . . . with his hoods*: Śeṣa is the thousand-hooded serpent upon whom Viṣṇu reclines in the ocean of milk. He incarnates as Balarāma.
22. *Yama the lord of death*: Yama is the Hindu equivalent of Pluto. He judges souls and determines their appropriateness for dwelling in the various heavens and hells of Hindu cosmography.
23. *as the ocean did . . . the goddess of fortune*: In the Rāmāyaṇa Epic, the ocean allows Rāma to cross over to Laṅkā on a bridge made of stones, in order to retrieve his wife, the captive Sītā.

24. *as he was before*: Kaṃsa had shackled Devakī and Vasudeva in 1.66.

CHAPTER 4
Kaṃsa's Encounter with the Goddess and his Council with his Ministers

1. *and bore the bow . . . and club*: According to the Devī Māhātmya (2.19ff.), Vāyu gave her the bow and arrows, Śiva the trident, Kāla the sword and shield, Varuṇa the conch and Viṣṇu the disc.
2. *Even the gods . . . mortals*: This is a reference to the disembodied voice that told Kaṃsa that the eighth child of his sister Devakī would kill him (X.1.34).
3. *The notion of difference . . . this truth*: With the notable exception of the commentator Madhva, one of the main tenets of Vedānta philosophizing is that there is some sort of oneness, *advaita* (literally non-duality), underlying all reality. This oneness, of course, is understood quite differently by Vedānta commentators such as Śaṅkara, Rāmānuja, Nimbārka, Vallabha and Baladeva. To perceive reality as separated from the one absolute truth is accepted by all these commentators as being illusion.
4. *thinks that the self is killed . . . ignorant person*: Compare with Gītā (II.19): 'One who thinks [the soul] is the killer and one who thinks it is killed, neither of them understand.'
5. *then we will today kill . . . pastures*: The similarities between this story and that of Herod in the New Testament caused some early Indologists to suppose that the Hindus had borrowed the narrative from early Christian sources. Eventually, however, it was pointed out that there was evidence to prove that the Kṛṣṇa story predated the common era.
6. *You do not kill . . . have stopped fighting*: There are certain codes of conduct incumbent on the *kṣatriya*, or warrior caste, in battle, which include injunctions such as these.
7. *who resides in hidden places*: Viṣṇu, as God, dwells within the heart of all living things.
8. *the Vedas*: The Vedas are the oldest texts that have been preserved from the Indo-Aryan, or Vedic people (and, indeed, the oldest Indo-European texts). There are four Vedas, three of which, the Ṛgveda, Sāmaveda and Yajurveda, primarily consist of hymns to be chanted in the performance of sacrifice. A fourth Veda, the Atharvaveda, is also chanted in sacrificial contexts, but contains material – spells, incantations, etc. – that is significantly different in nature from the other Vedas.

9. *assume any form at will*: *Yogīs* as well as powerful demons can transform their form at will.
10. *rājasic dispositions*: According to the Bhagavad Gītā (XVIII.23), action in *rajas* is characterized by self-interest and excessive endeavour. Those with such dispositions are passionate, desirous of the fruits of their actions, greedy, violent-natured, impure, and subject to joy and sorrow (XVIII.27). They cannot discriminate between wrong and right (XVIII.31), and tend towards duty, pleasures and wealth, desire and attachment to the fruits of action (XVIII.34). The happiness they attain is like nectar in the beginning, but like poison in the end (XVIII.38).
11. *bewildered by tamas*: The Bhagavad Gītā (XVIII.24) describes action in *tamas* as characterized by illusion. It disregards consequences and loss or injury to others, as well as to the performer's own capabilities. Those with such dispositions are undisciplined, vulgar, obstinate, wicked, deceitful, lazy, despondent and procrastinating (XVIII.28). They are enveloped in darkness, see everything in a perverted fashion, and imagine wrong to be right (XVIII.32). They are prone to sleep, fear, grief, depression and conceit (XVIII.35). The happiness they attain is delusive, and springs from sleep, indolence and negligence (XVIII.39).

CHAPTER 5
The Meeting of Nanda and Vasudeva

1. *sūta, māgadha and vandī bards*: *Sūtas* recite the Purāṇic histories, *māgadhas* the glories of royal lineages, and *vandīs*, that which is appropriate for the occasion.
2. *Ramā, the goddess of fortune*: The goddess of fortune is Viṣṇu's eternal consort and is typically called Śrī, or Ramā, in this text.
3. *cycle of saṃsāra*: *Saṃsāra* is the cycle of birth and death.
4. *dharma, artha and kāma*: *Dharma* involves abiding by one's religiously prescribed duties. As a consequence of this, *artha*, or prosperity, results, which, in turn, leads to *kāma*, or the satisfaction of desires. Since these three goals ultimately leave the human spirit unfulfilled, they lead to a fourth goal, *mokṣa*, or the desire for liberation from worldly existence.

CHAPTER 6
Pūtanā's Arrival in Vraj

1. *devotional activities . . . Sātvatas*: The path of *bhakti yoga*, or devotion to Viṣṇu/Kṛṣṇa, contains nine processes: hearing about the stories of the Lord, reciting them, remembering them, serving

the deity of the Lord, worshipping him, praising him, developing friendship with him, developing an attitude of service to him, and fully surrendering to him.

2. *all the directions*: See chapter 3, note 1.

3. *like Vṛtra struck by the thunderbolt*: This is a reference to the famous Ṛgvedic story where Indra battles the serpent Vṛtra and kills him with his thunderbolt.

4. *waving a cow's tail around him*: Such acts are considered auspicious, and ward off evil.

5. *on twelve different parts of his body*: Vaiṣṇavas mark their body with sacred clay in twelve different parts – the forehead, throat, chest, belly, left and right sides, left and right shoulders, left and right biceps, and top and bottom of the back – uttering a different name of Viṣṇu for each spot.

6. *bīja seed mantras*: A *bīja* seed *mantra* usually consists of the essential letter or syllable – generally the first letter followed by a nasal sound – of a deity's name, or of the entire name. This is followed by a formula invoking the deity's presence or protection in a particular part of the body.

7. *'May the unborn one protect your feet'*: This and the following four verses contain various names and references to Lord Viṣṇu.

8. *ḍākinīs . . . vināyakas*: These are all types of malevolent entities: *ḍākinīs* are a class of women who can perform magic with the use of *mantras*, and *yātudhānīs* and *kuṣmāṇḍās* are types of witches. *Piśācas* are very evil beings created by Brahmā, *rākṣasas* are demoniac beings created from Brahmā's anger, and *yakṣas* from his hunger. *Vināyakas* are another demoniac type of being.

9. *sadgati, the destination of saints*: *Sadgati* can refer to liberation. However, in verse 38 we are informed that Pūtanā attained *svarga*, which is the celestial realm, but still within the domain of *saṃsāra*, the cycle of birth and death.

10. *These feet . . . his devotees*: Offering respect and worship to a deity's feet is a very common devotional practice in Hinduism. In everyday life, touching someone with one's feet is an act of disrespect in India, since the feet, coming in contact with the pollutions of the streets, are the lowest part of the anatomy. Acknowledging that a deity's feet are sacred and worthy of worship, in contrast, underscores the purity and transcendence of the deity.

11. *Govinda [Kṛṣṇa]*: Govinda is a name of Kṛṣṇa meaning 'tender of cattle'.

CHAPTER 7
Deliverance from Tṛṇāvarta

1. *the twice-born*: After the sacred thread ceremony undertaken by the higher castes, members of Āryan society are considered to be 'twice-born'.
2. *when Rudra pierced the city with an arrow*: This is a reference to Lord Śiva's piercing of the three aerial cities called Tripura constructed by the celestial architect Maya. The demons had been granted a favour that these cities could only be destroyed when they were all in alignment, and then only by one arrow. Śiva accomplished this feat. See Śiva Purāṇa (Rudrasaṃhitā, Yuddhakhaṇḍa).
3. *Adhokṣaja [Viṣṇu]*: Adhokṣaja is a name of Kṛṣṇa and Viṣṇu and can mean 'one who is beyond sense perception'. According to the Mahābhārata (*uttara parva*, 70.10), it means 'one who is never diminished'.

CHAPTER 8
The Vision of the Universal Form

1. *the yuga*: A *yuga* is a period of time in Purāṇic cosmology. There are four *yugas* in a *caturyuga*, or four-*yuga* cycle: *satya yuga*, a golden age; *tretā yuga*; *dvāpara yuga*; and the present degenerate age of *kali yuga*. There are different incarnations of Viṣṇu, each one with a different complexion for each *yuga*. These are called *yugāvatāras* and are described in the eleventh book of the Bhāgavata (5.20 ff.).
2. *Vāsudeva*: There are various rules for the creation of patronymics in Sanskrit grammar, one of which is to extend the initial vowel of the father's name. Thus Vāsudeva is the son of Vasudeva.
3. *Nārāyaṇa*: Nārāyaṇa is generally used in the Bhāgavata as a synonym for Viṣṇu.
4. *līlā*: *Līlā* is the word used to refer to the sports or pastimes of Kṛṣṇa when he incarnates into the world. The term conveys an understanding that anything Kṛṣṇa does is determined by his own will, and for his own pleasure. It is not subject to the restrictions, control or expectations of the laws, norms and influences of this world (such as *māyā*, *dharma*, *karma*, *saṃsāra*, etc.) (see Introduction, pp. xxii–xxvi).
5. *She saw the circle . . . three guṇa qualities*: The senses, as well as the mind, intelligence, ego and the elements of matter – earth, water, fire, air, ether – all evolve from primordial matter, *prakṛti*

– as a result of the churning of the three *guṇas* (see Introduction, pp. xl–xliii).

6. *the three Vedas . . . Sātvata sages*: The Vedas are the oldest Indo-Aryan texts and are primarily hymns used in the sacrificial cult (see also chapter 4, note 8); for Sāṅkhya *yoga*, see Introduction, pp. xl–xliii; the Upaniṣads are the ancient philosophical texts of the late Vedic period; the *Sātvatas* are a tribe devoted to Kṛṣṇa.

7. *He, the greatly fortunate . . . became Yaśodā*: Sometimes the previous lives of characters in Kṛṣṇa's pastimes are noted, usually with a view to describing the types of activities they had previously performed that earned them the opportunity of associating so intimately with God.

CHAPTER 9
Kṛṣṇa's Favour to the Gopī *Yaśoda*

1. *guhyakas*: The *guhyakas* are a type of celestial being, and Kubera is the treasurer of the demigods.

CHAPTER 10
The Curse of Nārada

1. *grove of Kailāsa called Mandākinī*: Mount Kailāsa is the abode of Śiva.

2. *vāruṇī, an alcoholic drink*: This liquor is made from hogweed mixed with the juice of palm or date, and then distilled.

3. *the avyakta*: The *avyakta* (undifferentiated *prakṛti*) is the primordial material matrix before the evolution of the elements and the manifest world (see Introduction, pp. xl ff.).

4. *Sādhus*: *Sādhus* are ascetics who have given up all forms of material attachment such as family, home and the pursuit of sensual satisfaction, in the quest for truth and self-realization. Typically they wander around as ascetics with matted locks, wearing loincloths and carrying a staff and water pot.

5. *two celestial siddhas*: *Siddhas* are celestial beings. According to the Mahābhārata (*ādi parva* 70.15) they live in the Himālayas near the hermitage of Kaṇva.

6. *You are the mahat*: The *mahat*, also known as *buddhi*, is an evolute from *prakṛti*. It is cosmic (i.e. universal, undifferentiated) intelligence (see Introduction, p. xli).

7. *knower of the changes in all fields of activity*: In the Bhagavad Gītā, chapter 13, *prakṛti* (the material world) is known as *kṣetra* (the field), and *puruṣa* (the soul) is known as *kṣetrajña* (the knower of the field).

CHAPTER 11
The Killing of the Crane and Calf Demons

1. *Acyuta [Kṛṣṇa]*: Acyuta is a name of Kṛṣṇa or of Viṣṇu. It means 'one who does not fall down'.
2. *Daśārha [Kṛṣṇa]*: Daśārha is a name of Kṛṣṇa. Daśārha was a king of the Yadu dynasty, and his descendants are called the Daśārhas. Since Kṛṣṇa incarnated into this dynasty, he is sometimes called by this name.
3. *Bṛhadvana*: Bṛhadvana is another name for Gokula.
4. *Vṛndāvana*: Vṛndāvana means the forest of *vṛndā*. *Vṛndā* is another name for *tulasī*, a plant sacred to Vaiṣṇavas and related to basil. A *tulasī* leaf is always placed on the food offered daily to the deities in Vaiṣṇava temples and households.
5. *Balarāma*: Balarāma is sometimes called Baladeva in the text, here and elsewhere, but I have maintained the name Balarāma throughout to avoid confusion.
6. *kapitha tree*: The *kapitha* (the tree on which *kapis*, monkeys, are found) is the feronia elephantum.
7. *Bhagavān*: Although the term *Bhagavān* is generally used for God, it is, on occasion, used for a saintly person (see Introduction, pp. xix and lxxi, note 23).
8. *kathā*: *Kathā*, from the root *kath*, 'to speak about', refers to the public recitation of the activities of Kṛṣṇa.

CHAPTER 12
The Killing of the Demon Agha

1. *Thus, those boys . . . joyfully with Kṛṣṇa*: The merit to be able to take birth at the time of Kṛṣṇa's incarnation and participate in his *līlā* is understood as being the highest attainment of human life in the Vaiṣṇava *bhakti* schools. Such merit would have been accumulated throughout many past lives.
2. *sesame and water*: Sesame and water are offered as oblations to departed kinsmen. Agha is intending to kill the boys as an offering to his dead siblings.
3. *one yojana*: A *yojana* literally means the distance that can be covered in one harnessing, that is, without unyoking. It is typically considered to be about eight miles, although it is calculated variously.
4. *the ten directions*: See chapter 3, note 1.
5. *apsarās*: The *apsarās* are beautiful and seductive celestial nymphs.
6. *Hari's escape from death*: Śrīdhara notes that this escape from

death was only apparent. As the supreme, eternal being, Kṛṣṇa can never be threatened by death in reality; he creates these situations for the sake of *līlā* (see Introduction, pp. xxii ff.), and to enhance the devotion of his followers.

7. *atmāsāmya liberation*: There are five types of liberation in Vaiṣṇava theology: *sārūpya*, having the same form as the Lord; *sārṣṭi*, having the same opulence as the Lord; *sālokya*, living in the same abode as the Lord; *sāmīpya*, living close to the Lord; and *sāyujya*, merging with the Lord; *ātmasāmya* is *sārūpya*.

8. *lost the functions . . . Ananta [Kṛṣṇa]*: Śuka entered into an ecstatic state simply from thinking about Kṛṣṇa.

CHAPTER 13
Kṛṣṇa Manifests as the Calves and Cowherd Boys

1. *the enjoyer of sacrifices*: In the Bhagavad Gītā (5.29), Kṛṣṇa says that he is the enjoyer of sacrifices.

2. *'everything is the māyā of Viṣṇu'*: Śrīdhara does not provide the reference for this saying.

3. *The motherliness of the cows . . . without the illusion*: The motherly affection that the *gopīs* had previously had for their own sons did not change except that it was increased, since it was now directed to Kṛṣṇa himself, who had disguised himself as their sons, unbeknownst to them. Śrīdhara further explains that the conventional bonds of affection produced by illusion on the part of the cowherd boys, such as thinking 'this is my mother and I am her son', were absent with these cowherd boys since they were actually Kṛṣṇa himself.

4. *The affection of the people . . . as it had been for Kṛṣṇa*: Śrīdhara explains that previously the *gopīs* had more affection for Kṛṣṇa than for even their own sons, but now, since Kṛṣṇa had become their own sons, they had the same affection for these sons as they had previously had for Kṛṣṇa.

5. *rasa*: *Rasa*, literally 'taste', is the relishing of an aesthetic emotional flavour (see Introduction, pp. lx–lxi).

6. *why has she created this condition?*: Illusion, *māyā*, is a feminine entity. See also chapter 1, note 10.

7. *Lord of Vaikuṇṭha*: Vaikuṇṭha is the eternal *brahman* abode of Lord Viṣṇu, beyond the realm of *prakṛti*.

8. *Brahmā . . . merely an instant*: A *caturyuga* (the combination of the four *yugas*) is 3,600,000 human years. Seventy-one *caturyugas* equals a *manvantara*, the lifespan of Manu, the lawgiver of the universe. Fourteen of these, in turn, equal one day for

Brahmā, and his night is the same duration. Brahmā lives 100 years. A human year is thus only an instant for him.

9. *sattva and rajas*: The moon is compared with the *guṇa* of *sattva*, which is associated with pure white, protection and Viṣṇu, and the reddish colour of the eyes with *rajas*, which is associated with the colour red, creation and Brahmā.

10. *mystic powers . . . mahat*: There are eight primary mystic powers, *yogasiddhis*, attainable by the *yogī*, one of which is *aṇimā*, the power allowing one to shrink oneself down to atomic size. *Mahat*, or intelligence, is one of twenty-four derivatives evolving from the primordial matter of *prakṛti* (see Introduction, pp. xl–xliii).

11. *saṃskāras*: The *saṃskāras* are imprints of all the sense impressions and thoughts experienced in life after life that are recorded on the mental faculty. Memory and dream involve the ability to activate these impressions. They influence personality and are transmitted latently with the soul from body to body.

12. *truth, knowledge and unlimited bliss*: Viṣṇu and Kṛṣṇa have bodies that are not made from *prakṛtic* matter, but from *brahman* (see Introduction, pp. xxxvii–xxxix).

13. *the Upaniṣads themselves*: The Upaniṣads are ancient philosophical texts of the late Vedic period.

14. *from whom . . . manifests*: The last part of this sentence is almost identical to Muṇḍaka Upaniṣad, 2.2.10, and Śvetāśvatara Upaniṣad, 6.14.

15. *eleven senses*: The eleven senses are the mind, the knowledge-acquiring senses of hearing, sight, taste, touch and smell, and the working senses of legs, hands, tongue, anus and genitals.

16. *Thus he was unable . . . that which it is not*: In the Bṛhadāraṇyaka Upaniṣad (4.22), one heuristic process for arriving at an understanding of *brahman*, the absolute truth, is by eliminating everything known in the world: '*neti, neti*', it is 'not this', it is 'not that'. Another process is by affirming that '*sarvaṁ khalv idaṁ brahma*', 'all of this, indeed, is *brahman*' (Chāndogya Upaniṣad, 3.14).

17. *Ajita [Kṛṣṇa]*: Ajita is a name of Kṛṣṇa which means the unconquered one.

18. *without a second*: *advayam*, and similar terms, indicate that the ultimate truth is non-dual; everything emanates from Kṛṣṇa.

CHAPTER 14
Brahmā's Eulogy

1. *the essential nature of the self [ātmā] . . . unchangeable and formless*: The *ātmā* can only be known through itself, and not by any empirical means, since it is more subtle than the mind and senses. Its essential nature is pure awareness.
2. *an egg-like universe . . . and intelligence*: The universe, in Purāṇic cosmology, is enveloped by the eight sheaths of the material elements, each one ten times thicker than the preceding one. The fifth chapter of the Śrīmad Bhāgavata Purāṇa describes the structure of the universe, as well as the different planets and their inhabitants.
3. *You are endowed . . . like tiny atoms*: Viṣṇu lies upon the ocean of milk and from the pores of his skin millions of universes flow in and out with each of his inhalations and exhalations.
4. *Adhokṣaja [Kṛṣṇa]*: See chapter 7, note 3.
5. *But the statement . . . is not false*: Brahmā was born in a lotus grown from Nārāyaṇa/Viṣṇu's navel. Śrīdhara does not give a reference for this statement.
6. *Are you not Nārāyaṇa . . . the original man [nāra]*: This verse refers to a popular derivation of the name Nārāyaṇa.
7. *If this were true . . . disappear again?*: The third book of the Bhāgavata (chapter 8) describes how at the beginning of the creation Brahmā found himself sitting in the lotus growing from Viṣṇu's navel. Not understanding where he was or why he existed, he attempted to climb down the stem of the lotus for a long time in search of its origin. Failing to find this, he engaged in meditation, after which he was granted a vision of the primordial Viṣṇu.
8. *was by you revealed . . . in your stomach*: Yaśodā saw the universe in Kṛṣṇa's stomach when she looked in his mouth, in X.8.37–9.
9. *for the creation . . . for the destruction of the universe*: Brahmā creates the forms of the universe, Viṣṇu maintains them and Śiva destroys them at the time of annihilation. For Vaiṣṇavas, all three functions are performed under the auspices of Viṣṇu himself.
10. *your birth has occurred . . . animals and aquatics*: Viṣṇu incarnates among various species throughout the universe. Vāmana was an incarnation among the gods, Paraśurāma and Vyāsadeva among sages, Rāma and Kṛṣṇa among humans, Varāha among animals and Matsya among aquatics. The stories of these incarnations are recounted in earlier books of the Bhāgavata Purāṇa.

11. *The entire material manifestation . . . on a rope*: The illusion or ignorance of considering this world to be that which it is not is commonly compared (for example by the ninth-century teacher Śaṅkarācārya) to imagining a rope to be a snake. Through ignorance one thinks that the rope is a snake, thus experiencing fear and anxiety. However, on seeing the rope for what it is as a result of knowledge, the illusion of the snake disappears along with the fear and anxiety engendered by it, and one regains one's peace of mind and tranquillity. Likewise, seeing oneself as *ātmā* and the world as *brahman* is knowledge, but thinking oneself to be a body and the world to be matter is ignorance and engenders fear and anxiety.
12. *the eleven . . . the sense organs of those residents*: This is a reference to the eleven presiding deities, Śiva, Brahmā, etc., of the eleven senses. Since these control the functioning of the sense organs of all living beings, they also control the senses of the residents of Vraj. They therefore enjoy the *līlās* of Kṛṣṇa through the senses of the residents of Vraj.
13. *The most fortunate . . . [of the residents of Vraj]*: A typical devotional aspiration is to take birth as a blade of grass in Vraj so as to be touched by the dust from the feet of the Lord and his devotees. That even the dust from their feet is so desirable underscores both the sublimity of Kṛṣṇa and his devotees, and the humility required from the aspirant.
14. *Hṛṣīkeśa [Kṛṣṇa]*: Hṛṣīkeśa is a name of Kṛṣṇa that is construed in traditional sources as 'Lord (*īśa*) of the senses (*hṛṣīka*),' although, etymologically, it could mean 'one with bristly (*hṛṣī*) hair (*keśa*)'.
15. *Murāri [Kṛṣṇa]*: Murāri is a name of Kṛṣṇa and Viṣṇu. It means 'enemy of Mura', a demon who will be killed later (chapter 59).
16. *What Hari did . . . pauganḍa period [6–10 years]*: Since the cowherd boys were sleeping under the influence of Brahmā's *māyā* for an entire year, they did not recount the killing of the Agha demon, which took place when Kṛṣṇa was 5 years old, till the following year, when he had begun his *pauganḍa* period.

CHAPTER 15
The Killing of Dhenuka

1. *this universe is woven . . . my dear Parīksit*: The imagery of the universe being woven like a cloth on threads goes back at least to the Upaniṣads (e.g. Bṛhadāraṇyaka, III.8).

CHAPTER 16
The Banishment of Kāliya

1. *a distance of one hundred bows*: The longbow was a common unit of measurement in ancient India.
2. *ominous portents ... and on people*: Earth portents include earthquakes and other natural calamities, sky portents the raining of blood or meteors, and bodily portents the quivering of certain parts of the anatomy.
3. *footprints, which were marked with the signs of God*: Incarnations of God can be recognized by certain bodily characteristics. These include markings on the soles of the feet as described in the next verse.
4. *They perceived ... without their dear one*: See chapter 2, note 15.
5. *Garuḍa [Suparṇaka], the king of birds*: Garuda, the carrier of Viṣṇu, is a huge eagle. The name used for Garuḍa in this account is Suparṇaka.
6. *heaps of jewels on the serpent's head*: Certain serpents, such as the celestial *nāgas*, have jewels in their hoods.
7. *Nārāyaṇa*: Nārāyaṇa is another name for Viṣṇu among Vaiṣṇavas.
8. *Your incarnation ... the wicked*: See Bhagavad Gītā IV.8, where Kṛṣṇa says: 'To protect the righteous, destroy the wicked, and for the purpose of establishing *dharma*, I come *yuga* after *yuga*.'
9. *You are a sage accustomed to silence*: This is a reference to the incarnation of Viṣṇu in the form of Nārāyaṇa ṛṣi who spent many years in ascetic practice in the Himālayas with the sage Nara, who incarnated as Arjuna.
10. *Through your glance ... everything that exists*: At the end of each cosmic cycle, the *jīvas* who are still trapped in *saṃsāra* lie dormant within Viṣṇu until the next cosmic cycle begins. At this time, Viṣṇu reactivates their *guṇas* from their previous lives and they take up *saṃsāric* existence from where they left off.

CHAPTER 17
Deliverance from the Forest Fire

1. *the illustrious [Bhagavān] Garuḍa*: The term *Bhagavān* is used here for Garuḍa. Although overwhelmingly used as an epithet for Kṛṣṇa, it is occasionally used for other divine beings, and even for saintly or powerful mortals.

CHAPTER 18
The Killing of Pralamba

1. *Meru, king of mountains*: Meru is the golden-coloured mountain in the Himālayas that supports the celestial realm. It is a place of wonderful opulence, and the abode of all the gods.

CHAPTER 20
Description of Autumn

1. *the frogs ... religious observances*: This might be a reference to Ṛgveda VII.103.1, and Atharvaveda IV.15.13, where the croaking of the frogs is likened to the vociferous *brāhmaṇas* who recite the Veda after the *upākaraṇa*, or initiation ceremony, in the rainy season.
2. *just as the Vedas ... the influence of time*: In the present age of the *kaliyuga*, the meaning of the Vedas is considered to be obscured or lost because of the degenerative influence of the age and incompetence of the *brāhmaṇa* caste.
3. *The moon ... does not shine*: In most classical Hindu metaphysical thought, in addition to the five gross coverings of earth, water, fire, air and ether which produce the variety of different physical bodies in the universe, the soul is also covered by three subtle coverings – mind, intelligence and ego – which produce the variety of different psychological identifications in the universe. The ego is the covering which imposes false designations on the soul, such as imagining oneself to be black or white, male or female, Hindu or Christian, etc. (Śrīdhara gives the examples of thinking oneself to be a scholar, a generous person, a husband or a hero.) Such designations cause the soul to forget its own nature as pure consciousness and identify with such temporary, external characteristics. The ego is nonetheless *prakṛtic* [inert matter] (albeit subtle and invisible to the eye), and so can only appear to be animated because of the consciousness of the soul itself, just as the cloud can only appear to be illuminated because of the moon shining behind it. This simile points out that just as the light of the moon refracted through the clouds appears dim and coloured according to the nature of the cloud which is covering it, so the pure light of the self is refracted through the particular nature of the ego covering it in each individual. These ego coverings obscure the soul's awareness of itself as pure consciousness, and result in the plethora of false self-notions evident among people.
4. *and jambu fruits*: The *jambu* is the rose-apple tree.

5. *the āśrama*: In addition to the social division of society into four *varṇas* (see Introduction, p. xlix), ancient Hindu texts also divided the lifespan of individuals into four *āśramas* or stages. These are *brahmacārya* (studentship), *gṛhastha* (householder), *vānaprasthya* (forest dweller) and *sannyāsa* (homeless ascetic).
6. *the āgama [ritualistic texts]*: The *āgama* texts contain a variety of material, including detailed prescriptions as to how to perform ritualistic worship, generally to the deities of either Viṣṇu or Śiva or Devī.
7. *śabdabrahman*: *Śabdabrahman*, or sonic *brahman*, is the absolute truth manifest in the form of sound, especially the sound *om*. For Vaiṣṇavas, the names of Viṣṇu and Kṛṣṇa are considered *śabdabrahman*, and are repeated during meditation, which is called *japa*.
8. *āgrayaṇa ceremonies*: This is described in the Gṛhya Sūtras as the occasion when *navānna*, 'feeding on new rice', is celebrated.
9. *the two kalās . . . of Hari*: The Sanskrit term *kalā* indicates a part of something, and has a similar meaning to *aṃśa* (although some commentators claim that an *aṃśa* is more important, or embodies more of the potency or presence of the Godhead, than a *kalā*). Viśvanātha from the Gauḍiya school, which holds that Kṛṣṇa is the Godhead himself and not a partial incarnation, reads *kalābhyāṁ hareḥ* differently. He construes *hareḥ* as the moon, and *kalābhyām* as the two phases of the moon (see Introduction, pp. xix–xxii and lxxii, note 29.).
10. *snāta students*: A *snāta* student is one who has taken the ceremonial bath after completing his period of studentship, and is ready to return home and enter the period of *gṛhastha*, or householder.
11. *siddha yogis . . . appropriate time comes*: Śrīdhara notes that the *siddhas* are restricted by their spans of life, after which they obtain the fruits of their *yoga* by becoming celestial beings, etc. *Siddhas* are a type of celestial being, but when used in the context of *yoga* practice, the term denotes those who possess mystic powers.

CHAPTER 21
The Vision of Kṛṣṇa

1. *Madhus*: The Madhus is another name for the Yādavas.
2. *Kāma*: Kāma, the Hindu Cupid, is similar to his western counterpart. He is generally depicted as a naked youth who flies around piercing his victims with flowery arrows of love.

3. *a vaijayantī garland*: The *vaijayantī* garland is generally worn when anticipating victory. It has the quality of never fading.
4. *Dāmodara's [Kṛṣṇa]*: Dāmodara is a name of Kṛṣṇa which means 'he whose belly is bound'. It specifically refers to the *līlā* in chapter 9 of this text.
5. *The rivers . . . trees shed tears*: Śrīdhara explains that the rivers are like mothers to the bamboo flute – since bamboo is nourished by their waters – and so they are delighted that someone in their family has become a servant of *Bhagavān*, like any noble person would be. They experience the hairs rising in ecstasy on their skin in the form of lotuses growing from the surface of their waters. The trees, which are also related to the bamboo, are similarly ecstatic and shed tears of joy in the form of honey.
6. *noble Āryan people*: See Introduction, note 66.
7. *celestial air vehicles*: See Introduction, note 46.
8. *streams of flowers*: Śrīdhara notes that the streams of flowers refer to rain which resembled flowers.
9. *The Pulinda women . . . became contented*: Urugāya is a name of Kṛṣṇa or Viṣṇu that means 'One who takes wide steps', and refers to the story of the Vāmana dwarf incarnation. The meaning of this verse is that since this powder had touched Kṛṣṇa's feet (by the *gopīs* placing them on their breasts) the Pulinda women became ecstatic. The *kuṅkum*, although itself reddish, became further reddened from touching Kṛṣṇa's red feet.

CHAPTER 22
Kṛṣṇa Steals the Gopīs' *Clothes*

1. *great yoginī*: a *yoginī* is a female *yogī*.
2. *pūjā worship*: *Pūjā* is devotional ritual worship of a deity, typically including the offering of incense, flowers and ghee lamps, that is often performed informally or at home.
3. *Bhadrakālī*: Bhadrakālī and Kātyāyanī (verse 4) are different names and forms of the goddess.
4. *Śyāmasundara [Kṛṣṇa]*: Śyāmasundara is a name of Kṛṣṇa and means 'the beautiful black or dark-blue one'.
5. *Seeing that they were virgins*: Śrīdhara takes *āhatāḥ* to mean with 'unbroken vaginas', that is, virgins.
6. *deviation from their vow*: There is a play here between 'deviation', *cyuta*, and one of Kṛṣṇa's names, Acyuta, 'he who does not deviate'.
7. *The desire of those . . . sprouting*: The sense here is that desire for enjoyment in the world of *saṃsāra* results in activities that

plant seeds of *karma*. These then sprout, bear fruit and then produce further seeds in turn, and so the cycle of *saṃsāra* is perpetuated. However, focusing one's desires on Kṛṣṇa is highly desirable, since God is the appropriate object of all desire, and doing so causes one to lose interest in all other worldly or self-centred desires. Desire which is centred on Kṛṣṇa no longer produces seeds of further *karma*, and old *karma* is burnt up, just as fried grain can no longer produce seeds that sprout. *Bhakti yoga*, the path of devotion, involves fixing the mind on Kṛṣṇa, rather than trying to still the mind or withdraw it from thoughts.

CHAPTER 23
The Deliverance of the Wives of the Sacrificers

1. *They fell on the ground . . . like sticks*: The term *daṇḍavat*, 'like a stick', which has come to mean 'thank you' in Hindi, means falling down with a straight body fully extended like a stick, in order to offer maximum respect (as opposed to other types of obeisance such as that offered with the knees bent).
2. *The eating of food . . . sautrāmaṇī sacrifice*: The Aitareya Brāhmaṇa (VI.9) says that in an animal sacrifice, the eating of grains by one who has been consecrated should not occur until the performance of the sacrifice. The *sautrāmaṇī* sacrifice is a four-day sacrifice to Indra as protector.
3. *mantras, tantra rituals, ṛtvik priests*: In the Vedic period, the *mantras* are the sacred formulae uttered at the sacrifice. In later times, a *mantra* denotes any sacred utterance, particularly one containing the name of a deity. *Tantra* in the same period denoted the use of an expression that was valid for several consecutive oblations. In later times, it refers to non-Vedic esoteric practices usually associated with Śaivite and Śakta sects. A *ṛtvik* was an officiating priest at the Vedic sacrifice.
4. *patnīśālā*: The *patnīśālā*, the women's quarter, is situated in the south-west corner of the *vedi*, or sacrificial arena.
5. *the four types of food*: Foods are divided as to whether they are licked, swallowed, chewed or sucked.
6. *with your participation*: The participation of the wife was required in Vedic sacrifices.
7. *Abide by your own doctrine*: Kṛṣṇa makes numerous statements such as: 'Abandon all types of *dharma* and simply come exclusively to my shelter, I will free you from all sin, do not worry' (Bhagavad Gītā, XVIII.66); and 'Those who take shelter of me,

even if they be of sinful birth, women, merchants or labourers, attain the supreme destination' (Bhagavad Gītā, IX.32).

8. *the wives . . . sacrificial enclosure*: This contrasts with the *gopīs*, who, in chapter 29, refuse to be persuaded by Kṛṣṇa to go home.
9. *that birth which is threefold*: Śrīdhara considers these to be *śauklam* (birth from pure parents), *sāvitram* (initiation as a *brāhmaṇa* in the sacred thread ceremony) and *daikṣam* (initiation for the performance of sacrifice).
10. *the saṃskāra purificatory rites of the twice-born*: The *saṃskāras* are various rites of passage undergone throughout one's lifetime. Twelve of these are enjoined for *brāhmaṇa* males.
11. *the goddess of fortune . . . of her own nature*: Śrīdhara explains that these faults are pride and fickleness. One of the names of Śrī, the goddess of fortune, is Cañcalā, 'the fickle one', since fortune and wealth never stay with the same person for long.
12. *but they did not go, out of fear of Kaṃsa*: The *brāhmaṇas*' unwillingness to face danger in order to see Kṛṣṇa, even after they had repented and recognized his status, contrasts with the attitude of their wives (and, even more so, of the *gopīs*), who were prepared to face any obstacle to be with Kṛṣṇa.

CHAPTER 24
Kṛṣṇa Diverts Indra's Sacrifice

1. *this act of yoga*: *Kriyā yoga*, or *karma yoga*, is explained throughout the Gītā (especially chapter 3) as the performance of one's duty without desire for the result.
2. *the threefold goals of life*: These are *dharma*, religious duty; *artha*, prosperity; and *kāma*, enjoyment.
3. *A brāhmaṇa . . . service to the twice-born*: The social system of ancient India is divided into four castes. The *brāhmaṇas* are the priestly caste, the *kṣatriyas* the warrior caste, the *vaiśyas* the merchant and landowning caste, and the *śūdras* the labouring caste.
4. *mutual interaction*: Śrīdhara takes 'mutual interaction' to be the union between the sexes.

CHAPTER 25
Kṛṣṇa Lifts Mount Govardhana

1. *the annihilation of the universe*: The universe undergoes partial as well as complete annihilation at the end of various cycles of time before being re-created anew. At these terminal points of the cycle, the universe is inundated with water from rain clouds.

2. *my elephant Airāvata*: Airāvata, a white elephant produced when the gods and demons churned the ocean of milk, is Indra's carrier.
3. *Maruts*: Indra, as the god of rain, is often accompanied by the Maruts, who are storm gods.
4. *Tumburu*: Tumburu is the best musician amongst the *gandharvas*. (There is also a sage by this name who visited Rāma in the forest during his exile.)

CHAPTER 27
Indra's Eulogy

1. *Surabhi . . . Goloka*: A *surabhi* is a celestial cow which provides milk for the gods and sages whenever required. Goloka, which means the place of cows, is the name for Kṛṣṇa's eternal abode.
2. *Your dhāma [form]*: *Dhāma* can also mean abode. Śrīdhara glosses this with *svarūpa*, form.
3. *composed of virtue*: Śrīdhara glosses *tapomaya*, which generally means 'consisting of religious penance', as *pracurjñāna*, 'full of knowledge'.
4. *Bhagavān dispenses discipline . . . miscreants*: See Bhagavad Gītā, IV.8, where Kṛṣṇa says that he appears in every *yuga* in order to protect the *sādhus*, destroy the miscreants and establish *dharma*.
5. *Maghavan*: Maghavan (literally 'possessing gifts', 'bountiful') is another name of Indra.

CHAPTER 28
Kṛṣṇa Reveals his Abode

1. *Varuṇa, lord of the waters*: Varuṇa is one of the *lokapālas*, 'guardians of the universe'. He resides within the waters.
2. *the guardian of the world*: There are four *lokapālas*, 'guardians of the universe': Indra, Agni, Yama and Varuna.
3. *Brahmahrada*: *Brahmahrada* means 'lake of *brahman*'. Śrīdhara says that *brahman* is like a lake because of the unique experience of awareness of those who are immersed in it. He also notes that *Brahmahrada* refers to the place in the Yamunā where Akrūra had a similar vision.
4. *immersed . . . consciousness*: Śrīdhara states that they were immersed, and then aroused from *samādhi*, the ultimate state of pure awareness, by Kṛṣṇa.
5. *the abode of brahman, Vaikuṇṭha*: Śrīdhara glosses the *loka* of *brahman*, or abode of *brahman*, with Viṣṇu's realm of Vaikuṇṭha.
6. *Akrūra . . . Balarāma*: Akrūra's vision of Kṛṣṇa's abode in the Yamunā occurs later in the narrative of the text (see chapter

39). Śrīdhara points out that *purā* [previously] relates to Śuka's retelling of events to Parīkṣit long after these events had taken place.

CHAPTER 29
The Description of the Rāsa *Pastime*

1. *Rāsa Pastime*: The *rāsa* pastime refers to Kṛṣṇa's dance with the *gopīs*. It should not be confused with *rasa* (see Glossary).
2. *Kāma*: See chapter 21, note 2.
3. *[The karma] from ... through meditation*: Both impious deeds and auspicious deeds are the source of bondage, since both require that the performer undergo rebirth in order to experience the good or bad results that accrue from such deeds.
4. *in the same way as ... Hṛṣīkeśa*: Any kind of meditation upon God, even in hatred, results in the purification and ultimate liberation of the meditator. This underscores the purity and potency of God.
5. *Tulasī*: Tulasī is another consort of Viṣṇu, who takes the form of a plant. All Vaiṣṇava temples and households in India grow this plant, since Viṣṇu and his incarnations will not accept food offerings unless a leaf of *tulasī* is placed upon the food on the offering plate. Kṛṣṇa often wears a *tulasī* garland.

CHAPTER 30
Searching for Kṛṣṇa in the Rāsa *Pastime*

1. *O earth ... performed?*: The sense is that the earth is most fortunate since it is constantly being touched by the feet of Kṛṣṇa. The trees are the hair of the earth, and they are described here as standing erect with bliss. The earth therefore must have performed intensely austere practices in previous births to have earned this privilege.
2. *Urukrama?*: Urukrama is Vāmanadeva, the dwarf incarnation of Viṣṇu. See chapter 3, note 19.
3. *Varāha?*: Varāha is the boar incarnation of Viṣṇu, who lifted the earth from the ocean where it had fallen because of the agitation of the demons. The accounts of these and other previous incarnations are narrated in earlier books of the Bhāgavata Purāṇa.
4. *worshipped*: The word for 'worshipped' here is *ārādhitaḥ*, the past passive participle of the verb *ārādh*, 'to worship'. Gauḍīya commentators of the Chaitanya school of Vaiṣṇavism see this as a veiled reference to a nominal form of this root, Rādhā, which

is the name of Kṛṣṇa's primary consort, who is otherwise not mentioned in the text.

5. *31a*: This verse is not found in Śrīdhara, but is found in a number of other editions.

CHAPTER 31
The Gopīs' *Song in the* Rāsa *Pastime*

1. *a yuga*: A *yuga* is 4,320,000 years.
2. *He who created eyelashes . . . locks of hair*: The sense, here, is that even blinking causes an unwelcome momentary interruption in gazing at Kṛṣṇa's face.

CHAPTER 32
The Gopīs' *Lamentation in the* Rāsa *Pastime*

1. *just as the Vedas . . . hearts' desire*: According to Śrīdhara: 'in their *karma kāṇḍa* [ritualistic sacrificial sections], the Vedas, not seeing the Supreme Lord, remain unfulfilled because of those attachments [to the fruits of the sacrifice] which are born of desire. But, in the *jñāna kāṇḍa* sections, after seeing the supreme soul, they are then filled with bliss and renounce the attachments produced by desire.' The sense of this is as follows: the *karma kāṇḍa* sections of the Vedas deal with the specifics of ritual sacrifice, which are performed in order to attain worldly benefits. Since Kṛṣṇa only appears to those who are free of all desire for worldly enjoyments, he does not appear in these sections of the Vedas. Thus, the Vedas, personified, who are devotees of the Lord, remain unfulfilled in these sections. The *jñāna kāṇḍa* sections of the Vedas, however, which stress detachment, discuss the supreme soul (correlated with Kṛṣṇa in the Bhāgavata), and thus the Vedas become blissful due to the appearance of the Lord in these sections.

CHAPTER 33
The Description of the Rāsa *Pastime*

1. *rāsa pastime*: See chapter 29, note 1.
2. *the chiefs of the gandharvas*: The *gandharvas* are celestial beings who are renowned for their beautiful singing.
3. *the circle of the rāsa*: The *rāsa* dance is a circle dance between Kṛṣṇa and the *gopīs*.
4. *Lakṣmī*: Lakṣmī is Śrī, the goddess of fortune and consort of Viṣṇu.

5. *dharma ... non-dharma*: *Dharma* encompasses religious and moral as well as social duty. *Adharma* is its antonym.
6. *just as one who is not Śiva ... the ocean*: When the gods and the demons churned the ocean of milk, poison was produced as well as various valuable things. Śiva drank the poison, as a result of which his throat turned blue. The story is narrated in the eighth book of the Bhāgavata (chapters 6–9).
7. *When the duration of Brahmā's night had expired*: Brahmā's night lasts 4,320 million years, as does his day. He lives for 100 years of such days and nights.

CHAPTER 34
The Killing of Śaṅkhacūḍa

1. *guhyakas*: The *guhyakas* are *yakṣas*, a class of demigods.

CHAPTER 35
The Song of a Pair of Gopīs

1. *and lightning ... his chest*: Śrīdhara notes that the lightning is a reference to Lakṣmī, the goddess of fortune, who only remains in one place fleetingly, except for on the chest of Lord Viṣṇu, where she can always be found.
2. *she remains ... motionless*: Śrīdhara explains that the river has little piety, like the *gopīs*, because they both cannot attain Kṛṣṇa. As the *gopīs* remain with their arms trembling with love, so do the rivers with their waves; as the tears remain motionless in the eyes of the *gopīs*, so do the waters of the river.
3. *their bodies bristling ... streams of honey*: The trees here are manifesting the bodily symptoms of ecstasy, one of which is to weep.
4. *tilaka*: *Tilaka* is sacred clay worn on the forehead.
5. *O chaste lady*: In the bewilderment of their love, the *gopīs* seem to be addressing these words sometimes to individual *gopīs*, sometimes to several *gopīs* and sometimes to Yaśodā in her absence.

CHAPTER 36
The Dispatching of Akrūra

1. *slapped his arms*: Slapping the arms or thighs is a habit of Indian wrestlers when they are preparing to fight.
2. *the potent sage Nārada*: The term *bhagavān*, which can be translated as 'potent', is used here for Nārada (see chapter 17, note 1).

3. *These men . . . those two boys*: Most of the demons who attacked Vraj were either sent by Kaṃsa, or were his friends.
4. *Bho! Bho!*: *Bho!* is a common exclamation in classical Sanskrit.
5. In Vijayadhvaja's and Vīrarāghava's commentaries, thirty-three verses are added here explaining the circumstances of Kaṃsa's conception. In these verses, Kaṃsa explains that his chaste mother, the wife of Ugrasena the king of the Bhojas, was once strolling in the palace gardens. A celestial *gandharva* assumed the form of her husband and approached to enjoy her. After their union, she discovered that he was not her real husband but an impostor. Enraged at the deceit and that her chastity had been violated, she cursed the *gandharva*'s son, the fruit of their union, to be a cruel sinner. When the *gandharva* found out about the incident, he added a further curse against the coming child, namely that he would be inimical towards his relatives. As a result of this, the sinful Kaṃsa was born with a deadly grudge against his family.
6. *The bow sacrifice*: In his commentary, Vallabha states that Kaṃsa wanted to counter the power of Viṣṇu inherent in Kṛṣṇa by propitiating Śiva. He notes that in the Śiva *tantra*, Śiva is worshipped as presiding over the bow, which would thereby accomplish victory in battle. This ritual is called *dhanuryāga*, 'the bow sacrifice' (quoted in Tagare, 1978, 1478).
7. *Akrūra*: Akrūra is an uncle and devotee of Kṛṣṇa.

CHAPTER 37
The Killing of the Demon Vyoma

1. *the demonic pramathas and rākṣasas*: *Pramathas* are a type of demonic being, as are *rākṣasas*. During creation, when various species in the universe were born from various aspects of Brahmā, *rākṣasas* were born out of his anger. They devour cows and *brāhmaṇas*.
2. *the gods*: The term used for gods here is *animiṣa* [unblinking]. Gods can be identified because they do not blink, they wear garlands that do not fade, and their feet do not touch the ground.
3. *the marriage of the daughters of the heroes*: See chapter 60 for Kṛṣṇa's marriage to 16,000 princesses simultaneously.
4. *the city of Kāśī*: Kāṣī is the modern city of Varanasi.
5. *the akṣauhiṇī battalions*: An *akṣauhiṇī* consists of 21,870 elephants, 21,870 chariots, 65,610 horses, and 10,350 foot-soldiers. Nārada is here referring to the Mahābhārata war.

CHAPTER 38
The Arrival of Akrūra

1. *the deer are passing me on the right*: This is an auspicious omen.
2. *These are created ... his glance*: This is a reference to Viṣṇu depositing the *jīvas* into *prakṛti* through his glance at the beginning of each new cycle of creation.
3. *that is the abode ... the goddess of fortune*: Śrī is always to be found on Viṣṇu's chest.
4. *Kauśika ... the three worlds*: Śrīdhara glosses Kauśika as Indra, but does not elaborate on this reference, simply noting that Kauśika delivered something to Viṣṇu at some point. Bali's offering, in VIII.8–9, consisted of water, which he gave to the dwarf incarnation of Vāmana at the time of granting him three steps of land. See chapter 3, note 19.
5. *As knower of the field of the body*: In the thirteenth chapter of the Gītā, Kṛṣṇa describes the relationship between *kṣetra* [the field of *prakṛti*, or matter] and *kṣetrajña* [the knower of the field, the *ātmā* or soul]. Kṛṣṇa is also the knower of the field.
6. *the kalpavṛkṣa tree ... is solicited*: The *kalpavṛkṣa* tree of the gods bestows whatever object is requested from it.
7. *The pure dust ... of all the planets*: The sense here is that such rulers bow down their heads at Kṛṣṇa's feet.
8. *They were youths*: The term for 'youths' here – '*kiśora*' – refers to the period between eleven and fifteen.
9. *of black and white complexion [respectively]*: Kṛṣṇa is black and Balarāma white.
10. *an offering of madhuparka*: In Purāṇic times, *madhuparka* consisted of a mixture of honey and milk, and was offered to guests.

CHAPTER 39
The Return of Akrūra

1. *Śauri's [Kṛṣṇa] words*: Śauri is another patronymic of Kṛṣṇa. Śūra was Kṛṣṇa's grandfather.
2. *Akrūra ... [krūra]*: An *a* placed before a noun in Sanskrit negates that noun (as it does in certain instances in English, e.g. 'theistic' and 'atheistic').
3. *the night was like a moment for us*: There is a play here, between 'night' [*kṣaṇadā*] and 'instant' [*kṣaṇa*]. This is an *alaṅkāra*, or poetic embellishment, known as *yamaka* (see Introduction, p. lxiv).
4. *Ananta*: Ananta is a thousand-headed serpent who supports the

world on his hoods and upon whom Lord Viṣṇu reclines in the ocean of milk, Śvetadvīpa. Balarāma is an incarnation of Ananta.

5. *Mitra*: Mitra is one of the twelve Sūryas born to Aditi, the mother of the gods. The Sūryas are associated with the sun.
6. *The lord of serpents*: Ananta (Śeṣa) (see note 4).
7. *Śveta, the white mountain*: There is a reference to the Pāṇḍavas crossing this mountain when they were exiled in the forest (Mahābhārata, *uttara kāṇḍa*, *vana parva*, 139.1).
8. *sacred thread*: *Brāhmaṇas* wear a loop of thread (made of several strands) draped over their right shoulder and extending down to their left side. The thumb of the right hand is encircled by this thread when they chant the sacred *gāyatrī mantra* three times a day.
9. *Sunanda and Nanda*: Śrīdhara does not indicate who Sunanda and Nanda are.
10. *Sanaka and the others*: This refers to the four Kumāras (boy sages): Sanaka, Sanandana, Sanātana and Sanat. According to the Bhāgavata, when, even though still children, they were asked to produce offspring by Brahmā, they refused. From Brahmā's resulting anger, Śiva was generated. The four Kumāras also cursed the two gatekeepers of Viṣṇu's transcendent abode, Vaikuṇṭha, for failing to respect them.
11. *Brahmā and Rudra*: In the Bhāgavata Purāṇa (III.12), Rudra, 'the wailer', gets his name because he was born wailing from the forehead of Brahmā after the latter was angry with the four Kumāras.
12. *nine . . . brāhmaṇas*: Śrīdhara identifies these nine sages as Marīci and company (although Marīci is elsewhere listed, along with Aṅgirā, Atri, Pulastya, Pulaha and Kratu, as one of six sages born from Brahmā's mind).
13. *Prahlāda*: Prahlāda is the great child devotee of Hari. He survived a number of murderous attempts by his demonic father, Hiraṇyakaśipu, by taking refuge with Lord Hari, who eventually incarnated as the half-man, half-lion Nṛsiṃha to save his devotee. His story is described in the Bhāgavata (VII.7–11).
14. *Vasu*: Śrīdhara identifies this Vasu as Uparicaravasu, 'the Vasu travelling above', so named because he was given an aerial conveyance by Indra as a result of his intensely austere practices. There are eight Vasus identified variously in different texts.
15. *He was attended by . . . Māyā, illusion*: These are all different forms and qualities of the goddess.

CHAPTER 40
Akrūra's Eulogy

1. *earth, water . . . all the sense objects*: These are all ingredients of the universe according to the Sāṅkhya school.
2. *supplementary bodies of knowledge*: These supplementary bodies of knowledge, *vidyās*, including the six *vedāṅgas*, or limbs of the Vedas – astronomy, etymology, phonetics, grammar, metre and knowledge of the ceremonies – are accessories to the proper performance of the sacrifice.
3. *the three sacred fires*: The standard form of Vedic sacrifice included three sacred fires which were placed in fire altars, or open fires placed in enclosures of various shapes made with layers of bricks around a central space on a brick base: the *dakṣiṇāgni*, 'southern fire', placed in a sacrificial fire-altar of semi-circular shape, situated on the southern side of the ritual enclosure, which protected the ritual from malignant influences; the *gārhapatya*, 'domestic altar', a sacrificial fire altar of circular shape situated on the western side of the ritual enclosure, in which the domestic fire was installed and the oblations were cooked; and the *āhavanīya*, the square offering-altar situated on the eastern side of the ritual enclosure, in which the offering fire was installed and the oblations offered.
4. *the prescriptions presented by you*: Śrīdhara identifies these as the *pañcarātra*, the ritualistic texts expounding the details of Vaiṣṇava worship and practice.
5. *And still others . . . many teachers*: There are many Śaivite sects such as the Kāpālikas, Kālāmukhas and Pāśupatas.
6. *Those who are . . . O master*: Compare this with Bhagavad Gītā (IX.23): 'Even those who worship other gods with faith actually worship me, but they do so in ignorance.'
7. *Just as the rivers . . . in the end*: Compare this with the Chāndogya Upaniṣad (VI.1.10): 'These rivers, my dear, flow from the east to the east, and from the west to the west. They just go from sea to sea. They become the sea itself.'
8. *Prajāpati*: In order to facilitate creation, Brahmā created *prajāpatis*, 'lords of offspring', as secondary creators.
9. *forms you assume for sport*: The incarnations that are listed in the following verses are described in detail in earlier chapters of the Bhāgavata Purāṇa (as well as in other Purāṇas).
10. *Matsya, the fish incarnation*: Once, the Vedas were stolen by a demon who hid them at the bottom of the ocean. Viṣṇu, in the

form of Matsya, a fish, retrieved them. This incarnation also features in another narrative strikingly similar to the Biblical one. When the world was once inundated with water, Vaivasvata Manu made a huge boat within which he placed seven sages and various seeds. The earth was deluged by rain, and everything was destroyed except the seven sages and the seeds in the boat, which was towed to safety by the Matsya *avatāra*. The story is narrated in the Bhāgavata (VIII.24).

11. *pralaya, the dissolution of the universe*: There are two major *pralayas*, a complete one at the end of Brahmā's life, and a partial one at the end of his day. During these *pralayas*, clouds rain incessantly, immersing the creation in water.

12. *who appeared . . . [Hayagriva]*: According to the Skanda Purāṇa, Brahmā and the other gods conducted a test to see who was the greatest among them. When Viṣṇu easily won, a curse was put upon him by Brahmā that he would lose his head. He consequently attached a horse's head in its place to attend a sacrifice conducted by the gods, after which he regained his own head.

13. *Madhu and Kaiṭabha*: Madhu and Kaiṭabha were two demons born from the ear-wax of Viṣṇu, who attempted to steal the Vedas from Brahmā. Although they had been granted a favour by Devī, the goddess, that they could never be killed on land, they were eventually killed by the trickery of Viṣṇu on the water. Slightly different variants of this story are narrated in the Mahābhārata (*śānti parva*) and the Devī Purāṇa (chapter 1).

14. *who bore the Mandara mountain*: When the gods and demons churned the ocean of milk to obtain the nectar of immortality, they used the Mandara mountain as the churning stick. It was supported by Kūrma, the tortoise incarnation. This story is narrated in the Bhāgavata (VII.6–7).

15. *a boar [Varāha] . . . the earth*: The Varāha incarnation rescued the earth from the clutches of the demon Hiraṇyāksa (Bhāgavata III.13 and 19).

16. *the amazing lion [Nṛsiṃha] . . . people*: Nṛsiṃha, mentioned earlier, is the half-man, half-lion incarnation who saved the child devotee Prahlāda from his murderous father. Since the latter had received an assurance that he could not be killed by either man or beast (nor under a variety of other conditions), Viṣṇu assumed this hybrid form and thwarted the various conditions to kill the demon. This story is narrated in the Bhāgavata (VIII.2–10).

17. *Vāmana . . . the three worlds*: Vāmana is the dwarf incarnation of Viṣṇu. See chapter 3, note 19.

18. *[Paraśurāma] . . . warriors*: Paraśurāma exterminated the proud warrior race twenty-one times. This is narrated in the Bhāgavata (IX.15–16).
19. *[Rāma] . . . Rāvaṇa*: This is the well-known Rāma of the Rāmāyaṇa Epic, who rescued his wife Sītā after she was kidnapped by the demon Rāvaṇa. The story is only briefly referred to in the Bhāgavata (IX.10–11).
20. *Vāsudeva . . . Aniruddha*: Vāsudeva, Saṅkarṣaṇa, Pradyumna and Aniruddha form the *catur vyūha*, the four derivative forms of Viṣṇu that are prominent in the Pañcarātra texts, and in the theologies of Vaiṣṇava sects, particularly that of Rāmānuja. In the tenth book, Vāsudeva is Kṛṣṇa, Saṅkarṣaṇa is Balarāma, Pradyumna is Kṛṣṇa's son from Rukmiṇi, and Aniruddha is Pradyumna's son, Kṛṣṇa's grandson.
21. *the pure Buddha*: The Buddha is considered an incarnation of Viṣṇu in several Purāṇas, but, unlike the other *avatāras* whose stories are recounted, he is only fleetingly referred to. This suggests to scholars that he was subsumed into the list of *avatāras* at a late stage.
22. *the daityas and dānavas*: The *daityas* are the demons born of Diti, and the *dānavas* of Danu, both wives of Kaśyapa. Desiring a son, Diti once interrupted her husband's early morning meditation to solicit sex. Kaśyapa asked her to wait for a few minutes, warning that dawn was an inauspicious time for such acts since this was the time Śiva returned from the cremation grounds with his ghoul followers, but she would not desist and seduced him. Kaśyapa consequently informed her that she would be the mother of the demons Hiraṇyakaśipu and Hiraṇyākṣa. The story is narrated in the Śrīmad Bhāgavata (III.14).
23. *Kalki*: The Kalki *avatāra* is the last in the list of *avatāras*, and has yet to come. He will ride a white horse, and exterminate the degraded mass of humanity at the end of *kaliyuga*, the present world age. A description of his activities is outlined in the Agni Purāṇa (chapter 16).
24. *mlecchas*: The Mahābhārata (*ādiparva*, 174.38) describes the *mlecchas* as people born from the tail of Vasiṣṭha's celestial cow, who defeated the army of his rival Viśvāmitra. Generally the term is a derogatory one referring to foreigners or to people living outside the norms of the Vedic social system.
25. *aham mama ['I and mine']*: *Aham* ['I'] refers to the false notion of thinking oneself to be what one is not, namely, the body and

mind (since the *ātmā*, or real self, is distinct from these), and *mama* ['my'] of imagining that one actually owns objects in this world.

CHAPTER 41
The Entrance into the City

1. *the great Bali . . . pure goal*: Bali was the king of the demons, who was approached by Viṣṇu in the guise of a dwarf mendicant (see chapter 3, note 19).
2. *the sons of Sagara went to heaven*: The 60,000 sons of king Sagara were searching for the sacrificial horse, when they found it tied to a pole near the meditating sage Kapila. Thinking he had stolen it, they were preparing to attack the sage when he opened his eyes and burnt them to ashes. Eventually, the Gaṅgā river was brought down from heaven by the penances of Bhagīratha, a descendant of Sagara, so that the purificatory rites for these sons could be performed and they could attain heaven. However, Śiva was the only being capable of breaking the fall of the river as it struck the world. Pleased with Bhagīratha's penance, Śiva agreed to receive Gaṅgā's fall on his head.
3. *Kṛṣṇa, the elder brother of Gada*: Vasudeva had seven wives apart from Devakī. Gada was one of six sons born to one of these, Rohiṇī. He was thus a half-brother of Kṛṣṇa.
4. *sārūpya*: For the five types of liberation in Vaiṣṇava theology see chapter 12, note 8.
5. *arghya water*: *Arghya* is water offered to guests for washing the hands.

CHAPTER 42
Description of the Wrestling Arena

1. *rasa*: For a discussion of *rasa*, see Introduction, p. lx–lxi.
2. *the bow*: See chapter 36, note 6.
3. *separation . . . departure*: See chapter 39, verses 23–5.

CHAPTER 43
The Killing of Kuvalayāpiḍa

1. *you are no boy or youth*: The period of *kiśora* is from eleven to fifteen years of age.

CHAPTER 44
The Killing of Kaṃsa

1. *the lotus-navelled Lord*: At the time of a new cosmic cycle of existence, a lotus stem rises from Viṣṇu's navel. Brahmā, the creator, appears in the lotus flower.
2. *whose weapon is the disc*: Viṣṇu always holds a disc weapon in one of his four hands.
3. *he attained . . . to achieve*: According to the Vaiṣṇava schools, there are five different types of liberation (see chapter 12, note 7). One of these involves obtaining the same form as the Lord where he eternally dwells. Thinking constantly of the Lord, even with hostility as was the case with Kaṃsa, is considered to be the highest form of meditation.
4. *After releasing . . . imprisonment*: Kaṃsa had shackled Vasudeva and Devakī again (see chapter 36.19–20; also 1.66, 3.52, and 4.24).

CHAPTER 45
The Retrieval of the Guru*'s Sons*

1. *goals of life*: There are four *puruṣārthas*, or 'goals of human life', each one triggering the next. They are: *dharma*, religious duty; *artha*, material prosperity; *kāma*, sensual enjoyment; and *mokṣa*, liberation from the cycle of birth and death.
2. *the curse of Yayāti*: When Yayāti asked his son, Yadu, to transfer his youth to him, Yadu refused. Yayāti then laid a curse on Yadu and his descendants that they would never enjoy kingship.
3. *the Vedas, along with their supplementary literature*: The six *vedāṅgas*, or supplementary limbs of the Vedas, are: astronomy, etymology, phonetics, grammar, metre and knowledge of the ceremonies. These contribute to the proper performance of the Vedic sacrifice.
4. *the dharma literature*: The *dharma* literature, such as the Manusmṛti, prescribes the codes of conduct for human beings in terms of gender, caste, age, stage of life and other criteria.
5. *the knowledge of polity, which is of six kinds*: The sixfold aspects of polity consist of alliance, warfare, marching, encampment, duplicity and taking refuge.
6. *they learned as many arts*: Śrīdhara notes that these sixty-four arts are listed in the Śaivatantra. They are: (1) singing; (2) playing instruments; (3) dancing; (4) drama; (5) painting; (6) body-painting; (7) preparing designs with rice and flowers; (8) prepar-

ing a bed of flowers; (9) painting one's teeth, limbs and clothes; (10) inlaying a floor with gems; (11) preparing a bed; (12) making sounds with a water pot, and 'beating' water; (13) performing magical feats; (14) preparing garlands; (15) arranging head-dresses; (16) arranging garments and decorations; (17) drawing on the ears; (18) applying ointments; (19) arranging ornaments; (20) juggling; (21) adopting disguises; (22) sleight of hand; (23) preparing various types of comestibles; (24) preparing drinks and their colouration; (25) needlework and weaving; (26) puppetry; (27) playing stringed instruments and drums; (28) solving riddles; (29) creating images; (30) uttering tongue-twisters; (31) reciting books; (32) dramatic arts, narration and staging; (33) solving enigmatic verses; (34) fashioning arrows from reeds and cloth; (35) spinning with spindles; (36) carpentry; (37) architecture; (38) evaluating precious metals and stones; (39) metallurgy; (40) knowledge of colouring gems; (41) mineralogy; (42) science of trees; (43) organizing ram and cock fights; (44) teaching parrots and *śārika* birds to mimic speech; (45) driving out [an enemy?]; (46) hair-washing and dressing; (47) divining the contents of words and of a closed fist; (48) [refuting] the misconceptions of foreign sophistry; (49) knowledge of regional dialects; (50) knowledge of making flower carts; (51) inscribing magical formulae on amulets; (52) the art of conversation; (53) composing poetry mentally; (54) lexicography; (55) prosody; (56) performance of sacrifice; (57) performance of animated song; (58) disguising garments; (59) various types of gambling; (60) dice-playing; (61) children's games; (62) knowledge of war-chariots; (63) predicting victory; (64) knowledge of the science of sorcerers.

7. *The two great charioteers*: A great charioteer [*mahāratha*] can fight 10,000 foot-soldiers.

CHAPTER 46
The Removal of Nanda's Distress

1. *Bṛhaspati*: Bṛhaspati is a preceptor of the gods.
2. Some editions include the following line: 'I cherish them; for my sake they have renounced the world as well as *dharma*.'
3. *those two ... these entities*: In the Bhagavad Gītā (XV.15), Kṛṣṇa says: 'I am seated in everyone's heart and from me come knowledge, memory and forgetfulness.'
4. *A person who has ... the supreme destination*: In the Bhagavad Gītā (VIII.5–7), Kṛṣṇa says: 'Whoever remembers me at the time of giving up the body, comes to my state; there is no doubt about

this. One will attain to, and be transformed into, whatever state of being one remembers at the time of leaving the body. Therefore remember me at all times ... with mind and intelligence fixed, and thus you will definitely come to me.'

5. *is the colour of ... brahman*: The Īśa Upaniṣad (XV-16) speaks of the 'face of truth' covered by a golden disc. The worshipper prays to Pūsan, the sun, to remove it so that he can see the truth. Vaiṣṇavas hold the supreme truth to be Viṣṇu or Kṛṣṇa. See Gonda (1969: 25–8) for references to associations of Viṣṇu with the sun.
6. *Just as the ground ... that is doing things*: Although the ground remains immobile, it appears to go round and round when one has vertigo. Similarly, although the soul is pure awareness and does not act, it appears to act when awareness is focused on the active mind; but actually, it is the mind which is acting and not the soul.
7. *Will Kṛṣṇa ... by means of us?*: Śrīdhara states that the *gopīs* wonder whether Kṛṣṇa was killing them by his absence so as to be able to offer them as funerary oblations to his master, king Kaṃsa.

CHAPTER 47
Uddhava's Return

1. *One of them*: The Gauḍīya commentators take this *gopī* to be Rādhā, Kṛṣṇa's primary consort in the theology of this sect.
2. *She spoke as follows*: The passage that follows is an exceptional piece of love poetry. Gauḍīya commentators consider it to be an example of *citrajalpa*. This takes two forms: *sañjalpa*, the declaration of a lover's ingratitude; and *avajalpa*, the declaration of the unworthiness of the hero's love on account of his hard-heartedness. From a theological perspective, an outburst of *citra-jalpa* such as that contained in this passage is considered to reveal one of the highest attainable levels of love for Kṛṣṇa.
3. *'O keeper of honey'*: This is an example of *dhvani* (see Introduction, pp. lxv–lxvi).
4. *Lord of the Madhu dynasty*: There is a play, here, between *madhupa*, a bee or keeper of honey, *madhu*, and Madhupati, the lord of the Madhus.
5. *the remnants [prasāda]*: *Prasāda* is the remnants of offerings made to deities, such as food or flowers, that are distributed to devotees.
6. *he shot a monkey with his bow*: This is a reference to Rāma, a

previous incarnation whose story is told in the famous Rāmāyaṇa epic. Rāma shot Vālī with an arrow during the latter's battle with his brother, Rāma's ally. Since Rāma did so from behind a tree, when he was concealed and not personally involved in the combat, he was accused of breaking the principles of *dharma* for warriors.

7. *he disfigured a woman who lusted after him*: Rāma cut off the demoness Śūrpaṇakhā's nose and ears when she, enamoured of Rāma, threatened Śītā. However, according to the principles of *dharma*, a woman is not to be punished. Moreover, a warrior should satisfy anyone who surrenders to him.

8. *Bali*: In the story of Vāmana and Bali (see chapter 3, note 19) Bali was so magnanimous that, disregarding the warnings of his advisers, he offered Vāmana any three favours he cared to choose. Despite this, Vāmana took advantage of his highmindedness by accepting two of the favours offered and then having him arrested for being unable to fulfil the third.

9. *The tendencies towards . . . Kṛṣṇa*: Almost all schools of Vedāntic philosophy perceive all reality as a manifestation of the one supreme truth, and therefore as non-dual. According to the Bhāgavata, the ignorance of perceiving reality as being separate from the supreme truth, Kṛṣṇa, can be overcome by the *yoga* of *bhakti* – hearing about Kṛṣṇa's *līlā*, etc.

10. *From myself . . . my own māyā*: The sense here is that since everything is God, the apparent creation and destruction of things take place within God and by God's power.

11. *The ātmā [soul] . . . the fluctuations of māyā*: The soul is distinct from the mind, but, due to *māyā*, the self is identified with the activities of the mind – waking, deep sleep or dream. Nonetheless, its presence can be perceived as the awareness behind the mind's *vṛttis* [fluctuations]. The Māṇḍūkya Upaniṣad speaks of the four states of consciousness. The fourth state, *turīya*, is pure awareness of the self as distinct from its usual absorption in the other three states of waking, dream or deep sleep.

12. *Yoga and Sāṅkhya*: Yoga and Sāṅkhya are two of the six orthodox schools of Indic thought. Sāṅkhya is a metaphysics of *prakṛti*, the material universe (see Introduction, pp. xl ff.), and *yoga* a psychosomatic technique for extricating *puruṣa*, or the self, from its entanglement in this *prakṛti*.

13. *Even the unchaste Piṅgalā . . . desire*: The story of Piṅgalā the prostitute is recounted in the Bhāgavata Purāṇa (11.8). One night, Piṅgalā waited seductively at her door for a wealthy customer. When no one paid her any attention throughout the whole night,

she became disgusted with her desires, aspirations and petty goals, and took refuge with Kṛṣṇa.

14. *and worshipped Uddhava*: This phrase could also read: 'they worshipped Uddhava, recognizing him as Adhokṣaja himself'.
15. *What is the use . . . Brahmā*: This could also read, 'What is the value of births as a *brāhmaṇa* . . .'
16. *the king of medicines*: Śrīdhara glosses *agadarājah* ('king of medicines') with *amṛta* ('nectar'), possibly referring to the nectar of immortality that was sought by both gods and demons when they churned the ocean of milk.
17. *the Āryan code of conduct*: Śrīdhara glosses *āryapatha* ('the Āryan path', i.e. code of conduct) with *dharma* (the rules outlining social and familial duties).

CHAPTER 48
Kṛṣṇa Satisfies Trivakrā and Meets Akrūra

1. *As a sādhu . . . [respectfully]*: In certain contexts it is considered inappropriate for a junior person to sit on the same level as a senior, hence, since Kṛṣṇa was seated, Uddhava humbly sat on the floor, but touched the seat offered to him out of respect.
2. *The unfortunate woman*: Śrīdhara notes that she was unfortunate because she was not as engrossed by Kṛṣṇa as were the *gopīs*. But, of course, she was extremely fortunate to have such an intimate occasion with Kṛṣṇa. The story also illustrates that *bhakti* knows no bars – anyone can attain the highest good by simply offering themselves to Kṛṣṇa sincerely.
3. *sensual objects*: The word used here for sensual objects, *manogrāhya*, literally means 'that which is grasped through the mind', namely the objects of the senses.
4. *Sprinkling . . . on his head*: Sprinkling the foot-washing water of someone on one's head is a sign of extreme respect for that person.
5. *Because impositions . . . in reality*: Birth and death, and the dualities inherent in matter such as body and self, or 'I/mine' and 'other', etc., do not exist in the pure soul, or in *brahman*.
6. *You act out of your own free will*: Śrīdhara notes that although it may seem that Kṛṣṇa was bound to the mortar, or liberated from Kāliya in the Yamunā, these acts were performed from his own free will.
7. *We have heard that . . . to his own city*: The full story of the saga of the Pāṇḍavas is narrated in the huge Mahābhārata Epic. The Pāṇḍavas are Kṛṣṇa's paternal cousins – his aunt's children. As

brother of Pāṇḍu, Dhṛtarāṣṭra was the paternal uncle of the Pāṇḍavas and ruler of Hastināpura. His sons usurped the kingdom from their cousins, humiliated their wife (due to a quirk of fate, the Pāṇḍavas shared a wife, Draupadī), and banished them to the forest for thirteen years. These acts provoked the Mahābhārata war and constitute the central plot of the Epic.

CHAPTER 49
Akrūra Visits Hastināpura

1. *Dhṛtarāṣṭra . . . and Pṛthā [Kuntī] there*: Bhīṣma is the grandfather of the Kuru dynasty, the uncle of Pāṇḍu and Dhṛtarāṣṭra and Vidura, their half-brother. Pṛthā [Kuntī] is the mother of the Pāṇḍavas.
2. *Bāhlīka . . . Suyodhana [Duryodhana]*: Bāhlīka was an ally of Duryodhana, eldest son of Dhṛtarāṣṭra; Droṇa was the teacher of martial skills and the science of warfare both to the Pāṇḍavas and to the sons of Dhṛtarāṣṭra; and Kṛpa was Droṇa's son-in-law. Karṇa is Kuntī's son and hence in actuality the half-brother of the Pāṇḍavas. As a young girl, Kuntī, the mother of the Pāṇḍavas, was granted a boon from a sage that she could summon any demigod at will. Curious to try the incantation, she summoned the sun god. Once present, however, he impregnated her. The young girl resolved to hide her transgression and abandoned the child, who came to be known as Karṇa. Karṇa, a truly tragic character in the Epic, thus grew up without knowing that he was the eldest brother of the Pāṇḍavas (see note 4 below), and ended up opposing them in the great Mahābhārata battle.
3. *the unpleasant acts . . . poison*: This refers to various episodes in the Mahābhārata. Durodhana tried to kill the sons of Pāṇḍu in a number of ways such as attempting to poison Bhīma and plotting to burn them all to death in a house of lac when they were in exile in the forest.
4. *the reasons for the births of her sons*: Śrīdhara says that Kuntī is reminded by Akrūra of the special births of her sons from various gods such as Indra and the wind god. Kuntī had been granted the power to summon any god at will. Because her husband, Pāṇḍu, could not engage in sexual intercourse because of a curse, he asked her to summon Dharma, who begot Yudhiṣṭhira in her, Vāyu the wind god, who begot Bhīma, and Indra, who begot Arjuna. Her co-wife begot the twins, Nakula and Sahadeva, from the twins Aśvins. The five boys were considered the sons of Pāṇḍu, and hence known as Pāṇḍavas.

5. *Other people . . . sustenance*: Śrīdhara glosses such people as sons, etc.

PART TWO

CHAPTER 50
Entrance into the Fort

1. *My incarnation . . . sadhus*: In the Bhagavad Gītā 4.8, Kṛṣṇa says that he descends in every age in order to protect the *sādhus*, destroy the miscreants and establish *dharma*.
2. *I assumed . . . course of time*: Kṛṣṇa is referring here to previous incarnations.
3. *Ancient divine weapons . . . spontaneously*: This seems to refer to the weaponry used by Viṣṇu in previous incarnations.
4. *You remained hidden*: Śrīdhara takes this as referring to Kṛṣṇa being concealed inside everything. Alternatively, it could refer to Kṛṣṇa remaining hidden from Kaṃsa throughout his childhood in Vraj.
5. *the god Varuṇa*: Varuṇa, one of the twelve sons of Aditi, is one of the eight guardians of the quarters, and lord of the ocean. He carries a noose.
6. *A yavana hero*: *Yavanas* are foreigners who were once *kṣatriyas*. They are descended from Turvasu, son of Yayāti.
7. *mlecchas [barbarians]*: *Mlecchas* are basically people outside of the Āryan social order. The term is often used for foreigners. See also chapter 40, note 24.
8. *the śilpa manuals*: The *śilpa* text deals with architecture as well as with other mechanical or manual arts and crafts.
9. *the four varṇas*: The *varṇas* are the four castes, or social divisions, of ancient India (see Introduction, p. xlix).

CHAPTER 51
The Eulogy of Mucukunda

1. *Kārttikeya*: Kārttikeya, also known as Skanda or Subrahmaṇya, is the son of Śiva. He was the only one capable of killing the demon Tārakāsura, who was otherwise invincible and was tyrannizing the three worlds. He was installed by the gods as their commander-in-chief.
2. *are no longer alive*: Time passes much more slowly in the planets of the gods (as was seen in the Brahmā *līlā*, where Brahmā left for a moment of his time, which was a full year of human time).

Therefore, when Mucukunda returned to earth, it was a different era.

3. *(The king . . . said the gods.)*: This section is not in all editions, and is in brackets in the Chaukambha edition that I have used for translation.
4. *the three gods of gods*: The three gods of gods are Brahmā, Śiva and Viṣṇu.
5. *Ikṣvāku*: Ikṣvāku is the son of Vaivasvata Manu. He is mentioned in the Bhagavad Gītā (IV.1) as one in the line of authorities through which the Gītā was transmitted in a previous era.
6. *They call me Vāsudeva . . . Vasudeva*: See chapter 1, note 17.
7. *Remembering the words of Garga*: The question arises as to how Mucukunda could have possibly heard the words of Garga – at least those spoken by Garga to Nanda earlier in the text. Śrīdhara accounts for this by noting that the king had heard the words of Garga in some previous unspecified time when the latter prophesied that Kṛṣṇa would incarnate in the twenty-eighth *yuga*.
8. *this body . . . or wall*: The sense here is that the body is made of material elements, as are pots and walls.
9. *prāṇāyāma*: *Prāṇāyāma* (breath control) is the fourth step of Patañjali's eight-stepped *yoga* process.
10. *do not have their subconscious memories erased*: In *yoga* psychology, a *vāsanā* is a mental impression, or memory, recorded in the *citta* or subtle body (which consists of the mind, intelligence and ego). Every thought or sensual act performed throughout the myriad of lifetimes of the individual is recorded on the *citta*. Even when the sensual apparatus is closed down, such as in sleep or in the preliminary stages of meditation, the *vāsanās* recorded on the *citta* remain active. The goal of Patañjali's *yoga* system is *cittavṛttinirodha*, or the cessation of the constant churning of these thoughts and impressions. When this is accomplished, the *puruṣa*, 'self' (more commonly referred to as *ātmā* in other schools of Hinduism), can finally be perceived as the real self, distinct from these coverings of thought. Kṛṣṇa here is saying that only *bhakti* can erase these *vāsanās*. Other processes such as breath control may temporarily quell them, but they eventually reactivate.

CHAPTER 52
The Marriage of Rukmiṇī

1. *the kaliyuga . . . the northern direction*: Things are supposed to shrink in size in the *kaliyuga*, the last and most degenerate of the four world ages. The northern direction indicates the Himālayan

mountains, which are the destination of those seeking liberation.

2. *Gandhamādana*: Gandhamādana is a famous mountain lying to the east of the Himālayas. Many famous sages practised their ascetic disciplines there.
3. *Badarikāśram*: This is the famous site in the Himālaya mountains in northern Uttar Pradesh state, one of the four *dhāmas*, 'abodes of God', in Hindu pilgrimage.
4. *Pravarṣaṇa*: Pravarṣaṇa is the peak of the mountain Gomanta.
5. *a svayaṃvara marriage ceremony*: There are six types of marriage recognized in the Purāṇic period. The *svayaṃvara* is when the bride chooses her own husband. See verses 18 and 41 in this chapter.
6. *Garuḍa, snatched the nectar*: Garuḍa defeated all the gods and stole the pot of nectar that had been produced from the churning of the ocean of milk, despite the fact that it was formidably guarded. Viṣṇu was impressed with his achievements and granted him a favour. Garuḍa requested that he be allowed to be Viṣṇu's carrier, and his request was granted.
7. *the rākṣasa system of marriage*: The *rākṣasa*, or demoniac, marriage is when the bride is snatched away by brute force by the suitor (see note 5).
8. *a kāmadhenu exists for him*: The *kāmadhenu* is a heavenly cow that fulfils all wishes. The sense here is that the resoluteness of a dutiful *brāhmaṇa* results in all his wishes being fulfilled.
9. *the rākṣasa system*: See notes 5 and 7. In this instance with Rukmiṇī, however, the element of *rākṣasa* is blended with an element from the *gāndharva* type of marriage. A *gāndharva* marriage is a love marriage where both suitors choose each other. So this is a *gāndharva* marriage disguised as a *rākṣasa* one.
10. *the goddess Girijā*: Girijā, 'mountain-born', is another name for Śiva's consort Pārvati (also known as Umā, as in the next verse), daughter of the Himālaya mountains.

CHAPTER 53
The Abduction of Rukmiṇī

1. *the outcaste*: The term for outcaste here is *apasad*. There are six types of offspring produced from *apasad* marriages: those from a *brāhmaṇa* woman with a man from the three lower castes, the *kṣatriya*, *vaiśya* and *śūdra* castes; those from a *kṣatriya* woman with a man from the two lower castes, the *vaiśya* and *śūdra* castes; and those of a *vaiśya* woman with a man from the lowest caste, the *śūdra*.

2. *purohita*: Family priest.
3. *the three yāmas, or watches*: A *yāma* is a period of three hours, or one-eighth of a day.
4. *closed her eyes ... the appropriate time would be*: Śrīdhara explains that Rukmiṇi knew that it was not yet time for Kṛṣṇa to come. So she took courage and closed her eyes, which were filled with tears.
5. *Bhavānī [Ambikā]*: Ambikā and Bhavānī are other names of Umā (Pārvatī), the wife of Śiva. See also chapter 52, note 10.
6. *the remnants [of the offerings]*: The remnants of food offered to deities is called *prasāda* [God's grace] and is thought to be purifying if consumed.
7. *Her complexion was dark [śyāmā]*: *Śyāmā* can also mean a woman who has not yet borne children. Śrīdhara takes it to mean that Rukmiṇī was pre-pubescent.
8. *the bimba-fruits of her lips*: *Bimba* fruits are red.

CHAPTER 54
The Festivities at the Marriage of Rukmiṇī

1. *This dharma ... prajāpati Brahmā*: A *kṣatriya* must do his duty, even if it means killing his own family if they are engaged in non-*dharma*, as Kṛṣṇa reminds Arjuna in the second chapter of the Bhagavad Gītā. Brahmā himself is the first *prajāpati*. See also chapter 40, note 8.
2. *The soul is neither ... and the objects of forms*: The soul is the cause of everything unreal, and therefore is neither the same as the world (since it is pure soul) nor separate from it (since ultimately everything emanates from *brahman*). Through the consciousness of the soul, the world is perceivable, just as the sun is the condition both of sight and of the illumination of the forms that can be perceived, while not being the same as them.
3. *Kṛṣṇa, the husband of Śrī ... [Śrī, the goddess of fortune]*: Viṣṇu's eternal consort is Śrī. Just as Viṣṇu incarnates as Kṛṣṇa, so too does Śrī in the form of Rukmiṇī.

CHAPTER 55
Reflections on the Birth of Pradyumna

1. *He had formerly ... Rudra [Śiva]*: At one time, a great demon, Tāraka, was terrorizing the gods, strong in the knowledge that he could only be vanquished by Śiva, or his son. Śiva himself was uninterested in worldly affairs and was absorbed in meditation in the Himālayas. Hoping that he might at least beget a son to

vanquish Tāraka, the gods sent Kāma, the god of love, in a bid to arouse Śiva's passion and interest in Pārvatī, who was undertaking austere disciplines in order to receive Śiva as her husband. But Śiva simply became annoyed at being disturbed, and burnt Kāma to ashes with the power of his third eye.

2. *Śambara . . . would be his enemy*: Śambara was the son of the great demon Hiraṇyākṣa, and brother of Śakuni. He had been granted a favour by Śiva that contained a clause noting that he would die soon after Kāma was reborn on earth. He discovered that Kāma had been born to Kṛṣṇa.

3. *'and my left arm is twitching'*: The twitching of the left arm is an auspicious omen.

CHAPTER 56
The Story of the Syamantaka Jewel

1. *Syamantaka jewel*: The Nirukta, a traditional etymological work ascribed to Yāska in the fifth century BCE, refers to this jewel in what might be one of the earliest literary references to the Kṛṣṇa story (2.1.2).

2. *eight bhāras*: A *bhāra* is a measure of weight. Śrīdhara quotes a verse stating that four grains of rice are one *guñja*, five *guñjas* one *paṇa*, eight *paṇas* one *karṣa*, four *karṣas* one *pala*, one hundred *palas* one *tulā*, and twenty *tulās* one *bhāra*.

3. *He fought with. . . his own master*: Jāmbavān had formerly been a devotee of Rāma. Rāma had been helped in his mission to retrieve Sītā by bears and monkeys.

4. *Because you cast . . . fell to the ground*: The story of Rāma, a previous incarnation, is given in detail in the famous epic, the Rāmāyaṇa. The incidents mentioned in this passage refer to the time Rāma was preparing to cross the sea to Laṅkā to retrieve his spouse, Sītā, who had been kidnapped by the demon Rāvaṇa. Rāma prayed to Varuṇa, god of the waters, for passage, and when Varuṇa did not initially present himself, Rāma scorched the ocean. Eventually, his devoted monkey warriors built a bridge of rocks and mountain tops over the sea, the city of Laṅkā was razed to the ground, and the demon and his army exterminated.

CHAPTER 57
The Story of the Syamantaka Jewel (Continued)

1. *the Pāṇḍavas had been burnt*: Duryodhana was so jealous of the Pāṇḍavas that he had a palace made of highly flammable lac built for them, and conspired to make the Pāṇḍavas reside there, with

the intention of burning them. However, the Pāṇḍavas were informed of his plan, and escaped unrecognized. Since a tribal woman and her five sons happened to be sleeping in the building when it was set on fire, and were consequently burnt to death, the Kurus and others took their remains to be those of the five Pāṇḍavas. Thus, everyone thought the Pāṇḍavas were dead and performed their funeral rites.

2. *Bhīṣma . . . Droṇa*: See chapter 49, notes 1 and 2 for Bhīṣma, Kṛpa, Vidura and Droṇa. Gāndhārī was the wife of Dhṛtarāṣṭra (for whom see chapter 48, note 7).
3. *Duryodhana, the son of Dhṛtarāṣṭra*: Duryodhana, the oldest of the scheming 100 sons of Dhṛtarāṣṭra, was expert in club fighting. Balarāma was affectionate and well-disposed towards him.
4. *piṇḍa oblations*: *Piṇḍa* is an oblation made of rice, periodically offered to the departed soul.

CHAPTER 58
The Marriage of Eight Princesses

1. *the Pāṇḍavas, who had reappeared*: Śrīdhara notes that although they had vanished, the Pāṇḍavas reappeared at the residence of king Drupada to try their hand for his daughter, Draupadī, at her *svayaṃvara* (see note 8) marriage ceremony (Mahābhārata, *ādi parva*). This was their first public appearance after they were commonly assumed to have been burnt in the house of lac.
2. *Phālguni [Arjuna]*: Arjuna was born under the constellation of Phālguni.
3. *Remembering those numerous difficulties*: This is a reference to the ordeals undergone by the Pāṇḍavas and their mother during their period of exile in the forest, as described in the Mahābhārata Epic.
4. *Gāṇḍīva bow*: This was one of the three divine bows made by Brahmā, along with the Vijaya and Śārṅga bows, and could kill 100,000 opponents at a time.
5. *śarabha deer*: In later texts *śarabhas* are conceived of as eight-legged creatures which inhabit snowy mountains and are stronger than lions or elephants.
6. *He became . . . the god of fire*: The burning of the Khāṇḍava forest is told in the Mahābhārata (*ādi parva*). In these verses Śuka is relating different events, narrated in the Mahābhārata, that took place during Kṛṣṇa's absence from Dvārakā.
7. *Saved from the fire . . . in that hall*: Maya is the architect of both gods and demons. The Mahābhārata (*ādi parva*) relates how he

was saved from the Khāṇḍava forest fire by Arjuna, and *sabhā parva*, chapters 1–3, how he came to build the assembly hall for Arjuna. The assembly hall was built in such a way that the ground could be confounded with water, and water with ground. Duryodhana was humiliated when he unwittingly fell into a pool of water that he had mistaken for ground, and this further enhanced his hatred of the Pāṇḍavas. This is described in the Mahābhārata (*sabhā parva*).

8. *her svayaṃvara marriage*: A *svayaṃvara* marriage is when the bride chooses her own husband. Vindhya and Anuvindhya opposed their sister's choice of Kṛṣṇa.

CHAPTER 59
The Seizing of the Pārijāta *Jewel and the Killing of Naraka*

1. *Bhauma's [Naraka's] activities . . . seized [by Bhauma]*: Bhauma, or Naraka, was causing devastation and terror in the three worlds, and the gods were not able to withstand him. He carried away the earrings of Aditi, Indra's mother, as well as Indra's large white royal umbrella. Indra went to Dvārakā to inform Kṛṣṇa of these depredations.
2. *the pāñcajanya conch*: This conch was once inhabited by a demon who stole the son of Kṛṣṇa's and Balarāma's teacher, Sāndīpani. Kṛṣṇa killed the demon and took possession of the conch, the sound of which became one of his distinctive features in battle (see Bhagavad Gītā I.15).
3. *Thus Naraka . . . the earth*: When the demon Hiraṇyākṣa in the form of a boar carried the earth on his tusks to the Pātāla nether worlds, the earth became pregnant as a result of this contact and gave birth to a demon of tremendous power. The offspring of this inauspicious union was Naraka.
4. *who had been generated from the ocean of milk*: The Bhāgavata Purāṇa (VIII.7) describes how the ocean of milk was churned by the gods and demons intent on obtaining the nectar of immortality. Various valuable items were produced from this churning.
5. *the vaijayantī garland*: The *vaijayantī* garland has the quality of never fading.
6. *a great jewel [all of which had been stolen by Bhauma]*: Śrīdhara takes '*mahāmaṇi*' to refer to the peak of Mount Mandara rather than 'great jewel'.
7. *Airāvata*: Airāvata was another by-product of the churning of the ocean milk (Bhāgavata Purāna, 8.7). He is Indra's mount.

8. *Aditi*: Aditi was the wife of Kaśyapa and the mother of Indra. She had thirty-three sons, known as the Āditeyas.
9. *the pārijāta tree*: The *pārijāta* tree, whose scented flowers never fade, was another fabulous by-product of the churning of the ocean of milk. It only grows in the realms of the gods.

CHAPTER 60
The Conversation between Rukmiṇī and Kṛṣṇa

1. *sages ... ascetic staffs*: *Sannyāsi* mendicants, members of the fourth *āśrama* stage of life, carry a *daṇḍa* staff. Certain mendicants, however, renounce even this external symbol of status.
2. *kings – such as Aṅga ... and Gaya*: The stories of these kings are described in earlier books of the Bhāgavata.
3. Rukmiṇī is here referring to her manifestation of *prakṛti* – unformed material energy – which, in Vaiṣṇava theology, is impregnated with souls by the glance of Viṣṇu, resulting in the cyclical manifestation of the universe. As mentioned in the Introduction, pp. xl ff., *rajas* is employed in the evolution of the various elements from *prakṛti*.
4. *Ambā*: At the beginning of the Mahābhārata, Ambā, along with her two sisters, was carried off by Bhīṣma as a bride for his brother Vicitravīrya. However, Ambā had already set her heart on Śālva. When Bhīṣma learnt of this, he attempted to return her to the man she loved, but Śālva would not take her back since she had been touched by another. Ambā then carried out austere practices to get revenge against Bhīṣma. The repercussions of this are pivotal to one of the important narrative plots of the Mahābhārata.
5. *the disfigurement of your brother ... the gambling assembly*: This will be described in the next chapter.

CHAPTER 61
Rukmī's Death at Aniruddha's Marriage

1. *Yogīs see the future ... beyond the senses*: These abilities are among the eight *siddhis*, mystic powers, attainable by *yogīs*. See chapter 87, note 28.
2. *Ananga [Kāma] himself*: The apparent contradiction in terms between *Anaṅga*, Kāma (literally, the limbless one), and *aṅgayutas*, reincarnated (literally, endowed with limbs) is an example of the *alaṅkāra*, or poetic embellishment known as *virodhābhāsa* (see Introduction, pp. lxiv–lxv).
3. *despite being sworn ... contrary to dharma*: Śrīdhara quotes

popular opinion that 'charity from an enemy should not be enjoyed, and one should not dine in the presence of an enemy'.

CHAPTER 62
The Binding of Aniruddha

1. *the great soul Bali . . . the dwarf incarnation*: See chapter 3, note 19. Bali's story is described in the Bhāgavata (VIII.15–23).
2. *the elephants [who support] the cardinal points [of the earth]*: These elephants stand at the four quarters of the sky and support the earth.
3. *Śūra*: Śūra was the father of Vasudeva and grandfather of Vāsudeva [Kṛṣṇa].

CHAPTER 63
The Escorting of Aniruddha

1. *[Kārttikeya]*: Kārttikeya (also known as Skanda or Subrahmaṇya) was the commander-in-chief of the gods.
2. *the pramathas*: Śrīdhara glosses the *pramathas* with the *gaṇas*, the ghouls and ogres who are Śiva's companions.
3. *the bhūtas . . . brahmarākṣasas*: The *guhyakas* are a type of *yakṣa* god, the *ḍākinis* a class of women proficient in magic; the *bhūtas* are ghosts, the *yātudhānas* a type of *rākṣasa* demon; the *vetālas* are evil spirits; the *vināyakas* a type of demon; the *pretas*, departed spirits; the *mātās*, bloodthirsty female spirits associated with Kālī in later texts; the *piśācas*, a class of malevolent beings; the *kuṣmāṇḍas* are another class of demoniac beings, as are the *brahmarākṣasas*, who are particularly powerful.
4. *Brahmāstra [clashed] against brahmāstra*: The *brahmāstra* is considered to be the most powerful weapon in the Purāṇic arsenal. It was a type of heat weapon.
5. *the cycle of seed and shoot*: According to the law of cause and effect of *karma*, every seed bears a shoot which in turn bears a seed. Thus the cycle of existence is perpetuated.
6. *He whose navel is the sky . . . made manifest in the world*: A similar cosmic description of the Virāṭ Puruṣa, God in the form of the universe, occurs in the Bhāgavata, II.6 1–45.
7. *You are the fourth state of consciousness – transcendence*: The Māṇḍūkya Upaniṣad speaks of the four states of consciousness: waking, dream, deep sleep and the fourth – that which is beyond all these – namely, pure awareness.
8. *One whose senses . . . to be pitied*: According to the theory of reincarnation, the soul attains to the human form of life after

uncountable births in various species of *saṃsāra*. It is only from this rare human form that liberation from *saṃsāra* is possible (except in rare cases such as that of Gajendra the elephant: Bhāgavata VIII.2–4).

9. *the chief of the demons*: Śrīdhara considers this to be Prahlāda (Bhāgavata, VII.4–10). But it could also refer to Bali (VIII.15), who actually was the chief of the demons (Prahlāda was the son of the powerful demon, Hiraṇyakaśipu). Both Prahlāda and Bali were devotees of Viṣṇu despite being born into the families of demons, illustrating that anyone is qualified to engage in devotion, irrespective of birth.

CHAPTER 64
The Story of Nṛga

1. *hālāhala*: When the ocean of milk was churned by the gods and the demons in order to obtain the nectar of immortality, poison called *hālāhala* was also produced. Only Śiva could remove this, which he did by drinking it. As a result, his throat turned blue.

CHAPTER 65
The Dragging of the Yamunā at Balarāma's Triumph

1. *Madhu and Mādhava*: *Madhu* and *Mādhava* are spring months.
2. *Kāntī*: Śrīdhara glosses Kāntī with Lakṣmī (Śri, the goddess of fortune).

CHAPTER 66
The Killing of Pauṇḍraka and Others

1. *Give up my insignia*: Pauṇḍraka is referring here to the disc, club, conch and lotus which Viṣṇu holds in his four hands.
2. *at the end of the cycle of yugas*: The end of the cycle of *yugas* is known as *pralaya*, when the entire universe is torched by intense fire. *Brahmapralaya* occurs at the end of 1,000 sets of four *yugas*, or one day of Brahmā.
3. *the horrific pleasure grove of the Lord of ghosts*: This is a reference to Śiva, who frequents burial and cremation grounds with his ghastly associates.
4. *[By] assuming ... Hari's nature*: As noted in the Introduction (p. xxxvi), even if one constantly meditates on Kṛṣṇa in enmity, one nonetheless reaps the fruits of one whose consciousness is fully absorbed in God. Pauṇḍraka attained *sārūpya*, the type of liberation consisting of having the same form as the Lord.
5. *the dakṣiṇa sacrificial fire ... ṛtvik priest*: The *dakṣiṇa* sacrifice,

situated on the south side of the ritual area, consists of a series of three butter oblations, and accompanies the distribution of remuneration for the priests. The *ṛtvik* priest is an officiant of the sacrifice.

6. *pramathas*: See chapter 63, note 2.
7. *pralaya at the annihilation of the universe*: See note 2 above.

CHAPTER 67
The Killing of Dvivida

1. *Sugrīva . . . Mainda*: Mainda was one of the monkeys in the Rāmāyaṇa who helped Rāma search for Sītā. Sugrīva was another prominent monkey in the Epic who also helped Rāma in his mission, after Rāma assisted him in his feud with his brother, Vālī.

CHAPTER 68
Saṅkarṣaṇa's [Balarāma's] Victory as Manifested in the Dragging of Hastināpura

1. *Dhṛtarāṣtra . . . Duryodhana*: See chapter 49, notes 1 and 2 for details of these.
2. *defeated one single man . . . and then bound him up*: According to the *dharma* of *kṣatriyas*, combat should take place one to one, and between equals.
3. *the fly-whisk . . . and bed*: These are royal regalia.
4. *who brought the pārijāta tree of the gods and enjoys it*: See chapter 59, note 9.
5. *You who playfully . . . thousand-headed one*: Balarāma is an incarnation of Śeṣa, the thousand-headed snake upon which Viṣṇu reclines in the ocean of milk. Śeṣa bears the worlds upon his hoods.
6. *You uphold sattva . . . protection*: See Introduction, pp. xl ff.

CHAPTER 69
The Vision of Kṛṣṇa's Householder Life

1. *Peacocks . . . and cried out*: Peacocks always cry before rain. This verse is an example of the *alaṅkāra*, or poetic convention, known as *bhrāntimān*, 'the mistaken', when something is perceived as being other than it is.
2. *the three sacred fires*: See chapter 40, note 3.
3. *the five sacrifices*: According to the Manusmṛti (3.69–71) the *mahāyajña*, or 'great sacrifice', consists of five offerings – to Brahmā, the gods, the forefathers, humans and ghosts.

4. *eating their remnants*: As noted earlier, eating the remnants of food offered to the deity or to saintly persons is called *prasāda*, and is considered purifying.
5. *japa mantras*: *Japa* is meditation upon the repetition of the name of a deity.
6. *dharma, artha or kāma*: The fulfilment of *dharma*, *artha*, *kāma*, along with *mokṣa*, liberation, are the four *puruṣārthas*, or goals of human life. See chapter 5, note 4.

CHAPTER 70
A Message from the Kings Imprisoned by Jarāsandha

1. *Brāhmamuhūrta*, the period before sunrise, is considered the most suitable time for meditation and other religious pursuits. The mind is rested, and hence alert, but also less distracted than during other periods of the day, since the world has yet to awaken.
2. *meditated . . . his own being*: This sentence could also be construed as: "He meditated with peaceful mind on himself."
3. *the brahma [gāyatrī] mantra*: This is a *mantra* to the sun god chanted by *brāhmaṇas* three times daily on the sacred thread.
4. *He looked . . . gods*: These are auspicious ways to start the day.
5. *The six waves [in the ocean of saṃsāra]*: Śrīdhara does not enumerate these six waves [*ṣaḍ ūrmayaḥ*], but they are typically identified as hunger, thirst, grief, delusion, old age and death.
6. *digvijaya [conquering of the directions]*: During a *digvijaya*, 'conquering of the directions', a king wishing to be installed as emperor would release a horse to roam around the various adjacent kingdoms at will. Any king not accepting the jurisdiction of the would-be emperor could capture the horse and thereby provoke a confrontation. Others, who allowed the horse to traverse their kingdom, thereby acknowledged their subservience, and would be expected to pay tribute.
7. *Our perspective . . . saṃsāra*: From a Vedāntic perspective, everything ultimately rests on *brahman* and hence the dualities of the world are illusory. To be fearful, or to see the world in terms of dualities such as fear/security, love/hate, hot/cold, etc., is not the sign of an enlightened disposition.
8. *your devotee [Yudhiṣṭhira]*: Yudhiṣṭhira is the eldest of the five Pāṇḍava brothers, protagonists of the Mahābhārata. He is an older cousin of Kṛṣṇa (Kuntī, the mother of the Pāṇḍavas, is the sister of Kṛṣṇa's father, Vasudeva).
9. *the rājasūya*: The *rājasūya* is the sacrifice performed at the

inauguration of a king. The *rājasūya* sacrifice of Yudhiṣṭhira is described in the Mahābhārata.

10. *it is known . . . the Gaṅgā here*: When the Vāmana incarnation took the promised second step of land from Bali, as outlined previously (see chapter 3, note 19), his toe burst through the covering of the universe, causing water to pour in. This water is known by different names in different realms.

CHAPTER 71
Kṛṣṇa's Journey to Indraprastha

1. *A rājasūya sacrifice . . . O master*: Before the performance of the *rājasūya* horse sacrifice, a king wishing to be installed as an emperor would perform a *digvijaya* (see chapter 70, note 6).
2. *the wolf-bellied Bhīma*: Bhīma had a voracious appetite.
3. *They are also singing about . . . your parents*: In the Śrīmad Bhāgavata (III.4) Viṣṇu delivers his *bhakta*, the king of elephants, Gajendra, from the crocodile. Rāma freed Sītā from Rāvaṇa in the Rāmāyaṇa Epic, and Kṛṣṇa his parents from Kaṃsa in chapter 44 of this book.
4. *the principal vital air*: There are five vital airs, of which the *prāṇa* is the principal.
5. *He embraced his maternal cousin with a smile*: The five Pāṇḍava brothers, protagonists of the Mahābhārata, consist of Yudhiṣṭhira and Bhīma, who are older than their cousin Kṛṣṇa, Arjuna, who is his equal, and the twins Sahadeva and Nakula, who are his juniors.
6. *the Khāṇḍava forest . . . had been built*: The Khāṇḍava forest was offered to Agni, the god of fire, as a feast. As Agni was devouring all the human and animal inhabitants, Maya, who was hiding there in disguise, appealed to Arjuna for protection, which was granted (Mahābhārata, *ādi parva*). In return for this, Maya built the Pāṇḍavas a magnificent palace (Mahābhārata, *sabhā parva*).

CHAPTER 72
The Killing of Jarāsandha

1. *the rājasūya sacrifice*: The *rājasūya* is the sacrifice performed at the coronation of a king.
2. *the celestial kalpataru tree*: The *kalpataru* is a tree that has the power of providing any object one desires. It was another by-product of the churning of the ocean of milk, according to the Agni Purāṇa (chapter 3).

3. *Your brothers . . . deities of the world*: Yudhiṣṭhira is an incarnation of the god Dharma; Arjuna, of Indra; Bhīma, of Vāyu; and the twins Sahadeva and Nakula, of the twin Aśvins.
4. *Hariścandra . . . the hunter and the pigeon*: In order to keep his word, Hariścandra gave his entire kingdom to the sage Viśvāmitra. When this did not suffice, he sold his wife, his son and, finally, himself, resorting to earning a livelihood by cremating corpses. Eventually Viṣṇu, Śiva and Brahmā appeared and heaped rewards on him. Rantideva was renowned for his generosity, engaging 20,000 people just to cook for the guests who visited his palace both by day and by night. He donated all his wealth to *brāhmaṇas*. Uñchavṛtti was a poor *brāhmaṇa* who lived by begging. On one occasion he sat down with his family and was about to eat the day's gleanings – some pulverized food grains which he divided among his family – when the god Dharma visited him in disguise. Uñchavṛtti immediately gave him his own portion. When this did not satisfy the guest, he gave him his family's portion as well. Dharma took the family to the celestial realms in appreciation of his generosity. King Śibi's fame was legendary and so the gods decided to test him. Agni appeared to him in the form of a dove seeking shelter from Indra, who was pursuing him in the form of a hawk. When Śibi granted the dove protection, the hawk complained that he had been deprived of his legitimate food. Śibi then weighed the dove and carved off an equal measure of flesh from his own body to offer the hawk in compensation, but the dove's weight kept increasing until Śibi placed his entire body on the scale. The two gods then revealed themselves and blessed the noble king. The story of Bali is given in the Bhāgavata Purāna eighth book (and see chapter 3, note 19 above). It is also referred to in verses 24–25 of this chapter. Śrīdhara narrates that the pigeon and his mate treated a hunter as a guest and gave him their own flesh. For this, they were transported to heaven in a celestial vehicle. The hunter was impressed by their generosity and disgusted at himself. At the moment of death, his body was burnt in a forest fire and became freed from sin so that he, too, ascended into heaven. These stories illustrate the Purāṇic ideal of giving charity unconditionally to guests, and the benefits that accrue thereby.
5. *despite being restrained [by his own guru, Śukrācārya]*: Bali's guru, Śukrācārya, told Bali that the mendicant boy was in fact Viṣṇu, the enemy of the demons, and that his request should

not be granted. He even provided scriptural justification for the breaking of a promise, but Bali was true to his word, and as a token of his gift began to offer water from a pot. Śukrācārya entered the spout of the pot as an insect in order to obstruct the flow of water, but Vāmana pushed a piece of *darbha* grass into the spout, piercing Śukrācārya's eye. From that time on, the latter was blind in one eye.

6. *In the nights, they behaved like friends*: It was customary for soldiers on opposing sides to fraternize in the evening, after the day's battle, as occurred in the great war of the Mahābhārata.
7. *how he had been brought back to life by Jarā*: Jarāsandha, literally 'he who was joined together by Jarā', was created by the demoness called Jarā by joining together two halves of a child.

CHAPTER 73
Kṛṣṇa's Meeting [with the Kings]

1. *Ghanaśyāma [Kṛṣṇa]*: Ghanaśyāma is a name of Kṛṣṇa and means 'dark as a cloud'.
2. *Haihaya . . . because of wealth*: Śrīdhara states that Haihaya is Kārtavīrya. Kārtavīrya's minister tried to steal the divine cow from Paraśurāma's *āśrama*, on his master's bidding, killing the latter's father in the process. When Paraśurāma saw this, he killed Kārtavīrya and took a vow to wipe out the *kṣatriya* caste twenty-one times. This is described in the Bhāgavata Purāṇa (IX.15). Nahuṣa was once elected by the gods to fill the post of Indra temporarily when the latter went into hiding to get remission from the sin of killing Vṛtra, a *brāhmaṇa*. But once there, he desired Indra's wife, Indrāṇī, as a result of which he was cursed by the sage Agastya to become a python. He regained his original form upon seeing the Pāṇḍavas. Veṇu's story is described in the Bhāgavata Purāna (IV.14). He was a wicked king, hostile to the *brāhmaṇas*. When he prohibited the performance of sacrifice and the giving of alms, he was assassinated by the *brāhmaṇas*. Rāvaṇa's story is well known from the famous Rāmāyaṇa Epic. He was killed by Rāma, after abducting his wife, Sītā, and his kingdom was destroyed. Naraka's story is recounted in chapter 59 of this text.

CHAPTER 74
The Killing of Śiśupāla

1. *[He chose] Dvaipāyana . . . and Kṛtavraṇa*: These are all famous sages from the Vedic, Epic and Purāṇic literatures.
2. *just as those of Varuṇa had been previously*: Varuṇa once performed a *rājasūya* coronation sacrifice on the banks of the river Yamunā (Mahābhārata, *śalya parva*).
3. *On the day that the soma is extracted*: The *soma* is extracted on a particular day of the sacrifice, generally before the conclusion of the ceremonies. The *soma* plant was pressed between stones, strained, mixed with other ingredients, and then offered as libation to the gods.
4. *The schools of . . . highest goal*: Sāṅkhya and Yoga are two of the six schools of orthodox thought, and their influence pervades Purāṇic metaphysics. There is an atheistic system of Sāṅkhya, and a theistic one, referred to here.
5. *Their lineage was cursed by Yayāti*: Yayāti asked his eldest son, Yadu, to exchange his youthfulness for his own old age. When Yadu refused, Yayāti cursed his progeny, declaring that they would never become kings.
6. *for three consecutive births . . . hatred*: The story of the fall from Vaikuṇṭha of the two doorkeepers, Jaya and Vijaya, is narrated in the Śrīmad Bhāgavata (VII.1). When the four young celibate Kumāras, who had arrived at the gates of Vaikuṇṭha to visit Viṣṇu, were stopped by Jaya and Vijaya, they cursed the doorkeepers. As a result, Jaya and Vijaya took three consecutive births as demons. In the last of these births, the pair was born as Śiśupāla and Dantavakra.
7. *one's state of mind determines one's rebirth*: See chapter 1, note 33.
8. *The account of the birth . . . in great detail*: See note 6 above.

CHAPTER 75
The Crushing of Duryodhana's Pride

1. *O Bhagavān*: Here the term *Bhagavān* is used for Śuka.
2. *had merged into the feet of Kṛṣṇa*: As noted in 74.46, Śiśupāla attained the type of liberation called *sārūpya*, having the same form as the Lord.
3. *the patnīsaṃyāja ritual*: The *patnīsaṃyāja* ritual consists of four oblations offered to Soma, Tvaṣṭā, Agni and the wives of the gods.
4. *to remove the burden of the earth*: The burden of the earth refers

to the build-up of military power noted in I.17. The primary reason for Kṛṣṇa's incarnation, as outlined in the first chapter, was to remove this threat. By aggravating Duryodhana he was precipitating the great war that was to come.

CHAPTER 76
The Battle with Śālva

1. *the three cities*: On one occasion, the demons were given three aerial cities, made of gold, silver and iron respectively, as a boon by Brahmā. They could travel around the worlds in these with immunity, since they could only be destroyed when all three cities happened to be in the same place, and then only by one arrow. Śiva eventually accomplished this feat.

CHAPTER 78
Preparations for the Killing of Balvala and the Adventures of Balarāma

1. *You, our maternal cousin, Kṛṣṇa*: Dantavakra's mother, Śrutaśravā, was the sister of Kṛṣṇa's father Vasudeva.
2. *Kaumodakī mace*: The Kaumodakī mace was given to Kṛṣṇa by Varuṇa, god of the water, at the time of the burning of the Khāṇḍava forest.
3. *Romaharṣaṇa, the disciple of the great sage*: As noted in the Introduction (p. xv), the great sage Vyāsa compiled a Purāṇa Saṃhitā, or *ur*-Purāṇa text, from the tales, lore, anecdotes and songs from the ages and taught this to his disciple Romaharṣaṇa. Romaharṣaṇa, in turn, divided it into six parts and taught these to his six disciples.
4. *born from an improper marriage*: The *sūta*, charioteer, was a caste which some texts consider to be made up of the offspring of a *kṣatriya* father with a *brāhmaṇa* mother.
5. *the land of Bhārata [India]*: The story of Bhārata, after whom India is named in the Purāṇas, is narrated in the Bhāgavata (V.7–12). The land of Bhārata is described in the Purāṇas as consisting of nine concentric circles of land, each one surrounded by an ocean.

CHAPTER 79
An Outline of Balarāma's Pilgrimage

1. *He approached Prayāga ... ashram of Pulaha*: Prayāga is modern-day Allahabad. Pulaha is one of the *prajāpatis*, or progenitors of mankind, and son of Brahmā.

2. *He saw Balarāma . . . on Mount Mahendra*: Paraśurāma made Mount Mahendra his abode after slaughtering the *kṣatriyas*. See also chapter 82, note 2.
3. *Śrīraṅga, where Hari is present*: Hari is considered to be eternally present in certain holy places such as Śrīraṅga.
4. *Setu, the bridge across the ocean*: Setu is the place where Rāmacandra built a bridge of stones across the ocean to attack Laṅkā.
5. *the southern ocean, where . . . Kanyā*: The place in south India where the goddess is worshipped is Kanyākumārī, a very ancient holy place since it is mentioned frequently in the Mahābhārata, and was even known as such in the *Periplus* of Herodotus. The place is so named after the ascetic practices of Puṇyakāśī, daughter of Mayāsura and devotee of Śiva.
6. *the account of the annihilation . . . Pāṇḍavas*: After the great Kurukṣetra war, only a handful of combatants, including the Pāṇḍavas, remained alive.
7. *He had abstained from all engagement in the war*: Unlike Kṛṣṇa, Balarāma did not participate in the Kurukṣetra war, being sympathetic to both the Pāṇḍavas and the Kurus.
8. *Bhagavān Balarāma . . . pervades this universe*: Balarāma is being presented in these verses as ontologically the same as Kṛṣṇa, since he is a direct manifestation from Kṛṣṇa.

CHAPTER 80
The Story of Śrīdāmā

1. *two types of manifestation*: I translate *ubhaya liṅga*, which Śrīdhara takes to refer to moving and non-moving entities, as 'two types of manifestation'.

CHAPTER 81
The Episode of the Flat Rice

1. This verse is identical to Kṛṣṇa's statement in the Bhagavad Gītā (IX.26).

CHAPTER 82
The Meeting of the Gopas *and the Vṛṣṇi Clan*

1. *the kalpa world age*: A *kalpa* is a period of time consisting of 1,000 *caturyugas* (see chapter 8, note 1), or one day of Brahmā. This corresponds to 4,230,000,000 human years.
2. *Paraśurāma . . . purging the earth of the kṣatriya caste*: Paraśurāma is an incarnation of Viṣṇu who incarnated to destroy the corrupt *kṣatriya* caste. He is said to have exterminated the corrupt

kṣatriya caste eighteen times (in the Mahābhārata, *aśvamedha parva*, the number given is twenty-one times). His story is related in the Bhāgavata (IX.15–16).

3. *the coverings of their souls were destroyed*: In Hindu thought the embodied soul is considered to be enveloped in various coverings or sheaths (see chapter 87, note 7).

CHAPTER 83
The Queens Relate their Stories

1. *swan-like ascetics*: Saints are often compared to swans since the latter are reputed to be able to extract milk from a mixture of milk and water, just as saints are supposed to extract truth from illusion.
2. *my army of four divisions*: The four divisions are elephants, horses, chariots and infantry.
3. *Just as a fish . . . visible in water*: This story is related in the Mahābhārata, *ādi parva*. The king had set a near-impossible feat for the prospective suitors of his daughter, Draupadī. A small target (a fish) had been placed on top of a tall pole. Beneath it was a horizontal rotating plate with one small hole in it. An arrow had to be shot from below through the hole at the precise moment that it was aligned with the target. Moreover, the king had determined that this feat had to be accomplished using a particular bow that an ordinary man could barely lift. Whoever accomplished this task would win the hand of his daughter.
4. *a garland of dazzling jewels and gold*: In a *svayaṃvara* marriage ceremony, the bride places a garland over the neck of the man she has chosen as her spouse.
5. *The city is glorified . . . obscured the sun*: This is an example of the *alaṅkāra* known as *atiśayokti*, or hyperbole.

CHAPTER 84
Description of the Pilgrimage

1. *They were: Dvaipāyana [Vyāsa] . . . Vāmadeva and others*: These were all famous sages from the Vedic, Epic and Purāṇic periods.
2. *Brāhmaṇas are the venerable abode . . . source of the scriptures*: The sense here is that the *brāhmaṇas* teach scriptures, and the scriptures embody Kṛṣṇa. Therefore the *brāhmaṇas* are the abode of Kṛṣṇa.
3. *the mental covering of the soul*: The soul, in Vedāntic philosophy, is covered by an internal organ, the *antaḥkaraṇa* or *āśaya* of

mind, intelligence and ego (in addition to being covered by the external organs of the body). These coverings prevent the soul from realizing its true nature.

4. *that karma can be eradicated . . . with sacrificial oblations*: Reactions inherent in all *karma* (work) can be destroyed by offering one's *karma*, in this case the performance of Vedic sacrifice, to Kṛṣṇa. Gītā (V.10) states that: 'One who gives up attachment to one's acts, and offers them to the supreme being, is not affected by sin, like a lotus leaf by water.'

5. *the initiation ceremony*: Prior to the performance of a Vedic sacrifice, the sponsor of the sacrifice, in this case Vasudeva, undergoes an initiation ceremony called *dīkṣā*.

6. *When Vasudeva . . . [with butter]*: Śrīdhara states that *aktam* refers to daubing with mascara, and *abhyaktam* refers to smearing fresh butter on all limbs of the body.

7. *the post-sacrifice avabṛtha ablutions and the patnīsaṃyāja sacrifices*: The *avabṛtha* rites include a sacrifice to Varuṇa, god of water, the washing of the implements, and the bath of the sponsor of the sacrifice. The *patnīsaṃyāja* is a series of four *ghee* offerings to Soma, Tvaṣṭā, Agni and the wives of the gods.

CHAPTER 85
Fetching the Deceased Elder Brothers

1. *You are the eternal . . . into syllables*: Śrīdhara connects these four stages of sound with *vāc*, *pasyantī*, *madhyamā* and *vaikhari*, respectively. In the philosophical schools of the grammarians, the absolute truth is conceived of in terms of sound, *vāc*, also named *śabdabrahman*, 'sound *brahman*'. The system is a kind of sonic idealism wherein the entire world is an evolution from this original matrix of *śabdabrahman*. In the derivative ontological state of *pasyantī*, there is pure potentiality, but no differentiation of the sound. In the next state, *madhyamā*, *śabda* (sound) starts to become sequential and manifests as the mental sequence of thoughts. The next stage, *vaikharī*, corresponds to the externalization of words, and the external objects to which they refer. In this way, reality evolves in a type of sonic parallel to Sāṅkhya.

2. *You are the essence . . . the primordial matter*: Śrīdhara connects the material elements with ego under the influence of *tamas*; the senses with ego under the influence of *rajas*; and the gods with ego under the influence of *sattva* (see Introduction p. xli) on the Sāṅkhya of the Bhāgavata for further clarification.

3. *pradhāna [material nature] and the puruṣa [soul]*: In the Sāṇkhya

and Yoga schools, *pradhāna* is *prakṛti*, the universe of matter, and the *puruṣa* is the *ātmā*, or soul. The goal is to extricate the latter from the former.

4. *daityas, dānavas . . . nāyakas*: These are all different types of divine and demoniac beings.
5. *to the same extent [as those bound by hate]*: The demons hate Kṛṣṇa so intensely that their meditation upon him is even more unwavering than that of the gods.
6. *the first manvantara*: Śrīdhara glosses *antara* with *manvantara*. A *manvantara* is a reign of Manu, the progenitor of humans. The life span of a Manu is 71 *caturyugas*, or cycles of four ages.
7. *Brahmā . . . with his daughter*: Sarasvatī was Brahmā's daughter, born from his heart. Brahmā fell in love with her, but she tried to avoid the lecherous glances of her father by moving to his right. At this, a face appeared from his right, and, as she continued to walk around him in an attempt to avoid his amorous look, two more faces appeared, one after the other. Hence Brahmā has four heads. When Sarasvatī resorted to leaping into the sky, a fifth head appeared on Brahmā's head, turned upward (which was eventually severed by Śiva). Sarasvatī finally yielded to Brahmā, and became his wife. In the Bhāgavata (III.12.29–33) his sons, led by the sage Marīci, pleaded with their father not to perform such an act.

CHAPTER 86
Grace Bestowed on Śrutadeva

1. *a tridaṇḍa staff*: The *tridaṇḍa* staff consists of three sticks. The Manusmṛti, XII.10, states that 'the man is called a *tridaṇḍī* in whose mind control over three things – speech, thoughts and body – is firmly fixed.'
2. *our dynasty of king Nimi*: Nimi's dynasty is described earlier in the Bhāgavata (IX.13).
3. *the caused and uncaused characteristics*: Śrīdhara glosses the 'uncaused' with *prakṛti*, and the 'caused' with those things that evolve from it (see Introduction, pp. xl ff.).

CHAPTER 87
The Praise by the Vedas in the Exchange between Nārada and Nārāyaṇa

1. *who were born from the mind [of Brahmā]*: Mahābhārata, *ādi parva*, 65.10 names six sages born from the mind of Brahmā.
2. *after withdrawing into himself . . . previously created*: According

to the Bhāgavata, at the end of each full world cycle, the universe is dissolved back into *prakṛti*, and ultimately withdrawn into Viṣṇu.

3. *you awaken those who inhabit moving and non-moving forms*: When the universe is withdrawn into Viṣṇu all souls are put into a sleeping state, and their *karmas* and *saṃsāras* suspended. Everything is reactivated at the beginning of the next world cycle.

4. *but it remains unchanged . . . just like clay*: Clay can be transformed into objects, which eventually dissolve back into clay, but the clay itself does not change in nature. The Chāndogya Upaniṣad (VI.1.4) states that: 'Just as all things made of clay can be known by one lump of clay – any transformation of it [e.g. a pot] is just a label produced by speech, O dear boy, but the truth is that it is just clay.' In other words, just as a clay pot is ultimately just a transformation of clay, so the things of this world are simply transformations of Kṛṣṇa/Nārāyaṇa/Viṣṇu's energy.

5. *How can people's footsteps . . . on the earth*: Śrīdhara explains that just as, wherever people place their feet, they are ultimately placing them on the earth, similarly, whatsoever the Vedas describe in this world is simply a transformation of Viṣṇu, and therefore ultimately Viṣṇu.

6. *primordial intelligence . . . egg of a universe*: Intelligence (*mahat*) and ego (*ahaṅkara*) are the first and second products evolving from *prakṛti* during the creative formation of the world. When the latter is influenced by the various *guṇas*, the remaining ingredients in the physical universe evolve (see Introduction, pp. xl ff.).

7. *the different forms of people . . . annamaya*: Śridhara connects the different kinds of people with those conditioned by the five sheaths – the different layers of personhood, or coverings of the self. They are outlined in the Taittirīya Upaniṣad (II.1–5) as *annamaya*, the food sheath; *prāṇamaya*, the sheath of vital air; *manomaya*, the sheath of mind; *vijñānamaya*, the sheath of the intellect; and *ānandamaya*, the sheath of bliss.

8. *You are beyond both being and non-being*: Here, and in verse 24, Śrīdhara glosses *sad* (being) with the gross elements, and *asad* (non-being) with the subtle ones.

9. *those with gross vision*: Śrīdhara takes *kūrpadṛś* to mean 'having gravel in the eye', that is, with gross vision. *Kūrpa* means the space between the eyebrows, raising the possibility that this might be a reference to the *yogic* practice of focusing the eyes between the eyebrows during meditation (since the verse discusses meditational techniques).

10. *From the paths . . . the highest destination*: The meditation outlined in this verse seems to correspond to *tantric* practices, especially associated with the Śaivite and Śakta schools, but adopted by certain Vaiṣṇava sects as well. In these, the *kuṇḍalinī* or serpent energy, understood as a manifestation of the goddess in the form of *śakti*, rises up the central *suṣumnā* channel of the psychic body and through the seven *cakras*, or subtle vortexes of energy situated in various parts of the body, including the stomach, heart and head. When it reaches the topmost *cakra*, the *sahasrāra* in the brain area, she meets her Lord, in this case Viṣṇu (but, more typically, Śiva in the other *tantric* schools), who dwells there on a 1,000-petalled lotus, and the *yogī* has attained the goal.
11. *the flocks of swan [like devotees]*: See chapter 83, note 1.
12. *both hosts of gods came after Brahmā, in turn*: Śrīdhara takes the two classes of gods to be the *ādhyātmika* gods, who preside over the body and mind, and the *ādhidaivika* gods, who preside over the celestial bodies.
13. *Those who declare . . . the business transaction [of karma]*: Śrīdhara identifies the Vaiśeṣika and Patañjali schools as those who believe in production from non-being, the Nyāya school as that which believes in the destruction of being (i.e., that liberation is the destruction of the twenty-one types of suffering), the Sāṅkhya school as that which sees distinction in the *ātmā*, and the Mīmāṃsā school as that which believes truth lies in business transaction (i.e., enjoying the fruits that accrue from the performance of *karma*). But one could associate different philosophical schools with these categories.
14. *teach erroneously*: Śrīdhara glosses *ārupitaiḥ* with *bhramaiḥ*, 'with errors'.
15. *People do not discard . . . nature as gold*: In parallel fashion to chapter 87, note 4 above, the Chāndogya Upaniṣad (VI.1.5) says: 'Just as all things made of gold can be known by one nugget of gold – any transformation of it [e.g. a ring] is just a label produced by speech, dear boy, but the truth is that it is just gold.' In other words, a gold ring might look like a distinct object, but in essence it is just gold. Likewise, the things of this world are simply a transformation of Kṛṣṇa/Nārāyaṇa/Viṣṇu.
16. *You bind the learned with your words [in the Vedas]*: The Bhagavad Gītā II.42–3 states: 'The ignorant proclaim these flowery words [of the Veda]. These abound in varieties of sacrificial rites,

bestow rebirth as the fruit of *karma*, and lead towards the goal of opulence and enjoyment. Delighting in these words of the Vedas, the ignorant claim that: "there is nothing other than this". Aspiring for the celestial realms, these people are, by nature, full of desires.'

17. *Moving and non-moving beings . . . through his glance*: When the time for a new creation arrives, *prakṛti*, or material nature, is impregnated with the souls of all beings by Viṣṇu's glance.
18. *If embodied beings . . . sovereignty [over them]*: In this rather dense verse, Śrīdhara explains that if souls were unlimited, permanent and all-pervading (as some schools of thought, such as the Nyāya, Jain and Vaiśeṣika, hold), they would be equal to God, and so not subject to his control (such as being placed in bodies according to their *karma*).
19. *a person must be . . . not separate from him*: In other words, since beings are created from God and dependent upon him, then he is their controller.
20. *Because of the defective nature . . . do not understand*: Śrīdhara notes that one cannot know the supreme being, because the supreme being is beyond the reach of thoughts and words.
21. This verse is similar to the Chāndogya Upaniṣad, VI.9.1.
22. *your triple-rimmed frown [time]*: The three rims of time are past, present and future.
23. *who attempt to control . . . and of the senses*: The *aṣṭāṅga yoga* system dedicates two of its eight *aṅgas*, or limbs, to controlling the senses (*pratyāhāra*) and controlling the breath (*prāṇāyāma*).
24. *such an argument . . . and sometimes false*: Śrīdhara notes that the son is produced from the father and yet can be different from the father, and therefore the argument can be faulty, and the mistaking of a rope (the cause) for a snake (the effect) shows that the argument can be false. The snake/rope analogy is a favourite one of the great non-dualistic teacher Śaṅkarācārya, for whom the entire created world is an illusory superimposition upon *brahman* (within which there is neither form, qualities nor differentiation). As a person coming upon a rope on the road imagines it to be a snake and experiences fear, so the fearful world of experience is an imaginary projection upon *brahman*. Therefore the cause (such as a rope) may be real, but the effect it produces (the rope's resemblance to a snake) may be false. See also chapter 14, note 11.
25. *The false notion . . . mundane affairs*: Śrīdhara states that this is

a reference to the views of the Mīmāṃsā school, a tradition that attempted to perpetuate and justify the performance of Vedic ritual well after the Vedic age.

26. *The rhetoric . . . sacrificial utterances*: One is reminded of Kṛṣṇa's comments in the Gītā (II.42–3) (see p. 484, note 16). In the post-Vedic age, there is a general move away from the materialistic nature of Vedic ritual, which promotes the enjoyment of the fruit of sacrifice. One of the primary teachings that emerges strongly in the Gītā – *karma yoga* – is that as long as one desires to enjoy the fruits of sacrifice or of any type of activity, one must experience the good or bad karmic reactions inherent in all activity, and thus one remains ensnared in the cycle of birth and death.

27. *whose essence*: The term used for essence is *rasa*.

28. *your eight [mystic] qualities*: The eight *siddhis*, or mystic powers, referred to in Patañjali (III.46) are the powers of: *aṇimā*, becoming minute; *laghimā*, becoming extremely light; *mahimā*, expanding one's size and/or becoming extremely heavy; *prāpti*, reaching anywhere or anything; *prākāmya*, fulfilling one's wishes; *vāśitā*, controlling others; *īśitā*, creating, maintaining and destroying; *kāmāvasāyitā*, changing the natural order of things.

29. *Multitudes . . . their coverings*: The universes in Hindu cosmography are encapsulated by seven coverings of various elements, each one ten times thicker than the previous one.

30. *the Vedas . . . is not truth*: One of the statements describing *brahman* in the Bṛhad Āraṇyaka Upaniṣad (IV.22), is '*neti, neti*' – *brahman* is 'not this', *brahman* is 'not that'. By this technique, all items in the universe can be eliminated as not fully representative of *brahman*. An opposite heuristic strategy adopted in the Chāndogya Upaniṣad (III.14) is represented by the statement '*sarvaṃ khalvidaṃ brahma*' ('truly, this entire world is *brahman*').

CHAPTER 88
The Release of Rudra

1. *He is ego . . . tamas*: In the Sāṅkhya system of the Bhāgavata, all material substances evolve from *ahaṅkara*, 'ego', depending on whether it is affected by *sattva*, *rajas* or *tamas* – mind manifests from *sāttvic* ego, the ten sense organs from the *rājasic* ego, and the five gross elements from the *tāmasic* ego (see Introduction, pp. xl ff.).

2. *the aśvamedha sacrifices*: The *aśvamedha*, 'horse sacrifice', is an ancient Vedic sacrifice which is performed by kings to establish

their sovereignty. Yudhiṣṭhira performed one during his *rājasūya*, or coronation ceremony.

3. *Rāvaṇa and by Bāṇa*: Rāvaṇa was the evil king of Laṅkā in the Rāmāyaṇa, who kidnapped Rāma's wife Sītā. Śrīdhara does not specify the story in which Śiva granted boons to Rāvaṇa. In the Rāmāyaṇa, Rāvaṇa's favour was received from Brahmā. Rāvaṇa practised ascetic disciplines for 10,000 years in the middle of five fires, after which he cut off nine of his ten heads, one by one, as a sacrifice to Brahmā. Confident of his invincibility among humans, Rāvaṇa requested and was granted a boon by which he could not be killed by any god, but only by a man. He was eventually killed by Lord Rāma in his incarnation as a man. Bāṇa meditated on Śiva in the Himālayas. When Śiva appeared and asked him what he wanted, Bāṇa requested 1,000 hands so that he could destroy all his enemies. For his defeat by Kṛṣṇa see chapter 63.
4. *After he had bestowed . . . in a severe crisis*: This is an example of the *alaṅkāra* known as *parivṛtti*, 'the exchange of unequal things'. Śiva's reciprocation is far in excess of his devotees' offerings to him.
5. *uttering "Om"*: The Gītā (XVII.23–24) states that acts of charity, etc., should be given while uttering '*Om tat sat*.' '*Om*' is the sound representation of *brahman*. Colloquially, '*om*' can simply signify 'yes'.
6. *Vaikuṇṭha*: Vaikuṇṭha is the transcendent and eternal abode of Nārāyaṇa, situated in *brahman*, beyond the realm of *prakṛti*.
7. *One who goes there never returns*: The Gītā (VIII.21 and XV.6) speaks of Kṛṣṇa's abode as a place from which one never returns to this world.
8. *He became a piśāca [demon] on account of Dakṣa's curse*: Dakṣa, the father of Satī, once entered the sacrificial hall of the gods and sages, and was incensed when Śiva, his son-in-law, did not rise to greet him. He ranted against Śiva, reviling his ghoulish associates and macabre appearance, and then cursed him, saying that he would never receive a share of the oblations (Bhāgavata IV.26). *Piśācas* are evil beings generated from Brahmā.

CHAPTER 89
Retrieving the Sons of the Brāhmaṇa

1. *just as fire ... produced from itself*: In Sāṅkhya, grosser elements are generated from subtler ones, so water is generated from fire (see Introduction, p. xli).
2. *Lord Maheśvara [Śiva] ... his brother*: There are a number of different stories connected with Śiva's birth. In the Bhāgavata (III.12), he is generated from Brahmā's anger, which emerged from between the latter's brows, and thus is Brahma's offspring. Bhṛgu is also a son of Brahma.
3. *the eight siddhis*: For these mystic powers see chapter 87, note 28.
4. *My son has returned ... of deceitful intelligence*: The idea here is that a king should perform his *dharma* so perfectly that no non-*dharma* can enter the kingdom. The fact that the *brāhmaṇa* had lost nine of his sons suggested to him that something was amiss in the administration of the kingdom.
5. *These kṣatriyas ... at a sacrifice*: The sense is that if a *kṣatriya* cannot afford protection, he might as well go and perform sacrifices like a *brāhmaṇa*.
6. *Those people*: Śrīdhara takes 'those people' to be those who are censuring Arjuna.
7. *After crossing ... the Lokāloka mountain range*: As noted previously, the world, in Hindu cosmography, is divided up into seven concentric circles of land, each surrounded by an ocean containing different types of liquids, and seven mountain ranges. The entire area is separated from *tamas* (darkness) by the Lokāloka mountain range.
8. *mahat [primordial matter]*: In Īśvarakṛṣṇa's Sāṅkhya, *mahat* is *buddhi*, 'cosmic intelligence', the first evolutionary product from *prakṛti*. In the Bhāgavata (where *ahaṅkara* is the first product), *mahat* refers to the state of *prakṛti* in its creative potential, rather than to any subsequent distinct product or category.
9. *Ananta, the fabulous great serpent, was inside*: Ananta, a manifestation of Saṅkarṣaṇa [Balarāma], is a 1,000-headed serpent who resides at the bottom of the universe and holds up the worlds on his hoods.
10. *kalā [partial incarnations] ... dharma*: See Introduction pp. xix–xxii for a discussion of *kalā*.
11. *Nara and Nārāyaṇa*: Nara and Nārāyaṇa are Arjuna and Kṛṣṇa in the form of hermits who reside in Badarikāśrama in the Himālayas, performing ascetic disciplines.

12. *'Om'*: *'Om'* is uttered in contexts of acceptance. See chapter 88, note 5.

CHAPTER 90
Description of Kṛṣṇa's Activities

1. *Aravinda [Kṛṣṇa]*: Aravinda is a name of Kṛṣṇa which means 'lotus'.
2. *O cakravākī bird . . . wail piteously*: The *cakravākī* birds are said to lament for their mates at night when they are separated.
3. *braid of hair*: The crest plumes of the *cakravākī* bird are being compared to a braid of hair in the imagery of this verse.
4. *Or have your personal possessions . . . Mukunda?*: According to Śrīdhara, the ocean's personal possessions were the Kaustubha gem, which Kṛṣṇa wears, as well as Śrī, the goddess of fortune (both of which were produced from the churning of the ocean of milk, an episode described in the Bhāgavata, Book VIII, chs 6–7). The queens were wondering whether the ocean was lamenting just as they were lamenting because Kṛṣṇa had taken away the *kuṅkum* powder from their breasts.
5. *the penance [they must have performed in previous lives]?*: The idea here is that they must have performed intensely austere disciplines in previous existences to have attained the privilege of having Kṛṣṇa as their husband (as was the case for Devakī and Vasudeva in chapter 1).
6. *dharma, artha and kāma*: See chapter 5, note 4. These three goals are pursued in domestic life.
7. *the club battle*: This refers to the intra-clan Yadu battle which will be described below.
8. *svarūpya [liberation]*: For the five types of liberation in Vaiṣṇava theology see chapter 12, note 7.

BOOK XI

CHAPTER 6
The Gods Visit Kṛṣṇa

1. *the vyūha forms*: In the Vaiṣṇava Pañcarātra theology, the *vyūha* forms are expansions of Viṣṇu. The four primary ones are Vāsudeva, Saṅkarṣaṇa, Pradyumna and Aniruddha (these are not the same as their namesakes in Kṛṣṇa's *līlā* – Kṛṣṇa and his sons – except in so far as they are expansions of Viṣṇu). Each of these transcendent *vyūha* forms has a specific function and cosmic jurisdiction.

2. *sārṣṭi, equal opulence [with you]*: This is one of five types of liberation. For the other types, see chapter 12, note 7.
3. *for the purpose of passing beyond the celestial realms*: One has to pass beyond the celestial realms, which are still within the realm of *saṃsāra*, in order to attain Viṣṇu's abode.
4. *the adhvara sacrificial fire*: The *adhvara* fire is part of the *soma* ritual, and involves an animal sacrifice.
5. *Niruktas*: The Niruktas are texts dealing with the etymologies of Sanskrit words.
6. *With their three steps . . . [the Ganges]*: The three steps refer to the story of the incarnation of Vāmana, who appeared as a dwarf *brāhmaṇa* in order to curb the power of the king of the demons, Bali, who was actually a great devotee, but who had usurped Indra's kingdom. As described previously (see chapter 3, note 19), Vāmana approached Bali asking for three steps of land in charity. Śrīdhara states that his second step was like a victory flag. Viṣṇu's toe burst through the shell of the universe on his second step, through which the Ganges poured forth, flowing down over the three worlds like a fluttering banner.
7. *They say that . . . and mahat*: After the soul is injected into the *avyakta*, or undifferentiated *prakṛti* in its state as *mahat* (cosmic intelligence), creation takes place.
8. *your three wheels*: According to Śrīdhara, the wheel of time is divided into the three four-month-long seasons. Alternatively, the three wheels could denote past, present and future.
9. *the golden egg [of the universe] with its external coverings*: As noted earlier, the universe is described in the fifth book of the Bhāgavata as being like an egg with seven coverings.
10. *the sense objects . . . in māyā*: The senses are an evolutionary product of *prakṛti*, which is churned by the *guṇas* (see Introduction, pp. xl ff.).
11. *[since they may again fall under their control]*: Śrīdhara notes that the memory of previous sense enjoyment remains with those who are endeavouring to control their senses. In other words, other entities are fearful that previous memories and habits may impel them to fall again under the control of sensuality. Such a predicament does not apply to Kṛṣṇa, who, as we have been told repeatedly throughout the text, does not need to look beyond his own self for enjoyment. Kṛṣṇa can therefore enjoy or show indifference to sense objects based on his own desire, and not because he is subject to their influence, past or present.
12. *the rivers produced from washing your feet*: This is a reference to

the story of Vāmana, mentioned earlier (see note 6 above), who burst through the coverings of the universe with his toe when taking his second step.

13. *The moon was once afflicted . . . in due sequence*: Dakṣa's twenty-seven daughters were married to Candra, the moon god. But twenty-six of them complained that Candra was showing particular attention to Rohiṇī. Dakṣa warned Candra to be impartial, but the daughters continued to complain. Consequently, Dakṣa cursed Candra with consumption. When the gods solicited Dakṣa on Candra's behalf, Dakṣa modified the curse so that Candra would only be afflicted for a fortnight. Candra went to Prabhāsa to bathe and slowly recovered. It is as a result of Dakṣa's curse that the moon, which has 27 phases, waxes and wanes.

14. *by eating the remnants of your food . . . you have enjoyed*: *Prasāda*, or God's grace, is any item (usually of food, but also of clothing or adornment) that has first been offered to and enjoyed by the deity, and then returned to the devotee. Partaking of *prasāda* purifies the devotee, and is an important feature of Hindu worship.

15. *sannyāsī sages who are śramaṇa ascetics*: *Sannyāsīs* are the members of the fourth *āśrama* or stage of life. There are various stages of *sannyāsa*, all of which involve renunciation of material attachments, including home and family. *Śramaṇas* are ascetic monks, some of whom renounce even clothing. The term is also associated with Buddhist monks.

CHAPTER 29
Kṛṣṇa's Final Instructions to Uddhava

1. *the practice of yoga . . . O Acyuta*: The *yoga* being referred to here is the *aṣṭāṅga yoga* system of Patañjali.

2. Compare this verse to Bhagavad Gītā (VI.34), where Arjuna complains that the mind is unstable, turbulent, powerful and obstinate, and as difficult to control as the wind.

3. *you yourself take pleasure from [being with] the animals*: This refers to the fact that Kṛṣṇa is a cowherd boy.

4. *in the form of the inner Lord*: Śrīdhara glosses *caitya* with *antaryāmī*, which I have translated as 'inner Lord'. Vaiṣṇavas consider the *antaryāmi* to be a manifestation of God within the heart that is eternally different from the individual soul. (The practitioners of advaita Vedānta, following Śaṅkara, do not accept any ultimate difference between the individual soul and God.)

5. *who has assumed the three forms*: The three forms are Brahmā, the creator, Viṣṇu, the preserver, and Śiva, the destroyer.
6. *A person should perform all dharmas for my sake*: The 'most confidential instruction of all' in the Bhagavad Gītā (XVIII.64) is given in XVIII.65–6, wherein Kṛṣṇa tells Arjuna: 'Fix your mind on me, become my devotee, sacrifice to me and offer homage to me. I promise that you will definitely come to me because you are my devotee. Abandon all *dharmas* and take exclusive refuge with me. Do not worry, I will protect you from all sins.' In the Uddhava Gītā, Kṛṣṇa gives more detail as to what exactly such surrender entails.
7. *one should delight in doing dharma to me*: *Dharma* is used in a different sense, here, from elsewhere. *Dharma* is used in a number of different ways, both diachronically throughout Indian thought, and synchronically by different schools (see Dasgupta 1922, vol. IV: 3–11 for discussion). It is generally understood to refer to an individual's occupational or social duties, but in the Bhāgavata, when connected with devotion to Kṛṣṇa, it entails the pure worship of and surrender to God with no ulterior motive. See verse 21 of this chapter for a definition.
8. *a member of the Pukkasa tribe*: The *Pukkasas* are considered to be a low-caste tribe.
9. *A paṇḍita . . . the gentle or the cruel*: Compare with Bhagavad Gītā (V.18): 'A *paṇḍita* sees with equal vision a *brāhmaṇa* who is endowed with humility and learning, a cow, an elephant, a dog and one who cooks dogs.'
10. *like a stick on the ground*: The term *daṇḍavat*, 'like a stick', means to prostrate oneself fully, with arms extended over the head such that the entire body is stretched out straight like a stick. The term means 'thank you' in modern north Indian languages.
11. *Until . . . body, mind and speech*: Worshipping God, but failing to see him in all creatures, is here considered to be less spiritually advanced.
12. *There is not the slightest loss . . . my dear Uddhava*: Compare this with Bhagavad Gītā (II.40): 'One's effort is not lost in this [enterprise], nor is any reverse to be found.'
13. *I give myself . . . among my devotees*: Compare this to Bhagavad Gītā (XVIII.69): 'There is no one doing more pleasing service to me among people than he [who teaches this], and no one else on earth shall be dearer to me.'
14. *One who recites . . . day by day*: Compare this with Bhagavad Gītā (XVIII.70): 'I will have been worshipped through the sacri-

fice of knowledge by anyone who will study this sacred dialogue of ours – this is my opinion.'

15. *And the person . . . is not bound by karma*: Compare this with Bhagavad Gītā (XVIII.71): 'A person who hears this faithfully and without scoffing, he also is liberated, and will attain the auspicious planets of the pious.'
16. *have you understood . . . been dispelled?*: Compare this with Bhagavad Gītā (XVIII.72): 'Has this been heard by you attentively, Arjuna, and have your ignorance and delusion been destroyed?'
17. *You should not pass on . . . non-devotees*: Compare this to Bhagavad Gītā (XVIII.67): 'This should not be taught by you to one who is without austerity, to one without devotion, to one who does not wish to hear, or to one who speaks ill of me.'
18. *You should tell . . . or women*: Compare this to Bhagavad Gītā (IX.32): 'Those who take refuge with me, Arjuna, even if they are born of sinful wombs, women, *vaiśyas* or *śūdras*, can attain the supreme destination.'
19. *the four goals of life*: The four *puruṣāthas*, 'goals of human life', are *dharma*, religious duty; *artha*, economic prosperity; *kāma*, sensual enjoyment; and *mokṣa*, liberation. Each one leads to the next.
20. *When a mortal . . . my same nature*: Śrīdhara takes this as the liberation of *sārṣṭi* – having the same opulence as the Lord.
21. *known as Badarī*: This refers to the holy site of Badarī *āśrama* in the Himālayas.
22. *to his devotee, is liberated, along with the world*: Śrīdhara states that the world can be liberated by association with such a devotee.

CHAPTER 30
The Destruction of the Yadu Dynasty

1. *attained the same [form] as him*: This is the liberation known as *sarūpa*.
2. *Madhudviṭ [Kṛṣṇa]*: Madhudviṭ is a name of Kṛṣṇa meaning 'enemy of Madhu'.

CHAPTER 31
Kṛṣṇa Returns to his own Abode

1. *He . . . fixed his mind on himself*: This phrase could also read: 'Kṛṣṇa . . . fixed his mind on the *ātmā*.'
2. *Without burning . . . yogic concentration*: A *yogī* can self-combust his own body through the power of mind, when he is

ready to leave it for his next destination. However, Kṛṣṇa entered his supreme abode in his self-same body. Vaiṣṇava commentators hold that this is because his body is not made of the material elements of *prakṛti*, but is pure *brahman*.

3. *he saved you . . . ultimate weapon*: As noted earlier (see chapter 1, note 9), the last remaining survivor from the Kuru side in the Mahābhārata war, Aśvatthāmā, attempted to kill Parīkṣit when he was in the womb with the fiery *brahmāstra* weapon, so as to eradicate the sole surviving offspring of the Pāṇḍavas, and hence their dynasty.

4. *When your grandfathers . . . the great journey*: In the Bhāgavata (I.15) the Pāṇḍavas and Draupadī shed their royal clothes for tree bark, and then, desiring to relinquish the world, keep heading north into the Himālayas, until they drop down dead one by one.

Glossary of Sanskrit Terms and Names

Names of Kṛṣṇa and Viṣṇu are in bold.

Acyuta, name of Kṛṣṇa or Viṣṇu meaning 'one who does not fall down'.
adharma, antonym of *dharma*, irreligion.
Adhokṣaja, name of Kṛṣṇa and Viṣṇu meaning 'one who is beyond sense perception'.
Aditi, wife of Kaśyapa; had thirty-three sons, known as the Āditeyas.
advaita, 'non-duality', a philosophical tenet.
āgama, texts containing details of ritualistic worship, generally to Viṣṇu or Śiva.
Agha, the serpent demon.
ahaṅkāra, the false ego that causes one to identify with what one is not – the body and mind, etc. – rather than with one's real self, the *ātma*.
Aho! A common explanation in Sanskrit, meaning various things, such as Alas! Hey! Just see!
Airāvata, Indra's elephant mount.
Ajita, a name of Kṛṣṇa meaning 'the unconquered one'.
Akrūra, uncle and devotee of Kṛṣṇa.
akṣauhiṇī, battalion consisting of 21,870 elephants and as many chariots, 65,610 cavalry and 109,350 infantry.
alaṅkāra, literary embellishment, or adornment.
Āḷvārs, south Indian saints, devotees of Viṣṇu.
Ambikā, the goddess, a name of Umā, also known as Pārvatī, the wife of Śiva.
aṃśa, incarnations of deities that embody a portion or aspect of their powers.
ānanda, bliss; a quality of *brahman*.
Ananta, also known as Śesa, the thousand-headed snake upon which Viṣṇu rests as he reclines on the ocean of milk. Also a name of Kṛṣṇa meaning 'without limit'.

Aniruddha, Pradyumna's son, Kṛṣṇa's grandson.
Aravinda, name of Kṛṣṇa meaning 'lotus'.
arghya, water offered to guests for washing the hands.
Ariṣṭa, the bull demon.
Arjuna, one of the five Pāṇḍavas, and son of Indra.
arjuna, a species of tree.
artha, prosperity; one of the four goals of life.
Ārya/Āryan, a civilized or refined person and follower of the Vedic culture.
āśrama, a hermitage; a stage of a person's life (there are four) in ancient India.
aṣṭāṅga yoga, system of *yoga* of eight *aṅgas*, 'limbs', or stages.
aśvamedha, 'horse sacrifice', performed at the time of the coronation of a powerful king.
Atharvaveda, one of the four Vedas chanted in sacrificial contexts; contains spells, incantations, etc.
ātmā, the innermost self or soul. Pure eternal consciousness.
avatāra, an incarnation of Lord Viṣṇu who periodically descends into the world to protect *dharma*, according to the needs of time and place.
avyakta, undifferentiated *prakṛti*, the primordial material matrix before the evolution of the elements and the manifest world.
Baka, crane demon.
Baladeva, a name of Balarāma, brother of Kṛṣṇa.
Balarāma, brother of Kṛṣṇa.
Bali, king of demons, who had usurped Indra's kingdom, but a great devotee of Viṣṇu; was subdued by the Vāmana incarnation.
Bhadrakālī, another name for the goddess.
Bhagavad Gītā, 'song of God', spoken by Kṛṣṇa to Arjuna.
Bhagavān, God, 'one possessing *bhaga*', namely, prosperity, dignity, distinction, excellence, majesty, etc.
bhakta, a devotee.
bhakti, devotion.
bhakti yoga, the *yoga* of devotion.
bhāra, a measure of weight.
Bhauma, also known as Naraka, a demon who fought Kṛṣṇa.
Bhavānī, the goddess, another name for Umā (Pārvatī), the wife of Śiva.
Bhīma, one of the five Pāṇḍavas and son of Vāyu.
Bhīṣma, ancestor of the Kuru dynasty, uncle of Pāṇḍu and Dhṛtarāṣṭra.
Bho!, a common exclamation in classical Sanskrit.
bhūta, ghost.

bīja, 'seed' *mantra* consisting of the essential letter or syllable of a deity's name.
Brahmā, the four-headed creator god who engineers the forms of this world.
Brahmamuhūrta, the period before sunrise, considered the most suitable time for meditation and other religious pursuits.
brahman, name for the absolute truth in the Upaniṣads and throughout Hinduism.
brāhmaṇa, a member of the scholarly and priestly class; one of the four castes in the Hindu social system.
brāhmaṇas, a genre of Vedic texts outlining details for the performance of sacrifice.
brahmarākṣasa, particularly powerful type of demon.
brahmāstra, very powerful weapon in the Purāṇic arsenal; type of heat weapon.
Bṛhadvana, another name for Gokula.
buddhi, intelligence.
Caitanya, ecstatic mystic, founder of the Gauḍīya (Bengal) school of Vaiṣṇavism.
cakra, Kṛṣṇa's disc weapon.
cakras, subtle vortexes of energy situated in various parts of the body.
cakravāka, birds said to lament for their mates at night when they are separated.
cāṇḍāla, outcaste.
Cāṇūra, wrestler who fought with Kṛṣṇa.
cāraṇas, a type of celestial being who sings angelically.
caturyuga, four-*yuga* cycle; one day of Brahmā or 3,600,000 human years.
cit, knowledge; a quality of *brahman*.
daityas, demons born of Diti, wife of Kaśyapa.
ḍākinīs, a class of women who can perform magic with the use of *mantras*.
Dakṣa, the father of Satī.
Dāmodara, name of Kṛṣṇa meaning 'he whose belly is bound'.
dānavas, demons, born of Danu, wife of Kaśyapa.
daṇḍavat, 'like a stick', falling down prostrate with a straight body in the offering of homage.
Dāruka, Kṛṣṇa's charioteer.
Dāśārha, name of Kṛṣṇa meaning descendant of Daśārha, a king of the Yadu dynasty.
dāsya, servitude, one of the five primary *bhakti rasas* in the Caitanya school of Vaiṣṇavism.

Devaka, father of Devakī and brother of Ugrasena, Kaṃsa's father.
Devakī, Kṛṣṇa's real mother.
Devī, the goddess.
Devī Bhāgavata, another Purāṇa, also known as the Bhāgavata, which upholds the goddess as the supreme absolute being.
dharma, prescribed religious codes of conduct for human beings in terms of gender, caste, age and other criteria; construed in the Bhāgavata as unalloyed devotion to Kṛṣṇa.
Dharma, name of a demigod, the personification of *dharma*.
Dhenuka, the ass demon.
Dhṛtarāṣṭra, blind father of the 100 Kurus, paternal uncle of the Pāṇḍavas and ruler of Hastināpura.
Draupadī, daughter of King Drupada and wife of the five Pāṇḍavas.
Droṇa, the martial arts teacher of both the Pāṇḍavas and the sons of Dhṛtarāṣṭra.
Duryodhana, the eldest of the scheming 100 sons of Dhṛtarāṣṭra.
dvaita, a dualistic school of Vedānta.
Dvārakā, Kṛṣṇa's capital city.
Dvivida, impudent ape who fought with Balarāma.
Gada, one of six sons born to one of Vasudeva's seven wives, Rohiṇī; a half-brother of Kṛṣṇa.
gandharvas, celestial beings renowned for their beautiful singing.
Gaṅgā, sacred river.
Garuḍa, the carrier of Viṣṇu, a huge eagle.
Ghanaśyāma, a name of Kṛṣṇa meaning 'dark as a cloud'.
Girijā, 'mountain-born', name of Śiva's consort Pārvatī, daughter of the Himālaya mountains.
Gokula, place near Vṛndāvana.
Goloka, divine realm within *brahman* exclusive to Kṛṣṇa himself in the theology of the Caitanya and Vallabha sects.
gopa, a male cowherd.
gopī, a female cowherd.
Govardhana, hill which Kṛṣṇa held up with his little finger.
Govinda, name of Kṛṣṇa meaning 'tender of cattle'.
guhyakas, type of celestial being.
guṇas, 'strands' or 'qualities' inherent in *prakṛti*: *sattva*, 'goodness'; *rajas*, 'action'; and *tamas*, 'inertia'.
guru, teacher.
hālāhala, poison produced when the ocean of milk was churned by the gods and the demons; drunk by Śiva.
Hari, name of Kṛṣṇa meaning one who takes away (evil, or sin).

Harivaṃśa, supplement to the Mahābhārata, narrating the story of Kṛṣṇa's life.
Hastināpura, capital city of the Kurus.
Hiraṇyākṣa, demon who carried the Earth to the Pātāla nether worlds.
Hṛṣīkeśa, name of Kṛṣṇa meaning 'Lord of the senses', or 'one with bristly hair'.
Indra, god of rain, and king of the gods.
Indraprastha, capital city of the Pāṇḍavas.
Īśvara, God, the supreme being, identified as Kṛṣṇa in the Bhāgavata.
Jāmbavān, bear devotee of Rāma who fought his master in the form of Kṛṣṇa unawares.
Janārdana, name of Kṛṣṇa or Viṣṇu meaning 'one who stimulates men'.
japa, meditation upon the repetition of a name of a deity.
Jarā, hunter who shot Kṛṣṇa in the foot.
Jarāsandha, king, who fought Kṛṣṇa eighteen times.
jīva, embodied soul.
kalā, 'portion', or 'partial incarnation' of a supreme deity.
kali yuga, present world age, the last and most degenerate of the four ages.
Kāliya, multi-headed snake who polluted the Yamunā river.
kalpavṛkṣa, also known as *kalpataru*, wish-fulfilling tree of the gods which bestows whatever object is requested.
Kāma, the Hindu equivalent of Cupid, the god of love; pierces his victims with flowery arrows of love; erotic pleasure.
kāma, the satisfaction of desires, sensual enjoyment, one of the four goals of human life.
kāmadhenu, heavenly cow that grants all wishes.
Kaṃsa, king of Mathurā, and sworn enemy of Kṛṣṇa. Lord of the Bhojas.
Kanyākumārī, the southernmost tip of India, and a very ancient holy place.
karma, 'work', or 'act' and the reaction that is generated from it.
karma yoga, the performance of one's duty without desire for the result.
Kārttikeya, name of Skanda, son of Śiva and commander-in-chief of the gods.
Kashmir Śaivism, monistic philosophical school devoted to Śiva.
kathā, the public recitation of the activities of Kṛṣṇa.
Kātyāyanī, name for the goddess.
kaumara, the period of childhood from birth to five years.
Kaustubha, jewel obtained from the ocean of milk, worn by Kṛṣṇa.

Keśava, name of Kṛṣṇa meaning 'having beautiful hair'.
Keśī, horse demon.
Khāṇḍava, forest burnt in the Mahābhārata as an offering to Agni.
kinnaras, type of celestial being.
kiśora, the period of life between eleven and fifteen years of age.
kṛṣṇa, black.
kṣatriya, warrior caste, one of the four social orders.
kṣetra, 'the field', namely, *prakṛti*, the material world.
Kubera, the treasurer of the demigods.
Kumāras, four boy sages: Sanaka, Sanandana, Sanātana and Sanat; sons of Brahmā.
kuṅkum, saffron powder.
Kuntī, mother of the five Pāṇḍavas.
Kūrma, tortoise incarnation of Viṣṇu.
Kuru, famous dynasty, forefather of both the Pāṇḍavas and the 100 sons of Dhṛtarāṣṭra, but usually used in connection with the latter.
kuśa, sacred grass used in ritual contexts.
kuṣmāṇḍas, type of demoniac being; a witch.
Kuvalayāpīḍa, huge elephant who opposed Kṛṣṇa's entrance into Mathurā.
lakṣaṇas, traditional characteristics of a Purāṇa.
Lakṣmī, Śrī, the goddess of fortune and consort of Viṣṇu.
līlā, sports or pastimes of Kṛṣṇa when he incarnates into the world.
lokapālas, four guardians of the universe: Indra, Agni, Yama and Varuṇa.
Mādhava, name of Kṛṣṇa meaning 'descendant of Madhu'.
Madhu and *Mādhava*, spring months.
Madhudviṭ, name of Kṛṣṇa meaning 'enemy of Madhu'.
madhuparka, beverage offered to guests; consists of a mixture of honey and milk.
Madhus, name for the Yādavas.
Madhusūdana, name of Kṛṣṇa meaning 'killer of Madhu'.
Madhva, famous Vaiṣṇava theologian in the thirteenth century.
māgadhas, royal bards who recited the glories of royal lineages.
Mahābhārata, 100,000-verse epic describing the saga of the five Pāṇḍava brothers and their wife.
mahāratha, 'great charioteer', who can fight 10,000 foot-soldiers.
mahat, also known as *buddhi*, first evolute from *prakṛti*; cosmic intelligence.
mahāvākya, a 'pivotal', 'most important', or 'representational statement' for the theology of a sect.

mālatī, a type of jasmine with fragrant white flowers.
mallikā, a type of jasmine.
manas, the mind.
mantra, sacred utterance, particularly one containing the name of a deity.
maruts, Indra's companions, the storm gods.
mātās, bloodthirsty female spirits associated with Kālī in later texts.
Mathurā, Kṛṣṇa's birthplace, adjacent to Vṛndāvana.
Matsya, fish incarnation of Viṣṇu.
Maya, celestial architect of the gods.
māyā, power of illusion that ensnares all entities in the world.
Mīmāṃsā, one of the six schools of orthodox philosophical thought; formulated a rationale for perpetuating the old Vedic sacrificial rites.
mlecchas, people outside the Āryan social order; often used for foreigners.
mokṣa, liberation from worldly existence.
Mucukunda, famous king who incinerated Jarāsandha.
Mukunda, name of Kṛṣṇa meaning 'the giver of liberation'.
Murāri, name of Kṛṣṇa meaning 'enemy of the demon Mura'.
Muṣṭika, wrestler who fought with Balarāma.
nāgas, celestial serpents which have jewels in their hoods.
Nakula, one of the five Pāṇḍavas and a twin son of the Aśvins.
Nanda, Kṛṣṇa's foster-father.
Nara Nārāyaṇa Ṛṣi, incarnation of Viṣṇu.
Nārada, devotee sage who travels through space constantly chanting the names of Viṣṇu.
Naraka, also known as Bhauma, demon enemy of Kṛṣṇa.
Nārāyaṇa, another name for Viṣṇu among Vaiṣṇavas.
Niruktas, texts dealing with the etymologies of Sanskrit words.
Nṛsiṃha, half-man, half-lion incarnation of Viṣṇu, who saved the child devotee Prahlāda from his murderous father.
Nyāya, one of the six schools of orthodox thought; focused on developing rules of logic.
Om, sound representation of *brahman*; uttered in contexts of acceptance.
pañcādhyāya, five chapters in Bhāgavata's tenth book dedicated to Kṛṣṇa's amorous pastimes with the *gopīs*.
Pañcarātra, ritualistic texts expounding the details of Vaiṣṇava worship and praxis.
Pāṇḍavas, five brothers, and Kṛṣṇa's cousins; their saga is narrated in the Mahābhārata Epic.

Pāṇḍu, father of the five Pāṇḍava brothers and brother of Dhṛtarāṣṭra.
Paramātmā, 'supreme Soul', understood by Vaiṣṇavas as a form of Viṣṇu.
parārdha, 100,000 billion years, half of Brahmā's life.
Paraśurāma, incarnation of Viṣṇu who exterminated the warrior caste twenty-one times.
pārijāta, tree in the celestial realms whose scented flowers never fade.
Parīkṣit, the last remaining male in the Pāṇḍava dynasty, to whom the Bhāgavata is addressed.
Patañjali, author of the Yoga Sūtras.
paugaṇḍa, period of youth from six to sixteen years of age.
Pauṇḍraka, foolish king who thought he was Kṛṣṇa.
Phālgunī, name of Arjuna, who was born under this constellation.
piṇḍa, a periodic offering made of rice and offered to the departed soul.
piśācas, very evil beings created by Brahmā.
Pradyumna, Kṛṣṇa's eldest son from Rukmiṇī.
Prahlāda, great child devotee; survived a variety of murderous attempts by his demoniac father, Hiraṇyakaśipu, by taking refuge with Lord Hari.
prajāpatis, beings created by Brahmā for the purpose of facilitating creation.
prakṛti, the primordial matter from which the entire creation evolves in Purāṇic thought; consists of three qualities – *sattva*, 'goodness'; *rajas*, 'action'; and *tamas*, 'inertia'.
Pralamba, a demon who infiltrated Vraj in the guise of a cowherd boy.
pralaya, the destruction of the universe; *brahmapralaya* occurs at the end of 1,000 sets of four *yugas* when the entire universe is torched by intense fire.
pramathas, Śiva's attendants.
prāṇāyāma, breath control, the fourth limb of the eight-limbed path of Patañjali's *aṣṭāṅga yoga*.
prasāda, 'God's grace', any item that has first been offered to and enjoyed by the deity and then returned back to the devotee.
Prayāga, modern-day Allahabad.
pretas, departed spirits.
Pṛthā, another name for Kuntī, mother of the Pāṇḍavas.
purāṇa, 'that which took place previously', namely, texts of ancient lore; there are eighteen Purāṇas, one of which is the Bhāgavata.
purohita, family priest.

puruṣa, the innermost self or soul; pure eternal consciousness. A term for *ātmā*.
puruṣārthas, 'four goals of life': *dharma*, religious duty; *artha*, material prosperity; *kāma*, sensual enjoyment; and *mokṣa*, liberation from the cycle of birth and death.
Puruṣa-sūkta, ancient Ṛgvedic hymn to the *Puruṣa*, 'supreme being', often recited by Vaiṣṇavas.
Pūtanā, demon who takes the form of a beautiful woman and tries to poison Kṛṣṇa.
Rādhā, Kṛṣṇa's consort.
rajas, one of the three *guṇas*: action in, or characterized by, self-interest, excessive endeavour and attachment to the fruits of action.
rājasūya, horse sacrifice, performed at the installation of a new emperor.
rākṣasa, demoniac being; also one of the six types of marriage recognized in Purāṇic times, when the bride is snatched away by brute force by the suitor.
Rāma, name of Balarāma; also the incarnation of Viṣṇu who rescued his wife Sītā after she was kidnapped by the demon Rāvaṇa.
Ramā, goddess of fortune, also known as Śrī.
Rāmānuja, famous Vaiṣṇava theologian of the twelfth century CE.
Rāmāyaṇa, epic narrating the story of Rāma, the incarnation of Viṣṇu.
rasa, 'taste', 'mood' or 'flavour'; in aesthetics, the relishing of an aesthetic emotional mood. For the full list of the eight *rasas*, see Introduction, p. lxi.
rāsa, pastime, Kṛṣṇa's dance with the *gopīs*.
Rāvaṇa, evil king of Laṅkā in the Rāmāyaṇa, who kidnapped Rāma's wife Sītā.
Ṛgveda, one of the four Vedas; consists of hymns to the gods, chanted during the performance of sacrifice.
Rohiṇī, a constellation.
ṛṣi, sage.
ṛtvik, one of the priests officiating at the sacrifice.
Rudra, name of Śiva.
Rukmī, Rukmiṇī's eldest brother.
Rukmiṇī, Kṛṣṇa's principal wife.
śabdabrahman, absolute truth manifest in the form of sound.
sādhu, wandering ascetic saint; an exclamation meaning 'bravo'.
sādhya, type of celestial being.
Sagara, famous king with 60,000 sons.
Sahadeva, one of the five Pāṇḍavas and twin son of the Aśvins.

sakhya, friendship, one of the five primary *bhakti rasas* in the Caitanya school of Vaiṣṇavism.
śākta, follower of Devī, the goddess.
śakti, power, usually associated with the goddess, or feminine power of a male divinity.
sālokya, living in the same abode as the Lord; one of the five types of liberation in Vaiṣṇava theology.
Śālva, Kṛṣṇa's enemy who attacked Dvārakā in the aerial city Saubha.
samādhi, the eighth and final stage of the eight-limbed path of Patañjali's yoga system, when the *ātmā* (soul) is realized.
Sāmaveda, one of the four Vedas; consists of hymns to be chanted in the performance of sacrifice.
Śambara, enemy of Kṛṣṇa.
sāmīpya, living close to the Lord; one of the five types of liberation in Vaiṣṇava theology.
saṃsāra, the cycle of birth and death.
saṃskāra, life-cycle ritual; in *yoga* psychology, a mental imprint in the subconscious.
Śaṅkara, famous monist philosopher who initiated the *advaita*, 'non-dualist', philosophical system in the eighth to ninth centuries.
Saṅkarṣaṇa, name of Balarāma, brother of Kṛṣṇa.
Śaṅkhacūḍa, demon in the form of a conch.
Sāṅkhya, one of the six schools of orthodox philosophical thought, which posited the created world as a union between primordial matter, *prakṛti*, and *puruṣa*, soul.
sannyāsī, wandering celibate mendicants; members of the fourth *āśrama* or stage of life.
sārṣṭi, having the same opulence as the Lord; one of the five types of liberation in Vaiṣṇava theology.
sārūpya, having the same form as the Lord; one of the five types of liberation in Vaiṣṇava theology.
śāstra, any sacred scripture.
sat, eternity (being); a quality of *brahman*.
sattva, one of the three *guṇas*, characterized by tranquillity, detachment and knowledge.
Sātvatas, name of a tribe who are devotees of Kṛṣṇa.
satya yuga, a golden age, one of the four world ages.
Saubha, the aerial city used by Śālva to attack Dvārakā.
Śauri, a patronymic of Kṛṣṇa; Śura was Kṛṣṇa's grandfather.
sāyujya, merging with the Lord; one of the five types of liberation in Vaiṣṇava theology.

Śeṣa, thousand-headed serpent upon whom Viṣṇu reclines in the ocean of milk; incarnates as Balarāma. Also known as Ananta.

siddha, celestial being; an accomplished *yogī* who has attained mystic powers.

siddhis, mystic powers.

Śiśupāla, enemy of Kṛṣṇa.

Śiva, a supreme being; derivative manifestation of Viṣṇu for the Bhāgavata and for the Vaiṣṇava sects.

smṛti, 'that which is remembered', sacred scripture or indirect revelation.

soma, intoxicating beverage extracted on a particular day of the sacrifice, and offered to the gods.

Śrī, the goddess of fortune and Viṣṇu's eternal consort.

Śrī, a courtesy title.

Śrīdāmā, poor *brāhmaṇa* devotee of Kṛṣṇa.

Śridhara, fourteenth-century commentator on the Bhāgavata.

śrīvatsa, tuft of hair on Viṣṇu/Kṛṣṇa's chest.

Śrutadeva, *brāhmaṇa* devoted to Kṛṣṇa.

śruti, 'that which is heard', sacred scripture or transhuman revelation not composed by humans.

śūdra, member of the labouring caste.

Śuka, original narrator of the Bhāgavata.

Śūra, Vasudeva's father and Vāsudeva's [Kṛṣṇa's] grandfather.

surabhi, a celestial cow which provides milk for the gods and sages whenever required.

Sūta, secondary narrator of the Bhāgavata.

sūtas, royal bards who recite the Purāṇic histories; charioteer caste.

sūtras, verses in a sacred text.

svarga, the celestial region, but still within the domain of *saṃsāra*.

svayaṃvara, one of the six types of marriage recognized in the Purāṇic period; when the bride chooses her own husband.

Syamantaka, jewel worn by Kṛṣṇa.

Śyāmasundara, name of Kṛṣṇa meaning 'the beautiful black or dark-blue one'.

tamas, one of the three *guṇas*; characterized by darkness, illusion, sleep, indolence and negligence. Also meaning anger in some contexts.

tantras, esoteric practices usually associated with the Śiva or Devī sects.

Tripura, the triple flying cities of the demons constructed by the celestial architect Maya.

Trivakrā, hunchback woman of Mathurā who fell in love with Kṛṣṇa.

Tṛṇāvarta, demon who takes the form of a whirlwind.

tulasī, or *vṛndā*, plant sacred to Vaiṣṇavas and related to basil.
Uddhava, Kṛṣṇa's devotee and messenger.
Ugrasena, king of Mathurā whose kingdom was usurped by Kaṃsa.
Umā, another name for Śiva's consort Pārvatī.
Upaniṣads, ancient philosophical texts of the late Vedic period.
Urugāya, name of Kṛṣṇa or Viṣṇu meaning 'one who takes wide steps'; refers to the Vāmana dwarf incarnation.
Urukrama, Vāmanadeva, the dwarf incarnation of Viṣṇu.
Uttamaśloka, name of Kṛṣṇa meaning 'one who is praised in the best of verses'.
vaijayantī, type of never-fading flower used in Kṛṣṇa's garland.
Vaikuṇṭha, the eternal *brahman* abode of Lord Viṣṇu, beyond the realm of *prakṛti*.
Vaiśeṣika, one of the six schools of orthodox philosophical thought.
Vaiṣṇava, follower of Viṣṇu/Kṛṣṇa.
vaiśya, member of the merchant and landowning caste.
Vallabha, sixteenth-century Vaiṣṇava theologian.
Vāmana, dwarf incarnation of Viṣṇu.
vandīs, royal bards who recite whatever is appropriate for the occasion.
Varāha, boar incarnation of Viṣṇu, rescued the earth from the clutches of the demon Hiraṇyākṣa.
varṇāśrama, religio-social system of ancient India divided into four castes (*varṇas*) and four stages of life (*āśramas*).
Varuṇa, one of the twelve sons of Aditi, lord of the ocean and one of the eight guardians of the quarters.
vāsanā, mental impression, or memory, in *yoga* psychology, recorded in the *citta* or subtle body.
Vasudeva, Kṛṣṇa's father.
Vāsudeva, patronymic for Kṛṣṇa as the son of Vasudeva.
vedāṅgas, limbs of the Vedas – astronomy, etymology, phonetics, grammar, metre and knowledge of the ceremonies – essential for the proper performance of the sacrifice.
Vedānta, one of the six schools of orthodox philosophical thought; concerned with the relationship between *brahman*, *ātmā* and the perceived world.
Vedas, set of four ancient texts: the Ṛgveda, Sāmaveda, Yajurveda, Atharvaveda; consist of hymns to be chanted in the performance of sacrifice.
vetāla, type of evil spirit.
Vidura, the half-brother of Pāṇḍu and Dhṛtarāṣṭra.
vidyādhara, type of celestial being.
vināyaka, demoniac type of being.

Viṣṇu, supreme God of all gods, incarnates among various species throughout the universe.
Vraj, the greater Vṛndāvana region.
Vṛka, demon who tried to kill his own benefactor, Śiva.
vṛndā, or *tulasī*, a plant sacred to Vaiṣṇavas and related to basil.
Vṛndāvana, 'forest of Vṛndā'; place where Kṛṣṇa spent his childhood.
Vṛṣṇi, king in the Yadu dynasty; the Vṛṣṇis is a term used more or less synonymously with the Yadus, Kṛṣṇa's dynasty.
Vyāsadeva, compiler of the Vedas and Purāṇas.
Vyoma, name of demon.
vyūha, four divine forms expanded from Viṣṇu in Pañcarātra theology: Vāsudeva, Saṅkarṣaṇa, Pradyumna and Aniruddha.
Yadu, one of the five sons born to Yayāti, and founder of the Yādava dynasty, with which Kṛṣṇa is associated.
Yajurveda, one of the four Vedas; consists of hymns chanted during the performance of sacrifice.
yakṣa, type of supernatural being.
Yama, Hindu lord of the dead; judges souls.
Yamunā, river in Vṛndāvana.
Yaśodā, Kṛṣṇa's foster-mother.
yātudhāna, type of demon.
yātudhānī, type of witch.
yavanas, foreigners who were once *kṣatriyas*; descended from Turvasu, son of Yayāti.
Yayāti, ancient king; asked his eldest son, Yadu, to exchange his youthfulness for his own old age.
Yoga, one of the six schools of philosophical thought.
yoga, a technique for extricating the *puruṣa*, soul, from *prakṛti*, matter.
yogamāyā, the power of 'divine illusion'. Used by Kṛṣṇa to facilitate his *līlās* during his incarnation.
yogasiddhis, the eight primary mystic powers, attainable by the *yogī*.
yogī, practitioner of *yoga*.
yojana, 'distance that can be traversed in one harnessing of oxen'; about eight miles.
Yudhiṣṭhira, one of the five Pāṇḍavas and son of Dharma.
yuga, period of time in Purāṇic cosmology; there are four *yugas*: *satya yuga*, a golden age; *tretā yuga*; *dvāpara yuga*; and the present age of *kali yuga*.

Pronunciation Guide

DIACRITICS USED IN THIS TRANSLATION:

ā ī ū ṛ ḷ ḥ ṃ ṅ ñ ṇ ṭ ḍ ś ṣ

The following pronunciation guide attempts to give *approximate* equivalents in English to the Sanskrit sounds used in this text.

Vowels

Sanskrit vowels have both short forms and lengthened forms (the latter are transliterated by a line over the vowel – *ā*, *ī*, *ū*), as well as a retroflex *ṛ* sound articulated by curling the tongue further back on to the roof of the mouth than the English r. Other Sanskrit vowels alien to English are noted below. Vowels are listed in Sanskrit in the following traditional order (according to their locus of articulation, beginning from the back of the throat to the front of the mouth):

a as in 'but'
ā as in 'tar'; held twice as long as short *a*
i as in 'bit'
ī as in 'week'; held twice as long as short *i*
u as in 'bush'
ū as in 'fool'; held twice as long as short *u*
ṛ as in 'rim'
ḷ no English equivalent; approximated by l followed by *ṛ*, above
e as in 'they'
ai as in 'aisle'
o as in 'go'
au as in 'vow'

ḥ (*visarga*) a final 'h' sound which echoes the preceding vowel slightly; as in 'aha' for *aḥ*

ṃ (*anusvāra*) a nasal sound pronounced like m, but influenced according to whatever consonant follows as in 'bi**ng**o', 'pu**nch**'

Consonants

Sanskrit consonants have both aspirated forms (*kh*, *gh*, *ch*, *jh*, etc.) and unaspirated forms (*k*, *g*, *c*, *j*, etc.); the former involve articulating the consonant accompanied by a slight expulsion of air. There is also a set of retroflexes (transliterated with a dot beneath them – *ṭ*, *ḍ*, *ṭh*, *ḍh*, *ṇ*, *ṣ*), which have no precise English equivalents, and these involve curling the tongue further back on to the roof of the mouth than the English dentals. Sanskrit dentals (*t*, *d*, *th*, *dh*) are articulated with the tongue touching the teeth, slightly further forward than their English equivalents. The consonants are listed in Sanskrit in the following traditional order (according to their locus of articulation, beginning from the back of the throat to the front of the mouth):

k as in 'pick'
kh as in 'E*ckh*art'
g as in 'gate'
gh as in 'di**g-h**ard'
ṅ as in 'si**ng**'
c as in 'charm'
ch as in 'stau**nch-h**eart'
j as in 'jog'
jh as in 'hed**geh**og'
ñ as in 'ca**ny**on'
ṭ as in 'tub', but with the tongue curled further back
ṭh as in 'ligh**t-h**eart', but with the tongue curled further back
ḍ as in 'dove', but with the tongue curled further back
ḍh as in 're**d-h**ot', but with the tongue curled further back
ṇ as in 'tint', but with the tongue touching the teeth
t as in 'tub', but with the tongue touching the teeth
th as in 'ligh**t-h**eart', but with the tongue touching the teeth
d as in 'dove', but with the tongue touching the teeth
dh as in 're**d-h**ot', but with the tongue touching the teeth
n as in 'no', but with the tongue touching the teeth
p as in 'pin'
ph as in 'u**ph**ill'
b as in 'bin'

bh as in 'rub-hard'
m as in 'mum'
y as in 'yellow'
r as in 'run'
l as in 'love'
v as in 'vine'
ś as in 'shove'
ṣ as in 'crashed', but with the tongue curled further back
s as in 'such'
h as in 'hope'

List of Primary Sources Mentioned in the Text, Introduction or Notes

Vedas (the hymnological and oldest texts of the Vedic corpus)

Ṛgveda
Sāmaveda
Yajurveda
Atharvaveda

Upaniṣads (the philosophical and latest texts of the Vedic corpus)

Bṛhadāraṇyaka Upaniṣad
Chāndogya Upaniṣad
Taittirīya Upaniṣad
Īśa Upaniṣad
Śvetāśvatara Upaniṣad
Muṇḍaka Upaniṣad
Māṇḍūkya Upaniṣad

Itihāsa (the two great epics of India)

Mahābhārata (the story of the saga of the Pāṇḍavas; subdivided into *parvans*, or sections)
Rāmāyaṇa (the story of Rāma and Sītā)

Dharmaśāstra (law books)

Manu Dharmaśāstra
Gautama Dharmaśāstra

Darśana (philosophical texts)

Vedanta Sūtras (commentators mentioned: Śaṅkara, Rāmānuja, Madhva, Nimbārka, Baladeva, Vallabha, the Chaitanya school)
Yoga Sūtras
Sāṅkhya Kārikās

Purāṇas (group of eighteen texts outlining traditional narratives and histories)

Śrīmad Bhāgavata Purāṇa (commentators mentioned: Śrīdhara, Madhva, Jīva Gosvāmī, Vijayadhvaja, Vīrarāghava)
Padma Purāṇa
Viṣṇu Purāṇa
Skanda Purāṇa
Devī Purāṇa
Śiva Purāṇa
Agni Purāṇa

Texts on dramaturgical and literary theory

Nāṭyaśāstra
Sāhityadarpaṇa
Dhvanyāloka
Kāvyaprakāśa

Other Texts
Devī Māhātmya (sectarian text glorifying the goddess)
Bhagavad Gītā (Kṛṣṇa's famous instructions to Arjuna from the Mahābhārata Epic)
Aitareya Brāhmaṇa (one of the Brāhmaṇa genre of Vedic texts outlining sacrificial details)
Gṛhya Sūtras (late Vedic texts outlining details for domestic rituals)
Harivaṃśa (early account of Kṛṣṇa's life written in the Purāṇic style)
Pañcarātra texts (Vaisnava sectarian texts)
Śaivatantra (Saivite sectarian text)
Rudrasamhitā (Saivite sectarian text)
Nirukta (oldest Sanskrit etymological dictionary)
Upavedas (auxiliary, post-Vedic texts)

Bibliography

Abbott, J. E. (1899) 'The Topographical List of the Bhagavata Purana', *The Indian Antiquary*, XXVIII: 1–7.

Abhedananda, Swami (1967) *The Great Saviours of the World* in *Complete Works of Swami Abhedananda*, vol. 5. Calcutta: Ramakrishna Vedanta Math.

Banerjee, P. (1951) 'Śrīmad Bhāgavata – the Place of its Origin', *Indian Historical Quarterly*, 27 (2): 138–43.

Bhandarkar, R. G. (1913) *Vaiṣṇavism, Śaivism and Minor Religious Systems*. Strasburg. Reprinted 1982, Bhandarkar Oriental Research Institute, Poona.

Bharadwaj, Shiv Prasad (1975) 'Poetic Imagery in Bhagavata Purana', *Vishveshvarananda Indological Journal*, 13: 29–36.

Bhattacharya, Siddhesvara (1960/1962) *The Philosophy of Śrīmad Bhāgavata*, vols I and II. Calcutta: Visva Bharati.

Biswas, Ashutosh Sarma (1968) *Bhāgavata Purāṇa: A Linguistic Study*. Assam.

Bonazzoli, Giorgio (1979) 'The Dynamic Canon of the Purāṇas', *Purāṇa*, 21 (2): 116–66.

Brown, C. M. (1983) 'The Origin and Transmission of the Two *Bhāgavata Purāṇas*: a Canonical and Theological Dilemma', *Journal of the American Academy of Religion*, 51: 551–67.

Bryant, Edwin F. (2001) *In Quest of the Origins of Vedic Culture: the Indo-Aryan Migration Debate*. New York: Oxford University Press.

— (2002) 'The Date and Provenance of the Bhāgavata Purāṇa and the Vaikuṇṭha Perumāl Temple', *Journal of Vaisnava Studies*, 11 (1): 51–80.

— *In Quest of the Historical Krishna*. New York: Oxford University Press, forthcoming.

— and Ekstrand, Maria (2004) *The Hare Krishna Movement: Post-Charismatic Fate of a Religious Transplant*. New York: Columbia University Press.

Buitenen, Van J. A. B. (1988) 'On the Archaism of the Bhāgavata Purāna', in L. Rocher (ed.), *Studies in Indian Literature and Philosophy*. Delhi: Motilal Banarsidass.

Dahlquist, Allan (1962) *Megasthenes and Indian Religion*. Delhi: Motilal Banarsidass.

Dasgupta, S. N. (1922) *A History of Indian Philosophy*, vols I–V. Cambridge: Cambridge University Press.

Filliozat, Jean (1962) 'Les Dates du Bhāgavatapurāṇa et du Bhāgavatamāhātmya', in *Indological Studies in Honour of W. Norman Brown*. New Haven: American Oriental Society.

Gonda, J. (1954, rep. 1969) *Aspects of Early Viṣṇuism*. Delhi: Motilal Banarsidass.

Hawley, John Stratton (1979) 'Krishna's Cosmic Victories', *Journal of the American Academy of Religion*, 47 (2): 201–21.

Hopkins, Thomas J. (1966) 'The Social Teaching of the Bhāgavata Pūraṇa', in Milton Singer (ed.), *Krishna: Myths, Rites and Attitudes*. Chicago: University of Chicago Press.

Hudson, Dennis (1995) 'The Śrīmad Bhāgavata Purāṇa in Stone', *Journal of Vaiṣṇava Studies*, 3 (3): 137–82.

Ingalls, Daniel H. H. (1968) 'The Harivaṁśa as a Mahākāvya', in *Mélanges d'Indianisme: à la Mémoire de Louis Renou*. Paris: E. de Boccard, 381–94.

Jaiswal, Suvira (1967) *The Origin and Development of Vaiṣṇavism*. Delhi: Munshiram Manoharlal.

Krishnaswami, Aiyangar, S. (1920) *Early History of Vaishnavism in South India*. London: Oxford University Press.

Matchett, Freda (2001) *Kṛṣṇa: Lord or Avatārā: the Relationship between Kṛṣṇa and Viṣṇu*, Richmond: Curzon.

Prasad, Sheo Sankar (1984) *The Bhagavata Purana. A Literary Study*. Delhi: Capital Publishing House.

Preciado-Solis, Benjamin (1984) *The Kṛṣṇa Cycle in the Purāṇas*. Delhi: Motilal Banarsidass.

Rao, T. A. Gopinath (1986) *Elements of Hindu Iconography*. New York: Paragon.

Ray, A. (1932) 'Domicile of the Author of the Bhāgavata Purāṇa', *Indian Historical Quarterly*, 8: 749–53.

Raychaudhuri, Hemchandra (1975) *Materials for the Study of the Early History of the Vaishnava Sect*. Delhi: Oriental Books Reprint Corporation.

Rocher, L. (1986) *The Purāṇas*. Wiesbaden: Otto Harrassowitz.

Rukmani, T. S. (1970) *A Critical Study of the Bhāgavata Purāṇa*. Varanasi: Chowkhamba.

Schweig, Graham (forthcoming) *Dance of Divine Love: the* Rasalila *of Krishna and the Cowherd Maidens of Vraj*. Princeton: Princeton University Press.

Sheridan, Daniel (1983) 'The Bhāgavata Purāṇa: Sāṅkhya at the Service of Non-Dualism', *Purāṇa*, 25 (2): 206–24.

— (1986) *The Advaitic Theism of the Bhāgavata Purāṇa*. Delhi: Motilal Banarsidass.

Sheth, Noel (1982) 'Kṛṣṇa as a Portion of the Supreme', *Purāṇa*, 24 (1): 79–90.

— (1984) *The Divinity of Krishna*. Delhi: Munshiram Manoharlal.

Tagare, Ganesh Vasudeo (1978) *The Bhāgavata Purāṇa*, part 4. Delhi: Motilal Banarsidass.

Vyas, Ramnarayan (1974) *The Synthetic Philosophy of the Bhāgavata*. Delhi: Meharchand.